Environmental Funding Guide

Susan Forrester, Dave Casson

DIRECTORY OF SOCIAL CHANGE

Published by
The Directory of Social Change
24 Stephenson Way
London NW1 2DP
Tel: 0171 209 5151, fax: 0171 209 5049
e-mail: info@d-s-c.demon.co.uk
from whom further copies and a full publications list are available.

The Directory of Social Change is Registered Charity no. 800517

First published 1989
Second edition 1993
Third edition 1998

ISBN 1 900360 21 7

British Library Cataloguing in Publication Data
A catalogue record for this book is available from the British Library

Cover design by Kate Bass
Designed and typeset by Linda Parker
Printed and bound by Biddles, Guildford, Surrey, and King's Lynn

Directory of Social Change London Office:
Courses and Conferences tel: 0171 209 4949
Charity Fair tel: 0171 209 1015
Research tel: 0171 209 4422
Finance and Administration tel: 0171 209 0902

Directory of Social Change Northern Office:
3rd Floor, Federation House, Hope Street, Liverpool L1 9BW
Courses and Conferences tel: 0151 708 0117
Research tel: 0151 708 0136

CONTENTS

Acknowledgements

The editors would like to give warm thanks to all the many people who have been so cooperative in providing information for this guide.

Particular warm thanks are owed to Ruth Pilch who assisted during the last days of the work before publication.

INTRODUCTION

INTRODUCTION

THE ENVIRONMENT

A definition
For the purposes of this guide a wide definition has been used for 'environment'. It covers the spectrum of activity within the built as well as the natural environment. It ranges from regeneration activities in urban conurbations to the restoration and care of major buildings, churches and cathedrals; from local work by wildlife, amenity and community groups to work on national and international policy issues. It does not cover funding sources for activities solely concerned with the welfare of domestic, farm and laboratory animals.

A FINANCIAL OVERVIEW

The figures shown on pp10-11 indicate the relative scale of funding from different sectors. This broad brush approach allows some useful comparisons which should assist readers, particularly fundraising 'newcomers', to direct their approaches and create a good balance of funding contributors for their organisation.

Significant new funding sources
The **National Lottery Charities Board** and the **Landfill Tax Credit scheme** have changed the pattern of funding priorities in 1997.

The **Landfill Tax Credit scheme** arranges for waste disposal companies to pay a proportion of their taxable revenue into funding environmental activities (see ENTRUST entry). Contributions into this scheme leapt from more than £9 million in September 1997 to more than £60 million by early 1998. Grants are administered in a number of ways: directly by a landfill operator; by new non-profit organisations either set up by the landfill companies themselves or by independents such as Enventure; and also by coordinatory environmental bodies such as the Wildlife Trusts which in Spring 1998 were administering a total of £7.5 million for ARC and Biffa companies alone.

By Winter 1998 it seemed that the Landfill Tax was rivalling the environmental funding from all the National Lottery distribution bodies. Then in Spring 1998 the **National Lottery Charities Board** announced grants of £50 million for community environmental activities from its Fifth Programme. This regrettably was a temporary funding programme. Funding for similar activities has been subsumed within the board's general support to community involvement.

The **Landfill Tax Credit scheme** certainly rivals the total funding from the governmental sources listed in the table on page 10.

It has also generated far more for the environment in one year than all the 300 charitable grant-making trusts documented in this guide. This documentation could now seem redundant and/or of little value to fundraisers, but most funders, whether public or private, prefer to be contributors to a project rather than sole providers. Readers of this guide will see that matching funding is a basic requirement for the majority of schemes. Furthermore, trust support of whatever scale helps to validate a project to other funding bodies.

ESTIMATES OF FUNDING

Governmental

Most government agencies fund the public as well as the private sector. Whilst their figures distinguish between the grant-aid they make to these sectors, the sum to the private sector is not broken down between private owners and voluntary organisations. The figures below can only be 'guestimates' of funding totals to the voluntary sector.

The contribution to the voluntary sector from the largest tranches of governmental funding – those within regeneration, development and enterprise programmes (particularly the Single Regeneration Budget) could not be estimated. Here public and private activities are closely entwined in working, financial partnerships. Many voluntary environmental schemes are partnerships within larger local authority partnerships. The case studies illustrate some imaginative usage of these sources – indeed the labels, 'social', 'community' and 'environmental' can often be interchangeable depending on what angle of work is being emphasised. The umbrella term 'sustainable' catches all these elements.

The National Lottery

Up to Spring 1998 the **Heritage Lottery Fund** was the major contributor to environmental activities amongst the Lottery distribution bodies, but from 1998/99 its annual grant total was sharply reduced by £100 million to £250 million.

During its formative years, most of its funding was given for a small number of major artworks, museums and galleries (one of its largest grants of £25 million was given to the Kennet and Avon Canal). This pattern of funding may change.

Although the built heritage, landscape and wildlife are central to the fund's aims, the proportion of its funding to voluntary sector activities is difficult to estimate. But there are useful indicators. Land projects, mainly land purchase and conservation schemes, have absorbed only about 7% of total grant-aid (an estimated £58 million in 1997/98 and £35 million the year before). The largest single wildlife site purchase award in 1997 was given to Woodland Trust to buy Glen Finglas in Perthshire (£2.8 million).

Generous block allocations have been made. The Wildlife Trusts (RSNC) received nearly £24 million over two years. In 1997 they negotiated five-year funding of £25 million for a Reserves Enhancement Scheme to safeguard key habitats and certain endangered species (£14 million had been distributed to individual trusts by Spring 1998). A further £10 million was also given for reserve acquisition.

The Heritage Lottery Fund, along with other distribution bodies, is increasing its development of partnerships, with both governmental agencies and major voluntary organisations, instead of simply reacting to applications from major national institutions. This should devolve considerable additional funding sources reaching down to small local groups e.g. the Countryside Commission's £40 million for *Local Heritage* should support work by many varied groups in villages, towns and cities with their treasures in countryside, seashore and urban sprawl.

Other schemes such as *Urban Parks* are of necessity led by local authorities. A total of 147 urban parks received £84 million in grants ranging from a few thousand to a few million pounds. All but 5% of these were from local authorities.

In Spring 1998 the **National Lottery Charities Board** announced the allocation of some £50 million under its Fifth Programme – Environmental Issues in the Community – to projects which involve people in the management of their local environment. This one-off funding joined helpful allocations made under its Voluntary Sector Development and International programmes. No information was available about its Small Grants Scheme before publication of this guide.

The Millennium Commission estimated that a third of its funding (excluding the Dome) was allocated to environmental projects. This was some £424 million for environmental projects and parallels the £400 million for the Dome itself, a nice comparison of values! The Commission's funding for major projects was completed during 1997 but the *Millennium Awards Schemes* are set to continue indefinitely beyond the year 2000. These provide useful new funding sources for competent individuals working on environmental schemes. These totalled nearly £9 million by Spring 1998. Then the Civic Trust started a new scheme, Civic Champions, and others relevant to environmental activists are sure to follow.

Environmental work crosses many administrative boundaries and most of the Lottery Boards have some potential for funding various types of environmental activity (a wildlife trust received Arts Lottery funding).

An interesting topic for speculation is the eagerly awaited **Environmental Fund** of the **New Opportunities Fund** – the next major new funding source. Luke FitzHerbert, the editor of the *National Lottery Yearbook* does not expect it to start until 2000 and then to contribute perhaps £60 million over a five year period (comparable to the Landfill Tax in its first year and a half.)

Charitable trusts

Overall, charitable grant-making trusts give a total of between £37 and £40 million each year to environmental activities. The greater part of this environmental funding (84%) is given by only 55 trusts (16%) – those which give £100,000 and more a year to environmental activities. These trusts also give a higher proportion of their total funding (20%) to environmental activities than other trusts.

Conversely, half the trusts listed, which make small contributions of under £15,000 a year, also give a smaller proportion of their total grant-aid to environmental work (14%).

Companies

The 140 companies in this guide have been further researched from the more than 500 companies in the new publication – *A Guide to UK Company Giving 1998*. This shorter listing shows a clear predominance of companies in Utilities and Financial Services, with a large number of companies in Extraction, including oil.

Companies keep their figures close to their chests. Of course their charitable donations have to be publicly quoted in their company reports but their sponsorship, so closely allied to marketing and advertising, is notoriously difficult to gauge. The Green advertising bandwagon of the late 1980s has broken down and since much of this was blatant self interest and overstatement it may be no great loss. There has been a more troubling trend of the disengagement of certain major companies from their long-term environmental sponsorships.

1. ESTIMATES OF GOVERNMENTAL FUNDING

(based mainly on 1996/97 figures)

Historic Buildings and Monuments   £19m

Includes: English Heritage, Heritage Grant Fund, Historic Scotland, National Heritage Memorial Fund, Cadw Welsh Historic Monuments, Northern Ireland – Heritage

International   £11m

Includes: Department for International Development, Darwin Initiative (DETR), Environmental Know How Fund (DETR/DfID)

Landscape and Wildlife   £7m

Includes: Countryside Commission, English Nature, Scottish Natural Heritage, Northern Ireland – Environment, National Forest Company
Excludes: Forestry Authority, Ministry of Agriculture, Fisheries and Food

Others – General   £12m

Includes:
DETR funding schemes – Environment Action Fund/Local Projects Fund, Special Grants Programme (Regeneration & Housing);
Government funding administered by voluntary agencies – Rural Action for the Environment, Forward Scotland, Environment Wales, NI2000, Yorkshire Dales Millennium Trust
Excludes: DETR energy and transport schemes

Taxation credit

Landfill Tax Credit Scheme/ENTRUST   £60m (1997 only)

2. THE NATIONAL LOTTERY

annual guestimates for environmental activities

Heritage Lottery Fund	£40-50m
National Lottery Charities Board	
Voluntary Sector Development	£1.5m
International	£4.5m
Community Development	£5-10m
(excludes one-off 1997/98 environmental programme of £50m)	
Millennium Commission	
Award schemes	£9m

3. TRUST FUNDING

	% of trusts	Total grant-aid £	Total to environment £	% of funding to environment
£100,000+	16	154.7m	31m	20
£99,999 - £15,000	34	109.3m	4.84m	4
under £15,000	50	7.66m	1.04m	14
Total	100	271.66m	36.88m	(13.6%)

4. COMPANY CHARITABLE DONATIONS
to environmental activities

Number of companies: 141
Total charitable donations: £90 million
Estimated 10% to environmental activities £9 million

THE EDITORS

Readers who wish to contact the editors with any questions or comments should note that they work from different DSC offices and have been responsible for different sections of this Guide.

Dave Casson – re: companies, other grants and awards
Tel: 0151-708 0136; Fax: 0151-708 0139

Susan Forrester – re: all other sections
Tel: 0171-209 4422; Fax: 0171-209 4130

FUNDING SOURCES

CHAPTER ONE

GOVERNMENTAL FUNDING

INTRODUCTION

Some cautionary words are necessary.

DEVOLUTION

This guide covers the whole of the UK. Significant changes may occur when the new Scottish Parliament and Welsh Assembly assume their powers and functions.

The Scottish Parliament is expected to be elected in May 1999. This will be followed by a six month transitional period before full assumption of powers in 2000. Whilst the Scottish Office held extensive powers before this change and could put bills through the Parliament in Westminster, it will assume the key power to raise/vary income tax. (Westminster has reserved its powers over the following functions: the constitution, foreign policy, employment legislation, fiscal policy, social security and defence.)

The formation of the Welsh Assembly is expected to follow a similar timetable. It will take over the powers of the Secretary of State for Wales and Welsh Office but will not have tax-raising powers.

COMPREHENSIVE SPENDING REVIEW

The editing of this section had to be completed well before the results of the Comprehensive Spending Review which has applied to all sectors of governmental activity. Obviously changes will take place from 1999 which could not be anticipated.

DEPARTMENTAL CHANGE

The New Labour government made some departmental changes. The main one is the large 'amalgamated' Department of Environment, Transport and the Regions. A new Department of International Development was born from an expansion of the former Overseas Development Administration of the Foreign Office. The Department of Culture, Media and Sport was a significant renaming of the former Department of National Heritage. The transformation of the Ministry of Agriculture, Fisheries and Food to a Ministry of Food and Countryside heralded in the media after the election has not taken place. In view of the number of agencies and powerful interests involved this has not been surprising, but a National Food Agency was created in 1998 and more changes may well occur.

Internal reorganisation of divisions and units within many departments will lead to further changes of address than those which have been able to be indicated as imminent.

REGIONAL GOVERNMENT

This is where some of the most significant changes within government in England will be taking place. Whilst a new tier of horizontal, interdepartmental government bureaucracy has been developing through the *Government Offices for the Regions (GORs),* its wider evolution is being ensured through the creation of nine new *Regional Development Agencies (RDAs)* in England. They will have the same boundaries as the current GORs, with the exception of the North-West which will be covered by one office including Merseyside. (The arrangements with London would also seem to pose particular problems.) RDAs will take up their powers in April 1999 with shadow operations in place as soon as possible, maybe by April 1998.

The White Paper *Building Partnerships for Prosperity* of December 1997 outlined New Labour's plans. The core responsibilities of the RDAs include economic development and regeneration coupled with sustainable development. This means they will administer the *Single Regeneration Challenge Fund,* take a lead role on *European Union* structural funds and also assume the regional regeneration functions of *English Partnerships* and the *Rural Development Commission.* The boards will be business led with members reflecting regional interests such as the voluntary sector, rural areas and tourism. Each board will include four local authority members.

The mechanics of how the agencies will operate were very unclear at the time of writing and the relationships with, and knock on effects on other agencies and local authorities will be complex.

The only metropolitan funding schemes covered in this guide are the *London Borough Grants Unit* and the *Association of Greater Manchester Authorities (AGMA) Grant Scheme.*

LOCAL GOVERNMENT

This guide cannot possibly cover the details of regional and local support but it is important for newcomers to environmental work to be aware that good relationships with their local authority are crucial to their successful local development.

Working Partnerships: The Single Regeneration Budget and European Structural Funding

One certain generalisation is that there is huge variability in the responses local authorities can make to their voluntary sector. However the scenario is not just a gloomy one of dwindling resources. As the potential for direct funding has declined, so the opportunities via joint initiatives/working partnerships have expanded. These include regeneration programmes at both regional and European levels (see separate entries). Local authority support is essential to success with these schemes.

In addition local groups should remember that the local authority itself needs to demonstrate its own close rapport with its community when proposing schemes. The local authority needs its local groups as much as they need it. This is what is meant by partnership – a mutual process of interchange in which the exchange of money is only one (and not the inevitable) part of a practical relationship. Shared services and gifts in kind from an authority can be just as important, and are often more cost-effective.

Local Agenda 21

Local Agenda 21 functions at local authority and community level but unfortunately the title conveys very little to ordinary people, smacking as it does of committee meetings and paper. The Rio Conference on Environment and Development 1992, called for an action plan for the 21st Century in AGENDA 21, which, translated into Local Agenda 21, brings these action plans to our neighbourhoods. Councils were called on to work with their communities to examine environmental, social and economic issues facing their areas and to initiate practical actions to make changes and improvements.

Apparently as many as 70% of local authorities in the UK have some activities under this *discretionary* programme. Local advisory groups have been set up and, in some authorities, people have been appointed on contract to help co-ordinate or initiate activities. To take an example, Lewisham's Local Agenda 21 programme has established five groups:

◆ Natural Environment
◆ Waste Management
◆ Built Environment
◆ Transport
◆ Energy.

These follow the main areas of Agenda concern. However, the pattern of putting these themes into practice differs according to the local authority, its elected members and the groundswell of local interest and involvement. So it is a piecemeal response with no funds from central government to support the cash-strapped local authorities. (Issues such as transport, pollution and waste desperately need national and regional impetus to make integrated sense, although some helpful initiatives can be taken locally.)

The Structure of Local Government

The structure of local government altered in 1997 with the wider introduction of *unitary* authorities. A unitary authority has sole responsibility for all areas of local government concern in its given area. Scotland, Wales and Northern Ireland now have just one tier of local government.

In England, unlike Scotland and Wales, there has been no consistent pattern to the introduction of unitary authorities. Some counties and districts have been abolished and replaced entirely by unitary authorities (Berkshire) whilst other counties remain (Surrey). In many counties new unitary authorities co-exist alongside the counties of which they had formerly been a part. For instance two new unitary authorities have been created from within Leicestershire – Leicester City and Rutland – leaving a smaller Leicestershire County Council with seven district councils.

No structural changes have needed to be made in Northern Ireland or to the metropolitan boroughs of England since these authorities were already in effect single tier/unitary authorities carrying out the full range of local government responsibilities.

So the local authority system in England has become extremely varied and is still readjusting financially and administratively. The population size of unitary authorities varies considerably as does their geographical area. The arbitrary changes in boundaries, powers and scope of responsibility in certain areas have caused considerable strain and readjustment. The altering patterns of responsibility have also had a knock-on effect on the support to, funding of, and partnerships with the voluntary sector.

The Two-Tier Structure

Since the two-tier structure of county and district councils will remain in many areas, it is important to distinguish their different responsibilities. The following table shows which level of local authority deals with what, draws attention to overlapping interests and also to those areas which are not always so obviously environment-related, but which can be important areas for interchange and working partnerships. These include:

- Planning departments (urban and rural development and Agenda 21);
- Economic development and tourism departments (strategies to attract visitors and inward investment particularly the Single Regeneration Budget and European funding);
- Education departments;
- Libraries and museums services (organisation of events as part of educational and outreach work);
- Social services (environmental activities for client groups).

Many authorities, both county and district, have European Officers (enquire of the Chief Executive's Department).

Main Functions of County and District Councils

County Councils

EDUCATION
- Most schools
- Special education
- Nursery, adult and community
- Planning and quality assurance
- Resource management

PERSONAL SOCIAL SERVICES
- Provision for the elderly, children, and those with disabilities (including care in the community)
- Policy planning and quality assurance

PLANNING
- Strategic planning
- Mineral and waste planning
- Highway development control
- Historic buildings

TRANSPORT
- Public transport
- Highways and parking
- Traffic management
- Footpaths and bridleways
- Transport planning

EMERGENCY PLANNING

ENVIRONMENTAL SERVICES
- Refuse disposal

RECREATION AND ART
- Parks and open spaces
- Support for the arts
- Museums
- Encouraging tourism

ECONOMIC DEVELOPMENT

LIBRARIES

POLICE

FIRE

District Councils

ELECTORAL REGISTRATION

COUNCIL TAX AND UNIFORM BUSINESS RATES

HOUSING

PLANNING
- Local plans
- Planning applications

TRANSPORT
- Unclassified roads
- Offstreet car parking
- Footpaths and bridleways
- Street lighting

EMERGENCY PLANNING

ENVIRONMENTAL SERVICES
- Refuse collection
- Building regulations
- General environmental services
- Street cleaning

RECREATION AND ART
- Parks and open spaces
- Leisure centres and swimming pools
- Museums and art galleries
- Support for the arts
- Encouraging tourism

ECONOMIC DEVELOPMENT

Source: Local Government Commission for England (a few functions such as allotments, smallholdings and cemeteries have been omitted)

Do not be surprised that the titles of departments, and the groupings of responsibilities and names of council committees, can vary greatly from authority to authority. That is their executive decision.

PARISH COUNCILS, NEIGHBOURHOOD COUNCILS AND COMMUNITY COUNCILS

Last, but very certainly not least, be sure to be aware of the most local of local representation – the parish councils in rural areas, and neighbourhood councils in some urban areas (community councils in Wales). Their statutory powers are not wide – mainly village halls, playing fields, car parking, street lighting – but, crucially for environmental concerns, they *have to be consulted about any local planning applications*. In addition, schemes that are generated in co-operation with them are more likely to be listened to at higher levels. They may not have the money themselves but they can help open doors to both public and private sources by giving additional credibility to new practical proposals.

The importance of using your networks

These networks can usually keep you up-to-date with any developments/changes arising with government schemes. Plumb the information resources of the various departments of your local authority and of your local library thoroughly and be sure to get placed whenever possible on any mailing lists.

Making contact with other similar groups elsewhere and exchanging experiences can greatly strengthen resolve and help to recharge inspiration as well as generate ideas to improve tactics and management.

A host of co-ordinatory bodies in the voluntary sector provide assistance and excellent information about local, regional and national changes in addition to the environmental organisations (see Support Organisations). They include:

- Councils of Voluntary Service in towns, cities and boroughs, themselves co-ordinated by the National Association of Councils for Voluntary Service;
- Rural Community Councils, of which there are 38 in rural areas. They are co-ordinated by ACRE (Action with Communities in Rural England);
- Community associations, which are co-ordinated by Community Matters;
- Development Trusts Association, for development trusts.

In addition to providing information about governmental schemes, these organisations are usually also able to inform you of related groups you should know about.

THE HASTINGS TRUST –
juggling regeneration resources

Voluntary organisations have to keep themselves constantly informed about the changes and developments in funding and partnership opportunities. Then they can 'seize the moment'.

The work of the Hastings Trust, in acquiring a new home and a base for a community resource centre, illustrates support from several of the programmes covered in this guide, and the tenacity, flexibility and conviction needed to nurse a project through delays and setbacks. The trust's achievements have included a UK 2000 Kitemark, a Wimpy Walks Award, a Community Enterprise Award from Business in the Community, and two BT/Civic Trust Environment Week awards.

A Profile of Hastings

Although within the affluent South East, the seaside resort of Hastings (population 85,000) has seen its traditional industries of fishing, agriculture and tourism fall into serious decline. Its economy was boosted in the late 60s and early 70s by the influx of 20,000 people from a London overspill programme and the building of six small-scale industrial sites to employ them.

The housing and industrial estates, built on the last areas of open land in the borough, are high-density, lacking in most social amenities, with poor public transport to the town centre. Most of the enterprises on the industrial estates offer low-wage, low-skilled employment.

By the mid-1980s, 30 years of neglect and blinkered vision produced the similar levels of social and economic deprivation to those found in inner city areas. It ranks above Tower Hamlets, in East London, on some social indices, and has some of the highest levels of deprivation and unemployment in the South East.

THE DEVELOPMENT TRUST

Against this background, the Hastings Urban Conservation Project was set up in 1986 as a conservation-led initiative jointly funded by East Sussex County Council, Hastings Borough Council and English Heritage.

After the withdrawal of its three-year funding, a series of consultation exercises was carried out across the community to find a way of tackling the wider issues of regeneration within Hastings. A development trust was seen as the only way forward and by early 1991 the Hastings Trust was established as a charitable company.

The trust's aims and objectives are wide and varied:
- to enable all those who live in, work in or visit Hastings to protect and enhance their environment;
- to promote and assist the sustainable economic and cultural development of Hastings;
- to promote and disseminate good practice in conservation and community regeneration locally and regionally.

They are encapsulated in its shorter mission statement: 'To create active partnerships between the public, private, voluntary and community sectors and to enable them to work together for the economic, environmental and social regeneration of Hastings'. (Words closer to current 'regeneration-speak', Editor.)

The trust undertakes a broad range of projects including strategic initiatives, area studies, community and youth projects, environmental enhancements, education and training, and provision of resource and advice centres.

Its environmental activities are varied. They include a Community Environmental Project, with an officer funded by English Nature, working borough-wide supporting schools, community groups and residents associations in transforming their natural environment. It manages physical projects and directly supervises volunteer projects and links with many other local partners (public, private and voluntary) notably the borough's Smarten Up Hastings Campaign. A derelict High Street site has become a fine courtyard garden; roads and pathways have been refurbished and signed; railings painted and walls decorated. Volunteers maintain the Local Agenda 21 database for East Sussex users and the Buildings at Risk Register as part of English Heritage's National Register.

By 1996/97 the trust was employing three full-time core staff, and four full-time and one part-time project staff, along with a team of office and project-based trainees and volunteers, all responsible to its board of 12 directors. Its cash turnover was £221,000 supported by a core grant of £50,000 from Hastings Borough Council, with the balance made up of grant-aid and earned income. The trust's 'hidden' volunteer and in-kind income was valued at more than £232,000.

THE DEVELOPMENT OF ITS ASSET BASE

The growth of the Hastings Trust over the last six years has taken place in a series of short-term rented buildings, mainly as a result of a series of funding battles. However, it was during this time that the trust developed its greatest asset – a terrific team of staff, trainees and volunteers – a resource which generated the wherewithall to keep the trust afloat and its values alive. The trust still needed a strong asset-base to secure its long-term future and this became a primary, rather than a secondary task.

Its First Opportunity – a large redundant building

The 42,000 sq ft of the former Observer Print Building, at one of the gateways to the town centre, had been empty for several years. In 1991 the infant trust latched onto this as a prime site for managed workspace – that magic generator of both a home *and* an income for development trusts. It would solve the trust's problems and be the engine of regeneration and provide the 'buzz' in the town.

Working with the owners, English Partnerships (EP), Charities Aid Foundation (CAF), the local authorities and Barclays Bank, the trust produced a seemingly good package. Surveys, drawings, costings, business plans were all produced. The building programme, management structures, likely tenants, support packages, and everything to justify the project's feasibility appeared viable. Even a sensitivity analysis at 75% occupancy worked. None of this labour was paid for in cash but was valued, conservatively, at £70,000.

The trust worked for four years and brought the project to a stage where it had secured an offer of nearly £1 million from English Partnerships' major fund, a fairly soft loan of £680,000 from Barclays Bank, grant-aid of £100,000 from East Sussex County Council and £120,000 from the Single Regeneration Budget Challenge Fund. The only problem was that all the partners in this project were wearing rose-tinted spectacles, and the rose soon became grey when the owners turned out to be crooks, with the grant-aid and soft-loans turning to £ signs in their eyes.

The Second Opportunity

Undaunted, the trust continued its search for an asset base. It fundraised to buy the elegant, six-storey Georgian town house it had been occupying during 1994/5. The owner had died suddenly, leaving his company bankrupt and the price was good. Then suddenly the building was sold out from under the trust and it was given four weeks notice to quit. The borough council was approached for help with accommodation. They offered a small portakabin for free (rather small for a staff of six and 28 volunteers!).

The Third Opportunity – CIF and CAPS

During 1995 the trust heard about the new English Partnerships Community Investment Fund (CIF). Here at last was government recognition that voluntary and community organisations need support to develop their asset bases to help ensure a sustainable future.

The trust found shop-front premises with offices above in the Old Town Conservation Area. This provided enough space for all its activities with extra to generate letting income. An added plus, it was dilapidated and eligible for a Conservation Area Partnership Scheme (CAPS) grant. And it was cheap. EP sent down their case officer. The project appeared to meet their criteria and the trust was off again: a survey undertaken, architects' drawings done, building works scheduled, costings produced and estimates obtained for conversion works. An application to CIF was made in July 1995. Unfortunately, the acquisition and conversion costs totalled £307,000. EP were unhappy with these despite a hefty CAPS grant and, try as the trust might, there was no realistic business plan for the project that did not jeopardise its long-term survival. The building was sold anyway: the trust's interest had ironically revived commercial interest.

The Fourth Opportunity – CIF and the Brewery

The searchlight next fell on an empty Victorian pub. Its cellar added another income stream to the trust's new business plan – a micro brewery and training courses. The business plan for the project's long-term sustainability worked. After the usual sequence of survey, drawings, schedules and costings, the project figure this time was just about right for the CIF at £128,000. All systems go, everyone was happy and the application went in during mid October 1995. Then the pub owner gave the trust two weeks to complete the deal or it would go to a higher bidder. The trust's interest had again spurred the estate agents' interest, and as English Partnerships doesn't move fast, the trust again lost out.

The Winning Formula – 35 Robertson Street

During Christmas 1996 the right combination materialised: an empty building, its owners short of cash, CIF keen to offer money, the launch of CAF's Investors in Society, and Round Three of the Single Regeneration Budget. Plus, the first recognition by the borough council that the trust was 'a good thing' and needed support.

The asset and benefits accruing to the trust

♦ Empty, town centre, semi-derelict, four-storey Victorian building (former restaurant) in secondary shopping street due for upgrading.
♦ Double-fronted shop, large enough for accessible community resource, first floor meeting and seminar room, offices above. Basement for training courses. Income earning potential from spare space.
♦ Former Crown Estates property sold to new owners. Price £69,500 open to offers.

- Property eligible for shop-front grants and future Conservation Area Partnership Scheme funding.
- Project adds to Single Regeneration Budget Programme outputs.
- Raises trust's profile.
- Trust's presence will spark off further acquisition of empty properties for its Building Preservation Project and Environmental Enhancement Programme.
- Business plan corroborates the project's long-term sustainability.
- Investors in Society loan element repayment costs less than trust's current rental.
- Asset base for future development use.

Diary of the development over 15 months

- **January 96:** Board approval to pursue acquisition and refurbishment with support from trustee working party. Local surveyors conduct survey on pay-later basis if funding obtained.
- **February 96:** English Partnerships visit building, project approved and an outline CIF application invited.

New Funding Approach

Income projections from the business plan and greater support from Hastings Borough Council gave the trust enough confidence to take out a loan from the CAF's new Investors in Society scheme. An initial soft loan of £30,000 over ten years at a flat rate of 5% was negotiated.

Discussions were held between CAF and Hastings Borough Council to determine its commitment to the trust. In an historic breakthrough, the Director of Technical Services acknowledged that emergent trusts need at least ten years to develop and stabilise. The trust's achievements convinced him to put our core funding into his revenue budget, and save the annual funding round arguments. The borough would not stand guarantor for the loan as it was confident the trust would succeed. CAF was persuaded that the trust was a 'good risk'.

- **March 96:** Trust lawyers on stand-by. Reduced price to £55,000 negotiated by director and EP with owners following long conversation about charities, their funding, time scales, poverty, good will etc. EP's intervention helped convince owners.
- **May 96:** Full application invited by EP.
- **June 96:** Architects appointed on a no-funding/no-pay basis. (In the event the trust, in the shape of the director, had to undertake the tendering process, appointment of contractors and project management).

- **July 96:** Second survey undertaken at EP's expense.
- **August 96:** Costing of building conversion works from friendly local builder. Final figure of £117,500 for acquisition and refurbishment.
- **September 96:** Indications that EP grant level would be reduced by £10,000 and £ for £ against any further funding obtained.

Third round of the SRB Challenge Fund in full swing. Application for funding to develop and expand its Community Resource Centre in the new building. Presenting the resource centre as a separate project, identified additional funding from the SRB programme – 'outputs' and the 'strengthening of the voluntary sector involvement in regeneration'. This approach seemed a good thing but had later cashflow and clawback drawbacks.

- **October 96:** Negotiations with EP over level of funding. Offer around £65,885 (£10,000 less than needed). Renegotiate CAF loan to £39,500.
- **November 96:** Applications for planning permission and building regulations.
- **December 96:** SRB Challenge Fund III announced. The trust had won three year's revenue funding, plus capital for Community Resource Centre outfit and new IT equipment. EP agree press release.
- **January 97:** Planning permission granted.
- **February 97:** Trust's lawyers scrutinise CAF loan document and EP agreement.

CAF's loan agreement required building insurance, key person insurance on the director with guarantee that she remained in post for at least two years, plus first charge on building if failure resulted. In return, an interest holiday negotiated on the loan until the building works finished.

The requirements of EP's grant agreement were even more exacting, including approval of the trust's board of trustees.

Tenders issued to three local builders, to be returned by March 1997.
- **March 97:** Board approved and signed both agreements. New building bank account opened. Large cheques arrive from EP and CAF. Trust buys building 31st March.
- **April 1st 97:** 12-16 week refurbishment programme not started as planned. Delay of seven weeks due to the intricate workings of SRB and the Government Office of the South East (GOSE).
- **April 97:** Building regulations approval obtained. Press launch cancelled due to EP embargo for General Election period. Renegotiate interest

holiday with CAF. Contract let. Small works contract signed. Construction (Design & Management) Regulations handed over to contractor.

◆ **End May 97**: Contractors start structural repairs. Dry rot and wet rot discovered. EP agree up to an additional £4,000.

◆ **June 1997**: Resource Centre Project appraised for SRB programme. New architect appointed for Shop Front Design, schedule of works and order of costs. Resource Centre Project approved. *16 weeks late.* Renegotiate interest holiday with CAF. Press launch. Good time had by all.

◆ **August 97**: Shop front out to tender. Application made for Shop-front Improvement Grant. Cashflow about to suffer. Borough Council step in as accountable body for SRB and offer to up-front £5,000 per month.

◆ **September 1997**: Negotiate with GOSE for monthly payments (instead of quarterly) in arrears. Shop front grant approved. Contract let to shop fitters.

◆ **October 97**: Community Service Unit undertake internal decoration. Building works finished.

◆ **November 97**: Borrow TAVR 4 tonner, hire Luton van and move in.

This article is an edited version of a talk given at the Development Trusts Association Conference 1997 by Christine Goldschmidt, Executive Director of the Hastings Trust, 35 Robertson Street, Hastings, East Sussex TN34 1HT (Tel: 01424-446373). We thank her warmly for allowing it to be used.

Regeneration and Sustainability – a case study

When this guide was being compiled changes were predicted for the structures of government funding for regeneration and development. The new Labour Government had wanted to take a new look at the massive programmes it had inherited, and like all new governments, would probably want to place its own stamp on the programmes. No information about any changes was available before April 1998 at the earliest (unfortunately too late for this guide).

The largest funding scheme in England in 1997/98, the Single Regeneration Budget (SRB), may change its name and refocus its priorities. The predictions were that it would focus more closely on specific disadvantaged areas and specific groups.

However this case-study, supported under the SRB in 1997, is an adventurous multi-cultural and transcontinental initiative which seems to herald the expected focus on specific groups in our population.

LAPIS – LUTON AND PESHAWAR INITIATIVE FOR SUSTAINABILITY

LAPIS is a Local Agenda 21 partnership between Luton Borough Council and the World Wide Fund for Nature UK, funded within the borough's Single Regeneration Budget (SRB) Challenge Funding. That is its organisational framework in this country. What makes it special is that a similar partnership has been forged between WWF Pakistan, IUCN Pakistan and the Civil Authorities of the North West Frontier Province. These are the formal organisations involved, but the project's success depends on ordinary people (young and old) being motivated to work co-operatively on ways to improve their own immediate lives and thereby the wider aims of sustainable development.

This imaginative and ambitious project first started in 1995. Luton has a large community, particularly in its inner urban area, derived from the Indian subcontinent. LAPIS aims to build a web of relations for learning and action: between neighbourhood communities and the local authority, and between the groups and their schools extending out to international links with Peshawar in the North West Frontier Region of Pakistan (where WWF UK has offices and contacts in community development).

The project's first goal has been to encourage the formation of groups and to help them develop *attainable* action plans for their own neighbourhoods. Officers and local people have been developing

Neighbourhood Action Groups or Community Consultative Fora as part of LA 21. Once this interest and involvement has been aroused, local schools are drawn in to the process so that they can start to learn about sustainability from living practical activities, many of which they will develop themselves.

The first phase of the programme ran from 1995 to 1997. The process is gradual and cannot be forced or hastened if the people the proposed community development aims to resource, facilitate and serve, are to develop and take the initiatives themselves. By the end of 1997 LAPIS could point to a series of achievements which hopefully will burgeon and expand:

- two neighbourhood action groups have formed and are developing their own local sustainability action plans;
- staff training programmes have been set up to support these groups;
- a LAPIS network of schools working on education for sustainability has formed;
- WWF UK has offered grants to schools to produce school development plans and curriculum material that reflect the aims of the project;
- curriculum materials have been developed and trialled in schools, also a newsletter;
- six representatives from Peshawari groups made a two-week visit to Luton and developed a shared agenda with their Luton counterpartners;
- SRB funding was secured for Phase 2 of the programme (five years from April 1997).

People are sharing experience across the continents – for instance a women's group in Bury Park is exchanging ideas and approaches with a Peshwari women's support group.

Distances can concertina, even seem to disappear, as more common ground grows between the two initiatives in Peshawar and Luton. It gives another dimension to 'think globally act locally'.

For further information contact Marek Lubelski, LAPIS, Bury Park Community Centre, 90 Dunstable Road, Luton LU1 1EH (Tel: 01582-450194; Fax: 01582-450194)

ALPHABETICAL INDEX OF FUNDING SOURCES

SUBJECT INDEX OF FUNDING SOURCES

Trees, woodlands, forestry

Waste/recycling

GOVERNMENT FUNDING SOURCES

Ministry of Agriculture, Fisheries and Food

Whitehall Place (West Block), London SW1A 2HH
Tel: 0171-238 3000
The Ministry of Agriculture, Fisheries and Food (MAFF) has no dedicated budget from which voluntary bodies can seek funding. However it does support a small number of national voluntary bodies with concerns close to its own objectives.

MAFF Grants to Voluntary Bodies – 1996/97
Conservation and Woodlands Policy Division
Room 539, Nobel House, 17 Smith Square, London SW1P 3JR
Budget officer: Frances Radcliffe
Tel: 0171-238 5668; Fax: 0171-238 6126

Farming and Wildlife Advisory Group (FWAG): a number of farm conservation advisors are supported with services in kind, including professional advice and free office accommodation. In addition, core funding, grant-aid and an annual subscription (£259,000) is made.

Deregulation, Agricultural Resources and Training Division
Room 718, Nobel House, 17 Smith Square, 17 Smith Square, London SW1 P 3JR
Budget officer: Geoff Webdale
Tel: 0171-238 5755; Fax: 0171-238 6553

National Federation of Young Farmers' Clubs, towards its agricultural education activities (£36,000).

Applications: Since there are no specific grant schemes for such support voluntary bodies should contact the MAFF division relevant to their work about potential funding where there is mutual benefit. This should be done at least nine months in advance of the time when a grant is required.

MAFF's Conservation Grant Schemes
Grant total: £50,193,000 (1996/97); £63,007,000 (1997/98 estimate)
Contact: Frances Radcliffe (see above)

These substantial schemes are directed mainly, but not always exclusively, at farmers. Charities and voluntary bodies which own and maintain farmland could be eligible to apply to them. Free conservation advice is available and a farm visit made on request by the Farming and Rural Conservation Agency (FRCA) of ADAS or FWAG (funded by MAFF or part funded by MAFF and DETR respectively).

Countryside Access Scheme (£80,000 1996/97) aims to increase opportunities for public access on land which is in the guaranteed set-aside option of the Arable Area Payments Scheme (AAPS) for a period of 5 years and is additional to those payments.

Countryside Stewardship (£12,225,000 1996/97) for conservation and enhancement of some key English landscapes, features and habitats, and where appropriate, public access to them. Targets include the countryside around towns including community forests, traditional field boundaries, traditional orchards, historic landscapes, old meadows and pastures, coasts, uplands, watersides, lowland heath and chalk and limestone grassland.

In 1998, MAFF plans to launch a pilot Arable Stewardship scheme to address the decline of wildlife on arable land. Farmers will be able to apply for aid in return for following specific land management options designed to benefit wildlife.

Farm Woodland Premium Scheme (£2,323,000 1996/97) operates throughout England and encourages the planting of new woods on currently productive agricultural land. These grants are additional to the Forestry Authority's Woodland Grant Scheme (see separate entry). A single application can be made for both. Packs are available from the Forestry Authority Conservancy offices.

Habitat Scheme: Former 5-year Set-Aside and Saltmarsh (£1,420,000 1996/97) Incentives to manage land to create or improve wildlife habitats.

Moorland Scheme (£104,000 1996/97) for upland farmers outside ESAs who want to reduce stocking density and manage their land to improve the upland moorland environment, especially heather moorland.

Organic Aid Scheme (£406,000 1996/97) for farmers wishing to convert in accordance with the rules of the UK Register of Organic Food Standards.

The five schemes below are available in specifically designated areas.

Objective 5b – a joint EU/UK funded rural development programme available in the six English areas designated under Objective 5b of the EC Structural Funds (see separate entries). These designations run from 1994-1999

Environmentally Sensitive Areas (ESAs) (£31,803,000 1996/97). In 22 ESAs in England farmers are encouraged to enter a 10 year agreement to adopt practices which protect and enhance the environment. They receive annual payments.

Habitat Scheme: Water Fringes Schemes for 10-20 year agreements operate in six pilot sites.

Nitrate Sensitive Areas (NSAs) (£3,645,000 1996/97). Farmers in the 32 NSAs are encouraged to enter five year agreements involving changes in their farming practice in order to stabilise and reduce nitrate levels and protect future drinking water sources.

Farm Waste Grants in Nitrate Vulnerable Zones (NVZs) are available in these designated zones to enable farmers to comply with restrictions on the spreading of livestock manures.

Applications: Contact the MAFF Regional Service Centres.

Anglia – Beds, Cambs, Essex, Herts, Norfolk, Suffolk – Tel: 01223-462727; Fax: 01223-455652

Carlisle – Cumbria, Lancs, Northumberland, Tyne & Wear – Tel: 01228-23400; Fax: 01228-23468

Nottingham – Derby, Leics, Lincs, Northamptonshire, Notts – Tel: 0115-9291191; Fax: 0115-9294886

Reading – Berks, Bucks, E & W Sussex, Hampshire, Isle of Wight, Kent, Gtr London, Oxfordshire, Surrey – Tel: 0118-9581222; Fax: 0118-9392198

Bristol – Avon, Dorset, Somerset, Wilts – Tel: 0117-9591000; Fax: 0117-9505392

Crewe – Cheshire, Gtr Manchester, Merseyside, Shrops, Staffs – Tel: 01270-69211; Fax: 01270-669494

Exeter – Devon, Cornwall, Isles of Scilly – Tel: 01392-277951; Fax: 01392-410936

Northallerton – Cleveland, Durham, Humberside, Yorks – Tel: 01609-773751; Fax: 01609-780179

Worcester – Gloucester, Hereford, Worcester, Warwickshire, W Midlands – Tel: 01905-763355; Fax: 01905-763180

Association of Greater Manchester Authorities (AGMA) Grants Scheme

AGMA Grants Unit, Chief Executive's Department, PO Box 532, Town Hall Extension, Manchester M60 2LA
Tel: 0161-234 3364
Contact: Grants Officer
Grant total: £70,000 for one-off grants (1997/98)

Policy: This scheme was established in 1996 following the dissolution of Greater Manchester Council to support Greater Manchester wide projects and organisations. One-off funding is available for the following areas of activity: social welfare, recreation and the arts, environmental conservation and improvement, economic development and job creation, advice services, racial and other forms of disadvantage and discrimination.

Priority is given to projects which promote the image of Greater Manchester, which provide a county-wide service (or form part of a county-wide service) and which provide coverage over the majority of the ten Greater Manchester districts. Groups must be properly constituted and non-profit making.

Grants for one-off funding only. It is the Grants Committee's policy to give priority to one-off funding for:
(i) grants/guarantees against loss on events of brief programmes
(ii) general fixed term project costs

It is not the Grants Committee's policy to fund:
(i) equipment/furniture/vehicle costs (except where the equipment requested forms an integral and small element of an overall project)
(ii) building or refurbishment costs
(iii) the on-going revenue costs of a project.

A recent example of funding is the £2,500 to enable North West Focus to stage a series of events aimed at giving the voluntary sector and the inner areas a voice in the environment and developmental debates in Manchester during Global Forum Week.

Applications: On a form available from the correspondent. There are three deadlines a year: end of January, end of May and end of September. The committee meets three to four months after each deadline. No retrospective grants are given.

The Built Heritage Pairing Scheme (a pilot project for the North of England)

ABSA (Association for Business Sponsorship of the Arts) North, Dean Clough, Halifax, West Yorkshire HX3 5AX
Tel: 01422-367860; **Fax:** 01422-363254
Contact: Ceri Thomas, Manager
Grant total: £150,000 (1997/98)

This pilot scheme, funded by the Department of Culture, Media and Sport, was launched in 1995. It is hoped the scheme will eventually be extended to cover the whole of the country but readers should check its status.

The scheme covers Yorkshire & Humberside, North West and Northern regions and is designed to encourage businesses to sponsor the built heritage. Awards to heritage organisations are available as:
◆ 100% match funding for first time sponsors of repair work to the built heritage or physical improvements to enable access to the built heritage by the less able bodied;

◆ 50% match funding to sponsors in their first three years of built heritage
   sponsorship;
◆ 25% match to sponsors who have been sponsoring the built heritage for at
   least three years.

The minimum amount of matching money available for each sponsorship is
£1,000 and the maximum is £25,000. Heritage organisations may receive a total
or £25,000 in awards in any one year. There is no restriction on the number of
times a business may apply. All awards are discretionary.

Eligible organisations are those who own, manage or are responsible for the built
heritage, or are in receipt of funding from a government funding agency (such as
English heritage) for the sponsored event or project.

Applications: Full details are available with application forms which must be received
eight weeks before the start date of the sponsored activity.

The DCMS is considering the possibility of continuing the scheme and extending
it to the rest of England in 1998. A decision is unlikely before the end of 1997.

The Countryside Commission

John Dower House, Crescent Place, Cheltenham, Gloucestershire GL50 3RA
Tel: 01242-521381; Fax: 01242-584270
Website: http//www.countryside.gov.uk
Contact: Corporate Planning Unit (but see regional offices below)
Grant total: £14,711,000 (1996/97)
Breakdown:
   Local authorities / public bodies – £11,020,000;
   Private persons / non-public bodies – £3,050,000 including grants to 'major
   voluntary partners'*;
   Groundwork – £641,000**
*No figures were made available. In the previous year £1.98 million was given to 7
organisations: BTCV £979,000; Woodland Trust £295,000; Country Wildlife Trusts
to 16 trusts £211,000; National Trust £209,000; RSPB £188,000; CPRE £68,000;
Council for National Parks £30,000.
**£2,175,000 in the previous year.

The Countryside Commission is funded by the Department of the Environment,
Transport and the Regions and is the government's principal adviser on landscape,
conservation and countryside recreation. It also raises funds from other sources –
the National Lottery, the European Union and business sponsorship. The
Commission gives grants and financial support for a range of countryside
conservation and recreation activities.

In 1996 the Commission produced *A Living Countryside* – its strategy for the next ten years. This sets out 7 main themes which will be developed depending on 'resources available and guidance from the Ministers'. Grant-aid is directed at projects which support the priorities identified in the Strategy and Corporate Plan. In summary these are:

◆ the encouragement of local pride so that local communities and public organisations strengthen the special character of each part of the English countryside;

◆ the promotion of sustainable leisure activities, including such features as 'Greenways' – links between town and countryside, 'Quiet Roads', 'Millennium Greens', rights of way, and green tourism, including doubling the area of woodland in England and promoting products from land managed to benefit landscape, wildlife and recreation;

◆ the achievement of long-term benefits from farms and woodlands by finding a sound basis for the stewardship of land;

◆ sustainable development in the countryside, including experiments and advice on managing transport;

◆ better information about the countryside;

◆ protection and promotion of the areas of finest landscape – national parks, areas of outstanding natural beauty and heritage coasts;

◆ improvement of the countryside around towns including 'Community Forests' and 'Green Corridors into the Cities'.

For many years the Commission promoted many different types of grant in separate leaflets. It now runs a more flexible arrangement which follows the strategy outlined above but also allows for the differing regional character and needs of the countryside. Regional offices may have their own particular priorities within these, depending on the pressures and issues affecting the countryside in their area. Interested applicants should be in contact with their relevant office. National, regional and local voluntary organisations are all eligible for support. Each application is assessed by a Project Officer in the relevant office. Grants of between 20% and 50% may be offered. The level of grant is discretionary and only in exceptional circumstances will it exceed 50%.

If the project has secured funding from other Exchequer sources (i.e. from other government agencies or departments but not including local authorities) then the combined grant cannot exceed 50%. All other sources of funding or involvement in other schemes must be set out in the application.

A grant cannot be made retrospectively for work already undertaken.

Applications: Obtain a copy of 'Grants and Payment Schemes Booklet CCP 422'. Approaches can be made at any time of the year. How quickly applications and grants are processed depends upon the size and complexity of the application. In all cases, preliminary enquiries can be made to the Commission's regional offices at the addresses listed below.

Regional Offices

Northern: Warwick House, Grantham Road, Newcastle upon Tyne NE2 1QF Tel: 0191-232 8252; Fax: 01242-584270

North West: 7th Floor, Bridgewater House, Whitworth Street, Manchester M1 6LT Tel: 0161-237 1061; Fax: 0161-237 1062

Yorkshire and Humberside: 2nd Floor, Victoria Wharf, Embankment 1V, Sovereign Street, Leeds LS1 4BA Tel: 0113-246 9222; Fax: 0113-246 0353

Midlands: 1st Floor, Vincent House, Tindal Bridge, 92-93 Edward Street, Birmingham B1 2RA Tel: 0121-233 9399; Fax: 0121-233 9286

Eastern: Ortana House, 110 Hills Road, Cambridge CB2 1LQ Tel: 01223-354463; Fax: 01223-313850

South West: Bridge House, Sion Place, Clifton Down, Bristol BS8 4AS Tel; 0117-973 9966; Fax: 0117-923 8086

South East: 4th Floor, 71 Kingsway, London WC2B 6ST Tel: 0171-831 3510; Fax: 0171 -831 1439

The Countryside Council for Wales

Plas Penhros, Fford Penrhos, Bangor, Gwynedd LL57 2LQ
Tel: 01248-385500; Fax: 01248-385505; http://www.ccw.gov.uk
Contact: Ruth Taylor, Grants Team Leader based in Newtown (see below) Tel: 01686-613400
Grant-aid: about £3 million annually to 2000, to be apportioned approximately as follows:

   Access and enjoyment – £1 million
   Biodiversity – £900,000
   Understanding – £600,000
   Landscape – £500,000

The Countryside Council for Wales (CCW) is accountable to the Welsh Office which provides its annual grant in aid. As the national wildlife conservation authority and the government's statutory advisor on 'sustaining natural beauty, wildlife, and the opportunity for outdoor enjoyment in Wales and its inshore waters', grants are made towards programmes and projects meeting its objectives.

The council's booklet *Priorities for Grant Aid 1997–2000* highlights it four themes for grant-aid. The proportion of CCW grant-aid to be allocated is given in brackets.
- Landscape – to conserve the natural beauty and amenity of Wales (17%);
- Biodiversity – to conserve the quality and richness of wildlife and habitats (30%);

- Access and enjoyment – to provide, improve and sustain opportunities and facilities for public access to, and enjoyment of the countryside (33%);
- Understanding – to promote understanding of environmental issues (20%).

Obviously many programmes will integrate all these priorities into their operations: conserved woodland benefits both the landscape and wildlife habitats, encourages owners to allow greater public access and increases enjoyment and greater understanding of the countryside.

Levels of grant are discretionary but do not exceed 50% of the eligible costs of any one scheme. Grants cannot be offered in retrospect and payment will not be made where a project has started prior to the CCW issuing a formal offer of a grant and its acceptance by the applicant.

A selection of grants made to voluntary sector organisations in 1995/96 follows to illustrate the range (with the first five being the largest made in that year):
- BTCV – for management work in non-designated areas (£42,500);
- National Trust – for management work in designated areas (South – £38,559; North – £60,255);
- RSPB – for management work in designated areas (£30,262);
- North Wales Wildlife Trust – for partnership programme (£37,450);
- Council for the Protection of Rural Wales – for partnership programme (£27,250);
- Wales Young Farmers' Club, rural life project (£12,500);
- Association of Welsh Wildlife Trusts, otter project (£7,456);
- Mammal Society – for information project (£4,000);
- Shell Better Britain Campaign (£7,650);
- Field Studies Council – for training (£3,356);
- RSNC – for lowland grassland booklet (£1,200);
- Botanical Society of British Isles – for coordination of plant recording (£1,046);
- Marine Conservation Society – for advisory service (£896);
- Black Environmental Network, partnership programme (£416).

Applications: Applicants are encouraged to consult CCW officers at their nearest office (see list below) at an early stage in the formulation of their project. Whilst applications can be submitted at any time, it is better for them to be received as early as possible before the planned start of a project. Funding programmes are negotiated in the autumn and are expected to be submitted by the January before the start of the next financial year. Regional Offices:

Abergavenny – Tel: 01873-857938; Fax: 01873-854753

Aberyswyth – Tel: 01970-828551; Fax: 01970-828314

Bala – Tel: 01678-521226; Fax: 01678-520534

Bangor – Tel: 01248-373100; Fax: 01248-370734

Cardiff – Tel: 01222-772400; Fax: 01222-772412

Dolgellau – Tel: 01341-423750; Fax: 01341-423739

Fishguard – Tel: 01348-874602; Fax: 01348-873936

Newtown – Tel: 01686-626799; Fax: 01686-629556

Stackpole – Tel: 01646-661368; Fax: 01646-661368

Swansea – Tel: 01792-771949/895; Fax: 01792-771981

Llandeilo – Tel: 01558-822111; Fax: 01558-823467

Llandrindod Wells – Tel: 01597-824661; Fax: 01597-825734

Martin's Haven – Tel: 01646-636736; Fax: 01646-636744

Mold – Tel: 01352-754000; Fax: 01352-752346

The Darwin Initiative for the Survival of Species

Environment Protection International Division, Department of the Environment, Transport and the Regions, Room A504, Romney House, 43 Marsham Street, London SW1P 3PY

Tel: 0171-276 8157; Fax: 0171-276 8883;

E-mail: 101657.1740@compuserve.com

Contact: Maria Stevens, Darwin Initiative Secretariat

Grant total: £3 million (1997/98 also in 1998/99 subject to Parliamentary approval)

The Darwin Initiative was set up after the Rio Earth Summit in 1992 to assist 'countries rich in biodiversity but poor in resources'. The funding helps UK biodiversity institutions carry out research and/or training with a partner in a developing country, thereby helping them to meet their obligations under the Biodiversity Convention. Five principal areas of project work are targeted:

♦ institutional capacity building;

♦ training;

♦ research;

♦ work to implement the Biodiversity Convention of 1992;

♦ environmental education and awareness.

Each project is under the direction of a UK educational or scientific institution which includes many universities and other organisations. In 1996/97 a total of 32 projects were assisted (out of 175 applications). Most were in South East Asia, Africa and Central and South America. Examples of organisations that received support are:

♦ Botanic Gardens Conservation International, to set up institutional capacity for sustainable use of plant resources in Tam Dao National Park, Vietnam (£121,000);

♦ Durrell Institute of Conservation and Ecology, to devise plans to resolve the conflict between wildlife and people in Masai Mara, Kenya (£123,000);

♦ Earthwatch Europe, training on biodiversity projects for 45 students, Southern Africa (£120,000);

- Fauna and Flora International, production and implementation of management plans in protected areas of Andaman Islands, India (£146,000);
- Foundation for International Law and Development, to develop capacity to implement Biodiversity Convention by practical measures and policies, South Pacific (£110,000);
- WWF-UK for study on fiscal incentives for biodiversity conservations with recommendations to policy makers, Brazil (£67,000).

Although grants may be up to 100%, encouragement is given for matching funding. Grants are typically around £40,000 each year for three years.

Applications: Full details and application forms are available from the above address. Applications closed in late November 1997 for projects commencing in April 1998. The covering letter with application details in 1997 asked applicants to note: 'Ministers' commitment to the goal of poverty eradication and the need to highlight the contribution, if any, their project would make to the achievement of that objective in the developing country(s) concerned'.

The Energy Design Advice Scheme

This Department of Trade and Industry discretionary initiative aims to improve the energy and environmental performance of the building stock by making low energy building design expertise more accessible.

All eligible applications are offered an initial one day consultancy paid for by the scheme after which further expert consultancy may be offered (without obligation). A proportion of these further costs can sometimes be reimbursed.

Design advice is offered via regional centres (see below) with more planned to cope with demand. Requirements are a minimum planned area (500 square metres in Summer 1997) and evidence of intent to build.

Applications: Contact the Energy Design Advice Scheme at the following addresses (being sure to add the scheme's title):

c/o Royal Incorporation of Architects in Scotland, 15 Rutland Square, Edinburgh, EH1 2BE Tel: 0131-2284414; Fax: 0131-2282188

c/o Bartlett School of Graduate Studies, University College London, Gower Street, London, WC1E 6BT Tel: 0171-9163891; Fax: 0171-9163892

c/o Department of Building and Environmental Engineering, University of Ulster of Jordanstown, Newtownabbey, Northern Ireland, BT37 0QB Tel: 01232-364090; Fax: 01232-364090

c/o University of Sheffield, PO Box 595, Floor 13, The Arts Tower, Sheffield, S10 2UJ Tel: 01142-721140; Fax: 01142-720676

English Heritage

Fortress House, 23 Savile Row, London W1X 2HE
Tel: 0171-973 3000
Contact: Christine Wall, Public Relations Manager
Grant schemes: £40.8 million (1996/97). These figures contrast with £99.1 million in 1993/94.

Breakdown (£m) 1996/97
Buildings & Monuments 26%
Conservation areas 23%
Churches 26%
Cathedrals 10%
Archaeology 14%
Parks, gardens, landscapes 0.5%

English Heritage is the national body created by Parliament in 1984, and is charged with the protection of the country's historic environment and promoting public access to, and enjoyment and understanding of it. As the government's official adviser on all matters concerning heritage conservation, it also provides substantial funding for conservation areas, the repair of historic buildings, and archaeology in England, with funds provided by the Department of Culture, Media and Sport. English Heritage has three main capital programmes:

◆ building rescues
◆ conservation of historic properties
◆ development of historic properties.

Since 1992 it has been operating with greatly diminished funding from government.

Historic Buildings and Monuments Grants

These grants help with repairs to the most significant of England's historic sites and buildings. Applications are assessed against the architectural and historic importance of the property, the urgency and nature of the work, and the need for financial help. Domestic, agricultural or industrial structures and many archaeological sites are considered, as well as more grand and famous places. Normally only properties which are legally protected as scheduled monuments or as grade I and II listed buildings will qualify. It may also be eligible for support under the London grant scheme or if it lies within a Conservation Area Partnership (see below).

Grants are for major structural repairs to an agreed standard of materials and workmanship. Grants are occasionally offered for repairs to interior features including the conservation of objects, such as sculpture. Grants are not available for routine maintenance, alterations, conversions, improvement or demolition.

Grants are made to private owners including trusts and companies, local authorities, parochial church councils and other similar bodies.

The demand for grants exceeds the funds available and the former standardised levels of grant no longer apply. Each application is carefully assessed and the grant rate varies to suit particular circumstances. Recipients are expected to ensure an acceptable level of public access and that the public investment in the property is properly protected.

Management agreements can be offered to occupiers of monuments in farmland and these usually include small grants. The amount paid is based on the monument's acreage, but capital costs can also be met.

Conservation Area Partnership Grants

Grants are given to repair buildings and to help preserve or improve the character and appearance of some of the country's 8,000 or more designated conservation areas. These grants are available where there are agreed schemes or programmes of work with local authorities. Repair work to the structure or external appearance of a building in such an area may be eligible and can include re-roofing, repairs to stonework or brickwork, treatment of dry rot and repairs of windows and doors. In some areas grants are concentrated on encouraging the use of traditional local materials. Routine maintenance, alteration and conversion are not eligible.

Contact your local authority planning department to find out if a Conservation Area Partnership scheme is operating in your neighbourhood.

Joint Church Grants Scheme

This scheme, started in autumn 1995, is run jointly with the Heritage Lottery Fund to help with repair to historic religious buildings used for public worship by any denomination. Where a church has moral objections to receiving Lottery Funds a 'traditional' English Heritage Church grant may be possible.

The criteria for funding again rely on historic importance, urgency and financial need. Some improvements such as lighting, heating and toilets may be eligible in certain circumstances. Where funding is sought for other than structural works, some benefit to the wider public normally has to be shown. Repairs to bells and pipe organs have their own special assessment arrangements.

Survey Grants for Presentation Purposes

Grants are offered towards the cost of archaeological investigation and recording before the unavoidable destruction of important ancient monuments and sites.

Projects are selected for assistance within the framework of the criteria used to define a monument as being of national importance and thematic strategies discussed with the period societies and other specialist groups.

London Grants

A special scheme operates to cover historic structures in London concentrated on Grade II listed buildings at risk. Contact the relevant office (see below) for further information. This is one of the less 'stable' parts of English Heritage's funding support and changes may occur in its operation particularly in view of the fact that the agency has had to reorganise and retrench so much in the past few years (see grant-aid totals above).

Applications: English Heritage organises its work into three regions all based at Savile Row. Guidance notes and application forms are available from the relevant division (see below). There are no specific deadlines, proposals are reviewed throughout the year. The annual report and other leaflets are available from the Commission.

West Midlands and North Region

Tel: 0171-973 3020
West Midlands: Hereford & Worcester, Shropshire, Staffordshire, Warwickshire, West Midlands
North: Cleveland, Cumbria, Durham, Northumberland, Tyne & Wear
North West: Cheshire, Greater Manchester, Lancashire, Merseyside
Yorkshire and Humberside: Humberside, North Yorkshire, South Yorkshire, West Yorkshire.

East and South West Region

Tel: 0171-973 3018
East Midlands: Derbyshire, Leicestershire, Lincolnshire, Northamptonshire, Nottinghamshire
Anglia: Cambridgeshire, Essex, Norfolk, Suffolk
Thames and Chilterns: Bedfordshire, Berkshire, Buckinghamshire, Oxfordshire, Hertfordshire
South West: Avon, Cornwall, Devon, Dorset, Gloucestershire, Somerset, Wiltshire, Isles of Scilly.

London and South East Region

Tel: 0171-973 3711
South East: East Sussex, Hampshire, Isle of Wight, Kent, Surrey, West Sussex
North and East London: Barking and Dagenham, Barnet, Camden, Enfield, Hackney, Havering, Islington, Newham, Redbridge, Tower Hamlets, Waltham Forest
Central and West London: Brent, Ealing, Hammersmith and Fulham, Harrow, Hillingdon, Hounslow, City of London, Richmond upon Thames, City of Westminster
Kensington and South London: Kensington and Chelsea, Bexley, Bromley, Croydon, Greenwich, Kingston upon Thames, Lambeth, Lewisham, Merton, Southwark, Sutton, Wandsworth.

English Nature

Northminster House, Peterborough PE1 1UA

Tel: National office switchboard: 01733-455000; Enquiry Service: 01733-455101; Fax: 01733 568834

Enquiry Service: 01733-433101 (for national grants; approach relevant local teams for local grants)

Contacts: Sharon Gunn, Team Manager, Communication & Grants; Margaret Robinson, Grants Officer

Grant-aid:	1996/97	1997/98
	£1,839,000	£1,704,000
National schemes:	£1,259,000	£1,373,000
Local projects:	£580,000	£331,000

English Nature is the government funded body set up by the Environment Protection Act 1990 to promote the conservation of England's wildlife and natural features. 'Biodiversity and sustainability are at the heart of its work.' It advises government and other bodies, implements European and other international agreements, notifies outstanding areas as Sites of Special Scientific Interest (SSSIs) or, additionally, as National Nature Reserves (NNRs) and Marine Nature Reserve (MNRs). It works closely with public, private and charitable landowners and occupiers in various forms of cooperative and partnership arrangements for improved land management and wildlife enhancement. It also runs an extensive research programme and a popular public enquiry service.

It runs a grants programme consisting of a number of targeted national schemes and support at Local Team level for local projects and volunteer action. The programme reflects the organisation's nature conservation priorities:

◆ SSSIs
◆ Species recovery
◆ Biodiversity Action Plan habitats and species
◆ Sustainability
◆ Natural Areas
◆ Habitats and species directives
◆ Increasing public opportunities for wider public involvement.

The agency was not happy to give any more detailed information about its grants programmes or examples of recent beneficiaries for use in this guide lest it become outdated and misleading to applicants. 'Schemes are sometimes changed or even cancelled and the accuracy or information given months in advance cannot be guaranteed...funding levels are also subject to our annual grant-in-aid'.

All interested groups and individuals are advised to telephone the enquiry line (see above) for grants information, or contact their local EN office (see list below) to find out the current situation. Local offices have interests specific to their own areas. It is important for potential applicants to build up a working relationship with them. All groups whether rural, urban or urban fringe may be considered, but priorities will of course vary according to the needs and natural features of the different areas.

Exclusions: work in National Nature Reserves (with some exceptions), building works, projects outside England (except GB projects in cooperation with Scottish Natural Heritage and Countryside Council for Wales), compensation payments, expeditions and student projects (except those eligible for fieldwork projects by final year undergraduates, HND students and one-year postgraduates doing Masters degrees). Grants are not normally offered for ongoing office and administration costs, survey, research or data collection, books and periodicals.

Applications: Potential applicants are advised to contact the Enquiry Service or appropriate Local Team as early in the project planning stage as possible. They can then receive specific advice on relevant schemes, eligibility, availability of funds and required procedures.

Voluntary organisations, local authorities, other non-profit-making organisations and individuals are eligible to apply for the discretionary grants provided they are able to find at least 50% of the project costs from non-exchequer sources. Grants are normally paid in arrears on satisfactory completion of objectives and there is usually a requirement to submit project reports with claims.

Local Area Teams
Bedfordshire, Cambridgeshire and Northamptonshire
Peterborough Tel: 01733-391100; Fax: 01733-394093

Cumbria
Kendal Tel: 01539-792800; Fax 01539-792830

Devon
Okehampton Tel: 01837-55045; Fax: 01837-55046

Cornwall & Isles of Scilly
Truro Tel: 01872-262550; Fax: 01872-262551

Dorset
Wareham Tel: 01929-556688; Fax: 01929-554752

East Midlands – Lincolnshire, Leicestershire, Nottinghamshire
Grantham Tel: 014765-68431; Fax: 014765-70927

Essex, Hertfordshire and London
Colchester Tel: 01206-796666; Fax: 01206-794466

London
Tel: 0171-831 6922; fax: 0171-404 3369

Hampshire and the Isle of Wight
Lyndhurst Tel: 01703-283944; Fax: 01703-283834

Gloucestershire, Herefordshire and Worcestershire (listed as 'Three Counties')
Eastnor Tel: 01531-638500; Fax: 01531-638501

Humber to Pennines
Wakefield Tel: 01924-387010; Fax: 01924-201507

Kent
Wye Tel: 01233-81252; Fax: 01233-812520

Norfolk
Norwich Tel: 01603-620558; Fax: 01603-762552

North and East Yorkshire
York Tel: 01904-435500; Fax: 01904-435520
Leyburn Tel: 01969-623447; Fax: 01969-624190

North West
Wigan Tel: 01942-820342; Fax: 01942-820364

Northumbria
Newcastle upon Tyne Tel: 0191-281 6316; Fax: 0191-281 6305

Peak District and Derbyshire
Bakewell Tel: 01629-815095; Fax: 01629-815091

Somerset and Avon
Taunton Tel: 01823-283211; Fax: 01823-272978

Suffolk
Bury St Edmunds Tel: 01284-762218; Fax: 01284-764318

Surrey and Sussex
Lewes Tel: 01273-476595; Fax: 01273-483063

Thames and Chilterns
Crookham Common/Newbury Tel: 01635-268881; Fax: 01635-268940

West Midlands
Shrewsbury Tel: 01743-709611; Fax: 01743-709303
Banbury Tel: 01295-257601; Fax: 01295-275180

Wiltshire
Devizes Tel: 01380-726344; Fax: 01380-721411

English Partnerships – Investment Fund and Community Investment Fund

16-18 Old Queen Street, London SW1H 9HP
Tel: 0171-976 7070; Fax: 0171-976 7740
or 3 The Parks, Lodge Lane, Newton le Willows, Merseyside WA12 OJQ
Merseyside
Tel: 01942-296900; Fax: 01942-296927
Contact: Jon Rouse, Policy and Planning Manager; Harriet Price, Policy and Planning Officer
Total grant-aid to partnership initiatives: £157 million (1996/97)
Breakdown 1996/97:
Grants, contributions: £119.6 million
Derelict Land Grant payments to local authorities: £25 million
Other project payments: £11.5 million
Leeds Development Corporation: £1 million
(figures taken from Annual Report).

English Partnerships was set up in 1993 to regenerate derelict, vacant and under-used land and buildings throughout England. Its task is to work in partnership in every English region to transform areas of need into quality places for people to live and work.

It aims to achieve this by enabling the public, private and voluntary sectors to work together to promote, effect and deliver economic development, job creation and environmental improvement. In applying its investment and expertise, the Agency tries to obtain the best value for money for the tax payer by maximising the level of private sector investment and making the best use of our human and physical assets. Its activity is focused on the following areas:

- long-term area regeneration
- individual land reclamation projects
- job creating investment opportunities
- community development.

The Agency is funded through the Department of the Environment, Transport and the Regions and has a network of regional offices (see below) each headed by a Regional Director.

English Partnerships Investment Fund

This promotes a broad range of projects from large-scale, regionally planned schemes through to local initiatives. It has wide powers to:

- assist developers and others to carry out regeneration and to offer necessary financial assistance closely linked to the needs of individuals projects;
- promote and enter into joint ventures;
- carry out development on its own account.

All English Partnership projects must achieve one or more of the following outputs:

◆ create jobs;
◆ safeguard jobs;
◆ develop floorspace for industry, commerce, housing or leisure;
◆ make land (and infrastructure) available for employment space or housing;
◆ bring land back into use or make it safe for green/recreational purposes.

Areas of Operation

◆ European Objective 1 and 2 areas
◆ Coal field closure areas
◆ City Challenge and other inner city areas
◆ Other assisted areas
◆ Rural areas of severe economic need, chiefly European Objective 5b.
(See the entries for the European Regional Fund and Single Regeneration Budget for information about the location of the numbered Objective Areas.)

The above list is not exhaustive. The agency has the flexibility to respond to urgent needs outside these areas and structural shifts in local economies. Each regional office identifies its own priorities as part of the corporate planning process.

Operation of the Investment Fund

A broad range of support is available: help and advice; joint ventures; rental guarantees; loan guarantees; gap funding and other forms of partnership investment; direct development.

English Partnerships Community Development Work

The agency has a commitment to engage and work with local communities to achieve its objectives and has acted upon this by:

◆ appointing Community Development Managers in each region to build links with local communities and involve them in setting investment priorities;
◆ enabling local authorities to participate in the decision-making process in many of its major projects;
◆ establishing a Community Investment Fund that distributes funds to capital projects devised by community groups.

Community Investment Fund – about £3 million annually
The fund is designed to help local communities participate more effectively in local regeneration. It recognises that community groups find difficulty in accessing small amounts of capital funding to realise their goals with land or property regeneration projects.

The fund is for projects which are:

◆ put forward by voluntary groups based in and involving local communities;
◆ non-profit-making;
◆ involve capital works to provide or improve land and buildings;

- need a contribution from EP that will usually be below £100,000;
- contribute to EP's regeneration aims;
- produce social and economic benefits at community level;
- tie in with and contribute towards other local regeneration strategies;
- practicable and financially sustainable.

No revenue funding is available. All projects must adhere to the criteria set out in *The Community Investment Guide*. Appraisal, selection and monitoring of projects takes place at regional level. Projects should not be able to go ahead without EP support, and separate, clear benefits should be attributable to it. Applications are restricted to local, grass-roots, community/voluntary, non-profit distributing organisations. They need not necessarily be registered charities.

The Land Reclamation Programme may support small environmental improvement schemes. Funding is available for land improvement schemes which become public open space. Guidelines prepared for local authorities may be obtained. Groundwork Trusts have helped instigate as well as support several schemes assisted from this programme.

Applications: Obtain the full guides from your regional EP office (see list below) and then contact the Community Investment Officer for further advice and to discuss your proposal.

South East
58-60 St Katharine's Way, London E1 9LB Tel: 0171-680 2000;
Fax: 0171-680 2040

South West
North Quay House, Sutton Harbour, Plymouth PL4 0RA Tel: 01752-234821;
Fax: 01752-234840

Midlands
Osiers Office Park, Braunstone, Leicester LE3 2DX Tel: 0116-282 8400;
Fax: 0116-282-8440

Yorkshire & Humberside
Hall Cross House, 1 South Parade, Doncaster, South Yorkshire DN1 2DY
Tel: 01302-366865; Fax: 01302-366880

North West
Lancaster House, Mercury Court, Tithebarn Street, Liverpool L2 2QP
Tel: 0151-236 3663; Fax: 0151-236 3731

North East
St George's House, Kingsway, Team Valley, Gateshead, Tyne & Wear NE11 0NA
Tel: 0191-487 8941; Fax: 0191-487 5690

Corporate offices are based in London, Merseyside and Gateshead (see address above).

ENTRUST (re Landfill Tax Credit Scheme)

154 Buckingham Palace Road, London SW1 9TR
Tel: 0171-823 4574; Fax: 0171-824 8699
Contact: Dr Richard Sills, Chief Executive
Landfill Tax contributions: over £67.5 million to end February 1998, from September 1996, contrasting with £9 million in September 1997. The dramatic rise was caused by the end of the Landfill tax year (which runs from end September to beginning March).

In 1996 the first green tax, the Landfill Tax, was introduced on waste disposal in landfill sites in the UK with the expectation that the industry will reassess and reduce waste and its associated problems. HM Customs & Excise will collect the tax at variable rates (£2/tonne or £7/tonne) depending on the type of waste.

An ingenious additional notion means that up to 20% of landfill operators' tax liability may be diverted to environmental organisations. The idea is related to the need for companies to improve their environmental image and local relations. Companies get no direct cash benefit. Instead they are invited to support approved environmental organisations with the lure that for every £1 they donate, £9 will be released from their tax liability up to a maximum credit of 20% of their annual liability.

ENTRUST is not a supplier of funds. Funding can only be obtained from a landfill operator who should be approached directly by an environmental body. However, environmental organisations have to meet criteria laid down in the Landfill Tax Regulations and be approved by ENTRUST the 'Regulator of Environmental Bodies under the Landfill Regulations' which is set up as a separate company limited by guarantee.

Approved work under this scheme includes:
◆ land reclamation for economic, social or environmental use;
◆ measures for pollution reduction;
◆ research into sustainable waste management;
◆ education on waste issues;
◆ provision of amenity facilities in the vicinity of a landfill site;
◆ reclamation and creation of wildlife habitats;
◆ restoration of buildings of architectural and heritage interest in the vicinity of a landfill site;
◆ provision of financial, administrative and other services to environmental bodies. 'Vicinity' is being interpreted loosely, at about a 10 miles radius.

Once enrolled, environmental organisations which must be non-profit making bodies, can spend the contributions they receive from landfill site operators on approved activities, including their running costs and the fees payable to the regulatory body (£100 in 1997). It is again emphasised that environmental bodies have to find their own landfill operator.

By November 1997, 502 approved organisations had enrolled with, and 1,600 projects had been approved by ENTRUST. Examples of approved work included:

◆ RSNC from ARC to expand its coordinatory work throughout the country by setting up and running a grant scheme for environmental projects (£3.5 million);
◆ Environmental Council from Biffa Waste Services for 'Conservers at Work' – information programmes and events called Reduce, Reuse, Recycle in the Workplace, to encourage employees to take initiatives (£25,000).

ENTRUST provides a list of exemplary recipients, but without information of the size of the funding involved. Organisations which have received funding include:

◆ North West Environment Trust, for a landfill odour control study;
◆ Kentish Stour Countryside Project, for improving public rights of way;
◆ Global Balance Trust, for unused plant recycling;
◆ Cory Environment Trust, Thurrock, for improvements to Grays Town Wharf;
◆ The Wise Group Ltd, for environmental story telling challenge;
◆ Somerton Community Association for green play areas.

Applications: A detailed application form is available from the above address including a supplementary one asking for information about all the associated trading partnerships. Two information leaflets are available setting out the conditions. A northern office was being set up in Glasgow at the end of 1997.

Landfill Tax Help Desk, HM Customs & Excise, Dobson House, Regent Centre, Gosforth, Newcastle-upon-Tyne NE3 3PF Helpline: 0645-128484 (local call rate); Fax: 0145-129595

The Environment Agency

Rio House, Waterside Drive, Aztec West, Almondsbury, Bristol BS12 4UD
Tel: 01454-624400; Fax: 01454-624409; Website: www.environment-agency.gov.uk

The agency has statutory duties to protect and enhance the environment of England and Wales. Its specific responsibilities include conservation and recreation as well as pollution prevention and control, water resources, flood defence, fisheries and navigation. It was established by the Environment Act 1995 and brings together the work of the National Rivers Authority, the Pollution Inspectorate, the waste regulation authorities, and some parts of the former Department of the Environment. About 30% of its total income of £570 million is in government grant and the remaining 70% is raised though charging schemes and levies.

Its corporate plan for 1997/98 refers to Local Environment Agency Plans (LEAPS) to reflect its closer contact with industry, the public and local government. 'Involvement of local communities and in particular local authorities will be important in establishing partnerships and ownership of the plans by local people.'

The agency is not a grant-making body but collaborates with others, including the voluntary sector, in environmental projects. These areas include:

◆ R & D projects where external funding adds around £5 million to the value of its internal programme;

◆ Recreation and Conservation projects – although internal funding is very constrained the agency helps local communities by its involvement in many small schemes where it is only one amongst many providers of funds and expertise.

Schemes with voluntary partners include:

◆ Redgrave and Lopham Fen, a water resources low flow project, in partnership with English Nature, Essex and Suffolk Water Company and the Suffolk Wildlife Trust, which also involved European LIFE funds (see separate entry);

◆ Merseyside Basin Campaign's funding alliance with the Agency and North West Water which are providing £90,000 a year to set up more local River Valley Initiatives (seven had been established by Autumn 1997).

The agency has a head office in Bristol, a base in London and operates through eight regions (each with a Regional General Manager) and 26 Areas across England and Wales.

Environment Wales

c/o The Prince's Trust-Bro, 4th Floor, Empire House, Mount Stuart Square, Cardiff CF1 6DN
Tel: 01222-471121
Contact: Sian Phipps, Coordinating Development Officer
Total funding from Welsh Office: £618,000 (1997/98)
Grant aid: £368,000 (1997/98)

Environment Wales (EW) is a 'Welsh Office initiative supporting voluntary action which contributes to sustainable development by helping to protect and improve the environment of Wales'.

Members of its development team work within each of the eight core partner offices: The Prince's Trust-Bro; BTCV (Wales); Groundwork (Wales); CSV in Wales; Keep Wales Tidy Campaign; the Wildlife Trust (Wales); the RSPB and the National Trust in Wales. In 1995/96 about 57% of the funding was given to core partners and the remainder to other voluntary organisations. The fund's aim is a 50:50 split.

A registration scheme is in operation which, along with other benefits such as information mailings, is a prerequisite for application to the following grant funds:

- Management Grant Fund towards the cost of project staff – £190,473 in 28 awards (1996/97);
- Project Grant fund towards the costs of project materials – £189,604 in 60 awards (1996/97);
- Training Support Grant for staff and volunteers attending training courses, etc – £6,159 in 38 awards (1996/97).

Additional grant support is given for which pre-registration is not a requirement:

- Pre-Project Grants – £21,099 in 8 awards;
- Start-Up Grants – £6,750 in 7 awards.

In 1996/97 examples of single project rather than core grants included:

- Newport Wastesavers, for a Recycling Coordinator (£13,600);
- Forest of Cardiff, for the Llandough Community Woodland (£6,200);
- Prince's Trust Volunteers, for the Scoulton Country Park Access project in Pembrokeshire (£6,500);
- Shared Earth Trust, for Denmark Farm in Ceredigion (£5,950);
- Tools for Self Reliance, for Crickhowell Tools Workshop in Powys (£3,150).

Grants generally range according to the part of the programme. Management funding may be agreed for up to six years in which case level funding is given for three years followed by three years in which the grant tapers off. Renewal bids are needed every year nevertheless.

Applications: A detailed Information Pack is available including detailed criteria and general conditions of grant offers. Applicants are encouraged to contact the Cardiff office and discuss their ideas at an early stage. However, applicants should also 'accept that the award of registered status is not a guarantee that funding will be available'. Management grants for project staff are invited in August with a deadline of the first week in November for grants starting in the following April.

If funds are being given by another organisation funded by the Welsh Office (Countryside Council for Wales, Welsh Development Agency, Wales Tourist Board, Development Board for Wales, Prince's Trust-Bro, WCVA's 'Volunteering in Wales' for example), funds from EW and the other funder should not exceed 50%. However up to 75% of eligible costs can be given when Environment Wales is the only grant-maker funded by the Welsh Office.

All grants must be spent in the financial year in which they are made and any underspend will be returned to the Welsh Office and lost to the voluntary sector.

The Grants Committee meets monthly on average. Applications can be made at any time but ones earlier in the financial year (starting April) are more likely to be successful. Funds are often completely allocated by December.

The Environmental Action Fund

Environmental & Energy Awareness Division, Department of the Environment, Transport and the Regions 7/F8 Ashdown House, 123 Victoria Street, London SW1E 6DE
Tel: 0171-890 6693/6654; Fax: 0171-890 6659
Contact: Andy Kirby, Environmental Action Manager
Grant total: around £4 million annually; £3.4 million in nearly 100 grants (1997/98)

The Environmental Action Fund helps voluntary groups in England to advance the government's environmental policies. Ministers set priority areas annually and grants are for up to three years, subject to annual review. In announcing the 1998/99 fund the Environment Minister said, 'since education is at the heart of our agenda, sustainable development education projects will be the top priority'. A later announcement by the Deputy Prime Minister in mid September strengthened this. £500,000 of the EAF for 1998/99 will be reserved for sustainable development educational projects and an expert panel chaired by Sir Geoffrey Holland will 'drive initiatives forward.... The amount of funding available from EAF for non-education projects will not decrease'.

This guide was published before the results of a special review of the EAF in 1998 were available. Consultation with a range of interests took place from early February with decisions taken from April 1998. These changes could not be incorporated.

Priority Areas for 1998/99

◆ Education of the general public, or specific groups within it, about the importance of sustainable development, and the promotion of sustainable behaviour;
◆ Encouragement of waste minimisation, recycling, reuse of materials and efficient energy use;
◆ Improvement of local environments and promotion of biodiversity.

A group may submit one core application and up to three project applications which must be listed in order of priority.

Core Funding – 1997/98

New core grant: £223,000 to 8 organisations
Renewed core grant: £1,750,000 to 26 organisations

This funding, administered by the DETR, supports 'those unavoidable costs of national and regional organisations which help them fulfil their overall objectives, i.e. salary and running costs essential to their continued existence'. 'Regional' is defined as covering most of a Government Office Region. The minimum grant is £10,000 with no pre-set upper limit. Local groups are not eligible for this support.

Organisations which received new core grant in 1997/98 included:
◆ Cycling Project for the North West (£15,000, 1st of 3);
◆ Tree Council (£60,000, 1st of 3);
◆ Black Environment Network (£20,000, 1st of 3);
◆ UNED-UK (£30,000, 1st of 2);
◆ Atmospheric Research and Information Centre (£28,000);
◆ Advisory Committee on the Protection of the Sea (£20,000).

Organisations which received renewed core grant in 1997/98 included:
◆ BTCV, strategic (£398,775, 2nd of 3);
◆ RSNC-Wildlife Trusts (£293,775, 2nd of 3);
◆ Farming & Wildlife Advisory Group (£215,000, 2nd of 3);
◆ Waste Watch (£99,259, 2nd of 3);
◆ Community Service Volunteers, strategic (£68,000, 2nd of 3);
◆ Forum for the Future (£50,000, 2nd of 3);
◆ Learning through Landscapes (£43,000, 2nd of 3);
◆ Environment Council (£25,800, 2nd of 3);
◆ Climate Action UK Network (£24,374, 2nd of 3);
◆ Green Alliance (£20,800, 2nd of 3);
◆ Sea Watch Foundation (£18,000, 2nd of 3);
◆ Open Spaces Society (£10,750, 2nd of 3);
◆ North East Sheffield Conservation Group (£7,514, 3rd of 3).

EAF Project Funding – £1.7 million (1997/98)

Contact: Andy Kirby, Environmental Action Manager

Project funding supports specific activities with defined, measurable outcomes and clear timescales, which clearly achieve a government objective. Grants range from £10,000 to £75,000 a year for up to three years. Applications should fall within at least one of the priority areas listed under Core Funding above.

In 1996/97, 14 organisations were awarded new project grants totalling £318,000 and ranging from over £74,000 to £13,000. They included:
◆ Soil Association (£74,000, 1st of 3);
◆ Forum of the Future (£34,673, 1st of 2);
◆ National Energy Action (£27,000, 1st of 2);
◆ Sheffield Wildlife Trust (£21,000, 1st of 3);
◆ Arid Lands Initiative (£20,000, 1st of 2);
◆ Silvanus Trust (£16,000, 1st of 3);
◆ Centre for Sustainable Energy (£14,000, 1st of 2);
◆ Pedestrians' Association (£14,000, 1st of 3).

In 1996/97 a total of 51 organisations were supported to renew their projects with grants totalling £1,161,000 and ranging from £75,000 to £10,000. These included:

- Nature's World at Botanic Centre (£75,000, 3rd of 3);
- Sustrans, Safe Routes to Schools (£39,000, 3rd of 3);
- Global Action Plan, volunteer programme (£23,325, 2nd of 3);
- Black Environment Network, youth project (£21,166, 2nd of 3);
- Youth Clubs UK, green themes (£17,000, 3rd of 3);
- Henry Doubleday Research Association, go organic (£17,897, 2nd of 3);
- Consumers in Europe Group, Small Changes (£15,679, 2nd of 3);
- Transport 2000 partnership programme (£12,058, 2nd of 3);
- New Economics Foundation, community indicators (£10,000, 2nd of 2);
- Combined Heat and Power Association, tenant energy advice (£9,504, 2nd of 2).

BTCV had four ongoing projects and CSV, five.

Project Funding is administered by the Civic Trust for the DETR (see also the separate entry for the Local Projects Fund for smaller grants from £500 to £10,000 for specific projects also funded by the DETR).

Exclusions: These provisos apply to both core and project funding. Projects are not eligible for support if they are funded by: Countryside Commission; English Nature; Groundwork; Rural Action; Rural Development Commission; Tidy Britain Group; Single Regeneration Budget; English Partnerships; local authorities or any other source directly or indirectly funded by the DETR or any other government department. They can be in receipt of government support through the Environmental Task Force and funding from the National Lottery which is not counted as public sector support in this instance. Grants cannot be awarded retrospectively or used for activities outside England, for party politics or for the purchase of land or buildings.

Applications: This information applies to both core and project funding. Full details, forms, guidance, conditions and assessment criteria are obtainable from the department. They are also available on the Internet during the application period. The annual time-table is as follows: call for applications – July; closing date – September; shortlisting and assessment visits – November; notification to applicants – February. Successful projects can begin from April.

Total public support, including EAF grant-aid, should amount to no more than half of total costs. Benefits in kind, such as goods or services received, can make up to half the total value of matching support.

Successful applicants must have a 'Green Housekeeping' policy statement.

Two free publications are available to help support projects: a newsletter, *Activate* and *A Guide to Good Practice in Managing Environmental Projects*, a resource for local groups.

The Environmental Know How Fund

Department of Environment, Transport and the Regions, Environmental
Protection Group, Central & Eastern Europe Branch, Romney House,
43 Marsham Street, London SW1P 3PY
Tel: See below
Contact: Jaime Reynolds, Head of EKHF (but see below)
Grant-aid: £2 million annually to 1997/98

The Environmental Know How Fund (EKHF), which started in 1992, is a dedicated
tranche of the Know How Fund. It makes available British experience and expertise
to the countries of Central and Eastern Europe, including the newly independent
states, to help them tackle the need for environmental protection. EKHF is funded
by the Department of the Environment, Transport and the Regions, and is managed
by DETR and the Department for International Development. EKHF projects are
designed to support the international strategy on environmental aid to Central and
Eastern Europe, the Environmental Action Programme, endorsed by European
Environment Ministers.

Whilst there are no country-specific strategies, priority sectors are:
- Central Europe including Baltic States and the Balkans: EU approximation,
  capacity building in environment ministries and NGOs, protected area
  management, public awareness;
- Eastern Europe, Transcaucasia and Central Asia: protected area management,
  water quality, air quality, public awareness.

By 1995/96 over £7 million from the EKHF had been committed to support over
200 projects. Assisted projects relevant to this guide have included:
- University of Cambridge, regional land-use planning summer schools held
  annually (£50,000 p.a.);
- Open University, for distance learning methods and materials for use in City
  University, Bratislava, Slovakia (£190,000);
- Welsh Development Agency and Oxford Brookes University, to develop strategy
  for sustainable development in Vilcea County, Romania (£50,000);
- Walt Patterson, Royal Institute for International Affairs, for energy study of
  Romania and publication with Earthscan (£80,000);
- Field Studies Council, to develop a management strategy with the National
  Environmental Education Centre, Warsaw (£176,000 over 3 years between 1993/
  96);
- Lancashire Wildlife Trust for work with the Upper Tisza Foundation in Hungary
  (£7,100 between 1992/95);
- TVE/WWF-UK, for environmental education and public awareness in Hungary
  (£29,750 in 1994/95);

- Conservation Foundation, environmental law summer school in Georgia, Russia (£3,150 in 1996);
- Living Earth, environmental education/NGO strengthening (£25,000 in 1996);
- National Trust for environment exchange with Russia (£17,700 in 1996).

Exclusions: Disaster relief.

Applications: EKHF projects are developed in one of three ways: by in-country applications to the British Embassy Know How Section; through applications to the EKHF in London, or through 'scoping' visits by EKHF staff to Central and Eastern Europe.

There is no application form as such, and no deadline for applications.

Be sure to get the most up-to-date information from the departments. This book was being edited at a time of considerable departmental change after the 1997 White Paper on International Development. The relevant units of both departments are likely to have different addresses and/or telephone numbers. It is possible the Environmental Know How Fund could get subsumed within the general Know How Fund.

Enquiries
For Department of Environment, Transport and the Regions: Environmental Protection Group, Central & Eastern Europe Branch, Romney House, 43 Marsham Street, London SW1P 3PY (could move to Ashdown House in 1998) Will Morlidge, Executive Officer Tel: 0171-276 8195

For Department of International Development: The Know How Fund, 24 Whitehall, London SW1A 2AF (address could change)

In 1997 all telephone numbers started with 0171-210, follow with the four digits as appropriate:
Central Europe and Baltic States:
Albania – 0004; Baltic States – 6003; Bulgaria – 0020; Czech republic – 0006; Hungary – 0007; FYR of Macedonia – 0012; Bosnia Herzegovina – 0001; Croatia – 0003; FR of Yugoslavia – 0003; Poland – 0005; Romania – 0008; Slovakia – 0006; Slovenia – 0003
Russia – 0028/0041
Eastern Europe, Transcaucasia and Central Asia:
Armenia, Azerbaijan, Georgia, Kazakhstan, Kyrgyzstan, Tajikistan, Turkmenistan, Uzbekistan – 0065; Belarus, Moldavia, Ukraine – 0029.

Fax for Central Europe: 0171-210 0010;
Fax for Russia, Transcausasia and Central Asia: 0171-210 0030/0107.

The Environmental Protection Research Programme

Sustainable Development Unit, Environmental Protection Group, Department of the Environment, Transport and the Regions, Room A130, Romney House, London SW1P 3PY
Tel: 0171- 890 3000 (general); 0171-8409 (direct)
Contact: Ken Nully
Grant total: £28.877 million (1997/98)

Of the above grant total, £8.37 million is for new work. Increased emphasis is being given to research which supports the requirements of the Environment Act 1995 for producing and reviewing a National Air Quality Strategy. Support is directed at work in universities and research institutes.

Forest Service, Department of Agriculture, Northern Ireland (DANI)

Dundonald House, Upper Newtownards Road, Belfast BTA 3SB
Tel: 01232-520100; Fax: 01232-524570
Contact: Brian O'Hara
Grant total for private planting: £907,000 (1995/96)

To encourage the establishment of woodland, the Northern Ireland Department of Agriculture offers two national grant schemes, both administered by the Forest Service and part funded by the European Community. In 1995/96 a total of 224 new establishment grants were paid.

Woodland Grant Scheme (WGS) – three types of grant

i) **Establishment Grants** to create woodland and restock existing woodland after felling or windblow, by planting or natural regeneration.
Enclosed land supplement for new planting on land previously enclosed and improved for agricultural purposes.

Natural regeneration, a discretionary payment on completion of approved work to encourage natural regeneration.

Community woodland supplement, for those planting new woodlands close to towns and cities which can be used for informal public recreation.

ii) **Annual Management Grants** help towards the cost of management work in special woodlands of high environmental potential. At least one of three criteria must be met: safeguarding or enhancing the existing special environmental value; bringing the site up to minimum Forest Service environmental standards; maintaining or creating public access to woodlands.

iii) Special Grants

Livestock exclusion – an annual premium in Disadvantaged Areas to farmers to promote natural regeneration of woods by positive management.

Woodland Improvement grant – a discretionary payment towards work in existing woodlands needing one-off remedial measures.

Farm Woodland Premium Scheme (FWPS)

This encourages the establishment of new woodland to enhance the environment and as a productive alternative land use. Applicants must first be accepted under the Woodland Grant Scheme.

Applications: Full details are given in an information booklet accompanying the application forms obtainable from the District Forest Offices and County Agriculture Offices.

Forest Service:
Antrim District – Balymena Tel: 01266-662888; Fax: 01266-662877
Down/Armagh District – Castlewellan Tel: 013967-71144; Fax: 013967-71762
Fermanagh District – Enniskillen Tel: 01365-325004; Fax: 01365-324753
Londonderry District – Limavady Tel: 015047-62547; Fax: 01504-68075
Tyrone District – Omagh Tel: 01662-251020; Fax: 01662-253440

County Agricultural Offices:
Armagh – Tel: 01861-524979
Ballymena – Tel: 01266-662800
Coleraine – Tel: 01265-41000
Downpatrick – Tel: 01396-618249
Enniskillen – Tel: 01365-325004
Omagh – Tel: 01662-251020

The Forestry Authority

231 Corstorphine Road, Edinburgh EH12 7AT
Tel: 0131-334 0303; Fax: 0131-316 4891; Website: www.forestry.gov.uk
Contact: Gordon Inglis, Grants and Licences Division
Grants to private woodland owners: £33 million (1996/97);
budgeted: £42 million (1997/98); £43 million (1998/99)

The Forestry Authority is part of the Forestry Commission, the government department responsible for forestry in Britain. Its other components are Forestry Enterprise and Forestry Research. The work of the Authority entails the setting of standards for the whole of the forestry industry, both private and public, including Forestry Enterprise. It is also responsible for ensuring compliance with the regulations for plant health and tree felling and the administration of grant schemes to help private landowners.

Woodland Grant Scheme (WGS)

The aims of this scheme are:
- to encourage people to create new woodlands and forest to increase the production of wood, to improve the landscape, to provide new habitats for wildlife and to offer opportunities for recreation and sport;
- to encourage good management of forests and woodlands, including their well-timed regeneration, particularly looking after the needs of ancient and semi-natural woodlands;
- to provide jobs and improve the economy of rural areas and other areas with few other sources of economic activity;
- to provide a use for land instead of agriculture.

All woodlands and forests can be considered for grants under the WGS, except those which are too small or too narrow. Normally the woodland must be a quarter of a hectare in area and at least 15 metres wide, but smaller woods may be eligible if the aims of the scheme are met.

Grants for New Woodlands

Planting Grants encouraging the creation of new woodland are paid as part of a contract in which the applicant agrees to look after the woodlands and do the approved work to reasonable satisfaction. Rates of grants:
- Conifers – £700 per hectare;
- Broadleaves and Native Scots Pine – £1,350 per hectare for woods up to 10 hectares; £1,050 per hectare for woods greater than 10 hectares.

Grants are paid in two instalments: – 70% after planting and 30% five years later. At least 2,250 trees per hectare must be planted to receive the full grant, except for an amenity woodland, a new native woodland or a poplar wood.

Supplements are paid in addition to planting grants to encourage planting in priority areas.
- Better Land Supplement for the planting on arable or improved grassland – £600 per hectare.
- Community Woodland Supplement where access is given to local people – £950 per hectare.
- Locational Supplement for new planting in specific areas over a limited period of time – £600 per hectare. Check for details with your local office.

Short Rotation Coppice for poplars and willows. Such planting may receive £600 per hectare on non set-aside land or £400 per hectare on set-aside land.

Farm Woodland Premium Scheme (FWPS) encourages the creation of new woodlands for certain types of farm land to enhance the environment and as a productive alternative land use. The Forestry Authority is responsible for administering the scheme (though payments are made from the Agriculture Departments).
A 1995 EU regulation allows farmers to count arable land entered into the WGS and the FWPS towards their set-aside obligations.

Four Challenge Funds have been launched to encourage the planting of new woodlands in specific areas of the country:

◆ Bracken land in Wales;
◆ Native Woodlands in National Parks (England and Wales);
◆ The Grampian Forest (North East Scotland);
◆ The Deeside Forest and the Forest of Spey (Cairngorms in Scotland).

These projects will run for three years. Each year, applicants are asked to 'bid' for the amount of money they require to carry out the planting. The bids are judged on a competitive basis.

Grants for Existing Woodlands

Restocking Grants towards the cost of replanting an existing wood – £325 per hectare for conifers and £525 per year for broadleaves.

Natural Regeneration Grants may be made as an alternative to planting. A Discretionary Payment, covering half the cost of the work, assists work to encourage natural regeneration. When adequate stocking is achieved, a Fixed Payment will be paid – £325 per hectare for conifers and £525 per hectare for broadleaves.

Annual Management Grants towards the cost of work to safeguard or enhance the special environmental value of a wood, improve woods which are below current environmental standards, or create, maintain or enhance public access – £35 per hectare per year.

Woodland Improvement Grants assist projects which provide public recreation in woodlands, to improve undermanaged woods, and enhance woodland biodiversity – 50% of the cost of the work with more in some areas where it is possible to bid for a 'challenge fund'. Check with your local office for details.

Livestock Exclusion Annual Premium is paid if agricultural stock are removed from and kept out of ancient woodlands in the uplands – £80 per hectare.

The rates for the schemes above were current during Autumn 1997.

Applications: Detailed guidance and application forms are given in the pack available from the above address or from the Woodlands Officer in your local Forestry Authority Office. Check your telephone directory or ring the following national offices for the contact you need in the conservancies in your country:

Scotland, Edinburgh office
For contacts in its 6 conservancies: Tel: 0131-334 0303; Fax: 0131-314 6152;

England, Cambridge office
for contacts in its 7 conservancies: Tel: 01223-314546; Fax: 01223-460699;

Wales, Aberystwyth office
For contacts in its 3 conservancies: Tel: 01970-625866; Fax: 01970-626177.

(For Northern Ireland see entry under Department of Agriculture, Northern Ireland -DANI)

Forward Scotland

c/o Scottish Power, St Vincent Crescent, Glasgow G3 8LT
Tel: 0141-567 4334; Fax: 0141-567 4339; E-mail: forward.scotland@virgin.net

Forward Scotland (FS), formerly UK 2000 Scotland, is a charitable company funded annually by the Scottish Office Agriculture, Environment and Fisheries Department from which it received £500,000 in 1997/98. It is committed to putting the concept of sustainable development into practice throughout Scotland and works with communities, voluntary organisations and others.

It works in partnership with the public, private and voluntary sectors. FS has changed the emphasis of its programmes from those which concentrate solely on the environment towards programmes which also address social and economic concerns. 'The range of actions undertaken... will follow closely the areas set out in LA 21 and the UK Strategy for Sustainable Development'.

Partnership Fund

Grant total: £260,000 budgeted (1997/98)
Contact: Andrew Lyon, Development Manager
With this fund FS plays a financial, advisory and partnership role in larger scale sustainable development projects and initiatives. It works proactively and monitors the achievements. Recent partnerships include:

- Sustainable Communities, for partnership community programmes with Stirling, Edinburgh, Glasgow and Renfrewshire Councils (£56,000);
- Scottish Wildlife Trust, towards 37 teams working on environmental issues, biodiversity training and community based initiatives at 18 different locations (£35,000);
- East of Scotland Waste Minimisation Project, a programme bringing together East of Scotland Water, British Oxygen Company Foundation, ScottishPower, Scottish Environmental Protection Agency, and the Environmental Technology Best Practice Programme (£15,000);
- Scottish Conservation Projects Trust, for 5 programmes of work: Glasgow Community Projects providing training and employment on environmental projects in areas of need; Dundee Waste and Environment Trust which was established to disburse landfill tax credits; Highland Environmental Network;
- Conservation Local Area Networks (CLAN) who assist small voluntary groups taking environmental action; Action Recycle, doorstep recycling service in central Scotland (£35,000).

Small Project Grant Fund

Grant total: £40,000 budgeted (1997/98)
Contacts: Alison Quinn and David Airlie
This fund gives support, advice and grants to community led projects. Most grants are around £500 with £1,000 being given in exceptional cases. An organisation

must be able to comply with FS's sustainability check-list and have the necessary permissions and community support.

Recent grants have included:
- Scottish Pensioner Power Welfare Services (£1,000);
- Dighty Environmental Group and North Arran Community Growers (£500 each).

Applications: Contact the address above for the introductory leaflet and contact form – 'Small Grants Big Ideas'.

The Heritage Grant Fund

Heritage 4, Department of Culture, Media and Sport, 3rd Floor, 2-4 Cockspur Street, London SW1Y 5DH
Fax: 0171-211 6382
Contact: Linda Godfrey, 0171 211-6368; Tania Field, 0171 211-6367
Grant total: £546,000 (1996/97 and 1997/98)

The Heritage Grant Fund (HGF) of the Department of Culture, Media and Sport assists voluntary organisations in England whose activities further its own policy objectives for the historic environment. This includes both buildings and their gardens. Normally, only organisations providing national coverage are considered for grant although 'local projects providing an exemplar of good practice with potential for wider application' are also considered.

The HGF is not available to support activities covered by other DNH funding, including grants for capital projects such as repairs to historic buildings and monuments from English Heritage, and the museums and galleries funding available from the Museum and Galleries Commission and the Museums and Galleries Improvement Fund.

The two main types of grant given are:
- project grants for innovatory or experimental projects
- management grants to help meet the administrative or start up costs.

Grants for 1998/99 were offered on a one-year basis, with those for future years dependent on the Department's Spending Review. The priorities for funding in 1998/99 will be for projects:
- identifying and recording neglected aspects of the historic environment;
- promoting high standards in conservation practice;
- promoting understanding and enjoyment of the historic environment and widening access for all.

Grants have ranged between £2,000 and £60,000. They are intended to provide support towards revenue costs. Grants are normally limited to 50% of costs, but may be tapered to reduce the percentage of the costs met by grant in later years. Awards for 1997/98 included:

- Civic Trust, for a programme of free public access to heritage properties over a weekend in September 1997 (£60,000);
- Architectural Heritage Fund, towards the work of a development officer to help building development trusts (£30,000);
- Association of Small Towns and Villages, to help set up a network of local societies to share information about historic buildings (£10,000).

Applications: Application forms and full grant guidelines are available. Closing date for applications was the end of October 1997, for support in 1998/99. Approach the contacts noted above for more detailed advice.

Highlands and Islands Enterprise Network

Head Office: Bridge House, 27 Bank Street, Inverness IV1 1QR
Tel: 01463-234171; Fax: 01463-244469
Contact: Dr John Watt

This is the enterprise network with a broad economic, social, training and environmental remit for the north of Scotland. Highlands and Islands (HIE) at its centre helps oversee and resource as necessary the ten Local Enterprise Companies (LECs), each of which has a board of directors drawn from local businesses and the local community. HIE's central office helps with technical and financial back-up for projects which cross LEC boundaries, are of strategic benefit to the region as a whole, or are beyond a particular LEC's individual resources.

Priority is given to distributing funds to remote areas with long-term problems of population decline, lack of employment opportunities, and poor infrastructure, and to areas with low employment prospects.

Expenditure on operations	£65,951,000	(1996/97)
Enterprise	£50,447,000	
Environmental Renewal	£3,708,000	
Skill-seekers	£6,202,000	
Training for work	£4,299,000	
Community Action Grants	£1,295,000	

Although primarily concerned with business start-up and support they can also help voluntary organisations though the Community Action Grant and associated programmes. The strategic priorities for social and community development are:

- greater integration of social, community and cultural development with economic development;
- development and testing of innovative projects;

- development of the arts and Gaelic language and culture as a means of raising self-confidence and stimulating economic and social development;
- improvements in community social and economic life. The creation or improvement of physical facilities and environments, the stimulation of cultural activities and the encouragement of voluntary effort – especially at the local level.

Network members:

Argyll & the Islands Enterprise
Lochgilphead Tel: 01546-602281; Fax: 01546-603964

Caithness & Sutherland Enterprise
Thurso Tel: 01847-896115; Fax: 01847-893383

Inverness & Nairn Enterprise
Inverness Tel: 01463-713504; Fax: 01463-712002

Lochaber Limited
Lochaber Tel: 01397-704326; Fax: 01397-705309

Moray, Badenoch & Strathspey Enterprise
Elgin Tel: 01343-550567; Fax: 01343-550678

Orkney Enterprise
Kirkwall Tel: 01856-874638; Fax: 01856-872915

Ross & Cromarty Enterprise
Invergordon Tel: 01349-853666; Fax: 01349-853833

Shetland Enterprise
Lerwick Tel: 01595-693177; Fax: 01595-693208

Skye and Lochalsh Enterprise
Portree Tel: 01478-612841; Fax: 01478-612164

Western Isles Enterprise
Stornoway Tel: 01851-703703; Fax: 01851-705130

Historic Scotland

Longmore House, Salisbury Place, Edinburgh EH9 1SH
Tel: 0131-668 8600
Contact: See below

Grant totals:	1996/97	1997/98	
Historic building repair	£11,591,000	£12,300,000	
Ancient monuments	£249,000	£215,000	
Rescue archaeology	£1,600,000	£1,600,000	(30% in grants, remainder contracts)

Historic Scotland aims to protect, present and promote Scotland's built heritage which includes ancient monuments and archaeological sites, historic buildings, parks and gardens, and designed landscapes. It was made an executive agency by the Secretary of State for Scotland in 1991.

Historic Buildings

Contact: Edward Tait, Grants Manager
Tel: 0131-668 8600; Fax: 0131-668 8788
Grant Enquiry Section: 0131-668 8797

Grants are made available for the repair of buildings of outstanding architectural and historic importance and buildings in outstanding conservation areas. Buildings in the most urgent need of repair are given priority. Only buildings in categories A and B and buildings of prominence within outstanding conservation areas are considered eligible for grants. Modest buildings within Town Schemes established within outstanding conservation areas (partnerships with local authorities) may also receive assistance with repairs.

The demand for grants regularly exceeds the provision and there can be a delay before monies are made available.

The need for a grant has to be demonstrated. Private owners normally receive up to 33% of eligible costs; trusts up to 40% and churches in use up to 60%.

There are no maximum or minimum grants sizes or inadmissible sources of matching funding. Partnership funding can include contributions from the European Regional Development Fund (ERDF), and the Heritage Lottery Fund, as well as schemes jointly funded by other government agencies, such as LECs, Scottish Homes or local authorities.

Recent examples of grants/partnerships include:
- Holmwood House, Glasgow – National Trust for Scotland (£447,000);
- Argyll Motor Works, West Dumbarton – private sector (£400,000);
- Alexander Scott's Hospital, Huntly – private trust (£78,000).

Applications: Two booklets provide guidance: 'Guide to Grant Applicants' and 'Notes for Professional Advisers'. Awards are only made to the owner of the property. Conditions include a measure of public access, as appropriate, and a requirement to notify of disposal within 10 years of the award. Claims are accepted quarterly, in arrears, as work proceeds.

Regional Offices
North – Inverness Tel: 01667-462777
Central – Stirling Tel: 01786-450000
South – Edinburgh, see above.

Ancient Monument Grants

Contact: A J Tasker
Tel: 0131-668 8775; Fax: 0131-668 8765

Applications are dealt with on a priority system according to the historical, archaeological and architectural importance of the monument and the feasibility of the proposed works. Whilst monuments do not necessarily have to be scheduled, in practice grants are only awarded to scheduled monuments or those of schedulable quality. Inhabited buildings and buildings in ecclesiastical use (including buildings undergoing restoration for such uses) are not eligible.

The need for a grant has to be demonstrated. There is no set maximum or minimum size of grant. Private owners and trusts normally get no more than 75% of eligible costs; local authorities, 50%. Partnership funding is the same as for historic buildings (see above).

Recent grants/partnerships have included:
◆ Uchdachan Bridge, Association for the Protection of Rural Scotland (£78,000);
◆ Dunure Castle, Strathclyde Buildings Preservation Trust (£18,000);
◆ Ancrum Old Bridge, private owner (£18,000);
◆ Amisfield Tower, private owner (£10,000);
◆ St Cuthbert's chapel, Moffat, private owner (£5,000).

Applications: A booklet, Grants for Ancient Monuments (1997) provides guidance. The conditions attached to grants may include an undertaking to allow a measure of public access, as appropriate, and to ensure future maintenance.

Rescue Archaeology

Contact: Gordon Barclay, Principal Inspector of Ancient Monuments
Tel: 0131-668 8758; Fax: 0131-668 8765

Grants are given for investigation of archaeological sites and landscapes under threat, applied research into site conservation, and contributions to costs of strategic conservation effects by others. Also see *State-Funded Rescue Archaeology in Scotland: Past Present and Future.*

Recent grants have included:
◆ Fordhouse Burial Ground, National Trust for Scotland, for cost of excavating burial ground suffering from severe damage from erosion and rabbits (£12,043).

Applications: Approach the contact above for more information. Applications need to be made the September before the financial year of expenditure.

Housing Action Trusts (HATs)

HATs were set up under the 1988 Housing Act to take over and regenerate inner city housing estates. There were a total of six trusts, three in London boroughs, as at November 1997.

The aim of HATs is to redevelop, refurbish and manage their housing stock and to improve the physical, social and environmental conditions in their areas. To achieve these aims HATs can give grants to individuals, organisations (including charities) and businesses.

Details are available direct from the HATs:
- Liverpool 0151-227 1099;
- Castle Vale (Birmingham) 0121-776 6784;
- North Hull 0148-285 6160;
- Tower Hamlets 0181-983 4698;
- Waltham Forest 0181-539 5533;
- Stonebridge (Brent) 0181-961 0278.

General information can also be obtained from the relevant government office for the region (see Single Regeneration Budget entry) or RD1(E), Zone 4/J10, Eland House, Bressenden Place, London SW1E 5DU.

The Department for International Development (formerly Overseas Development Administration)

Abercrombie House, Eaglesham Road, East Kilbride, Glasgow G75 8EA
Switchboard: 01355-844000 Fax: 01355-84 3457

On November 5th 1997 the Secretary of State introduced a White Paper with the government's intention to more than double Britain's aid spending. An increase in the department's budget is expected to start from 1999. Resources will also be redirected as from 1998. Receipt of British aid will be linked to the commitment to certain policies by the recipient countries. Preferred partners are expected to get increased long-term aid. Aid to other countries may not necessarily be cut but directed through charities and NGOs rather than through official government channels.

Non-Governmental Organisations Unit Head:
Robin Russell

Joint Funding Scheme
Total grant-aid: £40,214,000 (1996/97) Budgeted £36,156,000 (1997/98)
Contacts: First point: dial the switchboard number above and ask for extension 3445; second point x 3585
Christine Holland Tel: 01355-84 3144; E-mail: c-holland@dfid.gtnet.gov.uk

The Non-Governmental Organisations (NGO) Unit co-funds long-term projects in developing countries by registered UK charities. Projects in which indigenous NGOs or church/community groups play a major part are not ruled out, indeed they are encouraged, but the grants can only be made to UK charities which must carry out the formal grant agreements for reporting and accounting.

Any project which aims at improving conditions for the poorest groups of people in developing countries is eligible for support, provided that it is developmental in character rather than for the relief of immediate needs.

Grants, usually on a 50:50 basis, can be made for up to five years with a maximum contribution of £500,000. (The remainder must come from non British government sources.) In general, the department will contribute on a £ for £ basis, but the percentage of official support can relate to special circumstances. Only family planning and population projects can apply for grants of more than 50% of the total budget.

Whilst core funding is not given, the extra management and administrative costs of the project incurred under this scheme in the UK can be included in its budget (up to 10%).

Evidence from the applicant charity that its project is acceptable to the appropriate authorities in the country concerned must be included in the application. The Scheme will not contribute retrospectively towards a project, i.e. for expenditure incurred in previous financial years.

Block grants

£20,483,000 (1996/97); £16,973,000 (1997/98)
Five major organisations receive notification of their guaranteed annual funding (blocks grants) under this scheme prior to each financial year. The block grant allocation accounts for about 46% of JFS funding. These agencies allocations are:
Oxfam – £5,304,000
Save the Children Fund – £4,583,000
Christian Aid – £3,003,000
Worldwide Fund for Nature – £2,164,000
Catholic Fund for Overseas Development – £1,920,000
Total: £16,973,000 (In 1996/97 an additional £3.5 million was also disbursed to these five agencies towards the end of the financial year from underspend in other departmental budgets.)

Other grants

£19,730,000 (1996/97); £19,183,000 (1997/98)
The 'other grants' were made to over 430 projects undertaken by some 130 organisations and included the following examples with relevance to this guide:
- Birdlife International, for projects in the mountain forests of Cameroon (£121,000);

- International Trust for Nature Conservation for seabuckthorn project in Ladakh, India (£2,482);
- ITDG for 13 projects – East Africa 2; Kenya; Nepal; Peru 2; Sri Lanka 5; Zimbabwe 2; (£573,400 in total);
- King Mahendra Trust, for Annapurna conservation area project, Nepal (£66,000);
- Plan International for 14 projects in South America, Africa, India, S E Asia including a permaculture project in Thailand (£29,600), integrated recycling in Colombia (£98,000);
- Population Concern for 12 projects in Bangladesh; Ethiopia 4; India 3; Nigeria; Pakistan; Tanzania 2;
- Rainforest Foundation, to protect Dong Nah Tom Forest in Thailand (£9,238);
- SOS Sahel for community environment project in Mali (£89,800) and a forest management project in Niger (£69,000);
- WaterAid for 11 projects in Ethiopia 3; Ghana; India; Nepal; Tanzania; Uganda 2; Zambia; Zimbabwe;
- Y Care International, for centre for organic gardening at Salto Grande, Argentina/ Uruguay (£13,541);
- Zoological Society of London for ankole cattle project in Uganda (£9,563).

Appropriate Technology Programme Fund

£1,750,000 (1996/97); £1,500,000 (1997/98)

Grants are given to organisations such as ITDG.

Exclusions: Funds are not available for relief or welfare projects, i.e. those that are clearly unsustainable, nor in general for the following:
- projects involving major construction works;
- single items of equipment or vehicles, other than as part of a larger project;
- conventional curative medical projects not combined with health education, preventative medicine or community-based programmes;
- environmental conservation projects in which the main objective is to conserve flora and fauna for their own sake, rather than for the benefit of poor communities;
- scholarships, even if part of a wider project;
- projects where proselytisation is a theme.

Applications are not accepted for Eastern Europe or the former Soviet Union (for these see entry for the Know How Fund of the Foreign & Commonwealth Office).

Applications: Detailed guidelines on the Joint Funding Scheme are available from the NGO Section. New proposals can be submitted at any time until the end of the 30 November immediately preceding the financial year (beginning of April to end of following March) in which the project is scheduled to begin.

Early submission of applications is helpful. Applications outstrip resources and decisions are not made on a first come, first served basis.

Landfill Tax Credit Scheme
(see ENTRUST)

The Local Projects Fund
see also Environmental Action Fund

Grants Management Unit, Civic Trust, The View, 6th Floor, Gostins Building, 32-36 Hanover Street, Liverpool L1 4LN
Tel: 0151-709 1969; **Fax:** 0151-709 2022; **Website:** www.civictrust.org.uk
Contact: Catherine Haynes, Grant Fund Manager

EAF Project Funding
Contact: Andy Kirby, Environmental Action Manager (at DETR)
Project funding supports specific activities with defined, measurable outcomes and clear timescales, which clearly achieve a government objective. Grants range from £10,000 to £75,000 a year.

Applications (1998/99) should fall within at least one of the following priority areas:
- education of the general public, or specific groups within it, about the importance of sustainable development, and the promotion of sustainable behaviour;
- encouragement of waste minimisation, recycling, reuse of materials and efficient energy use;
- improvement of local environments and promotion of biodiversity.

The administration of this part of the Environmental Action Fund of the Department of Environment, Transport and the Regions (see separate entry) is assisted by the Civic Trust. Elaine Simmons was EAF Grants Officer at the Civic Trust in autumn 1997.

Local Projects Fund (LPF)
Grant total: £300,000 (1997/98)
Contact: Ian Jones, Grants Officer for LPF
This fund is financed by the Department of the Environment, Transport and the Regions (DETR), and is administered by the Civic Trust. It aims to support voluntary organisations carrying out practical work and projects in England that make tangible and sustainable improvements to the environment. Projects should provide for and demonstrate wide community involvement, benefit and access. Priorities are the same as for EAF Project Funding.

Applications (in 1998/99) should fall within at least one of the priority areas noted above for EAF Project funding.
Grants range between £500 and £10,000 and can be up to a maximum of 50% of the project cost, providing matching funding has been secured from non-public sector sources which can include some support in kind. Matching funding should

be in the form of cash from non-public sector sources, i.e. own fundraising activities, business sponsorship, charitable trusts, award schemes and National Lottery.

A total of 114 grants were made in 1996/97 and included the following examples which display the range of organisations and projects assisted:

- Resourcesaver Recycling Systems, Avon, for an office paper recycling scheme (£10,000);
- Mudchute Park and Farm, London, for environmental improvements (£5,560);
- John Wooton House Tenants, West Midlands, community planting around two tower blocks (£4,143);
- Milton Keynes Green Business Club, environmental training for local businesses (£4,307);
- Oasis Children's Adventure, sensory trail (£2,140);
- Grimethorpe Neighbourhood Watch & Community Association, for White City Safer Community Project ((£2,000);
- Friends of Handforth Station, adopt-a-station (£1,200);
- Wells Civic Society, Somerset, for wild flowers around Wells (£1,009);
- St Lewis' Green Scheme, Cheshire, for nature trail (£740);
- Burton YMCA, for Task Force (£603);
- Beatrice Tate School, London, for facelift project (£500).

Exclusions: Projects are not eligible for support if they are funded by: Countryside Commission; English Nature; Groundwork; Rural Action; Rural Development Commission; Tidy Britain Group; Single Regeneration Budget; English Partnerships; local authorities or any other source directly or indirectly funded by the DETR. They can be in receipt of government support through the Environmental Task Force. Funding from the National Lottery is not counted as public sector support in this instance.

Grants cannot be awarded retrospectively or used for activities outside England, for party politics or for the purchase of land or buildings.

Successful applicants are expected to have a 'Green Housekeeping' policy statement.

Applications: These have to be made on an application form. Potential applicants obtain this with full guidelines and example budgets and need to follow them carefully as 'regulations' are minutely drawn. This entry cannot cover all the points made.

Criteria
- Clear environmental focus.
- Undertaken by a voluntary group, charity or not-for-profit organisation.
- Show an innovative approach and sensitivity to wider environmental concerns.
- Have relevant planning permission/consents and reasonable public access.
- Demonstrate sustainable long-term management.

◆ Obtain 50% matched funding from non-public sector sources
◆ Be in England.

Applicants should check the current deadlines for applications. All eligible applications receive an assessment visit. Grant decisions are taken by a panel of representatives from environmental organisations and the DETR which meets regularly.

Grants awarded during, for instance, the financial year 1997/98 must be claimed by mid January in 1998 and all work must be completed by the end of March in 1998.

Two free publications are available to help support projects, a newsletter, *Activate* and *A Guide to Good Practice in Managing Environmental Projects*, a resource for local groups.

The London Boroughs Grants Committee

London Boroughs Grants Unit, 5th Floor Regal House, London Road, Twickenham TW1 3QS
Tel: 0181-891 5021 general enquiries; Fax: 0181-891 5874
Contact: Daniel Silverstone, General Manager, x240; Andy Ganf, x225; Davina Judelson, x255
Total grant-aid: £28,403,000 (1997/98);
Environment and Tourism Sector: £753,000

The grants unit was restructured in 1997. The Grants Committee approved a Business Plan for 1998/99 which emphasised the introduction of a 'policy framework and procedures for involving the committee in package funding deals with other funders and service providers.'

New priorities for funding with effect from July 1997:
◆ addressing Outer London needs;
◆ advocacy development;
◆ innovative bids to improve black and ethnic minority access to benefits from regeneration opportunities;
◆ refugees and asylum seekers;
◆ single homelessness.

At the time of editing (Winter 1997) policy reviews and funding strategies had taken place in:
◆ Environment
◆ Play
◆ Tourism
◆ Single homelessness
◆ Refugees and migrants.

Environmental organisations seeking support need to be working with at least one of the selected priority areas. Support is only given to organisations operating in two or more London boroughs.

Nine organisations relevant to this guide were supported in 1997/98:
- Friends of the Earth (£114,470);
- London Wildlife Trust (£93,757);
- BTCV (£89,374);
- Energy Conservation and Solar Centre (£51,711);
- South London Children's Scrap Scheme (£43,610);
- Federation of Heathrow Anti Noise Groups (£38,392);
- Common Ground (£26,264);
- Heritage of London Trust (£13,543);
- Aviation Environment Federation (£11,281).

Applications: A funding pack is available (ring the telephone line above). There are no deadlines for applications, or maximum or minimum grants. The committee now works on a 'rolling application system' with four quarterly meetings. Copies of the latest Business Plan can be obtained.

The National Forest Company (NFC)

Enterprise Glade, Bath Lane, Moira, Swadlincote, Derbyshire CE12 6BD
Tel: 01283-551211; Fax: 01283-552844
Contact: Dr Hugh V Williams, Grants and Land Management Advisor

The National Forest, devised by the Countryside Commission and announced in 1990, links the ancient forests of Needwood and Charnwood and spans three counties in the English Midlands – Derbyshire, Leicestershire and Staffordshire. Its mostly rural landscape of mixed farmland is one of the least wooded areas of the country. It also suffers from economic decline and dereliction from mining and clay working. Its principal towns are Burton upon Trent (brewing), Coalville and Swadlincote (mining) and Ashby de la Zouche (historic).

The National Forest Company was set up in 1995 to create the new forest. It aims to promote nature conservation and cultural heritage; assist provision for sport, recreation and tourism; encourage agricultural and rural enterprise; stimulate economic regeneration; encourage community and business participation. Central to its work are its partnerships with local authorities, farmers, landowners, companies, local communities and people all over Britain. Whilst the company receives grant-aid from government this is pump-priming finance and covers a proportion of the project's total costs. It has its own specialists to generate further funds, investment opportunities and together with other partners has made ambitious bids to the Heritage Lottery Fund and the Millennium Commission.

Listed below are some of its funding initiatives (as at January 1998)

A National Forest Tender Scheme: £1.5 million (1997/98)
The Tender Scheme was launched jointly with the Forestry Authority in 1995, for rapid conversion of farm and derelict land to forest. An estimated two thirds of the planting needed during the Forest's first 10 years will be achieved through this scheme. In Round 3 (1997/98), 13 out of 27 bids were successful. Many of these were from local farmers planting new woods and giving access for walkers and horseriders. Others were urban such as a new woodland around playing fields, or planting on land restored after mineral workings between a brick factory and a row of houses. In a previous round the Woodland Trust had received support for forest creation on a site close to Linton near its small community woodland.

Land Acquisition Fund: £100,000 (1997/98)
The company has funds to buy land itself or to assist others in acquiring it, as part of its work to develop a wide range of partners in its work.

Development Programme Fund: £150,000 (1997/98)
This fund allows for strategic acquisition of land and site management agreements. It also supports community and arts projects within the National Forest Areas with maximum grants of £2,000 and £3,000 respectively per project. Around 30 local projects are supported each year including parish-based wildlife surveys, heritage and art projects and specific features at Forest sites. Both BTCV and Leicestershire and Rutland Trust for Nature Conservation have received support under this fund.

Major Forest Related Bids
The company will act as a catalyst giving advice and assistance for national and European Union funding. The National Forest has obtained Millennium funding of some £6.75 million for the National Forest Millennium Discovery Centre.

The National Heritage Memorial Fund

7 Holbein Place, London SW1W 8NR
Tel: 0171-591-6000; Fax: 0171-591 6001
Contact: Rebecca Osbourne, Public Relations Manager
Grants: £6.75 million in 43 grants (1996/97)

The National Heritage Memorial Fund (NHMF) was set up in 1980 in memory of the people who have given their lives for the United Kingdom. It is now funded annually by the Department of Culture, Media and Sport, but was initially funded by the sale of land compulsorily purchased for military reasons in wartime. The fund's role is to protect land, buildings, objects and collections which are of outstanding interest and are important to the national heritage.

The NHMF has become the national distributor of the Heritage Lottery Fund (see separate entry in the National Lottery section) which has transformed this small organisation in terms of its size, powers and responsibilities. The Heritage Memorial Fund still carries out its original functions with which it enjoys wider grant-making powers than the Heritage Lottery Fund. It is able in an emergency to move with great rapidity. However, the government's grant-in-aid has been severely reduced (from £12 million for most years before 1996/97, to £8 million in 1996/97 and down to £5 million for 1997/98). Grants and loans are provided for buying items which:

◆ are at risk of being sold abroad, developed, damaged or lost;
◆ have a clear memorial link.

Funding has been provided for land, buildings, works of art, museum collections, manuscripts and items of transport and industrial history. It also provides grants and loans to maintain and preserve most of these items.

Applications should only be made as a last resort, after all other possible sources of funding have been tried. The fund will only pay for the total cost of a project in exceptional cases.

Projects, whether large or small, will only be considered if all the following points apply:

◆ projects to buy, maintain or preserve land, buildings, objects or collections of outstanding interest and importance to the national heritage;
◆ projects based in the UK;
◆ projects which have already received financial help from other sources of funding but which need more money to be finished off or projects for which no other funding is available;
◆ projects to which the public will have access, unless public access might reduce the value of the item;
◆ projects which will be financially secure in the long-term;
◆ projects where there is a genuine worry that the item is otherwise going to be lost or damaged.

Examples of projects relevant to this guide which were supported in 1996/97 include:

◆ Launde Abbey Woods, Leicestershire and Rutland Wildlife Trust (£57,000);
◆ Auckinleck House, Scottish Historic Buildings Trust (£50,000);
◆ Upper Square, Hynish, Isle of Tiree, Hebridean Trust (49,500);
◆ Upper Lugg Meadows, Norfolk Wildlife Trust (£30,000);
◆ The Lough, Thorganby, Carstairs Countryside Trust (£6,000).

Exclusions: Private individuals and businesses. Grants to repair or restore buildings. For such assistance contact: English Heritage, Cadw or Historic Scotland, the Department of the Environment Northern Ireland, or the relevant local authority.

Applications: These should be made in writing and sent to the head of the fund, signed by the chairman, director or chief executive, and with a full justification of the need for help from the fund including:

- the reason for the grant;
- a full description of the project;
- photographs of the item, and for land and buildings, a map showing exactly where the property is and a site plan;
- full financial details, including an account of the money already raised or promised from other sources;
- where appropriate, a formal valuation of the item;
- a description of the body applying for assistance, its finances, and plans to care for/manage the project in the future.

Applications are usually acknowledged within three working days. If the proposal meets all the conditions for applying for grants or loans, the applicant will be informed of the date when the trustees meet.

The Northern Ireland Environment & Heritage Service

HQ & Corporate Affairs, Commonwealth House, 35 Castle Street, Belfast BT1 1GU
Tel: 01232-251477; Fax: 01232-546660; E-mail: ehs@nics.gov.uk

The service became a 'next steps' executive agency of the Department of the Environment in 1996. This means that it concentrates on day to day operational responsibilities and on supporting work practices whilst policy and legislation remain with the core of the department.

The chief executive, Robert Martin, referred in first annual report to its 'growing holistic approach' and that he was 'particularly pleased that our partnerships with non-governmental organisations continue to flourish'. In 1996/97 it consulted this constituency about the natural heritage grants and was revising its priorities and procedures. The service is an adviser to the Heritage Lottery Fund and the EC LIFE programme (see separate entries).

Its three main areas of work are carried out in separately located offices:

Natural Heritage
See address, telephone and e-mail, above
General enquiries: 01232-546530
Contact: Dr John Faulkner, Director of Natural Heritage
Grant total: £1,081,000 to 232 schemes mainly to district councils (1996/97); £1,314,000 (1997/98).

Grants relevant to this guide totalled:

	1996/97	1997/98
Conservation grants (NGOs)	£351,000	£370,000
Access to countryside (NGOs)	£16,000	£14,000
EC grants	£297,000	£300,000

The service sees its primary role as encouraging district councils and easing public access to the countryside which the DANI (Department of Agriculture) access payments scheme also supports.

It also provides grants to voluntary conservation organisations for a wide range of initiatives: core funding; staff funding for specific projects; surveys; conferences and general interpretation with a conservation benefit. Grants are usually 50% of approved expenditure. Since the early 1990s a Schools Conservation Project Scheme (maximum grant £500) has also been provided for schemes involving pupils, and more recently grants to farmers to try to revive corncrake numbers under the Corncrake Protection Scheme. Support was given to 126 schemes totalling £351,000 in 1996/97.

Access grants to the countryside are paid to District Councils for works on public rights of way and long distance routes. Grants can also be paid to other bodies where their scheme has endorsement from the district council. Up to 1997/98 the National Trust was the only organisation supported under this scheme with £16,000 in 1996/97.

The service is also responsible for the administration of EC grants. The first programme, the Physical and Social Environment Programme (PSEP), ran from 1990 to 1993 and has been succeeded by the Tourism Sub-Programme. Under Measure 1.2.4 money is provided for access/conservation projects. Altogether 17 EC tourism grants totalling £297,000 were made in 1996/97.

Built Heritage

5-33 Hill Street, Belfast BT1 2LA
Tel: 01232-235000; Fax: 01232-54311; E-mail: hmb.ehs@nics.gov.uk
General enquiries: 01232-543061
Contact: Dr Ann Hamlin, Director of Conservation
Grant-aid 1996/97

Private grants	£1,406,000
Local authority	£100,000
Historic churches	£294,000
Conservation Area	£650,678

Historic Buildings Grant is available towards repair and maintenance of 'certain eligible items which constitute the historic fabric of the building'. Generally new works are not grant aided even if carried out in a sympathetic manner, but a grant may be paid when 'approved alterations replace previous inappropriate works'. Grants towards professional consultancy fees (up to 75%) are also given. Although there is no statutory grading of listed buildings in Northern Ireland, rates of grant vary according to an internal grading system within the service. Recent grants have included:

- Church of the Immaculate Conception, Strabane, for repairs and restoration of belfry louvres (£6,840);
- 4 Glenmore Terrace, Hilden, Lisburn, for general refurbishment (£3,565).

The Northern Ireland Committee of Building Preservation Trust was set up in 1996 with 10 trust members and the service is actively encouraging the formation of others.

The Environmental Protection Service

Calvert House, 23 Castle Place, Belfast BT1 1FY
Tel: 01232-254754; Fax: 01232-254865

This service performs a function similar to the Environment Agency in England and SEPA in Scotland although the Department of Agriculture also covers some of the services. Whilst it does not provide grant schemes as such it could be a useful source of information, advice and hopefully cooperation for voluntary environmental bodies.

Applications: Further information and grant application forms can be requested from the addresses above either in writing or by telephone. The country is split into geographic areas. Contact each of the main offices for the location of the relevant regional office. Further advice and support is available at this level.

Programme for Partnership, Urban Programme, Scotland

Scottish Office, Development Department, Urban Regeneration and Area Initiatives, Victoria Quay, Edinburgh EH6 6QQ
Tel: 0131-244 0808; Fax: 0131-244 0810
Contact: Ann McVie
Total funding: £18 million (1997/98); Indicative budget: £34 million (1998/99)

The Programme for Partnership promotes council-wide regeneration partnerships to improve social, economic and environmental conditions for those who live in the areas of worst deprivation in Scotland. Each partnership is made up of the Council, Scottish Homes, the local enterprise company, other relevant agencies, the private sector, the community and voluntary sector.

In November 1996, 23 partnerships were set up. Of these, 12 are Priority Partnership Areas (PPAs), designated for up to 10 years, and 11 are Regeneration Programmes

(RPs), designated for up to 5 years. Each partnership receives an annual allocation of Urban Programme funds and makes its own decisions on how to use them locally.

Voluntary organisations have traditionally been the main recipients of Urban Programme funding with 60% of projects being run by voluntary groups. A similar level of involvement from the voluntary sector was anticipated under Programme for Partnership, the current urban regeneration policy framework. The level of voluntary sector involvement is being monitored by the Scottish Office. Two examples of projects follow, both on Wester Hailes, a peripheral estate to the west of Edinburgh built in 1970, where the high-rise blocks have been demolished and the current reduced population of 13,000 people suffers from 27% unemployment, and all the other social, community and environmental problems experienced by large urban estates.

i) Agenda 21 started in 1995, a partnership of the Scottish Office, City of Edinburgh Council and the 26 neighbourhood councils of Wester Hailes in association with Westside Training Agency (the area LEC), to assist long-term unemployed adults and young people with a programme of activities paralleling Agenda 21, which aims to improve the local environment through local participation (£240,000 over four years).

ii) An Environmental Ranger as appointed in 1997 to work on environmental issues with local people, targeting young school children in particular (£75,000 over three years).

Priority Partnerships Areas
Ardler, Dundee Tel: 01382-433617; Fax: 01382-433871
Craigmillar, Edinburgh Tel: 0131-4693821; Fax: 0131-469 3574
North Edinburgh Tel: 0131-4693821; Fax: 0131-4693574
Glasgow East End Tel: 0141-5546252; Fax: 0141-5540323
Glasgow North Tel: 0141-2870329; Fax: 0141-2870431
Greater Easterhouse Tel: 0141-7719338; Fax: 0141-7713856
Great Northern, Aberdeen Tel: 01224-523035; Fax: 01224-522832
Inverclyde, Greenock Tel: 01475-731700; Fax: 01475-731800
Motherwell North Tel: 01698-302449; Fax: 01698-302489
North Ayr Tel: 01292-616180; Fax: 01292-616161
Paisley Tel: 0141-840 3228; Fax: 0141-889 5140
West Dunbartonshire Tel: 01389-737401; Fax: 01389-737512

Regeneration Programmes
Angus Tel: 01307-473004; Fax: 01307-461874
Dundee Tel: 01382-433617; Fax: 01382-433871
East Renfrewshire Tel: 0141-5773144; Fax: 0141-6200884
Edinburgh Tel: 0131-4693821; Fax: 0131-4693574
Falkirk Tel: 01324-506004; Fax: 01324-506061

Fife Tel: 01592-416162; Fax: 01592-416020
Glasgow Tel: 0141-2870308; Fax: 0141-2875997
North Ayrshire Tel: 01294-324113; Fax: 01294-324114
North Lanarkshire Tel: 01698-302449; Fax: 01698-302489
South Lanarkshire Tel: 01698-454202; Fax: 01698-454376
Stirling Tel: 01786-442677; Fax: 01786-442538

Regeneration Branch

Northern Ireland Department of the Environment, 5th Floor Brookmount
Buildings, 42 Fountain Street, Belfast BT1 5EE
Tel: 01232-251966; Fax: 01232-251 976

Urban Development Grant (UDG)
Total funding: £5.4 million (1997/98); £3.5 million (1998/99)
30% for new building and 50% for refurbishment
Contacts: Brendan McConville (01232-251927); Paul McLoughlin
(01232-251967)

The department administers the Urban Development Grant which aims to promote
job creation, inward investment and environmental improvement by the
development of vacant, derelict or underused land and buildings. UDG was available
during Winter 1998 within priority areas of Belfast and Londonderry. However it
is possible for the grant scheme to respond to urgent needs outside these priority
areas.

A grant is usually given to cover a funding gap or shortfall between the cost of the
development and value on completion. Applications are assessed against criteria
which include provisions regarding direct benefit to deprived areas as well as
environmental benefits. The minimum grant size is £100,000.

In 1997 a total of 72 projects were finalised. The total investment in them had
been £9.4 million of which £3.3 million grant-aid derived from this scheme.

Applications: Application forms and additional information can be obtained from:
Belfast Development Office based at the address above (Tel: 01232-251928;
Fax: 01232-251976);
Londonderry Development Office, Orchard House, 40 Foyle Street, Londonderry
BT48 8AT (Tel: 01504-319900; Fax: 01504-319700).

**Community Enterprise (CERS) and CRISP (Community Regeneration &
Improvement Special Projects)**
Contact: Margaret Langhammer (Tel: 01232-251966; Fax: 01232-251 976)

Research Councils

Polaris House, North Star Avenue, Swindon, Wiltshire SN2 1EU

The seven research councils based in Swindon are funded and coordinated by the Office of Science and Technology (OST). They also receive funding for commissioned research from government departments, industry and other agencies. An OST/research council working group reviews cross-council activities. A Soil Science Advisory Committee has been set up by BBSRC and NERC (see below) to advise on priorities in research and training and to identify emerging opportunities.

The Natural Environment Research Council (NERC)

Tel: 01793-411500; Fax: 01793-411501
Contact: David Brown, Grants and Training (Tel: 01793-411797)

NERC is the leading body in the UK for research, survey, monitoring and training in all the environmental sciences. Its Awards and Training section includes five Research Grant and Training Award Committees: Earth Observation; Earth Sciences; Freshwater Sciences; Marine and Atmospheric Sciences; Terrestrial Sciences. Four main routes are used to fund the best science in universities and in NERC's own research establishments.

Science funding 1995/96

Thematic Research £26,382,000
Relevant applications to selected themes, important, topical or under-investigated, within its mission.

Non-Thematic Research £31,854,000
Proposals (both research and training) in any area covered by NERC's mission.

Core strategic Funding £39,028,000
Longer term research, survey or monitoring carried out mainly at NERC's own establishments.

The occasional grant is made to a voluntary/charitable organisation with a recognised scientific research base. In 1995/96 grants included:
- Natural History Museum (£376,000 grant of which £38,000 for research contract);
- British Trust for Ornithology, for research contract/programme (£11,000);
- Game Conservancy Trust (£12,000 grant);
- Wildfowl & Wetland Trust, Slimbridge (£5,000 grant).

The Biotechnology and Biological Sciences Research Council (BBSRC)

Tel: 01793-413201; Fax: 01793-413201
Contact: Awards & Training
Research Grants and Awards: £158,200,000 (1995/96)

Nearly two-thirds of the research funding shown above was paid to universities, either as competitively awarded grants or as studentship and fellowship awards. The remainder was allocated to research at BBSRC-sponsored institutes (three former BBSRC research institutes are now independent companies) with both recurrent and capital grants.

Scientific areas covered:
◆ Agricultural systems;
◆ Animal sciences and psychology;
◆ Biochemistry and cell biology;
◆ Biomolecular sciences;
◆ Chemicals and pharmaceuticals;
◆ Engineering and physical sciences;
◆ Genes and developmental biology;
◆ Food;
◆ Plant and microbial sciences.

Road Safety Division

Department of the Environment, Transport and the Regions, Great Minster House, 76 Marsham Street, London SW1P 4DR
Tel: 0171-271 4723; Fax: 0171-271 4728
Contact: Hilary M Davies

Grant-in-aid: RoSPA (£270,000 reviewed every 3 years)
The division provides annual grant-aid to RoSPA, the Royal Society for the Prevention of Accidents.

Road Safety Small Grants Budget: around £40,000 annually
Criteria for grant-making are based on a 'hierarchy of benefits which reflect and complement' the work of the department. These include proposals which improve:
◆ new (especially new young) driver safety;
◆ child safety, especially pedestrian;
◆ driver attitudes to speed;
◆ safety of other vulnerable users – pedestrians, cyclists, motorcyclists;
◆ 'hard-core' drink/driving psychology.

The small budget is used for short-term projects, or those which need finance to get an initiative started but which have a reasonable prospect of self-financing. Examples in 1996/97 included:

- University of Strathcylde, for 'Kerbcraft, a Child Pedestrian Training Manual, and for its distribution costs to local authority road safety officers;
- Merseyside Young Driver competition;
- Child Accident Prevention Trust's Child Safety Week.

Rural Action for the Environment

Rural Action National Team, ACRE, Somerford Court, Somerford Road, Cirencester, Gloucestershire GL7 1TW
Tel: 01285-659599; Fax: 01285-654537; E-mail: ruralaction@acre.org.uk
Contact: Simon Brereton
Grant total: £750,000 a year

Policy: Rural Action is a partnership of organisations working for a better environment throughout England. It has a national office, but grants and advice are administered locally, usually by the rural community council. It is funded by the Countryside Commission, English Nature and the Rural Development Commission and managed by ACRE. Information will also be available from most county wildlife trusts, BTCV, many community and environmental organisations and local authorities.

Rural Action aims to make it easier for people in rural communities to undertake almost any project which benefits their local environment or increases understanding and care of it. Any group of people within a village, small town or parish can apply for a grant. They may be an existing group (WI, youth group, village hall committee, town or parish council, etc.), local people coming together for a specific project, or just a group of friends.

Projects must concern some aspect of the environment and be in a rural area of England. Local people must be actively leading and involved in carrying out the project and the expected benefits should be sustainable. For site-based projects there must be full public access.

Examples of the types of projects supported: local surveys (e.g. wildlife, trees, traffic), practical tasks (e.g. creating or managing woodlands, footpaths, rebuilding dry-stone walls), feasibility studies, setting up recycling and community composting schemes, tackling litter, graffiti or noise problems, management plans for wildlife areas, landscape improvements around community buildings, energy audits, creating parish maps etc.

The project grants they give can cover the cost of specialist help and training and can also help with publicity, feasibility studies, consulting other local people, obtaining maps and other materials for surveys, hiring equipment and venues for meetings etc. Grants cannot be used to buy equipment or tools, but may fund some materials as part of a package including advice, etc.

Rural Action can also put you in touch with people who can give expert advice and help your group develop the skills and knowledge needed for the project.

Project grants can be for up to £2,000, although most are smaller. Your group must provide 50% of the total value of the project, which can include the time you spend carrying it out (valued at £46 per day) and 'in kind' donations of materials and services, as well as cash raised from other sources.

If the project is tackled in stages (e.g. feasibility study, public meeting, skills training etc.) you can apply for a grant for each stage before applying for further funding.

Applications: The following is the procedure for approaching Rural Action for support.

1. If you have an idea for a local environmental project, or a problem you want to tackle, contact any of the organisations in the Rural Action network in your county. Try your local Wildlife Trust, BTCV or RCC.
2. Arrange an initial meeting with a Rural Action advisor to talk through your ideas and how Rural Action can help.
3. The contact will give you a Registration of Interest card and explain how to obtain a Rural Action Project Grant application form.
4. Send the completed application form to the Project Grant Administrator for your county.
5. Project grants are usually paid in advance, so once the application is approved you can start work right away. You will be asked to provide a feedback report within six months.
6. Repeat applications are welcome.

The Rural Development Commission

141 Castle Street, Salisbury, Wiltshire SP1 3TP
Tel: 01722-336 255; Fax: 01722-432773: Website: http://www.argonet.co.uk/ rdc; E-mail: rdc.general@argonet.co.uk
Contact: Judy Basset, Head of Information

London HQ: Dacre House, 19 Dacre Street, London SW1H ODH
Tel: 0171-340 2900; Fax: 0171-340 291

The Rural Development Commission is the government agency 'concerned with the well-being of the people who live and work in rural England'. It concentrates the largest share of its resources in Rural Development Areas (RDAs). These are the parts of rural England experiencing the greatest concentrations of economic and social problems and here the commission aims to diversify and strengthen their local economies, and also strengthen communities and help disadvantaged groups. The development of partnerships with public and private sectors is central to its strategy and exemplified in its two main programmes.

Rural Development Programmes

Funding total: around £13 million annually

It can provide advice and funding for a range projects with environmental/ conservation benefits. It supports varied types of projects from village halls, to voluntary transport services, re-use of redundant buildings, green tourism and the regeneration of small towns and villages, all of which have environmental/ conservation benefits.

With its focus on the needs of a local community and its economy, attractions important for residents as well as visitors, such as crafts, heritage and exhibition centres, museums, festivals and countryside education, may be assisted to develop.

Rural Transport Development Fund

Grant total: £1.7 million (1996/97)

Of the 140 projects supported 69 were community ones.

Rural Action

A joint scheme with English Nature and the Countryside Commission to involve communities in the care of their environment is definitely supported up to 1998/ 99 (see separate entry under ACRE).

Village Hall Grants Scheme

Grant total: £1.6 million (1996/97)

The Village Halls Loans Fund is administered for the Commission by ACRE (see separate entry), and helps village halls and community centres across rural England. This support has been expanded by a £10 million award from the Millennium Commission.

The Commission also provides funding to and works closely with Rural Community Councils.

Rural Challenge

Annual funding total: £2.82 million (1996/97); £5 million (1997/98)

Funding total up to Round 2 in 1995/96: £37 million for 11 successful projects.

Rural Challenge is a competition which provides prizes of £1 million each year for winning projects put forward by local partnerships within Rural Development Areas (RDAs). The prize is paid out over three years. RDAs compete in alternate years, except for the four largest which compete annually. The commission aims to coordinate with the Single Regeneration Budget (SRB) Challenge Fund (see separate entry) by running to a similar timetable for bids and joint evaluation of SRB bids with a significant rural component.

Examples of Rural Challenge winners with relevance to this guide and which include input from voluntary organisations are:

◆ Rochdale Canal Corridor, West Yorkshire. This £2.9 million project provides local training and employment for the canal's restoration and maintenance managed from the work skills centre at Callis Mill as well as a market area and canal technology centre at Hebden Bridge, an energy conservation scheme and a trans-Pennine National Cycleway link. The partners include: Calderdale Metropolitan Council, Rochdale Canal Trust, Calderdale & Kirkless TEC, Gordon Rigg Ltd, Calderdale College, Calderdale Cycling Promotion Group, XHX7 Ltd, Mayroyd Partnership.

◆ Woodland Enterprise Centre, a project on the High Weald of East Sussex, promotes every aspect of timber production and use, by reviving the traditional industry of the area, developing markets, supporting woodland and integrating technology with environmental best practice. Partners are: Woodlands Enterprises Ltd, East Sussex County Council, Timber Growers' Association Ltd, Plumpton College, Timber Management Ltd.

Applications: Contact the Salisbury address above for general information. For information about specific schemes and individual projects contact the relevant Commission Area Office. It is important to do this and to build up a relationship with your relevant officers to develop a mutual working partnership.

North – Cumbria, Northumberland, Lancashire
Hawesworth Road, Penrith, Cumbria CA11 7EH Tel: 01768-865752;
Fax: 01768-890414;

Cleveland, Durham, Tyne & Wear
Morton Road, Yarm Road Industrial Estate, Darlington, Co Durham DL1 4PT
Tel: 01325-487123; Fax: 01325-488108;

Yorkshire & Humber
Spitfire House, Aviator Court, Clifton Moor, York YO3 4UZ
Tel: 01904-693335; Fax: 01904-693288;

West Midlands
Strickland House, The Lawns, Park Street, Wellington, Telford, Shropshire
TF1 3BX Tel: 01952-247161; Fax: 01952-248700;

East Midlands
18 Market Place, Bingham, Nottingham NG1 8AP Tel: 01949-876200;
Fax: 01949-876222;

East Anglia
Lees Smith House, 12 Looms Lane, Bury St Edmunds, Suffolk IP33 1HE
Tel: 01284-701743; Fax: 01284-704640;

South West
3 Chartfield House, Castle, Street, Taunton, Somerset TA1 4AS
Tel: 01823-276905; Fax: 01823-338673;

27 Victoria Park Road, Exeter, Devon EX2 4NT Tel: 01392-421245;
Fax: 01392-421244;
2nd floor, Highshore House, New Bridge Street, Truro, Cornwall TR1 2AA
Tel: 01872-273531; Fax: 01872-275646

South East
Sterling House, 7 Ashford Road, Maidstone, Kent ME14 5BJ
Tel: 01622-765222; Fax: 01622-662102;
The Chantry House, 29-31 Pyle Street, Newport, Isle of Wight PO30 IJW
Tel: 01983-528019; Fax: 01983-825745

Scottish Enterprise National

120 Bothwell Street, Glasgow G2 7JP
Tel: 0141-248 2700; Fax: 0141-221 3217; E-mail: scotentcsd@scotent.co.uk

The Scottish Enterprise network comprises 13 local enterprise companies (LECs)
with their respective subsidiaries, in the southern half of Scotland. It delivers a
range of business development and training services, along with environmental
and regeneration programmes. Its work centres on commercial schemes. Scottish
Enterprise National undertakes national and strategic projects directly and is also
responsible for leadership of the network. (See the entry for Highland and Islands
Enterprise for the northern network.)

Expenditure 1996/97

Enterprise	£181 million
Environment	£77 million
Youth Training	£87 million
Adult training	£58 million

A range of grants, business loans, financial/marketing advice is available for businesses
and small or new firms. Each LEC operates its own schemes and these need to be
contacted for particular details.

RAPID (Resources & Action for Private Industrial Development) is a programme
common to all LECs operating in urban areas. It aims to help ensure that the
property needs, whether industrial, office, or retail, of Scottish businesses are met.
In some circumstances it also supports the property element of tourism projects.
Projects eligible for support must be viable long-term but unable to go ahead without
public-sector support. The funding available from RAPID is the minimum needed
to make the project happen. An earlier scheme, Local Enterprise Grants for Urban
Projects (LEG-UP) which stimulated economic development and environmental
improvement in urban areas of particular need has been subsumed within RAPID.

Financial assistance maybe given in a number of ways: grant; participating grant;
loan; equity. Projects are more likely to be successful in obtaining support the smaller

the percentage of public funding required; and a loan or some other form of pay back, rather than by a direct grant, can be made. Awards have ranged from £6,000 to £1 million.

LEC Offices

Enterprise Ayrshire
Kilmarnock Tel: 01563-526623; Fax: 01563-543636

Scottish Borders Enterprise
Galashiels Tel: 01896-758991; Fax: 01896-758625

Dumfries & Galloway Enterprise Company
Dumfries Tel: 01387-245000; Fax: 01387-246224

Dunbartonshire Enterprise
Clydebank Tel: 0141-9512121; Fax: 0141-9511907

Fife Enterprise
Glenrothes Tel: 01592-623000; Fax: 01592-623149

Forth Valley Enterprise
Stirling Tel: 01786-451919; Fax: 01786-478123

Glasgow Development Agency
Glasgow Tel: 0141-2041111; Fax: 0141-2481600

Grampian Enterprise
Aberdeen Tel: 01224-575100; Fax: 01224-213417

Lanarkshire Development Agency
Bellshill Tel: 01698-745454; Fax: 01698-842211

Lothian and Edinburgh Enterprise Ltd
Edinburgh Tel: 0131-3134000; Fax: 0131-3134231

Moray, Badenoch & Strathspey Enterprise
Elgin Tel: 01343-550567; Fax: 01343-550678

Renfrewshire Enterprise
Paisley Tel: 0141-8480101; Fax: 0141-8486930

Scottish Enterprise Tayside
Dundee Tel: 01382-223100; Fax: 01382-201319

Scottish Environment Protection Agency

Head Office: Erskine Court, The Business Park, Stirling FK9 4TR
Tel: 01786-457700; Fax: 01786-446885; website: http://www.sepa.org.uk
Emergency Hotline: 0345-737271
Contact: Mark Wells, Environmental Issues Manager

The agency, funded via the Scottish Office and through charges, carries out similar work to the Environment Agency in England and Wales (see separate entry).

Although the majority of its work is regulatory, SEPA undertakes a significant amount of education and influencing work, often in partnership with other bodies in the public, private and voluntary sectors. It has no grant-aid programme, but is able to advise and support partnership projects which help achieve its environmental objectives.

A joint publication with Scottish Wildlife and Countryside Link has been funded and, according to a report in *Green Futures*, assistance has been given to the Scholarship Programme of Forum for the Future.

For local projects, organisations are advised to contact the regional offices closest to them. For national and international projects, organisations should contact the head office in Stirling. Staff are often able to give information and guidance even when financial support is not available.

Scottish Natural Heritage

12 Hope Terrace, Edinburgh EH9 2AS
Tel: 0131-447 4784; Fax: 0131-446 2279
Contact: National Grants Officer at Battleby, Redgorton, Perth PH1 3EW
(Tel: 01738-444177; Fax: 01738-442060)
Grant-aid: £7 million (1997/98)

No set proportions are allocated annually to different sectors. The figures from 1995/96 when £7.89 million was given in grant-aid are probably indicative: Voluntary sector 29%; Public sector – 57%; Private Sector – 14%.

Scottish Natural Heritage (SNH) is the government agency working with others to conserve and enhance Scotland's wildlife, habitats and landscapes. It is responsible to and funded by the Secretary of State for Scotland (and replaced the Countryside Commission for Scotland and the Nature Conservancy Council for Scotland in the early 1990s). It advises on policies and promotes projects which improve the natural heritage and support its sustainable use. Grants are available for a wide range of projects which:
◆ improve the conservation of species, habitats and landscapes;
◆ promote public enjoyment of the natural heritage;
◆ increase awareness and understanding of the natural heritage.

SNH particularly fosters the development of working partnerships with all kinds of interested parties – voluntary bodies, other public sector agencies (including local authorities), individuals and businesses.

Community and voluntary action
Grants for environmental projects; establishing and promoting local community-based organisations; information and assessment of local sites of natural heritage value; volunteer involvement, travel costs and training, and project/development officers for voluntary groups.

SNH funds a number of national voluntary and community organisations which are able to offer further information and advice to groups: Scottish Conservation Projects, Scottish Wildlife Trust, Rural Forum, Highland Forum, and Scottish Wildlife and Countryside Link.

Environmental education and interpretation
Grants for site interpretation; demonstration and display areas; interpretative strategies/plans; visitor reception facilities; publications, exhibitions and campaigns; seminars, training and fieldwork courses; schools.

SNH supports the Scottish Environmental Education Council and Regional Environmental Education Forums (based at the Department of Environmental Science, Stirling University) which can give further advice.

Land managers, farmers and crofters
Grants for landscape features; nature conservation; geological features; species; access; recreation. Management agreements may be arranged for ongoing programmes.

Projects eligible for funding under other governmental schemes (agricultural, forestry or agri-environment) are not usually considered.

SNH supports the Farming & Wildlife Advisory Group, based near Newbridge, Midlothian, and encourages applicants to seek its advice.

Applicants for all schemes must demonstrate that they have sought resources of support in kind and/or moral support from other people. They also need to consider carefully whether any of the other agencies giving overlapping areas of grant-aid is more appropriate to their project, i.e. the Forestry Commission, SOAEFD, Scottish Tourist Board, Scottish Sports Council, Historic Scotland, Local Enterprise Company or local authority.

Grants rarely exceed 50% of the total eligible expenditure. Higher rates may be offered for a limited number of priority projects. Grants range in size from under £100 to £1 million.

Exclusions: Work undertaken prior to submission of, and during consideration of an application; expeditions, research projects, conferences; publications; work required for planning consent or other statutory obligation.

Applications: Guidelines and application forms are available. Applicants are encouraged to discuss their proposals with the area officer nearest their project (see below) before submitting an application there. Projects relating to Scotland as a whole, or covering more than one region, should be sent to the National Grants Officer at the Battleby office. There are no deadlines but applicants are strongly advised to apply as far in advance of the start date as possible. Successful applicants are expected to monitor their projects and present a report.

Main Regional Offices – additional offices are based in each of the sub-regions of the four areas

North Areas

Northern Isles
Lerwick – Tel: 01595-693345; Fax: 01595-692565

East Highland
Dingwall – Tel: 01349-865333; Fax: 01349-865609

North Highland
Golspie – Tel: 01408-633602; Fax: 01408-633071

West Highland
Fort William – Tel: 01397-704716; Fax: 01397-700303

Western Isles
Stornoway – Tel: 01851-705258; Fax: 01851-704900

East Areas

Grampian
Aberdeen – Tel: 01224-312266; Fax: 01224-311366

Tayside
Battleby – Tel: 01738-444177; Fax: 01738-442060

Forth & Borders
Dalkeith – Tel: 0131-654-2466; Fax: 0131-6542477

West Areas

Argyll & Stirling
Stirling – Tel: 01786-450362; Fax: 01786-451974

Strathclyde & Ayrshire
Clydebank – Tel: 0141-951 4488; Fax: 0141-951 8948

Dumfries & Galloway
Dumfries – Tel: 01387-247010; Fax: 01387-259247

Scottish Rural Partnership Fund

Agriculture, Environment and Fisheries Department, Scottish Office,
Pentland House, 47 Robb's Loan, Edinburgh EH14 1TY
Contact: Stuart Forbes

The Scottish Rural Partnerships Fund supports a system of national and local partnerships throughout rural Scotland announced in the Scottish White Paper on Rural Policy, 'People, Prosperity and Partnership'. It aims to 'move decision-making closer to the local level and encourage communities to self-start'. Three broad categories of partnerships can be identified: strategic, area or topic-oriented.

Rural Strategic Support Fund

Total grant aid: approximately £1.6 million (1997/98)
Contact: Stuart Forbes, Room 028 (at the address above)
Tel: 0131-2240469; Fax: 0131-244 4071; E-mail: ranh.so.ph@gtnet.gov.uk

Local Rural Partnerships
For those forming a Local Rural Partnership or providing assistance to such a partnerships.

A special guidance note on the formation of these partnerships is available. It cites the Moray Firth Partnership as an example of a topic-based partnership including local authorities, local enterprise companies, port authorities, wildlife, nature protection and environmental organisations, the Forestry Commission and RAF Kinloss. The partnership is developing an integrated management strategy of the natural, economic, recreation and cultural resources of the area.

Councils for Voluntary Service
Only for rural and semi-rural CVSs. New applicants should ensure there is no overlap with existing councils. The Scottish Office will contact those currently receiving a grant.

Scottish National Environmental Organisations
Organisations undertaking environmental improvement projects throughout Scotland which may apply for core funding.

The work must be wholly undertaken in Scotland.

Grants are 'limited to the minimum required for the undertaking to succeed' and are not expected to exceed £40,000 a year. Grants to environmental organisations do not exceed 50% of eligible costs. Grant to Local Rural Partnerships does not exceed 50% of eligible cost in year 1, 33.33% in year 2, and 16.7% in year 3.

Rural Challenge Fund (RCF)

Total grant-aid: £1,220,000 (1997/98)
Contact: Raymond Evans, Room 028 (at the address above)
Tel: 0131-244 6945; Fax: 0131-244 4071;
E-mail:raymond.evans@ so061.scotoff.gov.uk

This competitive fund is open primarily to applications from rural communities and voluntary organisations in Scotland, though commercial concerns may bid for innovative transport-related projects (formerly run as a separate funding scheme).

Rural communities and voluntary organisations will be expected to have applied to the 'normal sources of funding' for their projects before submitting a bid to RCF to close any funding gap. 'In essence the RFC is a source of funding of last resort.'

Guidance about sources of funding is available from:

Rural Forum, Highland House, 46 St Catherine's Road, Perth PH1 5RY

Tel: 01738-634565

or your local Council of voluntary service.

In 1997/98 a total of 30 grants were made for projects ranging from one to three years, and included the following relevant to this guide:

- Laggan Forestry Initiative, a community led scheme (£68,000 over 3 years);
- Swan Trust, a maritime heritage resource (£15,000 over 3 years);
- Ant-Sireadh Eu-commaasach, art and the environment (£12,675 over 2 years);
- Newton Stewart Initiative, for a River Cree walkway and footbridge (£50,000);
- Scottish Farm & Countryside Educational Trust, for rural environment information service (£15,000 over 3 years).

Applications: Bids for 1998/99 needed to be submitted by 28th November 1997.

Local councils with a population density of less than 100 persons per square kilometer – all of whose area is regarded as rural except for settlements with a population of more than 10,000 – are listed below:

Aberdeenshire: (excluding Fraserburgh, Peterhead)
Angus: (excluding Arbroath, Carnoustie, Forfar, Montrose)
Argyll & Bute: (excluding Helensburgh)
Dumfries & Galloway: (excluding Dumfries, Stranrae)
East Ayrshire: (excluding Kilmarnock)
Highland: (excluding Fort William, Inverness)
Moray. (excluding Elgin)
Orkney Islands;Perth & Kinross: (excluding Perth)
Scottish Borders: (excluding Galashiels, Hawick)
Shetland Islands
South Ayrshire: (excluding Ayr, Prestwick, Troon)
Stirling: (excluding Stirling)
Western Isles.

Single Regeneration Budget Challenge Fund

Department of Environment, Transport and the Regions, Regeneration Division 2, Regeneration Policy Unit, Zone 4/A6, Eland House, Bressenden Place, London SW1E 5DU

Tel: 0171-890 3801; Fax: 0171-890 3789

Contact: Anna Walters, Regeneration Policy Unit

> *IMPORTANT NOTE: The Single Regeneration Budget Challenge Fund has been the major source of urban funding in England contributing millions of pounds annually to a rolling programme.*

In November 1997 no details were available about future regeneration programmes whilst the government's Comprehensive Spending Review was underway. Decisions were expected in Spring 1998. It was believed a similar type of programme would continue, possibly with a different title, and that it would become more precisely 'needs based' and target specific areas within regions. Readers will have to check the situation with the Government Office for the Region relevant to them (see list below).

The Single Regeneration Budget (SRB), which started in 1994, combines under one banner the 20 or so separate programmes which had previously been operated from different government departments: the Departments of Environment, Education and Employment, Trade and Industry and the Home Office.

By mid Summer 1997, three rounds of SRB and more than 500 schemes were in operation. A fourth bidding round had been launched in April 1997 for which applications closed in September 1997. Sustainability had been indicated to be a 'key issue' for Round 4 bidders with the guidance containing suggestions for implementation.

The aim of SRB is to provide a flexible fund for local regeneration in a way which meets local needs and priorities. Earlier urban programmes which had formed part of the wider SRB included:
- Urban Development Corporations
- City Challenge (the forerunner to the SRB Challenge Fund and based on the same principles of partnership and competition and now paid via the Challenge Fund) – 31 City Challenge winners each received £7.5 million a year over a 5 year period for the social, economic and environmental regeneration of their areas.

Both these programmes had wound up by the end of March 1998.

Most of the budget for SRB is administered by the new Government Offices for the Regions which coordinate the main programmes and policies at local level and ensure that businesses, local government and voluntary agencies have just one port of call.

Challenge Fund

From 1995/96 a proportion of SRB has been devoted to its Challenge Fund (CF) which encourages local communities to come up with comprehensive programmes to improve the quality of life in their area. CF partnerships are expected to involve a diverse range of organisations in their management, and harness the talent, resources and experience of local business people, the voluntary sector and the local community. Bids are expected to achieve some or all for the following objectives and to aim to:
- enhance the employment prospects, education, and skills of local people, particularly the young and those at a disadvantage, and promote equality of opportunity;

- encourage sustainable economic growth and wealth creation by improving the competitiveness of the local economy, including support for new and existing businesses;
- promote and improve the environment and infrastructure and promote good design;
- improve housing and housing conditions for local people through physical improvements, better maintenance, improved management and greater choice and diversity;
- promote initiatives of benefit to ethnic minorities;
- tackle crime and improve community safety;
- enhance the quality of life, and capacity to contribute to regeneration, of local people, including their health, and cultural and sports opportunities.

Funding is made available in response to 'bids' submitted to the relevant regional offices. Bids are expected to generate the greatest possible investment from the private sector and support from European Structural Funds as well as involving local communities and drawing on 'the talents and resources of the voluntary sector'. A strong emphasis is placed on local partnerships between relevant bodies: local authorities, TECs, other public bodies, the private sector, the voluntary sector and the local community. Funding is available for bids lasting from one to seven years, resources permitting.

Small free-standing schemes, especially those which do not link into a local regeneration strategy, are unlikely to achieve, either locally or collectively, the impact which CF aims to encourage. However, CF resources can contribute to a comprehensive strategy concentrated on a relatively small area eg. a rundown town centre, one or more housing estates or a large, multi-faceted development site.

Advisory groups assist in each of the 10 regions (see list below) with voluntary sector representatives on each; for instance, the London Council for Voluntary Service serves on the London group.

Some examples of SRB Challenge Fund partnerships with environmental projects are:
- Huddersfield Pride, following the example of Kirklees Council, has built appraisal based on Agenda 21 into its assessment of development projects;
- the Luton and Peshawar Initiative for Sustainability within the Luton and Dunstable Partnership builds on work by WWF and targets young students in ethnic minority groups and involves them in both a linkage with Peshawar in Pakistan and practical environmental improvement work.

General information: 'The SRB Challenge Fund: A Handbook of Good Practice in Management Systems' is available from the Government Office of your region (see below);

'Involving Communities in Urban and Rural Regeneration', published by HMSO for DETR, £10.00; ISBN 185 1120 483

These publications cover general policy rather than the practical details of negotiations, work relationships and activities. Voluntary groups are advised to approach their own local coordinatory body, the council for voluntary service, for further information and assistance.

The Urban Forum was set up as the voluntary sector voice on regeneration policy and has over 300 local and national community and voluntary organisations as members, with associate members from other sectors. Its activities include an information service for members, representing the sector on urban policy issues and lobbying for increased community involvement in regeneration.

Coordinator John Routledge, c/o National Council for Voluntary Organisations (NCVO), Regent's Wharf, 8 All Saints Street, London NI 9RL Tel: 0171-7136161; Fax: 0171-713 6300.

Applications: Always approach your local Government Office for your region first to obtain full information and guidance about the details of the programme currently operating. Ask to be put on the mailing list for information about the new programme. (Up to the end of Round Four bidding rounds had opened in April for funding in the following year. Bids had to be submitted at the beginning of September.) When a new programme starts make sure to arrange a meeting to discuss the information and how to proceed further in forming a partnership.

Ask your GOR for contacts with other voluntary organisations in your region which are part of a successful bid/programme of activities. This should help strengthen your resolve if the processes seem difficult and laborious and you need greater understanding of official practices.

Also ask your GOR for any coordinatory services provided in their area to assist voluntary organisations, for example Pan London Community Regeneration Forum provides training, advice and support to organisations in the Greater London area (for more details see 'Supportive Organisations' section).

Government Office for the Eastern Region
Room 116, Heron House, 49-53 Goldington Road, Bedford MK40 3LL
Tel: 01234-796154; Fax: 01234-276252
Contact: Rom Hirst

Government Office for the East Midlands
The Belgrave Centre, Stanley Place, Talbot Street, Nottingham NG1 5GG
Tel: 0115-971 2444; Fax: 0115-971 2558
Contact: Pam Hough

Government Office for London
7th Floor, Riverwalk House, 157-161 Millbank, London SW1P 4RT
Tel: 0171-217 3062; Fax: 0171-217 3461
Contact: Malcolm Sims

Government Office for Merseyside
Cunard Building, Pier Head, Liverpool L3 1QB
Tel: 0151-224 6467; Fax: 0151-224 6470
Contact: Liz Gill

Government Office for the North East
12th Floor, Wellbar House, Gallowgate, Newcastle Upon Tyne NE1 4TD
Tel: 0191-202-3649; Fax: 0191-202 3768
Contact: Derek Burns

Government Office for the North West
Room 1225, Sunley Tower, Piccadilly Plaza, Manchester M1 4BE
Tel: 0161-952 4351; Fax: 0161-952 4365
Contact: Helen France

Government Office for the South East
Bridge House, 1 Walnut Tree Close, Guildford, Surrey GU1 4GA
Tel: 01483-882322; Fax: 01483-882309
Contact: Jane Couchman

Government Office for the South West
The Pithay, Bristol, BS1 2PB
Tel: 0117-900 1854; Fax: 0117-900 1917
Contact: Robin Morris

Government Office for the West Midlands
2nd Floor, 77 Paradise Circus, Queensway, Birmingham B1 2DT
Tel: 0121-212 51194; Fax: 0121-212 5301
Contact: Ruth Dudley

Government Office for the Yorkshire and Humberside
Room 1206, City House, New Station Road, Leeds LS1 4JD
Tel: 0113-283 6402; Fax: 0113-283 6653
Contact: Alison Biddulph

There are regeneration programmes in the other countries of the UK, each with different biases.

Scotland: See separate entry Programme for Partnership, Scottish Office Development Department.

Wales: See entry for Welsh Development Agency and the Strategic Development Scheme.

Northern Ireland: Northern Ireland Office, Brookmount Building, 42 Fountain Street, Belfast BT1 5EE
Tel: 01232-540065; Fax: 0123-540871
Contact: Eddie Hayes, Director, Regeneration

Special Grants Programme (SGP)

Department of Environment, Transport and the Regions, Regeneration Division 1, Zone 4/H10, Eland House, Bressenden Place, London SW1E 5DU
Tel: 0171-890 3726; Fax: 0171-890 3719
Contact: Charity McEvoy
Grant total: £1.287 million (1997/98)

SGP supports projects in England in the areas of regeneration and housing that fall with the department's policy interests. The following rules apply to both regeneration and housing projects.

Only national projects can be supported but these may incorporate local pilot projects.

Grants are intended to provide help with revenue costs, such as salaries and office running costs. They are usually offered for three years, renewable annually, but may be offered for shorter periods. They are normally limited to a maximum of 50% of costs and usually tapered in future years to reduce the percentage of the costs met by grant. Balancing income should come from non-public sources, eg. private sector funding, subscriptions, donations, fees.

SGP Regeneration Programme – £946,000 allocated to 19 schemes in 1997/98, (2 of which totalling £59,000, were cross-cutting bids and concerned both regeneration and housing initiatives)

The regeneration element provides support to establish or develop national voluntary organisations whose main activities complement the department's regeneration policy interests:
◆ improving the effectiveness and efficiency of organisations involved in local regeneration;
◆ improving the level and effectiveness of community involvement in local regeneration;
◆ fostering partnerships between the voluntary, private and public sectors in local regeneration;
◆ promoting good practice in urban management and in the creation, improvement, use and management of green and other open spaces in urban areas;
◆ developing long-term partnerships between the voluntary, private and public sectors and the local community to initiate and carry forward regeneration;
◆ providing high quality work placements for young people through the Environmental Task force;

◆ promoting good practice on ways in which high quality design can be secured in local regeneration.

In 1997/98 grants under the regeneration part of the SGP awarded to organisations of particular interest to readers of this guide included:

Umbrella Organisations
◆ Association of Town Centre Management, to establish a fully professional, self-financing organisation (£15,000);
◆ Development Trusts Association (£25,000);
◆ Urban Forum (£34,000)

Improving effectiveness and efficiency of voluntary organisations
◆ Planning Exchange, pilot of an independent information service for community groups, with tailor-made information sheets on local topics, enquiry service, meetings, seminars, etc. (£16,000);
◆ British Urban Regeneration Association, to set up regional urban regeneration networks as focus for contact with government and English Partnerships (£30,000);
◆ Civic Trust: Enterprising Communities, training, etc. on strategic planning, capital project management, fundraising, sustainability (£49,000)

Improving level and effectiveness of community involvement in local regeneration
◆ Free Form Design and Technical Aid Services, research on the attainment of realistic levels of community involvement in public and private infrastructure developments through research/pilot projects with engineering/construction companies and dissemination of best practice (£42,000);
◆ Civic Trust: Winning Partnerships Phase 11, improving skills of community representatives, staff and partners, to increase effectiveness and accountability (£35,000)

Promoting good practice in urban management and in the creation, improvement and use of open spaces in urban areas
◆ Urban Villages Forum, a national promotional campaign of seminars, technical advice and support, and creation and development of demonstration projects (£15,000);
◆ Civic Trust – Realising the Vision, demonstration projects developing new town management partnerships (£58,000);
◆ Association of Town Centre Management, a national accreditation scheme for local town centre management initiatives (£50,000)

Developing long-term partnerships between the voluntary, private and public sectors and the community
◆ Civic Trust: Market Towns, regeneration of selected market towns affected by industrial and other decline; development of best practice for national replication (£60,000)

Alternative sources of finance
- ◆ Charities Aid Foundation, to improve voluntary organisations' access to private finance (£12,000).

Cross-cutting bid
Improving effectiveness and efficiency of voluntary organisations involved in local regeneration and housing
- • Civic Trust: Bridging the Gap, advising lead partners on how to involve the third sector, working with them on developing these skills, promoting good partnership practice – dissemination via national conference and report (£43,000)

SGP Housing programme – £341,000 allocated to 13 schemes in 1997/98. The department's housing policy interests include:
- ◆ sustaining a healthy private rented sector
- ◆ developing policies on access to and management of, social housing
- ◆ developing policy on special needs housing and gypsy sites
- ◆ encouraging the involvement of volunteers in the housing area
- ◆ encouraging the wider provision of social housing in rural areas.

Exclusions: As a grant 'of last resort', SGP funds are not available for work which is eligible for support under any other government grant programme, or which could proceed without SGP support or be carried out to an adequate standard without this funding.

Applications: These are sought during the summer. For further information approach the contact given above.

Strategic Development Scheme

Urban and Rural Development Group, Welsh Office Division
Tel: 01222-822136; Fax: 01222-823797
Contact: Mrs J Maxwell
Grant total: £38 million annually
Statutory Authority: Grants are made under the Housing Grants, Construction and Regional Regeneration Act 1996.

The Strategic Development Scheme (SDS) supports projects which promote economic, environmental and social development and which benefit areas of social need.

From 1997/98 onwards all SDS resources are being gradually transferred to the new unitary authorities. These authorities are solely responsible for determining successful new bids, provided they meet SDS criteria set by Ministers. Within these criteria individual authorities set their own priorities.

Local authorities are required to allocate a minimum of 20% of their SDS funding to voluntary sector projects.

Applications: Further advice and guidance can be obtained from the Economic Development or Planning Department of your local unitary authority. Leaflets are also available published by the Wales Council for Voluntary Action, Llys Ifor, Crescent Road, Caerphilly CF83 IXL (01222-855 100).

Training and Enterprise Councils / TEC National Council

Westminster Tower, 3 Albert Embankment, London SE1 7SX
Tel: 0171-735 0010; Fax: 0171-735 0090;
E-mail: stephen.hall@tec-national-council.blinklincoln.btx400.co.uk
Contact: Godfrey Blakeley, Press Officer
Combined TEC contracts with government: £1.4 billion annually
Chris Humphries, Chief Executive

Training and Enterprise Councils (TECs) have responsibility for the delivery of youth and adult training, together with a number of other government programmes. There were 79 TECs, covering England and Wales, (as at November 1997) of which 13 have merged with Chambers of Commerce and are known as Chambers of Commerce Training and Enterprise (CCTEs). Contact details can be found in the local telephone directory. Acronyms can vary so if in difficulty ask at your local library or council offices. In Scotland, similar work is the responsibility of the network of local enterprise companies (LECs for which see separate entries for Scottish Enterprise and Highland and Islands Enterprise).

Each TEC is an independent company operating under a contract with the Secretary of State for Employment and Education. Each has a 15-member Board of Directors, two thirds of whom have to be appointed from the private sector, with the remaining places open to local government, education, trade unions and the voluntary sector.

'They manage Business Link partnerships, Education Business Partnerships, local education strategic forums and influence the local training market. They are partners in most Single Regeneration Budget projects, most European Social Fund projects and all inward investment schemes'. Report: March 1997.

Each TEC has its own priorities and methods of operating and links can be made by voluntary organisations in a number of ways. The main programmes through which they could work are:
◆ Training for work
◆ Youth training
◆ Investors in People, the staff development programme
◆ New business start-up schemes providing business skills training and support
◆ Business training schemes – specialist and high quality training.

Being part of the TEC network at a local level is vital to find out how decisions are made and priorities are determined.

Training for Work

TECs are free to deliver the mix of skills training, work preparation and temporary work they judge appropriate to the local labour market. Organisations providing services under the Training for Work scheme and other Employment Service schemes compete for TEC contracts. Decisions about the contracts and the structure and staging of payments is a matter for individual TECs to decide at the local level. The move to funding in arrears and performance-based contracts which allow a proportion of the funding to be paid on delivery of certain defined positive outcomes, makes matters more complicated. Training providers awarded contracts are paid a unit price per trainee week. Many voluntary organisations continue to provide training through contracts with TECs. Since many TECs are rationalising the numbers of training providers they contract directly, training organisations may find they have to carry out sub-contracts with the main contractors.

Training providers contracting with the TEC to provide services may apply for a loan through the TEC from the Working Capital Loan Fund to help overcome the difficulties in dealing with a retrospective system of payment.

Local Initiatives Fund

Each operational TEC has a Local Initiatives Fund which is used to support innovative projects in training and enterprise. This funding has to be matched from other sources, and contributions from other public sources are not eligible. The size of this fund varies from TEC to TEC. For further information about this contact your local TEC.

Small businesses start-up schemes

TECs each have a range of schemes to support new small businesses. Again, the schemes vary from TEC to TEC, and you should apply to your local TEC for details of those operating in your area.

Welfare to Work – Environmental Task Force

Department of Education and Employment, New Deal Policy Division,
6Q Sanctuary Buildings, Great Smith Street, London SW1P 3BT
Tel: 0171-925 6626; Fax: 0171-925 6185/6
Contact: Chris Winfield

The UK-wide Welfare to Work programme aims to get 18 to 25 year olds off benefits. Young people are given four options:
- employment in the private sector;
- employment in the voluntary sector;

- full-time education;
- participation in the environmental task force.

The young person will be paid an equivalent of benefit plus a grant of up to £400 in instalments over a six month period. Each job must be clearly for six months and during this period the organisation must arrange an equivalent of one day a week training for which the organisation will be paid £750.

Twelve pilot schemes started in January 1998. The programme went 'national' in April 1998. The programme has called for cross departmental coordination between the Department of Education and Employment, Home Office and Department of the Environment, Transport and the Regions.

Organisations can bid to become providers of ETF placement work as part of a consortium (either with one organisation in the lead, or as a joint venture), or on their own. The contracts will be awarded at a regional or local level and last a maximum of three years and be subject to annual review. The length of the contract awarded will be flexible and depend on the nature of the project/s.

Work placements will not be 'block-booked'. Young people are referred on an individual basis so organisations need to have a pool of placements from which appropriate choices can be made. Each young person will agree a Personal Development Plan with the organisation and the New Deal Personal Adviser. They will also agree an Individual Training Plan which includes a course of study working towards an approved qualification.

Contact: The Employment Service at District Level.

Welsh Capital Challenge

Urban and Rural Development Group, Welsh Office
Tel: 01222-823136; Fax: 01222-823797
Contact: Mrs J Maxwell
Statutory Authority: Grants are made under the Housing Grants, Construction and Regional Regeneration Act 1996.

The Capital Challenge aims to support an integrated approach to capital expenditure which promotes economic, environmental and social development and which benefits disadvantaged urban and rural areas of Wales. Whilst the scheme only supports capital projects, exceptional bids to support short-term revenue costs associated with them will be considered.

Local authorities where invited to submit a maximum of two bids in 1997/98. Only one of the bids can be a local regeneration strategy which consists of more than one project.

Voluntary organisations should submit bids to their relevant unitary authority in response to the annual Welsh Office circular.

Applications: Further advice and guidance can be obtained from the Economic Development or Planning Department at the relevant unitary authority or from the Welsh Office.

The Welsh Development Agency

Pearl House, Greyfriars Road, Cardiff CF1 3XX
Tel: 0345-775577
Contact: Tom Bourne, Environment Director (Tel: 01433-845513;
Fax: 01443-845588)

The agency is empowered to help build the economy of Wales and improve its environment. Its major priority is urban regeneration and development. It encourages partnership between the public and private sectors providing grant-aid and investment as appropriate.

The agency concentrates on large strategic schemes. Many small funding schemes previously run from the WDA have now been transferred to the local authorities. (See also the entries for Strategic Development Scheme and Welsh Capital Challenge.)

WDA has for several years administered grant and loans schemes under the headings of land reclamation, urban development, property development, rural development, and community enterprise. It is responsible for Derelict Land Grants in Wales.

Applications: Advice and information on the current state of affairs are available from headquarters and the regional offices based in the towns listed below.

North East Wales
Wrexham Tel: 01978-661011

North West Wales
Bangor Tel: 01248-370082

West Wales
Carmarthen Tel: 01267-235642

South Wales (West)
Swansea Tel: 01792-561666
Bridgend Tel: 01656-56531

South Wales (Valleys)
Treforest Tel: 01443-841131
Hirwaun Tel: 01685-811268

South Wales (East)
Newport Tel: 01633-244666

Business Development Centre
Pontypridd Tel: 01443-841777

Small Firms Centre
Cardiff Tel: 01222-396116

Welsh Historic Monuments – Cadw

Crown Building, Cathays Park, Cardiff CF1 3NQ
Tel: 01222 500200; Fax: 01222 826375
Contact: Mrs Janette Watson, Historic Buildings Administrator
(Tel: 01222-826460)
Grant total: £5,270,000 (1995/96)

Historic buildings	£3,987,000
Private owners	£1,032,000
Churches	£622,000
Town schemes	£465,000
Ancient monuments	£312,000
Archaeological	£878,000
Post-excavation work	£93,000

CADW is an executive agency of the Welsh Office and performs assistance very similar to that of English Heritage and Historic Scotland. It gives grants only to buildings of outstanding historic or architectural interest, and for certain work in conservation area. It makes grants for:

◆ historic buildings, for repair and restoration
◆ conservation areas, for external work only
◆ civic initiatives heritage grants.

The latter is of particular interest to civic societies or other local voluntary groups. It covers a range of activities and priority is given to those which increase awareness of the built heritage and promote its appreciation, such as exhibitions and publications. Grants can be up to 50% of the eligible costs with a maximum of £2,000 and a minimum of £150. Applicants are expected to raise the remainder themselves and not from other public sources.

For other schemes guidelines of rates are observed, but these can vary as every application is treated on its merits.

	Historic Buildings Grant	Conservation Area Grant
Churches/chapels	50%	40%
Residential	40%	30%
Commercial	30%	25%

Applications: Obtain a copy of *Historic Buildings Grants and Conservation Area Grants* and check for other useful advice leaflets. The grant case officers will be able to answer most general queries (see information above). Technical details should be discussed with a member of the architectural staff. Grants are made on the advice of the Historic Buildings Council for Wales, an independent panel which meets five times a year to consider applications.

Repairs to historic buildings may require listed building consent for which the planning department of your local authority will be able to give advice.

Further information in the Cadw booklet, Listed Building Consent.

Welsh Rural Transport Innovation Grant

Transport Policy Division (3), Welsh Office, Cathays Park, Cardiff CF1 2NQ
Tel: 01222-826516; Fax: 01222-823248
Contact: Mrs C Swindenbank

Grants are available towards up to 50% of the capital costs of providing new or improved public transport services in rural areas (of less than 10,000 population).

Yorkshire Dales Millennium Trust

Beckside Barn, Church Avenue, Clapham LA2 8EQ or PO Box 2000, Clapham, LA2 8GD
Tel: 015242-51002; Fax: 015242-51150; E-mail: info@ydmt.org;
Website: www.ydmt.org
Contact: Richard Witt, Director
Grant-aid: £8 million in total to 2001 (see below)

This interesting environmental initiative, set up as an charitable company, works with a range of partners to grant-aid conservation projects in the Yorkshire Dales. From 1997 to 2001 it will be implementing an £8 million programme of environmental and community improvements known as the Dales EnviroNet Project, with the support of £4 million from the Millennium Commission.

The project partners are Yorkshire Dales National Park Authority, English Nature, the Forestry Authority, the Environment Agency, the Rural Development Commission, the Yorkshire Rural Community Council, plus many other organisations, district and county councils, voluntary organisations, landowners and other supporters. Whilst these agencies have pledged support, the trust is also having to raise £100,000 each year from the general public to make up the matching £4 million sum.

The focus of the project is working with Dales people and organisations to find out what improvements they would like to see carried out to celebrate the millennium. Projects fall into 12 categories including woodland planting, repairing walls and barns, creating wildlife habitats and upgrading village halls. Projects must be accessible or visible to the public and make a significant contribution to the landscape or the community. A total of some 500 projects is anticipated.

The trust can grant-aid projects up to a maximum of 50% and applicants must raise the remainder. Grants from other sources can be used to make up the matching funding eg. the Forestry Authority may aid woodland applications and the National Park Authority may support footpath or river crossing projects.

In early August 1997 the trust announced its first nine grants totalling £72,000 and ranging between £280 and £10,725. The following are examples:
- Muker Meadows, Swaledale to lay a flagstone path through this SSSI to allow both for lesser damage and greater accessibility (£10,725);
- Austwick School Flagging Project, near Settle, removing concrete and replacing with traditional stone, flower beds and seating (£4,687);
- Dale Barn Stepping Stones, Chapel-le-Dale, to improve crossing point (£601).

Exclusions: Projects outside the Yorkshire Dales.

Applications: Obtain the trust's 'Simple Guide' and application form. A project officer will help with further guidance and assessment of the application.

CHAPTER TWO

LOTTERY FUNDING

INTRODUCTION

This section gives information about the main funding opportunities for environmental initiatives as of *Winter 1998*. New opportunities arise periodically as the Lottery boards keep their policies under continual review. Readers should be careful to get all current information from source.

Organisations should also be alive to the potential of **all lottery boards** to offer some form of environmentally related funding, depending on the angle from which they are approached. The entries which follow concentrate on the boards most obviously relevant to the majority of users of this guide. For instance, arts activities with an environmental message or environmental impact are funded via the Arts Council, for example, as are performing groups with an environmental mission, or public art works. The Sports Lottery funds projects with playing fields. Both the Arts and Sports Lotteries support high quality of design in capital projects.

Keep alert to the full range of **special awards schemes** run by other organisations for the **Millennium Commission.** Several are given in the text but others may have been developed since this was researched.

Most particularly two new channels of support were announced within the sixth good cause in the government's White paper (*The People's Lottery*, July 1997). The most significant promises to be the **New Opportunities Fund.** When the fund was announced, the environment was noted as a specific area to be addressed, but without further details (unlike the other chosen areas of this fund's programmes). Further practical developments are not expected before 1999.

The other channel, relevant to talented individuals, is to be the **National Endowment for Science, Technology and the Arts** (NESTA). See information under the entry.

No further information was available on either of these attractive sounding schemes by January 1998 but there may well be announcements shortly after publication of this guide (Spring 1998).

CONTACTS FOR GENERAL INFORMATION AND APPLICATION FORMS

Arts Councils

Arts Council for England
14 Great Peter Street
London SW1P 3NQ
Tel: 0171-312 0123;
Fax: 0171-973 6590
General web site;
www.artscouncil.org.

Arts Council of Northern
IrelandLottery Unit
Macmeica House
77 Malone Road
Belfast BT9 6AQ
Tel: 01232-667000;
Fax: 01232-664766

Arts Council for Wales
9 Museum Place
Cardiff CF1 3NX
Tel: 01222-388288;
Fax: 01222-221447
Specific web site:
acwlotteryunit@mail.relay.co.uk.

Scottish Arts Council
12 Manor Place
Edinburgh EH3 7DD
Tel: 0131-243 2443/4

Sports Councils

Sports Council for England
Lottery Unit
16 Upper Woburn Place
London WC1H 0QP
Tel: 0345-649649;
Fax: 0171-273 1768

Sports Council for Northern Ireland
Lottery Sports Fund
House of Sport
Upper Malone Road
Belfast BT9 5LA
Tel: 01232-667000

Scottish Sports Council
Lottery Sports Fund Unit
Caledonia House
South Gyle
Edinburgh EH12 9DQ
Tel: 0131-243 2443/4

Sports Council for Wales
The SPORTLOT Fund
Sophia Gardens
Cardiff CF1 9SW
Tel: 01222-388288

ALPHABETICAL INDEX OF FUNDING SOURCES

SUBJECT INDEX OF FUNDING SOURCES

Access

Biodiversity, wildlife

Built heritage

– including industrial, transport and maritime

International

Interpretation/education

Landscape

– including parks and gardens

Local community environmental action

Research

Voluntary action award schemes

LOTTERY FUNDING SOURCES

Heritage Lottery Fund

7 Holbein Place, London SW1W 8NR
Tel: 0171-591 6000; Fax: 0171-591 6001; Enquiry service: 0171-649 1345 (24 hours a day, 7 days a week)
Contact: Rebecca Osborne, Public Relations Manager
Grant total: £450 million to 607 projects (1996/97)

The Heritage Lottery Fund supports projects which protect, restore and preserve land, and improve public access in a sympathetic manner. Its remit covers the whole of the UK. The fund similarly supports projects pertaining to buildings, objects and important collections. To secure funding support, all projects must be of national, regional or local heritage interest, and bring an improvement to those communities' quality of life. With the introduction of the National Heritage Act 1997, the Heritage Lottery Fund will also be able to assist projects which are simply aimed at improving public access, understanding and enjoyment of our heritage.

The fund is administered by the National Heritage Memorial Fund (see separate entry). The two funds are separate and have different purposes, but they share operational premises and annual reports. The staff of the two organisations are also separate.

During calendar year 1996, grants of £1 million or more absorbed 78% of the total given. Only 7% of the money was given in grants of £100,000 or less. However, the emphasis on allocation is changing with the introduction of various umbrella schemes which encourage smaller grants to a greater number of projects. These include initiatives such as Tomorrow's Heathland Heritage, the Local Heritage Initiative, and the Urban Parks Programme, to name but three. There were further such schemes in the pipeline (as at winter 1997), so it is worth contacting the Information Team in the first instance in order to receive the correct application advice.

In its annual report for 1996/97 the fund states that 'over 54% of all our grants so far have been for less than £100,000 and a further 28% have been for between £100,000 and £500,000'.

Breakdown of grants in 1996 by heritage field

	Value	*Number of grants*
Museum/gallery collections	£178 million	146
Buildings	£93 million	270
Industrial, transport, maritime	£40 million	50
Land	£35 million	36

The figures above have been taken from the *National Lottery Yearbook* 1997 edition published by the Directory of Social Change and refer to the calendar year.

New powers were granted to the fund by the National Heritage Act 1997 which greatly increased the range of possible projects that can be supported from 1998 onwards. The main changes cover:

♦ the removal of the concept of the 'eligible owner' so that important heritage projects, such as comprehensive townscape schemes and national parks, can enjoy lottery support on their heritage merits regardless of ownership;

♦ the extension of HLF's powers to enable it to help improve access to heritage; the study, understanding and enjoyment of heritage; the maintenance and development of heritage skills; public exhibitions; the contemporary recording of heritage;

♦ clarification of the ways the HLF may assist nature conservation, IT projects and heritage interpretation.

During 1997 the fund held an extensive public consultation into the direction and bias of its funding in the light of these new powers.

All readers should be aware that the policies of the lottery distribution boards undergo continual review and revision and that new schemes, or modifications, will be launched during the lifetime of this guide. **BE SURE TO OBTAIN THE MOST UP-TO-DATE GUIDANCE.** It is expected that programmes for local groups and some individuals caring for any heritage asset will be created, in addition to the scheme with the Countryside Commission noted below. Announcements to this effect were expected during April 1998.

Urban Parks Programme

(launched late 1996)
Contact: Dr Stewart Haring, Policy Adviser
Over £70 million allocated by Summer 1997

This scheme only covers parks with 'historic heritage interest' so that, at the time of editing in Winter 1997, many local parks of essential value did not qualify for support. This stricture may alter in the future.

Examples of grants made during the early months of this scheme include:
- Sheffield Botanical Garden, plus new educational facilities (£5 million);
- Southampton's Central Parks, to improve disabled access (£3.4 million);
- Aberglasney Restoration Trust, to restore the historic gardens of this Elizabethan mansion including its gatehouse and ornamental lake (£600,000 to part of a £2.7 million scheme).

Townscape projects

(see also entry for English Heritage and the Conservation Area Partnership Scheme)
A new UK-wide initiative will be announced in 1998. A small selection of grants of the kind relevant to readers of this guide (and displaying their diversity) is given below.
- WWF UK, for a feasibility study on a countrywide ponds reclamation scheme (£130,000)
- Norfolk Wildlife Trust, scrub removal and better public access in Hickling Broad national nature reserve to help save the rare swallowtail butterfly and benefit other creatures including bitterns and otters (£373,500)
- Winskill Stones, bought by Plantlife to stop it being broken up, for site restoration and improved public access and education (£125,700)
- Hanna's Close River Development, Newry, Co Down (£124,500)
- Dissenters' Chapel, Kensal Green, London, for restoration and visitor facilities (£120,445)
- Sconser Estate mountain and coastal land, Isle of Skye (£82,500)
- Zulu Herring Drifter Research, St Ayles Harbourhead, Anstruther, Fife (£35,800)
- New Grove Farm Meadows, near Tellech, Gwent (£34,130)
- Lincolnshire Trust for Nature Conservation, to improve volunteer facilities (£29,000).

Local Heritage Initiative

This £40 million scheme, run in conjunction with the Countryside Commission, was launched in late 1997 with a series of 20 pilot projects leading up to a full scheme open throughout the UK. It brings heritage lottery funding closer to people's everyday lives in rural areas and towns and villages. It aims to help people record and care for their local landscape, landmarks and traditions.

Case work staff have been appointed to develop a better understanding of local needs. They cover the following regions/areas: Scotland and North East England; Yorkshire, Humber and North West England; East and West Midlands of England; Northern Ireland and South East England; Wales and South West England; London and Eastern England. Contact the Information Office for their names and numbers.

Information: A newsletter *HLF News* published three times a year gives some information about grants. *Lottery Update* is also available three times a year and gives information on policy development and a list of grants by region and country.

A Simple Guide gives a general overview. Six separate introductory leaflets deal with: nature and countryside; historic buildings and ancient monuments; industrial, transport and maritime heritage; collections; museums and galleries; archives and special libraries. More detailed information is contained in the Application Pack. A joint annual report of both the Heritage Lottery Fund and the National Heritage Memorial Fund is also available. Contact the Information Team for these publications on 0171-591 6041/2/3/4.

Applications: Applicants have been expected to contribute 25% towards the total costs of a project. This level of contribution has been reduced to 10% for projects costing £100,000 or less to encourage applications from local projects. Be sure to obtain the most up-to-date Information Pack. New funding guidelines are due to be published in 1998. The pack up to this time included:

♦ information with guidance on policies and procedures to help make an application;
♦ application form and checklist;
♦ how to prepare a business plan (for projects with total costs of £500,000 or more and for all projects which will result in significant new or additional running costs for your organisation);
♦ recommended brief for historic landscape consultants (for Urban Parks applicants);
♦ local authority notification form;
♦ feedback form.

Specialist advice is given in other publications:
♦ Building Preservation Trusts (detailed guidance to help their applications);
♦ Joint Grant Schemes for Churches and Other Places of Worship (separate application pack produced with English Heritage).

Millennium Commission

Portland House, Stag Place, London SW1E 5EZ
Tel: 0171-880 20001; Fax: 0171-880 2000;
Web: http://www.millennium.gov.uk
Contact: Erica Roberts, Head of Awards

The commission supports projects which mark the end of the second millennium and the beginning of the third. It has a three-fold funding strategy:
♦ Capital Projects allocation, £1.256 billion (applications now closed);
♦ Millennium Awards allocation, £200 million (£100 million up to 2000 and £100 million to be invested to carry on into the third Millennium);
♦ Millennium Experience/Exhibition, £200 million with additional grant following an extension of the Commission's life) and support for other celebratory activities in the Year 2000.

In late Summer 1997 the commission estimated that 33% of its funding was devoted to environmental interests, of which: Environment 21%; Sustainability 12%; Science and Technology 19%; Community 36%; Education 12%. The considerable overlap between categories can be seen from the examples below. Whatever the exact proportion to environmental work, activities on the ground and in local communities have been greatly assisted, and some splendid major projects have been born.

Capital Projects: Applications for these have now closed. Several of the 14 'landmark' projects receiving grants of up to £50 million have environmental importance:

- Earth Centre, Doncaster;
- Millennium Seedbank;
- International Centre for Life;
- Eden Project, Cornwall.

Others receiving over £15 million are:

- Dynamic Earth, Edinburgh;
- National Botanic Gardens of Wales.

Many of the successful applications have been for 'umbrella' schemes, for example:

- Millennium Greens with the Countryside Commission. This highly successful scheme has a closing date of July 1998, but has already received many applications likely to fulfil its target of 250 Millennium Greens. As of 1st November 1997 as many as 4,440 requests for information had been received, 439 completed proposal forms had been made, and 132 communities had been invited to apply for site preparation grants. Contact: Martin Lane, Project Leader, or Peter Burbridge, Information Manager, National Project Team, Countryside Commission, 1st Floor, Vincent House, Tindal Bridge, 92-93 Edward Street, Birmingham B1 2RA Tel: 0121-233 9393;
- Yorkshire Dales Millennium Trust (see separate entry);
- ACRE re: village halls (see separate entry);
- National Cycle Network;
- Woods on your Doorstep.

More localised schemes, also with a wide range of both public and private partners include:

- Black Country Urban Forest, an £8.5 million project in the heart of the West Midlands – a joint initiative of the National Urban Forestry Unit, BTCV, Groundwork Black Country, Urban Wildlife Trust, Dudley, Sandwell, Walsall and Wolverhampton metropolitan borough councils;
- Turning the Tide, a £9.9 million programme to restore the coastal area of County Durham which has suffered from 100 years of waste coal tipping – a partnership of the county and district councils, English Partnerships, Northumbrian Water Group, English Nature, Countryside Commission, the National Trust, the Wildlife Trusts and Groundwork East Durham (£4.5 million).

Millennium Awards

Total: £100 million to the end of 2000.
Contact: Erica Roberts, Head

These awards support individuals. The theme for the first three years has been 'You and Your community'. Organisations have applied to administer a discreet three year scheme. Many of these organisations have a wide ambit in their criteria and it is not only the most obvious 'conservation' or 'environmental' organisations that will consider a project with environmental relevance. By Summer 1997 there were 13 partners:

- BTCV, awarded more than £3 million to give 1,000 individuals throughout the UK the opportunity to enhance and develop their conservation and leadership skills. Tel: 01491-839766; Fax: 0141-839646;
- The Prince's Trust, awarded £2.7 million for 2,500 awards to disadvantaged young people between 14 and 25 to work on projects benefiting people in their local communities. Tel: 0171-543 1243; Fax: 0171 543 1258;
- Raleigh International, awarded £1.9 million to offer 360 young people from three cities (the first was Leeds) to work on community and environmental projects in their home cities and in developing countries. Tel: 0171-371 8585; Fax: 0171-371 5116;
- Royal Society/ British Association for the Advancement of Science, awarded £1.7 million to make 500 awards to improve awareness and appreciation of science and technology. Examples of awards relevant to this guide: an information pack for children visiting London Zoo; a centre on sea trout by conservation in Wester Ross, Highlands; test of over-wintering box for lacewings with help from a community farm in Cardiff and its volunteers. Tel: 0171-973 3500; Fax: 0171-973 3051; E-mail: ba.talk.science@mcrl.poptel.aug.uk;
- Earthwatch Europe, awarded more than £1.4 million to enable 550 teachers and educators from the UK to participate in international environmental field projects. Tel: 01865-516366; Fax: 01865-311383; E-mail: ewoxford@vax.oxford.ac.uk;
- Techniquest, the Science Discovery Centre in Cardiff, awarded a grant of more than £365,000 in 30 awards to science popularisers in Wales. Tel: 01222-475 475; Fax: 01222-482517: E-mail: melanie@tquest.org.uk;
- CSV Scotland plus Glasgow CVS, Glasgow Works and the Wise Group from Glasgow New Opportunities, awarded £565,000 to give 160 disadvantaged people the chance to shape their lives and help contribute to the city's future. Tel: 0141-2041618; Fax 0141-214 0668; E-mail: csvo@gn.apc.org.

Other awards partners: Birmingham Partnership for Change; Tyne & Wear and County Durham Foundations (see separate entry); Farmington Institute; Help the Aged; Mind; Arthritis Care.

Applications: The commission does NOT fund individuals itself. Contact the Awards Team Assistant for an up-to-date list of awards partners. The partners will themselves supply further information, guidelines, forms, and so on.

Voluntary organisations can apply to the commission to run a scheme as partners. The third round opened in January 1998. Tel: 0171-880 2030.

National Endowment for Science, Technology and the Arts (NESTA) (Lottery)

Announced with the People's Lottery White Paper (in Summer 1997), this scheme is to be set up as a trust independent from government, with a one-off endowment of £200 million. Grants of around £10 million a year are expected to be made from the interest on its investments.

It will have three objectives:
- helping talented individuals to develop their full potential in the creative industries, science and technology;
- helping to turn creativity and ideas into products or services which are effectively protected;
- contributing to the advancement of public education about, and awareness and appreciation of, the creative industries, science and technology, and new art forms and their contribution to the quality of life.

No further information was available as at February 1998.

National Lottery Charities Board

16 Suffolk Street, London SW1Y 4NL
Tel: 0171-747 5300; Enquiry Line: 0171-747 5299; Fax: 0171-747 5210;
Web site: www.nlcb.org.uk.
Contact: Gerald Oppenheim, Director UK and Corporate Planning
Chairman: David Sieff; Chief Executive: Timothy Hornsby

The overall aims of this Lottery distribution body are to meet the needs of those at greatest disadvantage in society and improve the quality of life in the community. It is a single body which covers all the UK (unlike the arts and sports). It has offices in Scotland, Wales, Northern Ireland and in nine English regions (as well as an England head office). It works with regional advisory panels in England. The board is composed of 22 members representing each of the four countries. However, it is the country committees which approve the grant applications. In addition to the four national committees, there is also the UK committee. The board's chairman, David Sieff, does not sit on any of the grant-making committees.

It may seem churlish to start an entry for this responsive and imaginative Lottery Board in a negative fashion but it is important to make sure that the exclusions, common to all the schemes, are placed where they are less likely to be missed by the reader.

The main exclusion comes under the heading of 'legal eligibility'. Only applications from organisations which are established for charitable, philanthropic or benevolent purposes can be considered. Applicants can request a special leaflet. Also, no grants will be awarded where existing statutory funding will or may be replaced, nor where the money will subsidise statutory provision, nor to make up a deficit on a service otherwise statutorily funded. All lottery awards must be additional expenditure. Other exclusions include individuals; trading/profit-making companies; retrospective funding; rent; endowments; loan payments; community charges and utilities; activities promoting religious beliefs. Fuller details are provided with the relevant application papers.

Themed grant programmes
Grant-aid per programme: about £160 million

The board is particularly keen to support projects with a strong element of self-help and management by the community of people it benefits. This interest is followed through in the scoring system used for the assessment of applications.

The board is more flexible in its grantmaking than the other Lottery Boards. Matching funding is not a requirement and a range of grant proposals are considered: one, two or three year funding; sole or partial funding; revenue costs (including core costs); capital costs; and matching funds for EU grants. For large applications of more than £200,000 a detailed business plan and financial projections must be submitted.

The board has so far defined six themed programmes which are expected to rotate in order once the full round has completed. (In addition it has a Small Grants Programme and an International programme – see below.)

Round 1 (completed 1995) Poverty
Round 2 (completed 1996) Low income/youth issues
Round 3 (completed 1996) Health, disability and care
Round 4 (completed 1997) New opportunities and voluntary sector development
Round 5 (1997/98) Improving people's living environment/voluntary sector development (applications closed 3 October 1997)
Round 6 (1997/98) Community involvement/voluntary sector development (applications opened January 1998)

The fifth of these rounds (see below) has most obvious relevance to organisations working for our environment but organisations need to be aware of all the programmes as they arise. Aspects of their activities may well be highly relevant. An example of this was Round 4, New opportunities and voluntary sector development, announced in late summer 1997. About 20 organisations working in environmental activities were supported. This is a fraction of the total 1,500 successful applicants, but the £1.5 million in support makes many other entries in this book pale into insignificance. Beneficiaries included:

- Urban Wildlife Partnership, Lincoln (£97,788);
- Community Technical Aid Centre, Manchester (£161,766);
- Furniture Resource Centre, Liverpool (£280,000);
- Speke Children's Environment Committee (£112,645);
- Moss Community Allotment Garden Project, Macclesfield (£56,969);
- Coventry City Farm (£58,170);
- Groundwork Coventry (£183,874);
- Tools for Self Reliance, Northampton (£22,500);
- Greater Nottingham & South Nottingham Green Network (£25,154);
- Surrey Wildlife Trust (£10,100);
- Bath Environment Centre (£137,873);
- Windmill Hill City Farm Limited, Bristol (£280,000).

Round 5: Improving People's Living Environment (grants to be announced in spring 1998)

- Homelessness and its effects;
- Environmental issues in the community 'we particularly wish to support groups with projects which provide better access to green spaces for disadvantaged communities and which involve people in the management of their local environment';
- Work with animals which benefits people.

Round 6: Community Involvement/ Voluntary Sector Development (opened January 1998)

- Increasing people's sense of belonging, involvement and volunteering in their communities;
- Encouraging involvement of people who are marginalised in society in rural and urban areas.

Applications: The only way to get an application pack for the main rounds is to call 0345-919191 during the relevant period for the round concerned. Full information, guidance, criteria and application forms for Round 6 were available from January 1998. Unlike previous rounds, there is no closing date for applications and the programme is expected to run for at least a year. There will also be further opportunities for groups to hold more than one grant.

Small grants scheme

Total grant-aid: About 15% of total funding available (£2 million allocated by June 1997)

This scheme is open to groups with an annual income of less than £10,000 and makes grants between £500 and £5,000. Larger requests have to be made via the major programmes. It was piloted in Wales in 1996 and extended to Scotland, North East and South West England in 1997. The programme will be extended to the rest of England and to Northern Ireland during 1998.

At the time of writing very few environmental groups had realised the potential of this new and exciting area of support. Applications are particularly welcomed from new groups which must have a constitution or set of rules, a bank or building society account, and be able to provide an estimate of income and expenditure if too 'new' to have annual accounts.

Only five groups concerned with the environment (listed below) were supported (out of 543) in the round announced at the end of May 1997. But this support looks far more promising and flexible for local groups with modest schemes, than many others run by or on behalf of government which are dogged by greater accountability strictures and annual Treasury budgets.

- Dighty Environmental Group, Dundee – clearing debris from a stretch of burn running through 7 housing estates, and school information resource (£1,915).
- Environmental Concern, Orkney – 500 pairs of gloves for the annual beach clean-up (£636).
- Arthurs Hill Agenda 21, Newcastle-upon-Tyne – creation of community garden in local school ground by sub-group of a residents' association.
- Penlee Valley Community ECO-Park, Plymouth to pay for ground maintenance and pond creation for community park and children's play area on a housing estate.
- Polgrean Place Residents' Association, Parr, towards costs of gardening equipment for environmental improvement on a housing estate.

Applications: NO DEADLINES. The application form is simpler and notification faster than for the main grants scheme.

International

Total grant-aid: £25 million (First round – May 1997). At least 130 grants made, totalling an estimated £4 million – 16% of total – were directly relevant to this guide.

This is an annual programme. At this stage the board is devoting about 5% of its funding to work relating to overseas development. In its first round support to UK-based agencies working abroad, the focus was on projects benefiting disadvantaged people in Africa, Asia, South and Central America and the

Caribbean. Some of the money was allocated to Eastern and Central Europe with the aim of strengthening the capacity of local NGOs in the area. The Board is advised by a grants advisory panel of 13 people with experience of overseas development work. The majority of grants are aimed at long term developmental projects.

Grants can be for both capital and/or revenue costs and for one to five years' funding (part or whole). In most cases matching or partnership funding is not a requirement.

The first grants, announced in May 1997, showed a welcome recognition of the crying need for sustainable development measures to address poverty. However the 16% of the total allocated is not a high proportion. Grants given in the first tranche of funding which are directly relevant to this guide are listed below.

- BTCV – to help non-governmental organisations in Central and Eastern Europe to improve the conservation and management of environmentally protected areas (£339,308 over 3 years).
- Fauna & Flora International – to develop sustainable livelihoods in horticulture for villagers in remote Northern Turkey (£96,177 over 3 years).
- Forest Management Foundation – to help train disadvantaged families in the Solomon Islands to manage their local forests in a sustainable way to improve their economic situation (£20,060 over 2 years).
- ITDG – developing food production and processing with disadvantaged people in Asia, Central & South America (£471,956 over 3 years).
- International Centre for Conservation Education – to improve the lives of rural villages in Malawi (£226,252 over 5 years).
- International Institute for Energy Conservation – for energy efficient housing in the Republic of South Africa (£357,000 over 3 years).
- International Planned Parenthood Federation – to improve family planning and education in Rajasthan, India (£498,643 over 4 years).
- Marie Stopes International – education and child health services in 2 districts of Zimbabwe (£75,000 over 3 years).
- Plan International UK – to restore and protect the land on which the majority rely by establishing Watershed Development Associations in Dharmapuri District, India (£164,290 over 3 years).
- Population Concern – education and training in sexual and reproductive health in East Africa (£493,877 over 3 years).
- Rainforest Concern – to promote sustainable livelihoods in Pichincha province, Ecuador (£84,727 over 3 years).
- SOS Sahel International (UK) – environmental management for sustainable resources in Sheikan province, Sudan (£508,994 over 3 years).
- Survival International – to promote greater understanding amongst the British public of the issues affecting tribal people worldwide (£90,312 over 2 years).

- Television Trust for the Environment – to inform farmers in developing countries about low-cost appropriate technology to improve living standards and conserve the environment ((£104,250).
- Tree Aid – to restore tree cover in African villages to secure food sources and livelihoods (£283,602 over 5 years).
- World Wide Fund for Nature (UK) – to strengthen the capacity of rural communities in Uganda, Kenya, Tanzania and Zimbabwe to manage and benefit from the natural resources (£283,589 over 4 years).

Exclusions: Relief work/immediate disaster response; religious promotion; high capital cost infrastructure projects.

Applications: Guidance information and assessment criteria are available. Check the current position before applying. A new short guidance leaflet was published in early December 1997.

CHAPTER THREE

EUROPEAN UNION FUNDING

INTRODUCTION

This section highlights the key avenues of funding from the European Union (EU) relevant to this guide. It should be regarded as an introduction, rather than an exhaustive survey of potential sources.

Ecu are used in the entries. Its value fluctuates but as a guide, in February 1998 it was worth about 66p. Normally the EU's grants are given for limited periods, usually one year. Once a grant has been agreed, the sum cannot usually be increased.

The work of the Commission is structured as a Secretariat General served by 24 General Directorates (Directorates General – DGs), a Statistical Office and an office for Official Publications of the European Communities.

The funding for environmental and heritage projects noted in this guide originates principally from five directorates:

◆ Environment, Nuclear Safety and Civil Protection (DGXI)
◆ Audiovisual Information, Communication and Culture (DGX);
◆ Energy (DG XVII)
◆ Development (DG VIII)
◆ Regional Policy (DGXVI).

In many entries the information had to be indicative rather than detailed, due to the fact that new programmes were awaiting announcement at the time of editing.

When support is obtained for a environmental project through the Regional Fund it needs to go hand-in-hand with local development work and community participation if it is to meet the regeneration theme for a chosen disadvantaged area. Proposals need to be worked up in partnership with other organisations, both public and private, to meet the range of criteria.

Organisations should also consider whether there may be scope for involving organisations carrying out similar work in other member countries. A European dimension to your work will increase the chances of receiving funding.

The addresses of the European directorates have been provided in most cases. However full guidance and application forms are usually best obtained (where these are shown in the text) from the relevant department in the UK which also acts as a 'gatekeeper' and first point for assessment before it forwards short-listed proposals to the Commission. This is a variable procedure, however. When requesting application forms for any of these schemes, ask for an indication of how long applications take to be processed and what the average size of grant is so you can pitch your application accordingly.

Decisions on allocation of funds are often made in January when the EU financial year starts so in those cases where no closing date is specified, it is important to submit applications by November at the latest for schemes requiring funding in the following year. However, pockets of money occasionally become available at other times and, as with government departments here, sometimes unspent money needs to be allocated quickly by the end of the financial year.

UK OFFICES OF THE EUROPEAN UNION

Representation for the UK
Jean Monnet House, 8 Storey's Gate,
London SW1P 3AT
Tel: 0171-973 1992;
Fax: 0171-973 1900

Office for Wales
4 Cathedral Close, Cardiff CF1 9SG
Tel: 01222-371 631; Fax: 01222-395 489

Office for Scotland
9 Alva Street, Edinburgh EH2 4PH
Tel: 0131-225 2058; Fax: 0131-226 4105

Office for Northern Ireland
Windsor House, 9/15 Bedford Street,
Belfast BT2 7EG
Tel: 01232-240 708;
Fax: 01232-248 241

Information about Calls for Proposals can be found in the **Official Journal** also consult the **Web site:** http://www.cec.org.uk

COORDINATORY GROUPS

A number of groups, particularly of international development organisations, make policy inputs to the EU, and also provide invaluable membership support services. They include:

◆ *The European Environment Bureau*
◆ *The Liaison Committee of Development NGOs to the European Union* with its United Kingdom sub-grouping – the *EC-NGO Network*
◆ *BOND, the British Overseas NGOs for Development Group.*

Contact details are given in the section on supportive organisations.

ALPHABETICAL INDEX OF FUNDING SOURCES

SUBJECT INDEX OF FUNDING SOURCES

EUROPEAN UNION FUNDING SOURCES

Environment in developing countries and TROPFOREST C – Operations to Promote Tropical Forests

There are two separate addresses for different regions of the world.

For African, Caribbean and Pacific countries: Development Directorate General, Unit VIII/D/5, Building Evere Green, Rue de la Loi 200, B-1049 Brussels, Belgium
Contact: Mr Tincani, Head of Unit
Tel: 00 32 2 295 9444;
Fax: 00 32 2 296 6472

For Asian, Latin American and Mediterranean countries: External Economic Relations Directorate General, Unit 1A/K/2 Building Science 14, Rue de la Loi 200, B-1049 Brussels, Belgium
Contact: Alban Villepan
Tel: 00 32 2 299 2321/0708;
Fax: 00 32 2 299 0914

Environment in Developing Countries

Budget: Ecu 15 million (1996)
This programme aims to put into action the principle of sustainable development, and integrate environmental and development work, whilst having improvement of living conditions as a priority.

In 1994 the Catholic Institute for International Relations (CIIR) received support for an environmental education project in the Dominican Republic.

TROPFOREST C – Operations to Promote Tropical Forests

Budget: Ecu 50 million (1996)
This fund helps funding and technical assistance for developing countries and regional organisations to promote the sustainable management of tropical forests which have a local importance – the protection of water basins, prevention of soil erosion, saving degraded areas, and those which are of vital importance for climate change and biological diversity.

Some contribution from partners is desirable, although in 1993 Farm Africa received total funding for a three year project in Ethiopia (Ecu 550,000).

Applications (both programmes): They may originate from a range of organisations: NGOs, governments of developing countries, international institutions, national organisations, decentralised services and regional bodies, public bodies, local or traditional communities, private business or industry, including cooperatives.

Environmental Protection, European Commission

Environment, Nuclear Safety and Civil Protection, DG X1. A.3, TRMF 00/74, Rue de la Loi 200, B-1049 Brussels, Belgium
Tel: 00 32 2 299 9332;
Fax: 00 32 2 296 9560
Contact: Saturnino Munoz Gomez, Head of Unit

Applications can be made each year to the funds below. Calls for proposals are published near the end of the year. Full details can be obtained from the office above which also keeps a mailing list.

1) Promotion of European non-governmental organisations whose principal activity is in environmental protection.

This fund targets representative European organisations in member states as well as countries in Central and Eastern Europe and neighbouring countries of the Mediterranean. Its priorities include the following considerations:
- the multiplier effect of an organisation's activities at European level;
- the geographical scope of the activities of the association at European level;
- the capacity to promote dialogue and cooperation;
- the commitment to publicise as widely as possible the EU's environmental policy.

Grant-aid is for a maximum of 60% of eligible expenditure which includes personnel costs, general overheads, travel costs, equipment costs and subcontracting costs.

Funding was given to 18 organisations in 1996, with by far the largest grant of Ecu 200,000 (67% of eligible costs) to the Coordination Européenne des Amis de la Terre (CEAT) based in Belgium. The next largest grant of Ecu 69,172 was considerably smaller and given to the Eurogroup for Animal Welfare, also based in Belgium. Five organisations were Belgium-based, three in the Netherlands, two in Sweden, and one each in Austria, Denmark, France, Germany, Greece, Hungary, Spain and the UK.

The UK grantee was Birdlife International (Ecu 57,932 or 30% of eligible costs. In the previous year it had received Ecu 38,841).

Applications: In 1997 there was a deadline of 11th April.

2) General measures to inform and increase awareness of environmental problems

This fund gives priority to projects dealing with:
- implementation of environmental legislation;
- integration of environmental questions in other sectors;
- economic/fiscal instruments and employment;
- water;
- waste;
- noise;
- nature conservation;
- international aspects of Community environmental policy.

A variety of initiatives can be considered including conferences, seminars, training courses, codes of good practice, pilot projects, audiovisual documentaries for a European audience.

Funding is unlikely to exceed 50% of costs and all projects must be completed within 18 months of the grant agreement.

In 1995, funding was given to the following UK organisations:
- Friends of the Earth, Scotland (Ecu 211,305);
- East West Environment (Ecu 150,000);
- Institute for Public Policy Research (Ecu 143,949);
- Prince of Wales Business Leaders' Forum (Ecu 85,328);
- Agriculture Reform Group (Ecu 36,520);
- Royal Commission on Environmental Pollution (Ecu 22,432).

In 1996:

- Prince of Wales Business Leaders' Forum (Ecu 95,201 – 40% of eligible costs);
- Cambridge University (Ecu 89,251 – 35% of eligible costs);
- Climate Action Network (Ecu 81,546 – 36% of eligible costs);
- Goulandris Natural History Museum (Ecu 67,300 – 75% of eligible costs);
- Institute for European Environmental Policy (Ecu 28,590 – 50% of eligible costs).

Exclusions: These include land projects; educational measures aimed at schools, students and teacher training; environment and aid for developing countries; fairs and exhibitions; projects solely concerned with setting up electronic databases and computerised networks; research/study proposals.

Applications: Applications closed on 30th April in 1997.

European Investment Fund
(see Loans and Financial Services)

European Regional Development Fund (ERDF)

Department of the Environment, Transport and the Regions, Zone 4/B6, Regeneration Directorate, Eland House, Bressenden Place, London SW1E 5DU
Tel: 0171-890 3793; Fax: 0171-890 3809
Contact: Garry White, Policy Adviser ERDF

The European Regional Development Fund (ERDF) is one of the European Union's Structural Funds – along with the European Social Fund (ESF) and the European Agricultural Guidance and Guarantee Fund (EAGGF). Its aim is to stimulate economic development in the least prosperous areas of the community. Money is only available within designated geographical areas; those with Objective 1, 2 or 5b status.

Current programmes from funding under these objectives end in 1999. Negotiations on proposals for funding in Europe from 2000 on, are currently underway.

Objective 1: to improve the development of regions which are lagging behind the rest of the EC. Only organisations within these designated areas may apply. At present there are three Objective 1 areas in the UK – Northern Ireland, Merseyside and the Highlands and Islands of Scotland.

Objective 2: to regenerate designated areas affected by industrial decline. Only organisations within these designated areas may apply. Priorities for Objective 2 include assistance for the development of small and medium-sized enterprises (SMEs), improving the image and attractiveness of a region, tourism, and research and development. At present there are a number of Objective 2 areas in the UK: West Midlands (including Birmingham); Yorkshire and Humberside; East Midlands and Manchester, Lancashire and Cheshire; North West England and West Cumbria; North East England; Industrial South Wales; East Scotland; West Scotland; East London and the Lee Valley Corridor; Thanet; Stoke on Trent; Burton on Trent; Plymouth; Barrow and Gibraltar.

Objective 5b: to promote the development of rural areas. The present Objective 5b areas are: the South West

(Cornwall and part of Devon); Dumfries and Galloway; Rural Wales; the Northern Uplands; East Anglia; English Marches; Lincolnshire; Midlands Uplands – Derbyshire/Staffordshire; Borders; Rural Stirling; Grampian; Tayside.

No applicant organisation can be in receipt of funding from more than one Objective Fund for a particular project at the same time. Match funding cannot contain any element of European money. ERDF is primarily a capital fund and is highly flexible. It works on match funding principles, with priorities for the fund and levels of intervention (proportion of costs which can be applied for) decided and monitored by a national representative committee. In general terms ERDF supports measures to improve the competitiveness of businesses and localities. Some examples of the types of activity that could be funded under ERDF are:

◆ new premises for businesses;
◆ new transport and communication infrastructure;
◆ new marketing and inward investment initiatives;
◆ technology transfer and innovation activities;
◆ strategic research and development activities;
◆ training and support for SMEs;
◆ export and trade expansion activities;
◆ improved coordination of economic regeneration activities;
◆ reclaiming derelict sites and land;
◆ environmental improvements.

The UK is a major beneficiary of the ERDF. Finance has been made available for tourism infrastructure projects with both environmental and cultural significance such as the ERDF-funded beautification of Birmingham's Chamberlain Square, and the restoration of the Beamish Museum. In East Wales

the fund has supported the Festival of the Countryside, with David Bellamy its steering group chairman and the Countryside Council for Wales chairing its executive committee.

Regional Contacts for ERDF (as at January 1998)

Readers need to be aware that alterations to the administration will occur with the advent of Regional Development Agencies, timed to be set up no later than April 1999 and possibly before.

Interested readers are strongly advised to contact the government office for their region first for full information and advice.

Government Office for the Eastern Region

Heron House
49/53 Goldington Road
Bedford MK40 3LL
Tel: 01234-796129; Fax: 01234-796081
Contact: Ann Stanford

Government Office for the East Midlands

Floor D, The Belgrave Centre
Stanley Place
Talbot Street, Nottingham NG1 5GG
Tel: 0115-971 2570; Fax: 0115-971 2404
Contact: Mike Meech

Government Office for London

7th Floor, Riverwalk House
157/161 Millbank
London SW1P 4RR
Tel: 0171-217 3006; Fax: 0171-217 3463
Contact: Malcolm John

Government Office for Merseyside

Cunard Building, Pier Head
Liverpool L3 1QB
Contacts: Katherine Hinsworth, for Objective 1 (Tel: 0151-224 6428); Alex Rea, for other initiatives and general policy finance (Tel: 0151-224 6348); Fax: 0151-224 4671 for both.

Government Office for the North East
Stanegate House, Groat Market
Newcastle Upon Tyne NE1 1YN
Tel: 0191-202 3867; Fax: 0191-202 3825
Contact: Nick Muse

Government Office for the North West
Room 2004, Sunley Tower
Piccadilly Plaza, Manchester M1 4BE
Tel: 0161-952 4378; Fax: 0161-952 4007
Contact: Sylvia Yates

Government Office for the South East
Bridge House, 1 Walnut Tree Close
Guildford, Surrey GU1 4GA
Tel: 01483-882540; Fax: 01483-882529
Contact: Christine Reid

Government Office for the South West
Mast House, Sheperds Wharf
24 Sutton Road, Plymouth PL4 OHJ
Contacts: Mike Armstrong for Objective
2 (Tel: 01752-635030); Rick Heywood
(Tel: 01752-635010); Fax: 01752-635 090
for both.

**Government Office for the West
Midlands**
77 Paradise Circus, Queensway
Birmingham B15 1SJ
Tel: 0121-212 4550; 0121-212 5185
Contact: Alistaire Reekie

**Government Office for the Yorkshire
and Humberside**
Room 2 East, 25 Queen Street
Leeds LS1 2TW
Tel: 0113- 233 8260; Fax: 0113-233 8301
Contact: Margaret Jackson

SCOTLAND
**Scottish Office Structural Funds, Policy
& Coordination**
Victoria Quay, Edinburgh EH6 6QQ
Tel: 0131-556 0692; Fax: 0131-244 0738
Contact: Jim Millard

WALES
Welsh Office
European Regional Development Fund
European Affairs Division
Cathays Park, Cardiff CF1 3NQ
Tel: 01222-823 128; Fax: 01222-823 900
Contact: Peter Higgins

NORTHERN IRELAND
Northern Ireland Office
Department of Finance and Personnel
Parliament Buildings, Stormont
Belfast BT4 3SW
Tel: 01232-521811; Fax: 01232-521749

LIFE

European Commission, DG X1, Room
115, 5th Floor, avenue de Beaulieu 5,
B-1160 Brussels, Belgium
Tel: 00 32 2 296 3423; Web site: http://
europa.eu.int/comm/life/home.html
Total Budget 1996 – 1999: Ecu 450 million
(shared equally between its two
programmes, Environment and Nature)

The LIFE programme aims to help
implement and develop the Community's
environmental policy. It is now in its
second phase, running from 1996 to 1999.
There are no national quotas but the
Commission tries to ensure a reasonable
distribution between member states whilst
also giving support according to merit.

LIFE Environment
Contact in Brussels: Brian Ross, UK
Desk Officer
Fax: 00 32 2 296 9561 (for info pack)
Contact in UK: Verity Sherwood
European Environment Division,
Department of the Environment,
Transport and the Regions, Room A107
Romney House, 43 Marsham Street,
London SW1P 3PY
Tel: 0171-276 8708; Fax: 0171-276 8877

Life Environment specifically supports the Fifth Environmental Action Programme, which gives priority to five sectors: industry; energy; transport; agriculture; tourism. This part of the programme covers:

- industry: innovative demonstration projects to promote sustainable development and the integration of environmental considerations into industrial activities;
- local authority: demonstration, promotional and technical assistance projects to help local authorities integrate environmental considerations into land use development and planning;
- preparatory actions: projects which support forthcoming community legislation and policy (particularly in the areas of coastal zone management, waste and water management, and air quality).

A maximum of 50% financial support is given for demonstration projects running between 1 and 5 years. Revenue-generating projects can receive a maximum of 30% funding. The Commission's contribution rarely exceeds Ecu 1 million (around £700,000). The total cost of the project must be more than Ecu 400,000 and less than Ecu 10 million.

The Cornwall LIFE project was a partnership between Cornwall Wildlife Trust, Cornwall County Council and the Société Pour L'Etude et la Protection de la Nature en Bretagne. It developed a local environmental information system using IT in the service of conservation and planning systems. It was 50% LIFE funded and ran between 1994 and 1997 (Ecu 844,143).

Nine UK projects were successful in 1997, receiving EU support of Ecu 4.1 million

or around £3 million. Six of these came from local authorities and three from industry. The largest grant was won by the London Borough of Camden for Playbus Interactive, a special transport scheme.

Applications: These must be presented according to the guidance given in the LIFE Environment information brochure and submitted initially to the Department of Environment, Transport and the Regions which evaluates and shortlists them according to detailed criteria. The shortlist, negotiated bilaterally with the Commission, which makes its own assessment, is then passed to a panel of technical experts from across Europe for a final assessment.

Applications had to be received by DETR by the end of November 1997 for funding under the 1998 programme. Applicants are informed about the results during July 1998.

For further information please contact: Maggie Morley, European Assistant, at the DETR address above; Fax: 0171-276 8877.

LIFE Nature

Grant total: Ecu 42.4 million announced in July 1997 (of which about 25% to NGOs and the remainder to public authorities)
Contact in Brussels: Micheal O'Briain, UK Desk Officer
Fax: 00 32 2 296 9556 (for info pack)
Contact in UK: Richard Chapman

European Wildlife Division, Department of the Environment, Transport and the Regions, Room 9/22, Tollgate House, Houlton Street, Bristol BS2 9DJ
Tel: 0117-987 8570; Fax: 0117-987 8182 (for information booklet)
This part of the programme particularly aims to support the conservation of

natural habitats and of wild fauna and flora of EU interest, i.e. the implementation of the two key European directives (Habitats and Birds Directives) and the attendant Natura 2000 programme – the network of protected sites across the EU. Assisted projects have to take place within the sites proposed or classified under these directives. Alternatively they may focus on maintaining or restoring the populations of species mentioned in the annexes of both directives, regardless of the site designation, when essential action has to be taken.

In 1997 the Commission supported 60 projects each of which meets at least one of the three criteria:
- conservation of sites under the Habitats Directive (31);
- conservation of sites classified as Special Protection Areas under the Birds Directive (23);
- conservation of species of flora and fauna of community importance (6).

Most projects entail awareness raising and information activities.

A press release in July 1997 from the Commission noted that three out of seven proposals submitted from the UK had been supported with a total of Ecu 5.67 million:
- Securing Natura 2000 objectives in the New Forest (Ecu 3.75 million);
- Restoration of Atlantic oakwoods (Ecu 1.7 million);
- Wild Ness: conservation of Orford Ness, Phase 2 (Ecu 0.22 million).

In 1996 two UK proposals received support:
- English Nature, for management schemes for 12 marine Special Areas of Conservation (Ecu 2.457 million – 50% of project costs);

- RSPB, for the recovery of the bittern in 12 sites in East Anglia and one in North west England, in partnership with other wetland management agencies, both public and private (Ecu 1.878 million – 50% of project costs).

Applications: These need to be made first through the department which evaluates proposals against detailed criteria set by the Commission to which it sends a shortlist of preferred projects. Contact the officer for up-to-date details. A maximum of 50% of project costs is normally offered and applicants need to show they can secure the funding balance. Applications with a total project cost of less than Ecu 200,000 (roughly £160,000 dependent on exchange rate at the time) are not usually considered.

Funding proposals need to be submitted to the DETR by the end of December for forwarding to the commission to meet the annual submission date of end of January.

NGOs – schemes in developing countries

Development Directorate General, Unit VIII/B/2, Astrid 1/18, Rue de la Loi 200, B-1049 Brussels, Belgium
Budget: Ecu 170 million (1997)
Grant total: For work in developing countries – 90% of budget
Tel: 00 32 2 299 2974;
Fax: 00 32 2 299 2847
Contact: Mr Bruscasco
Grant total: For public awareness campaigns in Europe – 10% of budget
Tel: 00 32 2 299 2972;
Fax: 00 32 2 299 2847
Contact: Mrs Karen Birchall

Applications have to come from NGOs. This budget line supports 'people-oriented' sustainable development work.

Non-nuclear Energy – Joule/Thermie

Total programme funding:
Ecu 1,067 million (1994-1998)

These programmes within the Fourth Programme have addressed the development and demonstration of effective, cleaner and more reliable non-nuclear energy technologies which contribute towards compatibility between energy usage, environmental protection and economic development.

The Fifth Programme should start in 1998/99 and may well have a different name and structure.

JOULE – Research projects

Europe DGXII, Rue Montoyer 75, B-1150 Brussels
Contact: Joule Helpline Tel: 00 32 2 299 3608
Fax: 00 32 2 296 6882

THERMIE – Demonstration projects

DG XVII, Avenue de Tervuren 226-236, B-1049 Brussels
Contact: Wiepke Folkertsma
Tel: 00 23 2 295 7485;
Fax: 00 32 2 295 0577;
E-mail: wiepke.folkertsma@bxl.dg.17.cec.be

Applications: Further information and application details may be obtained from Mike Brook, Energy Technology Directorate, Department of Trade and Industry, 1 Victoria Street, London SW1H 0ET, Tel: 0171-215 2813; Fax: 0171-8287969

Promotion of Renewable Energy Sources (known as Altener)

Total programme funding:
Ecu 4 million (1993-1997)

This programme, called Altener, aims to promote greater awareness and usage of alternative energy. Support has mainly been given to planning and dissemination projects from local authorities, universities and consultants. It is not part of the Fourth Framework Programme for research and development which extends over a period of four years. A new programme is expected to start in early 1998.

Applications: Contact from the UK should be made with Mike Brook, Energy Technology Directorate, Department of Trade and Industry, 1 Victoria Street, London SW1H OET, Tel: 0171-215 2813; Fax: 0171-828 7969

RAPHAEL

European Commission Directorate General X, Cultural Programmes Unit, 102 Rue de la Loi, B-1049 Brussels, Belgium
Tel: 00 32 2 296 4917;
Fax: 00 32 2 296 6974
Contact: A Bouratsis
Total grant for programme: Ecu 67 million (around £56 million)

The RAPHAEL programme is designed to encourage the preservation and enhancement of Europe's cultural heritage, both 'movable and non-movable'. It was allocated a budget (see above) and was scheduled to run from 1996-2000 but full commencement was delayed through lack of agreement by some member countries.

A series of pilot actions were launched in 1996, and in 1997 it notified support (with a closing date of mid October 1997) towards:

- development and promotion of the European cultural heritage;
- thematic networks and partnerships between British museums (one of the chosen themes in 1997 was the History of Landscapes);
- further training and professional mobility in cultural heritage preservation;
- cooperation on the study, preservation and enhancement of decorated facades;
- study, preservation and enhancement of the European pre-industrial heritage.

Applications: Full details and applications forms should be obtained from the address above or the commission's UK offices (see introduction). Key criteria, as with all programmes are a European dimension and cooperation between at least three countries, two of which must be from the European Union.

SAVE (Specific Actions for Vigorous Energy Efficiency)

Directorate General for Energy, DGXVII-C2, The European Commission, Rue de la Loi, B-1049, Brussels, Belgium
Tel: 00 32 2 295 0678;
Fax: 00 32 2 296 6283;
E-mail: cfstathios:dalamangas@bxl.dg17.cecbe
Web: www:http://europa.eu.int/en/comm/dg 17/save.html
Contact: Stathis Dalamangas, Administrator, Energy efficiency and renewables Unit

SAVE II 1996-2000
Total annual funding: Ecu 18.3 million (1997); Ecu 15.5 million budgeted (1998)

This programme aims to stimulate energy efficiency in industry, commerce and domestic situations by funding a range of studies and programmes. It focuses on the non-technological aspects of energy efficiency and complements the technology-based programmes such as JOULE and THERMIE. Support may be given towards applied research or demonstration projects which test, develop, write-up, and most particularly disseminate their results. Proposals generally come from local authorities, universities and consultancies, but some proposals have arisen from the voluntary sector.

The Commission issues an annual call for proposals (usually early in the year) and its guidelines usually list a number of priority areas which it would like applicants to address. This list varies from year to year, but whatever the case, proposals must have a genuinely transnational element involving two or more partners from other EU member states.

Successful pilot projects are generally those which tackle new approaches to priority areas, and show they are good value for money in their ability both to generate energy savings and to be copied/reproduced elsewhere.

Funding up to about 50% of the projects costs is given for pilot projects which aim to help solve bottlenecks in carrying out energy efficiency policies, and to help others do so through the dissemination of the results. The costs of developing technological solutions are not covered. Funding is also available to assist in the creation of energy management agencies at regional and urban levels.

Recent projects relevant to this guide have included the following examples, but remember that the priorities may no longer be similar:

- National Energy Action, Northern Ireland, for an assessment of the potential for energy savings in community buildings which included an energy audit of 100 community buildings and training in energy awareness;
- The Tavistock Institute and Oxfordshire County Council, a joint project to develop energy awareness in secondary school students with curriculum-integrated projects in 4 subjects, leading to practical savings in energy use and costs.

Applications: Calls for proposals are usually announced at the turn of a year with end March the closing date for applications. Get on the SAVE mailing list held by the Department of the Environment, Transport and the Regions in order to be sent details of the next call for proposals when they are published by the Commission: Energy Efficiency, Policy and Sponsorship Division, Room C11/14, Department of the Environment, Transport and the Regions, 2 Marsham Street, London SW1P 3EB
Contact: Sarah Cullum
Tel: 0171-890 6634; Fax: 0171-276 4739

CHAPTER FOUR

LOANS & OTHER FINANCIAL SERVICES

INTRODUCTION

This section covers a number of organisations providing loans and financial support, often from a particular ethical/community stance.

Voluntary organisations need financial services attuned to their ways of working. Indeed many environmental organisations set up as charitable companies also have separate but parallel businesses which help fund their charitable activities and also enhance their work profile within the private sector.

Cash-flow is an insidious problem with capital projects of all kinds. Problems are experienced by organisations taking part in, for instance, regeneration partnership schemes and/or developing capital projects with support from the National Lottery.

All organisations embarking upon such projects need to be aware of the delays in dealing with the formalities of accessing agreed funding. This is the case particularly from European and other structural funding. Administrators learn how to juggle work schedules and different types of funding support. Coping with these problems can be an art in itself.

The case study from the Hastings Trust on page 22 illustrates the skill needed to mesh the different strands of support, and also the tenacity, the 'never say die' approach, when well-laid plans fail to materialise.

This section makes no claim to be a comprehensive directory of all the organisations active in this area, but covers some of the key sources of support.

ALPHABETICAL INDEX

LOANS & FINANCIAL SERVICES

Aston Reinvestment Trust

The Rectory, 3 Tower Street, Birmingham B19 3UY
Tel: 0121-359 2444; Fax: 0121-359 2333;
E-Mail: reinvest@gn.apc.org.
Contact: Pat Conaty, Development Manager
Board members: Sir Adrian Cadbury, Chairman; David Brooks; Allister Marshall; Martin Hockly; Bert Nicholson; Eion McCarthy; Ian Clegg; Clyde Pile; Fleur Leach; Chris Robertson; Jane Slowey; Simon Tiwasi; Louise Kilbride.
Fund target: £500,000 by March 1998, aiming to raise £3.5 million by 2000

The Aston Reinvestment Trust (ART) was set up to generate investment and support for small and social businesses in Birmingham, particularly in the inner city.

A separate industrial and provident society, ART SHARE, was formed in 1997 to launch a share issue to provide seed capital for a Birmingham local investment fund. Investment funds are being raised from corporate, governmental, charitable and individual investors. NatWest, Barclays and Charities Aid Foundation are lead supporters, having contributed £20,000, £15,000 and £5,000 respectively to ART's revenue funding for 1997/98.

ART aims to finance loans from £2,000 upwards at affordable rates for:
◆ social businesses
◆ self-employment and small business finance

◆ energy efficiency
◆ affordable housing.

It lends to projects which are viable but do not yet have the assets or track record to attract conventional lenders.

Birmingham Energy Savers Fund
'Money saved on fuel bills can be used to improve services.' ART is working with the Energy Savings Trust (see separate entry) and local partners to establish this dedicated Birmingham fund to provide energy saving loans to businesses and the voluntary sector.

Community Investment Fund
(see English Partnerships under Government Funding)

Ecology Building Society

18 Station Road, Cross Hills, near Keighley, West Yorkshire BD20 7EH
Tel: 01535-635933; Fax: 01535-636166;
E-mail: info@ecology.co.uk
Contact: Paul Ellis, General Manager
Assets: £19.5 million (1996)

This singular building society, founded in 1981, strictly limits the type of property on which it is prepared to lend money and only provides a means of finance for properties with an ecological payback. These can include: small-scale workshops;

back-to-backs; homes for people running small businesses with an ecological bias; derelict but sound houses; renovation and construction of houses with energy saving or energy efficient systems; organic smallholdings and farms; properties, the use of which will help to promote the life of small communities. All less conventional schemes for which it is difficult to obtain finance from other sources.

Mutuality, control of the organisation by its investing members in the interests of the members, and its guiding ecological ethos, is central to its work.

Examples of schemes which have received support include:
- The Greenpeace Eco-house at Glastonbury Festival;
- The Undergrowth Housing Co-op in Wales, which has strong links with the Centre for Alternative Technology;
- The purchase of a 42 acre woodland in Co. Durham, by a couple who are now running courses in woodland management, charcoal burning and other crafts.

For further information telephone or write to Freepost at the above address.

EIRIS – Ethical Investment Research Services

(see Supportive organisations)

European Investment Fund 'Growth and Environment'

100 boulevard Konrad Adenauer, L-2950 Luxembourg
Tel: 00 352 4379 3234;
Fax: 00 352 4379 3294

The European Commission launched a loan guarantee pilot programme for environmental investments by small and medium-sized enterprises (SMEs) in partnership with the European Investment Fund (EIF) in June 1997. The EIF has delegated responsibility for the approval and administration of individual loans to intermediary financial institutions in the member states. Barclays Bank is the chosen UK financial institution.

Eligibility information supplied by Barclays in Autumn 1997:
- loans of between £15,000 and £250,000;
- a term of between three and seven years;
- new investment with tangible environmental benefits;
- businesses with fewer than 100 employees and net fixed assets of less than £50 million;
- preference for businesses with less than 50 employees.

Applications: For proposal form and further information about the loan facility and the environmental criteria contact. European Loans Unit, PO Box 256, Fleetway House, 1st Floor, 25 Farringdon Street, London EC4A 4LP, Tel: Tel: 0171-489 1995; Fax: 0171-832 3083.

ICOF Group

115 Hamstead Road, Handsworth, Birmingham B20 2BT.
Tel: 0121 523 6886; Fax 0121 544 7117;
E-mail: icof@icof.co.uk Website http://www.icof.co.uk
Contact: Martin Hockly, Company Manager

ICOF (Industrial Common Ownership Finance) was established in 1973 to provide investment finance to the worker cooperative movement. In 1976 government finance of £250,000 established ICOF as the national body for cooperative finance. In the 1980s and 1990s ICOF expanded by administering the cooperative revolving loan funds of many local authorities. ICOF also manages a number of other loan funds such as the Local Investment Fund (LIF) sponsored by the DETR and BitC (see separate entry).

ICOF Community Capital was set up as an Industrial and Provident Society in 1994 to provide a revolving fund to extend its advice and lending to all organisations which can be seen as part of the social economy. Loans range from £5,000 to £50,000. For new start lending ICOF will not normally provide more than 50% of the capital requirement.

'Sound business finance, coupled with equal opportunity, environmental concern and the pursuit of social justice continue to be the hallmarks of our policy and practice.'

Applications: For further information contact the HQ in Birmingham (see above); also Llandyfan, Carmarthenshire: Tel: 01269-851211; Fax: 01269-851095

Investors in Society, CAF Loans Service

Charities Aid Foundation, Kings Hill, West Malling, Kent ME19 4T
Tel: 01732-520000; Fax: 01732-520001;
E-Mail: mhayday@caf.charitynet.org;
Website: http://charitynet.org/
Contact: Malcolm Hayday, Director, Investors in Society
Fund capital: approaching £3 million (November 1997)

This new service, launched in autumn 1996, offers low-cost loans to charities. At present it is a fund of CAF which is a registered charity and not a bank or a member of the Banks' Deposit Guarantee Scheme. Its objective is 'productive borrowing' where the expected return from loans exceeds the cost of borrowing, eg. for short-term bridging finance, to assist diversification into related areas of activity, or to help purchase new fixed assets from equipment to buildings. It is NOT 'a lender of last resort'.

The fund's activities cover the whole of the UK including UK NGOs working overseas.

The capital fund is raised from individuals and companies lending money interest free. Contributors can make reusable loans, reusable donations or outright donations of £100 or more and receive a Social Investment Certificate. As the fund builds a track record it will consider applying to the regulatory authorities for approval to take deposits at interest. Contributors are regularly informed of the good work their money is assisting. NatWest has seconded a staff member and Barclays have contributed to the fund's capital base. A Founding Committee drawn from major charities, financial institutions and companies advises CAF trustees. Controls are exercised through two committees managing credit and financial risks/exposures.

A recent loan relevant to this guide was given to the March Almshouse & Pension Charities, Cambridgeshire.

Loans on offer as at Winter 1997, ranged between £5,000 and £75,000 and were for between 3 months and 10 years.

Applications: Applications are welcome at any time.

Local Investment Fund

c/o Business in the Community, 44 Baker Street, London WIM IDH
Tel: 0171-224 1600; Fax: 0171-486 1700
E-mail: lif@bitc.org.uk.
Contact: Roger Brocklehurst, Project Director
Fund capital: £3 million (1997/98)

The Local Investment Fund (LIF) is a charitable company set up by Business in the Community in 1994 as a partnership between the then Department of the Environment, providing a £1 million endowment grant, and the private sector, providing £2 million in grants and loans. NatWest has lead this initiative with £500,000. Its board of directors, chaired by Bill Hulton of Botts & Co. also includes Ian Peters from NatWest, Robin Heal from LENTA and Roger Matland of the North Kensington Amenity Trust.

The fund provides loan funding to support enterprises by local voluntary organisations in urban areas of England which are economically viable but which cannot raise loans from conventional sources because of lack of track record or an asset base. Borrowers must be able to pay interest and repay capital when these are due. The security and lending terms are tailored to each borrower.

LIF uses an established fund manager to assess applications – Enterprise Ventures Cox based in Preston. Loans have been offered to date over a 3 to 10 year period and borrowers have been charged at base rate plus 1.5% to 3%, plus administrative costs.

An after sales service giving free specialist advice is part of the lending package but some compensation may be asked by fund managers where the demand for advice is frequent and time-consuming. The fund also acts as a catalyst for other funding by assisting applications by the borrower, and reassuring the provider that the enterprise is commercially sound and well monitored.

Loans are expected to be a minimum of £25,000 and a maximum of £250,000. By October 1997 11 loans had been agreed totalling £1.1 million. During 1998 LIF expects to open regional offices in areas of greatest demand.

Exclusions: LIF cannot assist in funding housing projects.

Applications: Applicants are invited to submit a full business plan to be reviewed in detail by the relevant fund manager. Initial enquiries should be addressed to the Directors of the Fund.

National Association of Mutual Guarantee Societies

Scriven House, Richmond Road, Bowdon, Altrincham, Cheshire WA14 2TT
Tel: 0161-9295130; Fax: 0161-929 5133;
E-mail: nigel@scriven.nwnet.co.uk
Contact: Nigel Bottomley, Director of Operations

The association is a non-profit making organisation, set up in 1991 and funded partly by the European Commission, to implement schemes throughout the UK.

A MGS is a way of providing funding to SMEs by using the collective strength of a number of businesses in a region. When the companies have created a fund of savings, that fund is used as security to assist the members to raise loans. Each society is formed as an Industrial and

Provident Society, a form of cooperative used by building societies.

There were seven societies with about 300 members in 1997: Lancashire; County Durham; Tameside; Black Country; Leeds; Kent; and East London. Funding and support to them comes from Business Links, TECs, local councils, Co-perative Development Agencies and European Regional Development Grants. (It was estimated that by the end of 1997 there will be 500 member companies covering more than 10 societies.)

NCVO/NatWest Financial Management Advice Service

Regents' Wharf, 8 All Saints' Street, London N1 9RL
Tel: 0171-713 6161 ext 2190;
Fax: 0171-7136300
Contact: Haroon Bashir, Financial Management Adviser

This service, sponsored by NatWest, offers voluntary organisations, particularly small national groups and those advising local groups, free advice and information sheets on questions such as VAT, insurance, preparing for auditors, and bank accounts. Confidential one-to-one consultancy services at competitive rates are arranged and users are also directed to advice and support in their own area.

Shared Interest Society Ltd

31 Mosley Street, Newcastle upon Tyne NE1 1BR
Tel: 0191-261 5943; Fax: 0191-261 8759;
e-mail: post@shared-interest.co.uk.
Contact: Mark Hayes, Managing Director; Alison Barret, Promotions Officer

Shared Interest is a cooperative lending society which gives people the opportunity to invest positively in Third World enterprise that will benefit poorer people and their communities.

Triodos Bank

Brunel House, 11 The Promenade, Clifton, Bristol B28 3NN
Tel: 0117-973 9339; Fax: 0117-973 9303;
E-mail: mail @triodos.co.uk
Contacts: David Hawes and George Pflug, Loan Managers
Loans: £70.4 million, of which £10.4 million (14%) in UK (1996)
Number of loans: 1,400
Total staff: 62, of which 20 UK
UK Managing Director: Glen Saunders

This bank, founded in Holland, now has offices in the UK and Belgium. Its primary aim is to mobilise savings in order to invest in the social economy. Triodos Bank merged with Mercury Provident, a small ethical bank working with a Rudolph Steiner philosophy, in 1995.

Triodos is not a charity. It is a profit-making organisation but not a profit maximising one. It has a continental company structure with executive board and supervisory board and no non-executive function in the UK. Its shareholding is mediated by a special trust structure to ensure the social and environmental aims of the bank are protected. Five sectors are prioritised by Triodos:
- charities
- the environment
- social business
- community groups
- the developing world.

It has a good understanding of the voluntary sector in the UK. Mercury Provident had been set up over a decade ago (having started as a Provident Society in 1974). The bank produces a complete list of the UK projects to which it is lending money. They are grouped under the headings: Social Business; Fair Trade; Environment; Sustainable Agriculture; Community; Social Housing; Education; Adult Education; Special Needs; Health; Religious and Spiritual Groups.

Loans have ranged from £20,000 to £5 million. Triodos Bank provides a full banking service.

In Autumn 1997 loans relevant to this funding guide have included:

- Dandelion Trust, towards purchase of ancient woodland in South Devon for wildlife preservation, and refurbishing of Bethania Chapel in Wales;
- Henry Doubleday Research Association, which runs a demonstration organic garden near Coventry, for new building and new garden at Yaldring in Kent;
- National Federation of City Farms, for a Green House in Bristol, its HQ and demonstration centre;
- Save Waste & Prosper, environmental consultancy for Leeds office refurbishment;
- The Centre for Alternative Technology (CAT), Wales;
- Harlock Hill Ltd has developed a 5-turbine wind farm in Cumbria, the first substantially community owned wind farm in the UK. Local people are given precedence for shares in the cooperative buying the turbines. Electricity is provided for over 5,000 local consumers;
- Genesis Biofuels Ltd has developed a fuel pellet made from wood waste.

UK Social Investment Forum (UK-SIF)

1st Floor, Vine Court, 112 Whitechapel Road, London E1 1JE
Tel: 0171-377 5907; Fax: 0171-377 5720; e-mail: uksif@gn.apc.org
Web site: http://www.arq/co.uk/ethical/business/uksif/home.html
Contact: Penny Shepherd, Executive Director; Danyal Sattar, Assistant Director

The forum, founded in 1991, is the UK network of stakeholders in social and ethical investment. Directors serve in a personal capacity and not as representatives of their organisation. Its 150 members include ethical funds, banks, non-profit social finance organisations, other financial institutions, financial advisers, charitable foundations, NGOs and concerned individuals.

Core funders are the Charities Aid Foundation, Polden Puckham Foundation, Prairie Trust and Unity Trust Bank.

The network publishes a useful Membership Directory.

Unity Trust Bank

Head Office, 130 Minories, London EC3N 1NT
Tel: 0171-680 6400; Fax: 0171-481 3633
Contact: Mark Davies, Relationship Manager
Chairman: Sir Dennis Landau
Managing Director: Gordon Beesley

The bank aims to provide a special service for charities and voluntary organisations. It was set up by the trade union and cooperative movements in 1984 to provide low cost banking and financial services. Every Unity customer has a dedicated Development Manager.

It is also the founder of the UK Social Economy Forum which is 'dedicated to raising the profile, awareness and effectiveness of the not-for-profit sector. We are wholly committed to principled investment which supports job creation, house building and socially and environmentally sound development initiatives throughout the UK.' The social economy, or third sector, covers all people-centred and value-driven groups which trade for a social purpose. Sir Dennis Landau, the bank's Chairman, is also Chairman of the UK Social Economy Forum.

Unity Green Grants encourage smaller environmental charities to look at their communication and gives practical help with the specialist advice of Media Natura (see separate entry). Winners in 1997 were:

+ Scrapp, a Surrey recycling project;
+ Bryson House, Belfast;
+ Hebridian Whale & Dolphin Trust.

1996 winners were: Lincolnshire Wildlife Trust; Push Bikes Birmingham; Tourism Concern.

Regional offices:
London, East Anglia and South East: 0171-481 3110
Midlands: 0121-631 2743
South West and Wales: 01179-552561 or 01222-233080
North West: 0161-773 7644
Yorkshire: 01142-682260
North East: 0191-257 3229
Scotland: 0141-332 6924.

When the offices are unattended all calls are re-routed to the Customer Service Centre, 4 The Square, 111 Broad Street, Birmingham B15 1AR 0121-631 2743.

CHAPTER FIVE

GRANT-MAKING TRUSTS

Introduction

The financial information about the majority of these trusts has been obtained from a direct analysis of the individual accounts and reports of each trust. Most of this work was done by looking closely at the accounts and grant schedules of trusts held on the public file at the Charity Commission. The commission covers only England and Wales.

Charities in Scotland and Northern Ireland register their legal status for tax purposes with the Inland Revenue but there is no equivalent service to the commission in those countries. There are fewer trusts in these countries, and these are more difficult to identify, trace and research.

Over 600 trusts were researched but only 286 have been given detailed entries. These trusts give more than £5,000 annually to environmental causes. All trusts included in detail in this guide were sent a draft entry for comment and amendment. Only 59% of trusts replied. Their amendments are incorporated.

CHARITABLE GRANT-MAKING TRUSTS AND COMPANY GIVING

Many grant-making charitable trusts are set up within companies as part of their community relations work and as a tax-effective way of giving gifts. These trusts are usually dependent on an annual allocation from the company based on its business success. They are serviced by company staff and the board of trustees comprises top company executives. This funding is covered in the company giving section of this guide.

Where trusts are clearly separate from the company i.e. with an independent endowment and independent trustee board, they are included in this part of the guide. Many are familiar household names such as Laing, Wates and Sainsbury. In these cases it has been a personal decision by an individual or individuals to set aside some of their considerable wealth for charitable purposes. Their grant-making is not directly linked to the interests of the company from which the family members derive their wealth.

CATEGORIES OF GIVING

The environmental interests of trusts have been broken down into four broad categories to help grant-seekers find relevant trusts.

These are:

1. Built heritage – restoration, renovation and reuse of buildings, particularly, but not exclusively, work which contributes to our architectural and industrial heritage (171 trusts).

2. Natural world – biodiversity, wildlife and countryside conservation (217 trusts).

3. Urban activities – environmental and regeneration activities in built up areas by local development trusts, Groundwork Trusts, civic amenity societies, city farms, community groups, and so on (30 trusts).

4. Issue-related work – working at national and international level on environmental policy, population, energy use, waste, pollution, transport, appropriate technology, and so on (74 trusts).

Only those trusts which give several grants in any one category have been included in this listing.

Other guides provide very detailed breakdowns of environmental interests/ activities. Whilst this can seem helpful to the reader this close categorisation can be misleading. A very small proportion of trusts have clearly stated policies and priorities for their environmental support. The majority work in a more idiosyncratic way. Some may support particular causes and types of activity one year and not the next. Others adopt a set pattern of giving to an annual list of beneficiaries with little leeway for outside applications. Those trusts which categorise their environmental donations tend to list them as Culture and Heritage, others call it Conservation, or Environment and Conservation, others Preservation. Fine divisions would also be related to small sums of money – the total sum given by over a third of the trusts is less than £15,000 a year.

The individual environmental grants by trusts are listed so the reader can see exactly each trust's range and balance of interests during a year, the size and number of such grants, and gauge the likelihood of a trust being interested in their particular activities.

SCALE OF GIVING TO ENVIRONMENTAL ACTIVITIES

Trusts giving over £100,000 a year to environmental work (55 trusts)

AIM Foundation	Baring Foundation
Aribib Foundation	Bridge House Estates Trust Fund
Architectural Heritage Fund	George Cadbury Trust
Ashden Charitable Fund	Caritas
Baird Fund	Clothworkers' Foundation

Francis Coales Charitable Foundation
Sir James Colyer-Fergusson's Charitable
    Trust
Ernest Cook Trust
Marjorie Coote Animal Charity
Council for the Care of Churches
Dulverton Trust
Earth Love Fund
John Ellerman Foundation
Esmée Fairbairn Charitable Trust
Earl Fitzwilliam Charitable Trust
Gannochy Trust
Gatsby Charitable Foundation
J Paul Getty Charitable Trust
Headley Trust
Historic Churches Preservation Trust
Historic Churches Trust (local)
J J Charitable Trust
Rees Jeffreys Road Fund
Jones 1986 Charitable Trust
Ernest Kleinwort Charitable Trust
Kirby Laing Foundation
Maurice Laing Foundation

Lord Leverhulme's Charitable Trust
Linbury Trust
Manifold Trust
Marshall's Charity
Monument Trust
National Gardens Scheme
Rudolph Palumbo Charitable Trust
Pilgrim Trust
Cecil Pilkington Charitable Trust
Porter Foundation
Mr & Mrs J A Pye's Charitable Trust
Robertson Trust
Jacob Rothschild GAM
Rufford Foundation
Stanley Smith UK Horticultural Trust
Staples Trust
Bernard Sunley Charitable Trust
Vincent Wildlife Trust
Westminster Foundation
Garfield Weston Foundation
A H & B C Whiteley Charitable Trust
Whitley Animal Protection Trust
Wolfson Foundation

Trusts giving between £50,000 and £99,999 a year to environmental work (37 trusts)

H B Allen Charitable Trust
Aurelius Charitable Trust
C H K Charities Limited
George W Cadbury Charitable Trust
CLA Charitable Trust
John Coates Charitable Trust
John S Cohen Foundation
Duke of Cornwall's Benevolent Fund
Dennis Curry Charitable Trust
Drapers' Charitable Trust
10th Duke of Devonshire's Trust (1949)
Ecological Foundation
Alan Evans Memorial Trust
Beryl Evetts & Robert Luff
Hamamelis Trust
Heritage of London Trust Ltd
Idlewild Trust
Iliffe Family Charitable Trust
John Jarrold Trust

Sir James Knott Trust
Leach Fourteenth Trust
John Spedan Lewis Foundation
Mark Leonard Trust
Mercers' Charitable Foundation
P F Charitable Trust
Frank Parkinson Agricultural Trust
Peacock Charitable Trust
Polden-Puckham Charitable Foundation
Prince of Wales' Charities Trust
Ripple Effect Foundation
Rowan Trust
Scottish Churches Architectural Heritage
    Fund
David Shepherd Conservation Foundation
Steel Charitable Trust
29th May 1961 Charitable Trust
Mary Webb Trust

Trusts giving between £25,000 and £49,999 a year to environmental work (39 trusts)

Lord Barnby's Foundation
Blair Foundation

Chris Basher Trust
Bromley Trust

Jack Brunton Charitable Trust
William Adlington Cadbury Charitable Trust
Charities Aid Foundation
Chase Charity
Alice Ellen Cooper-Dean Charitable
   Foundation
Countryside Trust
Iris Darnton Foundation
Delves Charitable Trust
Douglas Charitable Trust
Simon Gibson Charitable Trust
G C Gibson Charitable Trust
Glass-House Trust
Golden Bottle Trust
Hadrian Trust
Hedley Foundation Ltd
Lady Hirst Trust
Cuthbert Horn Trust
Kintor Charitable Trust

Leche Trust
Loke Wan Tho Memorial Foundation
Lyndhurst Settlement
J H M Mackenzie Charitable Trust
Sir George Martin Trust
Gerald Palmer Trust
Hon Charles Pearson Charity
Radcliffe Trust
Ratcliff Foundation
Linley Shaw Foundation
Simon Population Trust
M J C Stone Charitable Trust
Summerfield Charitable Trust
Charles & Elsie Sykes Trust
Tedworth Charitable Trust
Underwood Trust
Mrs Waterhouse Charitable Trust

Trusts giving between £15,000 and £24,999 a year to environmental work (39 trusts)

Ajahma Charitable Trust
Benham Charitable Settlement
Charlotte Bonham-Carter Charitable Trust
Sir Felix Brunner's Sons' Charitable Trust
Christopher Cadbury Charitable Trust
Edward Cadbury Charitable Trust
Sir Richard Carew Pole 1973 Charitable
   Trust
Leslie Mary Carter Charitable Trust
Cathedral Amenities Fund
Chapman Charitable Trust
J Anthony Clark Charitable Trust
Cleopatra Trust
Coda Wildlife Trust
Holbeche Corfield Charitable Trust
Sir John Eastwood Foundation
Environment Foundation
Donald Forrester Trust
Gordon Fraser Charitable Trust
Helen & Horace Gillman Trusts
Goldsmiths' Company's Charities

Grocers' Charity
Walter Guiness Charitable Trust
Miss K M Harbinson's Charitable Trust
Hayward Foundation
John & Ruth Howard Charitable Trust
Jephcott Charitable Trust
Robert Kiln Charitable Trust
Laing's Charitable Trust
Allen Lane Foundation
Lankelly Foundation
Lindeth Charitable Trust
Millchope Foundation
Esmé Mitchell Trust
Ofenheim & Cinderford
Panton Trust
Pen-y-Clip Trust
Austin & Hope Pilkington Trust
Sylvanus Charitable Trust
R D Turner Charitable Trust

Trusts giving under £15,000 a year to environmental work (104 trusts)

Astor Foundation
Bruce Ball Charitable Trust
Balney Charitable Trust

Barbour Trust
Richard Baxendale Charitable Trust
Geoffrey Burton Charitable Trust

A S Butler Charitable Trust
J & L A Cadbury Charitable Trust
Richard Cadbury Charitable Trust
Ellis Campbell Charitable Trust
Carew Pole Charitable Trust
Thomas Sivewright Catto Charitable
    Settlement
Wilfred & Constance Cave Foundation
B G S Cayzer Charitable Trust
Roger & Sarah Bancroft Clark Charitable
    Trust
de Clermont Co Ltd
Lance Coates Charitable Trust
The Cobb Charity
George Henry Collins Charity
The Sir Jeremiah Colman Gift Trust
The Augustine Courtauld Trust
D A Curry's Charitable Trust
Sarah d'Avigdor Goldsmid Charitable Trust
D'Oyly Carte Charitable Trust
Dr & Mrs A Darlington Charitable Trust
Lesley David Trust
Dumbreck Charity
Gilbert & Eileen Edgar Foundation
Eling Trust
Keith Ewart Charitable Trust
Sebastian de Ferranti Trust
Russell & Mary Foreman 1980 Charitable
    Trust
Jill Franklin Trust
Frognal Trust
Maurice Fry Charitable Trust
Gem Charitable Trust
H M T Gibson's Charity Trust
G N C Trust
Godinton Charitable Trust
D S R Grant Charitable Trust
Greater Bristol Foundation
G B Greenwood Charitable Trust
Gunter Charitable Trust
William Haddon Charitable Trust
Lennox Hannay Charitable Trust
R J Harris Charitable Settlement
W G Harvey's Discretionary Settlement
Havenhope Trust
Mrs C S Heber Percy Charitable Trust
G D Herbert Charitable Trust
Dorothy Holmes Charitable Settlement
P H Holt Charitable Trust
Mrs E G Hornby's Charitable Settlement
Inverforth Charitable Trust
Emmanuel Kaye Foundation

David Knightly Charitable Trust
Mrs F B Lawrence 1976 Charitable
    Settlement
Earl of March's Trust Company
Marsh Christian Trust
Mitchell Trust
Peter Nathan Charitable Trust
Naturesave Trust
New Horizons Trust
Notgrove Trust
Oakdale Trust
Oldham Foundation
Olive Tree Trust
Paget Charitable Trust
Late Barbara May Paul Charitable Trust
Susanna Peake Charitable Trust
Bernard Piggott Trust
Sir John Priestman Charity Trust
Ptarmigan Trust
Claude & Margaret Pyke Charitable Trust
Sir James Reckitt Charity
Mrs E E Roberts Charitable Trust
Leopold de Rothschild Charitable Trust
Edmund de Rothschild Charitable Trust
Jean Sainsbury Animal Welfare Trust
Schuster Charitable Trust
Scotbelge Charitable Trust
Peter Scott Trust for Education &
    Research in Conservation
Scouloudi Foundation
R J Shaw Charitable Trust
Skinners' Company Lady Neville Charity
John Slater Foundation
Leslie Smith Foundation
South Square Trust
Kenneth & Phyllis Southall Charitable Trust
W F Southall Trust
Star Foundation Trust
Swan Trust (formerly Mrs E D Gibson's
    Charitable Trust)
John Swire (1989) Charitable Trust
Tolkein Trust
Wall Charitable Trust
William Webster Charitable Trust
James Weir Foundation
Humphrey Whitbread's First Charitable Trust
H D H Wills 1965 Charitable Trust
Woodward Charitable Trust
Yapp Education & Research Trust
Zephyr Charitable Trust
Konrad Zweig Trust

Not known (8 trusts)

W A Cargill Fund
Winston Churchill Memorial
Fishmongers' Company's Charitable Trust
Mickel Trust

Tudor Trust
Veneziana Fund
Welsh Church Funds
Will Charitable Trust

CATEGORIES OF GIVING

1. Built heritage – restoration, renovation and reuse of buildings, particularly, but not exclusively, work which contributes to the architectural heritage (171 trusts).

Arbib Foundation
Architectural Heritage Fund
Astor Foundation
Aurelius Charitable Trust
B G S Cayzer Charitable Trust
Baird Trust
Bruce Ball Charitable Trust
Balney Charitable Trust
Barbour Trust
Barnby's Foundation
Benham Charitable Settlement
Charlotte Bonham-Carter Charitable Trust
Bridge House Estates Trust Fund
Sir Felix Brunner's Sons Charitable Trust
Jack Brunton Charitable Trust
Geoffrey Burton Charitable Trust
C H K Charities Limited
Edward Cadbury Charitable Trust
George Cadbury Trust
J & L A Cadbury Charitable Trust
Richard Cadbury Charitable Trust
William Cadbury Charitable Trust
Ellis Campbell Charitable Foundation
Sir Carew Pole 1973 Charitable Trust
Carew Pole Charitable Trust
Caritas (the James A de Rothschild Charitable Settlement)
Cathedral Amenities Fund
B G S Cayzer Charitable Trust
Chapman Charitable Trust
Charities Aid Foundation
Chase Charity
Roger & Clark Charitable Trust

Clothworkers' Foundation & Trusts
Francis Coales Charitable Foundation
John Coates Charitable Trust
John S Cohen Foundation
Sir Colman Gift Trust
Sir James Colyer-Fergusson's Charitable Trust
Ernest Cook Trust
Alice Ellen-Cooper Dean Charitable Foundation
Majorie Coote Animal Charity Fund
Holbeche Corfield Charitable Foundation
Duke of Cornwall's Benevolent Fund
Council for the Care of Churches
Augustine Courtauld Trust
Sarah d'Avigdor Goldsmid Charitable Trust
Dr & Mrs Darlington Charitable Trust
Lesley David Trust
de Clermont Co Ltd
Douglas Charitable Trust
Drapers' Charitable Trust
10th Duke of Devonshire's Trust
Dulverton Trust
Dumbreck Trust
Gilbert & Edgar Foundation
John Ellerman Foundation
Esmée Fairbairn Charitable Trust
Alan Evans Memorial Trust
Sebastian Ferranti Trust
Fishmongers' Company's Charitable Trust
Earl Fitzwiliam Charitable Trust
Donald Forrester Trust
Gordon Fraser Charitable Trust
Gannochy Trust
J Paul Getty Charitable Trust
Simon Gibson Charitable Trust
G C Gibson Charitable Trust
H M T Gibson's Charity Trust
Glass-House Trust

G N C Trust
Godinton Charitable Trust
Golden Bottle Charitable Trust
Goldsmiths' Company's Charities
G B Greenwood Charitable Settlement
Grocers' Charity
Walter Guiness Charitable Trust
William Haddon Charitable Trust
Hadrian Trust
Lennox Hannay Charitable Trust
Harris Charitable Settlement
Havenhope Trust
Hayward Foundation
Mrs C S Heber Percy Charitable Trust
Hedley Foundation Ltd
Heritage of London Trust Ltd
Lady Hind Trust
Historic Churches Preservation Trust
Dorothy Holmes Charitable Settlement
P H Holt Charitable Trust
John & Howard Charitable Trust
Idlewild Trust
Iliffe Family Charitable Trust
Inverforth Charitable Trust
John Jarrold Trust
Robert Kiln Charitable Trust
Kintore Charitable Trust
Sir James Knott Trust
Kirby Laing Foundation
Lankelly Foundation
Leach Forteenth Trust
Leche Trust
Lord Leverhulme's Charitable Trust
Linbury Trust
Lyndhurst Settlement
J H M Mackenzie
Manifold Trust
Earl of March's Trust Company Limited
Marsh Christian Trust
Marsall's Charity
Sir George Martin Trust
Mercers' Charitable Foundation
Mickel Fund
Millichope Foundation
Esmé Mitchell Trust
Mitchell Trust
Monument Trust
Peter Nathan Charitable Trust
New Horizons Trust
Notgrove Trust
Oakdale Trust

Oldham Foundation
Olive Tree Trust
P F Charitable Trust
Gerald Palmer Trust
Rudolph Palumbo Charitable
Late Barbara May Paul Charitable Trust
Peacock Charitable Trust
Hon Charles Pearson Charity Trust
Pen-y-Clip Trust
Bernard Piggott Trust
Pilgrim Trust
Austin & Pilkington Trust
Sir John Priestman Charity Trust
Prince of Wales' Charitable Trust
Radcliffe Trust
Ratcliff Foundation
Leopald de Rothschild Charitable Trust
Edmund de Rothschild Charitable Trust
Jacob Rothschild GAM Charitable Trust
Alan & Babette Sainsbury Charitable Trust
Schuster Charitable Trust
Scotbelge Charitable Trust
Scottish Churches Architectural Heritage
    Fund
Scouloudi Foundation
Skinners' Company Lady Neville Charity
John Slater Foundation
Stanley Smith UK Horticultural Trust
South Square Trust
W F Southall Trust
Steel Charitable Trust
M J C Stone Charitable Trust
Summerfield Charitable Trust
Bernard Sunley Charitable Foundation
Swan Trust
John Swire (1989) Charitable Trust
Charles & Elsie Sykes Trust
Tolkein Trust
R D Turner Charitable Trust
Underwood Trust
Veneziana Fund
Vincent Wildlife Trust
Wall Charitable Trust
William Webster Charitable Trust
James Weir Foundation
Welsh Church Funds
Westminister Foundation
Garfield Weston Foundation
A H & B C Whiteley Charitable Trust
H D H Wills 1965 Charitable Trust
Wolfson Foundation
Woodward Charitable Trust

2. Natural world – biodiversity, wildlife and countryside conservation (217 trusts).

H B Allen Charitable Trust
Arbib Charitable Trust
Ashden Charitable Trust
Astor Foundation
Bruce Ball Charitable Trust
Balney Charitable Trust
Barbour Trust
Barnby's Foundation
Richard Baxendale Charitable Trust
Benham Charitable Settlement
Blair Foundation
Charlotte Bonham-Carter Charitable Trust
Chris Basher Trust
Bromley Trust
Sir Felix Brunner's Sons' Charitable Trust
Jack Brunton Charitable Trust
Geoffrey Burton Charitable Trust
A S Butler Charitable Trust
Christopher Cadbury Charitable Trust
Edward Cadbury Charitable Trust
George Cadbury Trust
George W Cadbury Charitable Trust
J & L A Cadbury Charitable Trust
William Cadbury Charitable Trust
Ellis Campbell Charitable Foundation
Sir Carew Pole 1973 Charitable Trust
Carew Pole Charitable Trust
W A Cargill Fund
Caritas (the James A de Rothschild Charitable Settlement)
Leslie Carter Charitable Trust
Thomas Catto Charitable Settlement
Wilfred & Constance Cave Foundation
B G S Cayzer Charitable Trust
Chapman Charitable Trust
Charities Aid Foundation
C L A Charitable Trust
Roger & Sarah Bancroft Clark Charitable Trust
Cleopatra Trust
Clothworkers' Foundation & Trusts
John Coates Charitable Trust
Cobb Charity
Coda Wildlife Trust
John S Cohen Foundation
Sir Jeremiah Colman Gift Trust
Sir James Colyer-Fergusson's Charitable Trust

Ernest Cook Trust
Majorie Coote Animal Charity Fund
Holbeche Corfield Charitable Settlement
Duke of Cornwall's Benevolent Fund
Dulverton Trust
Dumbreck Trust
Ecological Foundation
Gilbert & Edgar Foundation
John Ellerman Foundation
Esmée Fairbairn Charitable Trust
Alan Evans Memorial Trust
Beryl Evetts & Robert Luff Animal Welfare Trust
Keith Ewart Charitable Trust
Fishmongers' Company's Charitable Trust
Earl Fitzwilliam Charitable Trust
Russell & Mary Foreman 1980 Charitable Trust
Donald Forrester Trust
Gordon Fraser Charitable Trust
Frogal Trust
Maurice Fry Charitable Trust
Garnett Charitable Trust
J Paul Getty Charitable Trust
Simon Gibson Charitable Trust
GC Gibson Charitable Trust
Helen & Horace Gillman Trusts
G N C Trust
Godinton Charitable Trust
Golden Bottle Charitable Trust
D S R Grant Charitable Settlement
G B Greenwood Charitable Settlement
Grocers' Charity
Walter Guinness Charitable Trust
Gunter Charitable Trust
Haddon Charitable Trust
Hadrian Trust
Hamamelis Trust
Lennox Hannay Charitable Trust
Miss K M Harbinson's Charitable Trust
R J Harris Charitable Settlement
W G Harvey's Discretionary Settlement
Idlewild Trust
Iliffe Family Charitable Trust
Inverforth Charitable Trust
J J Charitable Trust
John Jarrold Trust
Jones 1986 Charitable Trust
Emmanuel Kaye Foundation
Robert Kiln Charitable Trust

Ernest Kleinwort Charitable Trust
Sir James Knott Trust
Kirby Laing Foundation
Maurice Laing Foundation
Laing's Charitable Trust
Lankelly Foundation
Mrs F B Lawrence 1976 Charitable
    Settlement
Leach Forteenth Charitable Settlement
Lord Leverhulme's Charitable Trust
John Lewis Foundation
Linbury Trust
Lindeth Charitable Trust
Lke Wan Tho Memorial Foundation
Lyndhurst Settlement
J H M Mackenzie Charitable Trust
Manifold Trust
Earl of March's Trust Company Limited
Marsh Christian Trust
Sir Martin Trust
Mercers' Charitable Foundation
Mickel Fund
Millchope Foundation
Mitchell Trust
Monument Trust
Peter Nathan Charitable Trust
National Gardens Scheme Charitable Trust
Naturesave Trust
New Horizons Trust
Notgrove Trust
Oakdale Trust
Ofenheim & Cinderford Charitable Trust
Oldham Foundation
Olive Tree Trust
P F Charitable Trust
Gerald Palmer Trust
Rudolph Palumbo Charitable Foundation
Panton Trust
Late Barbara May Paul Charitable Trust
Peacock Charitable Trust
Susanna Peake Charitable Trust
Hon Charles Pearson Charity Trust
Pen-y-Clip Trust
Cecil Pilkington Charitable Trust
Sir John Priestman Charity Trust
Prince of Wales' Charitable Trust
Ptarmigan Trust
Mr & Mrs J Pye's Charitable Settlement
Claude & Margaret Pyke Charitable Trust
Ratcliff Foundation
Sir James Reckitt Charity

Mrs E E Roberts Charitable Trust
Robertson Trust
Leopald de Rothschild Charitable Trust
Edmund de Rothschild Charitable Trust
Jacob Rothschild GAM Charitable Trust
Rowan Trust
Rufford Foundation
Jean Sainsbury Animal Welfare Trust
Schuster Charitable Trust
Scotbelge Charitable Trust
Peter Scott Trust for Education &
    Research in Conservation
Scouloudi Foundation
R J Shaw Charitable Trust
Linley Shaw Foundation
David Shepherd Conservation Foundation
Skinners' Company Lady Neville Charity
John Slater Foundation
Leslie Smith Foundation
Stanley Smith UK Horticultural Trust
South Square Trust
Kenneth & Phyllis Southall Charitable Trust
W F Southall Trust
Staples Trust
Star Foundation
Steel Charitable Trust
M J C Stone Charitable Trust
Summerfield Charitable Trust
Bernard Sunley Charitable Foundation
Swan Trust
John Swire (1989) Charitable Trust
Charles & Elsie Sykes Trust
Sylvanus Charitable Trust
Tedworth Charitable Trust
Tolkein Trust
R D Turner Charitable Trust
29th May 1961 Charitable Trust
Underwood Trust
Vincent Wildlife Trust
Wall Charitable Trust
Mrs Waterhouse Charitable Trust
Mary Webb Trust
William Webster Charitable Trust
James Weir Foundation
Westminster Foundation
Garfield Weston Foundation
Whiteley Animal Protection Trust
Will Charitable Trust
H D H Wills 1965 Charitable Trust
Wolfson Foundation
Woodward Charitable Trust
Konrad Zweig Trust

3. Urban activities – support to environmental and regeneration activities in built up areas by local development trusts, Groundwork Trusts, civic amenity societies, city farms, community groups, and so on (30 trusts).

Astor Foundation
Bridge House Estates Trust Fund
Wilfred & Constance Cave Foundation
Cecil Pilkington Charitable Trust
Charities Aid Foundation
Cleopatra Trust
Cobb Charity
George Henry Collins Charity
Dumbreck Charity
Sir John Eastwood Foundation
Esmée Fairbairn Charitable Trust

Frank Parkinson Agricultural Trust
Garfield Weston Foundation
Gatsby Charitable Foundation
Glass-House Trust
Goldsmiths' Company's Charities
Greater Bristol Foundation
P H Holt Charitable Trust
J J Charitable Trust
Robert Kiln Charitable Trust
David Knightly Charitable Trust
Laing's Charitable Trust
Lyndhrst Settlement
Marsh Christian Trust
Olive Tree Trust
Peacock Charitable Trust
Tudor Trust
Zephyr Charitable Trust
Konrad Zweig Trust

4. Issue-related work – Organisations working at national and international level on environmental policy, population, energy use, waste, pollution, transport, appropriate technology, and so on (74 trusts).

AIM Foundation
Ajahma Charitable Trust
Ashden Charitable Trust
Astor Foundation
Baring Foundation
Bridge House Estates Trust Fund
Bromley Trust
Jack Brunton Charitable Trust
C H K Charities Limited
George W Cadbury Charitable Trust
Richard Cadbury Charitable Trust
Willliam Cadbury Charitable Trust
Ellis Campbell Charitable Foundation
Chapman Charitable Trust
Charities Aid Foundation
Chase Charity
J Anthony Clark Charitable Foundation
Lance Coates Charitable Trust 1969
Cobb Charity
John S Cohen Foundation
George Collins Charity

Ernest Cook Trust
Dennis Curry Charitable Trust
Dr & Mrs A Darlington Charitable Trust
Iris Darnton Foundation
Drapers' Charitable Fund
Ecological Foundation
Gilbert & Eileen Edgar Foundation
Ellerman Foundation
Environment Foundation
Esmée Fairbairn Charitable Trust
Beryl Evetts & Robert Luff Animal
    Welfare Trust
Maurice Fry Charitable Trust
Gatsby Charitable Foundation
Gem Charitable Trust
Simon Gibson Charitable Trust
H M T Gibson's Charity Trust
Miss K M Harbinson's Charitable Trust
R J Harris Charitable Settlement
J J Charitable Trust
John Jarrold Trust
Rees Jeffreys Road Fund
Robert Kiln Charitable Trust
Maurice Laing Foundation
Allen Lane Foundation
Mark Leonard Trust
John Spedan Lewis Foundation
Lindeth Charitable Trust
Lyndhurst Settlement

Manifold Trust
Marsh Christian Trust
Mitchell Trust
Naturesave Trust
Network Foundation
Oakdale Trust
Frank Parkinson Agricultural Trust
Peacock Charitable Trust
Hon Charles Pearson Charity Trust
Pen-y-Clip Trust
Polden-Puckham Charitable Foundation
Porter Foundation
Mr & Mrs J Pye's Charitable Settlement

Ripple Effect Foundation
Robertson Trust
R J Shaw Charitable Trust
Simon Population Trust
South Square Trust
Staples Trust
Swan Trust
Tedworth Charitable Trust
Mary Webb Trust
Yapp Education & Research Trust
Zephyr Charitable Trust
Konrad Zweig Trust

TRUSTS WITH PARTICULAR GEOGRAPHICAL AREAS OF INTEREST

The following geographical index indicates trusts which give preference to a particular country, region, county or city. The list should be used as an indication only **not** as a substitute for detailed research. It should also be used in conjunction with the index of giving by subject and the trust entries. Inclusion in this list shows a trust's **preference** to applications from a particular area but does not necessarily mean it **only** gives there.

North East

J Paul Getty Trust
Westminster Foundation
William Webster Charitable Trust

Durham
Hadrian Trust
Sir James Knott Trust

Humberside
Hull
Sir James Reckitt Charity

Northumberland
Hadrian Trust
Sir James Knott Trust

Tyne & Wear
Baring Foundation
Hadrian Trust
Sir James Knott Trust

Yorkshire
Jack Brunton
Earl Fitzwilliam Charitable Trust
Charles & Elsie Sykes Trust
Bradford
Sir George Martin Trust
Leeds
Sir George Martin Trust

North West

J Paul Getty Charitable Trust
John Slater Foundation

Cheshire
Sebastian de Ferranti Trust
Lord Leverhulme's Charitable Trust

Merseyside
Baring Foundation
Richard Cadbury Charitable Trust
P H Holt Charitable Trust
Lord Leverhulme's Charitable Trust
Cecil Pilkington Charitable Trust
Austin & Hope Pilkington
Liverpool
Cecil Pilkington Charitable Trust

Lancashire
John Slater Foundation
Mrs Waterhouse Charitable Trust

Midlands

Christopher Cadbury Charitable Trust
Edward Cadbury Charitable Trust
Richard Cadbury Charitable Trust
William Adlington Cadbury Trust
George Cadbury Trust
Dumbreck Charity
G N C Trust
Ratcliff Foundation
29th May Charitable Trust

Derbyshire
10th Duke of Devonshire's Trust (1949)

Northamptonshire
Benham Charitable Settlement
Francis Coales Charitable Trust
Earl Fitzwilliam Charitable Trust
Bernard Sunley Charitable Trust

Nottinghamshire
Sir John Eastwood Foundation
Jones 1986 Charitable Trust
Lady Hind Trust

Birmingham
George Henry Collins Charity
Millichope Foundation
Bernard Piggott Trust
WF Southall

South West

Wilfred & Constance Cave Foundation
Duke of Cornwall's Benevolent Fund

Avon
G N C Trust
Bristol
Garnett Charitable Trust
Greater Bristol Foundation
Wall Charitable Trust

Cornwall
Sir Richard Carew Pole 1973 Charitable Trust
G N C Trust

Devon
Sir Richard Carew Pole 1973 Charitable Trust
Claude & Margaret Pyke Charitable Trust
Sidmouth
Dr & Mrs A Darlington Charitable Trust

Dorset
Alice Ellen Cooper-Dean Charitable
    Foundation

Dorothy Holmes Charitable Trust
David Knightly Charitable Trust

Gloucestershire
Ernest Cook Trust
C H K Charities Limited
Notgrove Trust
Oldham Foundation
Susanna Peake Charitable Trust
Summerfield Charitable Trust
Cheltenham
Notgrove Trust
Summerfield Charitable Trust

Somerset
Roger & Sarah Bancroft Clark Charitable
    Trust

Wiltshire
Wilfred & Constance Cave Charitable Trust

South East

Bedfordshire
Balney Charitable Trust
Francis Coales Charitable Trust
Robert Kiln Charitable Trust
Steel Charitable Trust

Berkshire
Wilfred & Constance Cave Charitable Trust
Gerald Palmer Trust
Leslie Smith Foundation

Buckinghamshire
Balney Charitable Trust
Francis Coales Charitable Trust

Cambridgeshire
Earl Fitzwilliam Charitable Trust

East Anglia
Leslie Mary Carter Charitable Trust
G C Gibson Charitable Trust
Simon Gibson Charitable Trust
John Jarrold Trust
Late Barbara May Paul Charitable Trust

Essex
Augustine Courtauld Trust

Hampshire
Charlotte Bonham-Carter Charitable Trust
Ellis Campbell Charitable Trust
Sir Jeremiah Colman Gift Trust
G N C Trust
Walter Guiness Charitable Trust
David Knightly Charitable Trust

Hertfordshire
Francis Coales Charitable Trust
Robert Kiln Charitable Trust

Kent
Sir James Colyer-Fergusson Charitable Trust
Sarah d'Avigdor Goldsmid Charitable Trust
Bernard Sunley Charitable Trust

Norfolk
John Jarrold Trust

Oxfordshire
C H K Charities Limited
P F Charitable Trust
Schuster Charitable Trust
Henley
Arbib Foundation
Oxford
Mr & Mrs J A Pye's Charitable Trust

Suffolk
Geoffrey Burton Charitable Trust
Sir James Colyer-Fergusson Charitable Trust
Newmarket
Simon Gibson Charitable Trust

Surrey
Hamamelis Trust
Godalming
Hamamelis Trust

Sussex
Ernest Kleinwort Charitable Trust
Mrs E E Roberts Charitable Trust

London
Baring Foundation
Bridge House Estates Trust Fund
Drapers' Charitable Fund
Fishmongers' Company's Charitable Trust
Goldsmiths' Company's Charities
Heritage of London Trust Ltd
Westminster
Westminster Foundation

Channel Islands
H D H Wills 1965 Charitable Trust

Wales
C L A Charitable Trust
Simon Gibson Charitable Trust
G C Gibson Charitable Trust
Lady Hind Trust

Historic Churches Preservation Trust
Dorothy Holmes Charitable Settlement
Marshall's Charity
National Gardens Scheme
Oakdale Trust
Pen-y-Clip Trust
Bernard Piggott Trust
Ratcliff Foundation
Welsh Church Funds

Scotland
Baird Trust
WA Cargill Fund
Douglas Charitable Trust
Gannochy Trust
Helen & Horace Gillman Trusts
Miss K M Harbinson's Charitable Trust
Kintore Charitable Trust
Mickel Fund
P F Charitable Trust
Scottish Churches Architectural Heritage
    Trust
James Weir Foundation
Kondar Zweig Trust

Ireland
Garnett Charitable Trust
Helen & Horace Gillman Trusts
Allen Lane Foundation
Esmé Mitchell Trust

International
Aim Foundation
Ajahma Charitable Trust
Ashden Charitable Trust
Aurelius Charitable Trust
Blair Foundation
Chris Brasher Trust
Bromley Trust
A S Butler Charitable Trust
George W Cadbury Charitable Trust
William Adlington Cadbury Charitable Trust
Leslie Mary Carter Charitable Trust
Thomas Sivewright Catto Charitable
    Settlement
Charities Aid Foundation
Roger & Sarah Bancroft Clark Charitable
    Trust
Cleopatra Trust

Clothworkers' Foundation and Trusts
Cobb Charity
John S Cohen Foundation
George Henry Collins Charity
Ernest Cook Trust
Majorie Coote Animal Charity
Holbeche Corfield Charitable Trust
Iris Darnton Foundation
Dumbreck Charity
Earth Love Fund
Ecological Foundation
Gilbert & Eileen Edgar Foundation
John Ellerman Foundation
Environment Foundation
Keith Ewart Charitable Trust
Russell & Mary Foreman 1980 Charitable
    Trust
Donald Forrester Trust
Jill Franklin Trust
Maurice Fry Charitable Trust
Gatsby Charitable Foundation
Gem Charitable Trust
Glass-House Trust
Walter Guinness Charitable Trust
William Haddon Charitable Trust
Miss K M Harbinson's Charitable Trust
Headley Trust
Mrs C S Heber Percy Charitable Trust
G D Herbert Charitable Trust
Inverforth Charitable Trust
J J Charitable Trust
John Jarrold Trust
Jephcott Charitable Trust
Emmanuel Kaye Foundation
Ernest Kleinwort Charitable Trust
Kirby Laing Foundation
Maurice Laing Foundation
Mrs F B Lawrence 1976 Charitable
    Settlement
Linbury Trust
Lindeth Charitable Trust
Loke Wan Tho Memorial Trust
Mark Leonard Trust
Marsh Christian Trust
Monument Trust
Peter Nathan Charitable Trust
Network Foundation
Oakdale Trust
Paget Charitable Trust

Rudolph Palumbo Charitable Trust
Cecil Pilkington Charitable Trust
Polden-Puckham Charitable Trust
Jacob Rothschild GAM Charitable Trust
Rowan Trust
Alan & Babette Sainsbury Charitable
    Fund
Peter Scott Trust for Education &
    Research in Conservation
R J Shaw Charitable Trust
David Shepherd Conservation Foundation
Simon Population Trust
Stanley Smith UK Horticultural Trust
Staples Trust
Bernard Sunley Charitable Trust
John Swire (1989) Charitable Trust
Sylvanus Charitable Trust
Tedworth Charitable Trust
Tudor Trust
Mary Webb Trust
Garfield Weston Foundation
Whitley Animal Protection Trust
Will Charitable Trust
Zephyr Charitable Trust

ALPHABETICAL INDEX OF TRUSTS

GRANT-MAKING TRUSTS

29th May 1961 Charitable Trust

c/o Macfarlanes, 10 Norwich Street, London EC4A 1BD
Tel: 0171-831 9222; Fax: 0171-831 9607
Contact: The Secretary
Trustees: V E Treves; J H Cattell; P Varney; A J Mead
Grant total: £2,969,000
Beneficial area: UK
'It has not been the policy of the trustees simply to augment resources of institutions which have substantial reserves.'

Grants may be divided into three principal categories:
a) Capital grants for projects in process of development or which are instigated by the trustees.
b) Recurrent grants (up to three years) to help ensure the viability of such projects.
c) Recurrent grants (up to three years) to assist the general finance of institutions in need.

In 1994/95, the trust had assets of nearly £59 million which produced an income of £3.4 million. Grants span from £250 to £450,000, and cover a broad range of charitable activity, with a special interest in the welfare of young people. Of the 300 grants, 178 (60%) were between £2,000 and £10,000. Only 35 grants were for less than £1,000.

Support for the Coventry area continued, but it seemed to have spread to other parts of the West Midlands.

Grants relevant to this guide totalled over £55,000 (2% of total grant-aid) in 1994/95 and were given to:
- National Playing Fields Association (£15,000);
- Sustrans (£10,000);
- Country Trust, and Farms for City Children (£5,000 each);
- CPRE, Droitwich Canals Trust, Friends of the Earth, Sudbourne Parish Church (£3,000);
- Friends of Christ Church Spitalfields, Learning Through Landscapes, Warwickshire Wildlife Trust (£2,000 each);
- Woodland Trust (£1,500);
- Castle Bromwich Hall Gardens Trust, Coventry City Farm, Discovery Docklands Trust (£1,000 each).

Exclusions: No grants to individuals.

Applications: To the secretary in writing. Applicants must enclose a copy of their most recent accounts. Trustees meet in March, June, September and December.

AIM Foundation

Farrer & Co., 66 Lincoln's Inn Fields, London WC2A 3LH
Tel: 0171-242 2022
Contact: Charles Woodhouse
Trustees: Ian Roy Marks; Mrs Angela D Marks; Charles F Woodhouse
Grant total: £650,000 (1996/97)
Beneficial area: UK and overseas

The foundation was called the Ian Roy Marks Charitable Trust until 1993. Mr Marks is also a trustee of the Ripple Effect Foundation (see separate entry). Both these charities have given support to the Network for Social Change (see separate entry). Mr Marks is also a trustee of two other proactive trusts, the Foundation for Integrated Medicine, which supports and promotes joint research initiatives by conventional and complementary medicine, and the Chiron Trust, which supports various forms of healing. The foundation is adamant that it initiates its own contacts and projects for support. Outside approaches are firmly discouraged.

In 1996/97 the foundation's assets of £5.5 million generated an income of £204,000, whilst grants of £650,000 were made. A total of 27 grants of over £1,000 were given and ranged between under £1,000 to £295,000 (for the Essex Community Foundation).

The foundation's grants for 1996/97 were grouped under the following headings: healthcare; community development including homelessness; environment; and miscellaneous interests including youth development. Grants directly relevant to this guide were:
- Sustrans (£100,000);
- Gaia Foundation (£5,000);
- Ecological Foundation (£3,200).

Other grants included:
- Network for Social Change (£36,000);
- New Economics Foundation (£6,000).

Exclusions: Individuals.

Applications: It cannot be stressed enough that this foundation does not wish to receive applications. 'The trustees initiate all their own projects and do not respond to unsolicited applications.'

The Ajahma Charitable Trust

4 Jephtha Road, SW18 1QH
Contact: Suzanne Hunt, Administrator
Trustees: Jennifer Sheridan; Elizabeth Simpson; James Sinclair Taylor; Michael Horsman.
Grant total: £251,000 (1995/96)
Beneficial area: UK and overseas.

In 1995/96 the trust had assets of £3.5 million, an income of £178,000 and have 41 grants totalling £251,000. Many

charities are regularly supported, and the trust has a particular interest in national and international work in development and justice. It grants show a willingness to help more 'radical' work and that which is to do with socio-environmental concerns.

Grants in 1995/96 with some relevance to this guide totalled nearly £21,000 – 8% of grant compared with £40,000 – 16% of grant-aid given in the previous year:
- Panos Tobacco Information Programme (£10,000);
- Population Concern (£8,000);
- Traidcraft £2,500.

Exclusions: No support for animal or religious appeals or individuals.

Applications: The trustees have recently decided not to consider any further applications for grants unless the organisation is personally known to one of the trustees. 'This change in policy has been made because of an increase, over recent months, in the number of applications we have been receiving.' The trustees meet twice a year to consider applications. No application form is available. Write with brief outline of project. If the trustees wish for further information, a format will be made available for applicants to follow.

The H B Allen Charitable Trust

Bolinge Hill Farm, Buriton, Petersfield, Hants GU31 4NN
Tel: 01730-265031
Contact: P B Shone
Trustees: H B Allen; P B Shone.
Grant total: £771,000 (1996)
Beneficial area: UK.

In 1996 the trust had assets of £9,703,000, an income of £688,000 and gave £771,000 in 39 grants, 28 of which were for £10,000 or more. The trust has said it has no typical grant size and that its donations can be recurring or one-off and for both revenue or capital purposes.

In 1996 six grants totalling £70,000 (9% of grant-aid) were directly relevant to this guide:

- WaterAid (£25,000);
- Intermediate Technology (£15,000);
- Tools for Self Reliance (Milton Keynes), Falklands Conservation – Penguin Appeal (£10,000 each).
- River Mersey Inshore Rescue Service, Habitat Scotland (£5,000 each).

Exclusions: Individuals, organisations not registered as charities.

Applications: In writing to the correspondent. Trustees meet in March, June, September and December. Because of its great number of applications acknowledgements cannot be expected.

The Arbib Foundation

The Old Rectory, 12 Thameside, Henley on Thames, Oxon RG9 1LH
Tel: 01491-417000
Contact: L R Sanderson
Trustees: M Arbib; A H E Arbib; Hon J S Kirkwood.
Grant total: £1,527,000 (1996/97)
Beneficial area: UK, preference for Henley. The trust was established 'in particular to support the establishment of a museum in the Thames Valley for the education of the general public in the history, geography and ecology of the Thames Valley and the River Thames'.

No list of donations has been filed with its accounts at the Charity Commission since 1993/94. Both 1995/96 and 1993/94 were exceptional years with massive donations received by the trust (£3.7 million in 1995/96 largely from Perpetual shares, Mr Arbib's highly successful investment company). This generous input was for the River & Rowing Museum Foundation which has received support of at least £8 million from this foundation. Grants in 1993/94 totalled £4,051,000 and included the following gifts relevant to this guide:

- River and Rowing Museum (£4,000,000);
- Global Action Plan (£5,000);
- Water Education Trust (£3,000);
- Henley & District Agricultural Association (£2,000);
- Open Spaces Society (£500);
- Wiltshire Wildlife Trust (£250).

In 1992/93, for instance, when grant-aid totalled £69,000 three grants relevant to this guide were:

- Thames Salmon Trust (£20,000);
- River & Rowing Museum (£10,000);
- BBONT (£1,000).

Applications: Only local environmental charities will be considered.

The Architectural Heritage Fund

27 John Adam Street, London WC2N 6HX
Tel: 0171-925 0199
Fax: 0171-930 0295
Contact: Hilary Weir
Trustees: Council of Management: Sir John James, Chairman; Nicholas Baring; Robert Clow; Malcolm Crowder; Sir Brian Jenkins; Peter Rumble; Maurice Stonefrost; Roy Worskett; Dr Roger Wools; William Cadell; Jane Sharman.
Grant total: £2,208,000 in loans contracted, £2,302,000 for loans offered (1995/96)
Beneficial area: UK.

Policy in brief: Low interest loans, advice and information to encourage and assist the preservation and rehabilitation of old buildings by preservation trusts and other charities. Loans supplement funds which groups raise themselves. Grants are also made for feasibility studies on potential projects.

Background: The Architectural Heritage Fund (AHF), a non-profit making company with charitable status, operates a revolving fund to provide low-interest working capital to buildings preservation trusts and other charities undertaking the restoration of old buildings. It was set up in 1976 after a Civic Trust report to the

Department of the Environment suggested a national fund be established to provide low-interest loans.

The AHF is controlled by a Council of Management, half of whom are appointed by the Department of Culture Media and Sport. The AHF's principal source of working capital over the years has been government grants supplemented by donations from companies, charitable trust and individuals.

Loans

'The AHF makes low interest loans to organisations with charitable status for projects involving a change in ownership or use of the building concerned. Only buildings which enjoy the statutory protection of being listed and/or in a conservation area are eligible. AHF loans are normally made for a period of two years and for up to 50% of the estimated cost of any qualifying preservation project (including acquisition, repair, rehabilitation and/or conversion to a new use), subject to a maximum of £250,000. Every borrower must provide adequate security in the form of a first charge (mortgage) on a property to which it has a free and marketable title (including the building for which the loan is required) or a formal repayment guarantee from a suitable corporate body (e.g. a bank). The AHF charges interest at 5% simple for the agreed period of the loan.'

The AHF is willing to lend up to 75% of estimated gross cost to buildings preservation trusts (BPTs) on its Register. If a first charge is to be provided as security, the amount of the loan will not exceed 70% of the estimated resale value of the property over which the charge is taken. The AHF's maximum loan is currently £325,000 for BPTs.

Feasibility Study Grants

'An AHF feasibility study grant is a tool for assessing the risks inherent in a particular project. It is neither the first stage of a project nor a developed scheme for the repair and rehabilitation of an historic building, but a separate and preliminary exercise undertaken to enable a preservation trust to decide whether to proceed further. Feasibility study grants of up to £5,000 are available to any organisation with charitable status established for the purpose of restoring an historic building or buildings, particularly new trusts preparing to embark on their first projects. The potential project must involve a building which is listed and/or in a conservation area, whose repair and rehabilitation would be likely to qualify for an AHF loan, and which the trust intends to acquire and repair should doing so appear to be viable.'

Project Administration Grants

'The purpose of an AHF project administration grant is to enable new or inactive buildings preservation trusts to employ a part-time administrator in order to progress a project from AHF loan offer stage to contract stage and beyond. Only organisations on the AHF's Register of buildings preservation trusts are eligible.

In addition, the organisation must:
a) be applying for an AHF loan either for its first project or for the first project to be undertaken for at least two years;
b) have a capital reserve of £5,000 or less; and
c) have neither a paid employee of its own nor administrative support from a local authority or other organisation.'

Other Activities

The AHF gives advice on the formation and activities of buildings preservation trusts across the UK. It is an active member of the United Kingdom Association of Preservation Trusts (APT) which it helped to found and to which it provides financial and practical support. Both on its own and with the APT, the AHF organises periodic conferences and seminars.

During 1996/97 the AHF contracted 17 new loans valued at £2.2 million and 20 loans valued at £2. million were repaid. (Since the AHF commenced business in 1976, 341 loans amounting to £23.9 million have been contracted and loans to the value of £18 million were repaid).

During 1996/97, feasibility study grants amounting to £114,611 were offered and the AHF's Register of buildings preservation trusts grew by 17 to 165.

Recent loans contracted by AHF include the North Craven Building Trust for the Folly in Settle, North Yorkshire, Cockburn Conservation Trust for the Manse and Granary in Leith, Edinburgh, and Gwynedd Building Preservation Trust for Gwendar Mill near Conway.

The AHF expects to contract a loan offered to Belfast Buildings Preservation Trust for St Patrick's Church Board School, Donegall Street, Belfast in 1997/98.

Exclusions: Applications from private individuals and non-charitable organisations. Applications for projects not involving a change of ownership or of use.

Applications: Detailed notes for applicants for loans and feasibility studies are supplied with the application forms. Applications are considered quarterly in March, June, September and December and should be submitted at least six weeks before the council meeting at which decisions are taken. Telephone enquiries are welcome. Applicants must provide evidence of charitable status, a description and photographs of the property, architect's drawings and specifications, details of estimated income and expenditure, and either an estate agent's written estimate of the property's resale value or the name of a repayment guarantor. The AHF budgets for an average commitment of over £1 million each quarter in new loan offers. Offers normally remain open for a period of six months.

The Ashden Charitable Trust

See entry for the 'Sainsbury Family Charitable Trusts'
Tel: 0171-410 0330
Contact: Michael Pattison
Trustees: Mrs S Butler-Sloss; R Butler-Sloss; Miss J Portrait.

Grant total: £487,000 grant approvals (1995/96)
Beneficial area: UK and overseas.

This is one of the more recently established Sainsbury family charitable trusts, with Lord Sainsbury of Preston Candover's daughter and her husband as its trustees. Its endowment was increased in 1994/95 with £5+ million of shares in J Sainsbury plc. In 1995/96 its investments had a market value of over £12 million which generated a gross income of £507,000.

Grants were given in the following fields:
◆ Environmental projects UK;
◆ Environmental projects overseas;
◆ Community arts;
◆ Urban rejuvenation;
◆ Homelessness;
◆ General.

The trustees are 'advised by consultants with appropriate expertise' and seminars in its fields of interest may be arranged.

This trust is remarkable amongst charitable grant-making trusts for its enlightened support for transport and energy initiatives and in its giving to revolving loan funds rather than confining itself to grants. It seems to be developing as a leader in progressive environmental funding even amongst the Sainsbury family charitable trusts. A couple of its beneficiaries are also supported by the related trusts of Mrs Butler-Sloss's siblings – J J and Mark Leonard charitable trusts. However there are overlapping interests and beneficiaries generally amongst the Sainsbury family charitable trusts.

Grant approvals are clearly listed and described in the annual reports. They show that £282,000 (58% of grant approvals) was allocated to environmental work in 1995/96. This was a considerable increase in both size and proportion from the previous year when £154,000 (47% of grant-aid) was allocated.

Environmental Projects UK – (£155,000 – 1995/96; £64,000 – 1994/95)

In the UK, 'support focuses on issues of transport policy, pollution, energy efficiency and renewable energy technology. Grants are made for pilot projects which seek to demonstrate alternative transport schemes, or to commission accessible and objective research to inform transport policy makers and the general public. The trust continues to fund environmental education linked to the demands of the national curriculum.'

Grants in 1995/96:
◆ Transport 2000 Trust, for a p/t co-ordinator to develop partnerships between statutory and non-statutory bodies which encourage alternatives to car use (£45,000 over 3 years, plus £13,000 in the previous year for seminars responding to the Royal Commission on Environmental Pollution's report);
◆ Institute of Education, towards a Schools Network on Air Pollution project (SNAP) (£32,500 with £10,500 in the previous year);
◆ Woodland Trust, for 'Woods on your Doorstep' millennium project (£25,000 over 5 years);
◆ National Energy Foundation, for a pilot South Midlands Renewable Energy Advice Centre (£15,000 over 3 years);
◆ Projects in Partnership, for an Energywise pilot project to promote domestic energy efficiency (£15,000);
◆ Institute of European Environmental Policy, to commission a briefing paper on company cars and towards phase one of a company car research project (£11,000);
◆ Transport bursaries, towards a competition for transport journalists to produce high-quality case studies of good practice for publication (£5,000);
◆ Car Free Cities Network, towards publication of a car-sharing document for the annual meeting of the network (£4,000);
◆ Cycling document, towards background research for a document on non-motorised transport (£2,000).

Environmental Projects – Overseas: (£127,000 – 1995/96; £90,000 – 1994/95)

'Grants are made for the support of community based renewable energy projects, including solar, biogas, micro-hydro, and in particular for piloting technology for potential wider dissemination. There is an increasing focus on developing the renewable energy infrastructure, which includes training for engineers, setting up credit mechanisms and informing renewable energy policy. A small number of grants have also been made to support grass-roots income generating activities and school buildings in remote areas.'

Grant approvals in 1995/96:
◆ Energy Alternatives Africa, Kenya, £25,000 towards a revolving loan fund to support income generation in the micro-enterprise sector using solar energy, and £15,000 towards a domestic solar energy project for low income households in rural Kenya (£40,000);
◆ Karendea Solar Training Facility, Tanzania, bursaries and apprenticeships for solar trainees and technicians, (£24,000 over 3 years);
◆ Tropical Wholefoods, Fruits of the Nile, Uganda, for revolving loan fund for small, rural dried fruit producers to use solar powered drying equipment (£20,000);
◆ Appropriate Development for Africa Foundation, Cameroon, R & D of solar technology for rural Cameroon and visit to solar training organisation (£15,000);
◆ East West Environment Ltd, towards a loan fund for environmental solutions to water and energy supply, for this pilot ecotourist project in south Albania (£15,000);
◆ Surplus People's Project, South Africa, to install solar technology in a community building in Witbank (£5,500);
◆ Traidcraft Exchange, to support an event in Tanzania (£5,000);
◆ National Agricultural Research Organisation, Uganda, to develop biogas technology (£2,500 with £27,000 in the previous year).

Under 'General' – £19,000 (1995/96)
Save the Rhino Trust in Namibia (£500)

Exclusions: No grants direct to
individuals.

Applications: An application to one of the
Sainsbury family trusts is an application to
all; see the entry under 'Sainsbury Family
Charitable Trusts' for address and
application procedure. In 1995/96 trustees
met five times to consider disbursements.

The Astor Foundation

5 Northview, Hungerford, Berks
RG17 0DA
Contact: Mrs J E Jones, Secretary
Trustees: Chairman R H Astor; Sir
William Slack; J R Astor; Lord Astor of
Hever; Dr H Swanton; C Money-Coutts.
Grant total: £78,000 (1996/97)

In 1995/96, the foundation had assets of
£2.7 million which generated an income
of £162,000 from which 91 grants
totalling £108,000 were given. 36 grants
ranged between £1,000 and £3,000 whilst
53 were for less than £1,000.

The priority of the foundation seems to be
to support national social welfare and
medical charities.

Nine grants relevant to this guide totalling
£4,500 were given in 1995/96 to:
- The Country Trust, National Playing
  Fields Association (£1,000);
- Television Trust for the Environment,
  Thames Salmon Trust, Society for
  Horticultural Therapy (£500);
- Church Restoration Trust, London
  Wildlife Trust, Marine Conservation
  Society, Glastonbury Abbey (£250).

Exclusions: No grants to individuals and
no salaries. Registered charities only.
Generally no 'bricks and mortar' grants
except in exceptional circumstances.

Applications: There are no deadline dates,
applications should be in writing to the
correspondent. If the appeal arrives too

late for one meeting it will automatically
be carried over for consideration for the
following. A reply will always be sent
irrespective of whether an appeal is
successful or not. No telephone calls.

The Aurelius Charitable Trust

Kidsons Impey, Spectrum House, 20-26
Cursitor Street, London EC4A 1HY
Tel: 0171-405 2088
Contact: P E Haynes
Trustees: W J Wallis; P E Haynes.
Grant total: £62,000 (1996/97)
Beneficial area: UK and overseas.

The settlor, Dr Marc Fitch, was
particularly interested in the conservation
of culture inherited from the past and in
the humanities, and since his death in
1994 these policies have been continued.
Assets in 1997 stood at £1.4 million
generating an income of £80,000 from
which grants totalling £62,000 were made.
From time to time the trust has funded
groups relevant to this guide e.g. the
Victorian Society (£4,000) and CPRE
(£1,000) in 1993/94 and smaller grants to
Cathedral Camps in 1995/96

Exclusions: Individuals.

Applications: In writing to the
correspondent. Trustees meet twice a year
and grants are usually made on the
recommendation of advisers. The
corespondent has stressed 'we do not seek
applications for funding in order to meet
and realise our objectives'.

The Baird Trust

182 Bath Street, Glasgow G2 4HG
Tel: 0141-332 0476
Contact: Angus Sutherland, Secretary
Grant total: £216,000 (1996)
Beneficial area: Scotland

The trust supports the construction and maintenance of Church of Scotland churches and halls, endows parishes and generally helps the work of the Church of Scotland.

In 1996 it had assets of £4.9 million generating an income of £271,000 from which over 60 grants totalling £216,000 were given to churches and parishes throughout Scotland. Grants ranged between £1,000 and £5,000, largely for repairs and improvements to existing buildings.

Applications: In writing to the correspondent.

The Bruce Ball Charitable Trust

Honington House, Woodlands Road, Great Shelford, Cambridge CB2 5LW
Tel: 01223-843264
Contact: B S Bruce-Ball
Trustees: J S Bruce-Ball; Mrs S L Bruce-Ball; J B Ball; Mrs A R Ball.
Grant total: £9,000 (1996/97)
Beneficial area: UK.

The trust gives grants under four headings. The recent year for which accounts were on file at the Charity Commission showed a total of £9,000 in grant-aid 1993/94:
- Industrial Archaeology – £3,100 in 4 grants
- Environment – £2,100 in 7 grants
- Mental Health – £1,270 in 5 grants
- Other – £2,100 in 6 grants

Most grants have ranged between £200 to £350 with the outstanding annual grant given regularly to the Ironbridge Gorge Museum Trust. In 1993/94 a total of £5,000 (56% of grant-aid) was relevant to this guide and given to:
- Ironbridge Gorge Museum Ltd (£2,500);
- RSPB, New Forest Owl Sanctuary, Wood Green Animal Shelter, Wildlife Hospital Trust, WWF UK, Countryside Restoration Trust (£350 each);
- Chichester Canals Trust, Cotswold Canals Trust (£200 each).

Most grants are recurrent.

Applications: In writing to the correspondent.

The Balney Charitable Trust

The Chicheley Estate, Bartelmas Office, Pavenham, Bedford MK43 7PF
Tel: 01234-823663
Fax: 01234 -825058
Contact: G C Beazley
Trustees: Major J G B Chester; Robert Ruck-Keene.
Grant total: £38,000 (1996/97)
Beneficial area: UK, particularly the northern areas of Buckingham and Bedfordshire.

The report for 1995/96 noted that the 'trustees have allocated mainly to local needs with a bias towards aiding local churches faced with the heavy costs of repairs to medieval buildings, to service charities and to supporting the production of a work of original research in art history...substantial donations are expected to the new John Bunyan Museum in Bedford and to the care of the elderly and the continuing needs of local churches'.

Nine grants relevant to this guide totalled £4,000 in 1995/6 (15% of grant-aid):
- St Laurence Chichely (£1,199 with £1,370 in the previous year plus a £500 regular grant);
- All Saints Emberton (£1,000);

Other regular grants included:
- National Trust (£400);
- Buckinghamshire Historical Churches, Beds & Herts Historical Churches Trust (£300 each);
- CLA Charitable Trust, Forestry Trust, FWAG (£100 each).

Please note funds for 1998/9 financial year are already allocated due to very heavy demand.

Applications: In writing to the correspondent.

The Barbour Trust

P O Box 21, Guisborough, Cleveland
TS14 8YH
Contact: Mrs A Harvey
Trustees: Mrs Margaret Barbour; Henry
Jacob Tavroges; Anthony Glenton; Miss
Helen Barbour.
Grant total: £209,000 (1994/95)
Beneficial area: Tyneside.

In 1994/95, the trust had an income of
£347,000 and gave grants of £209,000. Its
objects include a stated interest in the
protection and preservation of
environmental, historical or architectural
features in both city and countryside in
North East England. Four grants relevant
to this guide were given in 1994/95:
- National Trust inner city project
  (£5,000, also supported in previous
  years);
- North Pennines Heritage Trust,
  Woodland Trust (£1,000);
- St John's Restoration & Development
  Trust (£500).

Exclusions: Individuals, capital grants for
building projects, request outside the area.

Applications: In writing to the
correspondent with charity number,
accounts and full back-up information.

The Baring Foundation

60 London Wall, London EC2M 5TQ
Tel: 0171-767 1348
Fax: 0171-767 7121
Contact: David Carrington, Director
Trustees: Lord Ashburton, (Chairman);
Nicholas Baring; Mrs Tessa Baring; R D
Broadley; Lord Howick; Ms Janet Lewis-
Jones; Lady Lloyd; Sir Crispin Tickell;
Martin Findlay; Anthony Loehnis.
Grant total: About £2,500,000 annually
Beneficial area: UK (with a special
interest in the London, Merseyside and
Tyne and Wear and Cleveland areas for its
Strengthening the Voluntary Sector
programme). Also UK charities working
with NGO partners in developing

countries. Please see under 'Applications'
for more details.

The programmes now operational are not
for environmental activities as such but are
relevant to organisations within the
environmental movement. The director
has also helpfully commented: 'We do
interpret 'environment' in the broadest
sense so do fund activities (even in the arts
programme) which are 'environmental
grants'. We also include a specific reference
to environmental issues in the criteria
relating to the International programme'.

In 1996 the foundation introduced totally
new grants programmes following the
collapse of the Baring Bank, its former
major source of income. The foundation
plans to distribute £2.5 million in each of
the three years up to December 1999.
Prior to 1995 the foundation had been
allocating about five times this current
total to certain areas of charitable work –
social welfare, health, the arts, education
and conservation. The rethink of its grants
programme has lead to an interesting new
direction for its support – the
development of the voluntary sector.
The foundation still maintains its
particular support for work in the
London, Merseyside, Tyne & Wear and
Cleveland areas but applicants need to be
aware of new refinements. It has also
retained support for the arts within two
new small schemes (not covered here at
all). All interested readers are strongly
advised to obtain a copy of the guidelines
leaflet a.s.a.p.

Support is to be given under two headings:
- Strengthening the Voluntary Sector
- Strengthening the Voluntary Sector –
  Mergers & Joint Structures

The first is vailable for national voluntary
organisations (see definition in guidelines);
London voluntary organisations working
in several London boroughs or across the
whole of London; community and other
local organisations in the Merseyside
region (including Skelmersdale and
Halton) and the North East of England
(the former counties of Cleveland and

Tyne & Wear plus, in Northumberland and County Durham, primarily the former coalfield areas; UK charities working with partner organisations/community groups in developing countries.

Priority is given to organisations and activities 'considered to be difficult to fund or are unlikely to attract public support'.

Examples of fundable activities: shared training initiatives; consultancies re efficiency; co-ordination/collaboration initiatives; key staff release for strategic matters/planning; initiatives to stimulate participation in project management by those it aims to benefit; feasibility studies of new projects.

Single grants are expected to be up to a maximum of £12,000: most are expected to be for much less. Grants can be for two or three years if a good case is made. The second is for UK voluntary organisations considering a merger or other formal joint structure which wish to explore the possibility further, plus organisations which have decided on the steps they need to take and need help in their implementation. All such applications will be treated as confidential and beneficiaries will not be named in reports or other publicity except with mutual agreement.

The foundation also welcomes applications from organisations that do not want to merge, but do wish to devise some formal joint structure that protects their independence while sharing some costs and/or functions.

Examples of fundable activities include: consultancies; release of a staff member to examine the proposal; legal, or other associated professional costs. Grants are anticipated to be between £2,000 and £10,000.

Applications: Applications can be made by local and regional organisations anywhere in the UK; national voluntary organisations (see full definition in guidance note); UK charities working with partner organisations and community groups in developing countries.

An application can be made jointly by all the organisations involved or by just one (again see detailed requirements).

International grants programme

The Baring Foundation has always been committed to assisting communities internationally to apply accessible and affordable technical expertise and resources to the provision of clean water, food, shelter and sustainable livelihoods. In this aspect of its grant making, the Foundation has supported UK based charities that work in other countries in partnership with community organisations and NGOs and has given particular priority to initiatives that are intended to strengthen the further development of vigorous and resilient community based organisations and self help groups.

For its new international grants programme, the Baring Foundation has decided to concentrate its support on activities that will enhance the effectiveness of the voluntary and community sector, especially in sub-Saharan Africa and Latin America – in particular through the sharing and transfer of expertise, knowledge and skills within those regions and between them and other parts of the world.

Exclusions: The foundation will not usually support: the continued funding of activity that is already taking place; the repeat of an activity that took place in a previous year; the increase in the scale of an existing service.

Strengthening the Voluntary Sector Grants Programme – Individuals; expeditions; grant maintained, private or LEA schools, bursaries or scholarships; medical research; medical equipment; animal welfare charities; appeals or charities set up to support statutory organisations; the purchase, conversion or refurbishment of buildings; religious activity; general fundraising appeals.

Mergers and Joint Structures Programme – Initiatives intended to lead to better co-ordination or collaboration between organisations – but have no implications for the creation of new formal structure (such initiatives may be eligible for support within the foundation's main grants programme).

Exclusions above also apply.

Applications: All potential applicants are strongly urged first to obtain full details direct from the foundation. The above information does not cover all the conditions.

All applicants must complete a datasheet.... and send it to the foundation together with full and precise information the details of which are set out meticulously in it guidance note.

Strengthening the Voluntary Sector

Grants and the Mergers and Joint Structures Scheme

This grants programme has no deadlines: applications can be sent to the foundation at any time. All will be acknowledged within two weeks of receipt. The foundation's staff or advisers may need to telephone or visit the applicant organisation. A decision may take up to six months and the applicant will be notified of the outcome by letter.

The trustees meet (in full council or in committee) monthly except for August. Decisions on Arts programmes are taken in January, May and September and for Strengthening the voluntary sector and International programmes in February, July, October and December. Decisions about merger programmes are taken throughout the year. On completion of the activity for which a grant has been made, a recipient is asked to complete a simple form assessing the impact of the grant.

Lord Barnby's Foundation

c/o Messrs Payne Hicks Beach, 10 New Square, Lincoln's Inn, London WC2A 3QG
Tel: 0171-242 6041
Contact: The Secretary.
Trustees: Lord Newall; Sir Michael Farquhar; J L Lowther; A O Deas; George Lopes.
Grant total: £240,000 (1995/96)
Beneficial area: UK.

In 1995/96 the foundation had assets of some £3.2 million which generated an income from which £240,000 was disbursed in over 130 grants ranging between £500 and £25,000. Only 11 grants were for more than £1,000. Most were for £500 or £1,000. The foundation gives to a wide range of charitable activities.

In 1995/96 ten grants were relevant to this guide and totalled over £45,000 (19% of grant-aid):
◆ Game Conservancy Trust (£25,000);
◆ Countryside Foundation (£10,000);
◆ Reading University Rural History Centre (£5,000);
◆ St Mary's Riverhead, Historic Churches Preservation Trust, Carlisle Cathedral, Lincoln Cathedral (£1,000 each);
◆ Rockingham Forest Trust, Wildside Trust (£500).

Applications: In writing to the correspondent. Applications are usually considered in February, June and October.

The Richard Baxendale Charitable Trust

34 Margaret Road, Penworthan, Preston PR1 9QT
Tel: 01772-95555
Contact: Miss Olive Watson
Trustees: P S Baxendale; Miss O Watson.
Grant total: £17,000 (1995)
Beneficial area: UK.

The trust support charities generally and in 1995 gave 19 grants totalling £17,000. Five grants totalling £3,500 (21% of grant aid were relevant to this guide:

- Greenpeace, Tree Aid (£1,000 each);
- Environmental Investigation Agency, Survival International, Whale & Dolphin Protection Society (£500 each).

Applications: In writing to the correspondent.

The Benham Charitable Settlement

Hurstbourne, Portnall Drive, Virginia Water, Surrey GU25 4NR
Contact: Mrs M Tittle, Managing Trustee
Trustees: Mrs M Tittle; Mrs R A Nickols; Edward D D'Alton; Philip Schofield; E N Langley.
Grant total: £136,000 (1995/96)
Beneficial area: UK, with a particular interest in Northamptonshire.

The trust makes a large number of small grants (about 250) to a wide range of charities. In 1995/96 its assets of £1.9 million generated an income of £140,000 from which grants of £136,000 were made. It gave nine grants over £1,000, two of which were for £10,000. The remainder were between £100 and £500.

Over 15 grants totalling some £16,000 (4% of grant-aid) were relevant to this guide:

- Holy Trinity Church Sunningdale (£1,000 in 2 grants);
- BTCV, Hawk & Owl Trust (£400 each);
- Brecon, Carlisle, Chichester, Ely, Lincoln cathedrals, Cathedral Camps (£300 each);
- Holy Sepulchre Church Northampton, and a number of other churches (£300 each);
- Chelsea Physic Garden, Farming & Wildlife Advisory Group, ITDG, Open Spaces Society, Population Concern (£300 each);
- The Northamptonshire Victoria County History received grants of £3,000.

Exclusions: Individuals.

Applications: In writing to the correspondent at any time, but no charity will be considered more than once each year and repeated applications will be ignored for 12 months. Replies cannot be sent to all applicants neither can telephone calls be accepted.

The Blair Foundation

Smith & Williamson, Onslow Bridge Chambers, Bridge Street, Guildford, Surrey GU1 4RA
Tel: 01483-302200
Contact: Graham Healy
Trustees: Robert Thornton; Jennifer Thornton; Graham Healy; Alan Thornton.
Grant total: £94,000 (1995/96)
Beneficial area: UK and overseas.

The foundation was set up by Robert Thornton, of Blair House, Ayrshire, in 1989. For the first four years of operation the trust received income from a covenant, this ended in 1993. In 1995/96, the trust had assets of £425,000 which generated an income of £268,000 from which 15 grants totalling £94,000 were made. Grant levels fluctuate from year to year.

The foundation has given a major part of its support to Jewish charities but intends to reduce this and 'expand an interest in wildlife and environmental preservation'. It supports large organisations such as Manx Nature Conservation Trust and WWF UK but also helps 'small groups engaged in preserving our environment'.

During the next five years the following proportions will guide its allocations:

- Children's charities 40%
- Jewish/General 20%
- Wildlife 20%
- Environment 10%
- Educational/Cultural 10%

In 1995/96 grants ranged from £1,000 to £35,000. The largest two grants were to:

- Ayrshire Wildlife Services (£35,000);
- Scottish Wildlife Trust (£12,000);

Other grants relevant to this guide included:
- Lyminge Forest Appeal (£5,500);
- National Trust for Scotland (£5,000).

Applications: To the correspondent in writing. The correspondent did not want to be included in this guide: '..I have been inundated with appeals for help, which far exceed the resources available...the costs of administration are now becoming disproportionate to the funds available'.

The Charlotte Bonham-Carter Charitable Trust

66 Lincoln's Inn Fields, London
WC2A 3LH
Tel: 0171-242 2022
Contact: Sir Matthew Farrer
Trustees: Sir Matthew Farrer; Norman Bonham-Carter; Nicolas Wickham-Irving.
Grant total: £92,000 (1996/1997)
Beneficial area: UK, with emphasis on Hampshire.

Though the trust's objects are general, annual grants to the National Heritage Memorial Fund and the National Trust are both incorporated in the outline. The trustees state that donations are made to 'those charities with which Lady Bonham-Carter was particularly associated during her life or had a particular interest in, with an emphasis on Hampshire'.

In 1996/97, the trust had assets of £2.8 million and an income of £106,000, from which 42 grants totalling only £92,000 were made.

Eight grants relevant to this guide were given to:
- Ashmolean Museum;
- Cotswold Canal Trust;
- Council for the Protection of Rural England;
- Gainsborough House;
- Sustrans;
- Almhouse Association;
- Gilbert White Museum;
- BTCV.

The trust sent this more up-to-date information about its eight beneficiaries. In 1996/97 but gave no information about the size of the grants made. In 1994/95 six environmental grants had been given which ranged between £1,000 and £15,000 and also included BTCV and the Gilbert White Museum which had received £1,000 each.

Exclusions: No grants to individuals. The trustees are not anxious to receive unsolicited general applications as these are unlikely to be successful and only increase the cost of administration of the charity.

Applications: In writing to the correspondent. There are no application forms.

The Chris Brasher Trust

The Navigator's House, River Lane, Richmond, Surrey TW10 7AG
Tel: 0181-940 0296
Contact: C Brasher, Chairman
Trustees: C W Brasher; S J Brasher; Lord Chorley.
Grant total: £49,000 (1994/95)
Beneficial areas: UK and overseas.

The trust was established in 1988. Its objects include 'to provide, or assist in the provision of facilities (particularly in wild areas) for the recreation of people in the UK particularly those with special needs for facilities – youth, disablement, poverty... to ensure and protect for public benefit wild areas of the UK in their natural condition.'

In 1994/95 the trust had assets of £505,000 and an income of £83,000 from which 17 grants totalling £49,000 were made.

Grants relevant to this guide were given in 1994/95 to:

- John Muir Trust to acquire Strathaid Estate Skye (£25,000);
- Sustrans (£5,000);
- Magog Trust, Scottish Field Studies Association (£3,000 each);
- BTCV (£2,000).

In the previous year large grants had been made to the National Trust for Scotland (£150,000) and the National Trust (£70,000).

Applications: The trust has no staff and does not reply to unsolicited applications.

The Bridge House Estates Trust Fund

PO Box 270, Guildhall, London
EC2P 2EJ
Tel: 0171-332 3710
Fax: 0171-332 3720
Contact: Clare Thomas, Chief Grants Officer
Trustees: The Mayor and Commonalty and Citizens of the City of London.
Grant total: £14.29 million (1996/97); £10 million addition (budgeted 1997/98)
Beneficial area: Greater London.

This trust has now become the largest grant-making trust operating exclusively in London, and one of the largest throughout the UK. Its policies are still undergoing development and refinement. It expects to introduce revised policies in Spring 1997. During its first period of grant-making between September 1995 and the end of March 1996 it gave grants ranging between £1,500 and £485,000 for an enterprising range of both capital and revenue projects. The Bridge House Estate Trust Fund has a long history extending back to a Royal Charter granted in 1282. Its sole objective until recently has been to mend and replace the four bridges over the Thames in the City of London (London, Blackfriars, Southwark and Tower). Over the years the fund has grown far larger than these obligations and in 1995 its objectives were extended to enable any surplus funds to be used in one or both of the following ways:

- in or towards the provision of transport and access to it for elderly or disabled people in the Greater London area;
- other charitable purposes for the general benefit of the inhabitants of Greater London.

Income for 1996/97 was £34.1 million. Expenditure for the year totalled £26.4 million and included the repair and maintenance of the bridges, investment property expenses and some £14.8 million for grants and their administration. The overall increase in total reserves for the year including revaluation of managed investments and property investments was £24.374 million. The level of grant giving is reviewed each year in accordance with the projected annual surplus and a level of £10m has been set for 1997/98.

The first 236 grants totalling £7.13 million were allocated in the six months before the end of March 1996. These were given within its five present priority areas:

- Transport and access for elderly and disabled people
- Environmental conservation
- Innovative projects which assist young people in deprived areas
- Schemes which assist elderly people to stay within the community
- Provision of technical support to voluntary organisations

The trust fund adopted a wise approach during its first months and engaged the experienced and respected Baring Foundation to 'kickstart' its operations. Advice was taken from leading London grant-makers and the voluntary sector. This depth of understanding shows in the wide variety of organisations that are being supported and the range of problems that are already being addressed by its funding. A Policy Review and consultation process conducted over a six month period has further informed its grant-making.

Grants approved during 1996/97 were categorised as follows:

- Transport: elderly and/or disabled people £1.4m 27 grants;
- Access to buildings; elderly people and/or disabled people £0.6 million 15 grants;
- Access to opportunities; elderly and/or disabled people £2.6 million 53 grants;
- Environmental conservation £1.1 million 16 grants;
- Innovative projects for young people £4.4 million 82 grants;
- Technical support £1.5 million 32 grants;
- Assist elderly in the community £2.3 million 37 grants;
- Others £0.6 million 10 grants.

The trust has been prepared to give substantial grants to most of its beneficiaries, and give them a real opportunity to prove themselves. Only 31 of the 272 grants in 1996/97 were for less than £10,000. Thirty one awards were for £100,000 or more. Three of these major grants were given for environmental conservation (see below).

The second annual report of the trust fund provides interesting additional background to its initial thinking. Transport became its first priority because of the close connections of Bridge House Estates with transport. It chose to focus on transport for disabled and elderly people who are often excluded from a full life by inaccessible public transport.

Its choice of environmental conservation is an unusual, and welcome, priority for a major trust despite its significant growth as an important part of contemporary voluntary action.

The trust has identified two areas of interest, environmental education and organisations involving volunteers. The trust aims to support projects which sustain, protect and improve London's environment and help to create a better environmental future for London. The trust is particularly interested in projects which raise awareness and knowledge of environmental issues in the wider community and encourage the involvement of volunteers. Notable themes include maintaining London's 'biodiversity' or variety of life and ensuring that resources are used in the least harmful and most efficient way.

As part of the trust's commitment to developing an active role for organisations which do not have environment as their main focus, but nevertheless have a keen in the environment, the trust will allow these organisations to make a separate application for an environmental project in addition to a proposal addressing another of the trust's categories.

The 16 beneficiaries during 1996/97 received 7% of total grant aid.
- London Wildlife Trust to increase community participation in the conservation of London's natural heritage (£400,000 over 2 years);
- Learning Through Landscapes (LTL) towards the improvement of London's school grounds by involving young people in conservation projects (£162,000 over 2 years);
- Wildside Trust towards environmental youth and community outreach projects in London (£120,000 over 3 years);
- Rubbish Dump/Waste Not Recycling towards an Environmentalist in Residence to raise awareness in schools (£85,000),
- Woodland Farm Trust towards the creation of visitors and educational facilities on a renovated farm in Shooters Hill, Greenwich (£75,000);
- Groundwork West London towards a post to develop a nature conservation area in a park and to promote educational activities (£61,000);
- Spitalfields Farm Association towards a farm manager and running costs of a volunteer programme (£30,000);
- Abney Park Cemetery Trust to develop a multi-disciplinary environmental education centre. The Civic Trust towards a salary and running cost of a conference organiser for a festival on the environment (£25,000) each;
- Friends of the New River Walk for the installation of a circular system for the new river walk pond (£23,000);
- Hornbeam Environmental Centre towards a post to manage an environmental centre (£16,000);

- Council for the Protection of Rural England (CPRE) towards the London Footprints project to encourage the better management of land and resources in London (£15,000);
- Work & Play towards a recycling and education project (£14,000 over 2 years);
- Platform to create a solar powered display vehicle to raise awareness about local ecological issues (£9,000);
- Pumphouse Educational Trust to establish an out of school children's environment education and conservation club (£8,000).

Exclusions: Individuals other grant-making bodies; schools; universities for general educational purposes; medical or academic research; religious purposes; preservation of buildings.

Applications: Applications must be submitted on an application form with accompanying documentation. They can be received at any time since the trustees meet ten times a year. There are no longer deadlines for receipt of applications.

The Bromley Trust

Ashley Manor, King's Somborne, Stockbridge, Hants SO20 6RQ
Tel: 01794-388241
Fax: 01794-388264
Contact: Keith Bromley
Trustees: Keith Bromley; Anna Home; Alan P Humphries; Nicholas Measham; Lady Ann Wood; Peter Winfield.
Grant total: £138,000 (1996/97)
Beneficial area: UK and overseas

The aims and objects of the trust are to make grants to charitable organisations that:
- Combat violations of human rights, and help victims of torture, refugees from oppression and those who have been falsely imprisoned.
- Help those who have suffered severe bodily or mental hurt through no fault of their own, and if need be their dependents; try in some small way to off set man's inhumanity to man.
- Oppose the extinction of the world's

fauna and flora and the destruction of the environment for wildlife and for mankind worldwide.

In 1997/98 the trust's annual income is expected to be around £155,000.

The trust's objectives are clearly defined and it hardly ever departs from them. By far the greater part of the income goes to charities that are concerned with human rights; a comparatively small proportion is given to charities concerned with the preservation of the world environment. The main charities supported usually receive their grants in four quarterly payments. One-off grants are occasionally made, but are rare. Grants are only given to registered charities. Local projects are hardly ever within the trust's scope. The 29 mainstream charities in 1996/97 included nine organisations relevant to this guide.
- Population Concern (£8,000);
- Survival International (£7,000);
- World Land Trust (£6,000);
- Greenpeace Environmental Trust, Marie Stopes International (£5,000 each);
- Birdlife International, Fauna & Flora Preservation Society (£3,000 each);
- Butterfly Conservation, Wildfowl & Wetlands Trust (£1,000 each).

Exclusions: No grants for individuals.

Applications: In writing to the correspondent, but note above. The trustees meet twice a year; urgent appeals may be dealt with at any time.

The Sir Felix Brunner's Sons' Charitable Trust

2 Inverness Gardens, London W8 7EH
Contact: T B H Brunner
Trustees: J H K Brunner; T B H Brunner; H L J Brunner.
Grant total: £57,000 (1994/95)
Beneficial area: UK.

The trust had assets with a market value of over £2 million in 1995 which generated an income of £62,000 from which 16 donations totalling £57,000, and ranging between £1,000 and £10,000, were given.

Three donations totalling £17,000 (30% of grant aid) were relevant to this guide in 1994/95:
♦ National Trust (£10,000, also given in the previous year);
♦ Open Spaces Society (£5,000);
♦ St Giles' Oxford (£2,000).

In the previous year two grants were given for church restoration St John's (£2,500) and Friends of Burford Priory (£1,000) with support also to Survival International (£1,000).

Applications: In writing to the correspondent.

The Jack Brunton Charitable Trust

10 Bridge Road, Stokesley, North Yorkshire TS9 5AA
Tel: 01642 -711407
Contact: D A Swallow
Trustees: Lady Diana Brittan; Mrs A J Brunton; J G Brunton; B E M Jones; E Marquis; D W Noble; P Reed.
Grant total: £46,000 (1995/96)
Beneficial area: The Old North Riding of Yorkshire.

In 1995/96 the Trust had an income of £112,000 and made 35 grants totalling £46,000.

The trust makes regular grants to York Minister. In 1995/96 the grants relevant to this guide were spread over a wide area of conservation, urban and rural regeneration projects, including churches, village and community halls, as well as projects relating to woodland, horticulture and regeneration of country crafts, which totalled approximately £29,000 (62% of grant aid):
♦ York Minister (£15,000 in 2 grants);
♦ Christchurch Westerdale (£2,000);
♦ All Saints, Easingwold (£1,000);
♦ Holy Trinity, Little Ouseburn (£1,000);

♦ The Botanic Centre (£3,000);
♦ Northdale Horticulture (£2,000);
♦ The Old Farmstead (£2,000);
♦ Hutton Buscal Village Hall (£500);
♦ Castle Church Youth Club & Parish Rooms, Ingleby Greenhow Parochial Church Council (£250) each;
♦ Slingsby Village Hall (£500);
♦ Bankfield Community Centre (£1,000);

Exclusions: Rarely to individuals.

Applications: In writing to the correspondent. The trustees meet four times a year.

The Geoffrey Burton Charitable Trust

1 Gainsborough Road, Felixstowe, Suffolk IP11 7HT
Tel: 01394 -285537
Contact: E E Maule, Trustee
Trustees: E de B Nash; E E Maule.
Grant total: £41,000 (1996/9)
Beneficial area: UK, especially Suffolk.

In 1996/97, the trust had assets of £592,000 including £498,000 termed 'mortgages'. The income was £48,000 including £40,000 mortgage interest. Grants totalled £41,000.

Grants were given ranging from £75 to £15,000. Most of the grants were given in Suffolk, especially Needham Market.

Grants relevant to this guide in 1996/97 absorbed at least 30% of total grant aid and were given to:
♦ Suffolk Wildlife Trust, towards Butterfly Project £4,000, towards upkeep of Bonny Wood, £2,000, towards purchase of Foxburrow Farm £2,000 (£8,000);
♦ St John's Needham Market (£4,000).

Other beneficiaries included Thornham Field Trust, Mid Suffolk Light Railway, River Stour Trust and Felixstowe Citizens Advice Bureau. Other beneficiaries included Ipswich Museums Trust,

Needham Market Play Group and Mid Suffolk Citizens Advice Bureau.

Applications: In writing to the correspondent.

The A S Butler Charitable Trust

Studham Hall Farm, Studham, Dunstable, Beds LU6 2NP
Tel: 01582-872265
Contact: Carol Horton
Trustees: Carol Horton; Mrs V J Catzeflis.
Grant total: £7,000 (1994/95)
Beneficial area: UK and overseas.

This trust gives a large number of small grants to environmental interests. In 1994/95 a total of 44 grants totalling £7,000 were given almost all of which are for wildlife conservation, both plants and animals. Grants are also given for animal welfare.

The largest grants were to PTES (£450) and CPRE (£400). Smaller grants included FoE and Greenpeace, ITDG, Rainforest Action Costa Rica, Population Concern, the Tiger Trust and Hertfordshire and Middlesex Wildlife Trust.

Applications: In writing to the correspondent.

C H K Charities Limited
(formerly the Sir Cyril Kleinwort Charitable Trust)

PO Box 191, 10 Fenchurch Street, London EC3M 3LB
Tel: 0171-956 6246
Contact: N R Kerr-Sheppard, Administrator
Trustees: D A Acland; D A E R Peake; A C Heber Percy; Kleinwort Benson Trustees Limited.
Grant total: £520,000 (1995/96) but see below
Beneficial area: UK, with an interest in Gloucestershire and Oxfordshire.
This charity has become a larger funder though no information was available at the time of preparing this entry. Assets of £12.4 million have been transferred from the Sir Cyril Kleinwort Charitable Trust to C H K Charities Limited which itself has received £28.5 million from other Kleinwort family resources.

The total assets of the charity amount to over £40 million and it expects to distribute £1.4 million in grants during 1997.

'The trustees are particularly interested in the fields of education, job creation, conservation, arts, population control, crime prevention and youth development.'

The trustees will provide assistance towards start-up or capital costs and, with lower priority, towards on-going expenses. This will normally take the form of a grant for say three to five years following which support may be withdrawn to enable the resources to be devoted to other projects.'

Its beneficiaries are 'charities known or local to the trustees and substantial national charitable bodies (but not normally the local branches or off-shoots of these).'

The following is based on the accounts of the Sir Cyril Kleinwort Charitable Trust for the year ending January 1996. Then the settlement had assets of £12.4 million which generated an income of £523,000. 82 grants were awarded totalling £520,000, of which more than three quarters were for amounts between £1,000 and £5,000. There were eleven grants for £10,000 or more.

Grants relevant to this guide were given to:
◆ Margaret Pyke Memorial Trust (£20,000);
◆ National Trust, Population Concern, Wycombe Abbey Centenary Appeal (£10,000 each);
◆ Cannongate 300 Organ Appeal, Stepping Stones Farm, Sustrans (£5,000 each);
◆ BTCV (£3,000);
◆ Cotswold Canals Trust (£2,000);
◆ Duns Tew PCC (£1,000);
◆ Wye Agricultural College (£868).

There were probably very many more small grants made via the £60,000 given for distribution through the Charities Aid Foundation small grants system.

Exclusions: No grants to individuals nor to small local charities, e.g. individual churches, village halls, etc, where there is no special connection to the trust. Appeals from local branches or off-shoots of national charitable bodies are normally not considered.

Applications: To the correspondent. Appeals will usually be considered within three months, but may be referred for further consideration at board meetings which are held twice a year, normally in March and October.

Cadbury Charitable Trust (Incorporated)

Elmfield, College Walk, Selly Oak, Birmingham B29 6LE
Tel: 0121-472 1838
Contact: Mrs M Walton, Secretary
Trustees: Charles E Gillett, Chairman; Christopher S Littleboy; Charles R Gillett; Andrew S Littleboy; Nigel R Cadbury.
Grant total: £20,000 (1995/96)
Beneficial area: The West Midlands.

The trust gives its areas of interest as follows: the voluntary sector in the West Midlands including Christian mission, the ecumenical movement, interfaith relations and education. Considerable support is given to the Quakers. The trustees prefer to support small or new organisations and projects rather than large or national organisations. 'The size of grant varies but most are between £250 and £2,500 and are usually one-off, for a specific project or part of a project. On-going funding commitments are rarely considered.'

In 1996 the trust had assets of £20 million which generated an income of £839,000 (these assets included the remainder of the £4 million gift to Selly Oak Colleges not yet paid). 176 grants were made during 1995/96, 13 of which for £10,000 or

more, 80 between £1,000 and £5,000, and the majority of the remainder were between £250 and £500.

Grants relevant to this guide totalling over £20,000 (4% of total grant-aid) were given to:
- Avoncroft Museum of Buildings (£6,867);
- Birmingham Botanical Gardens, Population Concern (£5,000 each);
- Royal Agricultural Society, Global Care (£1,000 each);
- Green Wood Trust, Worcestershire & Dudley Historic Churches Trust, Wildfowl & Wetlands Trust (£500).

Exclusions: Registered charities only. No student grants or support for individuals. 'The trust is unlikely to fund projects which have popular appeal or fund things which are normally publicly funded.'

Applications: At any time, but allow three months for a response. Applications that do not come within the trust's policy as stated above will not be considered or acknowledged.

The trust does not have an application form. Applications should be made in writing to the correspondent, they should clearly and concisely give relevant information concerning the project and its benefits, an outline budget and how the project is to be funded initially and in the future. Up to date accounts and the organisation's latest annual report are also required.

The Christopher Cadbury Charitable Trust

New Guild House, 45 Great Charles Street, Queensway, Birmingham B3 2LX
Tel: 0121-212 2222
Contact: Roger Harriman, Trust Administrator
Trustees: Roger V J Cadbury; Dr C James Cadbury; Mrs V B Reekie; Dr T N D Peet; P H G Cadbury; Mrs C V E Benfield.

Grant total: £52,000 (1996/97)
Beneficial area: UK, with a strong preference towards the Midlands.

In 1996/97, the trust had assets of £1,27 million and an income of £65,000. Grants were given totalling £52,000. Recurring annual commitments, subject to annual review, total £52,000. The trust has usually given a high proportion of its funding to conservation work. The largest grants relevant to this guide in 1996/97 were:

- Royal Society for Nature Conservation (£14,500);
- Worcestershire Wildlife Trust (£4,000);
- Norfolk Naturalist Trust (£3,000).

Applications: No unsolicited applications are considered by the trustees.

The George Cadbury Trust

New Guild House, 45 Great Charles Street, Queensway, Birmingham B3 2LX
Tel: 0121-212 2222.
Contact: R Harriman, Administrator
Trustees: Peter E Cadbury; Annette L K Cadbury; Robin N Cadbury; Sir Adrian Cadbury; Roger V J Cadbury.
Grant total: £226,000 (1996/97)
Beneficial area: Preference for the West Midlands.

This trust, the George Cadbury Fund B Account, was set up in 1924 and maintains a strong financial interest in the Cadbury company. Total investment income for 1996/97 was £253,000.

Nearly 300 organisations received grants during the year totalling £226,000 many based in the West Midlands area. There is a preference for organisations of which the trustees have a direct knowledge or involvement, many are supported recurrently.

The largest grants were given to Cheltenham College (£32,000) and King's College Development Appeal (£18,000). The latter could be for architectural upkeep.

Grants in excess to environmental of £500 or more were named and these included in 1996/97 were: the WWF UK (£5,000). 45 grants totalling £71,000 were between £1,000 and £4,999. The majority (238) were small grants of £999 and less totalling £43,000.

Grants in excess of £500 to environmental interests in 1996/97 were:
- Marine Aid Environmental Appeal; Royal Horticultural Society; Task Force Appeal; WWF Save the Tiger Fund; CPRE (£2,000) each;
- National Trust – Neptune £1000;
- Royal Society for Nature Reservations £500;

Applications: In writing to the correspondent. It is understood that few new applications are supported.

George W Cadbury Charitable Trust

New Guild House, 45 Great Charles Street, Queensway, Birmingham B3 2LX
Tel: 0121-212 2222
Contact: Roger Harriman, Trust Administrator
Trustees: Mrs C A Woodroffe; Mrs L E Boal; P C Boal; Miss J C Boal; N B Woodroffe; Miss J L Woodroffe.
Grant total: £149,000 (1996/97)
Beneficial area: UK and overseas.

In 1996/97 the Trust had assets of £4.38 million generating an income of £226,000 from which grants of £149,000 were made. The trust gave its grants in the following proportions:
- UK £101,000 – 67.8%
- Canada £24,000 – 15.8%
- USA £24,000 – 16.4%

The Trust concentrates its giving on population control and conservation. Grants relevant to this guide were given in 1996/97 to:
- Brook Advisory Centres (£15,000);
- Birth Control Trust (£12,000);

- Planned Parenthood Federation of Canada (£9, 000);
- Belfast Brook Advisory Centre (£10,000);
- Planned Parenthood Federation of Toronto (£5,000);
- Maternity Alliance (£10,000);
- Conservation Council of Ontario (£5,000);
- WWF (£7,000);
- International Planned Parenthood Federation (£5,000);
- Family Planning Association (£3,000).

Applications: It is understood that unsolicited applications are unlikely to be able to be considered.

The J & L A Cadbury Charitable Trust

2 College Walk, Birmingham, West Midlands B29 6LQ
Contact: The secretary
Trustees: Mrs L A Cadbury; W J B Taylor; Mrs S M Gale.
Grant total: £43,000 (1995/96)

The grant total for 1995/96 was larger than usual (around £20,000 is more customary) because of special income of £26,000 from Cadbury Schweppes shares. The trust gave a very large number (about 180) of small grants most of which are between £100 and £200 and only seven of which rose to £500.

In 1995/96 over 25 grants were relevant to this guide and totalled over £4,000 (9 % of grant-aid):
- Birmingham Parish Church restoration, Gatliff Hebridean Hostels Trust, Radnorship Wildlife Trust (£500 each);
- Herefordshire National Trust (£300);
- Avoncroft Museum, John Muir Trust (£250 each);
- CPRE, Dodford Chidlren's Holiday Farm, FoE, Woodland Trust (£200 each);
- RSPB (£130);
- Carlisle Cathedral, Farming & Wildlife Advisory Group, Population Concern, Woodland Heritage, WWF UK (£100 each).
A further half dozen church restoration projects were also supported.

Applications: In writing to the correspondent.

The Richard Cadbury Charitable Trust

6 Middleborough Road, Coventry, West Midlands CV1 4DE
Contact: Mrs M M Eardley
Trustees: R B Cadbury; Mrs M M Eardley; D G Slora; Miss J Slora
Grant total: £67,000 (1992)
Beneficial area: UK with an interest in local charities in the West Midlands, Merseyside and Worcestershire areas.

The most recent accounts on file at the Charity Commission were for 1992 and 1991. The only other sets of accounts were for 1969 and 1975.

In 1996 the trust had assets of nearly £500,000 which generated an income of £36,000. A higher sum, £49,000, was donated in grants. The trust gave a large number (150+) of small grants, with 13 grants of £1,000 and almost all of the remainder between £250 and £500.

Over 16 grants totalling over £6,000 (9 % of grant-aid) were relevant to this guide in 1996:
- NCH, Oxfam, Greenpeace (£1,000) each;
- Cathedral Camps, ITDG, Iona Community, Marie Stopes International, Population Concern, Water Well, Spiceland Restoration Fund (£500 each);
- Tree Council (£300);
- Greycraigs Outdoor Centre, People's Trust for Endangered Species, Survival International, Woodland Trust (£250 each);
- Common Ground (£200).
A number of grants were given for church restoration. Animal welfare trusts, and an organisation called Swansong were also assisted.

Exclusions: Individuals.

Applications: In writing to the correspondent.

The William Adlington Cadbury Charitable Trust

2 College Walk, Selly Oak, Birmingham
B29 6LQ
Tel: 0121-472 1464 (am only)
Contact: Mrs Christine Stober
Trustees: Brandon Cadbury; Hannah H
Taylor; W James B Taylor; Rupert A
Cadbury; Katherine M Hampton; C
Margaret Salmon; Sarah Stafford; Adrian
D M Thomas; John C Penny.
Grant total: £419,000 (1996/97)
Beneficial area: UK, but mainly in the
West Midlands, and overseas.

In view of the large number of
applications received by the trust in the
last few years, the trustees have re-defined
their policy and will only consider
applications from charities working in the
following fields:
- Birmingham & west Midlands
- Society of Friends & other Christian
  churches; health care; social welfare;
  education & training; the environment;
  preservation; the arts; penal affairs.

UK

Society of Friends; UK medical research;
UK environmental education
programmes; preservation of listed
buildings and monuments; penal affairs;
cross community projects in Northern
Ireland.

International

UK charities working overseas on long-
term development projects.

'Applications are encouraged from ethnic
minority groups and women-led initiatives.'

In 1995/96 the trust had assets of nearly
£12 million which generated an income of
£356,000. It received 1660 applications
and awarded 275 grants.
It is clear from the list of grants that the
majority of grants go to organisations
serving the West Midlands as stated by the
trustees' policy. Only seven grants were for
£10,000 or more, and the majority, 175,
were for amounts of £500 or less.

Grants relevant to this guide totalling
£39,000 (10% of total grant-aid) were
given to 21 organisations:

Under Environment: Conservation
- Shropshire Conservation Development
  Trust (£8,000);
- Kilmartin House Trust, Scotland
  (£5,000);
- Camphill Village Trust Water Research,
  National Federation of City Farms,
  Herefordshire Nature Trust, Birdlife
  International (£2,000 each);
- Peck Wood Alvechurch Worcestershire,
  British Butterfly Conservation Society,
  Rockingham Forest Trust Peterborough
  (£250 each);
- Skye Environmental Centre (£100);

Under Preservation
- The Lunar society Soho House,
  Birmingham, Swanage Pier Trust
  (£2,000 each);
- Lancashire & Yorkshire Railway Trust,
  Fenland Archaeological Trust (£1,000
  each);
- The Guild of Handicraft Trust Gloucs
  (£500);
- Monimail Tower Preservation Trust
  (£100);

Under Overseas Projects
- Marie Stopes International (£5,000);
- Forest Management Foundation
  Solomon Islands (£3,000);
- Kambai Forest Conservation
  Programme Tanzania (£500);
- Tools for Self Reliance (£250).

Exclusions: No grants are made to
individuals or non-registered charities, to
projects concerned with travel or
adventure (e.g. expeditions and
conferences), or to local projects or groups
outside the West Midlands.

Applications: In writing at any time to the
correspondent. There is no formal
application form, but applicants should
include the charity's registration number, a
brief description of the charity's activities,
and details of the specific project for which
a grant is being sought. A budget of the
proposed work together with a copy of the

charity's most recent accounts should also be included. Trustees will also wish to know what funds have already been raised for the project and how the shortfall is to be met.

Trustees meet in May and November. Applications are not acknowledged unless a stamped addressed envelope is provided.

The Ellis Campbell Charitable Foundation

Shalden Park Steading, Shalden, Alton, Hampshire GU34 4DS
Tel: 01256-381821
Fax: 01256-381921
Contact: Michael Campbell
Trustees: Michael D C C Campbell, Chairman, Mrs Linda F Campbell; Mrs Doris Campbell; Jamie L C Campbell; Mrs Alexandra J Andrew; Trevor M Aldridge.
Grant total: £35,000 (1996/97)
Beneficial area: UK, with a preference for Perthshire and Hampshire.

'Special emphasis is placed upon donations towards youth, education, and conservation (historical, architectural, and constructional heritage including modes of transport) in Hampshire and Perthshire.' In 1996, the trust had assets of £905,000 and an income of £64,000 from which grants totalling £35,000 were made. Grants relevant to this guide in 1996 totalled over £3,000 (9% of total grant-aid) and included:
- Save Britain's Heritage (£2,000 in 2 grants);
- Scottish Tree Trust, and a Hampshire parish church (£500).

The proportion of giving to heritage interests varies considerably. For example in 1994 (and in the previous year) Winchester Cathedral Trust was given £10,000 and the Scottish Trust for Underwater Archaeology, £1,000.

Exclusions: No grants to individuals unless known by a trustee.

Applications: In writing to the correspondent. 'Applicants should observe the areas of special interest and should not necessarily expect to receive an acknowledgement.' Trustees meet in March, July and October.

The Carew Pole Charitable Trust

Messrs Dawson & Co, 2 New Square, Lincoln's Inn, London WC2A 3RZ
Tel: 0171-404 5941
Contact: J C Richardson
Trustees: J C Richardson; J R Cooke-Hurle.
Grant total: £22,000 (1994/95)
Beneficial area: UK, with a particular interest in Cornwall and Devon.

This trust was founded by Sir John Cawen Carew Pole, former Lord Lieutenant of Cornwall, and the leading member of the long established family based at Torpoint. It has the same objects, trustees and administration as the Sir Richard 1973 Carew Pole Charitable Trust and it is not easy to distinguish the two from the type of grants given. An interest is shown in the architectural heritage, gardens and horticulture by both trusts, though these are not the only environmental areas potentially supported. In 1994/95 the trust had an income of £24,000 from which £22,000 was disbursed in 32 grants ranging between £100 and £10,000 five of which were for £1,000 or more.

Three grants were relevant to this guide and totalled nearly £13,000 (59% of grant-aid):
- National Trust (£10,000 with £5,000 in the previous year);
- Cornwall Heritage Trust (£2,500);
- Churchtown Field Studies Centre (£250 also given in the previous year).

Exclusions: Individuals.

Applications: In writing to the correspondent. Trustees meet in March and September.

The Sir Richard Carew Pole 1973 Charitable Trust

Messrs Dawson & Co, 2 New Square,
Lincoln's Inn, London WC2A 3RZ
Tel: 0171-4045941
Contact: J C Richardson
Trustees: J C Richardson; J R Cooke-Hurle.
Grant total: £32,000 (1995/96)
Beneficial area: UK with a particular
interest in Cornwall and Devon.

The Carew Poles are a long-established
family based at Torpoint and the objects of
the trust specifically mention 'Cornwall or
the Cornish people' or 'Cornish
connections'. This trust shares the same
trustees and administration with the
Carew Pole Trust. In 1995/96 it had an
income of £52,000 from which 35 grants
totalling £32,000 were given. Grants
ranged between £50 and £8,500 with
seven grants for £1,000 or more, and the
majority between £100 and £500.

Nine grants totalling nearly £18,000 (56%
of grant-aid) were relevant to this guide:
- National Trust, plus Jackson-Stopps
  Appeal – £1,000 (£9,500 in 2 grants);
- Carew Pole Garden Trust (£6,650);
- Devon Historic Buildings Trust
  Haldon-Belvedere Appeal (£500);
- Coral Clay Conservation Trust,
  Churchtown Farm Centre, Cornish
  Maritime Trust, Survival International
  (£250 each);
- Garden History Society, Survival (£100
  each).

The eponymous garden trust and the
National Trust are regularly supported.

Exclusions: Individuals.

Applications: In writing to the
correspondent. Trustees meet in March
and September.

The W A Cargill Fund

190 St Vincent Street, Glasgow G2 5SP
Tel: 0141-204 2833

Contact: Mr Alexander C Fyfe
Grant total: Around £75,000
Beneficial area: Preference for Scotland.

At least two Cargill Funds are
administered by Mr Fyfe: the D W T
Cargill Fund and the W A Cargill Fund.

Some information is available about the
latter although scant. It had assets of
around £1.5 million in 1994 from which
grants of about £75,000 were made to a
range of charitable interests (the fund has
general charitable objects and can give as
widely or as narrowly as it likes).

It is known that the fund supported the
RSPB in 1994/95.

Applications: In writing to the
correspondent.

Caritas (the James A de Rothschild Charitable Settlement)

c/o Saffery Champness, Fairfax House,
Fulwood Place, Gray's Inn, London
WC1V 6UB
Contact: Julie Christmas
Trustees: Lord Rothschild; Lady Serena
Rothschild; M E Hatch.
Grant total: £358,000 (1994/95)
Beneficial area: UK and Israel.

This trust is largely included because of its
gifts to the National Trust for the restoration
and upkeep of its family home, Waddesdon
Manor in Buckinghamshire. It donated
£264,700 in 1994/95 and £798,500 in the
previous year. (See the Jacob Rothschild
GAM Charitable Trust for even larger
donations by the family to Waddesdon.)
There has been little leeway for further
'caritas' although small grants have been
given for the built and wildlife heritage. A
number of grants in 1993/94 were more
relevant to this guide:
- Landscape Foundation, National
  Council for the Conservation of Plants
  and gardens (£1,000 each);
- Heritage of London Trust, Jerusalem
  Botanic Gardens (£500).

Leslie Mary Carter Charitable Trust

Messrs Birkett, 20-32 Museum Street, Suffolk IP1 1HZ
Contact: S R M Wilson
Trustees: Miss Leslie Carter; Stephen R M Wilson.
Grant total: £38,000 (1995)
Beneficial area: UK, particularly East Anglia, and overseas.

This trust characteristically divides its giving between social welfare causes and environmental interests, particularly wildlife and countryside. In 1995 the trust gave 12 grants ranging between £2,000 and £4,000.

Grants relevant to this guide totalled £17,000 (45 % of grant-aid) and were given to:
◆ BTO Save the Skylarks, Fair Isle Bird Observatory (£4,000 each);
◆ Field Studies Council, Norfolk Wildlife Trust (£3,500 each);
◆ River Stour Trust (£2,000).

In previous years grants have included Friends of the Earth and Greenpeace.

Exclusions: No personal applications.

Applications: In writing to the correspondent.

The Cathedral Amenities Fund, Cathedral Fabric Commission

Fielden House, Little College Street, London SW1P 3SH
Tel: 0171-222 3793
Contact: Dr Richard Gem
Trustees: From members of the Cathedral Advisory Commission of the General Synod of the Church of England.
Grant total: £12,000 (1996/97)
Beneficial area: UK.

To preserve and improve the setting and grounds surrounding cathedrals and greater churches.

In 1995/96 the fund had assets of £238,000 (£134,000 in 1993/94) and gave 4 grants totalling £16,000 (£13,000 in 1993/94) ranging between £1000 and £6000.

Exclusions: Fabric repairs and visitor facilities.

Applications: In writing to the correspondent.

Thomas Catto Charitable Settlement

23 Great Winchester Street, London EC2P 2AX
Contact: Miss Ann Uwins
Trustees: Hon Mrs Ruth Bennett; Lord Catto.
Grant total: £83,000 (1995/96)
Beneficial area: UK and overseas.

In 1995/96 the trust gave 134 grants ranging between £100 and £5,000. 36 grants were for £1,000+. Most grants were for £250 or £500.

Grants relevant to this guide were given to:
◆ Royal Horticultural Society St John Gala (£3,200);
◆ WWF (£1,000 in 2 grants);
◆ BTCV, National Trust, Scottish Native Woods, CPRE, SOS Sahel (£500 each);
◆ Wild Side Trust, National Trust for Scotland, Scottish Wildlife Trust, Intermediate Technology (£250 each).

Applications: In writing to the correspondent.

The Wilfrid & Constance Cave Foundation

c/o New Lodge Farm, Drift Road, Winkfield, Windsor SL4 4QQ
Tel: 01344-890351
Contact: W C Varney
Trustees: Mrs T Jones; Mrs J Pickin; Rev P Buckler; F Jones.

Grant total: £76,000 (1995/96)
Beneficial area: UK, with a preference for Wiltshire, Berkshire and the West Country.

In 1995/96 the trust had assets of £1.35 million and an income of £141,000 from which 46 grants totalling £76,000 were made. Most grants were between £1,000 and £5,000 with only one grant higher (£13,000 to King's Hall).

Grants have shown a preference for the west of England especially Wiltshire.

Grants in 1995/96 relevant to this guide included:
- Quiet Garden Trust (£4,000); Brushford Oak Tree Appeal (£3,000);
- Coventry City Farms, Farms for City Children (£2,000 each);
- Cotswold Canal Trust (£1,000 and in the previous year);
- Kennet and Avon Canal Trust, West Country River Trust, Marine Conservation Society (£1,000 each);
- Harman's Water Meadow Trust (£250 and in the previous year);
- Support was also given to a number of animal welfare organisations particularly those working for horses.

Applications: In writing to the correspondent.

The B G S Cayzer Charitable Trust

Cayzer House, 1 Thomas More Street, London E1 9AR
Tel: 0171-481 4343 ext. 274
Contact: J I Mehrtens
Trustees: Peter N Buckley; Peter R Davies.
Grant total: £71,000 (1994/95)
Beneficial area: UK.

It is understood that the trust has been accumulating its income and formulating a policy to fund a few major projects. In 1994/95 the trust gave 33 grants all but three of which were for less than £1,000. A major grant was given to the Feathers Club (£45,000).

Grants relevant to this guide were given to:
- Game Conservancy Trust (£5,300);
- Royal Botanic Gardens (£1,000);
- West Galloway Fisheries (£600);
- Tewkesbury Abbey Appeal (£500);
- National Trust Chastleton House Appeal (£400).

In the preceding year Crarae Gardens Charitable Trust received £10,000.

Exclusions: Unsolicited appeals will not be supported.

Applications: The trust tends to support only people/projects known to the Cayzer family or the trustees.

The Chapman Charitable Trust

Messrs Crouch Chapman, 62 Wilson Street, London EC2A 2BU
Tel: 0171-782 0007; Fax 0171 782 0939
Contact: Roger S Chapman
Trustees: Roger S Chapman; W John Chapman; Richard J Chapman; Bruce D Chapman.
Grant total: £160,000 (1996/97)
Beneficial area: UK.
In 1997, the trust had assets of over £4 million and an income of £163,000. from which the trust made 117 grants (ranging from £250 to £10,000) totalling £160,000. In the past three years the trust has given its largest grants to Aldeburgh and the Field Studies Council.

Grants were categorised in the trust's annual report under the following headings. The number of grants is shown in brackets.
- Cultural and recreational £23,000 (6)
- Education and research £14,000 (4)
- Health £14,000 (18)
- Social services £92,000 (80)
- Environment and heritage £5,500 (7)
- Religion £2,000 (3)

Categorisation can be for grant-seekers. In 1995/96 It seems that as many as 13 grants were relevant to this guide totalling nearly £25,000 (16% of grant-aid):

◆ Field Studies Council (£12,000 with £10,000 for Juniper Hall and £2,000 for Epping Forest Field Centre);
◆ National Trust for Scotland (£5,000);
◆ CPRE, Campaign for the Protection of Rural Wales, Holy Trinity Plaistow, Latrobe Heritage Trust, National Trust Snowdonia appeal (£1,000 each);
◆ Fair Isle Bird Observatory Trust, Goring Methodist Church, Marine Conservation Society, Salem Chapel Porthmadog, SAFE (Sustainable Agriculture, Food & Environment (£500 each);

However this list includes two grants categorised under 'Religion' which it is assumed are for renovation and restoration work, but could well be for spiritual and community activities.

Exclusions: No grants to individuals.

Applications: In writing at any time. The trustees currently meet twice a year at the end of September and March. They receive a great many applications and regret that they cannot acknowledge receipt of them. The absence of communication for six months means an unsuccessful application.

The Charities Aid Foundation

Kings Hill, West Malling, Kent, ME19 4TA
Tel: 01732-520031
Website: http/www.charitynet.org
Contact: Judith McQuillan, Grants Administrator
Trustees: Grants Council: David Carrington, Chairman; Professor Naomi Sargant, Vice-Chairman; John Bateman; Rev Dr Gordon Barritt; Gillian Crosby; Andrew Kingman; Jane Lewis; Lawrence Mackintosh; Michele Rigby; Professor Peter Quilliam; Ceridwen Roberts; Yogesh Chauhan.
Grant total: £577,000 (1996/97)
Beneficial area: UK and overseas.

The foundation's guidelines for applicants read as follows:

'The Charities Aid Foundation makes grants to enable charities to improve their management and effectiveness, in order to strengthen the UK charitable sector.

Grants are made to assist a charity:
◆ to improve its effectiveness in meeting its objectives
◆ to improve its use of financial resources, facilities, members, staff or volunteers
◆ to improve its stability or effectiveness
◆ to move into new areas of need.

'Emergency grants may be given to meet an exceptional, unforeseen financial setback, or where a single injection of funds is required to restore the viability of the charity. 'The foundation is advised on applications by the Grants Council, which meets quarterly to consider applications.

'Applications will only be considered from registered charities or organisations within the United Kingdom approved for charitable status by the Inland Revenue. Grants are normally made to small and medium sized charities with a proven track record. Applications are encouraged from black and ethnic minority groups.

'Funds are limited. Grants are normally one-off and should be used within 12 months of receipt. Only in quite exceptional circumstances may funding be awarded provisionally for a period of up to 3 years, subject to an annual review.

'Grants do not exceed £10,000. The average award is less than £4,000 and only two thirds of applications are successful. Grants are seldom for the full amount requested.'

A total of 156 grants were given in 1996/97, most of which were for amounts between £1,000 and £5,000. No organisations received the maximum possible grant of £10,000. Fundraising was a dominant concern. Grants were given to both local and national organisations with the balance probably to the former.

Beneficiaries relevant to this guide in 1996/97:

- Paddington Farm Trust (£8,000);
- Trees for Life (£5,000);
- Bath Churches Housing Association, Dartington North Devon Trust (£4,000 each);
- Horticultural Therapy (£3,000);Global Action Plan, Trust for Urban Ecology (£2,000 each);
- Greater Nottingham & South Notts Green Network (£1,000)

Exclusions: The Grants Council does not consider applications to assist with Lottery bids for retrospective funding to clear debts or repay loans towards the regular, central core and administrative expenditure of the charity for training which is part of a charity core activity, for example organisations whose main function is to provide counselling services for the erection, repair or purchase of buildings, nor for the provision of furniture or office equipment (including computer hardware) for start-up costs of new charities for scientific, medical or educational research from individuals or for the direct benefit of individuals.

Grants are not provided in response to general appeals, no matter how worthwhile the cause.

Applications are considered at meetings in February, May, August and November for which applications need to be submitted at least two months before.

Applications: In writing to the correspondent. Grants are decided four times a year.

The Chase Charity

2 The Court, High Street, Harwell, Didcot, Oxfordshire OX11 0EY
Tel: 01235-820044
Contact: Ailsa Hornsby
Trustees: Council: A Ramsay Hack; Gordon Halcrow; Richard Mills; Mrs R A Moore; Claudia Flanders; Keith Grant; Ann Stannard.

Grant total: £214,000 (1996/97)
Beneficial area: UK, with special interest in rural areas.

In 1996/97 the charity had assets of £4.5 million which generated an income of £289,000. A total of 68 applications received support out of 1,2197 applications, a success rate of 1:19.

Grants – 1995/96
- Social Welfare £132,000
- The Arts £49,000
- Heritage £33,000
  Almshouses £15,000 2 grants
  Conservation & Museums £2,500 1 grant
  Historic Buildings £15,500 8 grants

The charity's principal concern is to 'reach those groups falling within our areas of interest who, for geographical or other reasons, find it particularly difficult to raise the funds they need to carry out their work.' It aims to spread its grants as widely as possible throughout the UK. It decided in its policy review of autumn 1996 to discontinue giving grants in the Greater London area though projects outside London organised by organisations based within London may be considered.

The following extracts from its guidelines are relevant to this guide:

Historic Buildings
a) Churches
   'Grants are restricted to small rural parishes charged with the care of a national treasure. Local effort is a vital factor.'
b) Almshouses 'Most of the charity's help is concentrated on historic buildings in rural areas.'
c) Other buildings

'Small, interesting buildings, again in rural areas, are of interest; however, preference is given to historic buildings which are used for community purposes.'

Examples of grants in 1995/96:
- Calverton Almshouses, Buckinghamshire, towards refurbishment of the first of three cottages (£5,000);

- Arvon Foundation Ltd, Yorkshire, towards restoration of the Bee-bole wall (£2,500);
- Gad's Hill School, Kent, for restoration of the conservatory (£2,500);
- Avoncroft Musuem Development Trust, Bromsgrove (£2,250).
- 11 grants between £1,000 and £3,000 were given to local churches.

Social Welfare

'The trustees are placing increasing emphasis upon the provision of social welfare services and community development in rural areas, but not to the exclusion of urban areas...

'In these areas of concern, the trustees recognise the problems of access, homelessness, young people at risk, mental health and the frail elderly, and help, though on a necessarily modest scale, in a variety of ways. They attach great importance to the breadth of local support and the involvement of both users of services and volunteers.'

This section of its policy is reproduced because of the meeting of environmental and social welfare concerns in issues such as isolation and homelessness.

Exclusions: The trustees do not contribute to large appeals. Generally, circular type appeals have little chance of success but they are scrutinised and answered, positively in special cases. Circular letters bearing a facsimile signature are not answered. Grants are not made to individuals, including students, but the trustees do make some provision for them through other organisations. Large national organisations and their branches fall outside the guidelines as do requests for revenue or salary support.

Applications: The charity does not use application forms. Applications should be made in letter form with as much relevant information, but as economically as possible. The following information should be included:

a) Brief information about origins and present company/charitable status.

b) A recent annual report where available.
c) An explanation of why help is sought.
d) A description of what is needed and, where necessary, the development plans to meet that need, including information about timescale.
e) Detailed up-to-date financial information, including audited accounts and estimates, which covers both the general work of the organisation and the particular need.

Trustees' meetings are held in February, May, August, October and November.

The Winston Churchill Memorial Trust

15 Queen's Gate Terrace, London
SW7 5PR
Tel: 0171-584 9315
Contact: The Secretary
Beneficial area: UK.

The trust awards travelling fellowships to UK citizens irrespective of background or age so that 'as a result of personal experience gained during their travels, they (are) able to make a more effective and valuable contribution to the life of this country and of their community.'

Each year the trust selects different subjects or categories in which candidates can propose study projects of their own choice. In many, indeed most, years a category of interest to people concerned about our environment is included.

Travel and living expenses abroad are covered for a period of usually about four to eight weeks.

Applications: Obtain the leaflet and application form from the trust by sending a SAE (22cm by 11cm) to the above address. Completed forms need to be returned between July and October each year.

The CLA Charitable Trust

Summerlea, The Street, East Knoyle,
Salisbury SP3 6AJ
Tel: 01747-830410
Contact: Colonel A F Mackain-Bremner
Trustees: A N G Duckworth;
P de L Giffard; M A Gregory.
Grant total: £77,000 (1996/97)
Beneficial area: England & Wales only.

The main object of the trust is: 'The relief
of persons who are mentally or physically
handicapped by the making of grants or
loans to landowners for the provision of
facilities for recreation and leisure time
occupation for such persons...'. This is a
collecting rather than an endowed trust,
working through the Country Landowners
Association with which it is closely linked.

Projects supported in the past include:
provision of flat-bottomed boats suitable for
wheelchairs; laying of hard paths and
suitable lavatories for disabled people; special
bird hides – including a wheelchair lift to
give access to a bird hide in a tree; Braille
trails, and greenhouses for an horticultural
project for mentally disabled people.

Applications: In writing to the
correspondent.

The J Anthony Clark Charitable Foundation

Box 1704, Glastonbury, Somerset
BA16 0YB
Contact: Mrs P Grant
Trustees: Lance Clark; T A Clark; J C
Clark; Caroline Pym; Aiden Pelly.
Grant total: £137,000 (1995/96)
Beneficial area: UK.

The foundation is interested in the work
of 'small, new or innovative projects' and
gives support in the areas of 'health,
education, peace and preservation of the
earth and the arts'.

In 1995/96 it had assets of some
£4.6 million and an income of
£171,000. It made about 38 grants
totalling £136,000 ranging from under
£100 to £20,000. Most grants were
between £1,000 and £4,000. Five grants
relevant to this guide totalling £15,000
were made in 1995/96:
◆ ARA (£5,500);
◆ Survival International (£2,000);
◆ Artists Agency (£3,500);
◆ ACCIS (£2500);
◆ Rural Resettlement of Ireland (£1,500).

Exclusions: Individuals; conservation of
buildings.

Applications: In writing to the
correspondent but it is understood that
the trust does no seek unsolicited
applications and does not reply to them.

The Roger & Sarah Bancroft Clark Charitable Trust

40 High Street, Street, Somerset
BA16 0YA
Contact: Mrs B L Gunson
Trustees: Eleanor C Robertson; Mary P
Lovell; Stephen Clark; S Caroline Gould.
Grant total: £63,000 (1994) see below
Beneficial area: UK and overseas,
preference for Somerset.

The trust has general charitable purposes
with a particular interest in the Religious
Society of Friends and associated bodies,
charities connected with Somerset and
educational support to individuals.

Twenty grants were relevant to this guide
in 1994 totalling £4,300 (7% of grant-
aid). The trust has two separate funds.

In 1994, the ERC Charitable Trust had
assets of £399,000, an income of £13,000
and gave 40 grants totalling £17,000.
Many of these were, of course, very small
with the largest taking the lion's share –
the University of Edinburgh (£11,000).

Grants relevant to this guide were given to:
- Architectural Heritage Society of Scotland (£1,500);
- Buildings of Scotland Trust (£200);
- APRS Roads & Bridges Committee (£100).

The SBC Fund had assets of about £1.7 million producing an income of £62,000 from which 140 grants totalling £46,000 were given. Grants ranged from £50 to £6,500, mostly under £500.

Most grants relevant to this guide in 1994 were small though in a previous year £1,000 was given to the Society for the Protection of Ancient Buildings:
- CPRE (£300); CPRE Somerset (£100);
- Cotswold Canal Trust, Wiltshire & Berkshire Canal Amenity Group, New Lanark Conservation Trust (£200 each);
- Marie Stopes International (£150);
- Lincoln Cathedral, National Trust Wessex Appeal, Nunney Bell Restoration, Oldham Parish Church, Open Spaces Society, Sustrans, Tree Aid (£100 each);
- Windmill Hill City Farm (£50).
- Three churches in Wales received £200 each.

Applications: In writing to the correspondent. There is no application form and telephone calls are not accepted. Trustees meet about three times a year. Applications will be acknowledged if a SAE is enclosed.

The Cleopatra Trust

c/o Charities Aid Foundation, Kings Hill, West Malling, Kent, ME19 4TA
Tel: 01732-520081
Contact: Mrs Barbara Davis, Senior Information Officer
Trustees: Dr Charles Peacock; Bettine Bond; Clare Peacock.
Grant total: £270,000 (1995)
Beneficial area: UK and overseas.

The trust had assets, mainly shares in Nurdin & Peacock plc which generated an income of £140,000 in 1995 whilst grants of £270,000 were made. (In the previous year the trust had made grants of only £48,000 from an income of £131,000.) The trust is related to the Epigoni Trust (see separate entry) with which it shares its investment policy and trustees.

Whilst the trust is predominantly interested in supporting medical work it shows an interest in environmentally involved work often from the therapeutic angle. In 1995 the trust gave three grants relevant to this guide totalling £20,000 (7% of grant-aid) to:
- Farms for City Children (£10,000);
- Tree Aid, Tools for Self Reliance (£5,000 each).

In 1993 grants were given to the Society for Horticultural Therapy (£10,000) and the Marine Conservation Society (£5,000).

Applications: In writing to the correspondent.

The de Clermont Co Ltd

Morris Hall, Norham, Berwick upon Tweed TD15 2JY
Contact: Mrs E K de Clermont
Trustees: Mrs E K de Clermont; H S Orpwood.
Grant total: £28,000 (1995/96)
Beneficial area: UK with a particular interest in Scotland and the Berwick area.

This trust likes to give a very large number of modest gifts to a very wide range of activities. In 1995/96 it had assets of £688,000 which generated an income of £27,000. Over 200 grants totalling £28,000, were made. These included 17 small grants to groups relevant to this guide. These totalled about £1,500 (5%) of total grant-aid.
- Kirknewton Church (£250);
- National Trust for Scotland (£200 in 2 grants);
- Game Conservancy, WaterAid, WWF UK, Berwick Swan & Wildlife Trust, Berwick Bridges Trust, National Trust, St John the Evangelist Spittal (£100 each);

◆ Small gifts of £50 included Foe, BTCV, Tree Aid, Naturewatch Trust, Northumberland Wildlife Trust, RSPB, Roslyn Chapel Trust.

Applications: In writing to the correspondent.

The Clothworkers' Foundation and Trusts

Clothworkers' Hall, Dunster Court, Mincing Lane, London EC3R 7AH
Tel: 0171-623 7041
Contact: M G T Harris, Secretary.
Trustees: The Governors of the Foundation.
Grant total: £3,080,000 (1996)
Beneficial area: UK and overseas.

These charities make about 100 new grants a year, covering almost all areas of charitable activity. Only a few are for more than £25,000 or for less than £2,000. Nevertheless those for £30,000 account for over half the money dispensed. Grants are usually towards projects or capital or equipment, rather than contributions to running costs. A few of the largest grants are paid over a period of years, but this is unusual.

The Clothworkers' Foundation has a number of associated charities which contribute about a quarter of the grants total given above. The foundation and some of the other charities are endowed, but a large part of the income of the foundation comes by way of annual gifts (£1.2 million in 1995) from The Clothworkers' Company itself, which is not a charitable body. The governors have been building up the endowment by reserving about 30% of their income each year which, by the end of 1995, was worth £29 million.

The foundation publishes a statement of its grant making policy: 'Preferential consideration is given to appeals received from self-help organisations and to charities requiring support to 'prime the pumps' for development and more extensive fund

raising initiatives. Also to appeals related to textiles and kindred activities.'

With the exception of hospices and churches, the grants concentrate on national rather than local bodies, though there are exceptions to this. However there are hardly any grants to local branches of national organisations.

Grants in 1996
The grant totals in 1995 are categorised in the following table (some figures approximate):
◆ Welfare/relief of need £540,000 18%
◆ Medicine/health £589,000 19%
◆ Clothworking £580,000 19%
◆ Education/science £462,000 15%
◆ Children/youth £384,000 13 %
◆ Overseas £228,000 7%
◆ The Church £120,000 4%
◆ Heritage/environment £131,000 4%
◆ Arts £55,000

Grants relevant to this guide in 1996 included:

The Church
The foundation made two grants for church repair, both in the City of London:
◆ St Olave's Church, St Paul's Cathedral (£5,000 each);

Heritage, environment
These included:
◆ Rockingham Forest Trust, (£25,000);
◆ Birdlife International, Pepys House Trust (£10,000 each);
◆ Council for the Protection of Rural England, (£6,000);
◆ Ramblers' Association, (£2,000);
◆ Northumberland Wildlife Trust, (£1,100);
◆ Metropolitan Public Gardens Association, The National Trust, (£1,000 each).

Under Overseas
◆ Intermediate Technology Development Group, SOS Sahel International UK, (£10,000 each);
◆ Royal Geographical Society, (£2,000).

Exclusions: Grants to registered charities only; no grants to individuals or for their sponsored activities. Support for churches and independent schools is restricted to those with close and traditional links to The Clothworkers' Company.

Applications: The foundation has long been a pioneer among city livery companies in publishing full information about its work. It also prides itself on being open to telephone enquiries from potential applicants. Many of these will be handled by David Smith, the charities administrator.

1a. Applications should be made in writing on the registered charity's official headed note paper. Ideally, the appeal letter itself should be no longer than two and a half pages of A4.
   b. Detailed costings or a budget for the project or projects referred to in the appeal letter should form a separate appendix or appendices and should provide the fullest possible detail.
   c. The latest annual report of the applicant charity, together with the latest full audited accounts, including a full balance sheet, should also accompany the written application.

2. \During the course of the application letter, applicants should endeavour to:
   a   Introduce the work of the charity; state when it was established; describe its aims and objectives; and define precisely what the charity does and who benefits from its activities.
   b. Comment on the applicant's track record since its inception and refer to its notable achievements and successes to date. Endeavour to provide an interesting synopsis of the organisation.
   c. Describe the project for which a grant is being sought fully, clearly and concisely and comment on the charity's plans for the future.
   d. Provide full costings or a budget for the project/projects to include a detailed breakdown of the costs involved.
   e. Give details of all other applications which the applicant charity has made to other sources of funding, and indicate precisely what funds have already been raised from other sources for the project.
   f. All applicants are, of course, perfectly at liberty to request a precise sum of money by way of a grant. However it can be more beneficial for the applicant to concentrate on providing accurate and detailed costings of the project concerned thereby enabling the foundation to make its own judgement as to the level of financial support to be considered.

3. Applicants can greatly help their cause by concentrating on clarity of presentation and by providing detailed factual information.

Trustees meet regularly in January, March, May, July, October and November.

Preliminary information required in support of any application must include the latest annual report and full audited accounts.

The Francis Coales Charitable Foundation

The Bays, Hillcote, Bleadon Hill, Weston-super-Mare, Somerset BS24 9JS
Tel: 01934-814009
Contact: T H Parker, Administrator
Grant total: £100,000 (1996/97)
Beneficial area: UK, especially Beds, Bucks, Herts and Northants.

The trust provides grants and loans for: the repair and restoration of any ecclesiastical or other buildings built before 1875 which are open to the public, including their contents; archaeological and other research into antiquarian sites, buildings or items (including the cost of books, theses and lectures); and the purchase and stocking of public libraries to provide a supply of books relating to historical buildings and objects.

The trustees give priority to buildings in Buckinghamshire, Bedfordshire, Hertfordshire and Northamptonshire, where most of the settlor's business was carried out. Buildings in other counties are only considered in exceptional cases, although grants are made for monuments in churches irrespective of location.

In 1995, the trust had assets of nearly £1.2 million generating a net income of £100,000 from which 88 grants totalling £121,00 were given. (Unallocated income stood at £94,000.)

The trust received 118 grant applications and considered 99. All but 11 were supported. 48 applications from the preferred counties received 53% of the grant value (20% less than 1994), 9% in value was awarded to churches outside the area, 17% was awarded for monuments and 21% for publications and miscellaneous applications. The latter, which has affected the 1995 percentages, includes £25,000 for Northamptonshire Victoria County History Trust payable over five years, a project deemed to be of great importance.

Most grants ranged from £1,000 to £5,000. £5,000 grants were made towards work undertaken on:
◆ Windsor Castle's Aerary;
◆ Kingston-on-Soar chantry tomb;
◆ Brixworth Northamptonshire, tower and spire;
◆ Lathbury in Buckinghamshire;
◆ Great Hampden, Buckinghamshire, monuments;
◆ Poyntz Monument, North Ockendon, Essex.

Applications: In writing to the correspondent for an application form.

The John Coates Charitable Trust

Crockmore House, Fawley, Henley-on-Thames, Oxfordshire RG9 6HY
Tel: 01491-573367
Contact: Mrs P L Youngman
Trustees: Mrs Gillian McGregor; Mrs Catharine Kesley; Mrs Phyllidas Youngman.
Grant total: £260,000 (1996/97)
Beneficial area: UK.

The trust has a particular interest in medical charities, preservation of the environment, especially architecture, and education. The most recent accounts on file at the Charity Commission were for 1994/95 when the trust had assets of nearly £6 million and an income of £221,000.

The trust has sent its grant list for 1996/97 which showed nine grants relevant to this guide totalling over £54,000 (21 % of grant-aid):
◆ Painshill Park Trust (£12,500);
◆ Royal Botanic Gardens Kew, Chichester Cathedral (£10,000 each);
◆ Winchester Cathedral; St Bride's Church, Ely Cathedral, Almshouses Association (£5,000 each);
◆ Wildfowl & Wetlands Trust (£2,000);
◆ Farmland Museum, Petersfield Church (£1,000 each).

Exclusions: Individuals.

Applications: To the correspondent in writing. Trustee meetings are held in January and July.

The Lance Coates Charitable Trust 1969

Springhill Centre, Cuddlington, Aylesbury, Bucks HP18 0AE
Tel: 01296-747157
Contact: Hugh L Coates
Trustees: H L T Coates, E P Serjeant, S M Coates.
Grant total: £12,000 (1995/96)
Beneficial area: UK.

In 1995/96, the trust had assets of £837,000 and an income of £29,000 from which seven grants totalling £12,000 were given. The trust retained a balance of £60,000 so future spending should again rise. The correspondent has informed us that the annual distribution will be very unlikely to exceed £25,000.

The trust regularly supports certain organisations including the Country Trust

(£5,000 with £15,000 in 1994/95, £10,000 in 1993/94, £15,000 in 1992/93 and £25,000 in 1991/92).

Applications: In writing to the correspondent.

The Cobb Charity

108 Leamington Road, Kenilworth, Warwickshire CV8 2AA
Contact: Eleanor Allitt
Trustees: F Appelbe; Mrs E J Allitt; Mrs C Cochran; Mrs M Wells.
Grant total: £24,000 (1996/97)
Beneficial area: UK and overseas.

The trust aims to support:
- Education – linked to conservation, a sustainable ecology, confidence building, disadvantaged children, and adults, imaginative solutions to problems;
- Environment – conservation, agricultural research, cycleways.

It prefers to support smaller charities.

In 1995/96 the charity had assets of £405,000 and gave grants of £27,000 all in sums of £750. Grants clearly relevant to this guide totalled £7,000 (26% of grant-aid) and were given to:
- Environmental Investigation Agency;
- E-scape;
- Learning through Landscapes;
- FoE, Forum for the Future;Garden Reach, the Greenhouse, Natural Energy Education Project;
- Network Whitby Resource Centre;
- National Federation of City Farms.

In the previous year Sustrans received £1,250 and grants varied in size, though not markedly.

Exclusions: Individuals; building restoration; student expeditions.

Applications: In writing to the correspondent in August and January.

The Coda Wildlife Trust

The Cottage, Oak Hill, Wethersfield, Braintree, Essex CM7 4AJ
Contact: Mrs J M Davis
Trustees: Mrs J M Davis, H N G Davis; H S Davis.
Grant total: £20,000 (1995/96)
Beneficial area: UK.

The trust aims to educate the public in conservation and preservation, in maintenance of native and broad-leaved woodland and to encourage the better protection of wild birds and animals by the provision of nature reserves.

In 1992/93 the trust purchased Brookes Reserve, Tumblers Green near Stisted which is managed by Essex Wildlife Trust.

In 1995/96 the trust received £100,000 in donations from which grants of £20,000 were made. Known beneficiaries were the RSPB and Butterfly Conservation but it is not known whether these were the sole ones.

Applications: In writing to the correspondent.

The John S Cohen Foundation

85 Albany Street, London NW1 4BT
Tel: 0171-486 1117; **Fax:** 0171-486 1118
Contact: Duncan Haldane, Administrator
Trustees: Dr David Cohen, Chairman; Elizabeth Cohen; Richard Cohen.
Grant total: £380,000 (l996/97)
Beneficial area: UK and overseas.

The trustees aim to seek out projects which have 'an unusual and innovative nature whilst maintaining support for a number of regular beneficiaries'. It has a particular interest in supporting the arts and Jewish charities. Its grants support work with a national relevance.

In 1995/96, 119 grants totalling £381,000 were given with grants ranging from less than £1,000 to £25,000. The foundation categorised its grants and the sums of interest to this guide were as follows

Grants in 1995/96 and 1994/95
Environment/wildlife
   £13,500 3.5%   £22,500 5%
Conservation/heritage
   £10,500 3%   £35,500 9%

Additional sums were also given under other categories to family planning and population.

Relevant grants in 1995/96 and 1994/95 included:
◆ Oxford University, Environmental Change Unit (£50,000, 5th of 5);
◆ CPRE, Marie Stopes International (£10,000 each);
◆ Museums & Galleries Commission, London Historic House Museums Trust (£5,000 each);
◆ Island Plants Conservation Appeal, Kew (£2,500);
◆ SAVE (Britain's Heritage), Society for the Protection of Ancient Buildings, William Morris Craft Fellowships (£2,000 each);
◆ Octavia Hill Museum Wisbech (£1,500);
◆ Population Concern (£1,400).

Exclusions: Grants to registered charities only; no grants to individuals; no further medical support.

Applications: No response is made to applications unless it is decided to make a grant. Applicants should state the purpose for which a donation is required briefly outlining related work and the financial circumstances. Trustees normally meet in March and October and applications need to be made at least a month before.

George Henry Collins Charity

St Philips House, St Philips Place, Birmingham, West Midlands B3 2PP
Contact: David Turfrey
Trustees: A D Martineau; Elizabeth A Davies; Andrew A Waters; Henry E Ashton.

Grant total: £54,000 (1994/95)
Beneficial area: UK and overseas, with a particular interest in the Birmingham area.

The charity gives to a very wide range of charitable activity but almost exclusively to charities in the Birmingham area. In 1994/95 about 100 grants were made ranging between £250 and £1,250. Eighteen grants were for £1,000.

Eleven grants totalling £6,575 (12% of grant-aid) were relevant to this guide:
◆ Birmingham Botanical Gardens, Castle Bromwich Gardens Trust, ITDG (£1,000 each);
◆ Dodford Children's Holiday Farm, RSPB, Marie Stopes (£500 each);
◆ Groundwork Black Country (£325);
◆ Four churches received a total of £1,750 for restoration/conservation work.

Applications: In writing to the correspondent.

The Sir Jeremiah Colman Gift Trust

Malshanger, Basingstoke, Hants RG23 7EY
Contact: Sir Michael Colman
Trustees: Sir Michael Colman; Lady Judith Colman; Oliver J Colman; Cynthia Colman; Jeremiah M Colman.
Grant total: £90,000 (1994/5)
Beneficial area: UK, with a preference for Hampshire especially Basingstoke.

The first of the trust's purposes is to make donations to any friends or relatives 'who may through no fault of their own be in indigent circumstances or in need of pecuniary assistance'. Another is to make grants to 'past, present or future employees of any club, institution or company of which Sir Jeremiah Colman may be or may have been President, Director or member'. (One of which was the London Brighton and South Coast Railway Company.) Other objects are the maintenance of churches and their ministers, the promotion of education and recreation. A particular interest in

Hampshire and the Basingstoke area is evident in its grant-making.

In 1995 The trust had assets of over £2.19 million. A total of £90,000 was given in 250 grants ranging between £50 and £2,500. Most grants were for £500. Many were recurrent.

Twelve grants totalling £12,000 (13% of grant-aid) were relevant to this guide (Small payments of under £100 are not listed).

Thirteen long-term donations were made and included:
◆ Kew Royal Botanic Gardens (£5,000, 4th of 5);
◆ Herbal Research Phytotherapy (£400, 1st of 4).

Other grants included:
◆ National Trust, St Paul's Cathedral via Lord Mayor's appeal, St Andrew's Gatton, Wootton St Lawrence Church (£1,000 each);
◆ Parnham Trust (£750);
◆ UK Centre for Economic & Environmental Development, Hants & Wight Trust for Maritime Archaeology (£500 each);
◆ National Trust, Scotland (£400);
◆ National Council for Conservation of Plants & Gardens (£300);
◆ CPRE, Sir Harold Hillier Gardens & Arboretum (£100 each).

Applications: 'The funds of the trust are fully committed and any unsolicited applications are most unlikely to be successful.'

Sir James Colyer-Fergusson's Charitable Trust

Farrer & Co (Solicitors), 66 Lincoln's Inn Fields, London WC2A 3LH
Tel: 0171-242 2022; Fax: 0171-831 6301
Contact: Mrs Judith Hill
Trustees: J A Porter; Sir Matthew Farrer; Hon Jonathan Monckton; Hon Simon Buxton.

Grant total: £728,000 (1994/95)
Beneficial area: UK, but in practice almost exclusively Kent and Suffolk.

The trust has been making increasingly larger amounts of grant-aid annually (from £293,000 in 1992/93 to £423,000 in 1993/94 and £728,000 in 1994/95).

In 1994/95 the trust had assets of £12 million which generated a net income of £758,000 from which grants of £728,000 were made. Its grants are given in three categories: Churches in Kent, charitable causes in Kent and other charitable causes. In previous years the trust gave a simple analysis under these categories:

	1993/94	1992/93
Churches in Kent	£337,000 80%	£143,000 48%
Charitable causes in Kent	£66,000 16%	£144,000 49%
Other charitable causes	£17,000 4%	£9,000 3%

These tables show that the amounts given to churches or other Kent charities varies considerably from year to year.

Now that a full list of individual grants has been given for 1994/95 this table has not been provided. However at least 52% (£378,000) was given in 49 grants to Kent churches. The vast majority of other grants was given to other organisations in Kent and some in Suffolk.

A total of 133 grants, ranging from £500 to £20,000, was given in 1994/95. Most were between £1,000 and £10,000. The two largest grants of £20,000 were both given to Kent churches.

Grants relevant to this guide which totalled over £425,000 included:
◆ All Saints Brenchley, St Martin's Parish Church Cheriton (£20,000 each);
◆ BTCV, Vale of Elham Trust (£10,000 each);
◆ Canterbury Oasthouse Trust, Kent Archaeological Trust, Woodland Trust (£5,000 each);
◆ Vintners Valley Park Trust (£2,500);

◆ Sustrans (£2,400);
◆ Kent Trust for Nature Conservation (£2,000).

Exclusions: No grants to charities outside Kent or Suffolk, other than small grants made from covenanted donations. No grants to students or other individuals.

Applications: In writing to the correspondent.

The Ernest Cook Trust

Fairford Park, Fairford, Gloucestershire GL7 4JH
Tel: 01285-713273; Fax: 01285-713417
Contact: John G K Malleson, Agent and Secretary (Mrs J R Malleson, Awards Administrator)
Trustees: Sir William Benyon, Chairman; Sir Jack Boles; C F Badcock; M C Tuely; A W M Christie-Miller.
Grant total: £487,000 (1996/97)
Beneficial area: UK and overseas, but with a special interest in Gloucestershire and in other areas where the trust owns land (see note below).

Background: The trust was founded in 1952 by Ernest Cook, who died in 1955 aged 90. 'He has been accurately described as one of the founding fathers of the conservation movement. Following the sale of his family business, the travel agent Thomas Cook & Sons, in the early 1930s he devoted his wealth and energy to the purchase and rescue of great houses and estates, and of the works of art which they contained.'

General: The trust's endowment, consisting of the country estates owned by Ernest Cook, and the income from these estates (some 17,000 acres held at Fairford, Slimbridge and Barnsley in Gloucestershire, Hartwell and Boarstall in Buckinghamshire, Little Dalby in Leicestershire and Trent in Dorset) plus income from other investments, forms the fund from which educational awards are made.

Grants in 1996/97

Countryside and environment: £265,000 – 54%
Environmental research: £28,000 – 6%
Arts, crafts and architecture: £53,000 – 11%
Other: £140,000 – 29%
Total: £487,000 – 100%

The following headings and introductory paragraphs are taken from the trust's leaflet of policies and procedures for applications which includes a schedule of grants for the 1995/96 period. Examples of grants have also been chosen from the trust's 1995/96 report which outlines the activities funded.

'Countryside and environment:
In view of the trust's association with the land emphasis is placed on schemes which benefit rural areas. Grants in this category are made for educational work concerning conservation of the ecology of the countryside, for schemes which lead to a greater understanding of the countryside generally and to encourage stability of rural communities. Support is also given to projects designed to increase an intelligent concern for the environment as a whole.'

In 1996/97 a total of 92 grants were made in this category. The majority were in the £1,000 to £5,000 range. Grants included:
◆ Elm Farm Research Centre, education for farmers on organic farming (£15,000);
◆ Landlife, towards national wildflower centre (£10,000);
◆ Earth Balance near Newcastle upon Tyne, an integrated renewable energy system for demonstration purposes (£5,000, 1st of 3);
◆ Earthwatch, towards bursaries for volunteers on international research projects (£5,000, 2nd of 3);
◆ Forum for the Future, towards Forum Scholarships (£8,000, 2nd of 3);
◆ Groundwork South Tyneside, towards its Eco Centre at Jarrow (£5,000);
◆ Oaks Millennium Trust (£5,000);
◆ West Country Rivers Trust, towards an education officer (£5,000);
◆ Green Alliance, towards research on the impact of biotechnology on sustainable agriculture (£3,000);

◆ Global Action Plan – UK, towards training of volunteers to help form local groups (£2,400).

'Environmental research: Grants for research are made to universities or other recognised academic institutions. Projects supported reflect the trust's concern for the rural environment.' The six grants in 1996/97 included:
◆ Oxford Forestry Institute, for student bursaries (concluding year, £10,000 p.a. since 1994)
◆ Centre for Agricultural Strategy, towards uncommissioned research (£5,000, 1st of 3)
◆ Allerton Research & Education Trust for research into the impact on songbirds of gamebird management (£3,000, 3rd of 3).

Other beneficiaries were Cranfield University, the Pesticides Trust and Sustainable Agriculture, food and Environment (SAFE).

'The arts, crafts and architecture: While it is not the policy of this trust to fund work connected with building, or with structural conservation, trustees encourage appreciation of architecture, and support organisations providing training in practical conservation skills. Support is also given to rural craft training schemes.' A total of 26 grants were given in this category in 1996/97. They ranged in size from a few hundred pounds to £15,000. Most grants were between £1,000 and £5,000.

'Other grants lying outside specific categories: A number of projects which lie outside the immediate areas of ECT concern are supported simply upon their outstanding merits as schemes, or because they show potential for small amounts of money to have maximum impact on worthwhile activities. Among these, consideration is given to particularly innovative programmes providing a combination of housing, education and training for homeless and unemployed young people. Inevitably, the number of awards committed in this category is a very small percentage of requests received.'

In 1996/97 a total of 51 grants was given in this category. They ranged between under £1,000 to £10,000. They included BTCV Lifestyle & The Hazard Safety Centre.

Exclusions: 'The trustees do not award grants for charitable purposes which are not educational, or to organisations which do not hold charitable status. Loans are not made. Projects allied to medicine and health are not supported. Requests for general funding or from individuals are not supported. Building, restoration and conversion programmes, sporting and recreational activities and overseas projects all lie outside the trust's usual field of interest. Because of the large number of Trusts for Nature Conservation and Farming & Wildlife Advisory Groups support for these organisations is largely restricted to those based in counties in which ECT owns land.'

'Although exceptions are of course made to the above restrictions, and to those mentioned under specific categories, these are made infrequently and under exceptional circumstances.'

Applications: A leaflet with guidance on policies and procedures and a full list of beneficiaries is available.

'Proposals may be submitted at any time. Trustees meet in the spring and autumn to consider proposals and in addition to these two main meetings, requests for smaller grants are considered at more frequent intervals. There is no set form in which requests should be made as it is considered that the content of a letter gives excellent guidance to trustees as to its merits, but relevant information, including financial details, should be restricted to four sides of A4 paper and proposals should be submitted by the person directing the project. All proposals accepted for submission to trustees will be acknowledged but it is regretted that those not being put forward will be acknowledged only when a stamped addressed envelope has been enclosed. Applicants are welcome to discuss a project on the telephone prior to submitting a request.

Policies: Applicants are advised to focus on a specific educational need within an overall programme as requests for general support are rarely successful.
'In cases where conditional awards are committed it is the usual practice of ECT to hold the offer of the grant open for a maximum period of 12 months.'

The progress and outcome of grant aided projects are reported to trustees at their meetings, and recipients of larger grants are asked to submit a written report within a year of receiving an award. Payment of subsequent instalments of grants committed for two or more years is dependent upon the receipt of a satisfactory report on work achieved in the previous year.'

'Funds simply do not run to helping all the good and suitable applicants, and if they complain, the answer has to be that demands are many and sometimes the cupboard has been emptied and takes some time to replenish. We do in fact have more applications than we can adequately fill and so are not seeking to fuel the zeal of a wider range of organisations that we cannot satisfy'.

Trustees' meetings are held in March and October and it is understood that applications should be forwarded at least two months before a meeting for consideration.

Alice Ellen Cooper-Dean Charitable Foundation

c/o Messrs Preston & Redman (Solicitors), Hinton House, Hinton Road, Bournemouth BH1 2EN
Tel: 01202 292424
Contact: Douglas J Neville-Jones
Trustees: Miss Sylvia A M Bowditch; Maurice A Edwards; Rupert J A Edwards; Douglas J E Neville-Jones.
Grant total: £285,000 (1995/96)

Beneficial area: UK, with a particular interest in Dorset.

This trust gives half its grants to organisations in Dorset. Its founder, Alice Ellen Cooper-Dean, lived in Bournemouth and Bridport and the trust continues her involvement with the county. Its report states that it has a 'policy of assisting local and national charitable bodies, mostly on a regular basis'.

In 1995/96 its assets generated an income of £368,000 from which 62 grants totalling £285,000 were given. The top nine grants ranged between £10,000 and £33,000 with the rest mainly between £1,000 and £5,000.

Nine grants were relevant to this guide and totalled £26,000 (9% of grant-aid):
♦ Animal Heath Trust, Beaminster Church, Salisbury Cathedral, St Basil's Toller Fratrum (£5,000 each);
♦ St John's Holdenhurst, St Mary's Stoke Abbott (£2,000 each);
♦ Game Conservancy, Salway Ash Church (£1,000 each).

In the previous year the trust contributed a handsome £30,000 to the restoration appeal of Lincoln College, Oxford and the Dorset Trust for Nature Conservation received £2,000.

There seems little opportunity for new organisations to be added to its grant-making list unless they are personally known to the trustees (see below).

Exclusions: No grants to individuals

Applications: In writing to the correspondent. The Trust has stated that its funds are fully committed and that unsolicited applications have little chance of success.

The Marjorie Coote Animal Charity Fund

Barn Cottage, Lindrick Common, Worksop, Notts S81 8BA
Contact: Sir Hugh Neill

Trustees: Sir Hugh Neill; Mrs J P Holah; N H N Coote.
Grant total: £123,000 (1996/97)
Beneficial area: UK and overseas

The trust was established for the benefit of five named charities working for animals, and of other charitable organisations caring for horses, dogs or other animals or birds. The trustees are currently concentrating their resources on animal health and research and on the protection of species, while continuing to apply a proportion of the income to general animal welfare including animal sanctuaries.

In 1996/97 the trust had assets of £2.2 million generating an income of £122,000 from which grants totalling £123,000 were given. The largest grant continued to be given to the Animal Health Trust (£26,000).

Beneficiaries relevant to this guide included:
- Cambridge University Veterinary School, Project Life Lion, University of Edinburgh – for new teaching hospital for small animals – (£5,000 each);
- National Trust (£2,000);
- Gentleshaw Bird of Prey Wildlife Hospital, Peakirk Waterfowl Garden Trust, World Owl Trust (£1,000 each).

Applications: In writing to the correspondent. Applications must reach the correspondent during September.

The Holbeche Corfield Charitable Settlement

Greenoaks, Bradford Road, Sherborne, Dorset DT9 6BW
Contact: C H Corfield-Moore
Trustees: C H Corfield-Moore; K Corfield-Moore; S J H Corfield.
Grant total: £36,000 (1994/95)
Beneficial area: UK and overseas

In 1994/95 the trust had assets of £537,000 which generated an income of £31,000. Altogether 23 grants were made totalling £36,000 and ranged from £100 to £9,000.

During this year 11 grants were relevant to this guide totalling £18,000 (50%) of grant-aid:
- Woodland Trust (£9,000);
- Ironbridge Gorge Museum Trust, National Trust (£2,000 each);
- RSPB, WWF UK (£1,500);
- English Heritage; National Trust for Scotland (£500 each);
- Hawk & Owl Trust, South Pennine Packhorse Trails Fund, St Mary's Dunsford, St Catherine's Caerphilly (£250 each).

A grant was also given to Wat Krabok Monastery (£1,500). The trust seems to have associations with Bangkok and Thailand.

It should be noted than this emphasis on environmental grants in 1994/95 seems atypical. In the two previous years only a small proportion of its grant-aid was directed to these interests.

Applications: In writing to the correspondent.

The Duke of Cornwall's Benevolent Fund

10 Buckingham Gate, London SW1E 6LA
Tel: 0171-834 7346
Contact: Angela Wise
Trustees: The Earl Cairns; J N C James.
Grant total: £71,000,000 (1995/96)
Beneficial area: South west England

The fund receives donations from the Duke of Cornwall (Prince Charles) based on amounts received by the Duke as Bona Vacantia (the casual profits of estates of deceased intestates dying domiciled in Cornwall without kin) after allowing for costs and ex-gratia payments made by the Duke in relation to claims on any estate.

Priority is given to charitable organisations in the south-west of England, in areas in which the Duchy has landed interests. The fund gives to education, religion, relief in need, the arts, and 'the preservation for the benefit of the public of lands and buildings'.

No list of grants has been filed with the accounts since 1992/93 when a far larger grant-aid total was given than in 1995/96 – £152,000 compared with £71,000. Then grants were divided into annual subscriptions of which there were three, including Business in the Community and the Thames Salmon Trust (£2,500 each). Annual donations of relevance to this guide included:
- St Anta & All Saints Church (£25,000);
- Devon Wildlife Trust (£10,000);
- National Council for the Conservation of Plants & Gardens (£5,000);
- Bath Abbey Trust (£3,000);
- Reading University Rural History Centre, St Mary-le-Strand (£2,000 each);
- Loggans Moor Appeal, Keddington Church Restoration, St Tomey PC, St Colomba's church (£1,000 each);
- Charmouth Heritage Coast Centre, Cornwall Heritage Trust, Vauxhall St Peter's Heritage Centre (£500 each).

Four other churches also received grants of £500 or less.

In 1992/93 grants to environmental interests covered by this guide totalled £51,000 (33% of grant-aid).

Applications: In writing to the correspondent. Applicants should give as much detail as possible, especially information of what amount of money has been raised to date, what the target is and how it will be achieved.

The Council for the Care of Churches, Conservation Committee

Fielden House, Little College Street, London SW1P 3SH
Tel: 0171-222 3793; Fax: 0171-222 3794
Contact: Andrew Argyrakis, Conservation Officer
Grant total: £150,000 (1997)
Beneficial area: UK

The conservation committee of the Council for the Care of Churches administers various block grants which have been allocated for the conservation of church furnishing and fittings of artistic and historic interest in Church of England churches in use. The largest sum comes from the Pilgrim Trust.

Exclusions: No support for the repair and redecoration of church buildings.

The Countryside Trust

John Dower House, Crescent Place, Cheltenham, Gloucestershire GL50 3RA
Tel: 01242-521381; Fax: 01242-584270
Contact: Sarah Store, Secretary
Trustees: Richard Simmons; Richard Wakeford; John L Evans
Grant total: £15,000 from Unrestricted Fund; £29,000 from Restricted Fund (1996/97)
Beneficial area: England.

The trust was set up in 1990 with the proceeds of a generous legacy to the Countryside Commission from Miss Marjorie Broadbent of Hebden Bridge in Yorkshire. It aims 'to promote the conservation, preservation and restoration of the natural beauty of the countryside of England for public benefit'. In 1996/97, the trust had assets of £657,000 split between its Restricted and Unrestricted Funds.

Four grants totalling some £29,000 were given from its Restricted Funds to initiatives closely associated with the Countryside Commission:
- Growing Together Initiative (£6,000);
- Thames Path National Trail (£11,000);
- Mersey Forest – £6,000 – £102,000 held;
- National Forest Project – £2,700 held;
- Greenwood Forest – £2,300 held;
- Xmas card recycling – £4,000 – a further £8,000 held;
- Thames Chase – £190 held.

Unrestricted Funds: The trustees also offer seed corn grants to community or voluntary organisations concerned with the care of the local countryside of

England. A total of £15,000 was paid from the Fund during 1996/97. The most substantial grants were given to:

- Sheffield Wildlife Action Partnership (2,000);
- Devon Wildlife Trust, Gloucestershire Wildlife Trust, Cornwall Wildlife Trust (£1,000) each.

These grants are for the specific purpose of financing fundraising appeals where the money raised is to be used for practical conservation projects in the countryside, but NOT in towns. Projects related to sites which provide access to the public or which serve educational groups are particularly favoured. Examples of fundraising projects which have attracted support include concerts, promotional leaflets, country fairs, sponsored events and legacy campaigns.

Grants are up to a maximum of £5,000, but usually range from £100 to £3,500.

Exclusions: Capital payments and the labour costs of carrying out conservation work.

Applications: On a (simple) standard application form together with a map and supporting material as appropriate. Application deadlines are the end of January and the end of June.

The Augustine Courtauld Trust

Messrs Birkett & Long, Red House, Halstead, Essex CO9 2DZ
Tel: 01787-475252
Contact: Richard Long, Clerk
Trustees: Lord Bishop of Chelmsford; Rev A C C Courtauld; Lord Braybrook; Col N A C Croft; J Courtauld.
Grant total: £76,000 (1995/96)
Beneficial area: UK, with a preference for Essex.

In 1995/96, the trust had assets of £940,000 and an income of £84,000. Added to the £78,500 surplus from the previous year and after expenses of £4,000

were taken into account, the trust had £158,000 available for distribution and gave 47 grants totalling £76,000. Support is usually given to charities/projects which the trustees or Courtauld family have a connection with or interest in.

Five grants relevant to this guide were given in 1995/96. All these beneficiaries had also been supported in the previous year:

- Friends of Essex Churches (£9,000);
- St Paul's Church, Knightsbridge (£2,000);
- Royal Geographical Society, expedition (£750);
- St Andrew's Church Yeldham, Ferriers Barn (£500 each).

In the previous year support had also been given to Essex Heritage Trust (£1,000), and Wrabness Nature Reserve Manningtree (£500).

Exclusions: No grants to individuals.

Applications: In writing to the correspondent.

The Dennis Curry Charitable Trust

Messrs Alliotts, 5th Floor, 9 Kingsway, London WC2B 6XF
Tel: 0171-240 9971
Contact: N J Armstrong
Trustees: M Curry; Mrs A S Curry; Mrs M Curry Jones; Mrs P Edmond.
Grant total: £74,000 (1995/96)
Beneficial area: UK.

The trust has general charitable objects with special interest in the environment and education; occasional support is given to churches and cathedrals. The four trustees receive an equal share of the distributable income.

The assets of the trust have been steadily rising and in 1995/96 had reached £2.6 million producing an income of £119,000.

Six grants were given totalling £74,000. Of these four grants were relevant to this guide and absorbed £54,000 (73% of total grant-aid):

- Open University Department of Earth Science (£30,200);
- Science and Technology Regional Organisation (£21,000);
- Council for National Parks (£2,000, with £62,600 in the previous year and £10,750 in 1993/94);
- Cumbria Wildlife Trust (£1,000).

In the previous year large grants were given to the Earth Science Teacher Association (£16,315) and the John Murray Downland Trust (£15,000).

Applications: In writing to the correspondent.

D A Curry's Charitable Trust

Messrs Alliotts, 5th Floor, 9 Kingsway, London WC2B 6XF
Tel: 0171-240 9971
Contact: N J Armstrong
Trustees: Mrs L E Curry; A Curry; N J Armstrong.
Grant total: £67,000 (1995/96)
Beneficial area: UK.

The trust's grant-aid has been steadily increasing in the past three years, from £20,000 in 1993/94 to £42,000 in 1994/95 to £67,000 in 1995/96.

In 1995/96 three grants were relevant to this guide:
- National Trust (£6,000);
- RSPB Estuaries Campaign (£1,000);
- South Hams Society (£100);
- Two grants were also given to animal welfare charities.

Applications: In writing to the correspondent.

The Sarah d'Avigdor Goldsmid Charitable Trust

Hadlow Place, Golden Green, Tonbridge, Kent TN11 0BW
Tel: 01732-851722
Contact: Mrs R C Teacher

Trustees: Lady Rosemary d'Avidgor Goldsmid; A J M Teacher; Mrs R C Teacher.
Grant total: £34,000 (1994/95)
Beneficial area: UK, particularly Kent.

In 1994/5 the trust had assets of £421,000 raising a gross income of £27,000. Grants of £34,000 were given (compared with £18,000 in the previous year when income had been £31,000). The trust runs two funds – G and P – both similarly funded and it is impossible for the "outsider" to distinguish the difference between them. Both give to causes within the scope of this guide and, in two instances in 1994/95, grant-aiding the same organisation.

The grants from the funds have been listed together as both support the architectural heritage, wildlife and countryside work. More funding was given from the P Fund and its major grants are indicated with*. In 1994/95 over £6,000 (18 % of total grant-aid) was relevant to this guide:
- Tudeley Parish Church*, Wildfowl & Wetlands Trust*, WWF UK* (£1,000 each);
- Kent Trust for Nature Conservation (£800 in 2 grants, with £700*);
- Canterbury Cathedral (£600 in 2 grants, with £500*);
- Woodland Trust (£500);
- Rochester Cathedral, Zoological Society of London (£250 each);
- Chenley Heritage League of Friends, East Malling Church restoration, Farming & Wildlife Advisory Group, St Clement's Sandwich, Pembury Old Church, Sandwich Bay Bird Observatory, Tradescant Trust (£100 each).

Applications: In writing to the correspondent.

The D'Oyly Carte Charitable Trust

1 Savoy Hill, London WC2R 0BP
Tel: 0171-836 1533
Contact: Mrs J Thorne
Trustees: J Elliott, Chairman; J McCracken; Sir Martyn Beckett; Sir John Batten; Mrs F Radcliffe; Mrs J Sibley.

Grant total: £102,000 (1995/96)
Beneficial area: UK.

The trust support "arts, medical welfare and the environment" and certain charities in which Dame Bridget D'Oyly Carte, the settlor, took an interest are supported on a regular basis. The greater part of its support is given to arts organisations.

Grants ranged between £250 and £5,000 and in 1994/95 ten grants totalling over £7,000 (8% of grant-aid) were relevant to this guide:

♦ CPRE, Woodland Trust (£1,500 each);
♦ Heritage of London Trust, (£1,000);
♦ BTCV, FWAG, Enhan Trust, RSNC, St Mary Abchurch, Brook Advisory Centres (£500 each);
♦ Young People's Trust for the Environment (£250).

All but four of these beneficiaries had been supported in the previous year so the chances for new applicants are very low.

Exclusions: Individuals.

Applications: In writing to the correspondent who has written: "It should be noted, however, that the resources of the trust are directed to specific charities from year to year, and the trustees are therefore restricted in considering new applications." The trustees meet twice a year, in June and December. Applications should arrive at least one month before these meetings.

The Dr & Mrs A Darlington Charitable Trust

Ford Simey Daw Roberts, 8 Cathedral Close, Exeter, Devon EX1 1EW
Tel: 01392 274126
Contact: V A Donson
Trustees: Lloyds Bank plc, V A Donson.
Grant total: £87,000 (1996)
Beneficial area: Particular interest in Devon, especially in the area of Sidmouth and East Devon.

The trust has assets of over £1.7 million and income of £82,000 and made 12 grants of £87,000 in 1996. It is interested in the elderly and the disabled as well as nature conservation and historic buildings.

In 1995 only 2 grants totalling £6,500 (8% of grant aid) were relevant to this guide:
♦ Devon Wildlife trust £6,000 with £1,500 in the previous year.

In the previous year grants were given to Bicton College of Agriculture and the Devon Rural Skills Trust (£1,000) each.
♦ Devon Historic Churches Trust (£500).

In 1993 Parishill Park Trust was given £4,000.

Exclusions: Applications from individuals, including students, are most likely to be unsuccessful.

Applications: In writing to the correspondent.

The Iris Darnton Foundation

Buss Murton Solicitors, The Priory, Tunbridge Wells, Kent TN1 1JJ
Contact: J Toth Solicitor
Trustees: J Teacher, Chairman; Miss A D Darnton; Mrs C Hardy; Mrs H Robinson.
Grant total: £26,000 (1994/95)
Beneficial area: UK and overseas.

This trust funds education and research into wildlife and habitat conservation. In 1994/95 it had assets of £302,000 and an income of £23,000 and made grants of £26,000.

The following seven beneficiaries in 1994/95, four of which had also been supported in the previous year, although not necessarily for the same amount, illustrate its range of giving:
♦ Dian Fossey Gorilla Fund UK, WWF for Sand Lizard project and Nigerian Conference (£5,000 each);
♦ Rhino Rescue Trust, Wildfowl & Wetlands Trust (£2,500 each);

• National Council for the Conservation of Plants & Gardens, Canterbury Christchurch Alders Projects (£2,000 each).

Applications: In writing to the correspondent.

The Lesley David Trust

38 Whitelands House, Cheltenham Terrace, London SW3 4QY
Tel: 0171 730 6030
Trustees: Mrs Lesley Lewis; Mrs J M Lewis.
Grant total: £12,000 (1996)
Beneficial area: UK.

The trust gives many "standing order payments and special grants for the arts, particularly architecture and church buildings generally, nature conservation and local charities generally". The majority of these payments are well under £100 since the trust gives about 100 grants. It had assets of about £200,000 in 1995.

Examples of grants given in 1995 which are relevant to this guide included:
• Georgian Group (£1,000 in 2 grants);
• Friends of Christ Church Spitalfields (£150 in 2 grants);
• Essex Heritage, Lincoln's Inn Chapel (£500 each);
• Historic Chapels Trust, Octavia Hill Museum, River Lea Tidemill, RSNC, Lincoln Cathedral, Wisbech Society (£100 each);
• River Thames Society (£100 each 2 grants);
• Wrabness Nature Reserve, Bat Conservation Society (£50 each);
• Large numbers of churches were given small gifts (a handful for £100).

Applications: In writing to the correspondent.

The Delves Charitable Trust

New Guild House, 45 Great Charles Street, Queensway, Birmingham B3 2LX
Tel: 0121-212 2222
Contact: Roger Harriman

Trustees: Mary Breeze; John Breeze; George Breeze; Dr Charles Breeze; Elizabeth Breeze; Roger Harriman.
Grant total: £193,000 (1996/97)
Beneficial area: UK.

In 1996/97, Trust had assets with a market value of £4.75 million and an income of £199,000 from which £193,000 was given in grants. The trust reported that it gives annual subscriptions to 41 organisations totalling £177,000, subject to annual review. One-off donations are usually made from previously unspent income.

Annual donations were given to:
• International Technology (£10,000);
• Survival International (£3,000);
• National Trust (£6,000 including £3,000 to its Neptune appeal);
• Woodland Trust (£4,000);
• IPPF (£2,000);
• CPRE (£1,000);

One-off donations were given to:
• Born Free Foundation for Save the Rhino (£1000);
• Cotswold Rural Trust (£300);
• Good Gardeners Association (£500);
• Historic Chapels Trust (£350);
• Intermediate Technology (£250);
• Rhino Rescue Trust (£450).

Applications: "The funds of the trust are currently fully committed and no unsolicited requests can therefore be considered by the trustees."

The Douglas Charitable Trust

Messrs Dundas & Wilson, Saltire Court, 20 Castle Terrace, Edinburgh EH1 2EN
Contact: The Secretary
Trustees: Rev Prof D Shaw; D Connell; E Cameron.
Grant total: £33,000 (1994/95)
Beneficial area: Scotland.

Preference is given to the universities of Edinburgh and St Andrews and church restoration projects in Edinburgh and St Andrews.

In 1994/95, the trust had assets of £264,101 and gave grants of £33,000. Grants ranged between £1,000 and £11,000 and included Holy Trinity Parish Church in St Andrews (£7,000).

Applications: Contact the correspondent for further details.

The Drapers' Charitable Fund

Drapers' Hall, Throgmorton Street, London EC2N 2DQ
Tel: 0171-588 5001; Fax: 0171-628 1988
Contact: Tom Wareham, Secretary
Trustees: The Court of the Drapers' Company.
Grant total: £752,000 (1995/96)
Beneficial area: UK, with a preference for the city of London.

This fund was established by the Drapers' Company in 1959. Its income for grants runs at about £1 million a year and most of this is already committed for a number of years. In 1996/97 about £100,000 is available for new grants. These new grants range between £250 and £5,000 and are usually one-off.

The fund prefers to support initiatives which are national and widespread rather than local. It also supports initiatives in the City of London and, occasionally, other areas of inner London.

"The purposes for which grants are given vary widely but fall into four broad categories:
- aid to the disadvantaged, particularly initiatives aimed at improving the quality of life of those disadvantaged by poverty, ill health or disability, or aimed at counteracting the effects of disadvantage
- education and training
- where there is a connection with the Drapers' Company or one of its related organisations
- culture"

Grants are not generally made for salaries and running costs.

In 1995/96 £194,000 was given in 155 grants, a large number of which were obviously for less than £1,000.

Grants relevant to this guide in 1995/96 included:

Termly grants:
- Hertford College, Oxford (£29,000);
- Pembroke College, Cambridge (£20,000);
- St Anne's College, Oxford (£10,000);
- Council & Care of Churches (£5,000);
- Historic Churches Preservation Trust (£3,000).

Once only grants:
- Miss Betensen's Almshouses (£2,000);
- St Paul's Cathedral Trust, National Playing Fields Association (£1,320 each);
- Wateraid (£1,000);
- River Lea Tidal Mill Trust, St Asaph Cathedral (£250 each).

Applications: The company had not wanted an entry in this guide. The correspondent has written the funds have "declined over recent years and as a result it has been decided that our strategy for grant giving should be re-organised. The trustees will no longer be considering unsolicited requests for funding. In future the trustees will be selecting specific fields of activity and will, at their discretion, approach selected organisations with a view to possibly making grant-aid available."

The 10th Duke of Devonshire's Trust (1949)

Messrs Currey & Co, solicitors, 21 Buckingham Gate, London SW1E 6LS
Tel: 0171-828 4091
Contact: Theresa Skelton, trustee manager
Trustees: Marquess of Hartington; R G Beckett; N W Smith.
Grant total: £1,132,000 (1993/94) but see below

Beneficial area: UK with a preference for Derbyshire.

In 1993/94 the trust's assets of over £7 million which generated an income of £234,000. Payments of over £600,000 were made from the capital account to cover high donations of over £1 million, most of which was paid to the Chatsworth House Trust (£1,100,000 in three grants). The family house is consistently the largest beneficiary of trust funds. The trust usually gives about £60,000 a year to the house and accumulates for occasional exceptional grants.

In 1993/94 – Other grants relevant to this guide were made to:
◆ National Trust (£5,000);
◆ Lincoln's Inn Chapel Appeal (£2,500);
◆ Tideswell Church Restoration (£1,000);

In 1992/93 -
◆ Chatsworth House (£60,000);
◆ Manchester Cathedral Development Trust (£2,500);
◆ Horticultural Therapy (£1,000);
◆ Sheffield Conservation Volunteers (£250).

Applications: In writing to the correspondent. Approaches can also be made to the Comptroller, Chatsworth, Bakewell, Derbyshire DE4 1PP.

✗ **The Dulverton Trust**

5 St James Place, London SW1A 1NP
Tel: 0171-629 9121
Contact: Major General Sir Robert Corbett, Trust Secretary
Trustees: The Hon Robert Wills, Chairman; Lord Carrington; Lord Dulverton; Colonel D V Fanshawe; the Earl of Gowrie; John Kemp-Welch; Sir Ashley Ponsonby; Lord Taylor of Gryfe; J Watson; Colonel S J Watson; Dr Catherine Wills; C A H Wills; Sir David Wills.
Grant total: £2,825,000 (1996/97)
Beneficial area: UK but limited support to parts of Africa, see below. Recently, some assistance has been given in South Africa.

Background: The trust was founded in 1949 by the 1st Lord Dulverton, whose

family had made their fortune in the tobacco industry. His endowment to the trust was made up of shares in the Imperial Tobacco Company, but the trust has since diversified its investments and has no more than a small holding in that industry. Five of the current 13 trustees are relatives of the 1st Lord Dulverton (Wills is the family name).

General: The trust reviews its policy every five years, and this was last done in 1993. The trustees state that "the main work of the trust should continue to be maintained in the broad fields of Youth and Education, Conservation and General Welfare. In the field of Religion the main emphasis would continue to be the promotion and development of religious education in schools.....To a lesser degree contributions are made in the categories of Industrial Relations, Peace and Security, Preservation and other causes determined by the trustees to be of special merit. Limited support is maintained for old contacts and associations in East and central Africa; more recently some assistance has been given in South Africa.

"The trust had assets of over £74 million in April 1997 which generated an income of £2,782,000. In 1996/97 the trust made the following grants relevant to this guide which totalled £403,000 (14% of total grant aid): Conservation £288,500 (18 grants) and Preservation £114,000 (7 grants).

Conservation: The trust has funded a chair at Bristol University in memory of the second Lord Dulverton and three organisations (WWF, CEED and Care International UK) are major long term components of the trust's conservation policy (Annual Report 1995/96).
◆ World Wide Fund for Nature (£58,000);
◆ Wildfowl & Wetlands Trust (£25,000);
◆ UK Centre for Economic & Environmental Development (£22,000);
◆ CARE International (UK), Atlantic Salmon Trust, Middleton Botanic Garden, Royal Botanic Gardens, Kew, (£20,000 each);

- National Council for the Conservation of plants & Gardens (£16,500);
- Food & Agricultural Research Management (£14,000);
- Scottish Wildlife Trust, Pensthorpe Waterfowl Trust, Scottish Conservation Projects, Crarea Garden Trust, West Country Rivers Trust (£10,000 each);
- Royal Society of Arts, Royal Society for Nature Conservation (£8,000 each);
- Bristol University – Chair of Environmental Studies (£5,000);
- National Memorial Arboretum Appeal (£2,000).

Preservation: The trust noted in its annual report 1995/96 that "These grants were made as exceptions to the exclusion of appeals for repair and restoration."

Grants in 1996/97 were given to:
- Old St Mary's Church Clonmel (£43,000);
- Peterborough Cathedral Trust (£20,000);
- Historic Churches Preservation Trust (£16,000);
- National Manuscripts Conservation Trust (£15,000);
- Scottish Churches Architectural Heritage Trust (£10,000 each);
- National Trust for Scotland, Scotland Churches Scheme (£5,000 each).

The trust's annual report does not give any information about beneficiaries within its grant making listed as 'minor appeals' from which £100,000 was given in 1996/97 in grants up to £1,500. In previous years beneficiaries have been relevant to this guide.

Exclusions: "The trust does not operate within the broad fields of medicine and health, including drug addiction and projects concerning the mentally and physically handicapped. Also generally excluded are projects concerning museums, churches, cathedrals and other historic buildings.

"The whole field of the arts is excluded together with projects for schools, colleges and universities. The trust very seldom operates within the Greater London area nor in Northern Ireland except for specific nominated charities.

"No grants to overseas charities, except for the limited activity on a reducing scale with old contacts and associations in Central and East Africa.

"Grants are not made to individuals or for expeditions."

Applications: Applications should be made in writing to the secretary. Trustee meetings are held four times a year – in January, May, July and October. There is no set format for applications, but it is helpful if they can include the background and a clear statement of the aims of the appeal together with the funding target and any progress made in reaching it. Applications should, if possible, be restricted to a maximum of three sheets of paper. Initial applications should always include a summary of the previous year's accounts.

The Dumbreck Charity

Messrs Price Waterhouse & Co, Cornwall Court, 19 Cornwall Street, Birmingham B3 2DT
Tel: 0121-200 3000
Contact: The Trust Department
Trustees: A C S Hordern; Miss B Y Mellor; H B Carslake.
Grant total: £86,000 (1994/95)
Beneficial area: UK, especially the Midlands, and overseas.

In 1994/95, the trust had assets of £1.5 million and an income of £68,000. It gave grants totalling £86,000. Most grants were for either £500 or £750. Local grants are generally given in the Midlands, especially the West Midlands. The grants list was divided into the following categories: Animal Welfare/Conservation, Children's Welfare, Care of Elderly and Physically/Mentally Disabled People, Medical, Miscellaneous.

The first four categories are effectively annual subscription lists. The recipient organisations hardly vary at all; the amounts given to them can. The only category where there is scope for new grants is the Extraordinary category within Miscellaneous. Some of the extraordinary grants become regular grants the following year onwards.

In 1994/95 the following grants relevant to this guide were given:

Under "Animal Welfare/Conservation"
- Rare Breeds Survival Trust, Wildfowl Trust (£750 each);
- Friends of Conservation, RSPB, Warwickshire Nature Conservation Trust, WWF (£500 each);

Under "Child Welfare"
- Farms for City Children (£500);

Under "Elderly/Handicapped"
- Hockley Part City Farm (£750);

Under "Miscellaneous"
- Intermediate Technology Development Ltd, Farming and Wildlife Trust, Ironbridge Gorge Museum Development Trust (£750 each);

Under "Extraordinary"
- Worcester Cathedral Appeal (£2,500);
- Worcester Cathedral Arts Appeal (£1,000).

Applications: In writing to the correspondent. The trustees meet annually. Unsuccessful applications will not be acknowledged.

The Earth Love Fund

57 Woodstock Road, Oxford OX2 6HJ
Tel: 01865-511297; **Fax:** 01865-311383;
e-mail: earthlove@gn.apc.org
Contact: Victor Coppersmith-Heaven, Co-ordinator; Helen Newing, Projects Co-odinator
Trustees: Kenny Young; Nicholas H Glennie; Herbert Girardet.
Grant total: £132,000 (1994/95)
Beneficial area: UK and overseas.

The enterprising and exciting fund was set up in 1989 by Kenny Young, the music producer and writer. It is "committed to raising funds and awareness for environmental issues, in particular the world's disappearing rainforests. Its aims are to create global awareness for these vital issues through music-related projects, educational documentaries, videos and supporting programmes. The charity has been helping to conserve the rainforests and its indigenous inhabitants by funding development projects which are directly involved in protecting and regenerating the forests" (1994/95 report).

In 1991 it was working on a fundraising album and enlisting support of further artists and an advisory council of eminent figures in international conservation. By 1992 it had set up a trading company, Earth Love Fund Records Ltd, and was finalising its Earthrise fundraising project. In 1993 the fund had received a loan of £150,000 from the record company and in the same year started sharing offices with Earthwatch in Oxford.

By 1993/94 it started its first major donation programme with £181,000 given to nine projects in Central America, South America, Africa and South East Asia. The actual sums to each are not known but they included a catalyst grants programme in Peru, an eco-forestry project in Papua New Guinea, two projects for legal support from Otro Futuro to indigenous organisations in Venezuela, support for the continued demarcation/consolidation of the multi-ethnic indigenous territory of the Beni region of Bolivia, support for the Green Belt Movement of the Kenya Tree Planting Programme, environmental education in Nigeria and Thailand, and tropical forest revitalisation in Brazil.

By 1994/95 it had assets of £241,000 (including £130,000 of accrued income and £70,000 donated by its associated record company). A total of £132,000 was given to the following 11 projects:
- Gaia Foundation, for a series of projects (£44,557);
- Institute of Ethnobiology for the Amazon (£26,153);
- Rainforest Alliance, for catalyst funding (£22,525);

- Ind. Environmental Bamboo (£8,529);
- Forest Management Foundation (£7,500);
- University of the Forest – Kayapo (£6,519);
- Limbe Botanical Gardens, Village Development Trust (£5,000 each);
- George Simon (£4,417);
- National Fish and Wildlife (£1,682);
- London Ecology Centre (£500).

The fund's applicant guidelines outline its emphasis on "community-based conservation projects in rainforest regions and endangered forests worldwide. Projects which promote and conserve ecological diversity and cultural and community integrity will be given priority."

The fund also publishes a newsletter annually which is lively and informative about the projects it supports and its other fundraising activities not only through its record albums but also through its network of supporters – "Artists for the Environment".

Exclusions: Categories of project unlikely to be awarded a grant include: health, development per se; English language publications; pure research, or research carried out from a non-local basis.

Applications: First write to or telephone the projects co-ordinator from whom current advice – criteria, guidelines and standard form – can also be obtained.

"Grants are usually to small groups who need a little start-up money, and are typically between £2,000 and £10,000. If the proposal is for part-funding of a larger budget, it must be clearly indicated which parts are being requested from ELF and how it is proposed to fund the rest." No more than one year's funding is possible and grants are usually one-off. It cannot guarantee funding to all projects which fulfil its criteria.

ELF's advisory council meets twice a year to consider applications which must arrive at least two months before the date of the meeting (dates to be checked with the projects co-ordinator).

The Sir John Eastwood Foundation

Burns Lane, Warsop, Mansfield, Nottinghamshire NG20 0QG
Tel: 01623-842581; Fax: 01623-847955
Contact: Gordon Raymond
Trustees: Sir John Eastwood; Mrs C B Mudford; Mrs D M Cottingham; Gordon Raymond; Mrs V A Hardingham.
Grant total: £260,000 (1994/95)
Beneficial area: UK, but mainly Nottinghamshire in practice.

The foundation concentrates its donations on charities in Nottingham and Nottinghamshire with most of its grants for amounts between £500 and £5,000. This seems to be a truly "local" trust covering a wide range of charitable activity and prepared to give generously to small local organisations as well as giving more modest awards.

The foundation had assets of £7.67 million in 1994/95 which generated an income of £333,000 from which grants of £260,000 were given. Its grant-aid has fluctuated greatly from year to year: £260,000 (1994/95), £174,000 (1993/94), £371,000 (1992/93), £170,000 (1991/92) and a massive £1.1 million (1990/91).

In 1994/95 a total of 132 grants were given ranging from less than £100 to £25,000. Six grants were £10,000 or higher. Most grants (65) were between £1,000 and £5,000 with a large number (57) of small grants of under £1,000.

Grants relevant to this guide were given to:
- Newark & Nottinghamshire Agricultural Society (£10,000);
- Ashfield & Mansfield Groundwork Trust (£5,000 in 2 grants);
- Farnsfield & District Horticultural Society (£2,000);
- Stonebridge City Farm (£1,000).

A number of grants were also given to animal welfare organisations.

Exclusions: No grants to individuals.

Applications: In writing to the correspondent.

The Ecological Foundation

Lower Bosneives, Withiel, Bodmin, Cornwall PL30 5NQ
Tel: 01208-831236; **Fax:** 01208-831083
Contact: J Faull, Director
Trustees: The Marquis of Londonderry; Sir James Goldsmith; John Aspinall; R Hanbury-Tenison.
Grant total: £97,000 (1995)
Beneficial area: UK and overseas.

In general the foundation funds its own projects and reports. Most of its income is received in annual donations. In 1995 it supported 14 projects:
◆ World Rainforest Project (£30,000);
◆ Public Outreach (£16,000 with £34,000 in the previous year);
◆ Kambai Project (£16,000 with £19,000 in the previous year);
◆ Plantations Project (£12,000 with £1,000 in the previous year);
◆ Climate Change, Potato Project (£5,000 each);
◆ Genetic Diversity in British Agriculture (£2,000 with £10,000 and £11,000 in the 2 previous years);
◆ Global Commons Institute (£2,000);
◆ St James' Alliance (£1,000);
◆ West Country Rivers Trust (£600).

Applications: In writing to the correspondent, but see above.

The Gilbert & Eileen Edgar Foundation

c/o Chantrey Vellacott, 23-25 Castle Street, Reading RG1 7BS
Tel: 0118 959 5432
Contact: Mrs Avril Hallam
Trustees: A E Gentilli; J G Matthews.
Grant total: £66,000 (1996/97)
Beneficial area: UK and overseas.

The trust is particularly interested in supporting medical research, the arts and young people. The settlor also expressed an interest in "the promotion of facilities for recreation or other leisure time occupation".

In 1996 grant-aid was £66,000 (£70,000 in 1995). A total of 144 grants were given mainly in small sums of £250 to £500. Of these 16 were listed in its accounts under a heading "Recreation, including Conservation and Heritage". These showed a range of interests relevant to this guide:
◆ Gap foundation (£1,000);
◆ Iona Community, Sustrans, Worldwide fund (£500);
◆ Atlantic salmon Trust, Skye Environmental Centre (£250);
◆ RSPB (£200).

Applications: In writing to the correspondent.

The Eling Trust
See the Gerald Palmer Trust

The John Ellerman Foundation

Suite 10, Aria House, 23 Craven Street, London WC2N 5NT
Tel: 0171-930 8566; **Fax:** 0171-839 3654;
E-mail: eileen@ellerman.prestel.co.uk
Contact: Dr Christopher P Hanvey, Director & Secretary
Trustees: Dennis G Parry; Sir David A Scott; R Alastair Lloyd; Peter Strutt; Angela Boschi; David D Martin-Jenkins; Peter C Pratt; A L Revell;
Grant total: £3,825,000 (1996/97)
Beneficial area: UK and overseas, other than Central and South America.

The foundation was created in 1992 from the amalgamation of the Moorgate Trust Fund and the New Moorgate Trust Fund, and it bears the name of the founder of those funds. In April 1996 the foundation had assets of £85 million which generated an income of £4,052,000 from which 320 grants totalling £3,416,000 were made. The largest grant was for £100,000. Most grants (129) were for £5,000.

"The foundation's remit includes medical research and medical care, social welfare and disability (including those with a mental illness or learning difficulty), the arts and the environment, and some overseas activities."

"The foundation prefers to provide funding for central bodies or head offices rather than for local groups or branches but would hope to encourage central bodies or head offices to distribute at least part of any funding provided by the foundation to such local groups or branches." This was confirmed in the list of grants for 1995/96 where only around 50 out of a total of 320 grants were easily identifiable as local projects.

The trustees have targets by areas of interest for their allocation of donations. The outcome for 1995/96, shown below, was very close to the targeted allocation:
- Medical research & medical care 43%
- Care of disabled people 18%
- Arts, culture & heritage 14%
- Community development & social welfare 10%
- Overseas activities 10%
- Conservation 4%
- Others 1%

Grants in 1995/96 relevant to this guide totalled £240,000 (7% of grant-aid). They were given to a wide range of environmental organisations, several of which work overseas, including those concerned with countryside and wildlife conservation, architectural heritage, appropriate technology and population growth, as well as national collections for the study of plants and natural history.
- Royal Botanic Gardens Kew Foundation (£50,000);
- Natural History Museum (£30,000);
- WaterAid (£20,000);
- Royal Society for Nature Conservation (£16,000);
- Brogdale Horticultural Trust, National Trust, World Wide Fund for Nature, Youth Hostels Association (£10,000 each);
- RSPB (£8,000);
- National Trust for Scotland, Wildfowl and Wetlands Trust (£6,000 each);
- BTCV, Central Scotland Countryside

Trust, Chelmsford Cathedral, Llandaff Cathedral, Falklands Conservation Penguin Appeal, Fauna & Fauna Preservation Society, Intermediate Technology, Painshill Park Trust, Population Concern, Scottish Conservation Projects, Sebakwe Black Rhino Trust, Trees for Life (£5,000 each);
- British Trust for Ornithology (£3,000);
- South African Foundation for the Conservation of Coastal Birds (£1,000).

Exclusions: Grants are made only to registered charities, and are not made for the following purposes:
- For or on behalf of individuals;
- Individual hospices;
- Local branches of national organisation;
- 'Friends of' groups;
- Education or educational establishments;
- Religious causes;
- Conferences and seminars;
- Sports and leisure facilities, and local sports groups;
- Purchase of vehicles (except for those used by aid transport);
- The direct replacement of public funding;
- Hospital radio stations;
- Deficit funding;
- Local arts, theatre, dance & music groups;
- Local youth groups;
- Local advice centres;
- Domestic animal welfare;
- Circulars (will not receive a reply).

Applications: Four copies of the application should be made on the Foundation's application form and sent by post to the above address. A copy of the applicant's latest report and audited accounts shall accompany any appeal. All applicants receive a response. The Trustees and staff recognise that the running of charities has become a highly complex operation in a rapidly changing world. In response to clear and concise information, the Foundation aims to help and support a broad cross-section of charities and seek pride in the work it does.

The Environment Foundation

9 Dowgate Hill, London EC4R 2SU
Contact: L A J Duthie, Secretary
Trustees: John Elkington (Chairman);
Michael Martin, Charles Muller; Dr
Robert Aickin; J A Arnold; Mrs Helen
Holdaway; Tim O Donovan.
Grant total: £22,000 (August 1995)
Beneficial area: UK and overseas.

The foundation was originally set up in
1983 as the Eras Foundation (named after
the acronym for Environmental Risk
Analysis System). It changed its name a
year later. Its objects are the "protection,
enhancement and rehabilitation of the
environment ...in particular to foster new
or improved technological methods of
abating environmental pollution", "to
advance the education of the public and
"to promote study and research".

Until 1992 it sponsored a scheme which
had started as the Pollution Abatement
Technology Awards run by the RSA with
the CBI and the DoE. These became the
Better Environmental Awards for Industry
and then part of the Queen's Awards for
Industry.

Since 1993 it has been giving a small
number of grants annually. In 1995 its
four grants were given to:
◆ St George's House, Windsor, for
  consultation on "Biotechnlogy: the
  Potential Contribution to Sustainable
  Agriculture" (£8,933);
◆ Mansfield College, Oxford for debates to
  inaugurate the Oxford Centre for the
  Environment, Ethics & Society (£6,500);
◆ Fundacion Moises Bertone, Paraguay,
  for study of medicinal plants in
  Mbaracayu Forest Nature Reserve
  (£5,000 with an additional £3,000
  payable after completion);
◆ Youth Clubs Scotland, for Grizzley
  Challenge whereby children devise ways
  to improve some part of their own
  natural world, make a building safer and
  brighter, or reduce pollution (£2,000
  with £12,000 in the preceding year).

In the previous year a grant of £5,000 was
given to Powerful Information to place top
quality environmental literature in key
public libraries in selected developing
countries. In 1996 it has supported the
Green Alliance.

Applications: In writing to the
correspondent.

The Alan Evans Memorial Trust

Coutts & Co, Trustee Dept, 440 Strand,
London WC2R 0QS
Tel: 0171-753 1000
Contact: The Trust Manager
Trustees: Coutts & Co; John W
Halfhead; Deidre Moss;
Grant total: £98,000 (1995/96)
Beneficial area: UK.

"Donations are given for the purchase of
land, the planting of trees, shrubs and
plants and for the restoration of
cathedrals, churches and other buildings of
beauty or interest to which the public have
access."

In 1995/96 the trust had assets of £2.3
million which generated an income of
£209,000 from which grants of £98,000
were made. Half its payments were for less
than £1,000 and the remaining 40 grants
ranged between £1,000 and £5,000.

Examples of its grants included:
◆ National Trust Yealm Estuary (£5,000 +
  £2,500 for its Prior Park Appeal);
◆ John Muir Trust (£5,000);
◆ RSPB (£3,000);
◆ North West Ecological Trust (£2,500);
◆ Wildlife Trusts in Bristol and
  Bedfordshire, Arkwright Society
  (£1,500);
◆ Ely, Rochester, Chichester cathedrals
  (£1,000 each).

Exclusions: No grants to individuals or
for management or running expenses.
Grants to registered charities only. Any
appeal falling outside the trust criteria will
not be acknowledged.

Applications: In writing to the correspondent. Trustees normally meet three times a year.

The Beryl Evetts & Robert Luff Animal Welfare Trust

294 Earls Court Road, Kensington, London SW5 9BB
Tel: 0171-373 7003
Contact: R C W Luff
Trustees: R C W Luff; Sir Robert Johnson; B Nicholson; R P J Price; M Tomlinson, Mrs J Tomlinson.
Grant total: £62,500 (1995/96)
Beneficial area: UK.

The trust's principle objective is "the funding of veterinary research and the care and welfare of animals" (1995 report).

In 1995/96 the trust had assets of £1.3 million and an income of £87,000 from which it gave nine grants totalling £62,500. Most of its funding was devoted to its two major annual payments: Royal Veterinary College (£26,000) and the Animal Health Trust (£25,000). This commitment leaves little leeway for other approaches. However small sums are available to activities relevant to this guide including:
- National Equire and Smaller Animals Defence League (£1,000);
- The Ramsey Raptor Rescue Trust, International Fund for Animal Welfare and the Wildfowl & Wetlands Trust (£100 each).

Applications: It is understood the trust does not like to receive unsolicited applications.

The Keith Ewart Charitable Trust

c/o Manches & Co, Aldwych House, 81 Aldwych, London WC2B 4RP
Tel: 0171-404 4433

Contact: Timothy K Robertson
Trustees: Mrs H D Ewart; T K Robinson.
Grant total: £3,500 (1994)
Beneficial area: UK and overseas.

This small highly specialist trust is concerned with the conservation of endangered species of psitticidae (parrots at risk). Its grant-aid is slender and has been lower in 1994 (£2,500) compared with £5,000 (1991) and £4,000 (1993).

Its support in 1994 was given to Birdlife International (ICPB) for its Wax Palm Forest Project in Colombia. Grants in 1993 were given to the World Parrot Trust and the Jersey Wildlife Preservation Trust for work on the St Lucia parrot.

Applications: In writing to the correspondent.

The Esmée Fairbairn Charitable Trust

7 Cowley Street, London SW1P 3NB.
Tel: 0171-227-5400; **Fax:** 0171-227 5401
Contact: Margaret Hyde, Director
Trustees: John S Fairbairn, Chairman; Jeremy Hardie, Treasurer; Sir Antony Acland; Ashley G Down; General Sir John Hackett; Mrs Penelope Hughes-Hallet; Martin Lane-Fox; Mrs Veronica Linklater; Lord Rees-Mogg; Andrew Tuckey.
Grant total: £11 million (1996)
Beneficial area: UK.

Summary: This is one of the largest grant-making trusts, and the amount given yearly in donations continues to increase. Its grants are restricted to five areas: social welfare, education, arts and heritage, environment, social and economic research. Grants range from a few hundred pounds to £250,000 or, in exceptional occasions, up to £1 million. They may be awarded for one year or phased, and they can be for revenue, capital or project expenditure.

Background: The trust was founded by Ian Fairbairn in 1961 and it is named after his wife who died in a bombing raid at the end of the last War. Mr Fairbairn was a leading City figure, and endowed the trust with shares in his company, now M & G Group plc.

Its guiding principles are clearly stated:

- "its area of interest is UK-wide. The trustees aim to give particular attention to less advantaged areas.
- favours projects which will contribute to the preservation and development of a free and stable society.
- prefers projects which are innovative, developmental, designed to make a practical impact on a particular problem and reflect the principles of market forces. Especially in the case of local projects preference is given to those which demonstrate active local participation and support self-help.
- welcomes applications from black and minority ethnic groups.
- will be alert to the needs of disabled people in all appropriate funding decisions.
- looks favourably on projects undertaken in partnership, for example with another charitable trust.
- attaches importance to the assessment and dissemination of the results of work it has funded, so that others might benefit."

General

In 1996 the trust had assets of over £292 million and an income of over £12 million.

In its 1996 report it stated that it is continuing its effort to direct more of its resources to Northern Ireland, Scotland and Wales, and to the more hard pressed English regions.

Apart from its main grants programme, that is grants in excess of £5,000, the trust also has a Small Grants Scheme covering grants up to £5,000. Preference is given to projects largely supported by this funding, rather than those where the grant would form part of a larger funding scheme. Local, district and smaller national organisations are particularly encouraged to apply.

Extracts from the trust's policy guidelines relevant to this guide are quoted as follows:

- Environment
- "The trust wishes to promote sustainable development principally through practical projects, research where this is geared to advancing practical solutions, and education.
- The preservation of countryside and wildlife, appropriately linked to public access.
- The reconciliation of the needs of the environment and the economy, i.e. projects which sustain the former and promote solutions to any adverse environmental effects associated with economic development.
- The development of alternative technologies that help attain these objectives."

Environment Grants Analysis 1996
- Grants over £10,000: £622,000
- Grants under £10,000: £362,000
Total Grants £984,098

- Percentage of total grants 9.4%
- Number of new grants 65
- Number of continuing grants 13
Total 78

Larger grants in 1996 were given to:
- Royal Society for Nature Conservation (£111,000);
- Pedestrians Association, towards core funding (£65,000);
- Plantlife, towards purchase of Winskill Stores (£40,000);
- Council for the Protection of Rural England (£35,000);
- Green Alliance Trust, Woodland Trust towards the 'Woods on your Doorstep' project (£30,000 each);
- Forum for the Future towards project funding for new initiatives, Natural Environment Research Council towards PhD Research Studentship – 3rd of 3 grants (£25,000 each);
- Arthur Rank Centre towards core cost of Living Churchyard and Cemetery Project 1st of 3 grants, Botanical Society of the British Isles towards Co-Ordinator post 2nd of 3 grants, Marine Conservation Society towards Senior Conservation Officer post 2nd of 2 grants, Mammal Society toward 'Look

for Mammals ' initiative 1st of 3 grants (£15,000 each);
- Dorset Wildlife Trust towards Nature Conservation Interest project 1 x 3 (£13,000);
- Scottish Conservation Projects Trust towards CLAN initiative 2 x 3 (£12,000);
- Herpetofauna Conservation International towards Frog Mortality Project (£11,000).

Smaller grants included:
- Groundwork Hackney, Kent Trust for Nature Conservation, Landlife, Liverpool John Moores University, Mudchute Association, National Caving Association, Norfolk Wildlife, (£10,000 each);
- Pesticides Trust (£7,000);
- Radnorshire Wildlife Trust Ltd. (£6,000);
- Herpetological Conservation Trust, Loftus Development Trust, London Wildlife Trust, Nature Workshop, Northwest Ecological Trust, Oxfordshire Woodland Group, Gaia Trust (£5,000 each);
- Preston Montfield Field Studies Centre, Gibberd Garden Trust (£4,000 each);
- Hafod Trust, London Historic Parks & Gardens Trust, Manchester Metropolitan University, Merlin Trust (£3,000 each).

Arts and heritage

"In the heritage field, the trust supports:

Significant acquisitions by provincial public museums and galleries (only limited support since the trust channels most its funding in this area through another grant-giving body, the National Art Collections Fund. Please consult the trust's secretary before applying).

The preservation of buildings of historic or architectural value where these are put to public use, and the conservation of artefacts."

Grants in 1996 relevant to this included:
- Kings College, Cambridge repairs and restoration costs of Chapel, National Trust (£50,000 each);

- Landmark Trust (£40,000);
- Historic Churches Preservation Trust (£25,000, 1st of 3);
- National Trust for Scotland towards restoration costs of Holmwood (£20,000, 1st of 3);
- Dunblane Cathedral Development Fund (£13,000);
- Iona Cathedral Trust, Ironbridge Gorge Museum Development Trust (£10,000 each);
- Friends of Christ Church Spitalfields (£5,000).

Social and economic research

"The trust wishes to encourage the application of new ideas (or the challenging of old ones) to contemporary socio-political and economic issues. It supports research to this end, especially that designed with practical applications in mind, principally through the medium of independent research institutions."

A grant in 1995 was given to the Institute of Public Policy Research, towards an Environmental Taxation project (£16,000, 1st of 3).

Exclusions: Grants to registered charities only. The trust is unlikely to support the following: charities whose operational area is outside the UK; large national charities which enjoy wide support; branches of national charities; individuals; schools; medical (including research) or health care; expeditions; conferences or seminars; general appeals; sports; commercial publications; overseas travel; individual parish churches; animal welfare; sectarian religions; the direct replacement of statutory funding.

Retrospective grants are not made.

Applications: All applicants should first obtain the trust's guidelines (send SAE).

Applications for grants over £5,000 should be in the form of a letter with supporting information where necessary. The following information is required:
1. A brief description of your organisation, its work, management and staffing structure, and current budget.

2. Description of the purpose of the project for which funds are required, the amount sought from the trust, who will manage the project, the project start/ finish dates and the results expected.
3. A budget for the project, details of funds already raised and other sources being approached.
4. How your organisation intends to monitor and evaluate the project.
5. Your plans for sharing information about the project and what you learn from it with others in the field.
6. The most recent annual report and audited accounts.
7. Your organisation's charitable status, mentioning the charity's registration number.
8. The contact name and address and telephone number.
9. In addition, please quote the code for the current guidelines (EFCT/G1 for the guidelines used for this entry in the autumn, 1996, Ed).

Applications for grants up to £5,000 (Small Grants Scheme) should be made on the trust's application form. Copies are available from the Secretary, Judith Dunworth, at the trust address (send SAE).

Both kinds of application can be made at any time of the year, but allow good time for the processing of it, before its consideration at the trustees meetings in February, May, July and November, since applications can take up to six months to process.

Once the application has been considered the trust does not usually accept another application from the same organisation within 12 months from the date of the decision.

The Sebastian de Ferranti Trust

Henbury Hall, Near Macclesfield, Cheshire
Tel: 01625-422101
Trustees: S B de Ferranti; Mrs Beryl Casswell
Grant total: £9,000 (1994/95)

Beneficial area: UK with a particular interest in the Cheshire area.

The trust had capital of £180,000 and an income of £6,000 in 1994/95. It gave over £9,000 in 32 grants ranging between £20 and £2,000.

Six grants totalling £1,250 (14% of grant-aid) were relevant to this guide in 1994/95:
◆ Garden History Society (£500);
◆ Tewkesbury Abbey Appeal (£250);
◆ Adventure Farm Trust, Game Conservancy, St Alban's Macclesfield (£200 each);
◆ Cheshire Historic Churches (£100).

Population Concern is known to have received support in the following year.

Applications: In writing to the correspondent.

The Fishmongers' Company's Charitable Trust

The Fishmongers' Company, Fishmongers' Hall, London Bridge, London EC4R 9EL
Tel: 0171-626 3531
Contact: K S Waters, The Clerk
Trustees: The Wardens and Court of the Fishmongers' Company.
Grant total: £1,045,000 (1996)
Beneficial area: UK, with a special interest in the city of London and adjacent boroughs.

The trust states its policy as follows: "In general, the company's charitable funds will be used for the relief of hardship and disability, education, the environment, heritage and fishery related charities. Applications will normally only be accepted from national bodies (with the exception of charities in the City of London and adjacent boroughs).

"Preference will be given to charities seeking to raise funds for a specific project or for research rather than for administration or general purposes.

"In the case of requests for help for cathedrals, abbeys, churches and other old buildings, priority will be given to St Paul's Cathedral and Westminster Abbey."

Of the £1,045,000 given in donations in 1996, £449,000 was listed as "donations approved by the Court", but there were no details about the beneficiaries. These donations are made on a one-off basis, and normally do not exceed £10,000 for general charitable purposes. The balance of the money goes to the funding of existing scholarships and the company's own almshouses, to support Gresham's School and to provide grants to individuals for educational purposes.

Exclusions: No grants are made to individual branches of national charities or to regional or local charities, other than those in the City of London and adjacent boroughs. No grants are awarded to individuals except for education. Educational grants are not awarded to applicants who are over 19 years old.

Applications: In writing to the clerk. Meetings take place three times a year in March, July and November and applications should be received a month in advance. Grants are made on a one-off basis. No applications are considered within three years of a previous grant application being successful.

The Earl Fitzwilliam Charitable Trust

Estate Office, Milton Park, Peterborough PE6 7AH
Tel: 01858 -545342; Fax: 01858 -545887
Contact: J M S Thompson (Secretary)
Trustees: Sir Philip Naylor-Leyland; Lady Isabella Naylor-Leyland.
Grant total: £143,000 (1996)
Beneficial area: UK, preference for areas with historical family connections chiefly in Cambridgeshire, Northamptonshire and Yorkshire.

The trustees tend to favour projects and charities that are in some way connected with or will benefit rural life and communities including churches.

In 1995/96 the Trustees awarded one grant of £25,000 to Peterborough Cathedral Development and Preservation Trust. In addition 5 grants of £10,000 were made and 36 grants of between £1,000 and £5,000 each. The principal beneficiaries included the following charitable organisations:

- Fitzwilliam Museum Trust;
- Peterborough Museum;
- The Countryside Foundation;
- University College London;
- Friends of the Aged;
- Malton Museum Foundation;
- Papworth Trust;
- Courtauld Institute of Art;
- Ryedale Council for Voluntary Action;
- Rockingham Forest Trust;
- Badminton Conservation Trust.

Exclusions: No grants to individuals.

Applications: In writing to the correspondent.

The Russell & Mary Foreman 1980 Charitable Trust

Royal Bank of Scotland, Private Trust & Taxation, 45 Mosley Street, Manchester M60 2BE
Contact: Senior Trust Officer
Trustees: Royal Bank of Scotland plc
Grant total: £650 (1995/96); £15,000 (1994/95)
Beneficial area: UK and overseas.

The trust has a particular interest in "children, animals, ecological and environmental issues"

The trust donates its funds in small grants. The very low disbursement of only £650 in 1995/96 seems atypical. The trust had £224,000 in its capital account and a balance of disposable income of £20,000 so a higher sum may be expected in 1996/97.

In 1994/95 nearly £15,000 was donated in over 100 grants. The largest was £470 and close on half the grants were for less than £100. Many beneficiaries were given two grants and most of these had also been supported in the previous year.

Over 20 grants were relevant to this guide. They totalled over £4,000 (28 % of grant-aid) and included:

- Dian Fossey Gorilla Fund, Care for the Wild (£400 in 2 grants each);
- Whale & Dolphin Conservation Society, RSPB Malltraeth Marsh (£350 in 2 grants each);
- World Parrot Trust (£300 in 2 grants);
- FoE (£250);
- Greenpeace, International Wildlife Coalition, Rhino Rescue Trust, (£200);
- People's Trust for Endangered Species, RSNC, Sebakwe Black Rhino Trust, Water Aid (£200 in 2 grants);
- Belize Programme, Worldwide Land Conservation Trust (£175 in 2 grants);
- Birdlife International, Reptile Protection Trust, Tusk Force, Wildlife Aid, Tree Aid (£100 each).

In addition about an equal proportion of grants, both in terms number and funding, were given to animal welfare work. Four small grants were also given to Cambridge expeditions

Exclusions: Individuals
Applications: In writing to the correspondent but a reply cannot be expected.

The Donald Forrester Trust

231 Linen Hall, 156-170 Regent Street, London W1R 5TA
Tel: 0171-434 4021
Contact: Ms Brenda Ward
Trustees: Anthony Smee; Michael Jones; Gwyneth Forrester; Wendy Forrester.
Grant total: £395,000 (1994/95)
Beneficial area: UK and overseas.

This trust concentrates its grant-making on support to organisations concerned with a wide range of physical disabilities.

A handful of grants show an interest in conservation and the environment The trust had assets of £3.9 million in April 1995, almost entirely held as investments in Films & Equipments Limited. It follows the sensible practice of giving all its grants within the range of £1,000 to £10,000 rather than scattering its funds in tiny grants.

In 1994/95 it made 96 grants totalling £395,000. The great majority of grants (70 totalling £350,000) was given in sums of £5,000, two grants of £10,000 were made, one of £2,000 and 23 of £1,000.

Grants relevant to this guide totalled £22,000 (65) of total grant-aid in 1994/95:

- CPRE, Hampshire Gardens Trust, Intermediate Technology, Woodland Trust (£5,000 each);
- Historic Churches Preservation Trust, Worcester Cathedral Appeal (£1,000).

Applications: The trust has written to say that applications are not considered and that all grants are "made at the discretion of the trustees". The trustees meet in February and September.

The Jill Franklin Trust

78 Lawn Road, London NW3 2XB
Tel: 0171-722 4543
Contact: N Franklin
Trustees: Andrew Franklin; Norman Franklin; Sally Franklin; Sam Franklin; Tom Franklin.
Grant total: £37,000 (1994/95)
Beneficial area: UK and overseas.

In 1994/95, the trust had assets of £618,000, an income of £48,000 and gave grants totalling £37,000. The policy of the trust, the categories it supports, and the division of its funds and beneficiaries has been the same as for the Norman Franklin Trust (now winding down so no separate entry is given). It is concerned particularly with:

- Culture and the environment
- Overseas relief and development
- Relief, subdivided into: Welfare; Disability; Prisoners.

The correspondent has written that "We do give grants for church restoration where the church is of architectural significance (half a page in Pevsner's Buildings of England is our criterion), but not for improvements."

Some grants have been given to city farms in the past but these kinds of grants are apparently no longer made.

Exclusions: Grants are not given where statutory funding is available; for restoration; to heritage schemes; animals; students; building appeals; religious organisations or endowment funds.

Applications: Telephone applications are not accepted, but enquiries may be made. Annual reports and accounts as well as a budget are essential if the request is to be taken seriously. "The trustees tend to look more favourably on an appeal which is simply and economically prepared; glossy, 'prestige' and mailsorted brochures are likely to find their way into the recycling bin." No acknowledgement is usually given to unsolicited applications, except where a SAE is enclosed. An application to this trust is also considered by the Norman Franklin Trust. Separate applications to both trusts are binned.

The Gordon Fraser Charitable Trust

Holmhurst, Westerton Drive, Bridge of Allan, Stirling FK9 4QL
Contact: Mrs M A Moss
Trustees: Mrs M A Moss; W F T Anderson.
Grant total: £125,000 (1997)
Beneficial area: UK.

The trustees have absolute discretion as to the charities to be assisted. Currently the trustees are particularly interested in help for children/young people in need, the environment and the visual arts. The trust states that "applications from or for Scotland will receive favourable consideration, but not to the exclusion of applications from elsewhere."

In 1996, the trust had assets of £1.8 million and an income of £117,000 (including donations). It gave over 200 grants mainly between £200 and £500. Only 40 grants were over £1,000.

Twenty five grants totalling £16,000 (13% of total grant-aid) were relevant to this guide:
- Buildings of Scotland Trust (£4,000, also given in the previous 2 years);
- Royal Botanic Gardens Edinburgh (£3000 with £2,000 in the previous year);
- National Trust for Scotland, Scottish Churches Architectural Heritage Trust Dunblane Cathedral Development, Water of Leith Conservation Trust (£1,000 each);
- The British Naturalists' Society, British Trust for Ornithology, Cathedral Camps, Care for the Wild, Friends of the Earth, Scotland, The Rosslyn Chapel Trust, Sustrans (£500 each);
- Horticultural Therapy (£400);
- Ely Cathedral Restoration Trust, The International Otter Survival Fund, Irish Peatland Conservation Council, Planning Aid for Scotland (£300 each);
- Christ Church Lochgilphead, The Clyde Maritime Trust, Parochial Church Council of Newburn Building Appeal, Society of Friends of Dunblane Cathedral (£250 each);
- Friends of Craigmillar, North Hull Playgroup Association, The Sea Watch Foundation (£200 each);
- California Playgroup, Care for the Wild (£100) each.

Exclusions: No grants for organisations which are not registered charities, or to individuals.

Applications: In writing to the correspondent. Applications are considered in January, April, July and October. Grants towards national or international emergencies can be considered at any time. All applicants are acknowledged; and should be accompanied by an SAE. Attempts to contact the trustees by telephone are discouraged.

The Frognal Trust

c/o Charities Aid Foundation, Coach & Horses Passage, The Pantilles, Tonbridge Wells, Kent TN2 5TZ
Tel: 01892-512244
Contact: The Grants Administrator
Trustees: Mrs P Blake-Roberts; J P Van Montagu; P Fraser.
Grant total: £71,000 (1994/95)
Beneficial area: UK.

The trustees have a preference for charities concerned with old people, children, blind and otherwise handicapped, medical research, environmental heritage".

In 1994/95 the trust had assets of £1 million which generated an income of £62,000 from which 52 grants totalling £71,000 were given. Grants ranged between £500 and £2,857.

Eight grants relevant to this guide totalled £9,857 (14% of total grant-aid):
- Woodland Trust (£2,857);
- Ecological Studies Institute, Learning Through Landscapes (£2,000 each);
- Sustrans (£1,000);
- Dolphin Society, Open Spaces Society, Environment Trust Ltd, Mudchute Park & Farm Ltd (£500 each).

Exclusions: The trust does not support charities concerned with animal welfare, religious organisations or charities for the benefit of people outside the UK. No grants are given for educational or research trips.

Applications: In writing to the correspondent.

The Maurice Fry Charitable Trust

13 Quay Walls, Berwick-upon-Tweed, Northumberland TD15 1HB
Contact: Mrs F Cooklin
Trustees: Mrs F Cooklin; L E A Fry; Angela Fry; Mrs Lisa Weaks.
Grant total: £26,000 (September 1995)
Beneficial area: UK and Overseas.

In 1995 the trust had assets of about £836,000 which generated income from which 19 grants, ranging between £200 and £3,000, and totalling £26,000, were made.

Four grants were clearly relevant to this guide totalling £9,000 (35% of grant-aid):
- Tree Aid (£3,000);
- ITDG, Marie Stopes International (£2,500 each);
- National Trust for Scotland (£1,000).
- A grant was also given to the Island Trust (£1,200) but its work is not known.

Grants are restricted to organisations known to the trustees.

Applications: Unsolicited applications will not be acknowledged.

The Gannochy Trust

Kincarrathie House Drive, Pitcullen Crescent, Perth PH2 7HX
Tel: 01738 - 620653
Contact: Mrs Jean Gandhi, Secretary
Trustees: Russell A Leather, Chairman; Stewart Montgomery; Mark Webster; James A McCowan.
Grant total: £2,065,000 (1994/95)
Beneficial area: Scotland, with a preference for Perth and its environs.

"The Gannochy Trust was founded in 1937 by Arthur Kinmond Bell, whisky distiller and philanthropist. A K Bell built the Gannochy Housing Estate in Perth consisting of 150 houses and completed in 1932. This model scheme was a significant element in the foundation of the trust." The trustees maintain the estate and their other properties. In recent years they have enlarged the estate and are in process of providing a further 21 sheltered houses.

The prime objects of its other charitable donations are the needs of youth and recreation, but the trustees are not confined to this. All donations must be within Scotland with a preference given to charities in Perth and its environs.

In 1994/95, the trust had assets of over £83 million, and an income of £3,976,000.

Charitable distributions totalled £2,065,000 during the year, and the trust also made commitments of £947,000 to specific charitable projects.

The trust categorised its donations as shown below; "in all sectors, the interests of youth were amply served":

- Education 17%
- Social welfare 19%
- Health 16%
- Arts 6%
- Recreation 35%
- Environment 7%

The amounts given in these categories varies greatly from year to year and it seems that they should not be taken as guidance to the trust's balance of interests.

No indication was given in its report of the number and size of its grants. It provided, in accordance with Scottish charity law, a short list if those which exceeded 2% of income, i.e. £79,500). One was relevant to this guide: Perth & Kinross Heritage Trust (£100,000, a regular recipient of support).

The trust has stated that it gives about 180 grants a year ranging from £200 to £10,000. Some of them are recurrent, and they are distributed throughout Scotland.

Exclusions: No grants to individuals. Donations are confined to organisations recognised by the Inland Revenue as charitable, and the trustees have absolute discretion in the choice of recipient.

Applications: In writing to the correspondent, including where possible a copy of the latest accounts. "It is the practice of the trustees to scrutinise accounts before making donations". The trustees meet "frequently, generally monthly" to consider applications.

The Garnett Charitable Trust

30 Queen Charlotte Street, Bristol BS99 7QQ
Tel: 0117-923 0220
Contact: J W Sharpe, Solicitor

Trustees: A J F Garnett; Mrs P Garnett; R W Smerdon.
Grant total: £51,000 (1995/96)
Beneficial area: UK with a particular interest in the Bristol area and in Ireland.

This trust gives to the arts as well as to environmental concerns. In 1995/96 it had assets of £529,000 which generated an income of £32,000 from which 62 grants totalling £51,000 were given.

Eleven grants (given to 9 organisations) were relevant to this guide and totalled £7,350 (14 %) of grant-aid.

- Irish Wild Bird Conservancy (£900 in 3 grants, one for the Corncrake Project);
- Irish Peatland Conservation Council (£500);
- FoE (£400);
- Pride of Bristol Trust* (£250);
- Badgerwatch, PTES Mammal Fund, RSPB (£100 each).
- A number of animal welfare charities were also supported.

* Grants decided by Mr Garnett.

Applications: In writing to the correspondent.

The Gatsby Charitable Foundation

See the entry for the "Sainsbury Family Charitable Trusts"
Tel: 0171-410 0330
Contact: Michael Pattison
Trustees: A T Cahn; Miss J Portrait; C T S Stone (but see below).
Grant total: £23,372,000 grant approvals (1996/97)
Beneficial area: UK and overseas.

The foundation is the vehicle for the philanthropy of Lord David Sainsbury, the chairman of J Sainsbury plc. The foundation had a massive asset value of 3393 million (a decrease from £447 million in 1995/96 when he had given the foundation a further gift of £9.58 million).

"It is the policy of the trustees to concentrate on a few subjects at a time and to develop and implement programmes for them, usually over a number of years.... the trustees actively seek out practical, developmental and innovative projects and are generally not able to respond to unsolicited appeals."

The information in the chart below is taken from the foundation's annual reports. The main programme areas were listed as follows with the value of new approvals. The number of grants was not given for 1994/95. This information shows how a "snapshot" of the approvals for only one financial year can be quite misleading about the emphasis of a trust's interest/giving.

The following information lists support allocated to work relevant to this guide. It needs to be emphasised that the foundation develops its programmes in close conjunction with chosen organisations and that there is very little leeway for "cold" approaches.

Basic plant science

The trustees are advised by two groups:
◆ Dr John Ashworth; Dr David Baulcombe; Professor Sir Tom Blundell; Dr Enrico Coen; Professor Ian Crute; Gerard Fairtlough; Dr Roger Freedman; Dr Jonathan Jones.
◆ Professor Dick Flavell; Dr Roger Freedman; Professor John Gray; Professor David Ingram; Dr Jonathan Jones; Richard Price.

The Gatsby plant science programme is geared to the development of basic research in the UK and also to encouraging more young people to develop an active career in research. The main vehicle continues to be the Sainsbury Laboratory at the John Innes Centre in Norwich. "The aims of the work are to derive new understanding about the fundamental processes of plant growth and development from an analysis of the diseased and disease-resistant state of plants."

Grants have included in 1996/97:
◆ Wye college (£33,380);

and in 1995/96:
◆ 7th International Congress of Plant Pathology 1998 towards its costs (£60,000);
◆ Imperial College, London, towards Dutch Elm Disease research (£119,000);
◆ Ethnoflora of Socotra (£12,250);
◆ Royal Botanic Gardens Edinburgh (£11,500).

Social Development

This new category was started in 1995/96 "to make a contribution towards practical developments to improve the environment and well-being of people living in run-down urban areas".

Category £'000 (no of grants)	1996/97	1995/96	1994/95
Basic plant science	£307 (10)	£1,431 (22)	£13,651
Development in Africa	£1,176 (9)	£214 (5)	£2,133
Economic and social research	£5,847 (12)	£945,000 (8)	£1,498
Technical education	£5,736 (12)	£4,533 (28)	£2,257
Mental health	£2,204 (14)	£3,033 (15)	£1,941
Children and young people	£1,319 (47)	£1,809 (59)	£682
Health care & service delivery	£850 (12)	£1,116 (11)	£508,000
Social development	£340 (7)	£1,744 ( )	–
Cognitive neuroscience	£64 (2)	£171 (9)	£262
General	£5,531 (36)	£1,997 (34)	£1,857
Total:	£23,372(172)	£16,994(194)	£24,800 (not known)

(The 1994/95 figures are somewhat distorted by the inclusion under "Basic plant science" of £12 million funding over seven years (1994-1999) for the Sainsbury Laboratory at the John Innes Centre in Norwich.)

The two grants included:
National Tenants' Resource Centre and the LSE, to work up a programme of small-scale community regeneration initiatives providing grants to tenant and resident groups for self-help initiatives, dependent on undertaking suitable training (£1,250,000 over 5 years from 1995/96).

Development in Africa

(Adviser: Laurence Cockroft)
"Over the past decade the trustees have sought to maximise the value of their support... by concentrating their resources in a limited number of countries in one continent. They have selected African countries with reasonable stability and have supported small scale wealth creation in agriculture and manufacturing, and primary health care in support of women and small children. They have sought to work through local people to develop sustainable projects genuinely responsive to local needs.

"The countries identified in the annual report are Cameroon, South Africa, Kenya, Tanzania and Uganda. The last three have their own Gatsby Trusts with local trustees.

In 1996/97 the university of Reading was supported over two years for a study of the Green Revolution in Africa (£77,000).

Social and Economic Research

In 1995/96 the Planning Exchange in Glasgow was helped with its core costs (£50,000).

Technical Education

Science and Plants for Schools (SAPS) towards the ongoing work of this organisation started by the foundation (£805,000 over 4 years from 1995/96).

General

Only one grant relevant to this guide was given in 1996/97: Kings College Chapel Foundation (£5,000).

Grants in 1995/96 included:
◆ Woodland Trust, towards the "Woodlands on Your Doorstep" Millennium appeal (£175,000 over 5 yrs);
◆ Hawk & Owl Trust (£45,000).

No relevant grants were given in the preceding year.

Exclusions: No grants to individuals, and no applications for building grants will be considered.

Applications: Unsolicited applications are rarely successful but all can expect an acknowledgement. They can be submitted at any time in writing with the latest report and accounts. They should be concise (1 to 2 pages), identifying aim, approach, justification and timeliness and the amount sought. Further communication will only take place if the appeal is being seriously considered. An application to one of the Sainsbury family trusts is an application to all. See the entry under 'Sainsbury Family Charitable Trusts' for address and application procedure.

The Gem Charitable Trust

Messrs Farrer & Co, 66 Lincoln's Inn Fields, London WC2A 3LH
Tel: 0171-242 2022
Trustees: N J Marks; I R Marks; C F Woodhouse.
Grant total: £65,000 (1993/94)
Beneficial area: UK and overseas.

This trust is prepared to support trusts providing an intellectual base to environmental interests.
In 1994/95, the trust had an income of £39,000 but seemed to give only two grants totalling £8,000 compared with grants totalling £65,000 in the previous year. These were:
◆ New Economics Foundation (£6,000, with £19,000 and £5,000 in the 2 previous years);
◆ Environmental Research Association (£2,000).

The trust has regularly supported the Dartington Hall Trust and WYSE. It has given large grants in 1993/94 to the C Foundation (£38,000) and in 1992/93 to Mansfield Max Neef via the Gaia Foundation (£50,000).

Applications: In writing to the correspondent.

The J Paul Getty Charitable Trust

149 Harley Street, London W1N 2DH
Tel: 0171-486 1859
Contact: Ms Bridget O'Brien Twohig, Administrator
Trustees: J Paul Getty Jr; Christopher Gibbs; James Ramsden; Vanni Treves.
Grant total: £1,505,000 (1996)
Beneficial area: UK, but see below.

The trust had assets of over £37 million by the end of 1996 which generated an income of £2.1m from which 220 grants were made totalling £1,505,000.

About 85% of the trust's funding is given to social welfare. Its particular interests are in mental health, offenders, communities, homelessness, job creation and ethnic minorities. However, it also funds the arts, conservation and environment.

The following extracts relevant to this guide have been taken from the trust's 1996 guidelines: "The trust aims to fund projects to do with poverty and misery in general, and unpopular causes in particular, within the UK. The emphasis is on self-help, building esteem, enabling people to reach their potential. The trustees favour small community and local projects which make good use of volunteers. Both revenue and capital grants are made, but please see "Exclusions" below.

"Priority is likely to be given to projects in the less prosperous parts of the country, particularly in the North of England, and to those which cover more than one beneficial area (area of interest, not necessarily geographical, Ed).

"Grants are usually in the £5,000 to £10,000 range, and those made for salaries or running costs are for a maximum of three years. Some small grants of up to £1,000 are also made."

Conservation

"Conservation in the broadest sense, with emphasis on ensuring that fine buildings, landscapes, and collections remain or become available to the general public or scholars. (Not general building repair work). Training in conservation skills."

Environment

"Mainly gardens, historic landscape and wilderness."

In 1996, 20 grants totalling £140,000 (9% of total grant aid) were relevant to this guide.

- Wordsworth Trust, Cumbria (heritage) (£20,000);
- Botanic Gardens Trust, BTCV Northern Ireland (tree planting), FWAG Scotland (habitat preservation), Garden History Society, Historic Chapels Trust, Kilmartin House Trust, Argyll (archaeological site) (£10,000 each);
- Vivat Trust (restores old buildings), Biddlestone Chapel, Northumberland, Common Ground (£8,000 each);
- Association of Garden Trusts, CPRE Upper Heyford, Glouc., Game Conservancy Trust, National Council for the Conservation of Plants & Gardens, Peterborough Cathedral, Thamesclean (£5,000 each);
- Covent Garden Residents Association (Phoenix Garden), Rockingham Forest Trust, Northamptonshire (£3,000 each);
- London Historic Parks & Gardens Trust (£1,000);
- Friends of Pallant House, Chichester (£500).

Exclusions: The trustees do not generally consider applications for the elderly, children, education, research, animals, music or drama (except therapeutically), conferences and seminars, medical care (including hospices) or health, medical equipment, churches and cathedrals, holidays and expeditions, sports or leisure facilities (including cricket pitches).

Residential projects or large building projects are unlikely to be considered. The trustees do not support national appeals or grant giving trusts such as community trusts. Headquarters of national organisations and 'umbrella' organisations are unlikely to be considered, as are applications from abroad.

No applications from individuals are considered. All projects must be from a registered charity or be under the auspices of one.

Applications: Please request from the trust a copy of the guidelines before applying. Applications can be made at any time and all letters of appeal are answered. "A letter no more than two pages long is all that is necessary at first, giving the outline of the project, a detailed costing, the existing sources of finance of the organisation, and what other applications, including those to statutory sources, have been made. Please also say if you have applied to or received a grant previously from this trust. Please do not send videos, tapes or bulky reports – they will not be returned. Annual accounts will be asked for if your application is going to be taken further.

"The project will also have to be visited before an application can be considered by the trustees. This may mean a delay, as it is only possible to visit a small part of the country between each quarterly trustee's meeting. Some small grants of up to £1,000 can be made without a visit, but only for specific purposes".

The G C Gibson Charitable Trust

Deloitte & Touche, Blenheim House, Fitzalan Court, Newport Road, Cardiff CF2 1TS
Tel: 01222-481111
Contact: Karen Griffin
Trustees: R D Taylor; William D Gibson; George S C Gibson.
Grant total: £416,000 (1995/96)
Beneficial area: UK, with interests in East Anglia and Wales.

The trust was founded by George Cock Gibson in 1969, and by February 1996 had assets of over £6.8 million which generated a high income of £524,000. 138 grants were made during 1995/96, most falling between £2,000 and £4,000. Four grants were for £10,000 each. There is

little scope for new organisations to receive support – only 25 grants totalling £88,000 were given to organisations not supported the year before.

Grants relevant to this guide, totalling £49,000 (12% of grant-aid) were given to:
◆ Llandaff Cathedral Restoration Appeal (£10,000 with £5,000 the year before);
◆ Ely Cathedral Trust, Gwent Wildlife Trust, Hereford Cathedral, RSNC, Wildfowl & Wetlands Trust (£5,000 each and in the preceding year);
◆ National Trust, Enterprise Neptune (£3,000 with £2,000 in the previous year);
◆ Campaign for the Protection of Wales, (£2,000);
◆ Brecon Cathedral, Friends of Flitcham Church, Farm Land Museum, Wales in Trust (£2,000 each and in the previous year);
◆ St Mary Burwell (£1,000 and in the previous year).

Only one grant out of the 14 given had not been given in the previous year.

Exclusions: Only registered charities will be supported.

Applications: To the correspondent in October/November each year. Trustees meet in December/January. Successful applicants will receive their cheques during January. "Due to the volume of applications, it is not possible to acknowledge each application, nor is it possible to inform unsuccessful applicants."

Simon Gibson Charitable Trust

Hill House, 1 Little New Street, London EC4A 3TR
Contact: Bryan Marsh
Trustees: Bryan Marsh; Angela Homfray; George Gibson.
Grant total: £300,000 (1995/96)
Beneficial area: UK with an interest in East Anglia, particularly the Newmarket area, and Wales.

The trust was established in 1975 by George Simon Gibson, the son of George Cock

Gibson who lived and farmed in Newmarket and made his money in shipping in Wales (see G C Gibson Charitable Trust). George Gibson, the trustee of the Simon Gibson Trust, is his nephew.

The trust had assets of £5.8 million in 1995/96 which generated an income of £321,000, from which £201,000 was distributed.

Six grants in 1995/96 totalling £26,000 (13% of grant-aid) were clearly relevant to this guide and included:
◆ Ely Cathedral Appeal Fund (£10,000 and also in the preceding 3 years with £25,000 in 1992);
◆ Filleigh Church Restoration Fund, Llancarfen Parish Church (£5,000 each);
◆ Exning Church; Ironbridge Gorge Development Fund, WWF (£2,000 each).

These show a continued concentration on the built heritage, although grants have been given in previous years to Sea Watch Foundation, and a few wildlife trusts as well as the WWF.

Exclusions: No grants for individuals.

Applications: In writing to the correspondent. Telephone calls should not be made. The trust has no application forms. It acknowledges all applications but does not enter into correspondence with applicants unless they are awarded a grant. The trustees meet in April.

Mrs E D Gibson's Charitable Trust

See entry for the Swan Trust

H M T Gibson's Charity Trust

Pollen House, 10/12 Cork Street, London W1X 1PD
Tel: 0171- 439 9061; Fax: 0171- 437 2680;
E-mail mailbox@m.f.s.co.uk
Contact: The Secretary
Trustees: The Cowdray Trust Limited
Grant total: £6,000 (1996/97)
Beneficial area: UK.

This trust has general charitable objects and a particular interest in the arts and conservation of the built environment. It gives regularly to Turners Hill Free Church and to Turners Hill PCC and to Worth PCC. It also gives small occasional grants to York and Chichester cathedrals.

The trust's disbursements have been steadily falling from £29,000 in 1993/94 to £12,000 in 1995/96 to £6,000 in 1996/97.

Exclusions: No grants to individuals. Registered charities only. Funds are fully committed.

The Helen and Horace Gillman Trusts

Drummond Miure W.S. 31/32 Moray Place, Edinburgh EH3 6BZ
Tel: 0131 - 226 5151; Fax: 0131 -225 2608
Contact: Miss E A Couper
Trustees: J K Burleigh; F Hamilton; Ian Darling.
Grant total: £23,000 (1996/97).
Beneficial area: Great Britain, Ireland, with an interest in Scotland.

The trusts, which were set up in 1982, have assets worth about £500,000.

The trustees support bird conservation and work closely with bird charities, particularly the Royal Society for the Preservation of Birds (RSPB). Grants range between £500 and £10,000. Recent grant recipients have included the RSPB, the Islay Natural Heritage Trust, Port Charlotte and the Isle of May Bird Observatory.

Applications: In writing to the correspondent.

The Glass-House Trust

See entry for the Sainsbury Family Charitable Trusts

Contact: Michael Pattison
Trustees: Alexander J Sainsbury; T J Sainsbury, Jessica Sainsbury; Miss J S Portrait.

Grant total: £646,000 grant approvals (1995/96)
Beneficial area: UK and overseas.

This is one of the "young" Sainsbury family trusts with the three children of Sir Timothy Sainsbury as trustees. The others are the Tedworth and Staples Trusts (see separate entries).

In 1995/96 the trust had assets of over £13 million (£11.8 million of which was held in shares in J Sainsbury plc. In 1995 Sir Timothy had given the trust a million ordinary shares of 25p in the company.) It approved grants of £646,000 with actual payments of £218,000 and commitments of £403,000 carried forward from earlier years.

Its main interests – Parenting, Family Welfare & Child Development – are similar to those of the Tedworth Trust, but "Environment" is not singled out as a particular interest, unlike the Tedworth and Staples Trusts.

At the time of writing (April 1997) only two organisations falling within the scope of this guide had been directly supported since the trust was established:

In 1995/96
- Civic Trust, for the Campaign for Livable Places (£30,000 approved over 2 years, with £20,000 paid in both 1994/95 and 1993/94);

1994/95
- Architecture Foundation (£5,000).

Applications: See the entry for "Sainsbury Family Charitable Trusts".

The GNC Trust

c/o Messrs Price Waterhouse & Co, Cornwall Court, Cornwall Street, Birmingham B3 2DT
Tel: 0121-200 3000
Contact: Mrs P M Spragg.
Trustees: R N Cadbury; G T E Cadbury; Mrs J E B Yelloly.
Grant total: £60,000 (1995)

Beneficial area: Preference for Avon, Cornwall, Hampshire and the Midlands.

In 1995, the trust's assets generated an income of £69,000. it gave about 80 grants to a wide range of organisations. Grants are seldom above £10,000. The majority are small and less than £1,000.

Twelve grants totalling £14,000 (20% of grant-aid) were relevant to this guide:
- Woodland Trust (£5,000);
- Downs Light Railway Trust (£2,500);
- Royal National Rose Society (£2,000);
- Game Conservancy Trust, Sustrans (£1,000 each);
- National Trust (£700);
- Barn Owl Trust (£500);
- English Heritage (£365);
- Royal Horticultural Society (£300);
- Whitchurch Silk Mill (£275);
- WWF UK (£150).

Applications: In writing to the correspondent.

The Godinton Charitable Trust

Godinton Park, Ashford, Kent TN23 3BW
Contact: A W Green
Trustees: Wyndham George Plumptre; Michael F Jennings; Moran Caplat; John D Leigh-Pemberton; Louis H Parsons.
Grant total: £179,000 (1995)
Beneficial area: UK.

In 1995 the trust had income of £267,000 and made donations totalling £179,000 to about 500 charities. Most grants were for £250 and £500 with a very small number between £1,000 and £5,000 with the largest grant given to Glyndebourne. Grants were given over a wide field of activities.

Some 35-40 grants totalling over £11,000 (6% of grant-aid) were relevant to this guide and included:
- Home Farm Trust (£2,000);
- Canterbury and Rochester Cathedrals (£500 each);

- Scottish Conservation Projects, Kent Trust for Nature Conservation (£500 in 2 grants);
- Dr Johnson's House, Buildings of Scotland, Scottish Civic Trust, Chichester Cathedral, Wakefield Chantry Chapel, Historic Chapels Trust, St Martin's in the Fields, grants were also given to several churches (£250 each);
- Barn Owl Trust, Mammal Society, Project Podocarpus 95, Shared Earth Trust, Wildfowl & Wetlands Trust, Wildlife Aid, WWF UK, Zebakwe Black Rhino Trust (£250);
- Cotswold Canals Trust, London Ecology Centre, Vale of Enham Trust, Romney Marsh Research Trust, Woodland Trust (£250 each);
- Windmill Hill City Farm, Stonebridge City Farm, Horticultural Therapy, Iona Community (£250 each).

Applications: In writing to the correspondent. The trustees meet monthly usually. The correspondent has written "the trustees face substantial new demands upon their available funds and regret that it is therefore no longer possible for them to accept unsolicited applications" (editor's emphasis).

The Golden Bottle Trust

C Hoare & Co, 37 Fleet Street, London
EC4P 4DQ
Tel: 0171-353 4522
Contact: Secretariat
Trustees: A S Hoare; H C Hoare; D J Hoare; R Q Hoare; M R Hoare; A M Hoare; V E Hoare.
Grant total: £225,000 (September 1995)
Beneficial area: UK.

In 1995, the trust had assets of £943,000 and an income of £242,000, including £200,000 in donations. No list of donations was supplied. In the previous year the trust gave 127 grants totalling £169,000. Grants were then given to a wide range of organisations – arts, disability, medical, welfare, and conservation.

Grants relevant to this guide in 1994 totalled over £37,000 (22% of total grant-aid of £169,000) included:

- Atlantic Salmon Conservation Trust, Scotland (£12,000 in 2 grants);
- National Trust (£8,270);
- Game Conservancy Trust (£5,000);
- Butterfly Conservation (£2,000);
- WWF UK (£1,250 in 2 grants);
- BTCV, Fauna & Flora Preservation Society, International Trust for Nature Conservation, Royal Geographical Society, Linnean Society, Surrey Wildlife Trust (£1,000 each);
- Hampshire Gardens Trust, Natural History Museum Development Trust (£500 each);
- Mudchute Association, CPRE, Scottish Wildlife Trust, Lincoln Cathedral, Countryside Education Trust, Field Studies Council Blencarth Appeal (£250 each).

The trust correspondent has seen this draft but not supplied more detailed information about its grants.

Exclusions: No grants for individuals or organisations that are not registered charities.

Applications: In writing to the correspondent, who stated "Trustees meet on a monthly basis, but the funds are already largely committed and, therefore, applications from sources not already known to the trustees are unlikely to be successful."

The Goldsmiths' Company's Charities

Goldsmiths' Hall, Foster Lane, London
EC2V 6BN
Tel: 0171-606 7010; Fax: 0171-606 1511
Contact: R D Buchanan-Dunlop, Clerk
Trustees: The Goldsmiths' Company.
Grant total: £1,222,000 (Sept 1995)
Beneficial area: UK, with a special interest in London charities.

These endowed trusts are part of the Goldsmiths' Livery Company in the City of London. They comprise three major and six minor charitable trusts of which the principal ones are the General Charity, the Goldsmiths Charitable Donation Fund and the John Perryn's Charity. They share the same trustees and correspondent.

The objectives, which fall into three main areas, are as follows:
- Support for the Goldsmiths' Craft
- Education: In addition to support for its craft the Goldsmiths' Company sponsors a number of general educational initiatives.
- General Charitable Support: The largest area of grant-making is towards general charitable needs, ranging from the disadvantaged in society and general welfare to the churches and the arts.

"Grants are made to London-based and national charities only; where charities are members or branches of an association, appeals are accepted from the governing body or head office only."

A total of 180 grants was listed for 1995. (Two of the charities did not list grants of £1,000 and less, and whilst the other did not list grants of less than £1,000.) Only nine grants were £10,000 and higher. Most grants were between £5,000 and £1,000. Many grants (well over a quarter of those listed) were recurrent.

Grants relevant to this guide in 1995 totalled over £24,000 (2% of grant-aid) and included:
- Council for the Care of Churches, Westminster Cathedral (£5,000 each);
- York Civic Trust, Royal Geographical Society (£4,000 each);
- Historic Chapels Trust, Guildford Cathedral (£2,000 each);
- Mudchute Association (£1,500);
- BTCV (£1,000).

Exclusions: Medical research; student grants; provincial local charities; endowment and memorial appeals; animal welfare.

Applications: Applications for all of the charities applying for general charitable support should be made on an application form and should be accompanied by the following information.
- an outline of the current work and experience of the applicant organisation including details of staffing, organisational structure and use of volunteers;
- the organisation's most recent annual report, if one is published;
- a detailed budget for the proposed activity;the organisation's most recent audited accounts (or financial report required by the Charities Act);
- the methods by which the success of the project will be evaluated;the income/expenditure projection for the organisation for the current year;
- other grant-making organisations appealed to for the same project and with what result;
- preference for a single or annual grant for up to three years. No organisation, whether successful or not, will have more than one appeal considered every three years.

Trustees meet monthly except during August and September.

The D S R Grant Charitable Settlement

c/o Messrs Cobden Board & Co Accountants, Fountain House, Bromsgrove Road, Sheffield S10 2LS
Tel: 0114-266 4491
Contact: The Secretary
Trustees: E Wilkes; J M Wilkes; R M G Ostrouskis
Grant total: £18,000 (1994/95)
Beneficial area: UK.

The trust had capital of £138,000 and made grants totalling £18,000 in 1994/95.

Three grants totalling £8,200 (45% of grant aid) were relevant to this guide:
- FoE (£5,000);
- RSPB (£3,000);
- Yorkshire Wildlife Trust (£200).

Applications: In writing to the correspondent.

The Greater Bristol Foundation

PO Box 383, 16 Clare Street, Bristol
BS99 5JG
Tel: 0117-921 1311; Fax: 0117- 929 7965
E-mail: Website: http:/
www.bristol.digitalcity.org/community/
gbj/index.htm
Contact: Ronnie Brown, Assistant
Director
Trustees: John Burke, Chairman; Jay
Tidmarsh; Richard Lalonde; Bishop Barry
Rogerson; David Parkes; Douglas Claisse;
Christopher Curling; George Ferguson;
Marion Jackson; David Kenworthy; John
Pontin; Hugh Pye; Tim Stevenson; Simon
Storvik; Andrew Thornhill; Dereth Wood.
Grant total: £209,000 (1996/97)
Beneficial area: Greater Bristol, within
ten miles of Bristol Bridge.

This is a fundraising as well as a grant-
making charity, building up an
endowment to help meet the charitable
needs of Bristol. It also serves as an agent
managing and distributing specific funds
on behalf of other donors. Emphasis is on
communities at a special disadvantage
through lack of opportunities, specific
discrimination or poverty.

In 1996/97 the foundation had accrued
assets of £3.2 million which generated
income of £448,000. The foundation's
grant-making work focuses on five key
areas:
- Safer community environments;
- Young people;
- Relief form isolation;
- Disabled groups;
- Support for homeless people.

Grants relevant to this guide in 1996/97
included:
- Dundry Hill Group (£2,300);
- Fun at the Farm (£1,000);
- Woodland Trust (£600);
- BTCV (£500).

Donor advised grants over £100 included:
- Bristol Civic Society;

- National Trust;
- St Werburgh's City Farm.

Grants in the previous year included:
- Troopers' Hill Environmental
  Improvements (£2,420);
- Avon Wildlife Trust (£1,000).

Exclusions: Grants will not normally be
given to general appeals, individuals,
general overseas travel, fee-paying schools,
direct replacement of public funds,
promotion of religious causes, medical
research and equipment, organisations
without a permanent presence in Bristol,
or sports without an identifiable charitable
element.

Applications: On the form available from
the Correspondent, whom potential
applicants are advised to speak to
informally in the first instance and who
will supply detailed guidelines.
Applications of up to £1,500 can be
considered at any time under the Express
Grants Programme. Applicants will
normally hear with four weeks whether or
not the application has been successful.

The G B Greenwood Charitable Settlement

No 1 Westgate, Otley, West Yorkshire
LS21 3AT
Contact: Mrs G W Atkinson, Secretary
Trustees: D B Greenwood; S W Urry; J A
Greenwood; Mrs P M Urry;
Grant total: £25,000 (1995)
Beneficial area: UK.

In 1995 the trust made 17 grants totalling
£25,000 and most of the funding was
given to the Woodhouse Grove School
(£14,000). The school had received small
project grants of a few hundred pounds in
previous years.

The previous year (1994), when £42,000
was donated seems more characteristic of
its approach. Then over 70 grants were
given, 16 of which were for £1,000+, the
largest being for £1,800.

Twelve beneficiaries were relevant to this guide in 1994 and had also received support in the previous year (which suggests little leeway for new unknown applicants). These grants totalled over £5,000 (12% of grant-aid):

- Game Conservancy Trust (£1,000);
- Atlantic Salmon Trust, Greenpeace, National Trust Lake District Appeal, Yorkshire Wildlife Trust, Population Services, St George's Crypt Leeds (£500 each);
- CPRE, Enham Trust, FoE, St Mary's Bingley, Whale & Dolphin Conservation Society (£250 each).

Exclusions: Individuals. Only churches in the Leeds and Bradford area are considered.

Applications: In writing to the correspondent.

The Grocers' Charity

Grocers' Hall, Princes Street, London EC2R 8AD
Tel: 0171-606 3113; Fax: 0171-600 3082
Contact: Miss Anne Blanchard, Charity Administrator
Trustees: The Grocers' Trust Company Ltd.
Grant total: £252,000 (1995/96)
Beneficial area: UK.

The following information has been supplied directly by the charity. Accounts and Annual Reports are available at the Charity Commission.

The Grocers' Charity had assets of £5.5 million in 1995/96 which generated £338,000 in income from which grants totalling £253,000 were made. The majority of the money spent under the heading "Education" was committed to funding internal bursaries and scholarships at various schools and colleges with which the charity has historic connections.

The balance was well spread, as shown in the following table. Both capital and revenue projects received support by way of non-recurring grants. Emphasis is placed on enabling people to transform the quality of their lives through grants to charities which are subsequently allocated to individuals.

- Education 43.3%
- Heritage and the Arts 5.3%
- Disabled 15.8%
- Relief of Poverty, Youth 17. 9%
- Churches 5%
- Elderly and Medicine 7.7%

Most grants are for £1,500 and less with the majority for £500. "It is rare for larger grants to be made and when they are it is because of some specific link with the Grocers' company."

Exclusions: Organisations which are not registered charities. Support for churches, educational establishments, expeditions, hospices and research projects restricted to those having specific close and long-standing connections with the Grocers' Company. It is unusual for grants to be made to individuals (including students).

Applications: In writing to the correspondent, accompanied by a copy of the latest accounts. Applications, which may be submitted at any time, are not acknowledged, but all are notified of outcome. The trustees meet four times a year, in January, April, June and November. Informal enquiry by telephone is encouraged.

The Walter Guinness Charitable Trust

Biddesden House, Andover, Hampshire SP11 9DN
Tel: 01264-790237
Contact: The Secretary
Trustees: Elisabeth, Lady Moyne; F B Guinness; Mrs R Mulji.
Grant total: £161,000 (1995/96)
Beneficial area: UK and overseas, with a preference for Wiltshire and Hampshire.

The trust states, "We are unlikely to be able to support anything unless there is a personal connection, a local connection or unless the organisation has previously been supported by our trust."

In 1995/96, the trust had assets of £2.8 million and an income of £138,000. Over 80 grants totalling £161,000 were given and ranged from less than £100 to £17,600. Only three grants were for £10,000 or more. Most grants were for £200 to £500. A clear interest was shown in local organisations in Hampshire and Wiltshire.

Grants relevant to this guide totalling £20,900 (13% of total grant-aid) were given to:
+ St James' Church Ludgershall (£10,000);
+ St Catherine's College, Oxford, building appeal (£5,000);
+ SOS Sahel (£2,000);
+ Countryside Workshops Charitable Trust, ITDG (£1,000 each);
+ RSPB (£600);
+ Marie Stopes International, Wiltshire & Berkshire Canal Amenity Group (£500 each);
+ Great Bustard Trust Fund, Green Alliance, Hampshire Wildlife Trust, Wildside Trust (£200).

Applications: In writing to the correspondent.

The Gunter Charitable Trust

4 John Carpenter Street, London EC4Y 0NH
Tel: 0171-615 8000
Contact: Adrian Messenger
Trustees: J de C E Findlay; H R D Bilson.
Grant total: £38,000 (1994/95)
Beneficial area: UK.

In 1994/95, the trust had assets of £1 million and an income of £95,000. The trustees gave grants totalling only £38,000.

Ten grants relevant to this guide totalling £5,350 (13% of total grant-aid) were given to:
+ Marie Stopes International (£2,000);
+ CPRE, Friends of the Earth (£1,000);
+ Association for the Protection of Rural Scotland (£800);
+ Scottish Wildlife Reserves Fund, Scottish Wildlife Trust (£500 each);

+ Hampshire & I o W Naturalists' Trust (£250);
+ Holy Island Project, ITDG, Women's Environmental Network (£200 each).

Applications: In writing to the correspondent.

The William Haddon Charitable Trust

Manor Garden, Sibbertoft, Market Harborough, Leics LE16 9UA.
Tel: 01858-880280
Contact: Miss M A Haddon.
Trustees: Margaret Haddon; Joyce Haddon; Celia Haddon, Catherine Johnson.
Grant total: £19,000 (1994/95)
Beneficial area: UK and overseas.

The trust has a particular interest in conservation of churches and of wildlife as well as work in the vicinity of Northamptonshire and neighbouring counties. In 1994/95 it had assets of £215,000 and an income of £14,000. It gave 39 grants ranging between £100 and £1,000 and totalling £19,000.

Twenty three grants were relevant to this guide and totalled over £11,000 (58% of grant-aid):
+ Ely Cathedral, BTCV, PTES, RSPB, Woodland Trust (£1,000 each);
+ Beds and Cambs Wildlife Trust, National Trust Scotland, Southorpe Meadow and Wildlife Trust, International Primate Protection League, Programme for Belize, Wildlife & Wetlands Trust (£500 each);
+ Hawk & Owl Trust; Leics Historic Churches Preservation Trust (£250 each).

In addition 10 further grants were given to churches and chapels with the largest to St Mary the Virgin Iffley (£450).

Exclusions: Individuals.

Applications: In writing to the correspondent.

The Hadrian Trust

36 Rectory Road, Gosforth, Newcastle-upon-Tyne NE3 1XP
Tel: 0191-285 9553
Contact: John Parker
Trustees: Richard Harbottle; Brian J Gillespie; John B Parker.
Grant total: £170,000 (September 1995)
Beneficial area: Northumberland, Tyne and Wear, Durham.

Most grants go towards the running costs of social welfare organisations in the area of benefit. The trust will support organisations which it feels are less likely to get grants from other trusts and will make grants to organisations which are not registered charities but which are doing charitable work. Applications for capital and revenue projects are treated equally. Repeat applications are considered. Crisis applications can be dealt with outside the quarterly meetings. National appeals are not likely to be considered, and almost without exception grants are limited to projects within the area of benefit. The trustees will consider applications from former statutory projects.

In the year to September 1995, grants were categorised as follows: Social services; Youth; Women; Arts; Elderly & disabled; Individuals; Schools & education; Ethnic minorities; as well as Environment and Churches.

Grants relevant to this guide totalled over £33,000 (19% of total grant-aid) in 1995 and were given to:

Under "Environment" -
◆ Bede Foundation, Newcastle upon Tyne Trinity House, Beamish Open Air Museum (£5,000 each);
◆ BTCV, Tyne & Wear Building Preservation Trust, Durham Wildlife Trust, Bailiffgate Alnwick & District Museum, Woodland Trust – East Sunniside Farm (£1,000 each);
◆ Community Environmental Education Development Sunderland, Cook Street Nursery Centre (£800 each);

Under "Churches" -
◆ Cathedral Camps (£1,000);
◆ 1 x £2,000; 8 x £1,000 and 3 x £500 grants to churches.

Most of the 162 grants made during the year were for either £500 or £1,000, although there was one of £10,000 to the Tyne and Wear Foundation, completing a five year commitment towards their start-up costs.

Grants of £5,000 were given to: Beamish Open Air Museum; Northern Sinfonia Development Appeal; Leonard Cheshire (local branch) Red Feather Appeal and the Marie Curie Foundation for Conrad House Hospice.

Grants are wide ranging e.g. at one quarterly meeting grants were given to: The Three C's South Shields (camping holidays for deprived children); Them Wifies (training weekend for women's group); Action on Disability (towards purchasing a van for assessing disabled drivers).

Grants are made to individuals via various organisations – social services, relief agencies, disability aid funds, citizens advice bureaux and probation services amongst others.

Exclusions: General appeals from large national organisations and smaller bodies working outside the beneficial area.

Applications: In writing to the correspondent setting out details of the project and the proposed funding. Applications are considered at meetings usually held in October, January, March and July each year, or as otherwise required.

The Hamamelis Trust

c/o Penningtons, Highfield, Brighton Road, Godalming GU7 1NS
Tel: 01483- 423003
Contact: Mrs F Collins, Secretary
Trustees: Michael Fellingham; C I Slocock; Dr Leslie Martin; Duncan Stewart.
Grant total: £135,000 (1995/96)
Beneficial area: UK, but with a special interest in the Godalming and Surrey areas.

Although the trust is a general trust, the trustees have followed the settlor's known interests in medical research and conservation of the countryside, each interest receiving half the grant-aid. Grants are for specific projects and usually in units of £5,000 or £10,000.

In 1995/96, the trust had assets of £1.8 million and an income of £92,000. Grant-aid totalled £135,000 and was given in 25 grants which ranged from £2,000 to £10,000. The four £10,000 grants were to Royal Botanic Garden, Edinburgh, Wey & Arun Canal Trust, Wexham Trust and Wiltshire Wildlife Trust. Recipients of lesser grants relevant to this guide included BTCV, Gaia Trust and Shropshire Ornithological Society.

In previous years the trust gave £112,000 in 32 grants which generally ranged from £500 to £10,000. These included:
◆ Durham Wildlife Trust (£10,000);
◆ Woodland Trust (£7,500);
◆ Magog Trust, Surrey Farming & Wildlife, Council for National Parks, BTCV, Royal National Rose Society (£5,000).

Exclusions: Projects outside the UK are not considered.

Applications: To the correspondent. All applicants are asked to include a short synopsis of the application along with any published material and references. Unsuccessful appeals will not be replied to. The trustees usually meet twice a year to consider applications.

Medical applications are assessed by Dr Leslie Martin, one of the trustees, who is medically qualified.

The Lennox Hannay Charitable Trust

25 Copthall Avenue, London EC2R 7DR
Tel: 0171-638 5858
Contact: Robert Fleming Trustee Co Limited

Trustees: Robert Fleming Trustee Co Limited; Walter L Hannay; Caroline F Wilmot-Sitwell.
Grant total: £126,000 (1995/96)
Beneficial area: UK.

In 1995/96 the trust had assets of £7.2 million, an income of £283,000 and gave 56 grants totalling £126,000. They ranged between £200 to £12,000, with most between £1,000 to £9,000.

Eight grants relevant to this guide totalled over £12,000 and were given to:
◆ Countryside Foundation (£8,000);
◆ CPRE, The National Trust (£1,000 each);
◆ Tewkesbury Abbey (£750);
◆ Gloucester Wild Appeal, APT Design & Development, Snowshill Parochial Church Council (£500 each);
◆ St Lawrence Bourton on the Hill (£200).

All beneficiaries had also been supported in the preceding year.

Exclusions: No individuals or non registered charities.

Applications: In writing to the correspondent.

Miss K M Harbinson's Charitable Trust

190 Vincent Street, Glasgow G2 5SP
Tel: 0141-204 2833
Contact: The Secretary
Trustees: A Maguire; G C Harbinson; R Harbinson.
Grant total: £171,000 (1993/94)
Beneficial area: UK and overseas, but with a preference for Scotland.

The trust had assets of £4.2 million in 1993/94 which generated an income of £180,000 from which 49 grants totalling £171,000 were given, ranging between £1,000 and £9,000.

Grants relevant to this guide included:
◆ ITDG, Marie Stopes International (£9,000 each);

- John Muir Trust, Scottish Wildlife Trust, (£2,000 each).

It is also known that the RSPB and WWF UK received support during 1994/95.

Applications: In writing to the correspondent.

The R J Harris Charitable Settlement

Messrs Thrings & Long, Midland Bridge, Bath BA1 2HQ
Tel: 01225-448494
Contact: J J Thring, Secretary
Trustees: H M Newton-Clare, Chairman; T C M Stock; J L Rogers; A Pitt.
Grant total: £73,000 (1996/97)
Beneficial area: UK, with a preference for West Wiltshire and North Wiltshire, South of the M4.

In 1996/97, the trust had assets of £1.48m and an income of £67,000 from which 90 grants totalling £73,000 were given, ranging between £100 and £5,000. The trust appears to support mainly south–west based organisations, particularly in the Avon and Wiltshire area. Unusually, very few grants are given to large, well-known national charities. Grants were categorised by the trust as follows: Grants are given to a wide range of charitable activities and its categorisation of grants includes two groupings relevant to this guide:
1. Nature Conservation – Archaeology.
2. Building Restoration & General Environment.

No grants were given to the former in 1996/97.£9,400 (13% of total grant aid) was given to the latter. No details of beneficiaries were available.

Grants in earlier years relevant to this guide were given:

In 1994/95 -
- Bath Abbey Trust (£5,000 and in the previous 2 years);
- 2 grants to local churches;

In 1993/94 -
- Wiltshire Farming & Wildlife Advisory Group (£1,000 with £1,500 in the previous year);
- National Trust, Parnham Trust, Holy Trinity church Trowbridge (£500 each).

Applications: In writing to the correspondent. Trustees meet three times each year.

W G Harvey's Discretionary Settlement

1a Gibsons Road, Stockport SK4 4JX
Contact: F A Sherring
Trustees: F R Shackleton; F A Sherring.
Grant total: £28,000 (1996/97)

The settlement promotes the well-being of and prevention of cruelty to animals & birds.

In 1996/97 the settlement had assets of £726,000 and an income of £29,000. It has a set pattern of giving. In 1996/97 eight grants were given, five of which were for animal welfare. Three grants totalling £8,500 were relevant to this guide:
- Care for the Wild Defence Fund (£4,000 and in the previous year);
- Wildfowl & Wetlands Trust for Martin Mere (£3,500 and in the previous year);
- Three Owls Bird Sanctuary and Reserve (£1,000 and in the previous year).

Applications: In writing to the correspondent but note above. They are unlikely to give to any new charities.

The Havenhope Trust

Hope Farm, The Haven, Billingshurst, West Sussex RH14 9BN
Contact: B L Murgatroyd
Trustees: B L Murgatroyd; Mrs A V O Murgatroyd.
Grant total: £11,000 (1994/95)

In 1994/95 the trust had an income of £12,000 and gave grants of £11,000. No list of its grants has been submitted with its accounts on file at the Charity Commission since 1991/92 when £18,000 was disbursed and four grants totalling £5,200 (28% of grant-aid) were relevant to this guide:

- National Trust (£3,000);
- Woodland Trust (£1,500);
- Boxgrove Church appeal (£500);
- Farming & Wildlife Advisory Group (£200).

The Hayward Foundation

45 Harrington Gardens, London SW7 4JU
Tel: 0171-370 7063
Contact: Mark T Schnebli, Administrator
Trustees: I F Donald, Chairman; Sir Jack Hayward; G J Hearne; Mrs S J Heath; Dr J C Houston; C W Taylor; J N van Leuven.
Grant total: £918,000 (1995)
Beneficial area: UK.

The main interests of the foundation are medical research, and social welfare, in particular projects dealing with people with special needs. Around 60 grants are given yearly for capital projects, generally one-off, and they range from £500 to £50,000. Most grants are for £10,000 or more.

"The arts and conservation form a small part of the foundation's budget, together with education, and the trustees have supported specific projects and will continue to do so."

"Priority is given to applications seeking capital grants and the trustees make grants for revenue and other recurring costs only in exceptional circumstances. The trustees are anxious not to take over duties of the state or local authority where these statutory organisations are withdrawing from these activities. "The growing practice of establishing contracts between local authorities and charities who are service providers has made itself felt, and where trustees have been approached to provide capital funding to such organisations, so as to make their tenders to local authorities more competitive, these have been turned down. The trustees of the foundation feel that the greatest support should go to those

organisations which can demonstrate a truly voluntary and charitable input where people freely give of their time and effort."

In 1995, the foundation had assets of over £27 million. From an income of £2.5 million, £918,000 was committed in 55 grants (552 applications were received). The list of grants in the 1995 accounts showed 67 grants paid out during that year totalling £918,000. The South-East had half of the grants.

Few grants relevant to this guide were given in 1995:

- Exploratory, Bristol (£15,000);
- Avoncroft Museum Development Trust (£640).

Exclusions: The trustees do not make grants to individuals nor for revenue, holidays, travel, churches, expeditions, vehicles, general appeals, deficit funding and what is properly the responsibility of a statutory body.

Applications: Applications should contain a brief outline of the benefits a grant would make, how many people will benefit or what savings would be achieved. A full set of the latest audited accounts must be included and the application signed by a trustee.

The trustees meet in January, April, July, and October.

The Headley Trust

See entry for the "Sainsbury Family Charitable Trusts"
Tel: 0171-410 0330
Contact: Michael Pattison
Trustees: Sir Timothy Sainsbury; Lady Susan Sainsbury; T J Sainsbury; J R Benson; Miss J Portrait.
Grant total: £3,901,000 grant approvals (1996)
Beneficial area: UK and overseas.

This trust shares a common administration with other Sainsbury family charitable trusts. It is regarded as being, among other things, a vehicle for some of the charitable interests of Sir Tim Sainsbury, the settlor of the trust. At the end of 1996 nearly 70% of the market value of the trust's investments (£62 million) was held in shares in J Sainsbury plc.

Support is given for social welfare, the arts, the environment, developing countries and education, with a reducing amount for medical work. No information is given with the 1996 annual report about the size of its grants but most are likely to be handsome gifts. The list of beneficiaries is an unusual combination of the mainstream and of lesser known organisations. Its grants are listed under programme headings and the totals given to each category remained similar for five years until 1996. Then nearly two thirds of approved funding was directed to arts and the environment.

Garden, Edinburgh; Woodland Trust. In addition regular support is given to cathedrals (six grants in 1996) and also to parish churches of architectural merit in small rural villages (52 in 1996).

Arts and the Environment (overseas)

Grants of relevance to this guide included:
- Church of St Saviour, Riga
- Croatian National Heritage Fund
- Sychrov Castle and Park, North Bohemia

Grants in the previous year included: Margaret Mee Amazon Trust; World Monuments Fund; School for Restoration and Conservation, Czech Republic; International Trust for Croatian Monuments; London Garden, Jerusalem. A grant was also given under "Developing countries" to Wateraid.

	1996	1995
Arts & environment (home)	£2,475,000 (63 %)	£575,000 (28%)
Arts & environment (overseas)	£105,000 (3%)	£137,000 (7%)
Health &social welfare	£753,000 (19 %)	£615,000 (30%)
Education	£282,000 (7%)	£151,000 (7%)
Developing countries	£193,000 (5%)	£351,000 (17%)
Medical	£93,000 (2%)	£238,000 (12%)
Total	£3,901,000	£2,068,000

The average grant size is about £20,000 in most categories, but there may be a wide variation. The cursory 1996 trustees' report notes that "many grants are payable over several years". Grants are given to national, regional and local organisations.

Arts and the Environment (home)

Only 25 of the beneficiaries were named in the annual report. These included the following with relevance to this guide:
- Kemp Town Conservation Society
- National Trust Scotland
- Parnham Trust
- All Saints, Hove
- St Barnabas, Hove.

Grants in the previous year included: Pinder Recreational Trust; Royal Botanic

Exclusions: No grants direct to individuals.

Applications: An application to one of the Sainsbury family trusts is an application to all (see the entry under "Sainsbury Family Trusts" for further information). However, it is emphasised that "unsolicited applications are rarely successful". Nevertheless there is nothing to stop applicants pointing the relevance of their project to other activities previously funded by a Sainsbury foundation. The trustees of this particular trust only meet three times a year to consider disbursements, so the process of grant approval is unlikely to be rapid, though the staff may have discretion to give approval for very small grants.

The Mrs C S Heber Percy Charitable Trust

c/o Kleinwort Benson Trustees Ltd,
PO Box 191, 10 Fenchurch Street,
London EC3M 3LB
Tel: 0171-956 6600
Contact: The Secretary
Trustees: Mrs C S Heber Percy; A C
Heber Percy.
Grant total: £50,000 (1995/96)
Beneficial area: UK, with a particular
interest in Gloucester, and overseas.

In 1995/96 the trust had assets of £1.3
million and an income of £73,000 from
which 35 grants totalling £50,000 were
given. These ranged between £100 and
£20,000. The trust has a current policy to
give preference to charities local to them
in Gloucestershire It also appears to have a
particular interest in medical, elderly and
overseas causes. In 1995/96 the largest
grant was given to Life Education Centres
which also received £80,000 from capital
for their work relating to alcohol abuse.

Six grants were relevant to this guide and
totalled nearly £6,000 (12 % of grant aid):
♦ WWF UK (£2,000 with £3,000 in the
  preceding year);
♦ Woodland Trust (£2,000);
♦ St Peter's Upper Slaughter (£1,000);
♦ St Michaels (£500);
♦ Save the Rhino, Friends of Macintyre
  Tall Trees (£200 each).

Exclusions: Individuals are not supported.

Applications: To the correspondent in
writing.

The Hedley Foundation Ltd

9 Dowgate Hill, London EC4R 2SU
Contact: P T Dunkerley, Secretary
Trustees: P H Byam-Cook, President; C
H W Parish, Chairman; Sir Christopher
Airy; D V Fanshawe; P Holcroft; N H
Pakenham Mahon; J F M Rodwell.

Grant total: £868,000 (1995/96)
Beneficial area: UK.

The foundation supports "education,
training and welfare of young people,
provision of specialist medical
equipment, construction of new hospices
and initial funding for specialist nursing
schemes. Additionally some appeals can
be accepted which support disabled
people and Christian church community
projects".

A small number of grants were given
outside its main policy areas to church
restoration organisations, conservation
work and arts activities.

In 1994/95 the foundation had assets of
over £19 million generating an income of
£1.4 million from which about 250
donations of £868,000 were made. Most
grants were between £1,000 and £5,000.
(Some organisations received multiple
grants which totalled more than £10,000.)

Sixteen grants were relevant to this guide
in 1995/96 and totalled £34,000 (4% of
grant-aid):
♦ National Trust Scotland, North
  Kensington Canalside Trust (£5,000
  each);
♦ Dorchester Abbey, Hebridean Trust,
  Lincoln's Inn Heritage Fund (£3,000
  each);
♦ Cathedral Camps (£2,000 given over
  several years);
♦ Country Trust, Dorset Expeditionary
  Society, Pensthorpe Waterfowl Trust
  (£2,000 each);
♦ Friends of Kent Churches (£1,000 and
  in the previous year);
♦ Chichester Cathedral, Friends of New
  River Walk, Gardening for the
  Disabled, Insh Village church,
  Nantwich Church Appeal, Rochester
  Cathedral (£1,000 each).

As conservation and the environment is
not a priority the giving is variable- in the
previous year only seven relevant grants
totalling £9,000 were given.

Exclusions: Grants cannot be made to
overseas charities or, under any
circumstances, to individuals.

Applications: In writing to the correspondent enclosing accounts. Applications are processed monthly.

The G D Herbert Charitable Trust

Tweedie & Prideaux Solicitors, 5 Lincoln's Inn Fields, London WC2A 3BT
Tel: 0171-2429231
Contact: J J H Burden, Trustee
Trustees: M E Beaumont; J J H Burden.
Grant total: £49,000 (1994/95)
Beneficial area: UK and overseas.

In 1994/95, the trust £47,000 made 30 grants £48,000. Most of the grants were for £1,500. A few larger grants of £3,000 were given. The trust supports a regular list of beneficiaries and there seems little leeway for new applications.

Grants relevant to this guide totalling £8,000 (16% of grant-aid) were given in 1994/95 to:
- National Trust (£3,000);
- CPRE, Canterbury Oast Trust, Woodland Trust (£1,500);
- Wiltshire Trust (£500).

Applications: In writing to the correspondent. No applications are invited other than from those charities currently supported by the trust.

The Heritage of London Trust Ltd

Room 110a, 23 Saville Row, London W1X 1AB
Tel: 0171-973 3809; Fax: 0171-973 3792
Contact: Julian Spicer, Director
Trustees: Board of Management: Chairman; Giles Shepard; Vice Chairman, Sir Hugh Cubitt; and eighteen others.
Grant total: £93,000 (1996/97)
Beneficial area: Greater London.

The principal activity of the charity is to support the conservation and restoration of buildings of architectural and historical interest in Greater London. It was founded in 1981. It is both a fundraising and a grant-making charitable company.

With the demise of the GLC, the trust lost its main public sector support which has been partly replaced by assistance from the London Boroughs Grants Scheme and links have been made with London boroughs, most of which are affiliated to the trust. It receives technical and administrative support from English Heritage. As part of its fundraising the trust is prepared to handle donations earmarked for particular areas, or types of scheme or scheme. One of its objectives is to extend its programme to the widest spread of London boroughs and local heritage trusts. Camden, Croydon, Merton, Westminster and Kensington & Chelsea have given funds devoted to their boroughs. Working relationships are forged with similar trusts and some City livery companies. The trust aims to obtain partners to match their own contribution wherever possible. The trust now finds it has an increased role as advisor and supporter for applicants for Heritage Lottery bids.

Grants given are rarely more than £10,000 and usually averaging around £5,000. It has assisted churches, churchyards, cemeteries, museums, galleries, theatres, art centres, hospitals, hostels, homes, schools, colleges, fountains, monuments and statues, clocks, gazeboes, wall paintings, historic garden cabmen's shelters, and so on.

In 1995/96, the trust had assets of £539,000 and an income of £317,000, and received £51,000 in grants/donations (half the sum of the previous year), of which £14,000 was a continuing sum from London Borough Grants Scheme for administration. £35,000 was spent on consultancy fees. Grants agreed since September 1996 include:
- St. Pancras Waterpoint, Camden; The Albert Memorial, (£5,000 each);
- The Weavers' Charity Almshouses, Wanstead, (£3,500);
- The Temple, Wanstead, (£3,000);
- St. Luke's Church, West Holloway. (£2,500).

Applications: In writing to the correspondent, after which a site visit may be made. Board meetings are held 3 times a year.

The Lady Hind Trust

c/o Eversheds, 1 Royal Standard Place, Nottingham NG1 6FZ
Tel: 0115- 950 7000
Contact: The Trustees
Trustees: Charles Barratt; William Whysall; Nigel Savory; Timm Farr.
Grant total: £281,000 (1996)
Beneficial area: England and Wales only, with a preference for Nottinghamshire and Norfolk.

The accounts at the Charity Commission in the winter of 1997 showed that the trust had assets of some £6 million at the end of 1995.

There has been no list of grants with the accounts since 1987 when the first edition of this guide was researched. Then grants were given either to national organisations or local organisations in Norfolk and Nottinghamshire. Parish church appeals were rarely supported unless in these two counties. In 1987 eight grants (out of 155) were relevant to this guide and totalled £33,000. Of these six were for the architectural heritage and included:
- Norwich Historic Churches Trust (£15,000);
- Thornage Hall Appeal (£12,500);
- Woodland Trust (£1,000);
- Stonebridge City Farm (£500).

Exclusions: Individuals.

Applications: Applications, in writing and with accounts, must be submitted two months in advance of meetings in March, June, September and December. Unsuccessful applicants are not notified.

Historic Churches Preservation Trust
(with the Incorporated Church Building Society)

Fulham Palace, London SW6 6EA.
Tel and Fax: 0171-736 3054
Contact: Michael Tippen, Secretary.

Trustees: Joint Presidents: The Archbishops of Canterbury and York. Chairman: Lord Nicholas Gordon Lennox.
Grant total: approx. £650,000 in grants and £200,000 in loans (1995/96)
Beneficial area: England and Wales.

The trust was set up in 1953 following a report which found a serious decline in church maintenance and repair caused by the virtual cessation of work on historic churches for several decades during the 1930's recession and during and after the war. It is a national, non-denominational charity which relies entirely on voluntary support and aims to provide funds to bridge the gap between the money raised within the local community and the total cost of the repair work. It is also responsible for the administration of the Incorporated Church Building Society (ICBS), which makes interest-free loans and complements the help given by the HCPT.

There are also 33 County Historic Churches Trusts which are independent charities raising money and helping repair churches and chapels within their own boundaries. (See separate entry under Historic Churches Trusts (Local), for full list of addresses.) They have no financial links with the HCPT, although in many cases the HCPT, the ICBS and the county HCT may help the same church.

Churches are considered for financial aid on condition that:
- they are at least 100 years old and in regular use as places of public Christian worship (but not a cathedral) and likely to remain so for at least 5 years
- they are in England, Wales, the Channel Islands or the Isle of Man
- the PCC has insufficient funds to carry out the repairs
- they are properly insured
- they have generally not received financial aid from the trust or ICBS within the last 3 years
- work has not started or been completed before the specification has been reviewed.

The proposed work must be:
- specified, directed and certified by a chartered architect

- to the fabric of the church and authorised by Faculty or Archdeacon's Certificate
- carried out in accordance with the specification

Churches must be of historic or architectural interest, and repairs must be carried out "using traditional methods and materials which are in sympathy with the character and quality of the building". The trust has helped Roman Catholic churches and historic Non-conformist meeting houses and chapels as well as Church of England parish churches.

The trust had assets of £4.2 million in 1995/96 generating a total income of £876,000 which included a significant contribution from legacies.

The HCPT helped 320 churches in 1994/95. Grants ranged from £250 to £6,000 and loans between £400 and £6,000. The maximum figure for both donations and loans was lower than in previous years when £10,000 had been awarded. About a quarter of all beneficiaries received both grants and loans, three receiving the maximum sum for both grants and loans.

Exclusions: The HCPT and ICBS will not fund re-ordering; church clocks; heating & lighting; stained glass; furniture and fittings; organ repair; murals; monuments; decoration (except in the wake of repair work); re-wiring; churchyards & walls; work that has already been started or completed.

Applications: A written approach should be made in the first instance to seek a preliminary assessment. The case is then referred to a Diocesan Advisory Committee. With its recommendation secured, an application form is sent with which full specifications etc. are required. Trustees meet in March, May and November.

Historic Churches Trusts (local)

The names and addresses of the 35 county level churches trusts follow:

Bedfordshire & Hertfordshire Historic Churches Trust
Mr Tomlins, 80 Beaumont Avenue, St Albans, Herts, AL1 4TP Tel: 01727 853933

Royal County of Berkshire Churches Trust
Mr Stebbings, 6 Whitelands Drive, Mill Road, Ascot, Berks, SL5 8LR

Buckinghamshire Historic Churches Trust
Mrs Keens, The Pound House, Wicken, Milton Keynes, Bucks, MK19 6BN Tel: 01908 571232

Cambridgeshire Historic Churches Trust
Mr Walker, 14 Clay Street, Histon, Cambs, CB4 4EY Tel: 01223 234150

Historic Cheshire Churches Preservation Trust
Mr Cummings, Birch Cullimore & Co., 20 White Friars, Chester, Cheshire, CH1 1XS Tel: 01244 321066

Cornwall Historic Churches Trust
Mr Purser, 17 Higher Trehaverne, Truro, Cornwall, TR1 3PW Tel: 01872 74081

Derbyshire Historic Churches & Chapels Trust
Mr Mallender, 35 St Mary's Gate, Derby, Derbyshire, DE1 3JU

Devon Historic Churches Trust
Mr Plumbley, Jarrah, Broadpath, Stoke Gabriel, Devon, TQ9 6SQ Tel: 01803 782444

Dorset Historic Churches Trust
Mr McClintock, Lower Westport, Wareham, Dorset, BH20 4PR Tel: 01929 553252

Friends of Essex Churches
Mrs Blaxhall, Box F E C, Guy Harlings, 53 New Street, Chelmsford, Essex, CM1 1AT Tel: 01245 354745

Gloucestershire Historic Churches Preservation Trust
Mr Page, 7 Dollar Street, Cirencester, Glos, GL7 2AS Tel: 01285 650000

Hampshire & The Island Historic Churches Trust
Mr Woods, Secretary Winchester DAC, Church House, 9 The Close, Winchester
Tel: 01962 844644

Herefordshire Historic Churches Trust
Mrs Gallimore, Orchard House, Credenhill, Hereford, HR4 7DA
Tel: 01432 760304

Friends of Kent Churches
N Whithead, Beemans, High Street, Cranbrook, Kent, TN17 3DT

Leicestershire Historic Churches Trust
Lay Canon Cocks, 24 Beresford Drive, Leicester, LE2 3LA Tel: 01533 703424

Lincolnshire Old Churches Trust
Lt Cdr Rodwell, Lincolnshire Old Churches Trust, PO Box 195, Lincoln, Lincs, LN5 9XU

Norfolk Churches Trust Ltd
Mr Fisher, 7 The Old Church, St Matthews Road, Norwich, Norfolk, NR1 1SP Tel: 01603 767576

Northamptonshire Historic Churches Trust
Mr White, 7 Spencer Parade, Northampton, Northants, NN1 5AB
Tel: 01604 233233

Northumbria Historic Churches Trust
Rev Canon Ruscoe, The Vicarage, South Hylton, Sunderland, SR4 0QB

Nottinghamshire Historic Churches Trust
Mr Stewart, c/o Mark Stewart Associates, 34a Musters Road, West Bridgford, Notts
Tel: 0115 9455787

Oxfordshire Historic Churches Trust
Mr Lethbridge, Fawler Manor, Charlbury, Oxford, OX7 3AH Tel: 01993 891373

Romney Marsh Historic Churches Trust
Mrs Marshall, Lansdell House, Rolvnden, Nr Cranbrook, Kent, TN17 4LW
Tel: 01580 241529

Rutland: Historic Churches Trust
Mrs Worrall, 6 Redland Close, Barrowden, Oakham, Rutland, LE15 8ES
Tel: 0157 287302

Shropshire Historic Churches Trust
The Ven G Frost, The Archdeacon of Salop, Tong Vicarage, Shifnal, Shropshire, TF11 Tel: 01902 372622.

The Dorothy Holmes Charitable Settlement

c/o Smallfield, Cody & Co, 5 Harley Place, Harley Street, London WIN 1HB
Contact: The Correspondent
Trustees: D S Roberts; S C Roberts; B M Cody; M E A Cody.
Grant total: £34,000 (1995/96)
Beneficial area: UK, with an interest in Dorset (Poole) and Wales.

The settlement assists a wide range of charitable activities with churches and the environment stated as amongst its interests.

In 1994/95 the settlement had assets of £595,000 and an income of £61,000 from which grants totalling £34,000.

A large number (100) of small donations were made, mostly of £100 to £500. Only one grant was larger with a single largest grant of £1,000. Several grants are recurrent.

About ten grants relevant to this guide were given in 1994/95 totalling £2,000 (7% of grant-aid):
- BTCV, FoE, Greenpeace (£200 each);
- Seven grants given to churches generally of £200 each.

Applications: In writing to the correspondent.

P H Holt Charitable Trust

India Buildings, Liverpool, Merseyside L2 0RB
Tel: 0151-473 4693; Fax: 0151-473 4663
Contact: Roger Morris, Secretary
Trustees: J Utley; J Allan; D Morris; T Boyce: T Marshall; K Wright
Grant total: About £300,000
Beneficial area: UK, with a preference for Merseyside.

The trust makes a very large number of mostly small grants, about three quarters of them in Merseyside. However a few large grants of up to £100,000 are also made, but they are normally payable over several years. The one-off gifts and the subscriptions were up to a maximum of £3,000 in Merseyside and £5,000 elsewhere. The period gifts ranged up to £10,000 a year over anything up to 10 years.

Grants relevant to this guide totalling over £8,000 (3% of total grant-aid) were given in 1995/96 to:

Subscriptions -
- RSPB (£1,000);
- Merseyside Building Preservation Trust (£750);
- CPRE, CPRW, Friends of the Lake District, John Muir Trust (£250 each);
- Ancient Monuments Society, Historic Churches Preservation Trust, Society for the Protection of Ancient Buildings (£200 each);

Other -
- Survival International (£1,000);
- Merseyside Environmental Trust (£800);
- Wildfowl & Wetlands Trust (£600);
- Northamptonshire Historic Churches Trust, Painshill Park Trust, Scottish Wildlife Trust (£500 each);
- Liverpool Environment Forum (£400);
- Orton Trust, Upper Severn Navigation Trust (£250).

Exclusions: No grants to individuals.

Applications: In writing to the correspondent at any time.

The Cuthbert Horn Trust

Royal Sun Alliance Trust Co. Ltd.,
40 Chancery Lane, London WC2A IJN
Tel: 0171-344 4188
Contact: S P Martin
Trustees: Alan H Flint; Alliance Assurance Co Limited.
Grant total: £65,000 (1996)
Beneficial area: UK.

In 1995 the trust had assets of £1.4 million, an income of £71,000 and gave 17 grants totalling £51,000, a considerable increase on its previous grant totals of £28,000 (1994) and £26,000 (1993).

The trust is a regular supporter of a wide range of environmental interests.

Thirteen grants totalling over £30,000 (60 % of grant-aid) were relevant to this guide in 1995:
- Wildfowl & Wetlands Trust (£12,000 with £5,000 and £1,500 in the 2 preceding years);
- National Trust (£5,000);
- Cotswold Canals Trust, Soil Association (£2,000 each and both given support in the 2 previous years);
- Bioregional Development Group, British Butterfly Conservation, Gaia Trust, SAFE, Staffordshire Wildlife (£2,000 each);
- Campaign for the Protection of Rural Wales (£1,000 and in the 2 preceding years);
- Charleston Farm House Trust, Farms for City Children (£1,000 each);
- Centre for Alternative Technology (£500).

Exclusions: No grants are made to individuals.

Applications: In writing to the correspondent.

Mrs E G Hornby's Charitable Settlement

Kleinwort Benson Trustees Ltd,
P O Box 191, 10 Fenchurch Street,
London EC3M 3LB
Tel: 0171-956 6600
Contact: Christopher Gilbert, Secretary
Trustees: N J M Lonsdale; Mrs P M W Smith Maxwell.
Grant total: £51,000 (1995/96)
Beneficial area: UK.

In January 1996 the settlement had assets of £1.4 million and a net income of £50,000. It made 25 grants ranging between £300 and £10,000 most of which were over £1,000.

It appears to support a number of organisations on a regular basis with little leeway for new applicants. Grants relevant

to this guide in 1995/96 totalled over £12,000 (24% of grant-aid) and included:
- Countryside Foundation (£10,000 with grants of £1,300 in the 2 previous year;
- Irish Draught Horse Society (£1,500 also given in the 2 previous years);
- Population Concern (£1,000 also given in the 2 previous years).

Exclusions: Individuals.

Applications: In writing to the correspondent, but see above. Trustees meet annually in March, but applications are considered throughout the year.

The John & Ruth Howard Charitable Trust

111 High Road, Willesden Green, London NW10 2TB
Tel: 0181-459 1125
Contact: Alec S Atchison, Chairman
Trustees: Alec S Atchison; John H Hillier; Nina Feldman; Richard Hobson.
Grant total: £59,000 (1993/94)
Beneficial area: England.

The trust was set up in 1991 with a £127,000 endowment and received a further £350,000 over the following year from the estates of J H Howard and Mrs R M Howard. The aim of the trust is to spread its support equally across four specified areas: archaeology; church music; preservation and protection of public buildings, and general charitable causes. Grants can only be given to organisations in England.

Grants are not usually evenly spread across the four specified areas in any one year. Sometimes sums may be promised on condition that further sums are raised by the recipient, or that work is completed to a point where the publication of results can be guaranteed.

In 1994/95, grants were given totalling £55,000 (£59,000 in 1993/94):
- Archaeology (£7,000; £33,000 in 1993/94)
- Buildings (£13,000; £9,000 in 1993/94)
- Choral (£20,000; £3,500 in 1993/94)
- General (£14,000 in both years).

Exclusions: No grants to large appeals.

Applications: In writing to the correspondent.

The Idlewild Trust

54-56 Knatchbull Road, London SE5 9QY
Tel: 0171-274 2266
Contact: Ms Victoria Haire, Administrator.
Trustees: Dr G W Beard, Chairman; Mrs Peter B Minet; Mrs F L Morrison-Jones; Mrs A C Grellier; Lady Judith Goodison; M H Davenport; Mrs A S Bucks; J C Gale.
Grant total: £218,000 (1996)
Beneficial area: UK.

In 1996, the trust had assets of £1.8 million and an income of £188,000. Grants ranging from £500 to £10,000 and totalling £218,000 were given to 74 organisations.

They were categorised as follows (% of grant-aid shown):
- Preservation & Restoration £82,000 25 grants (34%)
- Conservation £4,500 2 grants (3%)
- Museums & Galleries £43,000 10 grants (13%)
- Performing Arts £51,000 21 grants (28%)
- Education £24,000 13 grants (18%)
- Fine Art £12,000 2 grants (3%)
- Victoria & Albert Museum £10,000;
- English National Opera £5,000;
- Brighton Festival Society £5,000;
- National Youth Dance Trust £2,000;
- St Tegan's Church, Llandegai £2,000;
- Trestle Theatre Co. £1,000;
- Edward Barnsley Educational Trust £1,000.

In previous years the balance of giving has been more in favour of the performing arts.

Exclusions: Grants to registered charities only. No grants are made to individuals. The trust will not give to:

- Repetitive nationwide appeals by large charities for large sums of money;
- Appeals where all, or most of, the beneficiaries reside outside the UK;
- Appeals in respect of church or school buildings where the buildings have no distinctive and outstanding merit, except where the school provides very specialised training;
- Parochial appeals. In this context, parochial means that all, or most of, the beneficiaries reside within the applicant's immediate locality;
- Appeals from organisations whose sole or main purpose is to make grants out of the funds which they collect;
- Appeals received from an organisation within 12 months of a previous grant;
- Research grants, deficit funding or endowment funding.

Applications: In writing to the correspondent, including the last audited accounts. There is no formal application form. Meetings are usually held in April, August and December. Only successful applications will be acknowledged unless an sae is enclosed.

The Iliffe Family Charitable Trust

Barn Close, Yattendon, Newbury, Berks RG18 0UY
Tel: 01635-201255
Contact: J R Antipoff
Trustees: N G E Petter; J R Antipoff; Lord Iliffe.
Grant total: £116,000 (1995/96)
Beneficial area: UK.

In 1996 the trust had assets of over £1 million which generated in income of £150,000. Detailed information about the previous year, when £145,000 was disbursed in grant-aid, has shown that 79 grants were made ranging from less than £100 to £25,000. Only 29 were for £1,000 or more. The majority were for a few hundred pounds.

Ten grants totalling over £53,000 (37% of grant-aid) were relevant to this guide:
- Pangbourne Chapel Trust (£25,000);
- Coventry Cathedral Development Trust (£20,000);
- Museum of Garden History (£3,000);
- Holy Trinity Development Trust (£2,000);
- Parnham Trust, Trinity Hospital Garden Appeal, Yattendon Church (£1,000 each);
- Yatt Parochial Church (£400);
- National Gardens Scheme (£100).

Applications: In writing to the correspondent. Only successful applications will be acknowledged. The trust did not wish for an entry in this guide.

The Incorporated Church Building Society
See Historic Churches Preservation Trust

The Inverforth Charitable Trust

The Farm, Northington, Alresford, Hampshire SO24 9TH
Tel: 01962-732205
Contact: Adam Lee, Secretary and Treasurer
Trustees: Elizabeth Lady Inverforth; Lord Inverforth; The Hon Mrs Jonathan Kane; Michael Gee.
Grant total: £210,000 (1996)
Beneficial area: UK and overseas, although almost entirely mainland Britain.

The trust only gives to national charities covering the whole of the UK or of national significance. It does not give to small, localised charities, though it is interested in small national charities. The trust has continued its recent policy of drawing on its capital to make donations in excess of income. Its assets of £2.919 million in 1996 generated a gross income of £191,000, whilst grants of £210,000 were made.

The trust makes a large number (192) of small grants. In 1996 only two were greater than £2,500. Grants were given for health and mental health, handicapped & aged, hospices, music & the arts, youth & education.

Grants relevant to this guide in 1996 totalled £5,000 (2% of total grant-aid) and were given to:
- Cathedral Camps, Sustrans, Young People's Trust for the Environment and Nature Conservation (£1,000);
- Almshouse Association, Hampshire Wildlife Trust, Plantlife, Wilts & Berks Canal Amenity Group (£500).

In the previous year the trust had allocated double this grant-aid to relevant groups.

Exclusions: No unconnected local churches, village halls, schools. No small or localised charities, etc. (A charity with a relevant place name or the work 'community' in its title will not be likely to qualify.) No animal charities. No branches or affiliated 'subsidiary' charities. Charities only, no individuals. No repeat applications within a year. These guidelines are strictly enforced, and non-qualifying applications are not reported to the trustees.

Applications: In writing to the correspondent at least one month before meetings. No special forms are necessary, although accounts are desirable. A summary is prepared for the trustees, who meet quarterly in March, June, September and early December. Replies are normally sent to all applicants; allow up to four months for an answer or grant.

The correspondent receives over 1,000 applications a year, and advises of a high failure rate for new applicants.

The J J Charitable Trust

See entry for the "Sainsbury Family Charitable Trusts"
Tel: 0171-410 0330
Contact: Michael Pattison
Trustees: John Julian Sainsbury; Mark Leonard Sainsbury; Miss J S Portrait.

Grant total: £200,000 grant approvals (1995/96)
Beneficial area: UK and overseas.

The trust is named after John Julian Sainsbury, the elder son of Lord Sainsbury of Preston Candover. It received gifts from him of £1.5 million in 1994/95 and £1.7 million in 1995/96, bringing the market value of the endowment to £5.8 million. None of the shares appear to be held in J Sainsbury plc.

Grants are made under the following headings (with number of approvals shown in brackets):

1995/96 1994/95
- Environment – UK and overseas £151,000 (9) £57,000 (6)
- Literacy Support £37,000 (3) £45,000 (4)
- General £13,000 (5) – – –
- Total £200,000 (17) £102,000 (10)

Grants relevant to this guide were made to support "environmental education in schools, sustainable transport schemes and demonstration projects, tree planting and rural conservation". Grant approvals relevant to this guide in 1995/96:
- FARM Africa, for a forestation project in Northern Tanzania (£35,000 over 3 years);
- Institute of Education, for extension of the Schools Network on Air Pollution project (SNAP) (£32,516 with £10,500 in the previous year);
- CPRE, towards a woodland protection project (£30,000);
- Woodland Trust, towards its treeplanting schemes (£15,000 with £5,000 in the previous year).
- Clarendon College/Nottingham City Council, for a pilot project to reduce car commuting (£11,030);
- Centre for Sustainable Energy, to continue the Young Energy savers primary school project (£10,500 with £14,000 in the previous year);
- BTCV for a volunteering programme for disadvantaged young people (£7,500);
- Environmental Education: Support for Teachers, for a project to identify high quality materials and raise teachers' awareness of key issues (£5,000);

- Bootstrap Enterprises, towards the Eco-kitchen at the Rubbish Dump environmental education project in Hackney (£4,000).
- A small grant was given under its "General" category to Save the Rhino Trust in Namibia (£500).

Grants in 1994/95 had also included:
- Plantlife 'Back from the Brink' project (£12,500);
- Friends of the Earth (£10,000); Homerton Grove Adventure Playground (£5,000 each).

Many of the beneficiaries were also supported by the two other trusts of which Lord Sainsbury's children as trustees – the Ashden and the Mark Leonard Charitable Trusts. Overlapping interests and support had also occurred with the trusts where Sir Timothy Sainsbury's children are trustees – the Staples, Glass-House and Tedworth trusts. These trusts are noteworthy for their interest in "progressive" environmental concerns rarely supported by other charitable trusts, such as renewable energy and transport.

Exclusions: No grants to individuals.

Applications: An application to one of the Sainsbury family trusts is an application to all. See entry under the "Sainsbury Family Trusts, for other trusts, the address and application procedure. Trustees meet five times a year.

The John Jarrold Trust

Messrs Jarrold & Sons, Whitefriars, Norwich NR3 1SH
Tel: 01603-660211
Contact: B Thompson, Secretary.
Trustees: R E Jarrold; A C Jarrold; P J Jarrold; Mrs D J Jarrold; Mrs J Jarrold; Mrs A G Jarrold; Mrs W A L Jarrold.
Grant total: £183,000 (1996/97) Funds available for distribution are dependent upon dividends received.
Beneficial area: UK and overseas, with a particular interest in East Anglia.

In 1996/97 the Trust gave 18 grants relevant to this guide totalling over £54,000 (30% of grant aid). They included:
- H J Sexton, Norwich Art Trust Assembly House Appeal (£25,000);
- Norfolk Heritage Fleet Trust (£7,000);
- Queens College, Cambridge (£5,000);
- Burlingham House (£3,000);
- National Trust, Enterprise Neptune, Holy Trinity Church, Norwich (£2,000 each);
- Norwich & Norfolk NNI Sad Association, Norman Community Church, St Michaels & All Angels, Aylesham, Round Church, Cambridge, Royal Society for the Protection of Birds, The Woodland Trust, Wymmdham Abbey. (£1,000 each);
- Norwich City Council, Guildhall Clock (£1,450);
- BTCV Norfolk (£500);
- Wensum Valley Project (£375);
- Coral Cay Conservation Trust (£300);
- Norfolk Museum Service – Team Panhard (£250).

In addition another 12 churches were supported with grants less than £1,000. Many small grants of £100/£150 were given to young people on various expeditions e.g. Health Project Abroad, GAP and Raleigh International.

Exclusions: Individual educational programmes outside the scope of the trust.

Applications: In writing to the correspondent.

Rees Jeffreys Road Fund

13 The Avenue, Chichester, West Sussex, PO19 4PX
Tel: 01243-787013
Contact: B Fieldhouse, Secretary
Trustees: P W Bryant, Chairman; M Milne; Dr S Glaister; M N T Cottell; Mrs June Bridgeman; Sir James Duncan; W H P Davison.
Grant total: £400,000 (1997)
Beneficial area: UK.

The objects of the fund are to:
- Support and promote research into road transport and related issues;
- Contribute to the training of transport specialists through post-graduate bursaries;
- Provide funding for key university transport posts;
- Improve the roadside environment and provide rest areas for motorists;
- Fund innovative projects aimed at improving facilities and safety for pedestrians and cyclists.

The fund had assets of £6.1 million at the end of 1996. This produced an income of £252,000, higher than in the previous two years. In 1996, £247,000 were distributed in the following way:
- Educational bursaries and support for universities £153,000;
- Research and other projects £64,000;
- Roadside rests £30,000.

"The trustees are anxious to avoid core funding...and seek to ensure their support is project based".

The fund has started to make three years agreements with the universities it supports in order "to encourage the universities concerned to enter into longer term planning with the hope that the lectureships can be on a permanent basis when the fund's pump priming ends". The fund supports a chair at Southampton lectureships at the Universities of Bristol, Nottingham, and at the Centre for Transport Studies of the University of London. Post-graduate bursaries are awarded in open competition on the recommendation of their prospective universities.

The Fund made grants of £10,000 to the British Road Federation to research into enhancing the environmental performance of the Existing Road Network and supported publications on Safe Motorway Driving and on Speed Control. A grant of £10,000 to study the Effect of Visual Impairment on Transport Behaviour was made to Napier University

Applications: There is no set form of application for grants. Brief details should be submitted initially. Replies are sent to all applicants.

The Jephcott Charitable Trust

Gappers Farm, Membury, Axminster, Devon EX13 7TX.
Contact: Mrs Meg Harris, Secretary
Trustees: N W Jephcott, Chairman; Mrs M Jephcott; Dr P Davis; Judge A North; Mrs A Morgan.
Grant total: £175,000 (1996/97 15 month period)
Beneficial area: UK, developing countries overseas.

The trust typically supports smaller national and international projects, or part of a project (that is under £500,000). Currently one of the areas of interest is the improvement of the quality of life of the poor and developing countries. Grants are usually for a specific project or part of a project. Core funding and/or salaries are rarely considered. "Pump-priming" donations are offered – usually small grants to new organisations and areas of work for short periods of time. Monitoring of how the grant is spent is usually required.

The trust's assets have risen to close on £3 million. Several of its grants in recent years have been clearly relevant to this guide. However it is often not possible to guess how much the motive to support a project is environmental compared with people-centred (if such a distinction can be made with much appropriate development work) e.g. Pahar Trust Nepal (£8,500) and Quaruru Bolivia and the Spice Islands Project (£1,000) all in 1994/95.

Grants in 1996/97 included:
- Water Aid Ghana (£12,000 with £10,000 in the previous year);
- International Research Association (£2,000).

A major grant of £25,000 was given to the Antartic Environment Project in 1993/94 with a grant of £5,000 to Population Control also.

Exclusions: No grants to individuals, including students, or for medical research. No response to general appeals from large, national organisations nor from organisations concerning themselves with poverty and education in the UK. Core funding and/or salaries are rarely considered.

Applications: Guidelines are available on request. Applications should be in writing using a brief application form at any time to the correspondent. Trustees meet twice a year.

The Jones 1986 Charitable Trust

Eversheds, 1 Standard Place, Nottingham NG1 2FZ
Tel: 0115-936 6000
Contact: The Secretary
Trustees: J O Knight; R B Stringfellow.
Grant total: £804,000 (1994/95)
Beneficial area: UK, especially Nottinghamshire.

The trust gives widely across the range of charitable activity and has a particular focus on work in Nottinghamshire. It was set up by Philip Locke Jones in 1986 without any endowment and receives most of its income each year from five family settlements (£52,000 in 1994/95). It has built up assets of over £1 million since it was set up and in 1994/95 had an income of £829,000.

The trust likes to give substantial grants to its own chosen activities. In 1994/95 a total of £804,000 was given in only 36 grants. Many of its beneficiaries are regularly supported with the largest recurrent grant given to Nottingham University for Nottingham Health Authority (£193,000).

Its grants relevant to this guide were also given to two long-standing beneficiaries. They totalled £61,000 (8% of grant-aid):
* Nottinghamshire Wildlife Trust (£51,000 with £55,000 and £43,000 in the 2 preceding years);

* Intermediate Technology (£10,000, also given in the preceding 3 years).

There also an interest in horses and donkeys with regular support for three sanctuaries/resthomes totalling £50,000 a year.

Potential applicants should bear in mind that the trustees select their own projects and to not wish to receive applications. They would prefer details of past grants not to be included so as not to encourage charities to make applications which "will inevitably fail".

Exclusions: No grants to individuals.

Applications: The trustees identify their own target charities and do not encourage or acknowledge any applications.

The Emmanuel Kaye Foundation

Messrs Gouldens, 22 Tudor Street, London EC4Y 0JJ
Tel: 0171-583 7777
Contact: D P H Burgess
Trustees: Sir Emmanuel Kaye; Lady Kaye; John Scriven; Michael Cutler.
Grant total: £24,000 (1995/96)
Beneficial area: UK and overseas.

The founder's personal interest was medical research and he funded research at two London teaching hospitals. The trust will probably follow that lead.

In the four years up to 1990, the trust's income consisted of a £10,000 donation, with grants being given up to this figure. Since then the trust has regularly received a donation taking its annual income to well over £100,000. It appears that the trust is building up its assets, with a consistent surplus of income over expenditure. By 1993/94, assets had increased to £646,000 which is held as cash at the bank, possibly for future large projects.

Annual grant-aid fluctuates markedly with donated in £24,000 in 1995/96 to 14 beneficiaries and £71,000 in 1994/95 to 40 beneficiaries. There were no grant schedules for either of these years with its accounts.

In 1993/94, the most recent year for which detailed information is on public file at the Charity Commission, the trust had an income of £147,000 including a further donation of £65,000. Its 40 grants totalled only £45,000 and 16 were for £1,000 up to £10,000.

Four grants were relevant to this guide in 1993/94 and totalled close to £8,000 (17% of grant-aid).
- Thames Salmon Trust (£3,750);
- BTCV (£3,000);
- British Friends of the Council for a Beautiful Israel, Population Concern (£500 each).

Applications: In writing to the correspondent.

The Robert Kiln Charitable Trust

15a Bull Plain, Hertford SG14 1DX
Contact: Mrs Margaret Archer
Trustees: Mrs S F Chappell; S W J Kiln; Mrs B Kiln; Dr N P Akers; Mrs J E Akers; G M Kiln.
Grant total: £67,000 (1996/97)
Beneficial area: UK, with a special interest in Hertfordshire and Bedfordshire.

The trust was formed in 1970 by Robert Kiln, a Lloyd's underwriter, and the six present trustees are all members of his family. The trust supports organisations concerned with archaeology, environmental conservation and musical education. Grants are usually one-off or instalments for particular projects. Salaries are not considered. Grants generally range from £100 to £1,000.

In 1996/97 a total of over 60 grants were made ranging between £100 and £6,200. Nearly £20,000 (30% of total grant-aid) was given in 19 donations to archaeological and conservation work and included:
- Hertfordshire Archaeological Trust (£2,400);
- University of Newcastle (Archaeology Dept), University of Sheffield

(Archaeology Dept) (£2,000 each);
- East Herts Archaeological Society, (£1,000);
- Herts & Middx Wildlife Trust, Intermediate Technology, Rugby Archaeological Society (£500 each);
- Woodland Trust (£400);
- Agroforestry Research Trust, Devon, Chiltern Woodlands Project, High Wycomb, Raptor Rescue, Hertfordshire (£250 each);
- Wildfowl & Wetlands Trust (£200).

The trust supports a wide range of causes, local, national and international, with a preference for Hertfordshire and Bedfordshire-based organisations, some of which appear to be regular beneficiaries.

Exclusions: Applications from individuals, churches, schools or artistic projects (e.g. theatre groups) will not be considered. The trust will no longer acknowledge receipt of applications.

Applications: In writing to the correspondent, setting out as much information as seems relevant and, if possible, costings and details of any other support. Two distribution meetings are held a year, usually in Jan/Feb and July/August.

The Kintore Charitable Trust

Messrs Dundas & Wilson, Saltire Crescent, 20 Castle Terrace, Edinburgh EH1 2EN
Contact: The trustees
Trustees: The Countess of Kintore; Dundas & Wilson.
Grant total: £48,000 (1994/95)
Beneficial area: Scotland with a preference for Grampian.

The trust awards grants to projects involving young people, environmental groups and local projects in the Grampian area.

The trust's assets at the end of March 1995 were £438,260 which had generated an income of £53,346 from which 34 grants totalling £48,000 were given (£24,400 in 1993/94).

These grants ranged between £160 and £15,000. Beneficiaries included:

- Crail Museum, the Frigate Unicorn, Thirlestone Castle Trust (each received a Kintore Trust Conservation Award of £1,000);
- Royal Incorporation of Architects in Scotland (£1,000).

Applications: In writing to the correspondent.

Ernest Kleinwort Charitable Trust

PO Box 191, 10 Fenchurch Street, London EC3M 3LB
Tel: 0171-956 6600; Fax: 0171-956 6059
Contact: The Secretary
Trustees: Kleinwort Benson Trustees Ltd; Madeleine, Lady Kleinwort; the Earl of Limerick; Sir Richard Kleinwort; Miss M R Kleinwort; R M Ewing; Sir Christopher Lever.
Grant total: £1,074,000 (1994/95)
Beneficial area: UK and overseas, with a special interest in Sussex.

The trust was set up in 1963 with an endowment of shares in Kleinwort Benson, the merchant bank. These shares had a market value of £27 million in March 1995. In 1994/95 the trust's income was £1.3 million which was disbursed in 261 donations. A wide range of charities working at all levels, nationally, internationally and locally, concerned with the environmental conservation, disability, health and the interests and needs of the elderly and the young were supported.

Grants ranged from £50 to over £100,000. Four grants were for £50,000 or more, 20% of the grants were for £5,000 or more, whilst more than half were for a few hundred pounds. Many grants were recurrent. Environment and conservation organisations received grants totalling over £269,000 (25% of total grant-aid). Grants relevant to this guide were given:

In 1994/95
- WWF UK (£80,000);
- Wildfowl & Wetlands Trust (£35,000);
- Zoological Society of London (£25,500);
- Earthwatch Europe (£5,000);
- High Beeches Gardens Conservation Trust, Royal Botanic Gardens Kew (£2,500 each);
- RSPB (£1,250);
- British Trust for Conservation Volunteers, CPRE, Soil Association Ltd (£1,000 each);
- Historic Gardens Trust (Sussex), International Tree Foundation (£750 each).

16 additional grants between £250 and £500 were also given to conservation organisations in the UK £106,500 was given to organisations working internationally:
- Dian Fossey Gorilla Fund (£30,000);
- Tusk £25,000);
- WaterAid (£20,000);
- Falklands Conservation (£12,500);
- Rhino Rescue Trust (10,000);
- Jamaica Family Planning Association (£9,000);
- Care for the Wild's Turtle Conservation Project (£1,000).

At least 55 grants, mostly under £1,000, were given to wide range of organisations in Sussex and included a number of conservation organisations.

Exclusions: Local charities outside Sussex are normally excluded.

Applications: To the correspondent. International grants are for conservation and planned parenthood. Trustees meet in March and November.

The David Knightly Charitable Trust

The Fishing Lodge, Britford, Salisbury, Wiltshire SP5 4DY
Trustees: Miss J K Knightly, Chair; P G Jessop;C D C Jameson; A Lang; Mrs M Eve
Grant total: £9,000 (Jan 1995)
Beneficial area: Wiltshire, Hampshire, Dorset.

"Pride of Place" awards are given many to amenity societies making improvements in their local environments particularly in the three named counties. The accounts on file at the Charity Commission give little detail except that six grants were made in the year ending January 1995 totalling £9,000.

Exclusions: Individuals.

Applications: Applications should be sent to The Civic Trust, 17 Carlton House Terrace, London SW1Y 5AW.

The Sir James Knott Trust

16-18 Hood Street, Newcastle-upon-Tyne NE1 6JQ
Tel: 0191-230 4016
Contact: Brigadier J F F Sharland, Trust Secretary
Trustees: Viscount Ridley; Mark Cornwall-Jones; Oliver James; Charles Baker-Cresswell.
Grant total: £1,153,000 (1996/97)
Beneficial area: Tyne and Wear, Durham and Northumberland.

This energetic and thoughtful trust makes grants to registered charities in the North East of England. Its main interests are community welfare, and youth and children, but most charitable activity is supported. Over 300 grants are made each year, and they normally range from a few hundred pounds to £25,000, but can be much larger. About a third of its grants are to charities also supported in the previous year.

A part-time assessor has been appointed to carry out follow-up visits on a sample of recipients to verify that the trust grants have been "well targeted and spent wisely". Clear guidelines for applicants are available (see below).

By March 1996, the trust had assets of £25.5 million which produced an income of £1.2 million from which 317 donations totalling £967,000 were made. Of these

only 22 were for £10,000 or more. The largest grant was for £25,000. More than 150 grants were under £1,000.

Eleven grants were relevant to this guide and showed a particular interest in the architectural heritage, countryside and wildlife conservation. They totalled £87,000 (9% of grant-aid).
◆ Northumberland Wildlife Trust (£15,000);
◆ Berwick Parish Church Fund (£12,500);
◆ Durham Diocese, church repair & building fund (£12,500);
◆ Newcastle Diocese, church repair & building fund (£12,000);
◆ Northumbria Historic Churches Preservation Trust (£10,000);
◆ Berwick upon Tweed Preservation Trust, County Trust (NE), Countryside Foundation (NE), Wildfowl & Wetlands Trust, Washington (£5,000 each);
◆ St Mary the Virgin, Holy Island (£3,000);
◆ BTCV (NE) (£2,000).

Exclusions: The trust deed excludes Roman Catholic charities. No applications considered from individuals or from non-registered charities. Grants are only made to charities from within the North East of England, and from national charities either operating within, or where work may be expected to be of benefit to the North East of England (Northumberland, Tyne & Wear & Co. Durham North & Centre).

Applications: In writing to the correspondent. "Please be brief. Do not, for example, explain at great length why it is that a blind, starving, bankrupt, one-legged man from Jupiter, needs help".

Despite the plea for brevity, the trust requests that applicants should address the following questions, although "not all the questions necessarily apply to you, but they give an idea of the kind of questions that the trustees may ask when your application is being considered":
◆ "Who are you? How are you organised/ managed?

◆ What is your aim? What co-ordination do you have with other organisations with similar aims?

◆ What do you do and how does it benefit the community? How many people 'in need' actually use or take advantage of your facilities?

◆ How have you been funded in the past, how will you be funded in the future? Enclose summary of last year's balance sheet.

◆ How much do you need, what for and when? Have you thought about depreciation/running costs/replacement? If your project is not funded in full, what do you propose to do with the money you have raised?

◆ What is the overall cost, what is the deficit and how are you planning to cover the deficit? Is it an open-ended commitment, or when will you become self-supporting?

◆ If you will never be self-supporting, what is your long-term fundraising strategy? Have you even thought about it?

◆ Who else have you asked for money, and how have they responded? What are you doing yourselves to raise money?

◆ Have you applied to the National Lottery? When will you get the result? If you have not applied, are you eligible and when will you apply?

◆ What is your registered charity number, or which registered charity is prepared to administer funds on your behalf? How can you be contacted by telephone?"

Trustees meet in February, June and October. Applications need to be submitted two months in advance.

The Kirby Laing Foundation

Box 1, 133 Page Street, Mill Hill, London NW7 2ER
Tel: 0181-906 5200
Contact: Miss E A Harley
Trustees: Sir Kirby Laing; Lady Isobel Laing; David E Laing; Simon Webley.
Grant total: £1,513,000 (1995)
Beneficial area: UK and overseas.

The foundation gives grants under the following headings: Medical welfare; Education; Cultural and environmental; Overseas aid; Mental health; Child & youth; Religious organisations; Disabled.

In 1995 the foundation had assets of over £28 million and an income of £1.6 million from which £1,513,000 was distributed in 51 grants, half of them being for amounts between £10,000 and £20,000. 164 small grants were covered by a payment of £355,000 to the Charities Aid Foundation.

In 1995 the "Cultural and Environmental" category absorbed £147,000 (10% of total grant-aid) within which the following grants were relevant to this guide:
◆ Royal Albert Hall Trust (£100,000);
◆ Dorset Natural History and Archaeological Society (£10,000);
◆ National Trust (£5,000).

Other relevant grants were given also:

Under "Education"
◆ Centre for Environmental Strategy, Sussex University (£65,000);
◆ Parnham Trust (£5,000);

Under "Miscellaneous"
◆ Rothamsted International (£12,000).

Exclusions: No grants to individuals; no travel grants; no educational grants.

Gifts in the category 'Cultural & Environmental' are usually made to national organisations, grants are rarely made to local initiatives unless there is a direct relationship to the Trust or its Trustees.

This foundation is administered alongside the Maurice Laing Foundation and the Beatrice Laing Trust (see separate entries). An application to one will be treated as an application to all.

Applications: One application only is needed to apply to this or the Maurice Laing Foundation or Beatrice Laing Trust. Multiple applications will still only elicit a single reply. These trusts make strenuous efforts to keep their overhead costs to a minimum. As they also make a very large number of grants each year, in proportion to their income, the staff must rely almost entirely on the written applications submitted in selecting appeals to go forward to the trustees.

Each application should contain all the information needed to allow such a decision to be reached, in as short and straightforward a way as possible. Specifically, each application should say: what the money is for; how much is needed; how much has already been found; where the rest is to come from. Unless there is reasonable assurance on the last point the grant is unlikely to be recommended. The trusts ask applicants, in the interest of reducing costs, to accept a non-response as a negative reply; if more is sought, a reply-paid envelope must be sent with the application. The trust does not encourage exploratory telephone calls on "how best to approach the trust".

The Maurice Laing Foundation

Box 1, 133 Page Street, Mill Hill, London NW7 2ER
Tel: 0181-906 5200
Contact: Miss E A Harley
Trustees: David Edwards, Chairman; Sir Maurice Laing; Thomas D Parr; John H Laing; Peter J Harper; Andrea Gavazzi.
Grant total: £498,000 (1996)
Beneficial area: UK.

The foundation had assets of nearly £49 million at the end of 1995, 36% of them represented by shares in two of the Laing companies: Eskmuir Properties Ltd and Laing (John) plc. Its income from April to December 1995 was £2,2 million, from which over £1 million was distributed in charitable donations. The foundation has changed its financial year, and in the year to April 1995, it distributed £1.6 million. The foundation makes about forty grants a year, ranging from £5,000 to £100,000.

In 1995 its grants were categorised as follows:
+ Education and Religion (£392,500) 17 grants;
+ Health and Medicine (particularly complementary) (£298,000) 14 grants;
+ Cultural and Environment (£157,500) 4 grants;
+ Miscellaneous (£20,000) 2 grants;
+ Charities Aid Foundation – CAF (£186,500) for distribution through its small grants system;
+ The Charity Service – TD Parr (£10,000).

Two of its major grants totalling £68,000 (6% of total grant-aid) were given to causes clearly relevant to this guide.
+ World Wide Fund for Nature (£63,000);
+ Royal Botanical Gardens, Kew (£5,000);
+ The LSE received £80,000 for work related to environmental issues.

This foundation could give a greater sum to the environment if the CAF service (see above) allocates small grants in the same proportion as the foundation gives its main grants.

Exclusions: No grants to individuals for education or travel.

Applications: One application only is needed to apply to this or the Kirby Laing Foundation or the Beatrice Laing Trust. Multiple applications will only receive a single reply. The trusts ask applicants, in the interest of reducing costs, to accept a non-response as a negative reply; if more is sought, a reply-paid envelope must be sent with the application. The trust does not encourage exploratory telephone calls on "how best to approach the trust".

Each application should contain all the information needed to allow a decision to be reached, in as short and straightforward a way as possible. Specifically, they should cover: what the money is for; how much is needed; how much has already been found; where the rest is to come from. Unless there is reasonable assurance on the last point the grant is unlikely to be recommended.

Laing's Charitable Trust

133 Page Street, London NW7 2ER
Contact: D W Featherstone
Trustees: Sir Kirby Laing; Sir Maurice Laing; R A Wood; Sir J M K Laing; D C Madden.
Grant total: £528,000 for organisations (1996)
Beneficial area: UK.

The trust supports a wide range of charitable activity with grants normally ranging from £50 to £30,000. They are given for revenue or capital costs, and can be recurrent. In 1996, £528,000 was given to charitable organisations as follows:
- £470,000 133 grants over £500
- £17,500 73 grants under £500
- £24,000 in Charities Aid Foundation vouchers up to £300

Grants relevant to this guide totalled £45,000 (8%) of total grant-aid in 1996:
- Civic Trust (£30,000)
- World Wide Fund for Nature UK (£10,000);
- Groundwore, Hertfordshire (£4,000);
- Woodland Trust (£500);
- Heritage of London Trust (£250),
- Young Peoples Trust for the Environment & Nature Conservation (£250);
- Lancashire Wildlife Trust (£216);
- Environment Council (£215).

24 of the grants over £500 and 27 of the grants for less than £500 were matching grants to the sum raised by Laing Employees for the organisations of their choice.

Exclusions: No grants to individuals (other than to Laing employees and/or their dependants).

Applications: In writing to the correspondent.

The Allen Lane Foundation

6a Winchester House, Cranmer Road, London SW9 6EJ
Tel: 0171-793 1899; **Fax:** 0171-793 1989; **E-mail:** allen.lane@btinternet.com
Contact: Heather Swailes, Executive Secretary
Trustees: Charles Medawar; Clare Morpurgo; Sebastian Morpurgo; Christine Teale; Zoe Teale; Ben Whittaker.
Grant total: £485,000 (1996/97)
Beneficial area: UK and Republic of Ireland.

This foundation "wishes to fund work which is unpopular and innovative and where a relatively small grant can make a significant impact". It assists work with groups such as refugees and asylum seekers; black and ethnic minority communities, offenders/ex-offenders and travellers. It has also clarified six broad areas of work as priorities:
- provision of advice, information and advocacy;
- community development;
- employment and training;
- mediation, conflict resolution and alternatives to violence;
- research and education aimed at changing public attitudes or policy;
- social welfare.

In 1996/97 the foundation had assets of over £12 million which generated a gross income of £666,000. It made grants totalling £395,000 to 184 organisations in the UK, and 36 grants totalling £90,000 to organisations in the Republic of Ireland (only for women's groups).

Most grants are for a few thousand pounds. Very rarely are grants given e.g. £5,000 a year for a maximum of three years. In 1996/97 annual report showed the following grants relevant to this guide:

Under "Policy research and awareness raising"
- Council for the Protection of Rural England, research on traffic in rural areas (£4,000);

- Forum for the Future, research in sustainable economics (£5,000);
- SAFE charitable trust, research on rural employment and training (£2,000);
- OP information Network, work on the effects of organophosphates on humans (£1,000);

Under "Advice, information and advocacy"
- Environmental Law Foundation (£3,000).

Exclusions: These include building costs; restoration of buildings; animal welfare. (A full list is given with the guidelines.)

Applications: Obtain full guidelines direct from the foundation. Applications can be made in writing at any time. Trustees meet three times a year in February, June and October. Grants are normally made for one year only. though sometimes a maximum of three years may be offered.

The Lankelly Foundation

2 The Court, High Street, Harwell, Didcot, Oxfordshire OX11 0EY
Tel: 01235-820044
Contact: Peter Kilgarriff
Trustees: Cecil Heather, Chairman; Leo Fraser-Mackenzie; W J Mackenzie; Georgina Linton; Lady Merlyn-Rees; A Ramsay Hack; Shirley Turner.
Grant total: £2,760,000 (1996/97)
Beneficial area: UK, but see below.

The foundation makes about 12 grants a year for capital or revenue needs. Projects helping people with disabilities and for general social welfare account for more than three quarters of the total amount given each year. Grants are rarely for less than £5,000, and although 75% of them are on a one-off basis, support can be spread for up to five years.

The administration of the foundation is linked with the Chase Charity but they remain two quite distinct trusts to which separate applications have to be made.

In April 1997, the foundation had assets of over £34.5 million, including £3.6 million of accumulated income, which generated an income of £2.1 million.

The priorities of the foundation from 1996 to 1998 are:

"We shall be expecting to support community initiatives to meet local needs. We shall look for user involvement as well as the proper use and support of volunteers and you will have to provide evidence of sound management and a culture which fosters equal opportunities. We intend to concentrate upon smaller charities, many of whom will have only a local or regional remit. Grants to large national charities are likely to be rare.

"We shall be giving a lower priority than in the past to heritage and the arts. In these areas, as others, priority will be given to projects which involve local communities and groups who are isolated by place or culture, or disadvantaged by poverty or disability.

"We want our grants to be effective, to achieve something which otherwise would not happen, or sustain something which otherwise might fail, but we do not make grants to replace funds that have been withdrawn from other sources.

"We shall monitor the effectiveness of all grants but those made over a number of years will involve more detailed evaluation."

The foundation tries to spread its grants widely throughout the UK and is particularly keen to develop more support to Scotland and Wales. It has stopped making grants for projects in the Greater London area for at least two years from 1996. Charities based in London but organising projects elsewhere are still be eligible to apply.

In 1996/97 only two out of the 119 grants given fell within its "Heritage & Conservation" category. They were given to:
- Lincolnshire Trust for Nature Conservation, Swaethmore, Leeds (£10,000 each);

In 1995/96 relevant grants were given to:
- Farms for City Children, Wick Court, Gloucestershire, towards capital cost of creating a new farm (£20,000);
- Otter Trust, Suffolk, towards establishment of a new base in Yorkshire (£15,000);
- Thornham Field Centre Trust, Thornham Magna, Suffolk, towards the cost of establishing a horticultural project for people with learning difficulties (£10,000).

Exclusions: The foundation does not contribute to large, widely circulated appeals. More particularly, grants are not made in support of: the advancement of religion; conferences or seminars; festivals or theatre productions; publications, films or video; research and feasibility studies; sport; individual youth clubs; travel, expeditions or holidays; medical research; hospital trusts; formal education; individual needs; endowment funds; animal welfare; other grant-making bodies; and under fives (other than summer holiday schemes).

Applications: The foundation receives many more applications than it can help, and less than one in fourteen applicants are successful. "This inevitably means that we have to disappoint good schemes which meet our criteria".
The trustees meet in January, March, July & October. There are no application forms.

"Applications may be submitted at any time, but you should be aware that agendas are planned well ahead and you should expect the process to take some months. If we think we may be able to help, we will talk to you to clarify issues, give time for your plans to mature and for other funders to give an initial response.

"Two or three months before the trustees consider a formal submission one of the staff will arrange to visit you or meet you at our office.

"You will be notified of the trustees' decision as soon as possible and, if a grant is agreed, of any conditions that may have been attached to its release."

Applicants should include the following information with the initial letter:
- what you do and why you are seeking the foundation's help
- brief information about the origins and current company/charitable status of your organisation
- annual report and accounts
- answer to the following questions:
  how much do you need to raise?
  how soon do you need to raise it?
  what support have you already attracted?
  who else have you asked to help?

"All applications receive a written answer and we try to act as quickly as we can. The length of this process depends to some extent upon the size of the appeal but more upon your readiness to keep us informed." A separate application needs to be made to the Chase Charity which shares the same administration.

The Mrs F B Lawrence 1976 Charitable Settlement

c/o Haynes Hicks Beach, 10 New Square, London WC2A 3QG
Tel: 0171-465 4300
Trustees: M Tooth; G S Brown; D A G Sarre.
Grant total: £116,000 (1996/97)
Beneficial area: UK and overseas.

Our most recent detailed figures are for 1994/95 when the trust's assets had a market value of £1.9 million generating an income of £132,000 from which 66 grants totalling £86,000 were made. Two grants were for £3,000, 18 were for £2,000, 42 for £1,000 and four for £750 and £500.

Grants relevant to this guide included:
- BTCV (£2,000);
- Greenpeace Environmental Trust (£1,000);
- Wildlife Aid (£750).

Beneficiaries supported in previous years have included the Architectural

Association and the Tradescant Trust –
Museum of Garden History.

Exclusions: Individuals.

Applications: In writing to the
correspondent with a copy of latest accounts.

The Leach Fourteenth Trust

Nettleton mill, Castle Combe, Near
Chippenham, Wilts, SN14 7NJ.
Contact: Mr & Mrs Roger Murray-Leach
Trustees: W J Henderson; M A Hayes; Mrs
J M M Nash; Mr Roger Murray-Leach.
Grant total: £79,000 (1996/97)
Beneficial area: UK.

Although the trust's objectives are general,
the trustees are following the interest of
the founder, which was to support
ecological work.

In 1997, the trust had assets of nearly £2
million. About 7 charities receive regular
payments. The trustees prefer to give large
grants for specific projects rather than
small awards towards general funding.

In the past the Trust has bought some
cliffs, supported a nature reserve, and a
hostel for homeless people, as well as
supporting the work of wildlife
preservation. Grants are usually £500 to
£5,000, but can be as large as £50,000.

In 1996/97 beneficiaries relevant to this
guide were:
- Jersey Wildlife Preservation Trust;
- Bishop's Waltham Society;
- Project Christchurch;
- The Zoological Society of London;
- Wildfowl and Wetlands Trust;
- Diane Fossey Gorilla Fund;
- Countryside Restoration Trust;
- SAFE; The Country Trust, Suffolk;
- Whirlow Hall Farm Trust.

Exclusions: Only registered charities are
supported.

Applications: In writing to the
correspondent. Only successful appeals
can expect a reply.

The Leche Trust

84 Cicada Road, London SW18 2NZ
Tel: 0181-870 6233; **Fax:** 0181-870 6233
Contact: Mrs Louisa Lawson, Secretary
Trustees: Primrose Arnander, Chair;
Diana Hanbury; John Porteous; Sir John
Riddell; Simon Jervis, Ian Bristow.
Grant total: £121,000 (1995/96)
Beneficial area: UK.

The trust supports Georgian architecture,
the arts, particularly music, and individual
students. It was founded and endowed by
the late Mr Angus Acworth CBE in 1950
and by 1995/96 had assets of £4.8 million
which generated an income of £220,000.

The trust provides an outline of what it is
prepared to support and grants are
normally made in the following categories:
1. Preservation of buildings and their
   contents, primarily of the Georgian
   period;
2. Repair and conservation of church
   furniture, including such items as bells
   or monuments, but not for structural
   repairs to the fabric – preference is
   given to objects of the Georgian period;
3. Assistance to the arts and conservation,
   including museums;
4. Assistance to organisations concerned
   with music and drama and dance;
5. Assistance to music students of
   outstanding ability;
6. Assistance to students from overseas
   during the last six months of their
   postgraduate doctorate study in the UK.

Changes in the categories are made from
time to time and applicants should always
check for the current one.

In 1995/96 the trust reported that its
seven grants to historic buildings took
about 17% of its grant-aid. These
included:
- Chinese Pavilion, Stowe, Royal Society
  of Arts for its facade restoration (£5,000
  each);
- Gilbert White Museum, Selbourne
  (£3,000).

Grants to 18 churches absorbed 10% of its funding and included:

- St Michael's, Newton Purcell for restoration of marble monument (£1,600);
- St Michael's Buckland, Worcs for restoration of 18thc clock tower and chime (£1,000);
- St Andrew's Chinnor (£700).

Exclusions: No grants are made for religious bodies; overseas missions; schools and school buildings; social welfare; animals; medicine; expeditions, British students other than postgraduate music students.

Applications: In writing to the secretary; trustees meet three times a year.

Lord Leverhulme's Charitable Trust

Coopers & Lybrand, 1 Embankment Place, London WC2N 6NN
Tel: 0171-583 5000
Contact: The Joint Secretary
Trustees: A E H Heber-Percy; A H S Hannay.
Grant total: £759,000 (1994/95)
Beneficial area: UK, especially Cheshire and Merseyside.

The trust was set up in 1957 by the 3rd Viscount Leverhulme with general charitable objects. In 1995 it had assets of £13 million which generated a low income of £450,000.

It operates two separate funds: one generates £30,000 a year paid to the Merseyside County Council, the trustees of the Lady Lever Art Gallery; the second is the Lord Leverhulme's Youth Enterprise Scheme which sponsors young people in the Wirral and Cheshire areas.

Its major fund distributed £705,000 in 111 other grants. Eleven of them were large, ranging between £20,000 and £166,000, and 31 were between £1,000 and £17,000. More than half of the grants were for less than £1,000, the majority of these were

small subscriptions for less than £100, including five for £5. Although some of the larger grants showed continuing relationships, several were given to organisations not supported before.

In 1994/95 the following grants were relevant to this guide and totalled over £116,000 (15% of grant-aid):

- Cheshire Cathedral Development Trust, St George's Church in Thornton Hough (£50,000 each);
- Cheshire Historic Churches (£10,000);
- Handicapped Angler Trust (£5,000);
- National Trust for Scotland (£1,000);
- St Michael's Altcar (£50).

Small subscriptions of under £20 were given to: Cheshire Ploughing & Hedgecutting Society, Friends of Ness Gardens and CPRE Cheshire branch. Animal Health Trust (£29,800 with £28,000 the previous year. Lord Leverhulme is chairman of the executive committee of this trust).

The commitment to the Cheshire and Merseyside area was strongly evident with three quarter of grants given there. Grants were also made to national organisations: National Garden's Scheme (£3,900).

Exclusions: Non-charitable organisations.

Applications: "By letter addressed to the trustees setting out details of the appeal including brochures."

John Spedan Lewis Foundation

171 Victoria Street, London SW1E 5NN
Tel: 0171-828 1000
Contact: Ms B M F Chamberlain, Secretary
Trustees: S Hampson; M J K Miller; W L R E Gilchrist; D R Cooper; Miss C Walton.
Grant total: £54,000 (1996/97)
Beneficial area: Gt. Britain and Northern Ireland.

Foundation does not make grants to individuals (including students), to local branches of national organisations, or for medical research, welfare projects or building works.

Applications: Write to Secretary giving full details and enclosing, where applicable, latest report and accounts.

The Linbury Trust

See also entry for the "Sainsbury Family Charitable Trusts"
Tel: 0171-410 0330
Contact: Michael Pattison
Trustees: Lord Sainsbury of Preston Candover; Lady Sainsbury; Miss J S Portrait.
Grant total: £7,835,000 (1995/96)
Beneficial area: UK and overseas.

In recent years Lord Sainsbury and his wife, the distinguished former ballerina Anya Linden, have resumed their trusteeship which they relinquished a few years after its establishment in 1983. Its most high profile work to date has been the funding of the Sainsbury wing of the National Gallery in London. The largest recent payments have continued to be for unnamed capital projects, probably the Royal Opera House.

The Linbury Trust up to 1995/96 has remained one of the most "closed" of the Sainsbury family trusts. (It contrasts in this respect greatly with the trusts associated with his three children.) It has only given a simple list of its funding under category headings in its skeletal annual reports. No information at all has been forwarded about its individual beneficiaries, or the number and size of its grants. A comparative table of grant-aid payments is shown below.

Exclusions: No grants direct to individuals.

Applications: An application to one of the Sainsbury family trusts is an application to all; see the entry under "Sainsbury Family Trusts" for address and application procedure. The trustees meet 10 times during the year.

The Lindeth Charitable Trust

Currey & Co, Solicitors, 21 Buckingham Gate, London SW1E 6LS
Contact: The Secretary
Trustees: C J Scott; Mrs E J Scott; E R H Perks.
Grant total: £29,000 (1994/95)
Beneficial area: UK and overseas.

The Linbury Trust

Grant-aid was paid as follows in the two recent years and show a consistent level of giving within the categories:

	1995/96	1994/95
Environment and heritage	£250,000 (3%)	£184,000 (4%)
Major capital projects	£5,590,000 (71%)	£2,204,000 (53%)
Chronic Fatigue Syndrome research	£490,000 (6%)	£370,000 (9%)
Other medical categories	£147,000 (2%)	£125,000 (3%)
Social work & research	£479,000 (6%)	£350,000 (8%)
Arts/arts education	£355,000 (5%)	£191,000 (5%)
Overseas (including Third World)	£254,000 (3%)	£277,000 (7%)
Education	£157,000 (2%)	£141,000 (3%)
Drug Abuse	£59,600 (1%)	£202,000 (5%)
Old people	£52,000 (0.6%)	£106,000 (3%)
Total	£7,835,000 (100%)	£4,151,000 (100%)

This trust has a particular interest in ecological and related research. In 1994/95 it had assets of £293,000 and gave 25 grants totalling £29,000. Five grants totalling £21,500 (74% of grant-aid) were clearly relevant to this guide:

- Ecological Foundation (£18,000);
- Project Podocarpus 1995 (£2,000);
- Ibex 1995, Reading University Department of Botany, Sebakwe Black Rhino Trust (£500 each).

An unidentified grant was given to Sheffield University (£2,500 with £1,000 in the previous year). The trust is also known to have supported the Wildfowl and Wetlands Trust.

In 1993/94 grants included:

- Colombia 1992, Harrison Zoological Museum (£2,000 each);
- Rothamsted Institute (£1,000).

Three smaller grants were given to county wildlife trusts.

Applications: In writing to the correspondent.

The Loke Wan Tho Memorial Foundation

Coopers & Lybrand, 9 Greyfriars Road, Reading RG1 1JG
Tel: 01734-597111
Contact: The Trustees
Trustees: Lady McNeice; Mrs T S Tonkyn; A Tonkyn.
Grant total: £79,000 (1995/96)
Beneficial area: UK and overseas.

In 1995/96, the trust had assets of £954,000 and an income of £92,000 from which 16 grants totalling £79,000 were given. They ranged between £500 and £5,000. Its interests are mainly environment/conservation and medical.

The trust appears to make a small number of large grants sometimes for a number of years and a number of smaller one-off grants.

Nine grants relevant to this guide, totalling about £60,000 (76% of grant-aid), were made in 1995/96.

- Asian Wetlands Bureau (£21,000);
- World Wise Fund for Nature 'Malaysia' (£19,000);
- The World Wide Fund for Nature 'Chitral' (£5,000);
- Jersey Wildlife Preservation Trust (£5,000);
- Marie Stopes International (£5,000);
- Intermediate Technology, Oriental Bird Club, Scottish Conservation Projects Trust and Sustrans (£1,000 or £2,000 each).

Relevant grants made in 1994/95 included:

- Earthwatch Europe, Responsible Forestry, SOS Sahel (£2,000 each);
- National Federation of City Farms (£500).

In previous years the trust has distributed a far larger total annual grant-aid e.g. £102,000 in 1991/92, but had then spent well over its annual income in doing so.

Applications: In writing to the correspondent.

The Lyndhurst Settlement

c/o Bowker Orford & Co, 15-19 Cavendish Place, London W1M 0DD
Contact: Michael Isaacs
Trustees: Michael Isaacs; Kenneth Plummer; Anthony Skyrme.
Grant total: £163,000 (1996/97)
Beneficial area: Usually UK, but local or foreign applications are considered if there is a strong civil liberty component.

The policy of the Lyndhurst Settlement is to encourage research into social problems with a specific emphasis on safeguarding civil liberties, maintaining the rights of minorities and protecting the environment which the trustees regard as an important civil liberty. The trustees prefer to support charities (both innovatory and long established) that seek to prevent, as well as ameliorate, hardship.

Some recipients are regular beneficiaries. In 1996/97, the settlement made grants to 64 recipients totalling £163,000. They ranged between £500 and £7,000. Requests are considered throughout the year and about 1,000 are received.

While supporting some of the more famous national bodies it also supports an interesting range of local conservation work of all kinds (wildlife, countryside and buildings). It is the view of the trustees that an essential element in the protection of the environment is the limitation of population growth.
- Marie Stopes International (£6,000);
- Population Concern, Ironbridge Gorge Development Trust, Masham Trust.
- Survival International, (£3,000 each);
- Cotswold Canals Trust, Environmental Law Foundation, BTVC, Waste Watch, (£2,000 each);
- Kent Trust for Nature Conservation, Thomas Phillips Price Trust, (£1,000 each).

Exclusions: Grants are only given to registered charities. Grants are not given to individuals. The trustees do not normally support medical or religious charities.

Applications: Requests for grants should include a brief description of the aims and objects of the charity, and must be in writing and not by telephone. Unsuccessful requests will not be acknowledged unless a pre-paid self-addressed envelope is provided.

The J H M Mackenzie Charitable Trust

Mortlake House, Vicarage Road, London NW14 8RU
Tel: 0181-876 0331
Contact: The Administrator
Trustees: J H M Mackenzie; Mrs J H M Mackenzie; J A H M Mackenzie.
Grant total: £40,000 (1998/89)

This trust which has general charitable objects has not sent any accounts to the Charity Commission for nearly a decade (or none have reached the files). It still exists since its basic records were amended at the Commission in 1997.

Very musty information for 1988/89 showed that most of its grant-aid went to the Atlantic Salmon Trust (£34,000) with small grants of a few hundred pounds to Paisley Abbey, WWF UK and the Game Conservancy Trust.

Applications: In writing to the correspondent.

The Manifold Trust

Shottesbrooke House, Maidenhead SL6 3SW
Contact: Miss C C Gilbertson
Trustees: Sir John Smith; Lady Smith.
Grant total: £703,000 (1996)

The trust supports the preservation of buildings and to a lesser degree other culturally important activities: the environment, education, including museums and the arts. Most grants are between £500 and £5,000, although a number of larger grants up to £50,000 are also given.

There have been large fluctuations in total grant-aid between 1990 (over £2 million), 1993 (£850,000),1994 (£474,000) and 1995 (£1,032,000). But the trust comments in its 1995 report that its ability to make grants is declining since for many years its payments have exceeded its income, the trustees believing it better to meet the present need of other charities than to reserve money for the future. Its assets of nearly £28 million in 1995 generated an income of only £715,000 although grant-aid of £1,032,000 was given.

In 1995 its grants were categorised in the trust's report as follows:

Grants in 1995
- Preservation
  Historic Buildings £605,000 58%
  Churches £126,000 12%
- Education, including museums
  £112,000 11%

◆ Environment £49,000 5%
◆ Music, arts, social causes £140,000 14%
Total £1,032,000 100%

Multiple grants were given to the trust's sister charity, the Landmark Trust, also based at the above address. This trust restores, and organises holiday lettings of, historic and architecturally unusual buildings and annually receives the largest grant from the Manifold Trust. In 1995 its grant of £500,000 (in six allocations) absorbed almost half of the 1995 grant-aid.

In 1995 the trust gave 185 additional grants ranging between £500 and £50,000. Only 18 grants were for £10,000 or more, with the vast majority of grants between £500 and £5,000.

The trust favours local activities or the less usual causes. It seems that the larger national environmental organisations are less likely to be assisted with only smallish grants for specific projects given to, say, the National Trust and the CPRE. Over 81 parish church councils received grants ranging between £500 and £3,500.

Grants relevant to this guide included:

In 1995
◆ Friends of Gibraltar Heritage (£50,000);
◆ Bexhill Old Town Preservation Society, and Sustrans (£25,000 each);
◆ Historic Chapels Trust (£20,000);
◆ New College, Oxford (£18,500);
◆ Royal Incorporation of Architects of Scotland (£15,000);
◆ Airfields Environment Trust (£10,000);
◆ Avoncroft Museum of Buildings (£7,500);
◆ Dovedale Almshouses Trust (£5,000);
◆ Georgian Group, Heritage of London Trust (£2,500 each);
◆ Groundwork Southwark, Survival International, Tusk (£2,000 each); Wymondham Heritage Society, Wey and Arun Canal Trust, River Lea Tidal Mill Trust, Dorchester Abbey, the Country Trust, Lewisham Environment Trust, Forum for the Future, Open Spaces Society, Marie Stopes International (£1,000 each);

◆ Friends of Taunton Castle, the Firefly Trust, Sheffield Conservation Volunteers, British Butterfly Conservation Society (£500).

Applications: Applications can be made at any time (only registered charities can be considered) preferably on a single sheet of paper, with details of the project, the amount needed and the amount already raised. Grants are considered once a month. If the application is for funds to preserve a building, then a note on its history and a photograph should be sent as well. The trust points out that it is unable to reply to all unsuccessful applicants.

The Earl of March's Trust Company Limited

Goodwood House, Goodwood, near Chichester PO18 OPY
Contact: The Secretary.
Trustees: Duke of Richmond (Chairman); Duchess of Richmond; Sir Peter Hordern; Mrs C M Ward.
Grant total: £24,000 (1996/97)
Beneficial area: UK and abroad with a particular interest in Sussex and Chichester.

In 1995/96 this trust had assets of over £300,000 generating an income of £29,000 from which 44 grants totalling £24,000 were given. Grants ranged from under £100 to £2,5000. Ten grants were for £1,000 or more.

Eight grants relevant to this guide totalling £8,600 (30% of grant-aid) were given to:
◆ United Reform Church, Chichester (£2,500);
◆ Brent Lodge Wild Bird Hops, Chichester Cathedral Trust, West Sussex Countryside Studies Trust (£1,000 each);
◆ Boxgrove Lavant and Tangmere Parish Churches (£800 each);
◆ M C Rainforest Appeal, Population Concern (£500 each);
◆ RSPB, WWF UK (£250 each).

Applications: In writing to the correspondent. Grants normally only to charities known to the directors.

The Mark Leonard Trust

See entry for the "Sainsbury Family Charitable Trusts"
Tel: 0171-410 0330
Contact: Michael Pattison
Trustees: M L Sainsbury; Mrs S Butler-Sloss; J J Sainsbury; Miss J S Portrait.
Grant total: £90,000 grant approvals (1995/96)
Beneficial area: UK and overseas.

This trust, set up in 1994, is the namesake of Mark Leonard Sainsbury, the younger son of Lord Sainsbury of Preston Candover. During 1995/96 he made a gift-aid donation of £200,000, following £1.2 million in the previous year, to the trust's endowment. Investments with a market value of £1.5 million were held in 1995/96 none of which appear to be J Sainsbury plc shares.

Grants are made under the following headings: Environment; Youth Work; General. As with the other trusts where Lord Sainsbury's children are trustees – the Ashden and J J trusts – support is given to key environmental issues often neglected by charitable grant makers – sustainable energy, environmental education and work in less advantaged areas. Several beneficiaries are common to these three trusts. Overlapping interests are also held with the trusts associated with Sir Timothy Sainsbury's children, the Staples, Tedworth and Glass-House trusts.

In 1995/96 the following allocations were relevant to this guide and totalled £54,000 (60% of grant-allocations):

Under "Environment"
- BTCV, towards their environmental volunteering programme for disadvantaged young people (£7,500);
- Centre for Sustainable Energy, towards a study into the potential for community-level renewable energy projects (£7,000, with the same sum in the previous year to develop its Energy Club);
- Environmental Education: Support for Teachers, towards a project to support teachers, to identify high quality materials and raise awareness of key issues (£5,000);
- Imperial College – Dr Keith Barnham, towards fees for research post to encourage the involvement of British industry in Quantum Well Solar Cells research (£24,000 over 3 years with £2,000 in the previous year);
- Landlife, Liverpool, to develop wildflower seedbanks and seed catalogue (£10,000 over 2 years).

Under "General"
- Save the Rhino Trust, Namibia (£500).

In the previous year a grant was given for a children's environmental pack by Bootstrap Enterprises – The Rubbish Dump (£4,000). The Monument Trust has long supported this organisation.

Applications: See the entry under "Sainsbury Family Trusts" for address and application procedure. The trustees meet five times a year.

The Marsh Christian Trust

Granville House, 132-135 Sloane Street, London SW1X 9AX
Tel: 0171-730 2626; **Fax:** 0171-823 5225
Contact: The Secretary
Trustees: B P Marsh; M Litchfield; A B Marsh; R J C Marsh; N C S Marsh.
Grant total: £129,000 (1996/97)
Beneficial area: UK and overseas.

Only registered charities experienced in their field are supported. The trust prefers to give long-term core funding to appropriate work, subject to yearly re-submission and review. Single projects and sponsorship proposals are therefore not supported. Grants range from £100 to £5,000.

The trust had assets of around £2.9 million in 1996/97 which generated an income of £144,000 from which 225 grants totalling £129,000 were made. About half of these were recurrent from the previous year.

The causes supported are categorised within seven areas of work: Social Welfare; Environmental Causes/Animal Welfare; Healthcare & Medical Research; Education & Training; Arts & Heritage; Overseas Appeals Miscellaneous (beneficiaries have included Population Concern).

Nineteen grants totalling £10,000 (8% of grant-aid) were relevant to this guide in 1996/97:
◆ Kent Trust for Nature Conservation, Population Concern (£1250 each);
◆ Irish Peatland Conservation (£1200);
◆ British Ecological Society, London Wildlife Trust (£1,000 each);
◆ Rare Breeds Survival Trust (£800);
◆ Fauna & Flora Preservation (£600);
◆ Royal Geographical Society (£500).

Exclusions: No grants to individuals. No support for individual church buildings or cathedrals.

Applications: In writing to the correspondent, including a copy of the most recent accounts. The trustees currently receive about 1200 applications every year. Decisions are made at fortnightly meetings.

The trustees attempt to visit each recipient charity at least once every three years to review the work done, learn of future plans and renew acquaintance with those responsible for the charity concerned.

Marshall's Charity

Marshall House, 66 Newcomen Street, London SE1 1YT
Tel: 0171-407 2979
Contact: M Wightwick, Clerk to the Trustees
Trustees: B H Larkins; M J Dudding; F A G Rider; W E McConnell; W C Young; D M Lang; and others.

Grant total: £823,000 (1995)
Beneficial area: England and Wales.

The charity assists the Church of England and the Church in Wales by making grants or, in some circumstances loans, for the following purposes:
◆ In support of parsonages. Towards the building, purchasing, altering, dividing, modernising or exceptional repair of parsonages;\
◆ Towards the restoration, reparation or improvement of existing churches within the counties of Kent, Surrey or Lincolnshire;
◆ Towards the erection of new churches; and
◆ Support as patrons of the parish of Christ Church, Southwark."

During 1994 the charity decided "to suspend offering grants towards the erection or purchases of new parsonages".

The following details were supplied by the charity. The charity had assets of £11 million at the end of 1995, and 88% of its total income (£1,063,000) came from property rentals.

The following grants were made in 1995:
◆ Grants to parsonages: £574,000;
◆ Grants to old churches: £249,000;
◆ 78 grants were given to churches and ranged from less than £1,000 to £6,500. Most of these grants were between £2,000 and £5,000.

Exclusions: No grants to churches outside the counties of Kent, Surrey & Lincolnshire.

Applications: To the correspondent in writing. Trustees meet in January, April, July and October. Applications need to be sent by the end of January, April, July and October for consideration at the next meeting.

Sir George Martin Trust

Netherwood House, Ilkley, Yorkshire LS29 9RP
Tel: 01943-831019; 01943-831570
Contact: Peter Marshall, Secretary

Trustees: T D Coates, Chairman; M Bethel; R F D Marshall; P D Taylor.
Grant total: £242,000 (1996/97)
Beneficial area: Largely Yorkshire with particular emphasis on Leeds and Bradford. Some grants are made in other parts of the North of England, and occasionally major national appeals are considered.

The trust supports a wide range of charities in Yorkshire, particularly in Leeds and Bradford. Most grants are between £100 and £5,000.

The trust has a policy of supporting a wide range of inner city charities in West Yorkshire, mainly in Leeds and Bradford. It prefers grants for capital rather than for revenue projects and is reluctant to support general running costs. It prefers to adopt a one-off approach to grant applications. However the trust occasionally gives recurrent grants for a maximum of three years.

In 1995/96 the trust had assets of £5 million and an income of £350,000 from which grants of £254,000 were given. In 1995/96 a total of 206 grants were given with an average donation of £1,250. Only 13 grants were for £5,000 or more. Most grants were either for a few hundred pounds, or under £5,000 (in about equal proportions).

In 1995/96 a total of 11 grants totalling over £17,000 (7% of total grant-aid) were relevant to this guide:
- National Trust Yorkshire Moors/Dales (£7,500);
- Meanwood Valley Urban Farm (£2,500);
- Woodland Trust (£1,700);
- National Gardens Scheme (£1,500);
- Northern Horticultural Society, Field Studies Centre, South Pennines Packhorse Trails Trust, (£1,000 each);
- Horticare Wakefield, Kew Royal Botanic Gardens (£500 each);
- York Natural Environment Trust (£280).

Only a handful of small grants were given outside Yorkshire.

Exclusions: Support for individuals or for post-graduate courses. Support for publishing books or articles or seminars. The trust does not like to fund projects which were formerly statutorily funded.

Applications: The trust meets in December and June each year to consider applications. These should be made in writing to the secretary. Applications which do not qualify cannot now be answered due to substantial increase in postal costs. Applications that are relevant to the trust will be acknowledged and, following meetings, successful applicants will be told of the grants they are to receive. Unsuccessful applicants, following the meeting, will not be informed that they are unable to receive a grant. The trust is unable to consider applications from organisations without charitable status. Telephone calls are not encouraged as the office is not always manned – it is better to write.

The Mercers' Charitable Foundation

Mercers' Hall, Ironmonger Lane, London EC2V 8ME.
Tel: 0171-726 4991
Contact: H W Truelove, Education and Charities' Administrator
Trustees: The Mercers' Company.
Grant total: £1,092,000 (September 1996)
Beneficial area: UK.

The foundation gives a large part of its grant-aid to education particularly the establishments with which it has an historic relationship. It also gives more generally to higher education, schools and further education and other educational projects. In addition it supports social welfare and medical charities, the arts and church livings.

The foundation gives about 6% of its grant-aid to activities within the scope of this guide. Its grant-list for 1996 showed 49 grants totalling £88,000 ranging

These grants included:

- Heritage of London Trust Ltd, Painshill Park Trust Ltd, British Trust for Ornithology, Environmental Council, Kew Bridge Engines Trust (£2,000 each);
- Carstairs Countryside Trust, Central Scotland Countryside Trust, Civic Trust, Historic Chapels Trust, International Otter Survival Fund, Royal Society for Nature Conservation, Soane Monuments Trust, (£1,000 each).

The 116 grants under £1,000 totalling £50,000 were not listed. These cover all areas of the trust's interests.

Exclusions: The company does not respond to circular (mail shot) appeals. Unsolicited general appeals are considered but not encouraged. Grants are only made to individuals in the form of educational support – see the companion volume The Educational Grants Directory.

Applications: In writing to the correspondent. The charitable trustees meet every month; the educational trustees every quarter.

The Mickel Fund

McTaggart & Mickel Ltd, 126 West Regent Street, Glasgow G2 2BH
Tel: 0141-332 0001; Fax: 0141-248 4921.
Contact: J R C Wark
Trustees: D W Mitchell; D A Mickel; B G A Mickel; J R C Wark.
Beneficial area: Scotland.

It is understood this trust, set up by the McTaggart & Mickel firm of building contractors, will consider funding of wildlife conservation and the architectural heritage.

Preference is given to local charities though it is prepared to consider approaches from national bodies in Scotland.

Applications: In writing to the correspondent.

The Millichope Foundation

Millichope Park, Munslow, Craven Arms, Shropshire SY7 9HA.
Contact: Mrs S Bury
Trustees: L C N Bury; S A Bury; Mrs B Marshall.
Grant total: £120,000 (1994/95)
Beneficial area: UK, especially Birmingham and Shropshire.

The trust supports a range of charities with a preference for those in the Birmingham area and Shropshire.

In 1994/95 the foundation had assets of £1.8 million generating an income of £143,000 from which 163 grants totalling £120,000 were made. They ranged from under £100 to £5,000 (£10,000 in the previous year) and were made to a wide range of organisations. Less than a third of the grants were for £1,000 or more. Most grants were small, between £100 and £500.

Nineteen grants relevant to this guide totalling over £19,000 (16 % of grant-aid were given in 1994/95:

- National Trust (£5,000 + £1,000 for Shropshire Hills Appeal);
- Marie Stopes International (£3,000);
- Fauna & Flora Preservation Society (£2,800);
- Ironbridge Museum, Shropshire Conservation Development Trust, Kew Royal Botanic Gardens, National Trust Scotland (£1,000 each);
- Avoncroft Museum of Buildings, CPRE, Black Country Museum, Game Conservancy Council, Parnham, Dodford Children's Holiday Farm (£500 each);
- Crarar Glen Garden, (£250);
- Farming & Wildlife Trust, Save the Rhino Trust (£100 each).

Exclusions: No grants to individuals.

Applications: In writing to the correspondent. Only registered charities may apply and should send a SAE.

The Esmé Mitchell Trust

PO Box 800, Donegall Square West, Belfast BT2 7EB
Contact: The Northern Bank Executor & Trustee Co Ltd
Trustees: P J Rankin; Cmdr D J Maxwell; R P Blakiston-Houston.
Grant total: £66,000 (1993/94)
Beneficial area: Mainly Northern Ireland.

The objects of the trust are general charitable purposes in Ireland as a whole, but principally in Northern Ireland. It has a particular interest in culture and the arts. About a third of the trust's fund is set aside to help selected heritage bodies. The trust has, on occasion, given grants over a period of two or three years, but in general does not become involved in commitments of a long-term nature. No further information is available.

Exclusions: It is most unlikely that applications from individuals wishing to undertake voluntary service or further education will be successful.

Applications: Applicants should submit a description of the proposed project; a recent statement of accounts and balance sheet; a copy of the constitution; details of tax and legal or charitable status (including the Inland Revenue Charities Division reference number); a copy of the latest annual report; a list of committee officers; information on other sources of finance; a contact address and telephone number. It would be helpful for administration purposes if three copies of the appeal documentation were to be forwarded.

To avoid delay in considering applications the trust advisers require a copy of the most recent financial accounts and the Inland Revenue Charities Division reference number with the original application.

Mitchell Trust

Murray Lodge, Burton's Lane, Chalfont St Giles, Bucks HP8 4BL
Contact: R Mitchell
Trustees: Ronald Mitchell; Lynette Mitchell.
Grant total: £9,000 (1996/97)
Beneficial area: UK.

In 1994/95 the trust gave all its grants to interests relevant to this guide, predominantly for wildlife but also for church restoration. The trustees must be keen herpetologists as the trust's major support has recently been given to the Reptile Protection Society (£5,500 in 1994/95 and 1993/94). However none of its grants are recurrent. The trust also has an interest in work for children with special needs although this area received no obvious support in 1994/95.

Its ten grants in 1994/95 were given to:
- Reptile Protection Trust, Wildlife Trust for Northants for Barford Meadow, Scottish Wildlife Trust (£1,000 each);
- Chilterns Woodlands Project; Herts Naturalists' Trust; Lynx Educational Trust, Whale & Dolphin Conservation trust, PTES Endangered Mammals Fund (£500 each);
- Throssel Hole Priory (£500);
- St Mary's Haddenham, St Bartholomew's Blore Bay, Pennault PCC (£250 each);
- Moulsoe Parish Church (£200).

In the previous year only three relevant grants were given with the largest to the Woodland Trust (£3,000).

Applications: In writing to the correspondent.

The Monument Trust

See entry for the 'Sainsbury Family Charitable Trusts'
Tel: 0171-410 0330
Contact: Michael Pattison
Trustees: S Grimshaw; Mrs Linda Heathcoat-Amory; R H Gurney; Sir Anthony Tennant.

Grant total: £6,086,000 for grant approvals (1996/97)

Beneficial area: UK and overseas, with a probable special interest in Sussex.

This trust is the vehicle for the charitable giving of Simon Sainsbury, the brother of Lord Sainsbury of Preston Candover and Sir Timothy Sainsbury. Some years ago it committed £5 million for the restoration of "a listed building in Cambridge", the former Addenbrookes Hospital, to become a new Institute of Management Studies. In 1995/96 and 1994/95 payments of £909,000 and £2,790,000 respectively were made from capital to the Monument Historic Buildings Trust Ltd, a charitable company of which Simon Sainsbury is a director.

The trust had assets valued at £99.6 million at April 1997 (a decrease from £106 million in April 1996). Its net income was £4.26 million. In 1996/97 the trust produced a report and accounts with much fuller information about its grants to its beneficiaries and the activities supported. This is most welcome, compared with the very limited information previously given, and will enable the pattern of its interests can be more clearly discerned.

The table shows the grant approvals relevant to this guide for four years out of a six period.

Grant approvals – The Environment

Year	Amount	No of Grants	% of total grant-aid
1996/97	£437,000	20	(7%)
1995/96	£881,000	13	(16%)
1994/95	£314,000	10	(14%)
1992/93	£477,000	12	(14%)
1990/91	£810,000	19	(28%)

The larger approvals made in 1996/97 included:
- BTCV for core costs (£166,500 over 3 years);
- Painshill Park Trust for preparatory work for new visitor centre and to support extended opening hours (£100,000);
- Fairfield Mills, Sedburgh & District Buildings Preservation Trust, for conservation of the mills (£25,000);
- National Maritime Museum, towards Neptune Court (£25,000);
- Sir John Soane's Museum Society, towards the purchase of 14 Lincoln's Inn Fields (£25,000);
- Hestorcombe Gardens Trust, to restore the temples in Bampfylde Garden (£20,000);
- Winchester Theatre Appeal (£15,000);
- British Isles Bee Breeders Association for research on the Varroa mite (£10,000);
- Longparish PCC, towards church restoration (£10,000);
- Susex Historic Churches Trust, towards revenue costs (£5,000, with grants also made in the 2 preceding years).

Twenty one grants in all were made and eight of these were less than £5,000.

The bias of these grants is clearly towards the built heritage, with interest also in the natural heritage.

Applications: An application to one of the Sainsbury family trusts is an application to all; see the entry under 'Sainsbury Family Charitable Trusts, for address and application procedure. The trustees met five times a year.

Applicants should note that the 1996/97 report states: "Proposals are generally invited by the trustees or initiated at their request. Unsolicited applications are discouraged and are unlikely to be successful, even if they fall within an area in which the trustees are interested. The trustees prefer to support innovative schemes that can be successfully replicated or become self-sustaining. The trustees also support a number of arts and environmental developments of national or regional significance."

The Peter Nathan Charitable Trust

85 Ladbroke Road, London W11 3PJ
Contact: Dr P W Nathan
Trustees: Dr P W Nathan; Martin Starkie; Adrian Parsons; Felix Appelbe.
Grant total: £9,000 (1996)
Beneficial area: UK and overseas.

In 1994/95 the trust gave £11,000 in 59 grants, 33 of which were relevant to this guide. They ranged from very small gifts of £6 to £1,200. Grants were predominantly for wildlife, associated environmental causes and animal welfare.

Donations included:
- People's Trust for Endangered Species (£1,200);
- Isle of Man Basking Shark Project (£650);
- Ecological Foundation (£500);
- Survival Trust (£400);
- Clean Rivers Trust, RSPB, Care for the Wild (£300 each);
- Sebakwe Black Rhino Trust, Global Tiger Patrol, Gaia Trust (£250 each);
- London Wildlife Trust (£100).

Applications: In writing, concisely, to the correspondent.

The National Gardens Scheme Charitable Trust

Hatchlands Park, East Clandon, Guildford, Surrey GU4 7RT
Tel: 01483-211535; **Fax:** 01483-211537
Contact: Lt Col T A Marsh, Director
Grant total: £1.3m (1996/97)
Beneficial area: England and Wales.

The trust exists to support selected beneficiaries on a long term basis.

Of the £1.3 million distributed in 1997 the main beneficiaries were:
- MacMillan Cancer Relief (£700,000);
- Gardens Fund of the National Trust (£250,000);
- Queens Nursing Institute (£70,000);
- Nurses Welfare Service (£49,000);
- Charities nominated by Garden Owners (£128,000).

Applications: The trust has long-standing relationships with all its beneficiaries and makes no grants for other purposes. Applications are therefore not accepted.

The Naturesave Trust

42 Henley Street, Oxford OX4 1ES
Tel and Fax: 01865-242280; **E-mail:** naturesave@msn.com
Contact: Matthew Criddle
Trustees: Matthew Criddle; David Elliott.
Grant total: £10,000 (1996/97)
Beneficial area: UK only.

This trust was set up in August 1995 by Naturesave Policies Limited, an insurance intermediary providing buildings and home insurance policies from Lloyd's of London, of which Matthew Criddle is the director.

Its leaflet says that "10% of the premium generated from the sale of all policies goes to benefit environmental and conservationist organisations on specific projects". In addition a free environmental appraisal is offered to commercial and charitable organisations which are paid for also from trust funds. "The trust is keen to support those projects with a long-term benefit which deal proactively with the root of a particular problem as opposed to merely reacting to the effects. The projects considered must be from environmental and conservationist groups and organisations who seek funding for specific projects and not the general administrative costs of their respective organisations." The trust is particularly interested in supporting sustainable development activities and especially those projects which could eventually lead to a greater commercial application. David Elliott of the Energy & Environment Research Unit in the Faculty of Technology of the Open University is one of the trustees and well known for his work over many years on resourceful use of energy, both material and human.

No report and accounts of its work had arrived on public file at the Charity Commission by mid Summer 1997 but the founding trustee sent the following information that about 13 projects had been supported with the largest grant of £5,000 given to Parry People Movers towards an ultra light tram system. Other grants known to have been given include:

- The Energy Showcase, towards the building of energy-efficient and ecologically sound demonstration houses to encourage volume housing contractors to adopt the design as standard by the next century;
- The Wind Fund, for wind power infrastructure;
- Centre of Alternative Technology for a Solar Study Centre to promote awareness and usage of solar power;
- The Charcoal Initiative, towards woodland coppicing for charcoal generation;
- Kennet Otter Habitat Project;
- Dorset Wildlife Trust water vole survey;
- Energy 32;
- Barn Owl Trust;
- The Sanctuary.

Exclusions: Individuals.

Applications: Contact the trust for an application form.

The Network Foundation

BM Box 2063, London WC1 3XX
Contact: Vanessa Adams, Administrator
Trustees: Patrick Boase, Chair; John S Broad; Ingrid Broad; Samuel P Clark; Candia Gillett; Oliver Gillie; Manning Goodwin; Hugh MacPherson; Sara Robin.
Grant total: £601,000 (1995)
Beneficial area: UK and overseas.

The income of this unusual foundation, which does not seek applications, comes from donations by members of the associated company, the Network for Social Change Ltd, 'a community of wealthy individuals seeking to realise their visions in ways that enable others'.

It is understood from a 'recruitment bulletin' of the company that in 1993 grants of an average size of about £3,000 were given to about 80 projects/organisations. There is little more recent information. This bulletin explained how the foundation worked, at least at that time:

'The Network as a whole has no expressed policy on the types of organisation or projects it will back. The responsibility for bringing forward applications lies with the members. Because they are such a diverse group, so are the applications. However,....Network members' interests tend to lie in smaller projects and organisations, in backing the inspired project or individual who is in a good position to create wide ripples, and exclude relief work....Because the sponsorship...is in the hands of the members, rather than lying open to public application, the relationship...can be more of a partnership than is normal in a funder-funded situation."

1) The Network "Funding Cycle" takes place once a year and takes six months. Small groups of members assess the projects under one of four headings:

- Peace and Preservation of the Earth;
- Human Rights and Solidarity;
- Health and Wholeness;
- Arts and Media.

Once this is done a "package of projects" is presented to the membership. The members then allocate the funds they are donating under the four headings. They cannot allocate to individual projects.

2) The Network 'Informal Funding' process allows individual members to bring forward projects they intend to fund personally and which they want to invite others to join them in funding. These meetings are usually run four times a year with a quick turnaround of cash.

3) Network Major Projects, currently four of them, are ones in which the Network plays a significant funding role over several years. Most relate to development issues or economics.

Two three-day conferences are held in late Winter and early Autumn. Other meetings and smaller events are also arranged. Prospective new members are introduced either by meeting an existing member or attending a group introductory session held from time to time in London. They are then invited to a conference.

The 1994/95 accounts show expenditures of £382,000 for the main funding cycle, a further £97,000 through the informal funding cycle, £11,000 for 'major projects' and three named grants apparently made through the foundation, but probably in effect by individual members, to the New Economics Foundation (£10,000), for Third World debt (£40,000) and to the Opportunity Trust (£31,000).

Applications: The Network chooses the projects it wishes to support and does not solicit applications. Unsolicited applications cannot expect to receive a reply.

The New Horizons Trust

Paramount House, 290-292 Brighton Road, South Croydon, Surrey CR2 6AG
Tel: 0181-666 0201; Fax 0181-667 6037
Contact: The Secretary
Trustees: Michael Pilch CBE; Mrs Christine Pilch; Peter Miles; Tony Neale; Ms Kate Dibley.
Grant total: £28,000 (1996)
Beneficial area: UK.

The trust gives grants to groups of older people carrying out projects for the benefit of the community, not vice versa. Grants are given to any group proposing a good idea that will benefit the community provided that:
◆ There are at least 10 people in the group;
◆ At least half of them are aged 60 or over;
◆ The project is new and makes use of the knowledge and experience of group members.

Applications may be made by new or existing groups, but in the latter case they must show that it is an innovative departure and will be managed as an entirely separate project. Grants may cover any costs involved in planning, organising and running a project for up to 18 months for items such as rent, heating, light, furniture, office equipment, materials and supplies.

The trust raised support for its work from companies and trusts and some of its projects are specifically sponsored by a company. Grants are usually from £500 to £1,000. In 1996 the trust gave 30 grants totalling £28,000. Examples of projects relevant to this guide supported by the trust in 1996 included:
◆ Manton House, Newtown, Birmingham for garden creation for this sheltered housing scheme (£1,500);
◆ Milford Environmental Group, conservation of the Cam Valley outside bath (£1,000);
◆ Stafford churchyard Improvement (£1,000);
◆ Saltford Brass Mill, Bristol, for start of visitor programme (£968);
◆ Five Valleys Trust, for natural regeneration of brown trout near Bathampton (£500).

Exclusions: No funding is given to on-going projects. Grants are not given: to repay loans or to meet any previous obligations that may already have been incurred by a group before their project has been approved by the trust; to pay salaries, although legitimate expenses may be reimbursed to volunteers provided these do not form an excessive proportion of the total; for travelling expenses, although limited expenditure on transport may be approved where it forms an integral part of the project.

Applications: First write to the office if you think you fall within the scope of the trust's programme. Then you may be put in touch with the trust's nearest Area Officer who can provide an application form and further advice and information.

The Notgrove Trust

The Manor, Notgrove, Cheltenham,
Gloucestershire GL54 3BT
Tel: 01451-850239
Contact: David Acland, Trustee
Trustees: David Acland; Elizabeth Acland.
Grant total: £75,000 (August 1996/97)
Beneficial area: UK, but with a strong
interest in Gloucestershire.

"The trustees contribute to some local
Gloucestershire charities on a regular
basis." Our most recent detailed figures are
for August 1995 when the trust had assets
of over £1 million which generated an
income from which £64,000 was given in
29 grants. Grants ranged between £100
and £15,000.

Eight grants relevant to this guide totalling
£11,450 (18% of grant-aid) were given in
1995:
♦ Farms for City Children (£2,000 with
  £10,000 in the previous year);
♦ St Bartholomew's Notgrove Perpetual
  Fabric Fund (£8,000 with £20,000 in
  the previous year);
♦ Tiger Trust (£500);
♦ Cotswold Canals Trust, Countryside
  Workshops, Society for Environmental
  Exploration (£250 each);
♦ Gloucestershire Society (£200).

These grants show a care for Notgrove –
its Parish Church Council also received a
grant of £2,000 in 1995.

In 1994 a major grant of £10,000 was
given to the newly established Folly
Fellowship, which works for the heritage
in and around "follies, grottoes, and
garden buildings, monuments, ruins, sites
of historic interest or particular beauty".

Exclusions: The trustees discourage
speculative appeals from organisations,
either outside Gloucestershire or with no
established connection with the trustees.

Applications: Appeals will not be
acknowledged.

The Oakdale Trust

Tan-y-Coed, Panty-dwr, Rhayader, Powys
LD6 5LR
E-mail: oakdale@tan4.demon.co.uk
Contact: B Cadbury
Trustees: B Cadbury; Mrs F F Cadbury;
R A Cadbury; F B Cadbury; Mrs O H
Tatton-Brown; Dr R C Cadbury.
Grant total: £127,000 (1996/97)
Beneficial area: UK & overseas, with a
special interest in Wales.

The trustees have decided that they will
concentrate on making grants to charities
and causes in Wales, and not respond to
any new appeals from the rest of Britain.
This Quaker trust particularly gives to
aspects of penal reform, medicine,
children/youth, social work and
international aid.

In 1995/96 the trust had assets of £2.4
million. It gave 138 grants totalling
£127,000 ranging from less than £100 up
to £5,000.

Nine grants relevant to this guide totalling
£7,450 (6% of grant-aid) were made:
♦ Marie Stopes International (£3,000);
♦ Cwmdaiddwr Church Roof, Woodland
  Trust (£1,000 each);
♦ Vale View Allotments Association
  (£800);
♦ National Trust (£700);
♦ Shared Earth Trust (£500);
♦ Trust in Angling (£250);
♦ Barn Owl Trust (£200).

Two additional animal welfare grants were
given. In 1994/95 the RSPB gave £2,000
for a Scottish land purchase.

Exclusions: No grants to individuals or to
appeals from charities outside Wales unless
the work is international.

Applications: In writing to the
correspondent but owing to the lack of
secretarial help no acknowledgement can
be expected. Trustees usually meet in April
and September.

The Ofenheim & Cinderford Charitable Trusts

Baker Tilly, Iveco Ford House, Station Road, Watford, Hertfordshire WD1 1TG
Tel: 01923-816400
Contact: G Wright
Trustees: R J Clark; R Fitzherbert-Brockholes; R McLeod.
Grant total: £163,000 (1994/95)
Beneficial area: UK.

Since 1985, the grants given by the two trusts have been listed together since they are administrated together. The trusts support nationally known and well-established organisations of personal interest to the trustees. Most grants are given in the fields of health, welfare and the environment, with some to arts organisations. A large number are recurrent.

In 1994/95, the trusts had combined assets of over £3.4 million with an income of £164,000. The assets of the Cinderford Trust increased in recent years to £2.7 million, due to £1.16 million worth of investments willed by Dr Angela Ofenheim who died in 1992.

Both trusts give grants ranging between £1,000 and £10,000. The files of both trusts are held separately at the Charity Commission and it appears that the Cinderford gave £110,000 and the Ofenheim £53,000 during 1994/95. A total of 41 grants were made by the two trusts and included the following six grants totalling £19,000 (12 % of grant-aid) which are relevant to this guide:
- WWF UK (£7,000);
- Game Conservancy Trust, National Trust (£4,500 each);
- Fauna & Fauna Preservation Society, Tree Council, Wildfowl and Wetlands Trust (£1,000 each).

Applications: In writing to the correspondent. Unsuccessful applications will not be acknowledged.

The Oldham Foundation

Kings Well, Douro Road, Cheltenham, Gloucs GL50 2PT
Tel: 01242-236066
Contact: Dinah Oldham
Trustees: J H Oldham, Mrs Dinah Oldham, S T Roberts, Prof R E Thomas John Sharpe, John Bodden.
Grant total: £57,000 (1994/95)
Beneficial area: UK with a particular interest in the Gloucestershire area.

This trust gives to a wide range of environmental interests but its support fluctuates. in 1994/95 eight beneficiaries were relevant to this guide and given support totalling £10,750 (19 %) of grant-aid:
- Green College (£3,000);
- Parnham Trust (£2,800 in 3 grants);
- WaterAid (£2,750 in 2 grants);
- RSPB Maelltraeth Appeal (£1,500);
- Good Gardening (£400);
- City Farm Bristol, Gloucestershire Society, Horticultural Therapy (£100 each).

In the previous year total grant-aid of £65,000 was given but only 4 grants worth £2,950 were relevant to this guide. The largest was to Tewkesbury Abbey (£2,500) followed by the Mero Elephant Project (£250).

Applications: In writing to the correspondent.

The Olive Tree Trust

82a Huddleston Road, London N7 OEG
Contact: Miss C R Charity
Trustees: Caroline Charity; Emma Ranson; Jonathan Gillett.
Grant total: £7,000 (1995/96)
Beneficial area: UK.

This young trust set up in 1993 and had funds of £187,000 at the end of 1995/96 during which year it gave three grants to organisations in London:
- Environment Trust (£3,000);
- Community Self Build; Notting Hill Housing Trust (£2,000 each).

The correspondent has written that "The trust has been set up to give money to organisations that help those who are at the bottom of the social pile to be involved in projects that can improve their situation i.e. self building housing schemes, involvement in regeneration of an area, etc. This it is focused most upon people and communities and their relationships to involvement in improving their environmental state and in caring for the environment per se."

Applications: In writing to the correspondent. No replies given to unsuccessful applications.

The P F Charitable Trust

25 Copthall Avenue, London EC2R 7DR
Tel: 0171-638 5858
Contact: The Secretary
Trustees: Robert Fleming; Valentine P Fleming; Philip Fleming; R D Fleming.
Grant total: £980,000 (1995/96)
Beneficial area: UK, with apparent special interests in Oxfordshire and Scotland.

The trust gives to a very wide range of charitable work. Trust's own analysis of its donations in 1995/96 showed categories for Conservation, preservation, restoration etc: £88,000 – 9% (36 grants)

These included:
◆ Historic Churches Preservation Trust (£20,000);
◆ Scottish Churches Architectural Heritage Trust (£15,000);
◆ Countryside Foundation (£10,000 each);
◆ CPRE (£1,000 for Oxfordshire branch);
◆ Cathedral Camps, Central Scotland Countryside Trust, Chester Cathedral Building Appeal, Civic Trust, National Trust for Scotland, International Monuments Trust (£1,000 each);
◆ AWE Fisheries Trust, Habitat for Humanity GB, Holy Cross Church (£5,000 each).

Animals, birds, fish etc: £9,000 – 94% (13 grants).
These included:
◆ Berkshire, Buckinghamshire & Oxfordshire Naturalists' Trust (£2,500);
◆ Atlantic Salmon Research Trust (£1,000).

Exclusions: No grants to individuals or non-registered charities. Individual churches are now excluded.

Applications: To the correspondent at any time, in writing with full information. Replies will be sent to unsuccessful applications if a SAE is enclosed. Trustees meet monthly.

The Paget Charitable Trust

(also known as the Herbert-Stepney Charitable Settlement)

41 Priory Gardens, London N6 5QU
Contact: Joanna Herbert-Stepney
Trustees: Joanna Herbert-Stepney; Lesley Mary Rolling; Mrs Joy Pollard.
Grant total: £100,000 (1994/95)
Beneficial area: UK and overseas, particularly local activities in Loughborough area.

In 1994/95, the trust had assets of £2.3 million, an income of £117,000 and gave 86 grants totalling £100,000. They ranged between £500 and £6,000.

The largest grants go to overseas relief and development work. Other interests include: deprived children; elderly people; carers; organic farming and animal welfare.

Nine grants were relevant to this guide and totalled over £10,000 (10 % of grant-aid):
◆ Intermediate Technology, Survival International (£2,000 each with grants also in the previous year);
◆ Friends of the Earth (£1,000 with £2,000 in the previous year);
◆ APT Design & Development, Harvest Help, Heritage House, Marie Stopes International, Soil Association (£1,000 each);
◆ Tree Aid (£500).

Exclusions: Normally registered charities only. The trust does not support individuals, projects for people with mental disabilities or medical research.

Applications: In writing to the correspondent; there is no application form. The trustees meet in spring and autumn.

The Gerald Palmer Trust

Eling Estate Office, Hermitage, Thatcham, Newbury, Berks RG16 9UF
Tel: 01635-200268
Contact: C J Pratt
Trustees: C J Pratt; J M Clutterbuck; D R W Harrison; J N Abell.
Grant total: £115,000 (1995/96)
Beneficial area: UK, especially Berkshire.

The trust's main activity is the management of its Eling Estate though it also gives grants to charitable organisations. In 1995/96 it had assets of over £6 million and an income of £576,000. The size of its grant-making fluctuates, from £47,000 in 1993/94, to £90,0000 in 1994/95 and to £115,000 in 1995/96 when its largest grant was given to St Katharine's House (£20,000). In 1992/93 Hampstead Norreys Amenity Trust received (£30,000).

In 1995/96 at least eight grants were relevant to this guide and totalled £33,000 (29 %) of grant-aid. (This does not include the major grant to St Katharine's House as it is not known whether this would be for heritage work on, say a fine house or an almshouse, or if the grant is for social work like an old people's home.)

- National Trust (£10,000);
- Winterbourne Church Appeal, St George's Wash Commmon, St Mary's Hampstead Norreys (£5,000 each);
- Farming & Wildlife Advisory Group (£3,000, 1st of 2);
- Countryside Foundation (£2,500);
- Thames Salmon Trust (£1,500 with £2,000 in the previous year);
- Forestry Trust for Conservation & Education (£1,000).

Another small trust, the Eling Trust, is also administered from the same address and supports charities in Berkshire. It gave donations of about £8,000 in 1993.

Exclusions: No grants to individuals, or to small local charities far from Berkshire.

Applications: In writing to the correspondent.

The Rudolph Palumbo Charitable Foundation

37a Walbrook, London EC4N 8BS
Tel: 0171 6269236
Contact: T H Tharby
Trustees: Lord Mishcon; Sir Matthew Farrer; Lady Palumbo; T H Tharby; J G Underwood.
Grant total: £434,000 (1992/93)
Beneficial area: UK and overseas.

Peter Palumbo won the battle to replace the old Mappin & Webb listed buildings in the city of London with a more "progressive" building. Voluntary groups were allowed to use the undeveloped site rent-free. Palumbo's City Acre Property Investment Trust signed a four year covenant to pay the Rudolph Palumbo Charitable Foundation (named after his father) £350,000 a year from 1990. It is not known whether this covenant has been renewed after 1994.

The foundation has been concerned with: Advancement of Education; Conservation of the Environment; Relief of Poverty; General Purposes. Total income in 1992/93 was £371,000 which with funds brought forward left £701,000 available for distribution. Forty donations were made totalling £434,000 leaving £266,000 in hand. Of these 12 were over £10,000 including two huge grants of more than £100,000 each, and 20 were for less than £1,000.

The following grants totalling £243,000 (56% of grant-aid) were relevant to this guide:

- St Stephen's Church Walbrook (£123,000);
- Painshill Park Trust (£100,000);
- Natural History Museum (£20,000).

Exclusions: Applicants should remember that the position with this trust is extremely unclear. Up-to-date records have not been submitted to the Charity Commission.

Applications: The solicitors have written in reply to this draft that: "The funds of this charity are heavily subscribed, and I am not at present in a position to know when grants can resume." He wanted the charity omitted from this guide "until matters are more certain".

The Panton Trust

The Old Paddock, Oakdleigh Road, Hatch End, Pinner, Middx HA5 4HB
Contact: H J Garside
Trustees: H J Garside; R Craig; L M Slavin.
Grant total: £20,000 (1994/95) but see below

In 1995/96 the trust had assets of £183,000 but it's income from dividends was negligible compared with previous years (only £9,000 compared with £32,000 in 1994/95 and £35,000 in 1993/94). The trust has made no grants since 1993/94 when £20,000 was disbursed in thirteen grants ranging between £200 and £3,000.

The trust seems to have a particular interest in wildlife and countryside conservation.

Eight grants totalling £15,000 (75 % of grant-aid) were relevant to this guide:
- Soil Association (£3,000);
- Cotswold Canals Trust, International Primate Protection League, Woodland Trust, WWF UK (£2,000 each);
- BTCV (£1,500);
- Wildfowl & Wetlands Trust (£1,400);
- Warwickshire Nature Conservation Trust (£1,000).

Applications: In writing to the correspondent.

The Frank Parkinson Agricultural Trust

33 Prospect Lane, West Common, Harpenden, Herts AL5 2PL
Tel: 01582-761173
Contact: A D S Robb, Secretary to the Trustees
Trustees: Prof P N Wilson; Prof J D Leaver; W M Hudson; J S Sclanders.
Grant total: £77,000 (1996)
Beneficial area: UK.

The Trust has as its principal object the improvement and welfare of British Agriculture. In 1996 the Trust made the following grants:
- Capel Manor Horticultural & Environmental Centre (£40,000);
- Wye College, University of London (£20,000);
- Gorgie City Farm (£10,000);
- Nuffield Farming Scholarship Trust (£6,000);

Part of the grant to Capel Manor had originally been phased to have been paid in the previous two years. Other recent beneficiaries have been The Scottish Farm and Countryside Educational Trust, Caring for Life (a charity) and Orley College of Agriculture & Horticulture.

Exclusions: Grants are given to corporate bodies and the trust is not able to assist with financial help to any individuals undertaking post-graduate studies or degree courses.

Applications: In writing to the correspondent. The trustees meet annually in April.

The Late Barbara May Paul Charitable Trust

Lloyds Private Banking Ltd, south Midlands Area Office, 22-26 Ock Street, Abingdon, Oxon OX14 5SW
Tel: 01235-554000
Contact: The Manager

Trustees: LLoyds Bank plc.
Grant total: £90,000 (1995/96)
Beneficial area: UK, with a preference for East Anglia.

The trust gives generally and particularly supports the young, the elderly and medical care. Its grants are usually for £1,000 each and 75 grants totalling £90,000 were given in 1994/95. This total grant-aid contrasts with the previous year when £159,000 was disbursed although its yearly income had been only £30,000. (Larger grants of £5,000 to £10,000 have been sometimes given for capital projects.)

In 1994/95 five grants totalling £5,000 (7% of grant-aid) were relevant to this guide: Daws Hall Trust, National Trust, RSPB, St Andrew's Ipswich, Sutton Church (£1,000 each).

Applications: In writing to the correspondent.

The Peacock Charitable Trust

P.O. Box 902, London SW20 0XJ
Contact: Mrs Janet Gilbert
Trustees: W M Peacock; Mrs S Peacock; C H Peacock.
Grant total: £1,356,000 (1995/96)
Beneficial area: UK.

The trust has a stated interest in "medical research and disability, youth work and conservation". It is very much a family-run trust with a consistent pattern of giving to certain organisations, particularly those concerned with medical research and disability. It supports chosen organisations over a number of years and there appears to be little leeway for new applicants to be considered.

In 1995/96 the trust had assets of £8.9 m and gave nearly 120 grants ranging between £100,000 and £200 with most grants (87) between £1,000 and £10,000. Only a third of all beneficiaries (40) had not received support in the previous year. Those receiving the largest grants have

been supported over many years, though sometimes with a short break. In 1994/95 the top 21 grants of over £20,000 absorbed two-thirds of the total grant-aid (£785,000), and only three of these organisations had not been supported in the previous year. Very few grants were given to local groups and these concentrated in the south of London (Merton and Wimbledon) and adjacent counties.

In 1996/97 eight grants totalling £60,000 (4% of total grant aid) were relevant to this guide.

- National Trust (£20,000 with £10,000 in the previous 2 years);
- Marie Stopes International (£12,000 – with £10,000 in the previous year);
- Ironbridge Gorge Museum (£7,500 and in the previous year);
- British Trust for Conservation Volunteers (£7,000);
- BTCV (£6,000 with £10,000 in the previous year);
- RSPB (£8,000 – with £6,000 & £11,000 in the previous 2 years);
- Wildfowl and Wetlands Trust (£6,000 with £500 in the previous year);
- British Trust for Ornithology (£6,000);
- Magdalen College Oxford Development Trust; Marine Conservation Society; Upper Severn Navigational Trust (£5,000 each);
- CPRE (£3,000 with £5,000 in the previous year);
- Sustrans (£2,000);National Federation of City Farms (£1,000 and £2,000 in the previous year);
- Chichester Cathedral Trust (£1,500 with £1,000 in the previous year).

Exclusions: Individuals and students.

Applications: Registered charities only should apply in writing, preferably early in the year and accompanied by full accounts. "Applications should include clear details of the need the intended project is designed to meet plus any outline budget. Only applications from eligible bodies are considered, when further information may be requested. To maximise the use of funds beneficially, only applications being considered will receive replies."

The Susanna Peake Charitable Trust

PO Box 191, 10 Fenchurch Street, London
EC3M 3LB
Tel: 0171-956 6600
Contact: Kleinwort Benson Trustees Ltd
Trustees: Susanna Peake; David Peake.
Grant: £99,000 (1995/96)

This is a "Kleinwort family trust", a
number of which have entries in this guide.
In 1995/96 it had assets of £1.38 million
which produced an income of £109,000 (a
result of the "windfall" from the take-over
of Kleinwort Benson by Dresdner Bank).
In 1995/96 grants totalling £99,000 were
made (compared with £54,000, in the
previous year). These 46 grants ranged
between £500 and £2,000 and were given
for education, medical research and
disabled people.

In 1995/96 nine grants fell within the ambit
of this guide. They totalled over £13,000 (14
% of grant-aid) and were given to
- St James Longborough (£4,000 in 2 grants);
- Population Concern (£2,000 each and in
  previous years);
- Farm Africa (£2,000);
- BBONT, Chiswick House Friends,
  Gloucestershire Wildlife Trust,
  Horticultural Therapy, St Lawrence
  Bourton on the Hill (£1,000 each);
- Cameroon Rainforest Appeal (£500).

A regular grant is given to the Heythrop
Hunt Charitable Trust. In previous years
support has also been given to the
Zoological Society of London, Cotswold
Canals Trust and the International Centre
for Conservation Education.

Exclusions: No grants to individuals.

Applications: To the correspondent in
writing.

The Hon Charles Pearson Charity Trust

Pollen House, 10-12 Cork Street, London
W1X 1PD
Tel: 0171-439 9061; Fax: 0171- 437 2680;
E-mail: mailbox@m.f.s.co.uk

Contact: The Secretary
Trustees: The Cowdray Trust Ltd.
Grant total: £48,000 (1996/97)
Beneficial area: UK.

In 1995/96, the trust had assets of
£2.1 million and an income of £760,000
from which 13 grants totalling £69,000
were given. They ranged between £200
and £30,000.

Four grants with relevance to this guide
totalled £43,000 (62% of grant-aid):
- Population Concern (£10,000 with a
  similar grant in the previous year);
- Game Conservancy Scottish Research
  Trust (£30,000);
- Scottish Country Life Museums Trust
  (£2,000);
- Echt Church (£1,000).

Exclusions: No grants to individuals;
registered charities only.

Applications: In writing to the
correspondent. There are no application
forms or deadlines. Acknowledgements are
not sent to unsuccessful applications.

The Pen-y-Clip Trust

59 Madoc Street, Llandudno, Conwy,
LL 30 2TW
Tel: 01492-874391
Contact: The Secretary
Trustees: Philip G Brown; Mrs Janet E Lea.
Grant total: £17,000 (1996/97)
Beneficial area: North Wales.

In 1995/96, its seventh year, the trust had
assets of £256,000 and an income of about
£19,000 from which £17,000 was given in
four grants all for environmental work in
Wales and all relevant to this guide (100
% of grant-aid).
- University of Wales, Bangor,
  advancement of marine archaeology
  (£7,500);
- RSPB Plas Bog, Anglesey home of
  bittern (£5,000);
- North Wales Wildlife Trust for
  publication of butterfly book on
  Gwynedd (£2,500);

◆ Oriel Ynys Mon for Tunnecliffe exhibition (£2,000).

Applications: In writing to the correspondent.

The Bernard Piggott Trust

James & Lister Lea, 42 Bull Street, Birmingham B4 6AF
Contact: Derek Lea, Clerk
Trustees: The Ven W Thomas; R A Sabin; D C Morris Owen; M St George Arrowsmith.
Grant total: £29,000 (1994/95)
Beneficial area: UK with a particular interest in Birmingham and parts of North Wales.

The trust gives to a range of charitable activity. Grants relevant to this guide were shown by its grants schedules to be mainly for churches and this support may, or may not be, for conservation/restoration. Small amounts were also given to countryside conservation.

Grants in the most recent annual schedule were given to:
◆ St Mary's Dolgellau (£3,000);
◆ St David's Cathedral, Holy Trinity Sutton Coldfield, Lighthorne Church (£1,000 each);
◆ BTCV, St Alban's & St Patrick's Highgate (£500 each).

Exclusions: Individuals.

Applications: In writing to the correspondent.

The Pilgrim Trust

Fielden House, Little College Street, London SW1P 3SH
Tel: 0171-222 4723; Fax: 0171-976 0461
Contact: Georgina Nayler, Director
Trustees: Mrs. Mary Moore, Chairman; Neil MacGregor; Lord Jenkins; Lord Thomson; Nicolas Barker; Lady Anglesey; Sir Claus Moser; Lord Armstrong; Lord of Cornhill Bingham; Eugenie Turton; Lord Cobbold.

Grant total: £1,671,000 (1996)
Beneficial area: UK.

The trust makes grants, sometimes large and spread over a number of years, but seldom recurrent and usually for amounts between £5,000 and £10,000, in the fields of preservation, art and learning, and social welfare. Though there can be exceptions, grants are mainly for capital or specific project purposes, rather than revenue funding.

During 1996 the trustees reviewed their policy and agreed guidelines from which the following extracts are taken:

Preservation
◆ Preservation of architectural or historical features on historic buildings or the conservation of individual monuments or structures of importance to the surrounding environment. Trustees will not normally contribute to major restorations or repairs unless a discrete element of the project can be clearly identified as appropriate.
◆ Projects that seek to give a new use to obsolete buildings of outstanding architectural or historic interest.
◆ Dissemination of information about historic buildings and documents and their importance to the community.
◆ Cataloguing and conservation of records associated with archaeology, marine archaeology, historic buildings and landscapes.
◆ Churchyards – the Pilgrim Trust will consider applications for grants towards the repair and conservation of churchyard walls and exterior funerary monuments.

Art and Learning
◆ Repairs and improvements to non-national museums and galleries.
◆ Cataloguing and practical conservation schemes, including local community schemes.

In 1995 the trust's gross income was £2.3 million, down from £2.4 million the year before. In 1996 the trust received 1,166 applications and made 244 grants, a success rate of (1:6).

The division of grant authorisations in 1996 was as follows:

- Art and learning: grants totalling £383,644
- Social welfare: grants totalling £740,858
- Preservation: grants totalling £546,175
  Ecclesiastical buildings – £278,075
  Secular buildings – £203,100
  Countryside – £65,000.

There is also a Small Grants Fund for the secretary to authorise grants of under £1,000. Seven such grants were made in 1996, all of £500 or less.

In 1996 some 25% of the trust's funding was given in areas relevant to this guide. Half these funds were spent on the repair and conservation of church fabric and fittings largely channelled through annual grants to other funding bodies (see below). Grants included:

Under 'Ecclesiastical buildings':

- Historic Churches Preservation Trust, block grant (£80,000);
- Council for the Care of Churches, block grant (£75,000);
- Scottish Churches Architectural Heritage Trust, block grant (£20,000);
- Shrewsbury Abbey, towards the cost of repairs to the exterior stonework and stained glass windows (£5,000);
- St Mark's Church, Dundela, Belfast, towards the repair of the tower and west front of the church (£7,500).

The grants under the categories 'Preservation' and 'Arts and Learning' were spread widely throughout the UK.

Exclusions: No grants are made to individuals, profit distributing companies or projects outside the UK.

Applications: Guidelines and application forms are available from the Pilgrim Trust offices. All applicants should complete the application form and attach the information which is listed in the checklist at the end of the form.

1. Name, address and telephone number of the charity.
2. Charity number and date of registration.
3. Name and designation of contact.
4. Aims of the organisation.
5. Subject of this appeal. Where appropriate, give timescales for various phases of the work and dates for completion.
6. Financial details of the project. State the total cost of the project and the amount already raised or promised. Have any contributions come from statutory sources? State major contributors.
7. Sum appealed for from Pilgrim Trustees.
8. A copy of the latest report and accounts.

The Cecil Pilkington Charitable Trust

P O Box 8162, London W2 1GF
Contact: A P Pilkington
Trustees: Sir Anthony Pilkington; A P Pilkington; Dr L H A Pilkington; R F Carter Jonas.
Grant total: £138,000 (October 1996)
Beneficial area: UK and overseas with a preference for Liverpool and St Helens.

Grants from this trust are made mainly to conservation projects, together with support for third world development and Merseyside charities.

In 1996, the trust had assets of £4.9 million which generated an income of £169,000.

It made 20 grants of between £1,000 and over £29,000. Of these 12 were clearly relevant to this guide and totalled £102,000 (73% of grant aid):

- Forestry Commission (£30,000);
- Conifer Conservation Programme (£27,000);
- Intermediate Technology, and RSNC (£10,000 each);
- BTCV, Ness Botanical Gardens, Rare Breeds Survival Trust (£5,000 each);
- Groundwork Trust, Civic Trust (£3,000);
- RSPB (£2,000);
- Barn Owl Trust, and BBONT (£1,000 each).

Applications: In writing to the correspondent.

The Austin & Hope Pilkington Trust

PO Box 124, Stroud, Gloucester GL6 7YM
Tel: 01734-597111
Contact: Penny Jones, Secretary
Trustees: Dr L H A Pilkington; Mrs J M Jones; Mrs P S Shankar.
Grant total: £269,000 (November 1994)
Beneficial area: UK, with a preference for Merseyside.

In 1994 the assets of the trust were £4.9 million generating an income of £230,000. A total of £269,000 was given in 40 grants ranging between £1,000 and £60,000. Nine grants were for £10,000 and more, but most grants were between £1,000 and £5,000.

Four grants were relevant to this guide and totalled £18,750 (7% of grant-aid):
- National Trust Lake District Appeal (£10,000);
- Letheringsett Church Roof Restoration (£5,000);
- Intermediate Technology (£3,000);
- Groundwork St Helen's (£750).

All, except the church roof, had been assisted in previous years.

Exclusions: No grants to individuals. Grants for purely local organisations, except in the St Helens area, are excluded.

Applications: In writing to the correspondent.

The Polden-Puckham Charitable Foundation

PO Box 951, Bristol BS99 5QH
Contact: The Secretary
Trustees: Carol Freeman; Candia Carolan; David Gillett; Harriet Gillett; Jenepher Gordon; Heather Swailes; Anthony Wilson.
Grant total: £293,000 (1996/97)
Beneficial area: UK and overseas.

The foundation's policy guidelines are as follows.
- Peace: 'Development of ways of resolving international and internal conflicts peacefully, and of removing the causes of conflict.'
- Ecological issues: 'Work which tackles the underlying pressures and conditions leading towards global environmental breakdown; particularly initiatives which promote sustainable living.'
- Other: 'PPCF also supports work on women's issues, human rights and social change. It has a long standing link with the Society of Friends.'
- Underlying Approach: 'In its work the foundation aims to support projects that change values and attitudes, that promote equity and social justice, and that develop radical alternatives to current economic and social structures. It gives particular consideration to small pioneering headquarter organisations.'

In 1996/97 the trust had assets of £6.8 million which generated an income of £301,000 from which 63 donations of £273,000 were made to 54 organisations. Its grants ranged between £100 and £20,000 with most grants (42) between £1,000 and £5,000. Most grants are normally for one to three years.

Grants relevant to this guide totalled £76,000 (28% of grant-aid) in 1995/96:
- New Economics Foundation (£15,000);
- Women's Environmental Network (£6,600 in 2 grants);
- Association for the Conservation of Energy, UN Environment and Development – UK Committee (£6,000 each);
- Friends of the Earth Trust, Gaia Foundation, Green Alliance Trust, SOS Sahel (£5,000 each);
- Ecological Foundation – Ecologist Outreach, Gaia House Trust, Tourism Concern (£3,000 each);
- Gaia Foundation – Global Commons Institute (£2,500);
- Green Network Charitable Trust, SAFE Charitable Trust (£2,000) each;

- Conifer Conservation Programme, Institute for Environmental Policy, The Natural Step (£1,500 each);
- Centre for Alternative Technology – Green Teacher, Permaculture Association (£1,000 each);
- World Conservation Monitoring Service (£250);
- UN Environmental & Development Committee (£6,000 in 2 grants).

In 1996/97 it is known that grants included:
- Climate Action Network, Transport 2000 (£5,000 each);
- UN Environmental and Development Committee (£6,000 in 2 grants).

Exclusions: Grants to individuals; travel bursaries; study; academic research; capital projects; community or local projects (except innovative prototypes for widespread application); general appeals.

Applications: The trustees meet twice a year in late March/early April, and October. The foundation will not send replies to applications outside its area of interest.

Applications should be no longer than two pages and should include the following:
- a short outline of the project, its aims and methods to be used;
- the amount requested (normally between £500 and £5,000 for one to three years), the names of other funders and possible funders, and expected sources of funding after termination of PPCF funding;
- information on how the project is to be monitored, evaluated, and publicised;
- background details of the key persons in the organisation. Please also supply: latest set of audited accounts; a detailed budget of the project; annual budget if available; list of trustees or board of management; names of two referees not involved in the organisation; charity registration number, or name and number of a charity which can accept funds on your behalf.

The Porter Foundation

Dolphin House, St Peter Street, Winchester, Hants SO23 8BW
Contact: Paul Williams, Executive Director
Trustees: Dame Shirley Porter; Sir Leslie Porter; Steven Porter; David Brecher.
Grant total: £1 million (1996/97)
Beneficial area: UK and Israel.

The foundation was set up in 1970 by Dame Shirley Porter, a former leader of Westminster City Council and daughter of Sir John and Lady Sarah Cohen, and Sir Leslie Porter, former chairman and president of Tesco.

The Porter Foundation has developed a set of policy guidelines to help direct its activity. 'The majority of funding will be towards projects in four key areas: education, the environment, cultural activity, and health, welfare, and humanitarian assistance'.

'Grants can be made for capital projects or for specific programmes or activities with a measurable end result. Grants will not be made on a recurring annual basis, or to cover general running costs. There is no maximum grant. Matching funding applications are welcomed.'

In 1995/96 the foundation had assets of £23 million which generated an income of over £1 million.

Its environmental support has concentrated on the Porter Super Centre for Ecology and Environment and Technology at Tel Aviv University (£120,000 a year for eight years).

Exclusions: 'The foundation funds only charitable organisations and does not make grants to individual applicants or respond to circular appeals.'

Applications: In writing to the correspondent. Trustees meet in April, July and December.

The Sir John Priestman Charity Trust

Messrs McKenzie Bell & Sons,
19 John Street, Sunderland SR1 1JQ
Tel: 0191-567 4857
Contact: R W Farr
Trustees: J R Kayll, Chairman; J R
Heslop; R W Farr; T R P S Norton.
Grant total: £198,000 (1994)
Beneficial area: UK, but with a strong
emphasis on Durham and Sunderland.

The trust was set up by Sir John Priestman
with an endowment of shares in several
railway companies. In 1994 the trust had
assets of £2 million, an income of £251,000
and made grants totalling £198,000.

In all, the trust gave grants relevant to this
guide worth over £58,000 (29% of total
grant-aid) in 1994.

Of this, £48,640 was given to 26
churches, including Friends of Durham
Cathedral (£2,140) as one of the trust's
aims is the 'maintenance of churches and
church buildings'.

Eight other grants relevant to this guide
totalled over £9,000:
+ Castle Quay Heritage Project (£2,000);
+ Woodcock & Bowes Almshouses
  (£1,500);
+ Durham Wildlife Trust (£1,355);
+ Wildfowl & Wetlands Trust (£1,315);
+ Southwick Village Farm (£1,000);
+ BTCV, Cathedral Camps Durham,
  Consett Acorn Trust (£750 each).

Applications: In writing to the
correspondent. Trustees meet in January,
April, July and October.

The Prince of Wales' Charities Trust

The Prince of Wales' Office, St James'
Palace, London SW1A 1BS
Contact: The Secretary
Trustees: Commander Richard Aylard;
M Henry Boyd-Carpenter; the Earl Peel.
Grant total: £149,000 (1994/95).)
Beneficial area: UK

'The trustees are primarily concerned to
support the charities and charitable
activities in which the Prince of Wales has
a particular interest.' The trust has a
company which exploits certain of the
Prince's copyrights particularly his artistic
and literary work. The profits from these
are donated to the trust.

In 1994/95 the trust had assets of nearly £3
million, an income of £480,000 and made
grants of £149,000. This was considerably
lower than in previous years, £275,000
(1993/94) and £324,000 (1992/93) and
the trust seems to be building up its capital
base. It gave 63 grants in 1994/95.

Unfortunately its grant list only included
the name of the beneficiary, not the grant
made. In previous years the accounts had
included categorisation without the detail
of the recipient. These figures showed
considerable variation in emphasis but
with conservation remaining stable
compared with medical or social and no
listing for arts organisations which feature
in the 1994/95 list.

	1991/92	1992/93
Medical	£156,000	£11,000
Social, benevolent, welfare	£86,000	£362,000
Conservation	£70,000	£64,000
Miscellaneous	£10,000	£26,000
Youth, education, sports	£2,000	£882,000
The Church	£500	£2,000

Beneficiaries relevant to this guide in
1994/95 were:
+ Sustrans
+ Farmhand
+ Pesticides Trust
+ Landlife
+ Habitat Scotland
+ Lancashire Wildlife Trust
+ Gloucestershire Wildlife Trust
+ Prince of Wales' Institute of
  Architecture
+ SAVE
+ Gloucestershire Historic Churches
+ Friends of Flitchum Church
+ St Peter's Wolferton

◆ Friends of Wakefield Chantry Chapel
◆ Holy Trinity Church Tresillian Appeal
◆ Shipton Moyne PCC Church Restoration
◆ St Asaph Cathedral Organ Appeal
◆ St Bartholomew's, St George's and St Florence Churches
◆ Southern African Rural Development.

Exclusions: No grants to individuals

Applications: In writing to the correspondent. However the Prince has particular charitable interests of his own (see note above) and unsolicited applications or those unconnected with these are unlikely to be productive.

The Ptarmigan Trust

Dolesden Farm, Turville Heath, Henley-on-Thames, Oxon RG9 6TJ
Contact: A Nicholson
Trustees: Andrew Nicholson; K Nicholson; Rodney Stone.
Grant total: £6,000 (1994/95)

This small trust in 1994/95 had assets of £78,000 and an income of £4,000. Whilst it has general charitable objects its grants show a particular interest in arts and the environmental concerns.

Five grants in 1994/95 totalling £5,000 (83% of grant-aid) were relevant to this guide. The largest was to the Paper Recycling Education Trust in Malawi (£3,000), with grants under £1,000 each to ITDG, RSPB, Environment Investigation Agency and the Woodland Trust. This year is understood to be exceptional and interests are usually biased more towards the arts.

In the previous year £9,000 was given in 15 grants and included grants to each of the organisation listed above, so there appears to be little leeway for new approaches.

Applications: This small trust is unable to consider unsolicited applications and no replies can be made to them.

Mr and Mrs J A Pye's Charitable Settlement

c/o Messrs Darbys, 50 New Inn Hall Street, Oxford OX1 2DN
Tel: 01865-247294
Contact: See above
Trustees: G W F Archer; R H Langdon-Davies; G C Pye.
Grant total: £349,000 (1995/96)
Beneficial area: UK, particularly the Oxford area.

The settlement was created by Jack A Pye, an estate developer from Oxford, and his wife, for general charitable purposes. Its particular interests are stated as 'nutritional and medical research, mental health and education, child welfare, conservation and the arts, as well as national and local needs in various fields'.

In 1995/96 the settlement had assets of nearly £6 million in both property and investments which raised an income of £372,000 from which 188 grants of £349,000 were made. Only 10 grants were for £10,000 or more, 37 grants were between £1,000 and £3,500, and 140 grants were for £500 and less. About 40 grants were given in the Oxfordshire area and the major part of the funding was distributed there. The vast majority of beneficiaries (143) had been given grants in the previous year. This is a large increase from the previous edition of this guide when only 43 beneficiaries had received grants in the previous year.

Grants relevant to this guide totalled some £160,000 (49% of grant-aid) in 1995/96:
◆ The Elm Farm Research Centre, a mixed organic farm at Hampstead Marshall, near Newbury, a regular beneficiary of a grant over 3 times larger than others (£94,000);
◆ Parnham Trust (£25,000 with £10,000 in the previous year);
◆ British Trust for Conservation Volunteers (£15,000 and in the previous year);
◆ Plan International, for water project in Zimbabwe (£7,500);

- Town and Country Planning Association (£3,000);
- Lancaster University, Unit of Vegetation Science (£2,000 and in the previous year);
- Marine Conservation Society, Royal Botanic Gardens Kew (£1,000 and in the previous year);
- Henry Doubleday Research Foundation (£1,000);
- British Trust for Ornithology, Dry Stone Walling Association, International Council for Bird Preservation, Population Concern, Marie Stopes International, Forestry Trust for Conservation and Education, Whale and Dolphin Conservation Society (£500);
- 8 smaller grants of £200 – £250 were also given.

Exclusions: No payments to individuals.

Applications: In writing to the correspondent.

The Claude & Margaret Pyke Charitable Trust

Dunderdale Lawn, Penshurst Road, Newton Abbot, Devon TQ12 1EN
Tel: 01626-54404
Contact: C D Pike
Trustees: C D Pike; M Pike; J D Pike; Dr P A D Holland.
Grant total: £9,000 (1994/95)
Beneficial area: UK, with a particular interest in Devon.

This trust concentrates its support on the 'environment, tree planting and wildlife'. It is associated with the Woodlands Trust (a general charity) from which £10,000 was transferred during 1994/95 to cope with the 'very heavy demands' made on it during the year.

In 1994/95 it had assets of £154,000, and an income of £27,000 from which more than 30 grants totalling £9,000 were given. A full list was not given with its accounts but its report noted the following:

- Edinburgh Academy for planting trees, Devon County Agricultural Association Forestry Section, (£1,000 each);
- Royal Albert Memorial Museum Appeal (£500).

NOTE: The Woodlands Trust gives generally in the West Midlands, Herfordshire and London area and apparently to work involving young and elderly people. A detailed entry has not been made because its support to environmental work appears to be minor. In 1994/95 its grant-aid of £48,000 supported over 50 organisations of which only three grants of £500 each, to BTCV, LWT and the Responsible Forestry Programme, were directly relevant to this guide.

Applications: Applicants should note that this trust did not want an entry in this guide so it is most unlikely that unsolicited applications will be welcomed or receive a response.

The Radcliffe Trust

5 Lincoln's Inn Fields, London
WC2A 3BT
Tel: 0171-242 9231; Fax: 0171-831 1525
Contact: Ivor F Guest
Trustees: Sir Ralph Verney; Lord Wilberforce; Lord Quinton; Lord Balfour of Burleigh; Lord Cottesloe
Grant total: £307,000 (1995/96)
Beneficial area: UK.

The Radcliffe Trust has developed a policy to support a very precise range of activities in music and the crafts, with a small margin to look at activities outside its main concerns. It has a distinguished history and was founded in 1714 by the will of Dr John Radcliffe, the most prominent physician of his day, who left the income from his property to fund the trust. Its present trustees are all titled and three have served with national arts councils.

In 1995/96 the trust had a gross income of £385,000 from assets of £7.15 million. In this year it reduced its payments on its administrative costs to 22% of income (compared with 30% in the previous year).

Total crafts grants in 1995/96: £154,000 in 32 grants ranging between £600 and 20,000.

'In the area of crafts, the main thrust is the support of apprentices, mostly but not exclusively, in cathedral workshops. For other grants, the trustees' main concern is to achieve a standard of excellence in crafts related particularly to conservation. The trustees monitor the progress of projects for which grants are made, particularly those which are spread over periods of more than one year'. 'The trustees make small grants for the repair and conservation of church furniture, including bells and monuments. Such grants are made only through the Council for the Care of Churches; direct applications are not accepted.'

The largest grants were given to the Weald and Downland Open Museum (£20,000), Iona Cathedral Trust (£17,500), the Council for the Care of Churches (£7,500), the Royal Academy of Arts (£7,000), and the Scottish Museum (£6,500).

Total music grants in 1995/96: £52,000 in 13 grants.

Total miscellaneous grants in 1995/96: £26,000 in 10 grants ranging between under £50 to £12,500. These included two major grants to the Allerton Research and Educational Trust (£12,500) and the Buckinghamshire County Museum (£10,000).

Exclusions: No grants to individual applicants, for social welfare, for buildings, for medical research, or in the music field for performance sponsorship or organ restoration.

Applications: In writing to the correspondent before the end of February and August each year for music applications, and before the end of March and September each year for other applications.

The Ratcliff Foundation

Ernst & Young, Chartered Accountants, 1 Colmore Row, Birmingham B3 2DB
Contact: The Secretary
Trustees: Edward H Ratcliff; David M Ratcliff; Carolyn M Radcliff; Gillian Thorpe; James M G Fea; John B Dixon.
Grant total: £198,000 (1995/96)
Beneficial area: UK with a preference for local charities in the Midlands and North Wales.

In 1995/96 the foundation gave 90 grants ranging between £500 and £5,000. Most were between £1,000 and £3,000. Grants show an interest in health, social welfare, places of worship and the environment, particularly wildlife conservation.

Fourteen grants were relevant to this guide and totalled £25,000 (13 %) of grant-aid:
- St Nicholas Kemerton (£4,000);
- West Midlands Wildlife Campaign (£3,500);
- Warwickshire Wildlife Trust, Avoncroft Museum of Buildings (£3,000 each);
- Farming & Wildlife Group (£2,000);
- RSPB (£1,500);
- Burntwood Pathway Project, Devon Wildlife Trust, Gloucestershire Wildlife Trust, Hawk & Owl Trust, Worcestershire Trust for Nature Conservation; Seawatch Foundation; Wildfowl & Wetlands Trust, Tewkesbury Abbey (£1,000 each).

Applications: In writing to the correspondent. Trustees meet in March, June and October each year.

The Sir James Reckitt Charity

Cherry Cottage, 6 The Briars, Hessle, East Yorkshire HU13 9BE
Contact: J P Robinson
Trustees: Miss C Pollock, Chairman and eleven others, mainly descendants of the founder.

Grant total: £435,000 (1995/96)
Beneficial area: UK, especially around Hull and the East Riding of Yorkshire.

This trust mainly supports Quaker work and a very wide range of local charities working in the areas of Hull and the East Riding of Yorkshire. Most of its grants are small, ranging from under £1,000 to £5,000. The charity was established in 1921 and endowed with shares in the Reckitt company. In 1996 shares in the successor Reckitt and Colman still represented 60% of the total market value of its (£11 million) assets.

In 1995/96 only 6 grants totalling more than £6,000 could be identified as relevant to this guide. They included: RSNC (£2,400); Yorkshire Wildlife Trust (£1,400); ITDG (£1,000).

Exclusions: Local organisations outside the Hull area, unless their work has regional implications. No grants to causes of a warlike or political nature, or for single events such as geographical expeditions. Grants are not normally made to individuals other than Quakers and residents of Hull and the East Riding of Yorkshire.

Applications: In writing to the correspondent at any time. Applications need to arrive a month before the trustees' meetings, in May and November, to be considered.

The Ripple Effect Foundation

No.1 Epsom Square, Trowbridge, Wiltshire BA14 0XG
Tel: 01225-776677
Contact: J G Gilbertson
Trustees: Miss Caroline Marks; Ian Marks; Miss Mary Falk; Ian Wesley.
Grant total: £87,000 (1994/95)
Beneficial area: UK and the developing world.

The trust has continued its policy of making grants to 'effective charities' working in the broad fields of environmental work, third world development and empowering deprived young people in the UK. It is linked with the AIM Foundation (see separate entry), of which Mr R Marks is also a trustee and from which it received a donation of £130,000 in 1994/95, plus £14,000 gifted by the settlor.

The trust describes its chosen activities and its funding plans in detail in its annual report attached with its accounts on file at the Charity Commission. The following notes were extracted from these reports.

The Gaia Foundation received a one-off grant of £32,000 in 1993/94 and the first part of a three-year commitment of £5,000 for their representation of 'the opinions of the people of the Amazonian Forest and other Forest People to policy makers'.

It works with the Network Foundation (see separate entry) to which it has donated £67,000 for environmental and health projects including a permaculture-based community agriculture project in Nepal. It supports a number of projects based in the Third World including the Ashoka Trust in India.

It has also developed a relationship with the New Economics Foundation but no specific grant was named.

This trust is far more interesting than the majority as it takes a particular interest in certain groundbreaking organisations and their schemes and develops a relationship with them. It follows the more visionary but also planned approach to its support characterised by the Network Foundation.

Exclusions: Unsolicited applications from individuals and charities will not be considered nor acknowledged.

Applications: The trust is proactive in seeking applications from projects that meet their funding criteria and areas of interest. Full assessments are made of each application, and evaluated before a further year's funding is released.

The Mrs E E Roberts Charitable Trust

Messrs Cripps Harries Hall, Solicitors, Tunbridge Wells, Kent
Contact: C Hall
Trustees: E E Roberts; C Hall; N Evelegh.
Grant total: £27,000 (1995/96)
Beneficial area: UK, but with a particular interest in East Sussex.

Grant-aid of £27,000 was given in 26 donations in 1995/96 out of an income of £29,000.

Seven grants were relevant to this guide and totalled £5,500 (20% of grant-aid):
◆ South East Farming & Wildlife Advisory Group (£1,250);
◆ St Alban's Frant, South of England Agricultural Society (£1,000 each);
◆ National Trust Scotland, Sussex Wildlife Trust, King Charles the Martyr (£750 each);
◆ Royal Horticultural Society (£500).

Most of these grants are recurrent (except those to churches).

Applications: Applications should be made in writing to arrive in September each year.

The Robertson Trust

P O Box 15330, Glasgow G1 2YL
Tel: 0141-352 6620; Fax: 0141-352 6617
Contact: Sir Lachlan Maclean Bt, Secretary.
Trustees: J A R Macphail, Chairman; J J G Good; K D M Cameron; B McNeil; T M Lawrie.
Grant total: £123,000 (1996/97)
Beneficial area: Throughout the UK.

A note with the financial statements reported that in 1995/96 'the major areas benefiting included medical research, care of the elderly, the young and the infirm, education in universities and schools, the arts, public services and national heritage'.

The trust has listed, as required by Scottish law, its seven grants in excess of 2% of gross income made in 1995/96. These included: Scottish Conservation Projects Trust, £167,000.

These major grants account for only 35% of the trust's expenditure, leaving the main part of its grant-making hidden. The trust has said that it made over 250 donations in 1995/96. The majority were between £5,000 and £10,000 with about 10% (25) of the grants for £1,000 or less. There is no information at all about whether any of these were recurrent, or whether they were for capital, project or revenue purposes.

It is disappointing that this large trust should now be supplying less information about its activities than in previous years. However it is understood that the comprehensive information about its grant-making in 1992/93 still provides a useful picture of its work.

Grants in 1992/93
During the year a total of £2,778,000 was disbursed. Nine organisations received grants in excess of 2% of its gross income. These included: National Playing Fields Association £219,000.

An analysis of its grants showed over half the expenditure going to organisations in Scotland. Out of a total of £2.78 million about £1.29 million was donated to UK-wide organisations or organisations based outside Scotland. Of course it is not possible to tell if the sums disbursed to UK-wide organisations were earmarked for projects in Scotland.

They included:
◆ National Trust for Scotland (£27,500);
◆ Scottish Conservation Projects Trust (£15,000);
◆ Scottish Wildlife Association (£11,000);
◆ Winchester Cathedral (£10,000);
◆ International Bird Preservation Council (£4,000);
◆ Wildfowl Trust;
◆ Scottish Churches Architectural Trust, Scottish Civic Trust (£2,000 each).

A handful of parish churches also received support.

A total of £57,000 was given to Animal Welfare and Pet organisations. Beneficiaries included the Animal Health Trust (£13,000), the Fund for Replacement of Animals (£12,000), and the International Horse Protection League (£11,000).

NB The Robertson Trust has been noted in other guides as giving mainly to Christian charities. The objectives of the trust are much broader than this. The trust receives innumerable requests from church restoration projects throughout the UK. This note is to disabuse parish church councils that a large source of funding exists to assist them with their plans.

Applications: The trust has no guidelines for applicants. Medical research requests are now required to complete a basic application form. All applicants are expected to be registered charities and to send a copy of their accounts. The trustees meet six times a year in January, March, May, July, September and November.

The Edmund de Rothschild Charitable Trust

PO Box 185, New court, St Swithins Lane, London EC4P 4DU
Contact: The Trustees
Trustees: E L de Rothschild; N de Rothschild; Rothschild Trust Co Ltd
Grant total: About £16,000
Beneficial area: UK

In 1994/95 the trust had an income of £24,000 and gave over 50 grants, several to the same beneficiary. These were given to Jewish and other charities, particularly welfare and the arts. An interest in horticultural activities threads its giving. No less than 12 grants totalling more than £11,000 were given to Exbury Gardens, the family pride and pleasure.

Other grants relevant to this guide were given to:
◆ Museum of Garden History (Tradescant Trust) (£600);
◆ Parnham Trust (£500);
◆ Royal Horticultural Society (£320);
◆ Tree Council, Kew Foundation, Enham Trust, Wildlife Trust (£100 each).

Some smaller grants under £100 each were also given.

Note: The fine Exbury Gardens near Southampton are owned by the de Rothschild family and noted for having one of the best rhododendron displays in the country.

Applications: In writing to the correspondent.

The Jacob Rothschild GAM Charitable Trust

14 St James' Place, London SW1A 1NP
Tel: 0171-493 8111
Contact: Miss S A Gallagher
Trustees: Rothschild; Serena Rothschild; Hannah Brookfield; Beth Tomassin; Nils Taube; M E Hatch.
Grant total: £1,608,000 (1995/96)
Beneficial area: UK and overseas

Readers should not get too excited at the size of the grant-aid given by this trust. Almost all in 1995/96 (£1,569,000) was given to the National Trust for the splendid restoration and upkeep of the Rothschild family home, Waddesden Manor in Buckinghamshire. A similar amount was given in the previous year when the Botanic Gardens Conservation Secretariat received £10,000 and the National Heritage Memorial Fund (£3,000).

Applications: In writing to the correspondent.

The Leopold de Rothschild Charitable Trust

New Court, St Swithin's Lane, London EC4P 4DU
Contact: The Trustees
Trustees: E L de Rothschild; N de Rothschild; Rothschild Trust Co Ltd
Grant total: £30,000 (1995)
Beneficial area: UK

In November 1995 the trust had capital assets listed in its accounts of £616,000. Its income was surprisingly large at £111,000 from which £30,000 was given in about 100 small grants ranging between £25 and £500. Grants were given to activities in the arts, children and disability. Six grants were relevant to this guide:
◆ National Trust (£750 in 2 grants);
◆ Northlands Trust for Nature Conservation (£500);
◆ Exbury Gardens (£350);
◆ Countryside Education (£100).

Two churches were given grants totalling £400.

Note: The fine Exbury Gardens near Southampton are owned by the de Rothschild family and noted for having one of the best rhododendron displays in the country.
Applications: In writing to the correspondent.

The Rowan Trust

c/o Coopers and Lybrand, 9 Greyfriars Road, Reading RG1 1JG
Tel: 01734 597111
Contact: The Secretary
Trustees: D D Mason; A Baillie; H Russell.
Grant total: £386,000 (1995)
Beneficial area: UK, especially Merseyside, and overseas.

The trust gives two thirds of its money to overseas projects and one third to social welfare projects in the UK. Most grants range from £1,000 to £10,000, and they can be one-off or recurrent.

For the UK grants programme, 'the trust focuses on projects which will benefit disadvantaged groups and neighbourhoods'. Environmental improvement is one of its selected spheres. 'The trustees are interested in projects which are concerned with self-help or advocacy as well as service provision. They also look for: user and community involvement in the planning and delivery of the project, a multi-disciplinary approach, and emphasis on empowerment.

The trust has 'regularly given grants to a limited number of large national organisations and development agencies, but also gives smaller grants to much smaller organisations and locally based projects'.

For the overseas projects, the trust prefers projects which will benefit disadvantaged groups and communities in such spheres as agriculture, community development, health, education, environment, human rights, and fair trade.

The trust had assets of £4.3 million in 1995 which generated an income of £259,000. Altogether 77 grants totalling £386,000 were made, all for £1,000 or more. Half of the grants were given to organisations working in overseas relief and development, and associated environmental concerns. An interest in human rights, racial equality and general welfare in the Liverpool area could also be discerned from a review of the grants list.

Grants relevant to this guide in 1995 totalled £57,000 (15% of total grant-aid) and were given to:
◆ Intermediate Technology (£32,500);
◆ Leaf for Life (£5,870);
◆ SOS Sahel (£3,500);
◆ Oxfam Solar Ovens Project (£3,286);
◆ Sustrans (£3,000);
◆ Action Water, IPPF, Kamai Forest Conservation Programme – Tanzania, Technology Applied Practically – Uganda (£2,000 each);
◆ BTCV (£1,000).

Twenty-one organisations supported in 1993/94 were also given grants in 1994/95, including the Children's Society (£8,000), Tools for Self Reliance (£7,300), Barnardos (£6,000), Family Service Units, NSPCC, New Horizons Youth Centre (£5,000 each), and Sustrans (£3,000).

Exclusions: Grants are only made to registered charities. No grants are given to individuals, for buildings or building work, or for academic research.

Applications: In writing to the correspondent. No application forms are issued.

Applications should include: a brief (two sides of A4) description of, and a budget for, the work for which the grant is sought; the organisation's annual report and accounts; and an indication of the core costs of the organisation.

The applications need to provide the trustees with information about: the aims and objectives of the organisation; its structure and organisational capacity; the aims and objectives of the project; and how the project's progress will be monitored and evaluated.

The volume of applications received precludes acknowledgement on receipt or notifying unsuccessful applicants.

Trustees meet in January and July.

The Rufford Foundation

Rawlinson & Hunter, Vogue House,
1 Hanover Square, London W1A 4SR
Tel: 0171-493 4040; **Fax:** 0171-493 3333
Contact: Elizabeth Foster, Administrator
Trustees: J H Laing; A Gavazzi; C R F Barbour.
Grant total: £1,101,000 (1993/94)
Beneficial area: UK.

In 1993/94 the foundation had assets of over £44 million, which generated an income of £1.3 million from which 51 donations were made totalling £1.1 million.

In 1993/94 the foundation gave its support in handsome amounts with nearly half its grants (22) for £10,000 or more. It is not known if the trust intends to continue this approach. Two years earlier it had given £982,000 in 172 grants, most of which were between £1,000 and £5,000. Only 14 grants were for more than £5,000 in 1991/92. One major grant to the Carlisle and Settle Railway (£16,569) fell within the ambit of this guide. The following grants were made in 1993/94:

- World Wide Fund for Nature (£99,000);
- Royal Botanical Gardens at Kew (£53,000 plus a second grant of £28,000 to Friends of Kew);
- British Ecological Society (£30,000);
- Save the Redwoods League (£17,000);
- Woodland Trust (£10,000).

Exclusions: Only registered charities are supported. No grants to individuals. The foundation tends not to give grants for building costs.

Applications: In writing to the correspondent, including budgets, accounts and an annual report if available.

The Alan and Babette Sainsbury Charitable Fund

c/o Clark Whitehill, 25 New Street Square, London EC4A 3LN
Tel: 0171-353 1577
Contact: D J Walker
Trustees: Lord Sainsbury of Drury Lane; Simon Sainsbury; Miss J S Portrait.
Grant total: £355,000 (1994/95)
Beneficial area: UK and overseas.

The fund is noteworthy for supporting several organisations concerned with aspects of human rights. It also makes many recurrent grants and in 1994/95 three quarters of its grant-aid (£265,000) was given to 35 regularly supported causes, so there is little leeway for new applications which would be likely to be within the range of £1,000 to £5,000.

The fund's assets are held predominantly in J Sainsbury plc shares, with a market value of £8.7 million in April 1995. Income was £405,000 from which 59 grants totalling £355,000 were made. They were categorised under the following headings.

Grants 1994/95
- Health and Social Welfare – £107,000, 25 grants, 14 recurrent
- Overseas – £134,500, 9 grants, 8 recurrent
- Scientific and Medical Research – £73,000, 9 grants, 6 recurrent
- Education – £18,000, 7 grants, 3 recurrent
- The Arts – £16,000, 5 grants, 5 recurrent
- Environment – £14,000, 3 grants, 1 recurrent
- Religion – £7000, 3 grants, 2 recurrent.

The interest in the environment has received only minor financial support over recent years and has been given to support the conservation of churches e.g. Friends of Essex Churches.

Exclusions: No grants to individuals.

Applications: To the correspondent in writing.

The Jean Sainsbury Animal Welfare Trust
(formerly The Jean Sainsbury Charitable Trust)

Grants are only given to animal welfare charities, mostly domestic animals and pets, and wildlife sanctuaries. Former grants to city farms are now discontinued. The administrator has also stressed that wildlife conservation as such is not supported.

The Sainsbury Family Charitable Trusts

9 Red Lion Court, London EC4A 3EB
Tel: 0171-410 0330
Contact: Michael Pattison

Of the 16 Sainsbury family charitable trusts, 11 administered from the address above are shown by their donations to have environmental interests. Funding amounting to over £3.7 million in 1995/96 was allocated by these trusts to a wide range of environmentally related activities.

The trusts have their own overlapping but different trustees who meet separately at differing frequencies and who work to different policies and priorities. The trusts of the senior members of the Sainsbury family, with the exception of the Gatsby Charitable Foundation, give little information about their grants and in this respect contrast greatly with the trusts associated with the younger family members (marked with an asterisk in the list below).

Environmental approvals 1995/96
(and % of total for each trust)

Gatsby : £1,431,000 – plant science 8% (£307,000, 1% 1996/97)
Monument: £881,000 16% (£437,000, 7% 1996/97)
Linbury: £400,000 plus overseas (p) 5%
Ashden*: £282,500 58%
Staples*: £240,000 plus overseas 36%
Headley: £225,000 6%
J J*: £151,000 75%
Mark Leonard*: £54,000 60%
Tedworth*: £52,000 16%
Glass-House*: £30,000 5%
Woodward*: £3,000 0.5%
Total: £3,749,000
* younger family members, (p) grants paid.

The funding by the Gatsby Charitable Foundation has concentrated on support of the Sainsbury Laboratory at the John Innes Foundation. Its research into plant biogenetics could eventually have immense beneficial impacts on sustainability overseas as well as crop health/ development everywhere. Plant research schemes have also been supported in Africa itself. The environmental pay-back will be long-term. A new educational organisation – Science and Plants in Schools (SAPS) has also been established.

The trusts connected with other senior members of the family have, on the whole, been supporters of the more traditional aspects of environmental concern, the built heritage and conservation of nature.

The trusts connected with the younger family members (except for the Woodward Trust) show a lively interest in issues of wider long-term environmental and social importance. These have included aspects of public transport, research into environmental taxation, uses of solar energy, recycling, micro-credit schemes in Africa for sustainable development, forestry and community development.

The Alan and Babette Sainsbury Charitable Fund is not within this administrative group, though the trustees are senior members of the Sainsbury family. The Jean Sainsbury Animal Welfare Trust has no connection to the family (see separate entries).

Exclusions: No grants for individuals. In the past some of the trusts have had such programmes but it looks as if this is now channelled through other charities specialising in this kind of assistance.

Applications: Except in the case of the Gatsby Foundation, there is no specific information available about how to apply, beyond the sentence that 'an application to one of the Sainsbury family trusts is an application to all'. A courteous warning note is sounded in the reply sent to organisations enquiring about how to apply: 'the vast majority of unsolicited appeals are unsuccessful' because the trusts 'adopt a proactive approach to their grant making'. It is difficult to estimate the proportion of funds available to outside applications. It is certainly small and potential applicants should not be encouraged by the size of the total environmental funding unless their work sits well with the trust's interests and is known to the trustees and their advisers.

However the office is generally approachable, and a telephone call may well establish whether there is any point in submitting a formal application. They are all administered at the office

above and one letter is said to ensure that an appeal is considered by whichever of the trusts is thought most appropriate.

The Schuster Charitable Trust

Nether Worton House, Middle Barton, Chipping Norton, Oxon OX7 7AT
Contact: Mrs J V Clarke
Trustees: Mrs J V Clarke; R D Schuster; P D Schuster
Grant total: £24,000 (1994/95)
Beneficial area: UK with a particular interest in the Oxfordshire area.

In 1994/95 the trust gave 22 grants ranging between £100 and £5,000. Its income was slightly lower than its grant total of £24,000 as opposed to the grant-aid of £33,000 in the previous year. During 1993/94 the trust had given a major grant of £22,000 to Worton's PCC and £1,000 to Churchill Church Restoration Fund (£1,000).

Its environmental interests cover wildlife, countryside and the architectural heritage. Its five grants relevant to this guide in 1994/95 totalled over £8,000 (33% of grant-aid):

♦ Repair of church clock (£4,800);
♦ Game Conservancy Trust, Tusk Force (£1,000 each);
♦ Campaign for Oxford (£500);
♦ Oxfordshire Historic Churches Trust (£250).

Applications: In writing to the correspondent.

The Scotbelge Charitable Trust

Matheson Bank, Jardine House, 6 Crutched Friars, London EC3N 2HT
Tel: 0171-528 4000
Contact: Keith Galloway
Trustees: Simon L Keswick; Keith Galloway; Adrian T J Stanford; Aurelia S Weatherall,
Grant total: £46,000 (1995/96)
Beneficial area: UK.

This trust was set up in 1990 and in the past two years has given grant-aid close to £40,000. Its income was only £26,000 in 1995/96 though three grants totalling £46,000 were given. They included the following donations with relevance to this guide totalling £11,000 (24% of grant-aid):

- Kilmartin House Trust, WWF UK (£5,000 each);
- RSFS Forest Trust (£1,000).

In the previous year grants were given to:

- Lincoln Cathedral (£3,500);
- The Environmental Initiative (£1,000).

Applications: In writing to the correspondent.

The Peter Scott Trust for Education & Research in Conservation

The New Grounds, Slimbridge, Gloucester GL2 7BS
Tel: 01453-890333; Fax: 01453-890827
Contact: Lady Scott.
Trustees: Lady Philippa Scott; Cassandra Phillips; Dr Dafila Scott.
Grant total: £9,000 (1996/97)
Beneficial area: UK and overseas.

The trust was set up as a memorial to the renowned ornithologist and conservationist with his widow as the leading trustee. It is administered from the headquarters of the Wildfowl and Wetlands Trust which he established. Its aims are: "to conserve and protect for the future benefit of the public the environment as a whole and its animal and plant life in particular and to educate the public in natural history and ecology and the importance of conservation".

Our detailed information is for 1994/95 when a high proportion of the grant-aid (£3,250) was given to two research projects re geese and Bewick's swan organised by the Wildfowl & Wetland Trust which is often supported. Three

other grants were to overseas study expeditions e.g.:

- Anjouan Expedition (£900);
- Frontier Uganda Environmental Expedition (£400).

Applications: In writing to the correspondent.

The Scottish Churches Architectural Heritage Trust

15 North Bank Street, The Mound, Edinburgh EH1 2LP
Tel: 0131-225 8644
Contact: Mrs Florence Mackenzie, Director
Trustees: Lord Ross, Chairman; Donald Erskine; Magnus Magnusson; Rev Robin Barbour; Sir Jamie Stormonth Darling; Lady Marion Fraser; John Gerrard; Rev Malcolm Grant; Ivor Guild; Mrs Mary Millican; Rev Kenneth Nugent; Professor frank Willett.
Grant total: £93,000 (1996)
Beneficial area: Scotland.

The trust was established "to care for Scottish church buildings in use for public worship, principally by raising funds for their repair and restoration and by acting as a source of technical advice and assistance on maintenance and repair".

In 1996 the trust had an income of £116,000 including £74,000 in donations. Forty grants totalling £79,000 ranged between £750 and £6,000. Churches of all denominations were supported but by far the largest number of grants (28) were given to the Church of Scotland.

Applications: In writing to the correspondent, after which an application form will be sent. The grants committee meets four times a year.

The Scouloudi Foundation

c/o Hays Allan, Southampton House, 317
High Holborn, London WC1V 7NL
Tel: 0171-969 5600
Contact: The Administrators
Trustees: Miss S E Stowell; M E
Demetriadi; Miss B R Masters; J D
Marnham
Grant total: £200,000 (1996/97)
Beneficial area: UK, "but not for
activities of a purely local nature".

The trust splits its donations into three
categories, "regular" and "special"
donations, and historical awards.
Historical awards generally make up
around one half of total grants, and are for
individuals to fund research and
publications in the historical field.

"Regular" donations are made annually to
a basic list of some 91 national charitable
organisations, a list which is very unlikely
to be extended by the trustees. The
amounts are distributed by the Charities
Aid Foundation, and are usually for
£1,200 or less. A few "regular" recipients
occasionally get "special" donations.

"Special" donations are made to
organisations working in the fields of:
disasters; education; environment; overseas
aid and refugees; handicapped and
disabled; humanities; medicine and health.
These grants are the ones to apply for, and
are usually for £2,500 or under, but see
below. Most are not recurrent, and are for
capital projects only with the exception of
disasters.

In 1996/97 the foundation had assets of
£4.7 million generating an income of
£200,000 from which grants of £196,000
were made. Donations relevant to this
guide totalled over £12,000 (7% of grant-
aid) and were given to:

Special
- Lincoln Cathedral Library (£2,000);
- Ely Cathedral Restoration Trust (£1,500);
- Regular -National Trust (£1,200);

- CPRE, Environment Council, Historic
  Churches Preservation Trust, RSNC,
  Woodland Trust (£900 each);
- Architectural Heritage Fund, BTCV,
  Habitat Scotland, Textile Conservation
  Centre, Tree Council (£600 each).

Exclusions: Except for historical awards,
grants are only made to registered charities
and no grants are made to individuals. No
grants for activities of a purely local nature.

Applications: Only about 28% of grants
are uncommitted. Applications giving full
but concise details should be sent to the
correspondent. These applications are
considered once a year in April.

The Linley Shaw Foundation

National Westminster Bank plc, Financial
& Investment Services, London Branch,
62 Green Street, London W1Y 4BA
Contact: The Senior Manager
Trustees: National Westminster Bank,
London Branch (and see below)
Grant total: £50,000 (1995)
Beneficial area: UK.

1995 was the first year this young trust
gave out grants (£50,000 out of an income
of £52,000). It has general charitable
objects but also one particular stated
interest – conservation of the countryside.
The National Westminster Bank as
executors set up an advisory committee
with Frank O'Shea, Julian Sheffield and
Lady Anne Scott as members.

Its first report noted that it wanted to
widen its understanding and range of
giving so in future years its may show
support either to a wider range of
conservation activities or to a wider range
of general charitable activities (or both).

Grants relevant to this guide totalled
£41,000 (82% of grant-aid):
- BTCV (£18,000 in 2 grants);
- National Trust (£15,000);
- Sussex Wildlife Trust (£3,500);

- Woodland Trust (£2,750);
- Staffordshire Trust (£2,000).

Applications: In writing to the correspondent.

The R J Shaw Charitable Trust

Randall & Payne, Rodborough Court, Stroud, Gloucs GLS 3LR
Contact: Michael Anthony
Trustees: John Shaw; Elizabeth Graesser; Peter Shaw, Mrs J Shaw.
Grant total: £2,000 (1996/97)
Beneficial area: UK and overseas.

The trust was registered in 1990 and gives to overseas development, health and the environment. In 1993/94 it had an income of only £3,000 and made 31 grants of over £12,000. These ranged from £100 to £1,000. Five grants were for £1,000.

Grants relevant to this guide included:
- Centre for Alternative Technology, National Trust, FoE (£1,000 each);
- Population Concern (£500);
- SOS Sahel (£100).

Applications: In writing to the correspondent

The David Shepherd Conservation Foundation

61 Smithbrook Kilns, Cranleigh, Surrey, GU6 8JJ
Tel: 01483-272323; Fax 01483 -272427;
E-mail: DSCF@DSCF.demon.co.uk.
Contact: Melanie Shepherd, Director.
Trustees: Anthony Athaide; Sir Robert Clark; Peter Giblin; David Gower OBE; Avril Shepherd; David Shepherd OBE.
Grant total: £95,000 but see below (1995)
Beneficial area: UK and overseas.

The foundation was established by David Shepherd, the internationally successful wildlife artist. It supports and complements other wildlife and conservation charities associated with:
- The conservation and management of endangered mammals.
- Anti-poaching activities in Africa and elsewhere and the abolition of the illegal trade in endangered species.
- Education of young people in matters relating to the conservation of the world's wildlife, natural resources and wild places, but with an emphasis on endangered mammals."

In 1992 the foundation decided to "concentrate its focus on the world's major endangered mammals primarily, rhinos, elephants, tigers, for which David is best known as an artist and to which he owes much of his success". Funds are raised also in "Zambia, South Africa, India, Australia and Hong Kong for urgent causes such as conservation investigation, research and education in the above animals".

The foundation generates funds from membership, auctions, sponsorship, gifts and donations, fundraising events and sales of products derived from David Shepherd's work for the foundation.

It now has a "Young Friends" membership scheme with Gary Lineker as its "Captain". "The income is used to respond quickly and directly to the needs of organisations in the UK and overseas, with whose objectives it is in sympathy, where it believes its contribution will have a significant effect on the achievement of specific project aims, and when it has been satisfied that its funds will be effectively applied." £250,000 was raised in 1995. Grants actually paid out varies greatly from year to year (£95,000 in 1995 compared with £145,000 in 1994 and £49,000 in 1993).

Grants allocated in 1995 included:
- Zambia's Elephant Conservation Programme (£25,000);
- Humane Society of the United States, to the Investigative Network countering

Siberian Tiger poaching and developing the first such tiger sanctuary (£20,000);
- Save the Rhino Trust, Namibia (£15,500);
- Aaranyak Nature Club of Assam, to conserve the last stronghold of the Indian rhino (£12,000);
- Environmental Investigation Agency (£11,700).

Exclusions: Applications for grants must be related to the conservation of the world's major endangered mammals.

Applications: In writing, in detail, to the administrator.

The Simon Population Trust

23a Buckland Crescent, London NW3 5DH
Tel: 0171-722 9512
Contact: J D Smithard, Treasurer
Trustees: Dr Kathleen Kiernan, Chair; Dilys Cossey, Secretary; John Cleland; Tim Dyson; Sir Richard King; Dr Allan G Hill; Penny Kane; Dr John McEwan; Madeleine Simms; John Smithard; Wendy Savage.
Grant total: £109,000 (September 1996)
Beneficial area: UK and overseas.

The trust was set up to help relieve poverty and improve health standards worldwide through a better understanding of problems of world population and resources. It supports research, education and action which "may contribute to the adjustment of population to resources".

In 1996 the trust had assets of £440,000 and an income of £130,000 from which it made awards to scholars and individuals and grants to organisations.

In 1996 its major "project expenses" were given to the Birth Control Trust (£24,000), a continuing relationship. Nine grants of between £1,000 and £5,000 were given to "scholars" and a further 14 grants of between £250 and £6,000 were given to those termed "individuals".

Four organisations were given grants as well as the Birth Control Trust:
- Education for Choice (£7,000);
- Reproductive Health Matters (£3,000);
- Planet 21 (£1,000);
- British Society for Population Studies (£500).

Applications: In writing to the correspondent.

The Skinners' Company Lady Neville Charity

The Skinners' Company, Skinners' Hall, 8 Dowgate Hill, London EC4R 2SP
Tel: 0171-236 5629
Contact: The Clerk
Trustees: The Master and Wardens of the Worshipful Company of Skinners
Grant total: £174,000 (1994/95)
Beneficial area: UK.

In 1994/95 the trust had an income of £180,000 and gave the major part of its funds in its annual support to the three company schools (£146,000). The remaining £28,000 was disbursed in 135, mostly small, gifts. Six were annual grants including £5,000 to Lincoln College Oxford.

The general grants have been very widely given but have shown a particular interest in young people and education. Some 12 small grants totalling £2,000 (7% of funds available to outside applicants) were relevant to this guide. These included:
- National Trust Centenary Appeal (£250);
- Marie Stopes International, Learning through Landscapes, John Muir Trust, Royal Kew Botanic Gardens, Ironbridge Gorge Museum, (£200 each).

However, the committee is tightening its grant-making criteria to make fewer but larger grants in selected areas and the following information may be totally irrelevant.

Exclusions: Registered charities only. No grants to schools and almshouses other than those related to the Company.

Applications: Contact the company about most recent grant-making criteria (see above note). By letter to the clerk by the end of March and September enclosing a copy of the latest audited accounts. Applications are not usually acknowledged. A charity which has received a grant will not normally be considered again until over a year has elapsed.

The John Slater Foundation

Midland Bank Trust Co. Ltd., Cumberland House, 15-17 Cumberland Place, Southampton, SO15 2UY
Tel: 01703-531396
Contact: Chris Woodrow
Trustees: Mrs J Hume; T Hume; A Taylor; C Band.
Grant total: £125,000 (1994/95)
Beneficial area: UK, with a preference for the north of England especially West Lancashire.

In 1994/95 the foundation had assets of £1.9 million, an income of £118,000 and made 48 grants totalling £125,000 ranging between £500 and £8,000. Most grants were for £1,000.

Grants relevant to this guide totalling £9,500 (8% of grant-aid) were given to:
- RSPB (£4,000);
- St Michael's Cottingley (£2,000);
- United Reform Churches at Aldington and Firehaven, St Paul's Fleetwood (£1,000 each);
- Hartford House Fleetwood (£500).

Four grants totalling £8,000 were also given to support animal welfare activities.

Applications: Applications are considered twice a year on 1st May and 1st November.

The Leslie Smith Foundation

The Old Coach House, Sunnyside, Bergh Apton, Norwich NR15 1DD.
Contact: M D Wilcox
Trustees: M D Wilcox; Mrs E A Furtek.
Grant total: £195,000 (1996/97)
Beneficial area: UK, with a preference for Berkshire.

The trust prefers to support charities of which it has special knowledge or interest, with emphasis on research and treatment of addiction, arthritis/rheumatism and asthma, child care treatment, care of the elderly and bereaved, and children and youth charities, including schools.

In 1996/97 the trust had an income of £160,000. In 1996/97 nine grants totalling £195,000 grants were given. The trust has a minor, but continuing interest, in wildlife. In 1996/97 a grant was given to the Suffolk Wildlife Trust (£3,000), a similar grant having been made in 1995/6.

In previous years the trust has made several small grants to local charities in Berkshire.

Exclusions: Registered charities only; no grants to individuals.

Applications: In writing to the correspondent. Only successful appeals are acknowledged.

The Stanley Smith UK Horticultural Trust

Cory Lodge, PO Box 365, Cambridge, CB2 1HR
Tel: 01223-336278
Contact: James Cullen
Trustees: Christopher Brickell; John Norton; John Dilger.
Grant total: £122,000 (1995/96)
Beneficial area: UK and overseas.

The trust's objects are the "advancement of education in horticulture". This remit is broadly interpreted, but excludes assistance to students for courses (although bodies providing such courses have been supported).

In 1995/96 the trust had assets of £2.5 million and an income of £165,000 from which 40 grants totalling £122,000, ranging between £300 and £10,000, were made.

Grants are made to identified projects and in 1995/96 included:
- OTS Save the Garden Fund (£10,000);
- Painshill Park Trust (£6,500);
- Institute of Horticulture (£6,000);
- RHS Plantnet (£5,000 x2);
- Women's Farm & Garden Association, Pershore College Special Plant Unit, Oxford University Botanic Gardens, Hestercombe Pleasure Gardens, Botanic Gardens Conservation International (£5,000 each);
- Tree Register of British Isles (£4,000);
- National Council for Conservation of Plants & Gardens (£3,000);
- Bath Preservation Trust, Ironbridge Gorge Museum (£1,000 each).

Exclusions: No support for projects in commercial horticulture (crop production etc.).

Applications: In writing to the correspondent. There is no application form. Guidelines are available from the correspondent.

Applications are considered twice a year (April and October); closing dates are March 15th and September 15th respectively.

The South Square Trust

P O Box 67, Heathfield, East Sussex, TN21 9ZR.
Tel: 01435-830778; **Fax:** 01435-830778
Contact: Mrs N C Chrimes, Clerk to the Trustees.
Trustees: C R Ponter; A E Woodall; W P Harriman; C P Grimwade, D B Inglis.
Grant total: £160,000 (1996/97)
Beneficial area: UK.

In 1994/95, the trust had assets of £2.4 million and an income of £157,000 from which grants totalling £151,000 were made. This divided into:
- Annual Donations: £24,000 in 34 grants;
- General donations: £52,000 in 88 grants;
- Directly aided students, bursaries and scholarships: £75,000.

Eighteen grants relevant to this guide totalling over £12,000 (8% of grant-aid) were given in 1995:

As Annual donations:
- Suffolk Historic Churches Trust, Woodland Trust, WWF UK (£1,000 each);

As General donations:
- Friends of the Earth (£1,750);
- Christ Church Spitalfields, St Mary's Bildeston Appeal (£1,000 each);
- National Trust (£1,000 in 2 grants);
- London Wildlife Trust (£750);
- Common Ground, Intermediate Technology, Suffolk Wildlife Trust (£500 and in the previous year);
- Greenpeace Environmental Trust, Naturewatch Trust, Ramblers' Association, Survival International, Sustrans, Trees for London (£500 each);
- People's Trust for Endangered Species (£250).

Bursaries and sabbaticals totalling £47,000. Grants were given to five organisations, four of which received grants the previous year: Byam Shaw School of Art, St Paul's School, Textile Conservation Centre and West Dean College. The other grant went to the Slade School of Art.

Directly aided and single award payments totalling £20,000. These are grants to individual students.

Applications: In writing to the correspondent. Individuals should ask for an application form at least three months before funds are required.

The Kenneth & Phyllis Southall Charitable Trust

Messrs Rutters, Solicitors, 2 Bimport, Shaftesbury, Dorset SPY 8AY
Contact: S T Rutter
Trustees: Daphne Maw; C M Southall; D H D Southall.
Grant total: £24,000 (1994/95)
Beneficial area: UK.

This trust has an interest in Quaker charities, the West Midlands, education and social welfare as well as nature conservation, which has received predominant support recently.

In 1994/95 it had an income of £44,000 from which £24,000 was disbursed in 31 grants ranging between £300 and £2,500. Of these, 14 totalling £13,000 (54% of grant-aid) fell within the scope of this guide:
- WNCT (Worcs ? Warwicks) Nature Conservation Trust (£2,500);
- John Muir Trust (Ble Bheinn Appeal (£2,000);
- FWAG; Friends of the Earth; Scottish Conservation Projects Trust, Tree Aid, RSPB, WWF UK, Wildfowl & Wetlands Trust, Woodland Trust (£1,000 each);
- National Trust for Scotland, Open Spaces Society, Wildlife Trusts (RSNC).

Applications: In writing to the correspondent.

The W F Southall Trust

c/o Rutters Solicitors, 2 Bimport, Shaftesbury, Dorset SP7 8AY
Tel: 01747-852377
Contact: S Rutter, Secretary
Trustees: Mrs D Maw; C M Southall; D H D Southall; Mrs A Wallis; M Holtom.
Grant total: £172,000 (1994/95)
Beneficial area: UK, with an interest in Birmingham.

This Quaker trust divides its grants into the following categories:
- Central Committees of the Society of Friends Meeting House appeals;
- Other Quaker charities;
- Birmingham District Charities;
- Other charities.

Over 170 grants are given each year.

Nine grants relevant to this guide and totalling over £8,000 (5% of total grant-aid) were given in 1995 to:
- Woodland Trust (£2,500);
- Intermediate Technology (£1,500);
- Historic Chapels Trust, Sustrans (£1,000 each);
- Marie Stopes International (£800);
- International Tree Foundation (£200);
- Tree Council (£150).

Exclusions: No grants to individuals.

Applications: In writing to the correspondent.

The Staples Trust

See entry for the "Sainsbury Family Trusts"
Tel: 0171-410 0330
Contact: Michael Pattison
Trustees: Miss Jessica Sainsbury; T J Sainsbury; Alexander Sainsbury; Miss J S Portrait.
Grant total: £672,000 grant approvals (1995/96)
Beneficial area: UK and overseas.

This is another "young" Sainsbury family trust. It has as trustees three of the four children of Sir Timothy Sainsbury (see also the Glass-House and Tedworth trusts).

It had an endowment valued at £11.5 million in 1995/96 and upped the total of its approvals from £182,000 in 1994/95 to £672,000, of which at least £240,000 (36% of total) was of particular interest to readers of this guide. It is becoming one of the leaders of progressive giving in environmental activities.

The grant approvals in 1995/96 were classified under the following headings with "Women's Issues" as a new category (although women are also emphasised under the overseas development programme):

1995/96 1994/95
- Environment £137,000 (9 grants) £23,000 (3 grants to 2 orgs)
- Overseas development £357,000 (15 grants) £70,000 (6 grants)
- Women's Issues £121,000 (4 grants)
- General £57,000 (4 grants) £89,000 (3 grants)

Total £672,000 (32) £182,000 (16)

Under Environment

"Projects are supported in developing countries, Central & Eastern Europe and in the UK....for renewable energy technology, training and skills upgrading and, occasionally, research. In Central & Eastern Europe, trustees are interested in providing training opportunities for community/business leaders and policy makers and in contributing to the process of skill-sharing and information exchange. In the UK, trustees aim to help communities protect, maintain and improve areas of land and to support work aimed at informing rural conservation policy."

Grant approvals in 1995/96
- WWF, towards core costs of Udzangwa Mountains National Park, Tanzania, park protection by conserving forests and developing alternative fuel supplies with local communities (£44,000);
- Woodland Trust, towards "Woods on your Doorstep" national Millennium tree-planting project (£25,000 over 5 years);
- FoE, £14,000 to cover costs of work on the European Bank for Reconstruction & Development and researching the extent of its impact on environmental policy in Central & Eastern European countries, £4,000 to cover costs of skill-sharing visit by representatives of Polish and Czech FoE groups to the UK (£18,000);
- BTCV, youth volunteering and training programme (£15,000 over 3 years);

- Olkonerei Integrated Pastoralist Survival Programme, Tanzania, towards rehabilitation of a solar lighting system in an animal husbandry vocational centre (£13,723);
- Plantlife, towards purchase of Winskill Stones limestone pavement, Yorkshire, to prevent commercial exploitation and protect rare wildflower species (£10,000);
- ApTibet, solar water heating technology for refugee Tibetan communities in India (£6,448);
- SOS Sahel, for solar equipment for community radio station in Mali (£4,480).

Under Overseas Development

"Support tends to be focused in East & South Africa, South and South-East Asia and South America although projects from other areas are considered on their merits... Trustees are interested in a range of activities, including income-generation projects, with a particular emphasis on the role of women in communities, shelter and housing, sustainable agriculture and forestry and the rights of indigenous people.." and "development projects which take account of environmental sustainability and in many cases, the environmental and developmental benefits of the project are of equal importance."

Grant approvals in 1995/96 included:
- ITDG for a credit project to facilitate micro-hydro schemes for rural villages in Maranon region, Peru (£56,224 over 2 years);
- Survival International, £37,800 over 3 years for production of 2 Urgent Action Bulletins each year, plus £2500 to emergency appeal for the Maasai Iloodoariak people of the Rift Valley Province, Kenya (£40,300);
- CARE, to cover the cost of conservation education equipment for Development Through Conservation project, Uganda (£6,809).

Grants of £16,000 each were given to the Headley and Jerusalem trusts, both Sainsbury family trusts associated with Sir Timothy and Lady Susan Sainsbury.

Applications: An application to one of the Sainsbury family trusts is an application to all; see the entry under "Sainsbury Family Trusts" for address and application procedure.

The Star Foundation Trust

c/o Lloyds Bank, 83 Cannon Street, London EC4
Contact: Dr Elizabeth Frankland Moore
Trustees: A C Wilson; Dr Elizabeth Frankland Moore; J Crawford; Mrs J S McCreadie; Mrs J Cameron.
Grant total: £34,000 (1991/92)
Beneficial area: UK.

The most recent accounts on public file at the Charity Commission were for 1991/92 so the following information is very out-of-date. Three grants relevant to this guide totalling £7,500 were made in that year (22% of grant-aid):
◆ WaterAid (£5,000);
◆ Greenpeace, for dolphins (£2,000);
◆ Cambridge Primate Study Borneo (£500).

Two small grants were given to churches.

In 1990/91 grants were given to Borocco People of Brazil (£1,000) and Care for the Wild, for badgers (£500).

Applications: In writing to the correspondent.

The Steel Charitable Trust

Messrs Bullimores, 3 Boutport Street, Barnstaple EX31 1RH
Contact: The Secretary.
Trustees: A W Hawkins; J A Childs; N E W Wright; J A Maddox.
Grant total: £810,000 (1996/97)
Beneficial area: UK, with some preference for Bedfordshire.

This trust supports a wide range of charitable activities both local and national, however, three quarters of its grant-aid is given to social welfare, health and medical research.

The trust's donations out of income rose from £640,000 in the previous year to £810,000. It had assets of over £20 million in 1997 which generated a gross income of £937,000.

Six grants totalling £59,000 (7% of grant aid) were relevant to this guide in 1996/97:
◆ Campaign for the Protection of Rural England (£20,000);
◆ Friends of St Marys Church, Luton (£18,000);
◆ Beds & Herts Historic Churches Preservation Society (£10,000);
◆ Sustrans, Almshouses Association (£5,000 each);
◆ RSPB (£1,000).

The trust also regularly funds animal welfare charities.

Exclusions: Individuals, students, expeditions.

Applications: In writing to the correspondent including a copy of the most recent accounts. Meetings are held in January, April, July and October. Applications are not acknowledged.

The M J C Stone Charitable Trust

Estate Office, Ozleworth Park, Wotton under Edge, Gloucestershire GL12 7QA
Tel: 01435-845591
Contact: M J C Stone
Trustees: M J C Stone; Louisa Stone; C R H Stone; Nicola J Stone; A J Stone.
Grant total: £190,000 (1995/96)
Beneficial area: UK.

In 1995/96 the trust gave grants ranging between £100 and £75,000. Three grants were over £25,000, 20 grants were for £1,000 and about 40 grants for £500 or less. A further four grants were between £2,000 and £5,000.

Eleven grants relevant to this guide totalling over £39,000 (21% of grant-aid) were given to:

- Church of St Mary the Virgin (£25,000);
- National Trust, CPRE (£5,000 each);
- Castle Bromwich Hall Gardens Trust, Tiger Trust (£1,000 each);
- Atlantic Salmon Conservation Trust (Scotland), Game Conservancy Trust, National Trust for Scotland, North Atlantic Salmon Fund (UK) (£500 each);
- All Saints' Great Charfield, Wotten Heritage Centre(£100 each).

Applications: In writing to the correspondent.

The Summerfield Charitable Trust

PO Box 4, Winchcombe, Cheltenham, Gloucs. GL54 5ZD
Tel: 01242-676774; Fax: 01242-677120.
Contact: Mrs Lavinia Sidgwick, Administrator.
Trustees: The Earl Fortescue; Martin Davis; Gilbert Greenall; Mrs Rosaleen Kaye; Mrs Rachel Managhan.
Grant total: £293,000 (1996)
Beneficial area: UK, but particularly Gloucestershire and Cheltenham.

"The trustees are particularly interested in hearing from those involved with helping the elderly, the needy and the arts. Causes in Gloucestershire attract most attention: applicants from outside the county, where they are successful, are only likely to receive relatively small grants." Viewed especially favourably are:

- the needs of those living in rural areas;
- ventures which make a point of using volunteers (and which train volunteers);
- applicants who show clear indications that they have assessed the impact of their projects upon the environment;
- joint applications from groups working in similar areas who wish to develop a partnership;
- those who have a conscientious objection to applying for National Lottery funding.

"The trustees particularly welcome innovative ideas from small voluntary groups."

The trust is prepared to fund all kinds of work and to give its grant-aid to capital costs and equipment, projects and running costs. A few grants are spread over a three year period.

In 1996, 42 grants were for under £1,000, 71 grants were between £1,000 and £4,900, 10 grants were between £5,000 and £9,900 and seven grants were for £10,000 and more.

It increased the proportion of its grants given within Gloucestershire to 86% (92% of total money spent).

In 1996 the trust donated 21% of its total grant-aid (£48,000) to activities relevant to this guide. £20,000 was given in grants to "Churches, cathedrals, etc". 13 grants totalling £41,000 were given under its "Conservation & environment" category.

These grants included:

- Forum for the Future (£15,000);
- Rendezvous Society (£9,000);
- St Aldate's Environmental Centre (£5,000);
- Soil Association (£3,000);
- British Trust for Conservation Volunteers (£2,000);
- Prospects Trust (£1,500);
- Association of Small Historic Towns & Villages, Community Composting Network, Cotswold Canals Trust, Diocese of Gloucester Youth Office (£1,000 each);
- Earthwatch Europe, Shared Earth Trust, Stroud Preservation Trust (for Gloucestershire Buildings Recording Group) (£500 each).

Exclusions: Donations are not usually given to: medical research; London-based projects; national charities, where the trust has already supported a local branch; organisations working outside the UK; private education; animal welfare appeals.

Private organisations and individuals are only very rarely supported, students being more likely to find favour than those with other needs. In any event, the trustees urge individuals to use a specialist charity to sponsor their application.

Applications: Applicants are asked to fill in an environmental questionnaire. The trustees meet quarterly, in January, April, July and October when they consider all applications received prior to the end of the preceding month.

"Applicants should write to me stating in their own words what is required, the purpose of the application, a brief history, a financial summary and (where relevant) registered charity number. Further, please say if and when you have previously applied to the trust for a grant.

"It also helps if grant seekers say which other trusts they are approaching: we may consult them (or members of our informal panel of advisors), unless applicants specifically write to request us not to."

New applications are acknowledged and applicants informed of the trustees' decisions. SAEs are welcomed.

The Bernard Sunley Charitable Foundation

53 Grosvenor Street, London W1X 9FH
Tel: 0171-409 1199 Fax: 0171-409 7373
Contact: Duncan Macdiarmid, Director.
Trustees: John B Sunley; Mrs Joan M Tice; Mrs Bella Sunley; Sir Donald Gosling.
Grant total: £2,795,000 (1995/96)
Beneficial area: UK, mainly England, and overseas, with local interests in Ealing, Kent, Northamptonshire and Madrid.

In 1995/96 the foundation made 315 grant payments, few of them for less than £1,000 and going up to £200,000. Many of the larger payments were instalments towards a total award of up to £500,000. There is a preference for capital or equipment costs.

A large number of grants are made in Northamptonshire and Kent (14% of all the identified local grants) and seems to be related to where trustees have their country homes.

Grants relevant to this guide in 1995/96:

♦ Churches and chapels £225,000 (8% of total grant-aid)
♦ Westminister Cathedral (£100,000);
♦ St Paul's Cathedral (£50,000);
♦ Ely Cathedral (£10,000);
♦ Iona Cathedral, Southwark Cathedral (£5,000);
♦ SAVE Britain's Heritage (£1,500).

A number of other grants were also given to other cathedrals and churches. Wildlife and the environment £60,000 (2% of total grant-aid) including

♦ Kent Trust for Nature Conservation (£12,000);
♦ Wilderness Trust, Foundation for Ethnobiology (£10,000 each);
♦ Game Conservancy (£7,600);
♦ RSPB, the Country Trust (£5,000 each);
♦ Natural History Museum Development Trust (£3,000);
♦ National Trust (£2,000);
♦ Tusk (£1,000);
♦ Wildlife Trusts (£600);
♦ Plan International (£500);
♦ Save the Rhino International (£250).

It is understood the trustees generally seek to maintain over time the existing balance between categories of grant, both in their size, distribution and in the field of work to which they apply.

Exclusions: No grants for individuals.

Applications: In writing to the Director. The letter should give details as to the following points:

♦ For what project is the grant needed.
♦ How much will it cost?
♦ If it is for a building, some backup is required for the costs.
♦ The last set of audited accounts (or, presumably the new "independently examined accounts" required for smaller charities by the 1993 Charities Act, but this needs to be confirmed. Ed).
♦ Any appeal documentation.

Trustees meet in January, May and October.

The Swan Trust

(formerly Mrs E D Gibson's Charitable Trust)

Pollen House, 10/12 Cork Street, London W1X 1PD
Tel: 0171-439 9061; Fax: 0171-437 2680;
E-mail: mailbox@msf.co.uk
Contact: The Secretary
Trustees: The Cowdray Trust Limited
Grant total: £27,000 (1996/97)
Beneficial area: UK.

This trust has general charitable objects and a particular interest in the arts and the architectural heritage.

It had an income of £46,000 in 1996/97 from which nearly 50 grants totalling £27,000 were given. The largest grant was £5,000 to the Royal College of Physicians. Five other grants were for £1,000+.

More than ten grants were relevant to this guide and totalled over £7,000 (30 % of grant-aid):
◆ The Almshouse Association, Heritage of London Trust, London Historic House Museums Trust (£1,000 each);
◆ Historic Chapels Trust, Intermediate Technology Development Group (£250 each);
◆ Chelsea Old Church (£200);
◆ Friends of Textile Conservation Centre, The International Trust for Croatian Monuments (£100 each).

Exclusions: No grants to individuals. Registered charities only.

Applications: In writing to the correspondent. There are no application forms or deadlines, Acknowledgements are not sent to unsuccessful applicants.

The John Swire (1989) Charitable Trust

John Swire & Sons Ltd, Swire House, 59 Buckingham Gate, London SW1E 6AJ
Tel: 0171-834 7717
Contact: G D W Swire

Trustees: Sir John Swire CBE; G D W Swire; J S Swire; B N Swire; M C Robinson; Lady Swire.
Grant total: £114,000 (1996)
Beneficial area: UK and overseas.

Sir John established the trust in 1989. By 1996, it had assets of £1.3 million and an income of £153,000 from which donations of £114,000 were given. There have been surpluses after grant-aid during previous years (when totals of £80,000, £81,000 and £39,000 were given in 1994, 1993 and 1992 respectively).

It is possible the trust has been accumulating resources to fund a major project.

No grant-lists have been filed with the trust's accounts since 1991 when £21,000 was disbursed in 26 grants, nearly half in one major grant to Cancer Relief Macmillan Fund. Six grants totalling over £4,000 (4% of grant-aid) were relevant to this guide:
◆ Kent Gardens Trust (£2,500);
◆ River Derwent Appeal River, RSPB (£500 each);
◆ British Trust for Ornithology (£350 in 2 grants);
◆ Tradescant Trust (£275 in 2 grants);
◆ Winchester Cathedral (£250).

Applications: In writing to the correspondent.

The Charles and Elsie Sykes Trust

6 North Park Road, Harrogate, North Yorkshire HG1 5PA
Contact: David J Reah, Secretary
Trustees: John Horrocks, Chairman; Harold Bartrop; Mrs Anne Barker; Mrs G Mary Dance; Michael Garnett; Michael Moore; Lord Mountgarret; Geoffrey Tate; John Ward.
Grant total: £329,000 (1996)

The trust gives about 262 grants each year of which 49 were for £1500 or over and 6 were for £5,000 or over. These are divided almost equally between "annual" grants and "special" grants. In 1996 about £183,000 was available for new applicants. The trust seems to be mainly interested in medical research, disability, hospices and hospitals, children and youth and social and moral welfare. It only listed seven grants of over £5,000 with its 1995 accounts at the Charity Commission. These included the St George's Crypt "More than a Roof" Appeal (£10,000) which could possibly be relevant to this guide. However, given to "cultural and environmental heritage" with 7% in the previous year. Animals and birds received under 1%.

Exclusions: Applications for a local project from southern part of the UK, from registered charities only.

Applications: In writing to the correspondent including a SAE.

The Sylvanus Charitable Trust

5 Raymond Buildings, Grays Inn, London WC1R 5DD
Tel: 0171-242 8688
Contact: J C Vernor Miles
Trustees: J C Vernor Miles; A D Gemmill.
Grant total: £81,000 (1996)
Beneficial area: UK and overseas.

The trust was founded by Claude, Countess of Kinnoull, a resident of California, USA, who was primarily interested in animal welfare (which receives the greater part of its funding) and the Roman Catholic Church (a major annual grant of about £25,000 has been given to the Fraternity of Saint Pius X, Switzerland.

In 1996, the trust had assets of £1.6 million. Its 16 grants ranged between £1,000 and £25,000 though most were between £1,000 and £5,000.

Four grants relevant to this guide and totalling £20,000 (33% of grant-aid) were given in 1995:
♦ Mauritius Wildlife Appeal (£5,000);

♦ Lynx Education Trust (£4,000);
♦ Wildfowl & Wetlands Trust, Wildlife Trusts, WWF UK (£2,000 each).

Three of these beneficiaries were supported in the previous year as well.

Applications: In writing to the correspondent, but its report with its accounts states "income is substantially committed and the trustees are seldom able to provide support to new applicants who approach them".

The Tedworth Charitable Trust

See entry for the "Sainsbury Family Charitable Trusts"
Tel: 0171-410 0330
Contact: Michael Pattison
Trustees: T J Sainsbury; Alexander Sainsbury; Jessica Sainsbury; Miss J S Portrait
Grant total: £332,000 grant approvals (1995/96)
Beneficial area: UK and overseas.

This young Sainsbury family trust has the same trustees as the Staples and Glass-House trusts (see separate entries), each trusts of the children of Sir Timothy Sainsbury. This trust shows a particular interest in Parenting, Family Welfare and Child Development. It also states an interest in the Environment as well as giving "generally". The trust had a net income of £370,000 in 1995/96 with £542,000 available for distribution. Its largest commitment was £1 million over 10 years (£100,000 p a) to the Winnicott Research Unit into child psychology.

Five grants were relevant to this guide. These thoughtful gifts totalled £52,000 (16%) of grant-aid and showed a willingness to think more widely about environmental concerns than the vast majority of charitable grant-making trusts:
♦ Woodland Trust, towards its "Woods on your Doorstep" national treeplanting project for the Millennium (£25,000 over 5 years);

- Transport 2000 Trust, towards its Local Authority Network for Sustainable Transport Policies (£12,000);
- Forum for the Future, for its Ecological Tax Reform project, a study of the implications of various forms of environmental taxation (£10,000);
- Plantlife, towards the purchase of Winskill Stones, the limestone pavement in Yorkshire (£5,000).

In 1995/96 gifts of £16,000 each were given to the Headley and Jerusalem trusts, the trusts of Sir Timothy and Lady Susan Sainsbury. Similar gifts were also given by the Staples and Glass House trusts.)

Applications: See the entry for "Sainsbury Family Charitable Trusts".

The Tolkien Trust

1 St Giles, Oxford OX1 3JR
Tel: 01865-242468
Contact: Cathleen Blackburn
Trustees: John Tolkien; Christopher Tolkien; Priscilla Tolkien; Frank Williamson.
Grant total: £50,000 (1994/95)
Beneficial area: UK.

The residuary estate of J R R Tolkien, the eminent Anglo Saxon scholar and author of Lord of the Rings provides the trust with its income, and although there is no permanent endowment, there should for a long time be an income from its book royalties.

Royalties have fluctuated and generated £59,000 in 1994/95, compared with £44,000 in 1993/94 and £79,000 in 1992/93. Its total assets stood at £61,000 in 1994/95.

A total of 41 grants were given, ranging between £250 and £7,500, to both national and local organisations, most of which had received a grant in the previous year.

Four grants relevant to this guide, totalling nearly £4,000 (8% of total grant-aid) were made:
- CPRE (£1,550);

- National Trust (£1,500);
- Harvington Hall Restoration Trust (£500);
- Intermediate Technology (£300).

Applications: In writing to the correspondent.

The Tudor Trust

7 Ladbroke Grove, London W11 3BD
Tel: 0171-727 8522
Contact: Jill Powell, Grants Administrator
Trustees: Grove Charity Management Ltd, of which the Directors are: M K Graves; H M Dunwell; Dr. D J T Graves; A A Grimwade; P J Buckler; C J M Graves (the present Director of the trust); R W Anstice; Sir James Swaffield; C M Antcliff; L K Collins; E H Crawshaw; M S Dunwell; J W D Long; B H Dunwell.
Grant total: £17,936, 000 (1996/97)
Beneficial area: UK and overseas.

"The trust is a general trust and its recently issued Guidelines for Applicants 1997-2000 indicate the prime focus is on organisations whose main purpose is to help the following groups of people: drug & alcohol abusers; elderly very frail/mentally infirm; homeless; mentally ill; offenders; alienated young and families under pressure. The trust can sometimes help with community building and support workers which contribute to the needs of these groups. The trust can occasionally help charitable/not-for-profit schemes stimulating local economy and local projects engaging people in their environment, where these operate in localities which are under resourced with high levels of social disadvantage, where people are being encouraged to play a part in their community." Areas outside its current guidelines are carefully listed and include:
- Conservation/protection of buildings;
- Conservation/protection of flora and fauna;
- Community foundations;
- Community transport;
- Credit unions;
- Fabric appeals for places of worship;
- Research.

Exclusions: Individuals. See also above.

Applications: Interested readers need to be obtain the most up-to-date guidance. Applications need to be in writing, no forms are used.

The R D Turner Charitable Trust

1 The Yew Trees, High Street, Henley in Arden, Solihull, West Midlands B95 5BN
Tel: 01564-793085
Contact: J E Dyke, Administrator.
Trustees: W S Ellis; J R Clemishaw; DP Pearson; T S Lunt.
Grant total: £46,000 (1995/96)
Beneficial area: UK.

In 1995/96 the trust had assets of £702,000 and income of £50,000 and gave 22 grants totalling £46,000 which ranged from £50 to £9,000.

Nine of its grants were relevant to this guide and totalled over £21,000 (46 %) of grant-aid. But these beneficiaries have been recurrent over the past three years so there appears to be relatively little leeway for new approaches.
* Ironbridge Gorge Museum (£9,000);
* National Trust for Scotland (£4,000);
* National Trust (£3,500);
* CLA Charitable Trust (£1,500);
* St Peter's Upper Arley (£1,100);
* Wildfowl & Wetlands trust (£750);
* Scottish Churches Architectural Trust (£650);
* Dunblane cathedral (£600).

Applications: In writing to the correspondent, must include latest report and accounts.

The Underwood Trust

32 Haymarket, London SW1Y 4TP
Contact: Antony P Cox, Manager
Trustees: C Clark; R Clark; Mrs P A H Clark.
Grant total: £433,000 (1994/95)
Beneficial area: UK.

The trust was set up in 1973 by Robert Clark and Mrs M B Clark. It has stated: "Donations are only made to registered charities engaged in the activities covered by the following broad classifications: medicine and health; general welfare; education, sciences, humanities and religion; environmental resources.

The trust's income is committed to long term projects, therefore new applications are very unlikely to be considered. "Apart from a restricted list of annual donations, recurring donations are seldom made."

In 1994/95, the trust had assets of £2.5 million which generated an income of £549,000 from which grants of £433,000 were made. The accounts for the last three years have been skeletal, with no narrative report or list of grants.

In 1994/95 grants were allocated as follows:
* Medicine and health £204,000
* Welfare: £96,500
* Education, sciences, humanities and religion: £83,000
* Environmental resources: £49,000

The trust used to give grants ranging between £3,000 and £10,000, and may continue to do so, but this is speculation.

Exclusions: No grants to individuals under any circumstances. Grants are not made for expeditions, nor to overseas projects.

Applications: Applicants should note the statement above that new applications are very unlikely to be considered. Applications are not normally acknowledged.

The Veneziana Fund

c/o Pothecary & Barratt, White Horse Court, North street, Bishops Stortford CM23 2LD
Tel: 01279-506421
Contact: Mrs P H Miles, Administrator.
Beneficial area: Venice and the UK.

For a number of years Pizza Express has been making a Veneziana Pizza and those customers buying it have made a contribution to the Venice in Peril Fund. Now half the money so raised is given to Venice in Peril and the other half to restore historical buildings older than 1750.

Applications: By application form provided by the administrator.

The Vincent Wildlife Trust

10 Lovat Lane, London EC3R 8DT
Tel: 0171-283 2089
Contact: Terence O'Connor
Trustees: Vincent Weir, Chairman; Ronald Yarham; Michael Macfadyen.
Grant total: £150,000 (1995)
Beneficial area: UK.

The trust's aims include study, research and education in wildlife conservation and the establishment, control, development and maintenance of nature reserves. It is both an operational and a grant-making body. The trust itself carries out "mammal research, publishes survey reports and species leaflets and where possible seeks to purchase nature reserves when suitable sites become available". In 1995 the trust owned and maintained six reserves and employed 10 field staff all working on mammals.

In its 1995 annual report the trust outlined its strategic thinking "having taken into account the activities of other conservation bodies" which was to use its resources to support and establish "specialist bodies" which it believed are "necessary over and above the government agencies and the county wildlife movement". It excludes birds from its resourcing activities in view of the work of the RSPB and the BTO and concentrates on "the remaining area – mammals – until hopefully some form of central organisation can be established to reduce the present fragmentation in this field."

In 1995 ten grants were made:
- Herpetological Conservation Trust (£111,000 with £71,000 in the previous year);
- British Butterfly Conservation Society (£30,000 with a similar grant in the previous year);
- Bristol University, brown hares in woodland project (£6,000 with £8,000 in the previous year);
- National Museum of Scotland, preparation of polecat specimens (£3,000);
- A further 6 grants of less than £1,000 were also given.

In 1994 its 13 grants totalling £202,000 included -
- Plantlife (£55,000);
- Dr David Macdonald, Lady Margaret Hall, Oxford (£15,000 and in the previous year);
- Dr S Swift, study of natterers and daubetons in Scotland (£14,000).

In 1993 grant-aid totalling £131,000 was given in 42 grants.

Applications: In writing to the correspondent.

The Wall Charitable Trust

Meade-King, 24 Orchard Street, Bristol BS1 5DF
Tel: 0117-926 4121
Contact: P G B Letts
Trustees: P G B Letts; Orchard Executor & Trustee Company; P J Watkin.
Grant total: £96,000 (1996/97)
Beneficial area: UK with a preference for Bristol.

The trust supports a range of charities with a preference for the Bristol area. The trustees have stated that they are inundated with requests for support, receiving over 2,000 a year while giving 141 grants. Although the trust supports a number of charities on an annual basis, the greater part of the income is spent on one-off payments in response to appeals, particularly local charities.

In 1996/97, the trust had assets of £2.1 million from which "gross resources arising in the year" were £105,000. It made 141 grants with local appeals receiving 55% of total funding.

The accounts on public file at the Charity Commission show no lists of grants since 1992/93 when £101,000 was distributed in 100 grants out of which the following 10 grants, totalling nearly £8,000 (8% of total grant-aid) were relevant to this guide:

- National Heritage (£2,000);
- Avon Wildlife Trust, Dolphin Society, Kennet & Avon Canal Trust, Painswick Rococco Garden Trust (£1,000 each);
- All Saints' Church Long Ashton, Cotswolds Canal Trust, Windmill Hill City Farm (£500 each);
- Royal Geographical Society, Silvanus Trust (£200).

Exclusions: Only in exceptional circumstances will the trustees give grants to animal charities and never to individuals.

Applications: In writing to the correspondent. Applications are dealt with on a monthly basis, but requests will not normally be acknowledged in view of the additional administrative cost.

Mrs Waterhouse Charitable Trust

25 Clitheroe Road, Whalley, Clitheroe, Lancs BB7 9AD.
Contact: D H Dunn, Trustee
Trustees: D H Dunn; Mrs E Dunn.
Grant total: £289,000 (1995/96)
Beneficial area: UK, with an interest in Lancashire.

The trust channels its donations mainly, but not exclusively, to charities based in, or with branches in, the Lancashire area. It aims to provide funds on a regular basis so most grants are recurrent. It may also make a limited number of more substantial grants to finance capital projects.

In 1995/96, the trust had assets of £4.7 million and an income of £273,000. 70 grants were given totalling £289,000. The largest grant was of £35,000. The National Trust Lake District Appeal received £25,000 as it had in the previous year.

All the remaining grants were for £2,000 to £5,000 and most were to health and social welfare organisations in Lancashire. There were thirteen new recipient charities; the remainder were all recurrent from the previous year.

Applications: In writing to the correspondent. There is no set time for consideration of applications, but donations are normally made in March each year.

The Mary Webb Trust

Cherry Cottage, Hudnall Common, Berkhamsted HP4 1QN
Contact: Mrs C M Nash
Trustees: Martin Ware; Mrs Jacqueline Fancett; Mrs Cherry Nash.
Grant total: £951,000 (1995/96)
Beneficial area: UK and overseas.

The trust makes payments from both capital and income and appears to be prepared to expend its resources this way rather than confine itself to grants based on its income. In 1996 it had assets of £1.8 million held mainly in the money market (£2.6 million in 1995). Its income totalled £217,000, and grants far in excess of this were made – £951,000.

The trustees have said in the past that they prefer to make their own enquiries about the projects they support. No grant-list has been supplied with the accounts apparently to try to deter "unsuitable applications. A grant to one charity does not mean that another charity working in the same field will receive support."

The donations in 1995/96 were classified as follows (1994/95 given in brackets):

- Philanthropic £710,000 (£331,000)
- Environment £87,000 (£131,000)
- Health £77,000 (£142,000)
- Social Services £57,500 (£315,000)
- International £11,000 (£80,500)
- Culture & Recreation £4,000 (£15,000)
- Education & Research £4,000 (£29,000).

Total: £951,000 (£1,044,000)

Exclusions: No grants to individuals.

Applications: "The trustees are concerned that they receive so many appeals. They want to make their own enquiries and cannot cope with such a large number of documents and accounts sent to them unsolicited. Please note that no further information is required until asked for." If it is decided to make an application, it would seem sensible to keep it short and simple, in the first instance, as requested.

Grants given only to registered charities.

The William Webster Charitable Trust

Barclays Bank Trust Co Ltd, Executorship & Trustee Service, Osborne Court, Gadbrook Park, Northwich, Cheshire CW9 7RE
Tel: 01606-313173
Contact: The trust administrator
Trustees: Barclays Bank Trust Co Ltd.
Grant total: £122,000 (1994/95)
Beneficial area: The North East of England.

In 1994/95 the trust had income of £105,000 and gave some 75 grants ranging between £250 and £5,000. Its greatest support was given to the Tyne & Wear Foundation with two grants of £5,000 each.

In 1994/95 the trust gave of total of £7,500 (7% if grant-aid) to organisations relevant to this guide:
◆ Six churches (£6,500, all but one for £1,000);
◆ BTCV (£1,000).

Exclusions: Individuals, non-charitable organisations.

Applications: Applications should be sent by the end of May for consideration in July, by the end of September for consideration in November, and by the end of January for consideration in March. Applications should include detailed costings of capital projects, a note on the funding already raised, the latest annual accounts and charity registration number.

The James Weir Foundation

84 Cicada Road, London SW18 2NZ
Tel: 0181-870 6233
Contact: Mrs Louis Lawson, Secretary
Trustees: Dr George Weir, Simon Bonham; William Ducas.
Grant total: £132,000 (1995)
Beneficial area: UK, with a special interest in Scotland.

This foundation gives mainly to health, social welfare and academic research. Its donations to environmental interests are never very large and they vary in number and total amount greatly from year to year.

In 1995 the trust had assets of over £4 million and an income of £168,000 from which grants totalling £139,000 were given in over 100 grants with the largest grant to the Royal Society of Edinburgh.

Only two grants (1% of total grant-aid) were clearly relevant to this guide in 1995:
◆ National Trust for Scotland (£1,000 also supported in the preceding two years with £500 and £2,000);
◆ WWF UK (£1,000 with a similar grant in 1993).

In contrast during 1993 seven grants (amounting to 5% of its then grant total) were within the scope of this guide – see beneficiaries noted above plus the Scottish Wildlife Trust, Buildings of Scotland Trust, CPRE and the Farming & Wildlife Advisory Group (£1,000 each). The foundation also supports animal welfare.

Exclusions: Individuals; organisations not registered as charities.

Applications: In writing to the correspondent (who also administers the Leche Trust, see separate entry). Distributions are made in June and November.

The Welsh Church Funds

See below
Grant total: Over £1 million

There are eight county Welsh Church Funds. The Table below gives the latest figures available from the Charity Commission database.

Welsh Church Funds – income and grant total

County	Income	Grants	Year
Caernarvon	£400,000	£55,000	1993/94
Clwyd	£34,000	£24,000	1994/95
Dyfed	£228,000	–	1995/96
(total expenditure £212,000 including £5,000 to individuals)			
Gwent	£238,000	£95,000	1994/95
(a further £4,000 to individuals)			
Mid Glamorgan	£386,000	£290,000	1994/95
Powys	£88,000	£89,000	1994/95
(a further £11,000 to individuals)			
S. Glamorgan	£40,000	£28,000	1993/94
W. Glamorgan	£100,000	£630,000	1994/95

Each fund restricts its support to organisations in its county although some national (i.e. Welsh) charities may be supported where this will benefit people in the county.

The funds generally give grants for the following: listed buildings including churches, community groups, halls, Eisteddfodau, arts organisations, and a wide range of other charities. Grants may also be given to individuals, for example those with outstanding sporting ability, but this will vary from fund to fund.

Clwyd Miss C Lotoczko, Chief Executive's Department, Clwyd County Council, Shire Hall, Mold, Clwyd, CH7 6NR
Tel: 01352-752121

Dyfed: A Jones, Director of Legal & Administration Services, Carmarthenshire County Council, County Hall, Carmarthen, SA31 1JP
Tel: 01267-234567

Gwent: M J Perry, Secretary to the Trustees, Gwent County Council, County Hall, Cwmbran, Gwent, NP44 2XQ
Tel: 01633 832841

Caernarvon: C Morris, Corporate Finance Section, Gwynedd County Council, Shirehall Street, Caenarfon, Gwynedd
Tel: 01286-679593

Mid Glamorgan: Director of Finance, Rhondda-Cynon-Taff County Borough Council, Bronwydd House, Porth, Mid Glamorgan CF39 9DL
Tel: 01443-680500

Powys: A G Thomas, Chief Executive, Powys County Council, Powys County Hall, Llandrindod Wells, Powys, LD1 5LG
Tel: 01597-826000

South Glamorgan: County Solicitor & Treasurer, South Glamorgan County Council, County Hall, Atlantic Wharf, Cardiff, CF1 5UW
Tel: 01222-872261

West Glamorgan: Director of Finance, West Glarmorgan County Council, County Hall, Swansea, West Glamorgan, SA1 4SN
Tel: 01792-471410

Exclusions: These vary from fund to fund. Generally non-listed buildings including churches are not supported and grants are not given to individuals for education or training where funding has not been offered by the education authority.

Applications: Usually on a form available from the correspondent, but check with the individual fund.

The Westminster Foundation

53 Davies Street, London W1Y 1FH
Tel: 0171-408 0988
Contact: J E Hok, Secretary
Trustees: The Duke of Westminster; J H M Newsum; B A J Radcliffe.

Grant total: £1,058,000 (1995)
Beneficial area: England, North-East and London SW1/W1

The foundation held investments worth £24 million and producing an income of £888,000 in 1995. About half the grants are for £1,000 or less, but the largest awards can top £100,000. Almost all grants are to national organisations, except in Westminster and the North West. About half the organisations receiving grants of £10,000 or more had also been supported in the previous year, though often with differing amounts.

This foundation specifically excludes newly established organisations, according to the information it has supplied under "Applications" below but the support to the emergent Forum for the Future led by Jonathon Porritt is an interesting exception.

The following information is divided according to the categories used by the foundation's grant-list.

Conservation – £80,000 in 11 grants
- Forum for the Future (£30,000);
- National Museums and Galleries on Merseyside (£12,000);
- Game Conservancy Trust (£10,000);
- Architecture Foundation, Cheshire Wildlife Trust, Habitat Research Trust (£5,000 each);
- Lancashire Farming & Wildlife Advisory Group (£600);
- BTCV, Farming & Wildlife Trust (£500 each).
- 2 grants also to military museums.

Church – £208,000 in 15 grants
- Westminster Abbey (£120,000, with £20,000 the previous year) Westminster Cathedral 1995 Centenary Trust (£50,000).

Most of the smaller "church" awards were for parish church councils. At least two of these were Methodist congregations.

Under its "Social and Welfare" category the largest of the 70 grants was:
- Henry Doubleday Research Association (£100,000).

Its 18 "Education" grants included:
- Hooke Park College of the Parnham Trust (£50,000);
- The Country Trust (£5,000).

Its 17 "Youth" grants included:
- Farms for City Children (£10,000).

Exclusions: No grants to individuals. Unsolicited applications from individual youth clubs, from 'holiday' charities, student expeditions, and youth adventure training will be unsuccessful; so also from individual homes for the elderly; arts/theatre projects.

Applications: Well established registered charities only may apply in writing, giving their charitable registration number and enclosing an up-to-date set of accounts. Trustee meetings are held in February, May, September and November.

The Garfield Weston Foundation

c/o Weston Centre, Bowater House, 68 Knightsbridge, London SW1X 7LR
Tel: 0171-589 6363
Contact: Michael S E Carpenter, Secretary, Fiona Foster, Administrator.
Trustees: Garfield Weston, Chairman; Guy Weston; Galen Weston; Miriam Burnett; Barbara Mitchell; Nancy Baron; Camilla Dalglish; Jana R Khayat; Anna C Hobhouse; George G Weston.
Grant total: £22,430,000 (1996/97)
Beneficial area: UK and overseas.

The foundation published an annual report with its accounts for the first time in 1995/96. It provides some analysis of its grant-aid and a full list of grants but a clear grant-making policy and criteria for support are still lacking. This is all the more important because the foundations grant-making continues to grow substantially.

The foundation supports a broad range of activities in the field of education, the environment, the arts, health (including research) religion, welfare and other areas of general benefit to the community in the United Kingdom. "It gives the trustees as much pleasure to support requests from small charitable organisations where a grant from the foundation can make all the difference to contribute to large appeals of national importance", Annual Report 1996/97.

The foundation has assets of a massive £2,146 million in 1996/97 which generated an income of over £30 million from which 1,018 donations over £22 million were given. Twenty nine of its grants were for £100,000 and more.

35 Grants in 1996/97 were categorised under the heading "Environment" and totalling £339,000 only 1.5% of total grant aid. Four of these grants absorbed over £250,000.

Grants in 1996/97 were given to:
- National Trust for Scotland, to rescue Newhailes, East Lothian (£103,000);
- Royal Botanic Gardens (Kew) Foundation, to play a growing role in the Convention on Biological Diversity (£100,000);
- Population Concern, towards its UK Education Service to schools, Scottish Conservation Projects Trust (£25,000 each);
- National Trust (£10,000);
- Garden History Society, Heritage of London Trust, Landscape Foundation, Plantlife, Reforesting Scotland, Royal Society for the Protection of Birds (£5,000 each); Rockingham Forest Trust (£4,000);
- British Trust for Conservation Volunteers, Devon Wildlife Trust, Groundwork Ashfield & Mansfield, Scottish Wildlife Trust, Woodland Trust (£2,500 each);
- Campaign for the Protection of Rural Wales, Camphill Communities of Ireland, Castle Bromwich Hall Gardens Trust, Castlefield Management Company, Centre of the Earth, Flora for Fauna, London Historic Parks & Gardens Trust, Oxfordshire Woodland Group, River Stour Trust Limited, Suffolk Wildlife Trust, Tree Council, Wildlife Trust (Avon) (£2,000 each);

- Cotswold Canals Trust, Epping Forest Centenary Trust, Isle of Man Friends of the Earth, Learning through Landscapes, Montgomeryshire Wildlife Trust, Staffordshire Wildlife Trust (£1,000 each).

Exclusions: No grants to animal welfare charities, individuals or for individual research or study or from organisations outside the UK.

Applications: To the correspondent. Applicants must be registered charities. "Charities are asked not to apply within a 12 month period of an appeal to the foundation, whether they have received a grant or not. Grants are normally made by means of a single payment and the foundation does not commit to forward funding."

All applications must include the following information: the charity's registration number; a copy of the most recent report and audited accounts; an outline description of the charity's activities; a synopsis of the project requiring funding, with details of who will benefit; a financial plan; details of current and proposed fundraising.

Humphrey Whitbread's First Charitable Trust

34 Bryanston Square, London W1H 7LQ
Tel: 0171-402 0052
Contact: Secretary
Trustees: H Whitbread; S C Whitbread; C R Skottowe.
Grant total: £48,000 (1996/97)
Beneficial area: UK.

The trust supports a very wide range of charities. In 1994/95 the trust had assets with a market value of over £2 million generating an income of £72,000 from which £60,000 was given in 400, mostly very small, grants. Fifteen grants were for £1,000 or more.

Some 30 grants were relevant to this guide and showed a particular interest in conservation of cathedrals and churches with a lesser interest in other environmental, wildlife and countryside concerns. they totalled only about £5,500 (9% of grant-aid) and included:

◆ Lincoln Cathedral, St Margaret's Fire & Restoration Appeal (£1,000 each);
◆ Christ Church Spitalfields (£700 in 2 grants);
◆ Beds & Herts Historic Churches Trust (£510);
◆ St Alban's Cathedral Education Centre (£500);
◆ Woodland Trust urban appeal + general (£350 in 2 grants);
◆ Ely Cathedral Trust (£300);
◆ York Minster Fund (£200);
◆ Barn Owl Trust, CPRE, National Trust, RSPB, Survival International, Woodland Trust (£100 each);
◆ Bath Abbey Trust, Billings Church Appeal, British Historic Buildings Institute, Carlisle Cathedral, Elstow Abbey, Historic Chapels Trust, Lincoln Preservation Council, Friends of Redundant Churches, Shrewsbury Abbey (£100 each).

Many more small contributions of £50 and less included groups such as Population Concern and FoE.

Applications: In writing to the correspondent.

A H and B C Whiteley Charitable Trust

Regent Chambers, Regent Street, Mansfield, Nottinghamshire NG18 1SW
Tel: 01623-655111
Contact: Edward Aspley
Trustees: Not known.
Grant total: £385,000 (1994/95)
Beneficial area: UK, with a special interest for Nottinghamshire.

The trust was set up in 1990, and although it is supposed to give mainly in Nottinghamshire, the latest lists of grants show ample support for London based national organisations. In 1994/95 it had an income of £470,000, of which

£300,000 was from Gift Aid donations. Fifteen grants were made during that year, although only eleven organisations benefited, and of these only the Royal School for the Deaf (£10,000) had not been supported the year before.

The largest beneficiary was the Victoria and Albert Museum which received a total of £200,000 in two equal grants (the same was given the year before). The National Trust was given £35,000 (£70,000 a year earlier), and the Mansfield and Ashfield Friends of the Mentally Handicapped £30,000 as in the previous year. £25,000 was given to each of Mansfield Lions Club (same as before), Chatham's Hospital (£100,000 the year before), and Southwell 2000 (£80,000 in 1993/94).

Applications: None are invited. The trust does not seek applications.

The Whitley Animal Protection Trust

Edgbaston House, Walker Street, Wellington, Telford, Shropshire TF1 1HF
Tel: 01952-641651
Contact: M T Gwynne, Secretary
Trustees: E Whitley; Mrs P A Whitley; Mrs V Thompson; E J Whitley; J Whitley.
Grant total: £268,000 (1995)
Beneficial area: UK and overseas.

The trust supports animal care/protection and other related conservation projects. In 1996 the trust had assets worth some £6.5 million and income of £303,000 from which 26 grants totalling £268,000 were made.

The trust's title is slightly misleading. It now concerns itself primarily with animal/wildlife conservation rather than with the protection and care of domestic animals and pets. In 1995 the 16 grants relevant to this guide totalled £218,000 (81% of total grant-aid):

◆ RSPB Mondhuie Woods (£50,000);
◆ Tweed Foundation (£35,000);

- Shropshire Conservation Development Trust for 3 officers (£31,800);
- West Galloway Fisheries Trust (£31,000 for 4 projects);
- Oxford University WILDCRU (£21,000);
- Veterinary Pathology (Liverpool University?) (£20,000);
- Edinburgh Zoo (£15,000);
- HUT Education Officer (£13,000);
- Margaret Mee Amazon Trust (£8,000);
- Salmon & Trout Association, Friends of the Earth, Scottish Wildlife Trust, Birmingham Botanical & Horticultural Society, for Aviary (£5,000 each);
- WWF UK, for 2 projects – Coed Cymru & Jordan Hill (£2,000);
- Orangutan Foundation, Ramthanbhore Tiger Patrol (£1,000 each).

Applications: In writing to the correspondent.

The Will Charitable Trust

Farrer & Co Solicitors, 66 Lincoln's Inn Fields, London WC2A 3LH
Tel: 0171-2422022
Contact: Vanessa Reburn
Trustees: H Henshaw; P Andras; A McDonald.
Grant total: £801,000 (1995/96)
Beneficial area: UK and overseas.

"The trust provides financial assistance to charitable organisations whose activities fall within the following categories, mainly within the United Kingdom:
a. Conservation of the countryside in Britain, including its flora and fauna.
b. Care of blind people and the prevention and cure of blindness.
c. Care of and services for people suffering from cancer and their families.
d. The provision of residential care for mentally handicapped people in communities providing family environment and the maximum choice of activities and lifestyle"

"A proportion of the trust's income is devoted to assistance in other fields, but this is reserved for causes which have come to the attention of individual trustees and which the trustees regard as deserving. It is only in exceptional circumstances that the trustees will respond favourably to requests from organisations whose activities fall outside the categories listed above".

"It is unlikely that applications relating to academic research projects will be successful. The trustees recognise the importance of research, but lack the resources and expertise required to judge its relevance and value".

"Grants are awarded only to registered charities. Grants vary in amount and in the year 1995/96, apart from one exceptional grant, the smallest was for £3,000 and the largest for £40,000. Most grants fall within the range of £15,000 to £30,000 and are made to substantial organisations having proven records of successful work in their fields of operation."

No further information is available about the trust's work except that Will Woodlands, an associated charity, had purchased the Glen Feshie Estate in the Cairngorms. The price was estimated in the press as £5 million. Its 1994/95 report says that it had completed a "separate special project", probably a reference to Glen Feshie, and had transferred £7 million of its capital to Will Woodlands for further work by that charity on the creation, regeneration and improvement of woodlands. Will Woodlands also received an initial grant of £150,000 from income.

Exclusions: See above.

Applications: To the correspondent in writing. There are no application forms. The trust normally distributes income twice yearly. Grants are made in March to organisations whose activities fall within categories (b) and (d) above and applications should be received by 31st January at the latest. Grants are made in October to organisations operating within categories (a) and (c) and applications should be received by 31st August at the latest.

The H D H Wills 1965 Charitable Trust

12 Token House Yard, London EC2R 7AN
Tel: 0171-588 2828
Contact: Mrs I R Wootton
Trustees: J Kemp-Welch; Lord Killearn; J B Carson; Lady E H Wills; Dr C M H Wills.
Grant total: £74,000 (1994/95, but see below)
Beneficial area: The United Kingdom, the Channel Islands and the Irish Republic.

This trust has, over the years, been the vehicle for extensive charitable donations by members of the Wills family. Its on-going General Fund income was only £121,000 in 1994/95, but its newly established Martin Wills Fund had £265,000. This came mainly from the farming profits of two estates left to the fund by Mr Wills, and this fund looks being the main source of grants in the immediate future.

The arrangements for the distribution of its awards are unusual, with different organisations to benefit in each year of a seven year cycle, as follows
- 1st Year (92/93) Magdalen College, Oxford
- 2nd Year (93/94) Rendcomb College, Gloucestershire
- 3rd and 4th Years (94/96) Wildlife conservation
- 5th Year (96/97) Ditchley Foundation
- 6th and 7th Years (97/98) At the Trustees' discretion.

The cycle then repeats over subsequent seven year periods.

The smaller General Fund gave over 130 grants in 1994/95, most of them of £250 or less. There were two larger grants, of £19,000 to Ditchley Park Conference Centre (another Wills family foundation) and of £10,000 for the Cambridge Foundation.

The small grants were widely spread, mainly among national charities and local organisations, most though not all of them in the south of England (Oxfordshire especially) and Scotland.

Grants relevant to this guide in 1994/95 included:
- Sandford St Martin Church (£1,000);
- Countryside Foundation, Westminster Abbey (£500 each);
- Barn Owl Trust, Bath Abbey, Care for the Wild, Iona Abbey, Scottish Wildlife, Suffolk Wildlife, Tusk (£250 each);
- Heritage of London Trust, Population Concern (£200).

Exclusions: No grants are given to individuals.

Applications: In writing to the correspondent.

The Wolfson Foundation

18-22 Haymarket, London SW1Y 4DQ
Tel: 0171-930 1057; Fax: 0171-930 1036
Contact: Dr Victoria Harrison, Executive Secretary
Trustees: Lord Wolfson; Lady Wolfson; Lord Quirk; Lord Quinton; Sir Eric Ash; Lord Phillips; Lord McColl; Professor Sir Leslie Turnberg; Mrs Janet Wolfson de Botton; Mrs Laura Wolfson Townsley; Sir Derek Roberts.
Grant total: £19,000,000 (1996/97)
Beneficial area: Mainly UK and Israel.

A small number of large grants (usually to universities and spread over a number of years) account for a large proportion of the value of awards. A relatively large number of smaller grants are made to a wide variety of bodies, including voluntary organisations. Grants are normally made under umbrella programmes which usually last for three years, and are most often, but not exclusively, for buildings and equipment.

"Grants are given to act as a catalyst, to back talent and to provide support for promising future projects which may be currently underfunded... Eligible applications from registered charities for contributions to appeals will normally be considered only when at least 50% of that appeal has already been raised... Grants to universities for research and scholarship are normally made under the umbrella of designated competitive programmes in which vice-chancellors and principals are invited to participate from time to time."

The foundation had an income of £21.3 million in 1996/97. New awards during this year amounted to £18,581,000 and they are described below. However, the sum actually paid out during that year was £12.4 million.

New awards for 1996/97
Arts and humanities: £2,506,000 in 54 grants
- Cathedrals and churches: £86,000 in 22 grants including: Exeter Synagogue (£8,000);
- All the remainder were churches.

Heritage: £1,685,000 in grants including:
- National Maritime Museum, Greenwich (£700,000);
- Royal Botanical Gardens, Kew (£250,000);
- Dulwich Picture Gallery (£125,000);
- Scottish United Services Museum (£100,000).

Exclusions: Individuals. Grants are not normally made for:
- research or other projects considered to be the proper responsibility of another funding body (such as a research council or the NHS); the costs of running or attending meetings, conferences, lectures, exhibitions, concerts, expeditions, etc;
- non-specific appeals (including circulars) and requests for contributions to endowment funds; the making of films or videos;
- overheads, running or administrative costs, VAT or professional fees; charities which redistribute funds to other charitable bodies; research involving live animals; the purchase of buildings.

Applications: It is essential to first obtain the detailed printed guidelines. Prospective applicants are encouraged to explore their eligibility by submitting in writing a brief outline of the project with one copy of the organisation's most recent audited accounts. There is no application form but detailed proposals (preferably no longer than 1000 words excluding appendices) should be in the format set out in the guidelines.

Applications can be considered if they come within an active umbrella programme. These evolve from time to time and those seeking support are advised to contact the director before making a full application. The same appeal cannot be considered by both this trust and by its sister body, the Wolfson Family Charitable Trust. An application to one may, however, be referred to the other at the discretion of the trustees. Unsuccessful applications cannot normally be reconsidered. Nor, usually, can further applications from the same body be considered until one year has elapsed, in the case of unsuccessful applicants, or five years if a grant has been awarded.

Trustees meet in June and December and applications have to be made by 15th March and 15th September.

The Woodward Charitable Trust

See entry for the "Sainsbury Family Charitable Trusts"
Tel: 0171-242 1212
Contact: Michael Pattison
Trustees: Mrs Camilla M Woodward; Shaun Anthony Woodward; Miss J S Portrait.
Grant total: £554,000 (1996)
Beneficial area: UK.

The trust is of particular interest to the Sainsbury "twitchers". It has only entered the fold of Red Lion Court in 1997 having been administered by its accountants from its registration in 1988.

Mrs Camilla Woodward is the daughter of Sir Timothy Sainsbury who in 1993 gave 2 million ordinary 25p shares in J Sainsbury plc, not as a contribution to the trust's own permanent endowment, but as a "restricted fund" and followed up with a further gift in 1995 of another 1 million in ordinary 25p shares without the proviso. Her husband, Shaun Woodward, has an interesting career which has already spanned working on "That's Life" to directing communications for the Conservative Party and backing Stephen Dorrell in its leadership contest.

By 1996 the trust's assets had grown to over £13 million and generated an income of £496,000. A total of £554,000 was paid in about 180 grants most of which were small and under £1,000. Its interests are broad but the lion's share of giving is made to opera and unlike other "young" Sainsbury family trusts little interest has been shown in environmental activities. A mere five grants totalling £3,000 were clearly relevant to this guide in 1996. The largest being to the Woodland Trust (£1,000). A grant was also made to Jesus College possibly for restoration (£10,000).

Exclusions: No grants direct to individuals.

Applications: See entry for the "Sainsbury Family Charitable Trusts".

The Yapp Education & Research Trust

Kidd Rapinet, Solicitors, 14-15 Craven Street, London WC2N 5AD
Contact: Ms Claire Bowden-Dan.
Trustees: P W Williams; Rev T C Brooke; Miss A J Norman; M W Rapinet; P G Murray.
Grant total: £91,000 (September 1991)
Beneficial area: UK.

Grants are given to schools, universities, colleges of higher education and hospitals, for the advancement of education and learning, and of scientific and medical research. A few grants are also made for environmental causes.

In 1995 the trust had assets of £2 million and income of £89,000 and made grants of £81,000. In 1991, the most recent year for which a schedule of grants was filed with the Charity Commission, the trust had assets of £1.44 million, an income of £104,000 from which grants totalling £91,000 were made.

Five grants totalling nearly £7,000 (7% of grant-aid) were relevant to this guide:
◆ Stepping Stones Farm (£3,000);
◆ FoE (£1,500);
◆ Learning through Landscapes (£1,000);
◆ Earthwatch Europe (£750);
◆ Birmingham Botanical Gardens & Glasshouses (£500).

Two grants were also given for animal welfare activities.

Exclusions: The trustees do NOT make grants within the following categories:
◆ Applications made by, or on behalf of, individuals;
◆ Applications made by non-charities in the name, or under the auspices, of a third party with charitable status;
◆ University expeditions;
◆ School building or development funds;
◆ Applications where the total amount of the appeal exceeds £100,000 (unless the balance of the appeal at the date of application is less than this figure);
◆ Applications from any applicant who has already received a grant from either the trust or the Yapp Welfare Trust (see following entry) within the preceding THREE YEARS.

Applications: In writing to the correspondent. Applicants are invited to complete and return a short standard application form. The trustees also expect to receive a copy of the applicant's latest accounts. Annual reports, newsletters or brochures should also be included with any application, but such supporting documentation should be kept reasonably brief. Applicants must include five copies of any supporting documents, and "applications submitted without the necessary supporting documents will be rejected automatically".

The trustees meet three times a year (usually in the middle of March, July and November) to consider grant applications. The list of applications is closed six weeks before the date of each meeting, and any application received after the closing date for one meeting is automatically carried forward to the next. All applicants will be notified of the outcome of their appeal.

The Zephyr Charitable Trust

New Guild House, 45 Great Charles Street, Queensway, Birmingham B3 2LX
Tel: 0121-212 2222
Contact: Roger Harriman
Trustees: Elizabeth Breeze, Chair; Roger Harriman; David Baldock; Donald I Watson.
Grant total: £25,000 (1996/97)
Beneficial area: UK and overseas.

This trust gives the major part of its support in subscriptions and reserves only a small amount for one-off grants. In 1996/97 it had an income of £29,000 from which grant-aid of £25,000 was disbursed. Thirteen charities received annual subscriptions totalling £21,000 in 1996/97 with only £3,800 given in grants. Its donations are "based on the continuing interests of the trustees" and its investments are made using the services of EIRIS, the Ethical Investment Research Information Service.

Four grants totalling £6,600 (26.5 % of grant-aid) were relevant to this guide:
◆ Intermediate Technology (£3,000);
◆ Survival International (£1,600);
◆ Pesticides Trust (£1,300);
◆ Paddington Farm Trust (£750).

All had received similar grants in the previous year.

Applications: In writing to the correspondent but see information above.

The Konrad Zweig Trust

House with Arches, Ormiston Hall, Ormiston, East Lothian EH35 5NJ
Tel: 01875-340541
Contact: Mrs Francesca Loening
Trustees: Ulrich Loening; Francesca Loening; Professor Aubrey Manning; Abigail Marland; Myrtle Ashmole; Annelie Rookwood.
Grant total: About £15,000 a year.
Beneficial area: UK, with a preference for Scotland.

The trust was set up in 1985 by the daughter and son-in-law of the late Konrad Zweig. It aims "to support ecological, social and economic projects concerned with the establishment of a sustainable and equitable balance between people and the environment".

Projects that the trust will support may be "academic, practical or may combine both approaches. They should be based on environmental and social concerns and must comply with the requirements and conditions of the trust".

Grants in the 1996/97 included:
◆ Scottish Borders Forest Trust (£3,000);
◆ Sustrans Safe Routes to Schools (£2,000);
◆ Black Environment Network (£1,500 1st of four);
◆ Youth Clubs Scotland (£1,500);
◆ Research Lecturer, Napier University, Sustainable Lobster Fishery Project (£1,000).

Applications: Trustees will be pleased to discuss projects with potential applicants and expect to be kept in touch with the progress of funded projects.

In the first instance applications, which can be from both organisations and individuals, should give a brief outline of the project, not exceeding two pages.

CHAPTER SIX

COMPANIES

INTRODUCTION

The information for this section has been collected by researching those companies known to have given a degree of support to the environment and those identified in the annual reports and publications of some of the main environmental organisations. We have tended to concentrate on donations but information on the sponsorship of environmental activities is also included.

It is important to be clear about the distinction between the two. While for any donation given, most companies will expect some kind of public recognition (for example coverage in the local press), where sponsorship is concerned, they are likely to demand it. Sponsorship is a relationship between two parties – often each with quite different interests – who come together to support a particular activity for quite different reasons. Usually the charity is looking to raise funds for its work and the sponsor company hopes to improve its image, to promote and sell its products or to entertain its customers. Sponsorship is a formal, contractual relationship, with VAT implications that should be carefully checked out. Such contracts are usually negotiated by the marketing or recruitment division of a company. One way to identify the appropriate budget holder is to ask the community relations department to provide you with a name or an introduction.

Please note that the figure given in company entries of this book is that for total charitable donations in the UK, not just for environmental support. Even for those companies that specify the environment as one of their focus areas, the actual amount given in donations to environmental organisations may only be about 10% of this total. Were all the companies listed giving 10% of the charitable donations budget to environmental charities, even this would total only about £9 million. However, some companies will be giving much greater amounts through sponsorship and other forms of support.

The policies of companies change often, sometimes annually. There is a current trend for companies to relate their community support more directly to their business activities than was once the case. While for some, such as utility companies, this may mean that greater emphasis is placed on environmental issues, for others this has resulted in a move away from environmental concerns. There are also general trends in support by companies. While a few years ago the environment was a popular funding area, it is now less so as the emphasis shifts towards causes related to children and youth projects.

The contacts and addresses in the entries were all as correct as possible at the time of going to print. Inevitably some of these will change in the life of this guide. We strongly urge potential applicants to check current names and addresses before applying to any company.

ALPHABETICAL INDEX OF COMPANIES

SUBJECT INDEX OF COMPANIES

This index shows the main areas that companies work in. Many are large holding companies which consist of companies which may work in different fields. An example is the Kingfisher group whose interests range from B&Q to Time Retail Finance.

COMPANIES

3i Group plc

91 Waterloo Road, London SE1 8XP
Tel: 0171-928 3131
Correspondent: Sabina Dawson, Assistant
Company Secretary
Charitable donations: £350,000
(1996/97)
Nature of business: Investors in industry.

Policy: The company gives its charitable
donations through the 3i Charitable Trust,
which favours charitable initiatives with
which members of staff are personally
involved, as well as local charities where 3i
has an office. It prefers to support smaller
charities where a grant will have a
significant impact. Although preference is
given to the arts, culture and quality of
life, higher education and self-help,
especially in inner cities, support may also
be given to a range of other causes
including the environment. Grants range
from about £20 to £10,000. A total of 64
organisations received grants of £1,000 or
more in 1995/96, including the Wildfowl
and Wetlands Trust and Business in the
Environment, the latter being one of three
recipients of £10,000.

Applications: In writing to the
correspondent. The Board of the 3i
Trustee Company Limited meet regularly.

3M UK Holdings plc

3M House, PO Box 1, Bracknell
RG12 1JU
Tel: 01344-858000
Correspondent: Tony Bellis, Corporate
Communications Manager
Charitable donations: £148,354 (1996)
Nature of business: Industrial, consumer
and healthcare products.

Policy: Support is only given to national
charities, local charities in areas of
company presence (16 locations
nationwide), and appeals relevant to the
company's business, with a preference for
charities in which a member of company
staff is involved. Support is given to
environmental causes, with a major
recipient in 1997 being the Earthwatch
Teaching Awards. Grants to national
organisations range from £1,500 to
£35,000. Grants to local organisations
range from £25 to £5,000.

Applications: In writing to the
correspondent. Policy guidelines
Corporate Charity & Community
Relations Policy are available from the
correspondent.

AEA Technology plc

329 Harwell, Didcot, Oxfordshire
OX11 0RA
Tel: 01235-433648
Fax: 01235-432123
Correspondent: Cathy Wright, Corporate
Community Involvement Manager
Charitable donations: £34,415 (1995/96)
Nature of business: Science and
engineering services.

Policy: The company focuses its support
on the environment and on creating
awareness and understanding in education
of the value of science, engineering and
technology. Emphasis is given in these
areas to activities which are close to the
company's sites or involve employees.
Grants range from £1,000 to £4,000.

Applications: In writing to the
correspondent.

Albright & Wilson plc

PO Box 3, 210–222 Hagley Road West, Oldbury, Warley, West Midlands B68 0NN
Tel: 0121-429 4942
Correspondent: J Stratton, Public Affairs
Charitable donations: £103,000 (1996)
Nature of business: Chemical and allied products.

Policy: Most support is given in areas of company presence, including assisting local community groups, education, the arts, enterprise/training, environment/heritage and science/technology initiatives. The Black Country Business Environment Association was one of the main beneficiaries in 1996.

Applications: In writing to the correspondent.

Allied Domecq PLC

24 Portland Place, London W1N 4BB
Tel: 0171-323 9000
Correspondent: Clive Burns, Secretary, Charitable Trust
Charitable donations: £748,000 (1996/97)
Nature of business: International spirits and retailing group.

Policy: The environment is one of the three main areas focused on by the company, the others being education and the arts. In general, there is a preference for local charities in areas where the company operates and appeals relevant to company business. Subsidiary companies have their own budgets and are encouraged to become involved with local organisations.

In 1996/97, the group committed over £3.5 million worldwide to community activities including direct donations to charities, donations in kind, secondments and sponsorships.

The charitable donations in the UK of £748,000 included £650,000 to the Allied Domecq Trust, which itself gave some £612,000 to a wide range of charitable

causes. Recent support for environmental causes includes grants of £10,000 to the University of Cambridge to fund a series of public lectures to promote academic development of environmental issues.

A major project is also under way with the Groundwork Foundation in the UK. The first development has been the regeneration of a ten mile stretch of canal and the £100,000 spent has helped provide access for the disabled as well as improving wildlife habitats. The fund of £300,000 is a three year partnership to encourage local Allied Domecq companies to develop schemes for lasting environmental improvements with their local Groundwork trusts.

Applications: Appeals to head office should be addressed to the correspondent. It may be more beneficial to apply to one of the subsidiary companies, especially if there is a local connection. Sponsorship proposals should be addressed to Ian Oag, Corporate Affairs Manager.

Amerada Hess Ltd

33 Grosvenor Place, London SW1X 7HY
Tel: 0171-823 2626
Fax: 0171-8872199
Correspondent: Public Affairs Department
Charitable donations: £71,000 (1996)
Nature of business: Oil and natural gas.

Policy: Although the environment is not stated as one of the company's favoured areas for support, it has supported the Grounds for Learning project in Scotland, which launched its initiative to encourage best practice in the development of school grounds to increase their environmental and educational amenities. It is also a member of the Green Alliance.

The company prefers to support local charities in areas of company presence with head office (London) supporting mainly charities working in London, and the Aberdeen office dealing with appeals relevant to that region. Support tends to be given to specific projects and employee involvement is encouraged.

Applications: Appeals from national charities should be addressed in writing to the correspondent. The Aberdeen office (Scott House, Hareness Road, Altens, Aberdeen AB1 4LE 01224-243000) deals with appeals relevant to that region.

Amersham International plc

Amersham Place, Little Chalfont, Buckinghamshire HP7 9NA
Tel: 01494-544000
Correspondent: Group Corporate Affairs
Charitable donations: £89,766 (1996/97)
Nature of business: Healthcare and life science products.

Policy: At local (in areas of company presence), national and international level, the company directs its giving towards healthcare, education and the environment (with occasional support going to other causes). Company operating sites in the UK are south Buckinghamshire, Cardiff and Gloucester. The company is a member of The Environment Council. In addition to charitable donations the company gave over £80,000 in other community contributions in 1996/97, including gifts in kind and expertise put at the service of community programmes.

Applications: In writing to the correspondent.

Amway UK Ltd

Ambassador House, Queensway, Bletchley, Milton Keynes MK2 2EH
Tel: 01908-363000
Fax: 01908-363222
Correspondent: Sharon Norman, Manager of Public Relations
Charitable donations: Not available
Nature of business: Household cleaning products; cosmetics.

Policy: The environment/conservation is one of the company's favoured areas of support for both donations and sponsorship. The Natural Environment

Research Council has received regular support.

Applications: The company stated that its funding for environmental projects has been committed for the foreseeable future.

Anglian Water plc

Anglian House, Ambury Road, Huntingdon, Cambridgeshire PE18 6NZ
Tel: 01480-443000
Correspondent: Mrs Glynis Hammond, Sponsorship Manager
Charitable donations: £106,377 (1996/97)
Nature of business: Water supply and sewage treatment.

Policy: The company supports a wide range of causes and charities in the Anglian Water area and, in common with other utility companies, several environmental initiatives are undertaken. Two of note are the development of a new nature reserve at Bowthorpe and Earlham Marshes near Norwich, and the launch of a five-year programme to reintroduce ospreys to Rutland Water.

The company also runs Caring for the Environment Awards to encourage environmental projects in the region, with the prize fund doubled to £40,000 in 1996/97. It has developed a partnership with In Bloom, which organises the annual competition for communities which use flowers and planting to improve the quality of their local environment. It also supports organisations such as the RSPB and Woodland Trust.

Applications: In writing to the correspondent.

Apple Computer UK Ltd

6 Roundwood Avenue, Stockley Park, Uxbridge UB11 1BB
Tel: 0181-569 1199
Fax: 0181-569 2957
Correspondent: Russell Brady, Corporate Relations Manager
Charitable donations: Not available

Nature of business: Personal computers.

Policy: The company provides gifts in kind in the form of computer equipment and offers expert knowledge or assistance. It is a supporter of the Dian Fossey Gorilla Fund to which it has previously given £30,000 worth of computer equipment for field staff, and in 1997 gave a cash donation described as 'generous'. Earthwatch has also been supported.

Applications: In writing only to the correspondent.

ASDA Group plc

ASDA House, Southbank, Great Wilson Street, Leeds LS11 5AD
Tel: 0113-243 5435
Correspondent: Christine Watts, Director of Corporate Affairs
Charitable donations: £100,000 (1996/97)
Nature of business: Supermarket retail.

Policy: Including charitable donations of £100,000, their total community contributions in 1996/97 totalled about £1 million. Donations are given through the ASDA Foundation which primarily supports causes recommended and supported by its store colleagues and customers. The focus areas are: children and education, women's health issues, grassroots local community activity.

In 1994/5, the trust had an income of £100,000 and gave grants totalling £81,000. Charitable status is a prerequisite for support. Grants normally range between £500 to £1,000. The grants made in 1994/95 included the categories: cathedrals and churches (£1,240); community problems, amenities and activities (£5,195); and environmental improvement (£500). One of the larger grants made was to the Groundwork Foundation (£4,150).

Applications: Charities should direct applications to the general store manager of their local ASDA.

BAA plc

130 Wilton Road, London SW1V 1LQ
Tel: 0171-834 9449
Correspondent: Rachel Rowson, Company Secretary
Charitable donations: £719,000 (1996/97)
Nature of business: Airport operators.

Policy: The company established its own charity – the BAA 21st Century Communities Charitable Trust – during 1996/97. It was set up to channel the company's donations to help local communities 'face the challenges of the new millennium, particularly in the areas of the three Es – education, economic regeneration and the environment'. With reference to the latter, the trust will help local groups nurture the physical environment.

Typical grants to organisations range from £50 to £20,000. Most support is given locally in south east England and in Scotland. Projects are also recommended by airport staff. The company supports a number of organisations concerned with conservation including Essex Heritage Trust and the wildlife trusts of Essex, Hampshire, Scotland and Sussex. In addition, Horley & Crawley Countryside Management Project received support from Gatwick Airport towards the running costs of a Land Rover.

The company have a night noise penalty which has been extended throughout the day; the fines are then donated to the local community.

Applications: Applicants are advised of the company's policy on charitable giving, if requested, and to write to the relevant airport.

Contacts for local appeals: *Heathrow Airport Ltd:* Community Relations Manager, Hounslow, Middlesex (0181-745 4494);

Gatwick Airport Ltd: Public Affairs, Gatwick, West Sussex RH6 0NP (01293-504192);

Stansted Airport Ltd: Community Relations Manager, Stansted, Essex CM24 8QW (01279-502710);

Scottish Airports Ltd: Head of Public Affairs, St Andrew's Drive, Paisley, Renfrewshire PA3 2ST (0141-848 4293);

Southampton International Airport: Public Affairs Manager, Southampton, Hampshire SO9 1RH (01703-629600).

Bank of Scotland

Public Relations Department, PO Box No.5, The Mound, Edinburgh EH1 1YZ
Tel: 0131-243 7058/ 243-7060
Fax: 0131-243 7081
Correspondent: Eric Scott, Manager, or Fiona Dawson, Assistant Manager
Charitable donations: £800,000 (1996/97)
Nature of business: Banking and related services.

Policy: In addition to charitable donations, the bank supports over 300 events throughout the UK through its diverse sponsorship programme. During 1996, the group contributed £3.9 million to the community, including donations of £0.8 million to charitable organisations.

Charitable donations: Contributions from this budget are made to organisations, large and small, which encompass a wide range of subjects including the homeless, education, the environment and wildlife, medical care and youth. In 1996, causes relevant to this guide which received support included Care for the Wild, the Farming & Wildlife Advisory Group and Tidy Britain Group.

Sponsorship: The bank maintains a sponsorship portfolio which is wide ranging, both in geographic terms and content. It is broken down into three major categories – sport, community (including environmental projects) and the arts. A great deal of emphasis is placed on encouraging young people and on grassroots development, as well as projects which have a wide public appeal.

Sponsorship is only undertaken on a commercial basis and the bank does NOT sponsor individuals, societies, charities or fundraising events for charities, conferences other than by the provision of wallets, etc., publications, videos, films or recordings.

Applications: Donations are decided upon by a donations committee which meets as required. Appeals should be addressed to R E Scott for sponsorship requests or Miss Fiona Dawson in the case of charitable appeals.

Barclays PLC

Community Affairs Department, 8th Floor, 54 Lombard Street, London EC3P 3AH
Tel: 0171-699 2657
Fax: 0171-699 2685
Correspondent: Mrs Angela Tymkow, Community Manager
Charitable donations: £4,400,000 (1997)
Nature of business: Banking, financial and related services.

Policy: In 1997, total contributions by the group were £15.1 million, including £13.5 million in the UK and £1.6 million through local offices overseas.

Support is only given to registered charities or for clearly charitable purposes. One of the five main categories supported is the environment.

Support is given through Barclays SiteSavers, a scheme run in partnership with the Groundwork Foundation to transform derelict and neglected land into new recreational facilities. This leaves very little scope to support other environmental charities. However, in the last couple of years grants have also been given to well known organisations such as Council for the Protection of Rural England, Countryside Foundation and Environment Trust. The bank has also undertaken a £500,000 four year sponsorship called Barclays Countryfocus, supporting the greater enjoyment of

National Trust countryside. From 1996 to 1999, the funds will provide for a range of projects including footpath repairs, new bridlepaths and cycle tracks, disabled routes, a disabled facilities booklet, family fun days, the annual week of Christmas walks, and information leaflets.

Applications: Appeals to head office should be sent to the Community Manager. Local appeals should be sent to regional offices which have their own budgets. Contact should be made in the first instance with the local branch manager whenever possible.

BASF plc

PO Box 4, Earl Road, Cheadle Hulme, Cheadle, Cheshire SK8 6QG
Tel: 0161-485 6222
Fax: 0161-486 0891
Correspondent: Barry Mansfield, Director of Public Affairs
Charitable donations: £51,613 (1996)
Nature of business: Manufacture of audio/video tapes; chemical company.

Policy: The areas of support favoured by the company are the arts, community, education and environment/conservation. It is one of the sponsors of the Young Environmentalist of the Year Awards (£6,667 in 1996/97). The largest UK manufacturing site is on Teesside, where the company is a founder member of Industry Nature Conservation Agency and a member of the wildlife trust.

Applications: In writing to the correspondent.

Bass plc

20 North Audley Street, London W1Y 1WE
Tel: 0171-409 1919
Fax: 0171-409 8501
Correspondent: Walter J Barratt, Charities Administrator, Bass Charitable Trust
Charitable donations: £1,100,000 (1996/97)

Nature of business: Hotels, leisure retailing and branded drinks.

Policy: The Policy Guidelines of the company state:

1. Bass supports a wide range of charities and in particular seeks to work with charities for mutual benefit. Charities in which Bass employees are actively involved are also supported through the Bass Community Award Scheme.

2. The main impetus of funding effort is directed to four broad areas – community, youth and education, environment and the arts. Within the environment category, Bass supports projects and programmes of work to protect and/or improve the physical landscape and the urban environment, with particular emphasis on areas where the company has a significant presence. Special consideration is given to appeals originating in areas where the company has a substantial presence and/or with which an employee has a close and active association. Many donations are given in response to appeals initially made to Bass operating companies.

Grants to local organisations range from £250 upwards and to national organisations from £1,000 upwards. Major support will be given over the next three years (1998–2000) to Millennium Greens.

Applications: In writing to the correspondent. Local appeals should be addressed to the public relations manager at the appropriate regional office. Established charities should always send up-to-date audited accounts with any appeal. Policy guidelines are available from the correspondent.

BG plc

100 Thames Valley Park Drive, Reading RG6 1PT
Tel: 0118-935 3222
Correspondent: Dr Mary Harris, Director Designate, BG Foundation
Charitable donations: £2,200,000 (1996)
Nature of business: Gas suppliers.

Policy: BG has wide ranging community interests, including maintenance and improvement of the environment. Organisations sponsored include BTCV, RSPB, Green Alliance, Groundwork, Tree Council and Sustainability. Transco is also a sponsor of the Mersey Basin Campaign. Details of the Transco Grassroots Action Scheme, which awards up to £100,000 in grants to schools, charities and voluntary organisations to fund local practical projects aimed at improving the local environment, can be found in the Awards section of this guide.

The Exploration and Production business supports the Wildlife Trusts Rockwatch, and a club for young geologists.

Applications: In writing to the correspondent. The unit at headquarters handles all requests which have national implications.

BHP Petroleum Ltd

Neathouse Place, London SW1V 1LH
Tel: 0171-802 7000
Correspondent: Miss Justine Wood, External Affairs Assistant
Charitable donations: £60,000 (1996/97)
Nature of business: Oil and gas exploration and production.

Policy: The company prefers to support local charities which benefit the communities directly affected by its activities in the North West and north Wales area. It focuses its support on education, community welfare, medical research, youth, the arts and the environment.

In February 1996, the company set up The Lennox First Oil Fund to celebrate the flow of the first oil from its Lennox Field in the Irish Sea. This fund provides grants of up to £2,000 for projects which provide clear environmental or safety benefits to the Sefton community. Applications to this fund should be made to the Public Affairs Manager, BHP Petroleum Ltd, Point of Ayr Terminal, Hollywell, Flintshire CH8 9RD.

Applications: In writing to the correspondent.

Blue Circle Industries PLC

84 Eccleston Square, London SW1V 1PX
Tel: 0171-828 3456
Correspondent: Miss Sarah May,
Charitable donations: £247,486 (1996)
Nature of business: Cement and allied products.

Policy: Blue Circle's charitable donations were categorised as follows in 1996: social causes 18%; education 43%; medicine 10%; environment, the arts and sport 29%.

Of the grants given 80% were to local organisations and 20% to national. Grants range from £100 to £100,000 and are usually paid in CAF vouchers. Slight preference is given to projects in which a member of staff is involved, charities in areas of company presence and appeals related to company presence.

The company is currently contributing substantial funds to three national charities for a three year period.

For 1997 to 1999, support is being given to Construction Industry Trust for Youth, Cancer Research Campaign/Hospice Movement and Groundwork Kent Thameside, with monies being focused in areas of local business operations.

The company sponsors the Young Environmentalist of the Year awards (£6,667 in 1996/97).

Local community initiatives and a number of county wildlife trusts have also been supported. More recently Blue Circle has become a member of the corporate environmental responsibilities group set up by Earthwatch.

Applications: In writing to the correspondent. Grant decisions at head office are made by a donations committee. Sponsorship proposals to the correspondent. Local appeals to the relevant regional office.

BOC Group plc

Chertsey Road, Windlesham,
Surrey GU20 6HJ
Tel: 01276-477222
Tel: 01276-471333
Correspondent: Anne Leggatt,
Administrator – Appeals & Donations
Charitable donations: £612,000
(1996/97)
Nature of business: Manufacture and
supply of gases and related products;
healthcare products and services.

Policy: BOC prefers to maintain a small
number of long-term commitments,
preferably related to its activities. Some
preference is also given to appeals from local
organisations in areas where the group has a
plant. One of the four main categories of
support is the environment.

Environment projects are funded through
the BOC Foundation for the Environment
(an independent body), which spent about
£500,000 on projects in the year. The
Foundation provides funding for projects
which aim to demonstrate in a practical way
how pollution can be reduced in the UK.
So far it has focused mainly on issues of
waste management and water quality. It has
a particular interest in projects where partial
funding has already been obtained from
other sources.

The main criteria on which applications
will be judged are as follows.
1. Ideally projects should be capable of
completion in 6 to 18 months – though a
longer duration can be acceptable.
2. Projects must have clearly defined goals –
preferably with a series of milestones against
which progress can be measured.
3. Projects should involve research to be
carried out in Britain and to be concerned
with some aspect of environmental control
or pollution abatement.
4. More than one organisation may be
involved as long as responsibility is
effectively allocated.
5. If successful, the results or approach of
the project should have the potential for
replication

Applications: Appeals should be made in
writing to: The Director, The BOC
Foundation, c/o 70 Shenfield Road,
Shenfield, Brentwood, Essex CM15 8EW.

Body Shop International PLC

Watersmead, Littlehampton, West Sussex
BN17 6LS
Tel: 01903-731500
Fax: 01903-844021
Correspondent: Clive James, Foundation
Manager
Charitable donations: £750,000
(1996/97)
Nature of business: Skin and hair care
products.

Policy: The company does most of its
charitable giving through its registered
charity, The Body Shop Foundation,
which also receives donations from
franchisees, employees and friends of The
Body Shop. Its ongoing purpose is to give
financial and gift in kind support to
innovative, grassroots organisations
working in the fields of human rights and
environmental protection.

Human and civil rights: it is interested in
most issues ranging from land rights to
torture. There are, however, two areas that
it is particularly interested in – women
and indigenous people.

Environmental protection/sustainability:
the foundation tries to minimise the
consumption of energy and resources,
whilst supporting renewable energy
development.

In 1995/96, the foundation listed the 50
largest of the 208 grants given, which
ranged from £2,000 to £52,000. Seven of
these grants were of £20,000, and
included those to:

◆ Unrepresented Nations & Peoples
Organisation (UNPO) for ongoing
support costs, including fundraising
and computer acquisition, of this
Hague based organisation;

◆ the Academy for Socially Responsible
Business Foundation, for academic

set-up costs of the Academy's office including salaries, computers and other equipment;

◆ Mother Jones, a US based investigative magazine – which is part of the Foundation for National Progress – for research, publication and dissemination of projects on shrimp aquaculture, women's economic development and sustainable agriculture;

◆ Women's Environmental Network Trust (WENDI) – final instalment of three-year funding for the salary of the co-ordinator of an information hotline for consumer questions on the environment.

There were 13 grants of around £10,000 to £16,600 which included:

◆ Community Service Volunteers for production of an awareness raising video;

◆ Bioregional Development Group for traditional lavender oil production in South London;

◆ Forest Monitor towards research on logging in South East Asia and for legal assistance for communities in the Solomon Islands and Vanuatu;

◆ the Movement for the Survival of the Ogoni People for support of the then imprisoned Ken Saro-Wiwa.

Large grants were also given to: Parks and Recreation (Glasgow City Council) – 50% towards the costs of a sports coaching project with local primary schools, and Pathways Sheltered Workshop for a project making bird boxes and garden furniture. In addition, a separate Endangered Species Fund had £50,000 to help endangered animals around the world (it spent only £10,000 of this). Only around 1% of the 600 requests received each month are considered. Grants vary from around £1,000 to £50,000.

Campaigns: The Body Shop encourages regular interaction with campaigning organisations and decision-making bodies, particularly relating to human rights and environmental concerns. Recent campaigns have included support for the

Ogoni people of Nigeria, whose lands have been devastated as a result of oil drilling, and support for women's organisations against domestic violence.

Applications: The foundation has recently decided that it will no longer accept unsolicited applications. It is operating on a proactive basis, considering the issues it wants to address, then researching to connect with groups that meet its remit.

Bristol Water plc

PO Box 218, Bridgewater Road, Bristol BS99 7AU
Tel: 0117-966 5881
Fax: 0117-963 4576
Correspondent: Jeremy Williams, Public Relations Manager
Charitable donations: £20,000 (1996/97)
Nature of business: Water company.

Policy: The company supports environment/heritage causes including water-based schemes such as local pond wildlife projects. Grants range from £10 to £350.

Applications: In writing to the correspondent. Applications are considered quarterly.

British Airways plc

PO Box 10, Heathrow Airport, Hounslow, Middlesex TW6 2JA
Tel: 0181-562 5238
Correspondent: Jacky Ive, Community Relations
Charitable donations: £1,070,000 (1996/97)
Nature of business: Air transportation.

Policy: The telephone number given above puts callers through to the British Airways Community Relations Noticeboard, an answering service advising that unsolicited appeals will only be accepted in writing and that the company focuses on three broad areas: the environment; tourism and heritage; and youth development. Support is only given to appeals in areas in which the company operates, and which provide the opportunity for substantial staff involvement. Organisations supported in the last year include Birdlife International, Care for the Wild, International Centre for Conservation Education, National Trust and Woodland Trust.

Applications: Appeals should be addressed to: Jacky Ive, British Airways plc, Speedword House, S240P, Heathrow Airport, Hounslow, Middlesex TW6 2JA.

British Alcan Aluminium plc

Chalfont Park, Gerrards Cross,
Buckinghamshire SL9 0QB
Tel: 01753-233200
Correspondent: Corporate Affairs Department
Charitable donations: £103,000 (1996)
Nature of business: Chemical production and processing.

Policy: Priority is given to charities in need of funds rather than very well supported charities, and to charities close to British Alcan locations. Money is channelled through the British Alcan Charitable Trust, with environment and heritage listed as one of several preferred areas of support. Grants to national organisations range from £250 to £500, and to local organisations from £50 to £300.

Applications: Appeals to head office should be addressed to the correspondent. Grant decisions are made by a donations committee which meets bi-monthly. All divisions/subsidiaries channel appeals to the trust.

British Energy plc

10 Lochside Place, Edinburgh Park,
Edinburgh EH12 9DF
Tel: 0131-527 2000
Correspondent: Chrystall MacDonald, Communications Manager
Charitable donations: £220,000 (1996/97)
Nature of business: Generation and supply of electricity.

Policy: The company's policy is to (a) give corporately to specific appeals related to the company objectives, and (b) delegate local giving to location managers with the emphasis on matching funds raised by staff. There is a preference for children and youth, social welfare, medical, and environment. Grants to national organisations range from £1,000 to £10,000. Grants to local organisations range from £10 to £200. Nuclear Electric, now part of British Energy, was one of the sponsors of the Young Environmentalist of the Year awards in 1995/96.

Applications: In writing to the correspondent.

British Land Company plc

10 Cornwall Terrace, Regents Park,
London NW1 4QP
Tel: 0171-486 4466
Correspondent: John Ritblat, Chairman
Charitable donations: £78,000 (1996/97)
Nature of business: Property investment and development.

Policy: 'British Land is strongly committed to investing in the future by providing facilities for young people and children through arts, sport and education, and funding and fostering support for improvement of the environment.' The company supports the Civic Trust and particular support is given to charities involving young people, especially in activity-based projects.

Applications: In writing to the correspondent.

British Nuclear Fuels plc

Risley, H280, Warrington, Cheshire
WA3 6AS
Tel: 01925-832000
Correspondent: Robert Jarvis, Head of Community Involvement
Charitable donations: £2,400,000 (1996/97)

Nature of business: Nuclear fuel services and electricity generation.

Policy: Although the company is currently focusing support on youth-related activities it is also involved in various environmental schemes. These include The Yottenfews Environmental Project, West Cumbria; The Nature Trail at Springfields, Preston; an educational environmental hide at Pennington Flash, Leigh and Sustainability NW.

The company supports schemes and charities in the North West (including national appeals based in the North West). Within this, there may be a preference for West Cumbria. Typical national grants range from £100 to £15,000. Local grants range from £25 to £1,000.

Applications: In writing either to the correspondent above or to the Community Affairs Manager of the nearest factory. A donations committee meets monthly.

The British Petroleum Company plc

Britannic House, 1 Finsbury Circus, London EC2M 7BA
Tel: 0181-658 0712
Correspondent: Manager, Community Affairs
Charitable donations: £3,400,000 (1996)
Nature of business: Oil industry.

Policy: In 1996 the company gave £18.4 million in community support worldwide, including £6.2 million in the UK. Worldwide support was categorised as follows:
- community development – £6.9 million
- education – £6.1 million
- environment – £1.5 million
- arts – £2.0 million
- other – £1.9 million

The environment, education, and community development are the three core themes on which the company's future community affairs programmes will be concentrated. Within the environment category, the company seeks to use its expertise and resources in the fields of health, safety and the environment, wherever appropriate, through its community affairs programmes. It supports organisations which are involved in tackling fundamental environmental issues, environmental education, and practical conservation work.

An organisation seeking a financial donation should be a UK registered charity or recognised by the Inland Revenue as having charitable status, or be involved in community or charitable activities. Projects should be close to BP centres and/or be pilots which may be of national interest. They should have clear and measurable objectives which, ideally, are attainable within a specified period of time. Policy guidelines for applicants and reports on the charitable activities of the group are available from the correspondent.

The BP Conservation Programme promotes pioneering scientific projects worldwide working with BirdLife International and Flora and Fauna International. Projects are organised by teams of university students who work with local communities to investigate threatened animals, plants and habitats. The aim is to make long-term conservation gains and demonstrate how human needs can co-exist with environmental priorities. Every year, eight prizes are awarded to the best projects in the categories of: tropical forests; oceanic islands and marine habitats; wetlands, grasslands, savannahs and deserts; and globally threatened species. At least half the prize money is given to local organisations involved in the project. Over the last five years there have been 422 applications and 48 awards made. Long-term objectives are encouraged with a £10,000 award each year to the best follow-up proposal from a previous winner.

In the UK, BP sponsors the Grizzly Challenge in Scotland (see separate entry in the awards section of this Guide). It has also worked with Groundwork Trusts.

Applications: The company's other UK addresses are:

BP Exploration, Farburn Industrial Estate, Dyce, Aberdeen AB21 7PB
BP Chemicals, Grangemouth Factory, Bo'ness Road, Grangemouth, Stirlingshire FK3 9XH
BP Oil UK Ltd, Witan Gate House, 500–600 Witan Gate, Central Milton Keynes MK9 1ES.

British Steel plc

9 Albert Embankment, London SE1 7SN
Tel: 0171-735 7654
Correspondent: Richard J Reeves, Company Secretary
Charitable donations: £586,000 (1996/97)
Nature of business: Steel-making.

Policy: The company makes grants centrally, mainly to national appeals. It also has a preference for local charities in areas of company presence, appeals relevant to company business, and charities in which a member of staff is involved. Preferred areas are the arts, environmental projects and educational activities. Grants to national organisations range from £250 to £10,000. Grants to local organisations from £1,000 to £5,000. The Council for the Protection for Rural England and the Woodland Trust are among the organisations supported in recent years.

Applications: Grants from head office are decided by a Donations Committee, which meets quarterly. Applications (including sponsorship) should be in writing to the correspondent, although local appeals should be made through local offices of British Steel.

British Sugar plc

Oundle Road, Peterborough, Cambridgeshire PE2 9QU
Tel: 01733-563171
Correspondent: John Smith, Public Relations Manager
Charitable donations: £95,000 (1996/97)
Nature of business: Sugar and animal food manufacture.

Policy: Charitable donations are administered through the British Sugar Foundation. Support is focused on projects of particular benefit to the communities in which British Sugar operates and in which employees live and work. The policy guidelines published by the company include:

♦ the foundation has particular interests in projects in the following areas: health and healthcare; education; environment; enterprise;

♦ projects inspired by company employees will receive special attention.

In 1996/97 the Foundation had an income of £95,000, all of which was paid out in grants. Unfortunately, no list of grants was included with the accounts, but it is known that the British Trust for Ornithology, Landlife and RSPB have been supported in recent years. The company concern for the environment is also reflected in the fact that it preserves sites of special scientific interest on three factory sites.

Applications: In writing to the correspondent. The company produce a useful Policy & Guidelines for Applicants leaflet.

British Telecommunications plc

BT Community Partnership Programme, Room 3054, BT Centre, 81 Newgate Street, London EC1A 7AJ
Tel: 0171-356 5750
Correspondent: Stephen Serpell, Head of Community Partnership
Charitable donations: £2,700,000 (1996/97)
Nature of business: Telecommunications.

Policy: Through its Community Partnership Programme, BT supports a variety of organisations and good causes in partnership. The projects supported must:

♦ be of positive relevance to BT

- bring demonstrable benefit to the community

- offer clearly understood and recorded mutual benefits

- provide opportunities for BT people to be involved

- enhance BT's reputation.

BT has moved to a more proactive stance towards its community programme and has adopted the theme of access and communication, focusing increasingly on projects which relate to BT's own role in society. Support is given to a wide range of community initiatives, both local and national.

In 1995/96, BT gave over £15 million in contributions (including financial donations and other support)..

The general policy is to give a significant gift for a specific purpose rather than scatter smaller sums, and to give fewer but larger donations. Grants to national organisations range from £250 to £100,000, and to local organisations from £50 to £50,000.

Support is given to UK-wide environmental concerns as well as to the physical regeneration of destitute areas, conservation and national heritage. Its general practice is to develop a small number of environmental schemes, no more than two or three a year, which are worked up a long way in advance. For example, in 1998 BT had developed BT Countryside for All, a project promoting best practice for access into the countryside by disabled people. For this the Fieldfare Trust received £1/3 million of which £120,000 was allocated for an ongoing relationship with WWF-UK and support is also given to individual Groundwork and Wildlife Trusts.

The company has a particular interest in Education and Training with the focus of its work directed at Economic Regeneration.

Applications: Decisions on major grants are made at head office by the Board Community and Charities Committee which meets quarterly. Smaller grants can be made by staff of the relevant Community Unit at their discretion. Local appeals should be sent to the appropriate BT local office. (Each BT zone has its own community affairs staff operating a programme which reflects the needs of that area.)

Contacts: Roger Morton (0171-356 6842) and Gerard Darby (0171-356 6704) for environment and economic development.

Burmah Castrol plc

Burmah Castrol House, Pipers Way, Swindon SN3 1RE
Tel: 01793-614094
Correspondent: Secretary to the Appeals Committee
Charitable donations: £170,000 (1996)
Nature of business: Specialised lubricants and chemicals.

Policy: Burmah Castrol only supports projects which are close to areas of company presence either in the UK or overseas (i.e. within 20 miles of one of the company's larger operating units, generally Wiltshire, Broadstairs and Stanlow).

The company supports environmental projects through separate budget allocations: sponsorship and charity. In all cases, projects must be close to one of the company's operating locations. Grants to national organisations range from £500 to £3,500. Grants to local organisations from £50 to £3,000. In 1995/96 it was one of the sponsors of the Young Environmentalist of the Year awards (£5,000).

Applications: Requests for sponsorship should be directed to the Community Relations Executive, Burmah Castrol Trading Ltd, while charitable requests should be directed to the correspondent. The initial application need not be too detailed but should include a summary of the project, its objectives and costs. If you have any queries about the eligibility of a project, a preliminary telephone call would be advisable.

Cadbury Schweppes plc

25 Berkeley Square, London W1X 6HT
Tel: 0171-409 1313
Correspondent: The Cadbury Schweppes
Foundation
Charitable donations: £1,036,000
(1996)
Nature of business: Manufacture and
marketing of confectionery and soft
drinks.

Policy: Most requests to the company for
charitable donations are channelled
through the Cadbury Schweppes
Foundation, the company's charitable trust
in the UK. This has no endowment but is
funded by grants from the company each
year. Grants are made at the discretion of
the trustees whose current focus is on
selected projects and organisations in the
fields of education and enterprise; health
and welfare; and environment.

The trust plans its giving in advance for
each year; unsolicited appeals are not
encouraged. There is a preference for
charities relevant to company business, in
areas of company presence and with
company staff involvement. Grants to
national organisations range from £10,000
to £40,000, and to local organisations
from £1,000 to £5,000. The Tidy Britain
Group was among the organisations
supported in 1996.

Applications: Most grants are committed
in advance on an ongoing basis. Any
correspondence should be addressed to:
The Cadbury Schweppes Foundation at
the above address.

Calor Group Ltd

Appleton Park, Riding Court Road,
Datchet, Slough, Berkshire SL3 9JG
Tel: 01753-540000
Correspondent: Andrew Camp,
Marketing Manager
Charitable donations: £29,000 (1996)
Nature of business: Distribution of liquid
petroleum gas and gas burning appliances.

Policy: Calor's community programme is
focused on six areas, one of which is the
environment. The company has recently

given donations to National Federation of
City Farms and National Trust. The
company is committed 'to a sponsorship
programme which encourages better
stewardship of the natural environment'.
Its conservation and rural sponsorship
programme covers 45 events in 39
counties of England and Wales with
additional activities in Scotland. It
sponsors best kept village competitions
and other initiatives including best village
hall competitions, inter-village quizzes,
rural conferences and publications.

Applications: In writing to the
correspondent.

Cheltenham & Gloucester plc

Barnett Way, Gloucester GL4 3RL
Tel: 01452-372372
Tel: 01452-373975
Correspondent: Sharon Wynn, Marketing
Services Manager
Charitable donations: £50,000 (1996)
Nature of business: Financial services.

Policy: The company prefers to support
charities in Gloucestershire and the South
West. Although not listed as one of the
company's main areas of support, it does
support a Rural Initiative Fund set up by
Gloucestershire Rural Community
Council, with the Rural Development
Commission, to give small grants to a
wide range of local community projects.
Eligible projects include those concerned
with the environment and conservation.

Applications: Further details can be
obtained from Gloucestershire Rural
Community Council.

Chevron UK Ltd

Woodhill House, Westburn Road,
Aberdeen AB16 5XL
Tel: 01224-334000
Correspondent: Ruth Mitchell, Public
Affairs Co-ordinator
Charitable donations: £90,000 (1996)
Nature of business: Oil industry.

Policy: Most causes supported by Chevron are predetermined and therefore few additional requests for assistance are likely to be successful. Most support is given in north east Scotland, with the environment being one of the preferred fields. There is a preference for appeals relevant to company business and charities in which a member of company staff is involved. Grants to local organisations and to local sections of national organisations range from £50 to £1,000.

Recent beneficiaries have included the Scottish Wildlife Trust, Thames Salmon Trust, Art in Nature and support for various universities.

In America, company employees volunteer for numerous community projects to improve the environment, for example cleaning debris from beaches, and restoring National Park land.

Applications: In writing to the correspondent.

Christies International plc

8 King Street, St James', London SW1Y 6QT
Tel: 0171-839 9060
Correspondent: Mrs Robin Hambro, Charities Department
Charitable donations: £375,000 (1996)
Nature of business: Auctioneering.

Policy: The major portion of Christies' charitable donations goes to underwriting a broad scope of arts-related causes and projects on all economic levels. These range from the conservation of paintings and the fabric of small country churches, to the sponsorship of major exhibitions in national museums, arts centres or on the Christies premises at King Street. Grants to national organisations range from £200 to £5,000. Grants to local organisations from £100 to £500.

The company supports rural conservation and environment programmes. It is involved in the Westminster Council conservation activities. European sponsorship includes supporting the

International Castles Institute, Europa Nostra, and the World Monument Fund. It also sponsored the Garden of the Year Award in conjunction with the Historic Houses Association from 1985 to 1995.

Applications: In writing to the correspondent. Applications with particular reference to the company's charitable programme are submitted to a committee who make grant decisions.

Clydesdale Bank PLC

30 St Vincent Place, Glasgow G1 2HL
Tel: 0141-248 7070
Correspondent: Peter Ramsay, Public Relations Manager
Charitable donations: £80,000 (1996/97)
Nature of business: Banking.

Policy: The bank prefers to support Scottish organisations particularly those working in the fields of heritage, the environment and local natural disasters (i.e. in Scotland). National grants range from £100 to £10,000. Local grants range from £50 to £500. Deeds of covenant account for 50% of funds allocated. In 1994/95, major grant recipients included the National Trust of Scotland.

Applications: In writing to the correspondent. Applications are considered by a charitable donations committee.

Coca-Cola Great Britain

1 Queen Caroline Street, London W6 9HQ
Tel: 0181-237 3000
Fax: 0181-237 3700
Correspondent: Ian Muir, Manager of External Affairs
Environmental support: £240,000 (1997)
Nature of business: Soft drinks marketing.

Policy: The company sponsors both national and local events in the sport, entertainment and environment fields. It concentrates on two specific environmental issues: recycling through various areas; and litter – through support for the Tidy Britain Group, especially in the sponsorship of their People and Places Programme.

Educational activities have also tended to cover environmental matters with sponsorship either in whole or in part of such publications as 'Finding out About Packaging', 'Finding Out About Managing Waste' and the 'Dustbin Pack'. The latter was produced by Waste Watch, of which the company continues to be a major sponsor, having more recently supported the production of another publication 'Wise up to Waste'. Ian Muir, the Manager of External Affairs, is a Council Member of Waste Watch. An environmental guide for schools produced by the RSPB under the auspices of the Council for Environmental Education, 'Our World, Our Responsibility', was also supported by the company, and has now been supported by a Welsh language edition.

Applications: In writing to the correspondent.

Commercial Union plc

St Helen's, 1 Undershaft, London EC3P 3DQ
Tel: 0171-283 7500
Correspondent: Miss J Miller, The Appeals Officer
Charitable donations: £300,803 (1996)
Nature of business: Insurance and financial services.

Policy: Funds are allocated in the form of long-term support to a carefully selected group of charities in categories ranging from medical research and care, to arts and conservation, and from welfare of the elderly to education and support for the young. In addition, the company has sponsored several larger initiatives including the Thames Pathway Project led by British Trust for Nature Conservation Volunteers, and funding of an educational pack, aimed at schoolteachers, for the Natural History Museum. The company also supports a variety of international projects and charities through its overseas businesses.

Applications: Due to Commercial Union's committed support to a selected group of charities, very few donations are allocated to charities that apply in writing.

Conoco Ltd

Conoco Centre, Warwick Technology Park, Gallows Hill, Warwickshire CV34 6DA
Tel: 01926-404804
Correspondent: Louise Teboul, Secretary of UK Contributions Committee
Charitable donations: £536,000 (1997)
Nature of business: Oil company. In the UK its petrol is marketed under the brand name Jet.

Policy: The company supports a wide range of local charities in areas of company presence, such as Aberdeen, Warwick and Humberside. The environment is one of the main areas supported by the company. The company have produced a book and CD ROM entitled Understanding our Environment, and a teaching programme (in seven languages) for schools which helps pupils to learn about the natural world. It has also refurbished a nature observatory at Cleethorpes Discovery Centre, and the Conoco Natural History Centre to enable it to incorporate the University of Aberdeen's Natural History Museum and Cruickshank Botanic Garden. There are plans to support South Humber Bank Landscape Initiative to improve the area. Other environmental groups receiving support include Lincolnshire & South Humberside Trust for Nature Conservation, BTCV, RSPB, Wildlife Trusts, Wildfowl & Wetlands Trust, Marine Conservation Society and World Wide Fund for Nature.

Applications: In writing to the correspondent.

Co-operative Bank plc

1 Balloon Street, Manchester M60 4EP
Tel: 0161-832 3456
Fax: 0161-839 4220
Correspondent: Chris Smith, Group Public Marketing Manager

Charitable donations: £638,312 (1996/97)
Nature of business: Banking and financial services.

Policy: Community contributions totalled £1,375,000 in 1997 (over 3% of pre-tax profits), of which £638,000 was cash donations. This included £149,000 from the 'Customers Who Care' scheme, in which the bank donates a proportion of the its VISA income to charities. VISA users vote on how the money raised should be shared among nominated organisations.

Generally the bank makes only small charitable donations, with preference for local and national charities in the areas of company presence and appeals relevant to company business. Preferred areas of support are business ethics, environmental protection, inner city regeneration, equal opportunities, co-operatives, education and children and youth. The National Centre for Business & Ecology, Mines Advisory Group and RSPB were among the beneficiaries in 1997.

Banking services: The bank offers free banking to charities and community groups with an annual turnover of less than £250,000 if a minimum credit balance of £500 is maintained. For larger charities, banking services are negotiated on an individual basis with the bank's Charities Unit.

Applications: In writing to the correspondent.

Derbyshire Building Society

Duffield Hall, PO Box 1, Duffield, Derby DE56 1AG
Tel: 01332-841000
Fax: 01332-840350
Correspondent: Eric Walker, Head of Corporate Communications
Charitable donations: Not available
Nature of business: Financial services.

Policy: The company has a sponsorship budget of up to £100,000 of which about 40% is committed to conservation/environment projects. Support is only given locally, with recent beneficiaries including Derbyshire Best Kept Village Competition, Bronze Age Rock Art Preservation Programme, Groundwork Trust and Care for the Wild.

Applications: In writing to the correspondent.

East Midlands Electricity plc

PO Box 444, Wollaton, Nottingham NG18 1EZ
Tel: 0115-901 0101
Correspondent: Julian Evans, Corporate Relations Manager
Charitable donations: £46,200 (1996/97)
Nature of business: Distribution and supply of electricity.

Policy: Support is only given to organisations and projects within the East Midlands Electricity area and to appeals relevant to the company's business. The focus is on partnerships, with support in kind for real effect, rather than cash donations. Preferred areas of support are education, environment, elderly people and energy efficiency. Grants range from £25 to £5,000. In 1994/95, major grant recipients included Energy Awareness Project (Nottingham) and Energy for Wildlife Fund (RSNC).

Applications: In writing to the Community Affairs Manager.

Eastern Counties Newspapers Group Ltd

Prospect House, Rowen Road, Norwich NR1 1RE
Tel: 01603-628311
Correspondent: T Stevenson, Managing Director
Charitable donations: £19,000 (1996)
Nature of business: Newspaper publishing.

Policy: Preference for local charities in East Anglia, where the company operates. It prefers to support the arts, children and youth, education, elderly people, enterprise and training, environment and heritage, sickness and disability, social welfare, and sport. During 1996, main beneficiaries included: Norwich Historic Churches Trust, Norwich Cathedral, Suffolk Wildlife Trust, Norfolk Schools Outreach and Quidenham Children's Hospice.

Applications: In writing to the correspondent.

Eastern Group plc

PO Box 40, Wherstead, Ipswich IP9 2AQ
Tel: 01473-553409
Fax: 01473-554466
Correspondent: Peter Gray, Corporate Relations Manager
Charitable donations: £232,056 (1996/97)
Nature of business: Electricity and gas supply.

Policy: Total community contributions (including sponsorships, donations, secondments, placements, staff time and help/gifts in kind) were around £1.3 million in 1996/97.

The company gives preference to organisations helping the environment, children and youth, education, older people, sickness/disability, medical research, social welfare and fundraising events.

Around 200 local and regional sponsorship grants were made. The main environmental related beneficiaries were Wildlife Trusts – Special Places programme in the eastern region, team building conservation projects with the National Trust. Additional support was provided, among others to Hertfordshire Groundworks, The Broads Society and Thornham Walks.

An estimated 20% of Eastern's sponsorship activities in the community are with environmental organisations.

Applications: The company have policy guidelines which are available from the correspondent. Applications should be in writing but an application form is also available upon request. Sponsorship proposals should be addressed to: P Gray, Corporate Relations Manager and donations requests to M Faulkner, Secretariat Manager.

Elementis plc

One Great Tower Street, London EC3R 5AH
Tel: 0171-711 1400
Correspondent: Mrs H M Cowin, Elementis Charitable Trust
Charitable donations: £124,789 (1996)
Nature of business: Chemical.

Policy: The figures shown are for the group as a whole. Roughly half is dispensed through the Harrisons & Crosfield Charitable Fund and half through subsidiary companies and branches at local level.

The company supports local wildlife projects and is involved in the Timber Trade Federation initiative Forests Forever. This campaign aims to help safeguard the world's forests and Britain's timber supplies, and to promote the use of wood as a versatile and renewable product. The company has pledged to donate funds towards 'the public relations campaign, mounted to combat some of the negative and inaccurate publicity that has arisen following the increase in awareness about environmental issues'.

Applications: In writing to the Elementis Charitable Fund, but note that unsolicited applications are rarely considered.

Elf Exploration UK PLC

1 Claymore Drive, Bridge of Don, Aberdeen AB23 8GB
Tel: 01224-233000
Fax: 01224-233838
Correspondent: Sandra Ross, Public Relations Co-ordinator
Charitable donations: Not available

Nature of business: Oil and gas exploration and production.

Policy: The company is committed to supporting the arts, the environment, education, and social welfare groups within the communities in which it operates (principally Aberdeen and the Orkney Islands). It supports registered charities, with grants recently given to the RSPB and the National Trust for Scotland. The former was to establish First Nature, a field teaching programme on RSPB nature reserves for 5-7 tear olds, and Second Nature, an equivalent programme for 8-11 year olds. Annual major donations range from £1,000 to £20,000. Monthly smaller donations range from £50 to £500.

Applications: In writing to the correspondent.

EMI Group plc

4 Tenterden Street, Hanover Square, London W1A 2AY
Tel: 0171-355 4848
Fax: 0171-495 1307
Correspondent: Charity Committee, Corporate Affairs Department
Charitable donations: £3,700,000 (1996/97)
Nature of business: EMI Music and the HMV Group.

Policy: The Corporate Affairs Department considers projects primarily related to the individual businesses and which create learning opportunities and encourage improved environmental performance. The criteria are:

- the achievement of a well balanced programme which adequately reflects the current needs of today's society and environment. Support is divided between three key areas: employee Initiatives, charitable donations and sponsored projects;

- to support activities within the areas of education, environment and social responsibility. Benefiting organisations must be well-run registered charities and proposals for projects must be well-defined;

- to encourage and support the commitment, enthusiasm and participation of employees who are involved in voluntary activities within their local communities, and to give consideration to projects which they put forward and in which they become involved;

- financial donations must be tax efficient and therefore of maximum benefit to the recipient and maximum value for the company.

'Our policy relates to those activities supported from the Group's corporate headquarters in the UK. A committee meets regularly to consider all written requests against the above guidelines and on their merit. In addition, EMI Group's businesses decide individually where to focus their own charitable giving and sponsorship resources.'

Within the environment category support is given to organisations which seek to promote and raise awareness, educate and strive to improve the environment. Among those supported are Forum for the Future (£15,000), and BTCV and Westminster Initiative (£5,000 each).

Applications: Applications should be in writing to the correspondent. Sponsorship proposals should be addressed to Melanie Gant, Head of Corporate Community Involvement.

Enterprise Oil plc

Grand Buildings, Trafalgar Square, London WC2N 5ES
Tel: 0171-925 4000
Fax: 0171-925 4321
Correspondent: Mrs Jane Stevenson, Secretary, Donations Committee
Charitable donations: £228,300 (1996)
Nature of business: Oil and gas exploration and production.

Policy: Donations are given from head office only. There is a preference for projects in areas where the company operates and appeals where a member of staff is involved. Large national appeals are supported, particularly social welfare, medical, children and youth, education, environment and organisations concerned with disabled people.

In 1996, beneficiaries of relevance to this Guide included the Royal Botanic Gardens, Kew, CPRE, Young People's Trust for the Environment, Wildlife & Countryside Link, Scottish Wildlife Trust and The Wildlife Trusts.

Applications: In writing to the correspondent. A donations committee, consisting of the Chairman, Corporate Affairs Director, and Secretary meets several times a year.

Essex & Suffok Water plc

Hall Street, Chelmsford, Essex CM2 0HH
Tel: 01245-491234
Correspondent: Public Relations Assistant
Charitable donations: £52,900 (1996/97)
Nature of business: Treatment and supply of water.

Policy: The company supports local projects concerning water, environment or children. There is a preference for charities with company staff involvement. Donations are generally of £25 to £500, but can be for more. The Tidy Britain Group has been supported recently.

Applications: In writing to the correspondent.

Esso UK plc

Esso House, Victoria Street, London SW1E 5JW
Tel: 0171-834 6677
Fax: 0171-245 2201
Correspondent: P J Truesdale, Community Affairs Co-ordinator
Charitable donations: £1,495,351 (1996)
Nature of business: Oil industry.

Policy: The company gives priority to projects in areas which are its main UK employment points – the New Forest, Abingdon, Victoria and Leatherhead – or those involved with education (particularly environmental and scientific), the environment, and health and safety.

Esso proactively plans its programmes and likes to strike up long-term working partnerships with the organisations it works with in the voluntary sector. Almost all funds are committed at the beginning of the year, therefore unsolicited requests are rarely supported. The company carries out advertising and promotion on behalf of the charities it works with.

Esso works in partnership with a number of environmental organisations. Not surprisingly, support is given to 21st Century Tiger, London Zoo, Global Tiger Patrol and Tusk Force towards their tiger conservation programme. 1997 was the 10th year of the company's work with Groundwork, over which time it has contributed nearly £0.5 million. In 1997, it sponsored a major national Groundwork conference. It is also working with over 70 voluntary, public and private sector partners in the Trees of Time and Place campaign. Organisations supported in the last year include CPRE, the Tree Council, the Woodland Trust, BTCV and Learning through Landscapes.

Education initiatives relevant to this Guide include funding towards the Council for Environmental Education's 'Information in Action' strategy, including a series of training workshops for information and education officers on sources of information and support for environmental education.

Applications: The company responds to all appeals received, but in view of the policy outlined above unsolicited appeals are very rarely successful.

Eurotunnel plc

Customer Service Centre, Chevington park, High Street, Foxton, Kent CT19 4QS
Tel: 01303-273 3000
Correspondent: Public Affairs Manager
Charitable donations: £120,383 (1996)
Nature of business: Tunnel construction.

Policy: The company prefers to support local charities in areas of company presence and appeals relevant to the company's business. The environment and heritage are two of several preferred areas for support. The company has been involved in the White Cliffs Countryside Project, to which it has committed £40,000 a year. The site was awarded the 1997 SSSI Award from English Nature. It comprises 666 acres of which 133 are owned by the company and it is important for orchid and butterfly conservation.

Applications: In writing to the correspondent.

Fina plc

Fina House, Ashley Avenue, Epsom, Surrey KT18 5AD
Tel: 01372-726226
Fax: 01372-744515
Correspondent: N C P Vandervell, Corporate Affairs Manager
Charitable donations: c. £20,000 (1996/97)
Nature of business: Oil/petrol refinery.

Policy: The company supports local charities in areas of its operations particularly environmental organisations. Organisations supported recently include Surrey Wildlife Trust and the Royal Society for Nature Conservation.

Applications: In writing to the correspondent.

First Trust Bank

92 Ann Street, Belfast BT1 3HH
Tel: 01232-325599
Fax: 01232-438338
Correspondent: Amanda Loney, Public Relations Official
Charitable donations: Not available
Nature of business: Financial services.

Policy: The bank only supports local initiatives, with environment/conservation being one of several areas favoured.

Applications: In writing to the correspondent.

Ford Motor Company Ltd

Eagle Way, Brentwood, Essex CM13 3BW
Tel: 01277-253000
Correspondent: R M Metcalf, Director, Ford of Britain Trust
Charitable donations: £1,638,000 (1996)
Nature of business: Motor vehicle manufacturers.

Policy: In addition to the donations figure above, the company funds the Ford of Britain Trust. Recipient organisations should preferably be registered charities. The majority of donations are one-off grants to local charities in the areas where the company has a presence. There is also a preference for charities in which a member of staff is involved. Typical grants to national organisations range from £500 to £5,000, and to local organisations from £50 to £5,000. A wide range of causes are supported including the environment, which in 1996/97 received a total of £3,050 out of the overall total of £440,000. Birdlife International was one of the organisations supported.

In addition, Ford organises the Henry Ford European Conservation Awards which has a total prize fund of $500,000 and participants from 23 countries across Europe. It is operated in association with the Conservation Foundation, UNESCO and other leading conservation agencies in all participating countries (further details are given in the awards section of this Guide).

Applications: Applications to the Ford of Britain Trust should be addressed to the correspondent. The trustees met on three occasions in the year to 31st March 1994, July, January and March.

General Accident plc

Pitheavlis, Perth PH2 0NH
Tel: 01738-621202
Fax: 01738-621843
Correspondent: P M White, Assistant Secretary

Charitable donations: £450,272 (1997)
Nature of business: Insurance.

Policy: Support is mainly given to national charities, though charities in areas of local branches are also supported. Environment/heritage is one of several areas supported. The company provided financial support and volunteers to assist conservation projects during 1997 with the Scottish Conservation Projects Trust. Local charities are dealt with by local branches; many appeals are then referred to head office.

Applications: In writing to the correspondent, including full details of the work of the organisation concerned, its charitable status and a copy of its most recent audited accounts. Sponsorship appeals should be addressed to the Communications and Media Department.

General Electric Company plc

1 Stanhope Gate, London W1A 1EH
Tel: 0171-493 8484
Correspondent: The Hon. Sara Morrison, Director
Charitable donations: £824,000 (1996/97)
Nature of business: Electrical engineers.

Policy: The main areas of charitable support are young people, social welfare, environment/heritage, education and training. Preference is given to local charities in areas of company presence, appeals relevant to company business, and charities in which a member of staff is involved. Direct support is preferred. Grants to national organisations range from £1,000 to £5,000 and to local organisations from £500 to £2,000. Grant recipients during 1996/97 included the World Wide Fund for Nature.

Applications: Appeals (other than local appeals) should be made in writing to the correspondent and are considered by a donations committee which meets as required. Applications for local support should be made in writing to your local

GEC operating unit in the UK. These subsidiaries and operating units have their own grants budgets. Some of the units also operate a staff charity fund, where the staff collect and distribute money to charity on their own initiative.

Glaxo Wellcome plc

GlaxoWellcome House, Berkeley Square, London W1X 6BQ
Tel: 0171-493 4060
Fax: 0181-966 8237
Correspondent: Ruth Seabrook, Manager, Charitable Contributions
Charitable donations: £6,000,000 (1997)
Nature of business: Pharmaceutical manufacture.

Policy: All charitable donations made in the UK are agreed by the Group Appeals Committee, which is a Committee of the Board of Glaxo Wellcome plc. The company considers appeals that fall within four categories, of which one – preservation of national heritage, the environment and culture – is of relevance to this Guide.

As part of this support, £250,000 was donated to fund a millennium seed bank at the Royal Botanic Gardens Kew which aims to collect seeds from the entire UK flora and one tenth of the world's flora.

Landlife and the Green Alliance have also received support. The company is also a sponsor of the Young Environmentalist of the Year Awards (£5,000 in each of the last two years).

Applications: Appeals for charitable support on a national scale should be addressed in writing to the correspondent. Organisations seeking support for community projects within the locality or region of Glaxo sites should contact the relevant site to request the correct company contact. Applicants are asked to supply a concise summary of their aims, objectives and funding requirements, together with a copy of their most up-to-date audited accounts.

Guardian Royal Exchange plc

Royal Exchange, London EC3V 3LS
Tel: 0171-283 7101
Correspondent: C V Foster, Appeals
Secretary
Charitable donations: £287,272 (1996)
Nature of business: Insurance, financial
services and investment business.

Policy: All appeals should be made to the
Secretary of the GRE Charitable Trust.
Support is only given to local charities in
areas of company presence (west London,
Harold Hill, Dartford). In 1995, the trust
gave around 200 grants totalling £225,500.
About half the grants were for £1,000 to
£6,000 (the majority of which were for
£1,000 to £3,000) and the other half were
mostly for £500 to £750. Grants were
mainly for medical, then welfare charities.

However, a number of grants relevant to
this guide were made, including those to
Canterbury Cathedral (£2,500); Civic
Trust, CLA Charitable Trust, Heritage of
London Trust and Woodland Trust (all
£1,000); Association for the Protection of
Rural Scotland, Open Spaces Society and
Farms for City Children (all £750); with
smaller grants to Kent Trust for Nature
Conservation, Kings Lynn Preservation
Trust, Marine Conservation Society and
the National Trust.

Applications: In writing to the
correspondent. No decisions are made
independently of head office. Grant
decisions are made by a donations
committee which meets as necessary.

Guinness PLC

Note: Guinness Plc has merged with
Grand Metropolitan to form Diageo Plc.
All correspondance is dealt with from the
address below.
Diageo, 8 Henrietta Place, London
W1M 9AG
Tel: 0171-927 5200
Correspondent: Ann Quinn, Community
Support Manager, Diageo
Charitable donations: £4,500,000 (1996)

Nature of business: Brewers and distillers.

Policy: Diageo is expected to follow a
policy similar to that of Guinness Plc,
outlined below.

Support is given to registered charities only,
usually for projects in areas of company
presence. Specific areas are targeted in order
to achieve maximum impact; these are:
medical welfare, education, environment,
water of life and the arts.

In addition to the group's own
environmental policy and standards,
direct support is also given. In 1992,
Aberfeldy Distillery in Scotland bought
adjacent land and developed a woodland
nature trail. Working with local
environmental organisations, the
distillery helped to develop a long-term
plan to provide a secure haven for the red
squirrel, and indigenous Caledonian pine
has now been planted. In Ireland,
Guinness is one of the main supporters of
Oakglen – a broadleaf afforestation
project in the valley of Glencree in the
Wicklow mountains.

The Water of Life initiative was launched
in 1995, with £250,000 to support water-
related conservation and humanitarian
projects worldwide. It has supported
activities as diverse as turtle conservation
in Australia, canal clearance in Scotland,
clean water and sanitation in India, a
waterways handbook in the UK, and a
wetlands wildlife project in Ireland. Most
projects supported have been suggested by
operating subsidiaries.

Guinness Brewing Worldwide supports
the environmental charity Earthwatch,
sponsoring students from some of its key
markets to take part in scientific research
projects around the world.

Applications: Appeals and corporate
sponsorship proposals should be
addressed in writing to the
correspondent. Decisions are made by the
Donations Committee. However, the
company is taking an increasingly proactive approach to its community
programme, and therefore the number of
successful speculative applications is
extremely small.

Halifax plc

Trinity Road, Halifax, West Yorkshire
HX1 2RG
Tel: 01422-333333
Correspondent: Victoria Soye, Group
Community Affairs Manager
Charitable donations: £1,860,396
(1996)
Nature of business: Banking and financial
services.

Policy: The policy guidelines of Halifax
plc list eight categories of support, one of
which is the environment. Within this
category the policy is to support local
environmental projects. These can cover a
wide spectrum with help given to as many
schemes as possible, including drystone
walling, path laying, clearing derelict land,
woodland management and the creation
of inner-city gardens. The company is
keen to promote projects which involve
the communities themselves, so that local
people have the opportunity to contribute
ideas and have an interest in the success
and future development of the project
concerned. In the last year, funding was
provided for the development of BTCV's
training programme.

Applications: In writing to the
correspondent.

Hewlett-Packard Ltd

Cain Road, Bracknell, Berkshire
RG12 1HN
Tel: 01344-360000
Correspondent: Ian Ryder, Director –
Communications
Charitable donations: £74,000 (1996)
Nature of business: Electronic apparatus
manufacture.

Policy: All charities supported are selected
from nominations by employees, with
preference given to those which employees
give their time and efforts to, or which
directly benefit employees' families or
friends. Support is given to a wide variety
of organisations, particularly local,
community-based charities (within a 25
mile radius of the company's factories) and
selected national charities.

Preferred areas of support are children and
youth, social welfare, medical, education,
enterprise and training, and environment
and heritage. Recipient organisations must
be registered charities and donations are
increasingly given through the Charities
Aid Foundation.

The company also seeks to promote
awareness of wider environmental issues. It
currently sponsors the Margaret Mee
Amazon Trust and BTCV.

Applications: All charities are nominated
by company employees. Sponsorship
proposals should be addressed to the
correspondent.

The Highland Distilleries Co. plc

106 West Nile Street, Glasgow G1 2QY
Tel: 0141-332 7511
Correspondent: F S Morrison, Assistant
Company Secretary
Charitable donations: £133,000
(1996/97)
Nature of business: Malt whisky distillers.

Policy: The company supports a variety of
local charities and community activities
preferably in Scotland and particularly in
the more remote areas where its distilleries
are located. Environment/heritage is one
of several categories supported. Donations
are usually £100 to £1,000, but can be
larger in exceptional circumstances.

The company is also a member of Scottish
Business in the Community and supports a
joint venture with the Islay Council for
Social Service to train people to carry out
domestic energy conservation improvements
for low income families and elderly people
on the islands of Islay and Jura.

Applications: In writing to the
correspondent.

Hyder plc

PO Box 295, Alexandra Gate, Rover Way,
Cardiff CF2 2UE
Tel: 01222-500600
Correspondent: Jackie Roe, PR Manager

Charitable donations: £63,000
(1996/97)
Nature of business: Electricity
distribution and supply; water and
sewerage activities.

Policy: In addition to the quoted
charitable donations figure of £63,000, the
company annual report for 1996/97 states
that the group has also provided funding
to community projects and is involved in
Business in the Community initiatives.
The figure quoted above is for sponsorship
only; there is no separate figure for
charitable donations available. Preferred
areas of sponsorship include the
environment and heritage. Hyder includes
the major Welsh utility companies
SWALEC and Welsh Water. The latter is a
current sponsor of the Keep Wales Tidy
campaign, while the former has recently
supported the National Trust.

Applications: In writing to the
correspondent.

Imperial Chemical Industries plc

Imperial Chemical House, 9 Millbank,
London SW1P 3JF
Tel: 0171-834 4444
Correspondent: Margrit Bass,
Administrator Appeals Committee
Charitable donations: £700,000 (1996)

Policy: The responsibility for ICI's
charitable giving in the UK rests with the
Appeals Committee of the ICI Board at
the address above. Donations to registered
charities are normally paid through the
ICI Charity Trust. ICI regional businesses
also provide support at local level to the
communities in which they operate.
Direct support is preferred.

The priority areas of giving are education,
social welfare, youth, disability groups,
and the environment, with a preference for
national organisations (grants usually
range from £500 to £20,000), or those
located in communities where the
company has a strong presence (grants
usually range from £250 to £1,000).

In addition to ICI's support for local UK
communities, the individual subsidiary
businesses of ICI worldwide have their
own programmes of local support. The
company lists several areas of support,
with lists of relevance to this Guide
being:

♦ environment organisations that make a
positive contribution to the
improvement of the environment;

♦ churches of any denomination are
considered if they are in the vicinity of
an ICI site or are of national or
historical significance;

♦ building appeals will only be considered
for buildings of national or historical
importance.

Examples of organisations supported
include Birdlife International, Civic Trust,
CPRE, Green Alliance and Plantlife and
ICI Chemicals & Polymers support for the
Mersey Basin Campaign. The company
was also the first corporate sponsor of two
highly endangered British butterfly species
under an initiative to rescue 116
threatened native plant and animal species.
The company has committed £110,000
over two years, which will pay for
fieldwork by Butterfly Conservation.

Applications: In writing to the
correspondent. Individual operating units
have their own charitable budgets, and
should be approached directly. The Dulux
Community Paint scheme has an entry in
the Voluntary Organisations section of this
Guide.

Inchcape plc

33 Cavendish Square, London W1M 9HF
Tel: 0171-546 0022
Correspondent: Joanna Lavendar,
Assistant Manager Corporate Affairs
Charitable donations: £305,000 (1996)
Nature of business: Services and
marketing group.

Policy: The company gives support
through the Inchcape Charitable Trust. The
fund now makes fewer donations but
for larger amounts to very carefully

targeted charities with a specific focus on international aid. The three areas of support are:

- international flagship fund
- regular one-off donations
- staff related and special cases fund.

Inchcape looks to support carefully targeted organisations that are generally relevant to the group's businesses, principals and worldwide operations and to provide opportunities for employee involvement and for support with products made by principals and customers. From 1995, over £1 million, plus goods and services, has been committed in an initial five year partnership with Raleigh International entitled The Inchcape Initiative. 'In addition, Inchcape seeks opportunities where it can involve its employees and principles, and can strengthen its links with the communities where it operates.' The partnership with Raleigh International will enable more people to participate on a variety of environmental and community projects such as the expedition to Malaysia: 105 venturers from Britain, Argentina, Chile, China, Japan, Singapore and 18 Malaysians helping to construct fresh water wells, health clinics and a hanging bridge. In addition to supporting The Inchcape Initiative, group companies continue to support their local communities.

Applications: In writing to the correspondent.

Jaguar Cars Ltd

Browns Lane, Allesley, Coventry
CV5 9DR
Tel: 01203-402121
Correspondent: Val King, Secretary to the Charities Committee
Charitable donations: £33,576 (1997)
Nature of business: Luxury cars.

Policy: The company gives support mainly to local charities in the areas of company presence. The company will support national charities if they have a local branch, or can in some way benefit the groups' employees and their families.

Although the environment is not one of the company's main areas of support, it has given help to set up a Jaguar reserve in Belize, in conjunction with the World Wide Fund for Nature.

Applications: In writing to the correspondent. Decisions are made by a donations committee which meets quarterly.

Johnson Wax Ltd

Frimley Green, Camberley, Surrey
GU15 6AJ
Tel: 01276-852000
Fax: 01276-822688
Correspondent: Marie McCanna, Consumer Services Manager
Charitable donations: £200,000 (1996/97)
Nature of business: Household cleaning products.

Policy: The company prefers to support local charities in areas of company presence (mainly in Hampshire and Surrey), especially in the fields of children and youth, social welfare, the arts, medical, and particularly the environment.

Projects the company supports are often of a specifically environmental nature. The company's environmental mission statement says: 'We will support and participate in the development of public policy and in educational initiatives that will protect human health and improve the environment. We will encourage cooperation on this work with government, industry, suppliers, environmental groups, schools, universities and other public organisations'. Projects supported include reclamation of local natural beauty spots and canal improvements. In recent years work has been undertaken with the National Trust, Environmental Council, Woodland Trust, BTCV and CPRE.

Typical grants to national organisations range from £1,000 to £25,000, and to local organisations from £25 to £50,000.

Applications: In writing to the correspondent.

Kellogg's

The Kellogg Building, Talbot Road, Manchester M16 0PU
Tel: 0161-869 2601
Fax: 0161-869 2103
Correspondent: C H Woodcock, Manager, Corporate Affairs
Charitable donations: £485,000 (1997)
Nature of business: Manufacturer of breakfast cereals.

Policy: The company is committed to involvement in the communities in which it operates, especially the local communities. Two-thirds of total community support is focused on the North West and Clwyd (and in the Manchester and Wrexham areas in particular), the balance being spread nationally.

Of the community support which the company provides 50 – 60% is in cash donations, with particular emphasis on local community development and economic regeneration; the welfare of disadvantaged people; and extra learning opportunities for children.

The company is a registered supporter of the Environment Council's Business and Environment Programme and represented on the board of Groundwork Trusts in Salford and Trafford, Manchester and Wrexham.

Applications: All applications should be addressed in writing to the correspondent. Grant decisions are made by a donations committee which deals with applications when received. Appeals received by local plants are passed to head office with any comments that the local management wish to make.

Kingfisher plc

North West House, 119 Marylebone Road, London NW1 5PX
Tel: 0171-724 7749
Correspondent: Helen Jones, Company Secretary
Charitable donations: £987,793 (1996/97)

Nature of business: Retailing and property interests.

Policy: The company and its subsidiaries are contributors to a number of community projects, either in cash, in kind or by donation of human resources. The company focuses its activities on supporting opportunities which:

- are pioneering and innovative;

- fit well with and contribute directly to Kingfisher's mainstream business activities, customers and products;

- allow the company to add real value;

- give scope for company employees to become involved, develop their full potential or gain new skills and experiences;

- involve developing longer term relationships.

Efforts are concentrated on issues affecting the home and family and in particular education/youth development, the older generation, community safety and crime prevention, and equal opportunities and environmental issues.

The main group company associated with environmental issues is B&Q, which has a social responsibility budget of about £200,000. Specific environmental initiatives include the B&Q Stores Grant. As part of B&Q's environmental '1,000 day countdown to the new millennium' stores have been encouraged to be more involved in local environmental issues by being offered a green grant. Stores are asked to achieve certain standards on several areas of environmental management, such as waste management and energy efficiency compliance with legislation, staff and customer awareness of issues and litter control in the local environment. If stores reach a median grade they are encouraged to apply for a green grant which will provide funds for an environmental project. This could be on the store site or linked with another organisation such as a school, community centre, local authority, WWF or another locally based conservation organisation. Grants are typically in the low £100s.

WWF Education Project: B&Q is working with WWF on a project aimed at GNVQ students at schools and colleges. It is a CD ROM based package which focuses on how companies can be environmentally responsible. There are two major case studies – B&Q and a smaller specialist environmental retailer (Out of This World). The project is being trialled with educational specialists and will be launched to 2,000 plus schools and colleges in time for the next academic year. There will also be an Internet conference in October and scholarships (totalling £1,000) for the winning schools.

Capiz: B&Q is also working with WWF in the Philippines to improve both the diving conditions and the harvesting of this shell which is used in lampshades sold at B&Q.

In addition, B&Q is increasingly using only independently-certified well-managed forests for the sourcing of timber, and is currently leading an initiative encouraging all paint suppliers to reduce the solvents in paint.

Applications: In writing to the correspondent. Shortlisted applications are considered by the Social Responsibility Committee.

Applications to B&Q should be addressed to: Bill Whiting, Marketing Director, B&Q plc, Portswood House, 1 Hampshire Corporate Park, Chandlers Ford, Eastleigh, Hampshire SO5 3YX. Sponsorship proposals should be addressed to the group company secretary or to the marketing directors of the individual operating subsidiaries.

Kwik Save Group plc

Warren Drive, Prestatyn, Clwyd LL19 7HU
Tel: 01745-887111
Correspondent: Alan Foulkes, Head of Community Affairs
Charitable donations: £86,536 (1996)
Nature of business: Discount grocery retailer.

Policy: The company's support for the environment is limited to sponsorship of local environment projects with schools totalling £2,500. It has also supported the Tidy Britain Group.

Applications: In writing to the correspondent.

LASMO plc

100 Liverpool Street, London EC2M 2BB
Tel: 0171-945 4545
Correspondent: Nina Hamilton, Public Affairs Adviser
Charitable donations: £132, 024 (1996)
Nature of business: Oil and gas exploration and production.

Policy: To receive consideration by the appeals committee, appeals should be directed towards national causes or local charities in areas where the company has operations i.e. Aberdeen (through the Elf Consortium – see separate entry) and London. Local charities receive 90% of the company's support.

The environment/conservation is one of several favoured areas for support. Typical grants to national organisations range from £250 to £5,000, and to local organisations from £100 to £1,000. The Council for the Protection of Rural England and Woodland Trust were among the organisations supported in 1996.

Applications: Applications are considered quarterly in March, June, September and December. No progress report can be given outside of these review dates. Charitable appeals and sponsorship proposals should be addressed to the correspondent.

Legal & General plc

Temple Court, 11 Queen Victoria Street, London EC4N 4TP
Tel: 0171-528 6200
Correspondent: John MacCarthy, Communications and Resource Director
Charitable donations: £461,103 (1996)
Nature of business: Insurance.

Policy: Legal & General's policy regarding its sponsorship and donations programme is to give significant long-term support to a small number of projects which are directly related to the group's core businesses. Local programmes are used to support the community in places where large numbers of employees live and work.

At a national level, the group's policy is to support identifiable work in five defined areas, with donations or sponsorships of between £25,000 and £100,000 a year, usually for two or three years. This programme is run proactively and unsolicited appeals are not welcome, although information about organisations which work in the relevant areas is always useful.

The programme covers the following areas: social welfare; medical research; environment; crime prevention; and equal opportunities for women. Within the environment associated educational resource pack run by Living Earth. This is designed to encourage schools to develop environmental projects in partnership with business. (Contact: Warwick House, 106 Harrow Road, London W2 1XD 0171-258 1823).

At a local level, programmes fund a wide range of community activities in areas where employees live and work. Preference is given to projects in which employees are involved. Local programmes are run in Brighton and Hove, Cardiff and Surrey.

Applications: Information about national charities which meet the group's guidelines should be sent to the correspondent. Appropriate local appeals should be sent to:

Brighton & Hove: Gianna Dodd, Community Affairs, Legal & General, 2 Montefiore Road, Hove, East Sussex BN3 1SE.

Cardiff: Lynne Sheeney, Community Affairs, Legal & General, Knox Court, 10 Fitzallan Place, Cardiff CF2 1TL. Surrey: Rob Catt, Community Affairs, Legal & General, Legal & General House, St Monicas Road, Kingswood, Tadworth, Surrey KT20 6EU.

John Lewis Partnership plc

171 Victoria Street, London SW1E 5NN
Tel: 0171-828 1000
Correspondent: Mrs D M Webster, Secretary to the Central Charities Committee
Charitable donations: £1,030,000 (1996/97)
Nature of business: Department stores and Waitrose supermarkets.

Policy: The Partnership's Central and Branch Council is responsible for about half the total donations and gives to what can be broadly described as 'welfare' organisations. The chairman is responsible for the other half and gives to organisations which, in broad terms, fall into the categories of the arts, education and the environment. Last year more than half was given in support of musical activities, the rest being divided among drama, literature, painting etc., the conservation of buildings and the countryside, and teaching and research, including museums and natural history.

Beneficiaries of relevance to this guide included the Royal Geographic Society (to set up a Southern Region), a grant towards research into the life cycle of the large colony of herring and lesser black-backed gulls in Bristol, Civic Trust and Woodland Trust.

Applications: In writing to the correspondent. Applications are discussed quarterly. Local charities should deal with their local Partnership department store, production unit or Waitrose branch.

Littlewoods Organisation PLC

100 Old Hall Street, Liverpool L70 1AB
Tel: 0151-235 2713
Fax: 0151-476 5118
Correspondent: Jerry Marston, Group Community Affairs Manager
Charitable donations: £1,500,000 (1996/97)
Nature of business: Retail and leisure.

Policy: During 1996/97 community sponsorships and charitable funding amounted to more than £2 million. A new community investment strategy was drawn up and adopted in November 1997.

A key theme for future programmes will be regeneration. The emphasis will be on creating and sustaining jobs and prosperity in targeted communities, and on combining employee expertise and other company resources with cash donations to achieve greater impact. Organisations supporting disadvantaged groups will continue to receive funding, and employee fundraising and volunteering will be more actively promoted.

The company is one of the sponsors of the Young Environmentalist of the Year Awards (£6,667), and within its Merseyside regeneration programme, considers applications with an environmental focus. Examples include the Tidy Britain Group "Liverpools' picking up" campaign (£5,000), and sponsorship of Merseyside Environment Week (£5,000), the latter focusing on grants to schools and community groups.

Applications: In writing to the correspondent.

Lloyds TSB Group plc

See entry in the trusts section of this Guide.

London Electricity plc

Templar House, 81–87 High Holborn, London WC1V 6NU
Tel: 0171-331 3114
Correspondent: Jane Vine, Community Affairs Executive
Charitable donations: £500,000 (1996/97) – cash and in kind
Nature of business: Electricity supply.

Policy: The company generally supports London-based projects, in particular projects concerned with regenerating the capital, protecting and enhancing the environment, and with education in the broadest terms.

The company also organises and sponsors the Londoners of the Year Awards, created to reward a wide range of worthy projects in the capital. The focus is on supporting 'unsung heroes' of London and giving a helping hand to the capital's best start-up projects in the community. £25,000 prize money is made available annually.

Other major community projects include support for Learning Through Landscapes, a charity which aims to eradicate asphalt playgrounds in London and Trees for London, which is concerned with greening the capital.

Applications: In writing to the correspondent.

London Stock Exchange

London EC2N 1HP
Tel: 0171-797 1000
Correspondent: Corporate Affairs Department
Charitable donations: £113,000 (1996/97)
Nature of business: Organisation and regulation of markets in securities.

Policy: There is a preference for charities within the inner London area and the surrounding boroughs i.e. Tower Hamlets and Islington. The Stock Exchange concentrates its charitable giving in six areas, one of which is the environment. Donations tend to be made for projects in London whose aim is to improve the city environment or to educate city dwellers on environmental issues such as 'City Farm'.

Applications: In writing to the correspondent.

Manchester Airport plc

Wythenshawe, Manchester M90 1QX
Tel: 0161-489 3000
Correspondent: Manchester Airport Trust Fund Administrator
Charitable donations: £100,000 (1996/97)
Nature of business: International airport operation.

Policy: Manchester Airport has established a Community Trust, as a community based initiative to promote, enhance, improve, protect and conserve the natural and built environment in areas affected by the activities of Manchester Airport. Applications for grants will be assessed by a board of eight trustees who have been appointed by the local authorities of Stockport, Trafford, Manchester, Congleton, Macclesfield and Vale Royal along with Cheshire County Council and the Airport Company. The trustees will only consider applications from projects/organisations within the scheme boundary.

Applications: Trust brochures and application forms can be obtained by contacting the Trust Fund Administrator (0161-489 5281).

Marks & Spencer plc

Michael House, Baker Street, London W1A 1DN
Tel: 0171-268 4422
Fax: 0171-268 2260
Correspondent: Mrs Y Pennicott, Manager, Community Involvement
Charitable donations: £5,500,000 (1996/97)
Nature of business: Retail.

Policy: Marks & Spencer's community involvement policy is to support the communities in which the company trades through cash contributions and secondment of staff to a wide range of projects and voluntary organisations. Priorities are health and care, the arts, and community development and environment. Generally the company prefers to provide seedcorn support to smaller and less well known causes.

In the UK total contributions were £9.8 million in 1996/97, broken down as follows: health and care £2,200,000; community development and environment £1,500,000; arts and heritage £1,100,000; matching funds and local support for stores £700,000; secondment £2,600,000; departmental and support costs £1,700,000.

The environmental policy states: 'The public, in particular young people, are keen to find out more about the environment and explore practical ways in which they can become more involved. We therefore place emphasis on young people as we wish to develop in them an awareness, respect and responsibility for the environment, through education and personal involvement'.

Major funding is provided to a selection of initiatives. The objectives are:

- to consider, protect and improve the environment. Emphasis is placed on urban rather than rural areas;

- to provide impartial information and a signposting service to other projects to enhance and build on that knowledge;

- to educate young people;

- to promote sustainable regeneration including recycling waste and energy conservation;

- to make positive use of neglected environments;

- to reduce air and water pollution, and encourage more environmentally friendly transport.

The company are long-time supporters of the British Trust for Conservation Volunteers and provided private sector partnership funding for the National Pioneers Millennium Awards. The Marks & Spencer Youth Environment Programme is run with the Groundwork Foundation and aims to promote small-scale urban environmental projects undertaken by young people. Support has also been given to the National Federation of City Farms, Learning Through Landscapes and the Countryside Foundation and the company has continued its sponsorship of the Young Environmentalist of the Year Awards.

Criteria and priorities for support are: community benefit and the promotion of self-help; an efficient and cost-effective administration; achievable objectives; that the project be run by the right people for the right reasons; possible benefits to company staff. Staff often visit a project before making a decision to provide support.

Applications: The programme is administered from the London office by nine staff. The department receives some 20,000 letters each year, about 10,000 are appeals. All applications should be in writing to the relevant contact at the address above.

Mars UK Ltd

3D Dundee Road, Slough, Berkshire
SL1 4LG
Tel: 01753-693000
Correspondent: Jenny Ward, Charities Administrator
Charitable donations: £209,474 (1995)
Nature of business: Food manufacture.

Policy: The group at head office supports mainly national charities. The subsidiary companies (including Mars Confectionery and Pedigree Pet Foods) tend to support charities local to their sites. The company is a member of the British Trust for Conservation Volunteers and local ecology trusts and has recently supported the Civic Trust and Tidy Britain Group. It sponsors the Mars Awards for Environmental Achievement and the Mars Environment Awards for schools in Slough.

Applications: In writing to the correspondent. Approaches from local charities should be made directly to operating companies. The appeals committee meets four times a year.

McDonald's UK

11–59 High Road, East Finchley, London
N2 8AW
Tel: 0181-700 7000
Correspondent: Sarah Watkins, Consumer & Community Affairs Assistant
Charitable donations: £378,046 (1997)
Nature of business: Quick service restaurants.

Policy: The company gave details of its support in the 1996 Per Cent Club annual report, from which the following information is taken. The company

focuses support on child welfare, the environment and education. The company is an Environment Council member, sponsor of Earthwatch, and supports environmental initiatives including Groundwork and Tidy Britain Group's national Spring Clean campaign. For the latter, it sponsored leaflets, banners and tray-liners, as well as providing publicity.

Applications: In writing to the correspondent. Regional and local appeals should be directed to the appropriate marketing departments in London, Manchester (Salford) or Birmingham (Sutton Coldfield).

Meyer International plc

Aldwych House, 81 Aldwych, London
WC2B 4HQ
Tel: 0171-400 8888
Tel: 0171-400 8700
Correspondent: D Stovold, Assistant Secretary
Charitable donations: £49,300 (1996/97)
Nature of business: Building materials and timber.

Policy: Most of the group's community contributions in 1996/97, amounting to £150,000, were made up of donations in kind (especially supplying building materials, usually at cost price), the remainder (£49,300) being given in charitable donations. Support is given to national charities and charities local to the company's operations and appeals where a member of the group's staff is involved. There is a preference for those activities and projects concerned with children and youth, enterprise and training, environment and heritage – especially the preservation of buildings of national importance, education and overseas projects. The company gives grants to national and local organisations ranging from £50 to £6,500.

The grants list for 1996/97 included the following two categories of relevance to this Guide:

Environmental – 19 grants totalling £12,100. Initiatives supported include research into the preservation and regeneration of forests and their wildlife both in the UK and overseas, and the promotion of environmental education. The largest grants were £5,000 to the Woodland Trust and £1,000 to Frontier (East Usumbara Forest Research) for environmental exploration in Tanzania. The remaining grants ranged from £100 to £500.

Preservation of buildings – 2 grants totalling £1,500: Chiltern Open Air Museum (£500) and Westminster Abbey Trust (£1,000).

Applications: In writing to the correspondent. Telephone applications cannot be accepted.

Michelin Tyre plc

Campbell Road, Stoke-on-Trent ST4 4EY
Tel: 01782-402081
Tel: 01782-403372
Correspondent: P Niblett, Internal Communications Manager
Charitable donations: £41,566 (1996)
Nature of business: Tyre manufacture.

Policy: The company has a strong preference for local charities (i.e. north Staffordshire, east Lancashire, Tayside and Co. Antrim), especially those in which a member of staff is involved and appeals relevant to the company's business. Grants range from £10 to £500. Although environmental causes are not listed by the company as a preferred area of support, it is involved in local schemes to improve wasteland and school playgrounds, as well as running tree planting schemes at factory locations.

Applications: In writing to the correspondent.

Midland Bank plc

27–32 Poultry, London EC2P 2BX
Tel: 0171-260 8000
Correspondent: Richard Dear, Manager, Donations
Charitable donations: £1,600,000 (1996)
Nature of business: Banking, financial and related services.

Policy: In 1996 the company spent £5.9 million in support of community activities in the UK. This was in the form of donations, sponsorship, secondments and gifts in kind. £1.6 million was for charitable purposes, £250,000 of which was relating to the £1 for £1 staff charity scheme. Environmental support is limited and comes mainly through the National Trust Card (one of several affinity cards).

Applications: In writing to the correspondent. The company also has regional Charity Liaison Officers.

Midlands Electricity plc

Mucklow Hill, Halesowen, West Midlands B62 8BP
Tel: 0121-423 2345
Tel: 0121-423 1825
Correspondent: Sue Heritage, Community Relations Officer
Charitable donations: £419,416 (1996/97)
Nature of business: Distribution and supply of electricity and gas.

Policy: Preference is given to local charities in the Midlands, national charities and charities in which a member of staff is involved. A wide range of causes are supported including the environment, elderly people and the arts.

Over the last three years, £1.5 million has been donated to NEA, the national energy efficiency charity. Many smaller organisations are also supported.

Applications: In writing to the correspondent.

Mobil Holdings Ltd

Mobil House, 500–600 Witan Gate, Central Milton Keynes MK9 1ES
Tel: 01908-853000
Correspondent: R C Newstead, Manager, Media Relations
Charitable donations: £71,317 (1995)
Nature of business: Oil and petroleum products.

Policy: The company only supports registered charities, with one of the areas of support being the environment/heritage. Priority is given to charities in areas of company presence i.e. Milton Keynes, south Essex and Wirral. One recent initiative was the production of the Mobil Greensight pack – a resource pack developed by Living Earth and the Green Alliance to enable teams of students to produce a high quality video documentary about a local company's impact on the environment.

Applications: In writing to the correspondent.

Monsanto plc

PO Box 53, Lane End Road, High Wycombe HP12 4HL
Tel: 01494-474918
Correspondent: Karen Tait, Public Relations Manager
Charitable donations: £35,557 (1996)
Nature of business: Herbicides, pharmaceutical products and food ingredients.

Policy: The company supports local charities in areas of company presence, national charities and charities in which a member of company staff is involved. The company tries to help self-supporting projects. It has strong links with schools and education and matches donations raised for charities by employees. Grants to national organisations range from £250 to £1,000. Grants to local organisations range from £20 to £100. Much of the company's community support is given to conservation/environment causes. Current major projects are with the National Trust and Game Conservancy. The Farming & Wildlife Advisory Group was and Wrexham Groundwork Trust were also supported in 1996.

Applications: In writing to the correspondent. The charity committee meets four times a year and tends to exclude the more well-known charities.

The National Grid Group plc

National Grid House, Kirby Corner Road, Coventry CV4 8JY
Tel: 01203-537777
Correspondent: Trevor Seeley, Senior Public Relations Officer
Charitable donations: £2,300,000 (1996/97)
Nature of business: Electricity transmission.

Policy: National Grid implements a community relations programme which places particular emphasis on environmental initiatives. It supports national charities and local charities in areas of company presence. Major schemes involve the countryside and environment.

The company has also set up and run education centres with the active involvement of local education authorities. It has also recently launched three national sponsorships in partnership with the Local Government Board (National Grid Community 21 Awards for Local Authorities), the Tree Council (National Grid Tree Warden Scheme) and BTCV (National Grid for Wildlife).

Applications: In writing to the correspondent. Local appeals should be made to one of four area offices. Sponsorship proposals should be addressed to the correspondent.

National Power PLC

Windmill Hill Business Park, Whitehill Way, Swindon, Wiltshire SN5 6PB
Tel: 01793-877777
Correspondent: Catherine Springett, Assistant Company Secretary
Charitable donations: £419,322 (1996/97)
Nature of business: Electricity generation and supply.

Policy: The company makes donations through the National Power Charitable Trust. The trust supports a wide range of community, health and social causes, particularly initiatives which aim to alleviate suffering and deprivation and for the promotion of self help and voluntary work in the community.

Support is particularly given to charities with local outlets near company sites or with company staff involved. Although the environment is not an area supported by the charitable trust, the company is a member of the Woodland Trust, a sponsor of the Wood Hall Moated Manor Project, a supporter of local wildlife trusts and a member of the National Trust.

Organisations receiving support through the Landfill Tax Credit Scheme include Groundwork, Landscape Trust, Institute of Environmental Management and Business Environment Association.

Applications: In writing to the correspondent. Sponsorship proposals should be addressed to: Sponsorship Manager, Corporate Communications.

National Provident Institution

Grove Hill House, 21–27 Grove Hill Road, Tunbridge Wells, Kent TN1 1SB
Tel: 01892-705413
Fax: 01892-705611
Correspondent: Angela Gower, Public Relations Coordinator
Charitable donations: Not available
Nature of business: Pensions specialist.

Policy: The environment is one of the favoured areas of support of the company, both for donations and sponsorship. Its two major projects in this field are NPI Red Alert North West, a network of local groups throughout Cumbria and the Sefton Coast helping to conserve the red squirrel in North-West England, and NPI Treasures of Britain campaign. The company also supported the Woodland Trust in 1996.

Applications: In writing to the correspondent. The contact for sponsorship proposals is Sarah Royle, Communications and Sponsorship Manager.

Nationwide Building Society

Nationwide House, Pipers Way, Swindon SN38 1NW
Tel: 01793-455139
Correspondent: James McCormick, Community Affairs Manager
Charitable donations: £606,741 (1996/97)
Nature of business: Personal financial and housing services.

Policy: There are four broad themes within Nationwide's Community Affairs strategy and any activities should normally embrace at least one of these themes:

◆ homes – housing initiatives;

◆ initiative – training, youth projects, education/schools/preparation for life;

◆ caring – counselling and advice, disabled support/access, health, discrimination (various);

◆ heritage/environment – saving things (as well as money), green issues, conservation/recycling.

There is a preference for projects with the potential for staff involvement. Support is given to national and local charities.

Applications: Applications for donations or sponsorship should be sent to the correspondent. On a local basis, giving depends on the local area managers, who have small budgets for local community projects.

Nestlé UK Ltd

York YO1 1XY
Correspondent: Peter J Anderson, Community Relations Manager
Charitable donations: £932,000 (1997)
Nature of business: Food manufacture.

Policy: The company makes donations to registered charities through the Nestle Charitable Trust and also supports non-registered good causes locally. In addition to cash donations its main area of non-cash support is gifts in kind – the company provides support with product, furniture and equipment donations to local good causes.

The company considers donations in various fields including the environment. Support is given to properly managed activities of high quality in their particular field. However, a relevant link or connection with the company's business is usually looked for; this may be geographic (within the catchment area of company factories; there are over 30 locations throughout the UK), related to the food industry or through connections with university departments or employee activities. Employees involved with local voluntary groups may apply for a grant of up to £1,500.

Support for environmental organisations has ranged from the British Trust for Conservation Volunteers, to providing a trust in Halifax which offers low interest loans for companies wanting to improve the appearance of their properties in the inner city or providing a little money to convert a York school's playground into a garden.

Applications: Applications for support of local good causes should be made to the Manager of the nearest Nestle location, but for large scale donations or national charities the request should be sent to Community Relations Department, Nestle UK Ltd, Haxby Road, York YO1 1XY (01904-604924).

News International plc

PO Box 495, Virginia Street, London E1 9XY
Tel: 0171-782 6074
Correspondent: Jane Reed, Director of Corporate Affairs
Charitable donations: c. £1,000,000 (1996/97)
Nature of business: Printing and publishing of national newspapers.

Policy: News International's programme aims to achieve a balance between national projects and those in areas where the company has a presence. Nationally, donations are given to registered charities only, with the environment/heritage being

one of several areas supported. National grants range from £250 to £50,000. Local appeals from Merseyside and Scotland are dealt with at the company's plants in Knowsley and Kinning Park, Glasgow, respectively. For appeals from the Wapping area, support is normally given through the St Katherine & Shadwell Trust (details of which can be found in A Guide to the Major Trusts Volume 1). Local grants range from £250 to £10,000.

The group has been involved with Groundwork Trust in an initiative in Knowsley called Greenforce. It aims to improve the landscape within Knowsley, using help and assistance from local residents, schools and businesses as well as financing projects itself. It also launched the Greenforce Challenge, a competition for individuals, schools and community groups involved in environmental improvement projects.

Applications: In writing to the correspondent. The charities committee meets regularly. Unsuccessful applicants are given reasons and the corporate policy explained. Appeals to subsidiary companies should be made to managing directors, managing editors or editors. In some cases larger requests are referred to the charities committee. Sponsorship proposals to the group should be addressed to the Director of Marketing, News Group Newspapers, or the Director of Marketing, Times Newspapers.

Northern Electric plc

Carliol House, Market Street, Newcastle-upon-Tyne NE1 6NF.
Tel: 0191-221 2000
Correspondent: Julian L Kenyon, Community Affairs Officer
Charitable donations: £200,000 (1996/97)
Nature of business: Electricity distribution and supply.

Policy: The community contributions include in kind support, secondments and staff time, award schemes and community festivals, in addition to charitable donations. The company only supports local charities in its area of operation (i.e. Northumberland, Tyne & Wear, Cleveland, Durham and North Yorkshire) and of perceived value to the community. There is a fair spread throughout the region. The environment and heritage are included in the company's preferred areas of support. The company states that there is the 'possibility of high gearing (i.e. supporting an event that itself has a prospect of raising money from the public)', especially if there is good value for money in profile terms for the company.

In addition to the company's own initiative to promote awareness of environmental issues and energy efficiency, a range of local environmental organisations are supported including the Botanic Centre at Middlesbrough, Washington Wildlife Centre, local civic societies and wildlife trusts.

Applications: In writing to the correspondent.

Northern Ireland Electricity PLC

PO Box 2, Danesfort, 120 Malone Road, Belfast BT9 5HT
Tel: 01232-661100
Correspondent: D Davey, Northern Ireland Electricity Charities Committee
Charitable donations: £175,000 (1996/97)
Nature of business: Electricity supply.

Policy: The charities committee considers any registered charity, with a preference for local charities in areas of company presence, but national charities may be supported. The community affairs committee prefers sponsorship opportunities in several fields including environment and heritage. The Charities Committee prefers to give in kind support rather than cash. Several organisations of relevance to this Guide have been supported recently including Groundwork Northern Ireland, National Trust, RSPB Conservation Volunteers and World Wide Fund for Nature.

Applications: In writing to the correspondent.

Northern Rock plc

Northern Rock House, Gosforth, Newcastle-upon-Tyne NE3 4PL
Tel: 0191-285 7191
Correspondent: Maureen Rowbottom, Personal Assistant to the Managing Director
Nature of business: Financial services.
Charitable donations: Not available

Policy: The company undertakes community sponsorship, but in future most of its community support will be channelled through the Northern Rock Foundation, established by the company in 1988 with a £1 million donation. The company will covenant 5% of its pre-tax profits to the Foundation each year. The Foundation's primary objective is to help improve the conditions of those disadvantaged in society by age, infirmity, poverty or other circumstances. It will support causes primarily, but not exclusively, in the North East. Environmental projects which do not accord with the main objectives of the Foundation will not be considered for funding.

Applications: In writing to Fiona Ellis, Director, the Northern Rock Foundation, 21 Lansdowne Terrace, Newcastle upon Tyne NE3 1HP Tel: 0191-284 8412

Northumbrian Water Group plc

Northumbria House, Regent Centre, Gosforth, Newcastle-upon-Tyne NE3 3PX
Tel: 0191-383 2222
Correspondent: John Mowbray, Customer Relations Manager
Charitable donations: £134,660 (1996/97)
Nature of business: Water supply and sewage services.

Policy: The company supports local charities in its area of operation and appeals relevant to company business. The environment and heritage is one of the preferred areas of support. Most donations are for less than £1,000, averaging around

£200 to £300. The company has supported the Millennium Project for the restoration of the Durham Coastline, committing £150,000 to the project.

Applications: In writing to the correspondent.

Norwich Union plc

Surrey Street, Norwich NR1 3NG
Tel: 01603-622200
Correspondent: Group Corporate Affairs
Charitable donations: £276,000 (1996)
Nature of business: Insurance.

Policy: The company has a preference for appeals relevant to company business, community projects in the Norwich, Sheffield and Eastleigh areas, and charities in the fields of crime prevention, and health and safety. For the foreseeable future, the company is focusing its program on fewer key charities. The company has an environmental policy and actively supports a number of conservation initiatives.

Applications: In writing to the correspondent. Sponsorship proposals should be addressed to: Donna Barker, Sponsorship Co-ordinator, Group Corporate Affairs, 25–27 Surrey Street, Norwich NR1 3TA.

Nynex CableComms Ltd

Nynex House, Timpson Road, Off South Moor Road, Baguley, Manchester M23 9WX
Tel: 0161-283 5066
Fax: 0161-283 1040
Correspondent: John Knight, Head of Public Relations
Nature of business: Cable TV, telephones.

Policy: The main environment initiative undertaken is the commitment of £300,000 worth of sponsorship to the BTCV over three years. The money will be invested in conservation projects within Nynex's 16 franchise areas.

Applications: In writing to the correspondent.

OCS Group plc

79 Limpsfield Road, Sanderstead, Surrey CR2 9LB
Tel: 0181-651 3211
Correspondent: M H George, Treasurer
Charitable donations: £6,568 (1996/97)
Nature of business: Business services sector.

Policy: The environment is the main area supported, through both donations and sponsorship which are committed for long periods in advance. Although donations totalled only £9,000 in 1995/96, the Tidy Britain Group and WWF UK received £10,000, presumably in sponsorship. This support is ongoing.

Applications: In writing to the correspondent.

Orange plc

Foxholes Business Park, The Chase, John Tate Road, Hertford SG13 7NN
Tel: 01454-624600
Fax: 01454-618501
Correspondent: Denise Lewis, Head of Public Relations and Sponsorship
Charitable donations: £257,500 (1996)
Nature of business: Personal communications services.

Policy: As premier sponsor of the Millennium Seed Bank Appeal (a registered charity) organised by the Royal Botanic Gardens, Kew, the company made the first of ten annual payments of £250,000. One of the most ambitious international conservation projects ever undertaken, the project aims to store seeds from all of the UK's flora and from 10% of the worlds 250,000 plant species by the year 2010.

In addition, the group made charitable cash donations of £7,500 and provided sponsorship and gifts in kind to various community projects in Bristol, Hertford, and Darlington totalling around £130,000.

Applications: In writing to the correspondent. (N.B. The telephone number below is for head office in Bristol – they will automatically route you to the office in Hertford).

Panasonic UK Ltd

Panasonic House, Willoughby Road,
Bracknell RG12 8FP
Tel: 01344-862444
Correspondent: Gary Thomson,
Personnel Director
Charitable donations: £285,289
(1996/97)
Nature of business: Electrical equipment.

Policy: Each office/site has its own budget
to support local charities in areas of
company presence (Bracknell, Wakefield
and Northampton). The company
predominantly supports causes local to its
main office in Bracknell and other regional
sites. No cash donations are made by the
company. Instead it prefers to donate
equipment for either office use or
fundraising purposes wherever possible
and responds to requests received
accordingly. (The figure given above is the
cost of this.) The company is a patron of
the Berkshire Community Trust and has
sponsored local environmental and other
good causes including the Berkshire
Community Environmental Awards.

Applications: In writing to the
correspondent, although please note that
the company does not normally respond
favourably to unsollcited requests.

Pilkington plc

Prescot Road, St Helens, Merseyside
WA10 3TT
Tel: 01744-28882
Correspondent: David Roycroft,
Chairman, Grants Committee
Charitable donations: £109,236 (1997)
Nature of business: Producer of glass and
related products.

Policy: Pilkington supports local causes in
the communities where it operates,
especially St Helens and Merseyside. A
wide range of charities/projects are
supported through its charitable trust.
Grants range from £50 to £2,000.

In 1996/97, Mersey Basin Campaign
received £10,000. In previous years the
trust has also supported organisations such
as Brathay Exploration Group and
Lancashire Wildlife Trust. In addition, the
company provides non-cash support
through arts sponsorship, good cause
sponsorship and gifts in kind.

Applications: In writing to the
correspondent. Decisions are made by the
grants committee which meets every two
months.

PowerGen plc

Westwood Way, Westwood Business Park,
Coventry CV4 8LG
Tel: 01203–424000
Correspondent: Emma Grainger,
Communications Department
Charitable donations: £254,444
(1996/97)
Nature of business: Generation and sale
of electricity.

Policy: PowerGen's community support is
focused on areas relevant to its business
activities, in particular education, science,
technology and engineering, and the
environment. In 1996/97 its main grant
beneficiaries included: the Women's
Engineering Society, Drive for Youth/
Groundwork; Year of Engineering Success;
Going for Green; and a Senior Research
Fellowship in Energy Efficiency, St Hilda's
College, Oxford.

Applications: In writing to the
correspondent.

The Rio Tinto plc

6 St James's Square, London SW1Y 4LD
Tel: 0171-930 2399
Tel: 0171-930 2349
Correspondent: J H G Senior, Head of
Community Affairs
Charitable donations: £1,122,000
(1996)
Nature of business: International mining
company.

Policy: Group companies around the
world give active support to their local
communities, both directly and through
independently managed foundations. In

Britain the company focuses its community support on a limited number of significant projects in specific areas where it believes it can make a distinctive contribution.

There is a very focused and proactive approach to the type of organisation the company chooses to support, with the emphasis on education, the arts, environment and world affairs. Within the environment category, the company aims to support voluntary initiatives which sustain and improve the physical environment both in the UK and overseas, and to encourage debate and discussion on environmental issues.

Support continues to be provided to several major UK environmental organisations. These include BTCV, the Conservation Foundation, Earthwatch, the Green-IT project at Groundwork, Royal Botanic Gardens, Botanic Gardens Conservation International, Flora for Fauna and the World Conservation Monitoring Centre.

In general, Rio Tinto prefers applications which:

- are for specific projects and events
- have clearly stated objectives which are capable of being monitored and evaluated
- are short and concise, stating clearly the donation requested.

Applications: In writing to the Community Affairs Assistant. The company may require appropriate acknowledgement of its support in publicity and other material and will wish to receive periodic progress reports.

RJB Mining plc

Harworth Park, Blyth Road, Harworth, Doncaster, South Yorkshire DN11 6DB
Tel: 01302-751751
Correspondent: R J Budge, Chief Executive
Charitable donations: £1,085,751 (1996)

Nature of business: Coal mining and associated activities.

Policy: The company has a preference for supporting charities local to Nottinghamshire and Yorkshire, especially those connected with the arts, children/youth, environment/heritage, fundraising events, medical research, social welfare, and sport. No further information was available.

Applications: In writing to the correspondent.

The Royal Bank of Scotland Group plc

42 St Andrew Square, Edinburgh EH2 2YE
Tel: 0131-556 8555
Fax: 0131-558 3573
Correspondent: G P Fenton, Head of Sponsorship and Community Programme
Charitable donations: £2,081,352 (1996/97)
Nature of business: Banking, insurance and financial services.

Policy: The bank's community programme supports not for profit organisations with an involvement in environment and heritage, financial counselling and training, health and community. Organisations should be working for the benefit of communities in which the bank operates. Recent partnerships include working with the National Trust for Scotland, Young People's Trust for the Environment, Groundwork Foundation, Mersey Basin Campaign and Sustrans.

The bank considers supporting the headquarters of national organisations. Local groups should contact their local branch of the bank.

Applications: In writing to the correspondent, including if possible appropriate reports and accounts or financial statements.

Safeway plc

6 Millington Road, Hayes, Middlesex
UB3 4AY
Tel: 0181-848 8744
Correspondent: Sheila Underwood,
Community Relations Manager
Charitable donations: £46,000
(1996/97)
Nature of business: Food retailing.

Policy: The company supports projects
relating to families and children, including
education and environmental initiatives.
Support is also given to fundraising
initiatives organised by national and local
charities. There is a preference for national
charities and local charities near to trading
stores. Small, local appeals are usually
steered through district managers who
may then recommend the appeal to head
office. Store managers are able to make
small gifts in kind to local groups, both
charitable and non-charitable.

The group has supported, either through
sponsorship or donations, the Soil
Association, Green Consumer Week,
National Trust, Habitat Scotland, Council
for the Protection of Rural England and
Friends of the Earth. With the Edinburgh
School of Agriculture, the Scottish
Development Agency and the EEC,
Safeway has co-sponsored a model organic
farm to test how artificial fertiliser and
pesticide-free agriculture could work in
practice.

Safeway has also been involved with and
helped finance the introduction of organic
farming courses at Worcestershire College
of Agriculture and is supporting a similar
initiative at Reading University. It is also a
main supporter of the Brogdale Trust,
home of the national fruit collection, and
the Henry Doubleday Research
Organisation, a body devoted to organic
methods.

Applications: In writing to the
correspondent.

J Sainsbury plc

Stamford House, Stamford Street, London
SE1 9LL
Tel: 0171-695 6000
Fax: 0171-695 0097
Correspondent: Mrs S L Mercer,
Sainsbury Charitable Fund
Charitable donations: £2,000,000
(1997/98)
Nature of business: Retail distribution of
food.

Policy: The corporate community
investment programme is made up of the
Charitable Fund, arts sponsorship
programme, town centre management and
environmental departments, as well as
small donations through the stores at local
level and goods in kind.

Support is restricted to within the UK and
preferred beneficiaries are those concerned
with young families, the elderly and
disabled people. National and local
charities are supported, i.e. WWF (Marine
Stewardship Council), Kew Botanic
Gardens, Countryside International Trust,
Botanic Gardens International. Crisis
Fareshare is also supported on a food
donation project.

Applications: Appeals should be
addressed to Alison Austin in the
Environmental Affairs Department. They
can be received at any time and should
include details of aims and objectives,
target audience and links with at least one
Sainsbury store.

Corporate sponsorship requests should be
addressed to the Community Affairs
Department.

Schroders plc

120 Cheapside, London EC2V 6DS
Tel: 0171-658 6000
Correspondent: B Tew, Schroder Charity
Trust
Charitable donations: £606,000 (1996)
Nature of business: Merchant banking
and investment group.

Policy: Donations are channelled through
the Schroder Charity Trust. Only

registered charities are supported, with a tendency to support national appeals. Local branches of national charities may also receive help, but very little money is given to purely local charities. Within these broad areas of preference, each appeal is considered on its merits. Currently, particular attention is being given to the country's heritage and a substantial donation has been made to the Oxford Bodleian Library campaign. Grants are usually for £500 to £2,000, larger donations may be spread over four or five years. In 1995, it gave over 400 grants totalling £525,000. Westminster Cathedral received £8,000 and Prague Heritage Fund £5,000.

Other grants of relevance to this guide included those to National Trust (£2,500), WWF and World Society for the Protection of Animals (£2,000 each), Natural History Museum Development Trust (£1,300), Game Conservancy Council (£1,200), CPRE, Country Trust, Ferriers Barn, National Trust for Scotland and the Wildfowl and Wetlands Trust (all £1,000). Recipients of smaller grants included Berkeley Reafforestation Trust, Millennium Forest for Scotland and Scottish Conservation Projects Trust.

Applications: In writing to the correspondent. Grant decisions are made by a committee which meets monthly.

Scottish Hydro-Electric plc

10 Dunkeld Road, Perth PH1 5WA
Tel: 01738-455040
Correspondent: Carolyn McAdam, Head of Corporate Communications
Charitable donations: £89,798 (1996/97)
Nature of business: Electricity supply.

Policy: The company supports local charities in areas where the company operates i.e. Peterhead, Perth, Pitlochry, Aberdeen and Invernees, followed by the remoter communities of the Highlands and Islands and then Scotland-wide. The environment/heritage is listed as one of several preferred areas of support.

Applications: In writing to the correspondent.

Scottish & Newcastle plc

Abbey Brewery, Holyrood Road, Edinburgh EH8 8YS
Tel: 0131-556 2591
Correspondent: Linda Bain, Corporate Affairs Manager
Charitable donations: £525,000 (1996/97)
Nature of business: Brewing, retail and leisure.

Policy: The company mainly supports projects in communities where the company operates (in the North East and Scotland and the North West and South East). This support includes charitable giving, sponsorship activities, youth training, liaison with schools and management involvement in local bodies and organisations. Grants to national organisations range from £50 to £1,000 (occasionally as high as £50,000) and grants to local organisations from £50 to £5,000 (occasionally as high as £10,000).

Some of the larger donations made during the year were to environment-related causes. This included those to Glasgow Caledonian University (£50,000 in each of the last five years) to endow a Chair in environment research, and Scottish Wildlife Trust's River Valley Project (£30,000) bringing together different groups with an interest in river management and river area land use..

More than £30,000 was distributed for environmental projects to improve the countryside through the Theakston Heritage Fund, which operates in conjunction with the Countryside Commission. Local support has ranged from a scheme to devise a management plan for the entire length of a river, to a tree planting programme within a city green belt. Each Center Parc village has conservation rangers who run environment-based education activities.

Applications: In writing to the correspondent. A donations committee meets quarterly. Local appeals should be directed to the regional office.

Scottish Power plc

1 Atlantic Quay, Broomielaw, Glasgow
G2 8SP
Tel: 0141-248 8200
Correspondent: Rachel Sherrard,
Corporate Affairs
Charitable donations: £484,641
(1996/97)
Nature of business: Utility company.

Policy: Most donations are made within the group's three operating areas. Preference for charities involving children and youth, heritage, arts, and environment. UK charities are supported if they have Scottish offices.

Manweb, now a subsidiary of Scottish Power, is a supporter of the Mersey Basin Campaign and has also given grants to the National Trust in recent years.

Applications: In writing to the correspondent.

Sedgwick Group plc

Sackville House, 143–152 Fenchurch Street, London EC3M 6BN
Tel: 0171-377 3456
Correspondent: Ms Victoria Secretan, Community Programmes Manager
Charitable donations: £180,000 (1996)
Nature of business: Insurance.

Policy: The company supports national charities and charities local to its offices, especially local to Tower Hamlets. On a local level, the company participates in a number of community programmes and tends to focus on those which receive little general public attention. The company works in partnership with representatives of the community, central and local government, large national charities and small local initiatives. Grants to national organisations range from £200 to £5,000 (occasionally up to £10,000) and to local organisations from £100 to £2,500.

As well as the environment/heritage being one of several areas the company prefers to support, it also operates recycling schemes in its offices with income generated being donated to local charities and schools. Several offices also take part in Local Agenda 21 environmental initiatives and have joined a number of planting schemes. A series of 'Green Futures' lectures by well-known speakers on environmental issues, held at the City of London's Guildhall, was sponsored by Sedgwick in conjunction with London Guildhall University and the Corporation of London.

Overseas donations given from the UK are to alleviate the effects of specific disasters and to establish long-term development projects in developing countries. For example, in Botswana a chalet has been sponsored at a nature reserve to promote conservation of the environment through education programmes.

Applications: Applications need not be elaborate, but should include details of who benefits from the work, what the charity/organisation does, the aim of the project and how Sedgwick's help could make a difference. Basic financial information and an annual report or leaflet should be included. The company state: 'Remember that Sedgwick may be able to offer time and skills rather than money'. Grants to national and London charities are decided regularly by an appeals committee.

Applications should be addressed to the correspondent. Local appeals in Norfolk, Essex and East Anglia can be addressed to Debbie Hilton, Public Relations Officer, Sedgwick Ltd, Victoria House, Queen's Road, Norwich N1 3QQ. Sponsorship proposals should be addressed to Miss Julia Fish, Director, Corporate Communications at head office. Local appeals may also be sent to regional offices – larger offices are in Birmingham, Bristol, Cardiff, Edinburgh, Glasgow, Leeds, Manchester, Norwich, Reading, Slough and Witham (Essex).

SEEBOARD plc

PO Box 639, 329 Portland Road, Hove,
East Sussex BN3 5SY
Tel: 01273-428593
Fax: 01273-428494
Correspondent: Sally Hutchinson,
Community Affairs Executive
Charitable donations: £68,730 (1996)
Nature of business: Electricity supply and
distribution.

Policy: Seeboard's community
involvement concentrates mainly on youth
activities, generally involved with
education and enterprise/training. Support
is concentrated in the company's operating
area, which includes most of Kent, all of
East Sussex, large parts of West Sussex and
Surrey, and the London boroughs of
Croydon, Kingston and Richmond.
Grants range from £50 to £5,000.

Support is given in five categories, one of
which is the environment and countryside
projects. The company has worked with
the County Wildlife Trusts in the South
East to encourage volunteer activities. It
has also helped to establish and fund the
Alchemist Scrapstore which makes surplus
materials from local businesses available
for schools and community groups. The
Environmental Education Centre has also
received support.

Applications: Seeboard makes few major
sponsorship awards – worth between
£5,000 and £20,000 each – in each
financial year. Applications for these must
be made before the end of the previous
December. In most cases these run for one
year only, but longer programmes may be
considered with an annual review. Smaller
awards are made on a rolling programme.
These range from donations of small gifts
for fundraising events, through donations
of electrical appliances to financial support
of up to £5,000.

To apply please write, giving brief details
of your organisation and your request to
the correspondent. The correspondent
stated: 'Seeboard makes every effort to
reply to all appeals. We do, however,
receive a large number of applications and
can support only a small proportion of
them'. Telephone and faxed applications
cannot be considered.

Severn Trent plc

2297 Coventry Road, Birmingham
B26 3PU
Tel: 0121-722 4544
Correspondent: Audrey Drew,
Community Affairs Executive
Charitable donations: £226,725
(1996/97)
Nature of business: Water and sewerage
services.

Policy: Generally support is given to
appeals from within the area of the Severn
Trent Group operations, occasionally
national charities are considered if they
can prove a local link. Grants generally
range between £500 and £1,000 but can
be up to a maximum of £10,000. Support
has been given to Business in the
Environment, Green Alliance and RSPB.

Applications: In writing to the
correspondent.

Shell UK Limited

Shell-Mex House, Strand, London
WC2R 0DX
Tel: 0171-257 3000
Correspondent: Miss L Duncan,
Manager, Arts & Environmental
sponsorship
Charitable donations: £1,024,544
(1996)
Nature of business: Oil industry.

Policy: Total community contributions in
1996 were £4.3 million including support
for various educational, enterprise,
environmental and arts initiatives. The
furtherance of voluntary endeavour and
projects of potential national significance
are also favoured. Central resources usually
benefit national concerns, while local ones
aid organisations active within the vicinity
of major installations. Shell offers discounts
on fuel cards for registered charities.

On the community environmental front,
the main thrust of Shell UK's efforts
continues to be concentrated on the Shell

Better Britain Campaign, which is now over 25 years old. The campaign encourages "action by local people to improve the quality of life at neighbourhood level, in ways which respect the earth's resources", through the provision of information, advice and grant aid. Further information can be found in the awards section of this Guide.

Applications: Enquiries should be addressed to the Shell Better Britain Campaign, Victoria Works, 21A Graham Street, Hockley, Birmingham B1 3JR.

South West Water plc

Peninsula House, Rydon Lane, Exeter EX2 7HR
Tel: 01392-446688
Fax: 01392-434966
Correspondent: H Weatherley, Corporate Communications Manager
Charitable donations: £30,000 (1996/97)
Nature of business: Water and sewerage services.

Policy: The company only gives to local charities in areas where it operates, with the environment and heritage being one of the preferred categories for support. Grants range from £500 to £1,000.

Applications: In writing to the correspondent.

SWEB Holdings Ltd

800 Park Avenue, Aztec West, Almondsbury, Bristol BS12 4SE
Tel: 01454-201101
Correspondent: Sharon Cross, Corporate Communications Officer
Charitable donations: £284,000 (1996/97)
Nature of business: Electricity supply.

Policy: In common with other utility companies, support is concentrated in the company's area of operation. Sponsorship of environmental courses is more common than direct donations. Projects include: a three year programme on farm conservation through the Farming & Wildlife Advisory Group, with the company sponsoring a professional adviser in each of Avon, Cornwall, Devon and Somerset and through them 'helping to organise newsletters, farm walks, demonstrations and visits, wildlife preservation schemes, tree planting, and flower and grass seed projects'; and a Tree Scheme, with the aim of planting native trees and shrubs throughout the region. In 1994/95, 60 projects were supported including schools, planting over 16,000 trees and shrubs and 1,500 metres of hedging.

Applications: In writing to the correspondent, between October and December. A committee considers all applications and a decision is based on relevance locally, the nature of the application and the geographical spread throughout the South West.

Southern Electric plc

Southern Electric House, Westacott Way, Littlewick Green, Maidenhead, Berkshire SL6 3QB
Tel: 01628-822166
Correspondent: Julian Reeves, Public Relations Manager
Charitable donations: £232,400 (1996/97)
Nature of business: Electricity supply.

Policy: The policy is to promote the company's activities in its own region, by supporting appeals relevant to company business and charities in which a member of company staff is involved. Priority is given to: schemes supporting training or increasing the employment prospects of disadvantaged young people; schemes promoting the welfare and well-being of the young or the elderly – particularly projects related to energy conservation and efficiency; schemes encouraging safety at work, in homes, schools and public places; and schemes promoting crime prevention, environmental care and conservation.

Applications: In writing to the correspondent, with a brief description of the project and the form of assistance being sought.

Tarmac plc

Hilton Hall, Essington, Wolverhampton
WV11 2BQ
Tel: 01902-307407
Correspondent: A C Smith, Group
Secretary
Charitable donations: £379,000 (1996)
Nature of business: Building and
property.

Policy: The company is especially
committed to the communities in which it
is based. It gives to a wide range of
projects and charities, including
environmental enterprises. Grants to
national organisations range from £250
to £5,000; grants to local organisations
from £50 to £5,000. The company has
sponsored a range of events including the
National Hedge Laying Championships,
the English Dry Stone Walling
Championships and the Best Kept
Village competition in East Staffordshire.
It is also a corporate member of the
Woodland Trust and regularly supports
the National Trust.

Applications: The company has stated
that it is currently not considering any
appeals for donations.

Tate & Lyle plc

Sugar Quay, Lower Thames Street,
London EC3R 6DQ

Tel: 0171-626 6525

Correspondent: G D Down, Assistant
Company Secretary

Charitable donations: £877,000
(1996/97)

Nature of business: Refining and
marketing sugar, syrups and other
sweeteners and starches.

Policy: The company gave the following
breakdown of its community support in
its 1996/97 annual report: education and
youth 35%; civic and environment 30%;
health and welfare 19%; arts 16%.
Grants to national and local organisations
range from £250 to £10,000. Registered

charitable status is desirable, but not
essential, for recipient organisations.
Donations are made through the Charities
Aid Foundation. The company has
sponsored the UK launch of the
Programme for Belize and is matching its
employees' contributions towards this
project with the aim of acquiring 160,000
acres of forest in Belize for conservation.

Applications: All appeals go through head
office and should be addressed to the
correspondent. Sponsorship proposals
should be addressed to D M Dale.

Taylor Woodrow plc

4 Dunraven Street, London W1Y 3FG
Tel: 0171-629 1201
Correspondent: Administrator, Taylor
Woodrow Charitable Trust
Charitable donations: £110,000 (1997)
Nature of business: Housing, property
and construction.

Policy: The company gives donations
primarily through the Taylor Woodrow
Charitable Trust which was endowed by
the company. It is the policy of the trust to
support mainly UK registered charities
operating on a national basis with the
environment/heritage being one of several
preferred areas of support.

Applications: In writing to the
correspondent.

Tesco plc

Tesco House, Delamare Road, Cheshunt,
Hertfordshire EN8 9SL
Tel: 01992-632222
Correspondent: Linda Marsh, Secretary
to the Charitable Trust
Charitable donations: £1,065,961
(1996/97)
Nature of business: Supermarket retailer.

Policy: Charitable support is channelled
through the Tesco Charitable Trust.
Support is given to national charities and
local community projects in areas of
company presence. Donations are
primarily targeted towards educational

projects and charities working for the welfare of children, elderly people and people with disabilities.

Environmental initiatives, although not a main area for support, have included sponsorship of the National Society for Clean Air round table initiative on cleaner automobile fuels, to examine the contribution clean fuels can make to reducing air pollution. The company has also embarked on a joint venture with the RSPB to help to save the skylark. The package consists of £100,000 a year (potentially for three years) to fund conservation action by the RSPB, including research and survey work, provision of advice to the farming community and policy, advocacy and public awareness campaigns.

Applications: In writing to the correspondent.

Texaco Ltd

1 Westferry Circus, Canary Wharf, London E14 4HA
Tel: 0171-719 3000
Correspondent: Paul Bray, Public Relations Manager
Charitable donations: £54,226 (1996)
Nature of business: Oil industry.

Policy: The company prefers to support local charities in areas where it operates, in the fields of children and youth, education, environment and the arts. It chooses to support activities, projects and organisations which bring long-term benefits.

Applications: Applications should be made in writing and sent to the address above, to the relevant contact. Charities from the east London/Docklands area should write to David Robinson, General Manager of Company Affairs; Swindon and Pembroke charities should write to Paul Bray, Public Relations Manager, and if you are in the Aberdeen area write to Sean Galvin, Manager of Corporate Communications.

Thames Water plc

Nugent House, Vastern Road, Reading, Berkshire RG1 8DB
Tel: 01734-593690
Correspondent: Julian Le Patourel, Assistant Secretary
Charitable donations: £117,000 (1996/97)
Nature of business: Water and sewerage services.

Policy: The company gives almost exclusively to organisations working in its area of operation (Thames Valley) and charities in which a member of staff is involved. The main exception being an annual grant to WaterAid (£37,000 in 1994/95). Most grants (and money) are given in the fields of recreation and culture, with other preferred areas of support being public health, education, environment and heritage. It will consider supporting projects which deal with the water environment (especially science ponds in schools), the River Thames, water use in homes and gardens, and the civic environment (especially where water is involved). Grants to local organisations range from £150 to £5,000. The RSPB was supported in 1996/97.

Applications: The charity committee meets to consider applications in February and October. Applications should be in writing to the correspondent. Sponsorship proposals should be addressed to Frances Scaddan, Secretary & Legal Department, RBHG.

Unilever

Unilever House, Blackfriars, London EC4P 4BQ
Tel: 0171-822 6303
Correspondent: R A Harcourt, Appeals Committee
Charitable donations: £4,000,000 (1997)
Nature of business: Branded consumer goods.

Policy: Unilever supports a number of environmental organisations and initiatives. It is currently contributing £100,000 a year to the World Wide Fund for Nature, to support a Marine Stewardship Council to halt the decline in global fish stocks. In 1996/97, it was one of the sponsors of the Young Environmentalist of the Year Awards (£7,700). It is also a partner in the Mersey Basin Campaign and supports organisations such as CPRE and the Green Alliance, as well as local Groundwork and Wildlife Trusts. Unilever supports the upkeep of the Port Sunlight village (founded as a model community for the Lever workers and now a major tourist attraction on the Wirral).

Applications: In writing to the correspondent. R A Harcourt is responsible for corporate sponsorship while the individual company marketing directors are responsible for brand sponsorship. A donations committee meets quarterly. Local appeals should be addressed to the local plant or branch. A J George is responsible for education liaison.

United Utilities PLC

Dawson House, Great Sankey, Warrington WA5 3LW
Tel: 01925-234000
Fax: 01925-233364
Correspondent: Sandra Palmer, Communications Manager
Charitable donations: £814,986 (1996/97)
Nature of business: Water industry and electricity supply.

Policy: The company will work in partnership with organisations for mutual benefit to protect and improve the environment in areas that are relevant to the company business.

Environmental initiatives include supporting a partnership between North West Water, the Environment Agency and the Mersey basin campaign, a 25 year programme to clean up the River Mersey system. Partnerships have also been established with organisations such as Wildlife Trusts, Wildfowl & Wetland Trust, BTCV, Forests for the Community, RSPB, Groundwork, Landlife and the Peak and Lake District National Parks.

Applications: In writing to the correspondent.

Waste Management International plc

3 Shortlands, Hammersmith International Centre, London W6 8RX
Tel: 0181-563 7000
Correspondent: Angela Paleomwiliges, Secretary in Corporate Affairs
Charitable donations: £94,000 (1996)
Nature of business: Waste management and related services.

Policy: The company has some preference for charities related to the environment, the field in which it operates. They do however support a range of other charities. UK Waste Management Ltd are one of the major business sponsors of Waste Watch. In 1995/96, it supported the Cycler outreach project, the Affordable Solutions conference and a special version of the publication Good Riddance. The company also sponsors the UK WasteSavers programme working with Groundwork Foundation to involve young people in identifying ways to reduce waste in their community and school.

Applications: In writing to the correspondent.

Wessex Water plc

Wessex House, Passage Street, Bristol BS2 0JQ
Tel: 0117-929 0611
Correspondent: Alan Crofts, Company Secretary
Charitable donations: £109,000 (1996/97)
Nature of business: Water and sewerage services.

Policy: The company supports registered charities operating in the area administered by Wessex Water plc. In addition to direct donations, £35,000 was given by way of sponsorship to local, environmental and water-related activities and gifts in kind. This includes support for nature conservation trusts.

Applications: In writing to the correspondent. The Community Involvement Committee meets monthly.

Whitbread plc

Chiswell Street, London EC1Y 4SD
Tel: 0171-606 4455
Fax: 0171-615 1009
Correspondent: I S Anderson, Community Investment Programme Manager
Charitable donations: £721,233 (1996/97)
Nature of business: Food, drinks and leisure company.

Policy: The company supports a wide range of charities, through its charitable trust, under six broad headings: medical and health; welfare; education; humanities; environmental resources; and the arts. Each year the company highlights a number of priority areas to support, which may vary slightly from year to year. A priority is also given to local appeals in areas where the company has a strong trading and employment presence (donations of around £200 are given to charities when staff members or pensioners are involved). The typical level of support for local appeals is £50 to £500. Appeals should be initially directed to the Company's Charity Co-ordinator who will consult with a Regional Community Affairs director on the merit of each application.

Initiatives in 1996 included a fundraising promotion on behalf of the Countryside Foundation. The Wayside Inns division organised local walks to raise funds to supply copies of an educational resource pack for 7-11 year olds (The Lychford File) for local schools. Whitbread is also one of the sponsors of the Young Environmentalist of the Year Awards (£7,700).

Whitbread is an acknowledged leader in the encouragement, support and recognition of employee volunteers, and has 35 operational site committees across its various businesses. For the past 14 years it has run the Whitbread Volunteer Action Awards to promote volunteering and raise public awareness of volunteering generally. Awards of £1,000 are made to winners from Wales, Scotland, Northern Ireland and seven English regions, as well as the Young Volunteer Award and the Changemaker Award for schoolchildren. In partnership with the Home Office these Awards are now being extended to recognise organisations supporting volunteers.

Applications: All appeals must be made in writing accompanied by a copy of the organisations current annual report and accounts and should be sent to Paul Patten, Charities Co-ordinator. Appeals should initially be directed to the Company's Charity Co-ordinator who will consult with a Regional Community Affairs Director or Regional Education Manager on the merit of each application. The company has 10 regional Community Affairs Directors who are responsible for promoting and implementing the company's involvement with local communities.

Wickes plc

Wickes House, 120–138 Station Road, Harrow, Essex HA1 2QB
Tel· 0181-901 2000
Fax: 0181-424 9937
Correspondent: Karina Donaghey, Personal Assistant to the Managing Director
Charitable donations: £69,000 (1996)
Nature of business: DIY retail.

Policy: The company prefers to support projects by awarding gifts in kind and cash donations to support local charities in areas of company presence. The company remains the principal sponsor of Project Barito Ulu, in the Kalimantan province of Indonesia. The project is supported by the Indonesian Ministry of Forestry, the Smithsonian Institute and Cambridge University, and is investigating the regeneration of tropical forests and related issues. It has supported the project for eight years..

Applications: In writing to the correspondent.

John Wood Group plc

John Wood House, Greenwell Road, East
Tullos, Aberdeen AB12 3AX
Tel: 01224-851000
Correspondent: Shirley Muir, Head of
Corporate Communications
Charitable donations: £48,000 (1996)
Nature of business: Engineering, oilfield
logistics and supplies.

Policy: The company only supports local
community projects in areas of company
presence and projects in which employees
are directly involved. Grants range from
£50 to £10,000, but may more often be for
around £1,000. In general the company
will consider supporting charities which fall
into seven categories, one of which is
conservation projects. Donations are
dependent on existing local government
support and towards specific needs which
would not normally be met by central
funds. They should not be obscure causes.

Applications: In writing to the
correspondent.

Woolwich PLC

Watling Street, Bexleyheath, Kent
DA6 7RR
Tel: 0181-298 5000
Fax: 0181-298 4737
Correspondent: Gail Johnson, Public
Relations Co-ordinator
Charitable donations: £449,000 (1996)
Nature of business: Banking and financial
services.

Policy: The society's Community
Involvement Programme provides support
for national charities and organisations
within the areas of the head offices in
south east London and north Kent. The
society will consider appeals for funding
and resources for projects submitted by
charities, voluntary organisations, and
educational organisations, situated within
the above areas. The major community
affairs programme covers enterprise and
the built environment, education and the
national curriculum, and training for
unemployed people.

Specific donations to charitable and
voluntary bodies cover wide interests: help
for disadvantaged young people and
elderly people; medical projects and
appeals of national importance; building;
housing and conservation concerns. It
prefers to support specified projects rather
than core funding. Grants to national
organisations up to £20,000, and to local
organisations up to £5,000.

Support has been given to Kent Thames-
side Groundwork Trust, Kent
Environment Newspaper and Kent
Schools 'Green' Envelope Scheme. In
1996/97, the company was one of the
sponsors of the Young Environmentalist of
the Year Awards (£5,000) and supported
the Tidy Britain Group.

Applications: In writing to the
correspondent. Applications should specify
the project for support and give full
information on the funding required.

Yorkshire Bank plc

20 Merrion Way, Leeds LS2 8NZ
Tel: 0113-247 2000
Correspondent: The Secretary, Yorkshire
Bank Charitable Trust
Charitable donations: £148,000
(1995/96)
Nature of business: Banking.

Policy: The donations of £148,000
include those made directly by the bank
and those made through the Yorkshire
Bank Charitable Trust. Recipients must be
registered charities and within the area
covered by branches of the bank i.e. in
England from north of the Thames Valley
to Newcastle-upon-Tyne. Charities
considered for support include those
engaged in youth work, facilities for less
able-bodied and mentally disabled people,
counselling and community work in
depressed areas, with some support also
being given for the arts and education.

The trustees are unlikely to make more
than one donation to a charity within any
12 month period. Grants are usually one-
off for a specific project or part of a
project, ranging from £100 to £1,000.

In 1996, the trust had an income of £240,000 including £200,000 from donations and gifts. Grants totalled £122,000 including the categories: buildings £1,250; conservation/environment £11,102.

The bank also helps schools to stimulate interest in extra-curricula activities through a conservation grants award scheme administered by the British Trust for Conservation Volunteers. This scheme is available to all schools operating a Yorkshire Bank Savings Scheme. Schools involved in environmental or conservation projects undertaken on school premises may apply for grants of up to £100 and additional special cash awards are made for projects of particular merit.

Applications: In writing to the correspondent, including relevant details of the need the intended project is designed to meet. Grants decisions are made by a donations committee which meets twice a month; responses may take three or four weeks to process. Requests for community involvement should be addressed to the Secretary to the Yorkshire Bank Charitable Trust and for arts sponsorship to the Corporate Communications Manager.

Yorkshire Electricity Group plc

Wetherby Road, Scarcroft, Leeds LS14 3HS
Tel: 0113-289 2123
Tel: 0113-289 5466
Correspondent: Mrs Angela Gault, Community Relations Manager
Charitable donations: £77,740 (1995/96)
Nature of business: Energy utility.

Policy: The company, in common with other regional utility companies, has a preference for local charities in areas of company presence and appeals relevant to company business.

Environmental projects supported recently are: the Poles & Trees Campaign – in which the company aims to plant at least one native tree for everyone of the new 2,000 poles it uses each year to bring electricity supply to homes; Kirklees Countryside Unit – a partnership with Kirklees Metropolitan Borough Council on a programme of environmental education work to promote greater access to the countryside, and a better understanding of tree cycles and local rivers; Kirklees Environmental Awards designed to reward local communities, schools and business for their commitment to the local environment.

Applications: Applications in the form of a sponsorship proposal should be made in September/October for the following financial year budgets (April – March).

Yorkshire Water plc

PO Box 500, Western House, Western Way, Halifax Road, Bradford BD6 2LZ
Tel: 01274-691111
Correspondent: Cheryl Wright, Community & Education Manager
Charitable donations: £100,000 (1996/97)
Nature of business: Water and sewerage services.

Policy: The annual budget is divided between charitable giving and sponsorship. Support is given to a wide range of appeals, especially water-related, from Yorkshire and North Humberside, the only exception being support for WaterAid. Preferred areas of support are children and youth, social welfare, environment, arts and water-based sports. Grants range from £10 to £20,000 and in previous years have included £12,600 to the National Trust, as part of a five year commitment totalling £63,000, to fund an education centre at Fountains Abbey, and £3,000 to Yorkshire Wildlife Trust.

Support is also given through the company's environmental awards scheme.
Together with the Environment Agency and English Nature, the company has undertaken a four year study and management plan of the River Derwent. The river supplies 10% of Yorkshire's drinking water, but is also an important wetland habitat.

Applications: In writing to the correspondent.

CHAPTER SEVEN

Other Grants & Award Schemes

INTRODUCTION

This section covers two different types of support. Firstly, grants available from independent non-governmental organisations whose main function is not grant-making; and secondly, award schemes and competitions run by various organisations. The existence of the latter often depends on the promotional and publicity policies of sponsoring companies. Some run for several years; some for only one year.

We have aimed to cover the more established schemes and those which appear to have a good chance of continuing. Some reward work completed; others provide grants on the basis of project proposals. It is important to check before applying.

ALPHABETICAL INDEX OF GRANTS & AWARDS

INDEX BY BENEFICIAL AREA

This index shows the *main* areas other awards and grants cover but does not necessarily mean that they exclude other categories.

OTHER GRANTS & AWARD SCHEMES

Age Resource Awards

Age Resource, 1268 London Road,
London SW16 4ER
Tel: 0181-679 2201; Fax: 0181-679 6069
Contact: Emma Aldridge

Policy: 1997 was the seventh year of these awards, sponsored by Unigate, which recognise the achievements of people still going strong after 50 years. There are five categories, all of which relate to projects involving volunteers over 50 years old, in their design and management.

The category of relevance to this guide is Environment Action. This covers initiatives which encourage adults and children to work together on the renewal and conservation of urban and rural areas.

Applications are divided into seven regions, with regional winners from each category receiving £250 and a citation. One project from each category than receives a national award worth £1,000. The regions are:
- Midlands, Wales and East Anglia
- North East and Yorkshire
- North West (including Cumbria)
- Scotland
- Northern Ireland
- South East and London
- South West and Channel Islands.

Applications: Information is available from the address above.

Association for the Protection of Rural Scotland (APRS)

Gladstone's Land, 3rd Floor, 483 Lawnmarket, Edinburgh EH1 2NT
Tel: 0131-225 7012/3; Fax: 0131-225 6592
Contact: Awards Administrator

Policy: The association started an annual award scheme in 1975 to mark European Architectural Heritage Year. The purpose of the scheme is to encourage good planning, architecture and landscape, and to recognise particularly fine examples of structures, reclamation sites or works, newly-built or renovated, in a rural setting. These should enhance Scotland's natural heritage and be in harmony with their landscape setting. The awards take the form of plaques and diplomas.

Applications: The deadline for entries is the end of May and awards are presented in October. All entries are visited by the judges.

Best Kept Village Competitions

CPRE, Warwick House, 25 Buckingham Palace Road, London SW1W 0PP
Tel: 0171-235 9481

Policy: Best Kept Village competitions are organised in virtually every shire county in England and Wales – in most cases by the county rural community council or county branch of the Council for the Protection of Rural England. Some district councils also run equivalent competitions. Most county competitions are sponsored by Calor Gas Ltd.

The competitions are designed to encourage rural communities to maintain and improve the local environment and to foster community spirit. They are not intended to reward "the most beautiful, most ancient or most picturesque – just the best kept". The awards themselves are usually a sign or plaque which is held for a year and either a modest cash prize or goods such as a bench, bulbs or trees. There may be specific categories for particular areas such as churchyards, or buildings such as village halls. The competitions are increasingly sensitive to conservation requirements (e.g. grass is not always expected to mown short) and some include a special Conservation Award for particular environmental improvements.

Applications: Entry is normally on a simple form, usually available in early Spring. Parish councils, amenity services, women's institutes and other community groups may enter "their" village or town. Judging takes place through the summer.

Black Environment Network

UK Office, 9 Llainwen Uchaf, Llanberis, Gwynedd, Wales LL55 4LL
Tel: 01286-870715
Contact: Pam Green, Co-ordinator
Grant total: £1,000 (1996/97)

Policy: The Network aims to inform, support, link and represent the wishes of the ethnic minority communities in environmental action. It provides a range of training, advice, information and consultancy services and works to develop partnerships with national organisations.

It also operates the Ethnic Minorities Award Scheme, which supports environmental projects that have a significant number of participants from ethnic communities.

EMAS operates as:

1. An advice service sign-posting ethnic minority environmental projects to other sources of funds or support.
2. A small grant scheme giving grants only to:
 ♦ innovative projects which are unlikely to gain support from other large grant schemes.
 ♦ initiatives which need small amounts of money urgently in order to spur strategic developments.

Grants range from £50 to £500, averaging £150. Projects supported have included grants towards involving young people in particular localities to take part in environmental youth exchange in Europe at short notice, a heating unit urgently needed for winter for a conservatory project for black elderly in Wandsworth towards the end of the financial year when funds have run out in most grant schemes, a trip for a youth leader from Sheffield to meet with nature reserve wardens in North Wales to familiarise himself with facilities and opportunities available for young people there, exhibition materials for an Asian youth project wishing to share their experience of an environmental exploratory trip to Pakistan.

Applications: Initially in writing to the correspondent.

British Ecological Society

26 Blades Court, Deodar Road, Putney, London SW15 2NU
Tel: 0181-871 9797; Fax: 0181-871 9779
Contact: The Executive Secretary

Policy: The society has several award schemes, each with the aim of promoting ecology and research as widely as possible. Many relatively small awards are made, together totalling about £45,000.

1. Small ecological project grants

To promote all aspects of ecological research and ecological survey. Grants are given to individuals rather than organisations. Grants are not normally given for expeditions, since this is covered by a separate scheme.

Up to £1,000 may be given, to cover for example, travel costs, the employment of short-term assistance, equipment costs etc. Grants are not given to full-time students or to cover your own wages. Closing dates are January 1st, April 1st, July 1st and October 1st.

2. Research travel grants

To cover travel from the UK or Irish Republic to another country or vice versa. Funding is available for any type of work so long as the research is not part of a degree course. Grants are made on the basis of scientific merit, research record, experience and publication record.

The maximum grant is £2,500 and can cover all or part of the costs of travel, subsistence and insurance, together with a contribution to a "bench fee" charged by host organisations. Closing dates: March 1st and September 1st.

3. Research grants for schools

Grants can be given to teachers for research in schools which involves the pupils. The grants are intended to cover any special equipment costs, but the equipment will become the property of the society rather than the school. The maximum grant is £750. Closing dates: January 31st, April 30th and September 30th.

4. Expedition grants

These cover costs of expeditions that further the education of young ecologists by extending experience overseas. Expeditions must consist of at least three people who are preferably undergraduates or sixth form students. The maximum grant is £1,000. Closing date January 31st.

Applications: Each of the programmes has a number of other specific guidelines and an application form, available from the correspondent.

The council considers applications at its quarterly meetings.

BT Countryside for All Awards and Grants

The Fieldfare Trust, 67a The Wicker, Sheffield S3 8HT
Tel: 0114-270 1668; Fax: 0114-276 7900

Policy: The Fieldfare Trust promotes countryside recreation and access for people with disabilities and manages the BT Countryside for All Awards and Grants schemes.

Awards are given to existing projects which demonstrate good practice in access provision. You can apply for an award to celebrate the work you've done to date and, if successful, receive further publicity for your project.

Grants are financial contributions to new or on-going projects which are designed to improve countryside access for everyone. There is about £165,000 available under the scheme for 1997/98.

Applications: On a form available from the Fieldfare Trust.

Community Enterprise Scheme – RIBA

66 Portland Place, London W1N 4AD
Tel: 0171-580 5533
Contact: Bernadette Hammerson-Wood

Policy: These annual awards recognise the achievements of local people who are working to improve the quality of life in their communities. This is an annual competition to highlight, encourage and publicise the most imaginative development initiatives, particularly where local enthusiasm and drive has been advanced with support, assistance or advice from all sectors of the community including local residents, voluntary organisations, businesses and professions, and local authorities.

Entries are invited from England, Northern Ireland, Scotland and Wales.

Awards are made in six categories:
- The Chartwell Land/HACT Award for Housing and Homelessness
- The Community Enterprise Award for Community Buildings
- The Marks & Spencer Award for Community Services
- The Times Award for Improvements to the Local Environment
- The United Biscuits Award for Business Development & Training
- The Touche Ross Award for Young Enterprise

In addition, there is a special award, supported by the RDC, for the best example of an initiative which addresses a particular rural issue.

A wide range of projects is eligible, including refurbishment and renovation, urban farms and environmental improvements. Specific categories (and their sponsors) and the level of awards (cash) vary from year to year.

Applications: On a form available from the correspondent, together with supporting material including a feasibility study if possible.

Co-op Care Grants Scheme

PO Box 53, New Century House, Manchester M60 4ES
Tel: 0161-834 1212
Contact: David Croft, Manager, Customer Services Department

Policy: This scheme, started in 1992, is run and funded by Co-operative Wholesale Society Ltd. It provides grants totalling £150,000 for voluntary groups in the UK, aiming to encourage the groups to carry out projects in a way which will benefit the community.

Grants range from £500 to £5,000. There are five categories of support, one of which is for organisations trying to make improvements to the general environment of their community. The projects could include saving endangered species, organising a recycling scheme, renovating historical buildings, wildlife conservation or forming an environmental action group. "We are looking for new, exciting ideas to help the environment locally."

Applications: On a form available from the correspondent. The closing date is the end of July each year.

Council for the Care of Churches

Fielden House, Little College Street, London SW1P 3SH
Tel: 0171-222 3793
Contact: Dr Thomas Cocke, Secretary
Grant total: About £200,000 a year

Policy: The Council is a permanent Commission of the Church of England's governing body, the General Synod. Its main function is to help the parishes and guide and co-ordinate the work of the local (diocesan) committees for the care of churches.

It has a statutory duty to provide information and views on the architectural and historic qualities of every church being considered for redundancy, and to provide advice if requested in particular cases, especially those involving demolition, or the proposed alienation of historic treasures. As well as the care of ancient buildings, the Council is also concerned with the encouragement of contemporary arts and design.

The Council offers grants for the conservation of important furnishings and fittings in Anglican churches. These include bells and clocks, organs, metalwork, monuments, paintings, books and manuscripts, textiles, woodwork and furniture and wall paintings.

The Council also advises English Heritage, the Heritage Lottery Fund and other bodies on funding in these categories.

Applications: Application forms are only made available when outline information concerning a particular case has been received. Potential applicants should check the dates of the committee dealing with the specific category of interest, as they only meet once or twice a year.

Dulux Community Projects

PO Box 343, London WC2E 8RJ
Contact: Dulux Community Projects Office

Policy: This well-established scheme provides community groups with free paint – around £180,000 worth is given away each year. The scheme is designed to "provide help and encouragement to recognised voluntary groups who wish to carry out painting projects for the benefit of the community". The only requirement is that the painting is done by unpaid volunteers.

In addition, cash awards are made to twenty selected projects which offer "the greatest potential in terms of creativity and benefit to the community".

Applications: On the official application form (available on receipt of a 49p A4-sized sae) which specify exact requirements in terms of type of paint, colour and quantity. The form is available from Easter to May with the closing date for receipt of application forms being the end of May/early June.

Enventure Ltd

Ilkley, Otley, North Yorkshire
Tel: 01943-850089
Contact: Dr Maggie Bignall, Director

A group of non-profit companies, Enventure Ltd, Enventure Northern Ltd Enventure Southern and Yorventure, have been set up covering different parts of the country to act as professional fund managers for the companies contributing to the Landfill Tax Credit Scheme. They apparently organise the arrangements for appropriate organisations and projects to receive funding.

Each company handles the quarterly payments made from the credit scheme for a number of landfill companies except for Enventure Northern Ltd which handles credits for just one operator in Humberside.

A figure of the total annual funding via these organisations was not available but the funding from Enventure Northern is thought to be about £1.5 million a year.

Applications: Environmental organisations should contact the address above to find out about funding via these intermediaries.

Environmental funding schemes from Landfill Tax Credit
see Enventure and Wildlife Trusts

Europa Nostra Awards

Lange Voorhout 35, 2514 EC The Hague, Netherlands
Tel: +31 70 35 60 333;
Fax: +31 70 36 17 865
Contact: Marijnke de Jong, Awards Officer

Policy: Europa Nostra/IBI is a European association of non-governmental organisations active in the field of heritage. The main aims are the protection and enhancement of the European cultural heritage, both architectural and natural, as well as the encouragement of high standards of architecture and of town and country planning in the service of the European heritage.

One of its activities is the organisation of the Europa Nostra Award Scheme, which recognises projects which make a distinguished contribution to the conservation and enhancement of Europe's architectural and natural heritage.

Eligible projects include the restoration of buildings; the adaptation of old buildings to new uses, preserving their original character; the restoration and conservation of parks and gardens as well as preservation of landscape, having a particular cultural or historical value; and new construction in conservation areas, harmonising sympathetically with the older environment, or which pays due respect to the environment in areas of outstanding natural beauty.

They are open to both the private and commercial sector and from national, regional and local authorities.

Recognition can be given in two categories: medals for the most outstanding entries and diplomas for the other winners. In addition, all award winners will receive a wall plaque.

Applications: On a form available from the correspondent. The deadline for entries is normally the 1st of June.

Fauna and Flora International

Great Eastern House, Tenison Road, Cambridge CB1 2DT
Tel: 01223-571000
Contact: Abigail Entwistle, Manager, 100% Fund
Grant total: About £25,000

Policy: The society supports conservation projects worldwide through the 100% Fund. This fund was established to provide grants for projects involving endangered species and/or habitats. Most grants go to support projects outside the UK. They range from about £200 to £5,000.

The society states that special importance is attached to: value in terms of addressing threats to species or area; viability for conservation management and/or education; feasibility in terms of personnel and technique; local involvement, and fundraising and publicity potential and possibility for future follow-up work.

Grants will not be given for: undergraduate expeditions; further education studies or higher degrees; individuals taking part in commercially organised projects. Research will not normally be supported, unless it is clearly shown that it will lead to an immediate conservation benefit.

However, applications seeking support for conservation activities recommended in Action Plans from the Specialist Groups of the IUCN Species Survival Commission are welcome, as are projects involving lesser known or "unpopular" species.

Applications: On a form available from the correspondent. Guidelines for applicants are also available. Potential applicants will be informed of the return date when they are sent a form (which relates to the Conservation Committee meetings). Applicants are informed of the decision about two months after this return date.

Ford European Conservation Awards

1 Kensington Gore, London SW7 2AR
Tel: 0171-823 8842
Contact: Conservation Foundation

Policy: This scheme offers cash prize awards in four categories: natural environment; heritage; young people; conservation engineering.

The awards run in all European countries, with the national winners from each country going forward to the European competition.

In 1996/97, UK winners were:
Natural environment
The Restoration of Radgrave and Lopham Fen, one of the most important wetlands in Britain.
Heritage
◆ Fox Talbot Museum.
◆ Gatton Park – Parkland Restoration.
Engineering
Sustainable Village Project at West Lothian.
Young people
The High Cross of Donaghmore.

Applications: On the form available from the above address. The deadline for applications is normally September.

Glenfiddich Living Scotland Awards

The Glenfiddich Distillery, Dufftown, Nr Keith, Banffshire AB55 4DH

Tel: 01341-820373

Policy: These financial awards were set up in 1985 to help projects involved in the conservation of Scotland's heritage in its widest sense. Environmental projects are considered if they are seen to incorporate sustaining resources and/or are of benefit to the community and/or historical education.

Awards are generally given to smaller projects or identified segments of a large project and can range from £100 to £4,000. About £30,000 is available each year.

Applications: On a form available on written request from the Glenfiddich Distillery. The end of June is the closing date each year, with awards presented in September/October.

Improve Your Local Environment

Keep Scotland Beautiful, 7 Melville Terrace, Stirling ST8 2ND
Tel: 01786-471333
Contact: May Wright

Policy: These annual awards are sponsored by OCS Group Ltd in association with Keep Scotland Beautiful. The Challenge offers awards to local projects which improve the local environment. The projects can range from cleaning up a river bank or school playing field to painting a youth centre or repairing a swing park. Prizes are available to voluntary groups, schools and youth clubs.

Applications: On a form available from the correspondent. The closing date is normally the end of June each year.

Inland Waterways Association (IWA)

114 Regents Park Road, London NW1 8UQ
Tel: 0171-586 2510/2556
Contact: Neil Edwards, Executive Director
Grant total: £44,700 (1996)

Policy: The IWA was funded in 1946 for the retention, conservation, restoration and development of the inland waterways for the fullest possible commercial and recreational use. Grants or loans are made to Canal Trusts and Societies for furthering the above aims.

In 1996, the association had an income of £443,000, over £225,000 of which was from subscriptions and £143,000 from grants and donations. Expenditure totalled £392,000, this included:
Administration £60,000
Publications £51,000
Campaign costs £228,000

This latter figure includes £44,700 given in grants by the National Waterways Restoration & Development Fund. £10,000 was given to Montgomery Canal to which it gives ongoing support (it has received a legacy dedicated to the "Monty"). WRG Ltd received £22,500 with £10,000 to Swansea Canal and £2,000 in other grants. In previous years, grants have totalled £1.3 million with large grants including £384,000 to Montgomery Canal, 267,000 to WRG Ltd and £232,000 to Milton Keynes Projects on the Grand Union Canal.

Applications: In writing to the correspondent. There are no formal criteria and there is no standard application procedure – each case is judged on its merits. IWA's Restoration Committee may visit and give advice to projects seeking support. Applications are reviewed by the council which meets monthly.

Mersey Basin Trust

Sunley Tower, Piccadilly Plaza, Manchester
M1 4AG
Tel: 0161-228 6924
Grant total: £45,000 (1996/97)

Policy: The trust has five current
programmes for making grants, each of
which have their own criteria. With the
exception of the Green Action Grants all
the schemes apply to the whole Mersey
Basin Campaign area (i.e. Merseyside,
Greater Manchester, Cheshire and part of
Lancashire).

Green Action Grants

Contact: Mark Turner at the address above.

These grants are awarded for
environmental improvement activities
carried put by young people under 25 (e.g.
schools, youth organisations) and other
groups. The initiatives should aim to
enhance the environment surrounding the
River Weaver and associated areas in the
Runcorn and Northwich areas. Projects
include:
- studies and improvements to encourage
  wildlife
- creating footpaths and access for people
  with special needs
- improving the area for recreation
- clearing up litter/eyesores
- planting trees and managing woodlands
- organising environmental competitions.

Grants are for up to £1,000. They are
sponsored by ICI Chemicals and
Polymers. In 1996/97, 12 grants were
given totalling £7,300.

Stream Care Project Fund

Contact: Mark Turner at the address above.

Support is given to projects which
encourage the whole community to adopt
and improve their local watercourses. This
can include clearing litter, planting trees
and wildflowers, constructing footpaths,
designing leaflets and signs. 36 projects
received support in 1995/96, with grants
totalling £6,600. They are sponsored by
North West Water, the Environment
Agency and the Countryside Commission.

Waterside Revival Grants

Contact: Gwen White at the above address

Awarded for waterside improvements these
projects must:
- improve the appearance, use and
  management of publicly accessible
  waterside sites
- be organised and substantially carried
  out by local voluntary groups
- actively involve the local community
  and volunteers.

Projects may contribute to: nature
conservation, recreation and tourism,
tackle eyesores, pollution and neglect,
improve access, conserve the built
environment, increase public involvement
in waterside improvement.

Grants may be for up to £1,000. Any
voluntary group working in the
community and involving volunteers on a
project may apply. Eligible items include
building materials, hand tools, plants,
specialist equipment and labour. The costs
of specialist advice, fees, publicity and the
like should not exceed 15% of the grant.
In 1996/97, 31 groups were offered grants
totalling £24,000. However, from 1997
reduced funding of £8,000 a year only, is
available.

Other grants
Some financial assistance is available to
assist schools with travel to carry out river
studies.

Millennium Awards
*see under Lottery Funding,
The Millennium Commission,
for several schemes to support
the work of individuals in
their community e.g. BTCV,
Earthwatch Europe, tec. The
Civic Trust has also started a 3
year scheme –
'Civic Champions'*

National Grid Community 21 Awards

National Grid Community 21 Awards Office, Calverton House, 2 Harpenden Road, St Albans, Hertfordshire AL3 5AB
Tel: 01727-850761
Contact: Nadir Meerza or Sarah Dennis

Policy: This scheme set up initially to run for three years (up to 1999), awards grants of up to £5,000 to help local authorities finance community projects which improve the social, economic and environmental quality of life in their areas and form part of their Local Agenda 21 strategy.

It is open to local authority schemes being run in partnership with groups such as schools, youth organisations, residents associations, local businesses, charities and other voluntary organisations. The awards will go to initiatives judged to be of most benefit to the local community.

Projects must be new schemes or developments of existing schemes, and address sustainability concepts such as efficient use of resources, promotion of good health for all, access to education and employment and caring for nature.

Applications: Must come from Local Agenda 21 co-ordinators. The closing date is 30th September.

Nature's Prize – Scottish Environmental Awards

Loch-na-leoba, Old Glen Road, Newtonmore PH20 1EB
Contact: Dick Balharry

Policy: These annual awards aim to encourage, recognise and reward the best projects working to help Scotland's natural heritage. Community groups, businesses, individuals, schools and groups of volunteers are all eligible to apply.

There are three categories: improving, understanding and enjoying the natural heritage (further details below). Nine chosen projects (three from each category) are the subject of a television programme broadcast across Scotland. Each receives 3600 to continue and expand their project. The winning project from each category also receives an award.

1. Improving Scotland's natural heritage

For projects which restore neglected habitats or areas of degradation, or enhance the quality of the Scottish natural heritage. For example, managing a native woodland for nature conservation, creating a patch of natural habitat from an old area of urban wasteland or simply improving the area around your office for wildlife.

2. Understanding Scotland's natural heritage

For projects which promote education and understanding of the Scottish natural heritage. For example, a drama production with an environmental theme, an information trail for local people or making a video or display about wildlife, habitats or landscape.

3. Enjoying Scotland's natural heritage

Projects which encourage public participation and enjoyment of the Scottish natural heritage. For example, organising a nature walk or programme of events, improving access to a local beauty spot or running an environmental playgroup for the children in your area.

Applications: On the official entry form.

NI2000

Nore Villa, 16 Knockbracken Health Care Park, Saintfield Road, Belfast BT8 8BH
Tel: 01232-403 779
Contact: Brendan McSherry

NI2000 is a charity set up to encourage and help groups and individuals to carry out projects which benefit the environment and the local community. It is a partnership of councils, government, business and voluntary organisations. Its funding is predominantly from government sources and in 1997/98 it received a total of £61,000-£41,000 from the Training & Employment Agency and £20,000 from the Environment and Heritage Service.

It is funded primarily to help job creation and environmental work by voluntary groups. It provides advice and guidance, and a networking service with other groups, as well as small start-up grants up to a maximum of £500. Work eligible for a grant must:

+ involve a specific practical environmental activity;
+ involve CWP or volunteer labour;
+ demonstrate community and environmental benefit.

Exclusions: Purchase of land or buildings.

Applications: For further information and help with completing the application form contact the Project Officer at the address above.

Pride of Place Awards

See The David Knightly Charitable Trust

RIAS Scottish Community Projects Fund

The Royal Incorporation of Architects in Scotland, 15 Rutland Square, Edinburgh EH1 2BE
Tel: 0131-229 7545; Fax: 0131-228 2188

Policy: This fund gives grants to community led organisations to employ an architect or other professional to produce a feasibility study for building and environmental improvement projects or employment initiatives.

Grants are for half the cost of the feasibility study, normally up to £1,500 (including VAT), but up to a maximum of £3,000.

Projects can include refurbishment, renovation, new building and associated landscape works, environmental projects, community plans and employment generating projects.

Applications: On a form available from the correspondent.

RICS Conservation Awards

Royal Institution of Chartered Surveyors, 12 Great George Street, Parliament Square, London SW1P 3AD
Tel: 0171-222 7000
Contact: Miriam Simpson, Communications Executive

Policy: The RICS runs a yearly Conservation Award Scheme designed to encourage and recognise outstanding achievement in the fields of conservation and enhancement of the built and natural environment. The nine categories range from Craftsmanship in Building Conservation to Efficient Building and Urban Renewal.

Applications: On an entry form available from the correspondent. No entry fee is required.

Right Livelihood Awards

PO Box 15072, S-10465 Stockholm, Sweden
Contact: Kerstin Bennett, Administrative Director

Policy: Introduced in 1980, these awards are to "honour and support those working on practicable and replicable solutions to the real problems facing us today". They recognise "vision and work contributing to making life more whole, healing our planet and uplifting humanity".

Nominations for the awards, which are made to individuals and organisations, may be made by anyone in the world. The awards involve cash to be shared by several recipients for specific projects and non-monetary recognition to an individual or individuals.

In 1997, the award of about US$240,000 was shared by five individuals from four continents for their contributions to a sustainable future for humanity, including ground-breaking work on people-centred development, nuclear dangers, toxic chemicals and nature conservation.

Applications: Further information is available from the address above.

Royal Institute for British Architects

PO Box 640, Newcastle-upon-Tyne NE99 1QY
Tel: 0191-232 9292
Contact: Joanne Watson, Administrator, Community Architecture Resource Centre

Policy: The Community Architecture Group of RIBA operates a Community Projects Fund to provide small grants for community-led organisations which want to employ an architect or other professional to produce a feasibility study for a building or environmental improvement project. Grants are available for projects in England only.

Schemes assisted have included housing (refurbishments, self build, new build), business workshops and managed workspaces, improvements to parks and playgrounds, church conversions to community use, community centres, village halls, city farms, sports and leisure projects and community arts centres.

Successful applicants receive a grant to cover 50% of the cost of a feasibility study, normally up to £1,000 inclusive of VAT but with a maximum grant of £3,000. The grant is not dependent upon the applicant finding the matching 50% but is a contribution towards the cost of the professional adviser's fee. Support is targeted to those projects considered unlikely to proceed without a CPF grant.

Applications: On the official application form. Grants are made throughout the year. The panel meets every six weeks to consider applications. Grants are paid on receipt of a copy of the invoice and the feasibility study. Guidelines for applicants and a leaflet on the scheme are available from the address above.

There is a network of regional co-ordinators able to advise on applications and the seeking of professional help. Contact names and addresses are available from the RIBA Community Architecture Resource Centre.

Rural Initiatives Scotland

Rural Forum, Highland House, St Catherine's Road, Perth PH1 5RY
Tel: 01738-634565
Contact: Sue Sadler, Head of Management Services

Policy: This is a small grant scheme supported by Shell UK Ltd and local authorities and administered by the Scottish Council for Voluntary Organisations and Rural Forum Scotland. It awards enabling grants up to a maximum of £1,000.

Projects must be new initiatives, and applications must be from non-commercial and non-statutory bodies in villages, townships or rural areas with a population of up to 2,000. Schemes must be administered by voluntary organisations recognised as charities.

Applications: The scheme for 1998 will be launched in August with the final date for applications being some time in January 1999. An application form is available from the correspondent.

Rural Wales Awards

Campaign for the Protection of Rural Wales, Ty Gwyn, 31 High Street, Welshpool. Powys SY21 7YD
Tel: 01938-552525

Policy: The Rural Wales Awards are given to county branches of CPRW for "practically anything that promotes environmental good practice, or displays design that is in harmony with the landscape, or that has served to restore an important landscape feature (natural or man-made) or that is innovative or promotes better environmental awareness and understanding". The awards do not involve cash prizes, but a wooden plaque and framed certificate.

Applications: Information will automatically be forwarded to CPRW county branches.

Shell Better Britain Campaign

Victoria Works, 21a Graham Street, Birmingham B1 3JR
Tel: 0121-212 9221
Contact: Peter Woodward, Campaign Manager
Grant total: £210,000 (1997)

Policy: The campaign, now over 25 years old, encourages "action by local people to improve the quality of life at neighbourhood level, in ways which respect the earth's resources", through the provision of information, advice and grant aid. There are two funds that make grants.

Grants of up to £2,000 totalling £160,000 (1997) are made from the Community Projects Fund for neighbourhood initiatives that benefit both the community and the environment. Most practical projects that will result in tangible improvement to the local environment are eligible for support and any community-based voluntary group may apply. The main requirements are that the project must be organised by a local group and be substantially carried out by volunteers, that it must be of benefit to the wider community, and that it must be capable of being completed within 12 months of receipt of the grant.

Grants up to £10,000 totalling £50,000 (1997) are made from the Partnership Innovation Fund for joint research/action projects that improve under-standing and test ideas about sustainable development at community level.

A free network supplies those who join with an information pack, a bimonthly newsletter and case studies.

Applications: On a form available from the correspondent.

Silver Lapwing Awards

Farming & Wildlife Advisory Group, NAC, Stoneleigh, Kenilworth, Warwickshire CV8 2RX
Tel: 01203-696699
Contact: Kate Bradshaw, Marketing Manager

Policy: These awards (formerly known as Farming & Wildlife Awards) are offered to farmers who have done most to encourage wildlife conservation on their farms within the constraints of successful commercial farming. Judges aim to ensure small farms are given equal opportunities with large farms, and arable with livestock.

Awards take the form of a cash prize, and for the winner a trophy.

Applications: On a form available from the correspondent, which should be sent to the local county Farming and Wildlife Advisory Group. The deadline for entries has been May.

Transco Grassroots 1998 Environmental Sponsorship Scheme

c/o Kallaways Ltd, 2 Portland Road, London W11 4LA
Tel: 0171-221 7883
Contact: Transco Grassroots Administration

Policy: This is a competitive sponsorship scheme offering money for planned conservation and environmental projects in England, Scotland and Wales. It is open to individual secondary and middle schools, conservation charities and community groups.

A total of £120,000 is available. The maximum award is £7,500. Typical projects eligible for funding range from improving pathways, restoring natural habitats, to creating city farms or environmental facilities for disabled people.

Applications: The entry brochure will be mailed to 7,000 schools and 3,000 voluntary groups and charities. An independent panel of judges includes senior figures from the environmental sector, media and education.

The entry period is April to May, with judging in June. Winners are notified in July.

Tree Council

51 Catherine Place, London SW1E 6DY
Tel: 0171-828 9928; Fax: 0171-828 9060
Contact: Robert Osborne, Director

Policy: The Tree Council has limited funds available to help well-planned tree planting projects and is keen to support local groups and individuals who seek to beautify their neighbourhood through the imaginative use and care of trees.

Applicants may be a voluntary organisation, school, parish or community council or a private individual. Projects should ideally be on land to which the public has access, or at least provide public benefit from an improved landscape. Projects for tree banks will be considered if the trees are intended for eventual use on public land. Applicants must ensure that adequate arrangements have been made for proper maintenance.

Eligible expenses include the cost of trees, labour for planting, fencing and any necessary supports to establishment, such as stakes and fertiliser.

Some direct contribution to the project is expected from the promoter, either in money or labour, preferably both. Grants are limited to a stated maximum figure or to 50% (75% for schools) of the eligible costs actually incurred, whichever is the lower. Applicants must therefore ensure they can meet the other 50% (25% for schools) of the funds to complete the project. Payment is conditional upon production of evidence that expenditure has been incurred within 12 months of the offer of a grant.

Applications: On a form available from the correspondent. This should be returned by 31st July for autumn projects.

Wessex Watermark Awards

The Conservation Foundation, 1 Kensington Gore, London SW7 2AR
Tel: 0171-823 8842; Fax: 0171-823 8791

Policy: Wessex Watermark was launched in 1993 in association with Wessex Water Plc. It helps finance environmental projects which have links with water in Somerset, Wiltshire, Avon and Dorset. 40 awards were given in 1996/97 ranging from £150 to £1,000.

Many of the organisations supported were schools with awards also given to a canal amenity group, parish council, Dorset Wildlife Trust, a scout association and a playgroup. Projects included various activities concerned with ponds, planting trees for protective screening, creating wheelchair access, work on a canal foot bridge and an education pack on rivers and ponds.

Applications: On a form available from the correspondent.

Whitbread Action Earth

CSV Environment, 17 Midland Road, St Pauls, Bristol BS2 0JT
Tel: 0117-908 1100
Contact: Sue Mennear

Policy: Action Earth is a seasonal campaign aimed at reducing the environmental damage caused during the festive season. It aims to encourage the launch of new environmental projects on the theme of "A Green Christmas".

The programme offers grants of up to £50 to voluntary organisations. Projects range from recycling Christmas cards, paper and trees to practical environmental improvements and educational programmes.

Applications: Application forms are available towards the end of the year.

The Wildlife Trusts – Biffaward Fund and ARC Environment Fund

RSNC, The Green, Witham Park, Waterside South, Lincoln LN5 7JR
Tel: 01522-574534; Fax: 01522-511616; E-mail: grants@wildlife-trusts.compulink.co.uk
Contact: Fund Manager

Biffaward Fund

Fund total: £4 million (1998/99)

ARC Environmental Fund

Fund total: £3.5 million (1998/99)

In early 1998 the Wildlife Trusts were administering two separate funding schemes on behalf of Biffa Waste Services Ltd and ARC. Only organisations which are first enrolled with ENTRUST, the regulatory body (see separate entry) can apply to these funds.

Both schemes expect applicants to be able "to provide from a third party 10 percent of the amount requested" which cannot be provided by "an Enrolled Body or a contractor to an Environmental Body". All applications for more than £5,000 must present a monthly cash flow plan for the project as well as a detailed expenditure budget.

Applications: Full guidance notes about each of the schemes and applications forms are available from the address above. Applications for both schemes can be sent at any time and also have to be submitted to its Fund Management Board which meets quarterly.

World Wide Fund for Nature (WWF–UK)

UK Project Management Unit, Panda House, Weyside Park, Catteshall Lane, Godalming, Surrey GU7 1XR
Tel: 01483-426444; Fax: 01483-426409
Contact: Bryony Chapman, UK Projects Officer
Grant total: £1,934,000 (1994/95 – UK Conservation programme)

Policy: The WWF UK Conservation Programme can provide funding for a wide range of conservation projects in addition to land purchase. The aim is to achieve the conservation of nature and ecological processes by:

- preserving genetic, species and ecosystem diversity
- ensuring that the use of renewable natural resources is sustainable now and in the longer term, for the benefit of all life on earth
- promoting actions to reduce to a minimum pollution and the wasteful exploitation and consumption of resources and energy.

The conservation strategic priorities are:

- international species and habitats
- UK's countryside and coasts
- living seas
- lightening the UK's ecological footprint abroad
- linking conservation and human needs
- conservation through partnerships.

Applications are accepted which address elements of these themes, by means of a variety of techniques including: management, research and survey, policy research, lobbying and public awareness initiatives.

Projects are assessed by external panels and grants approved may subsequently be displaced by commercial sponsorship funds.

WWF will normally fund long-term projects for a maximum of three years, with continued funding being conditional upon satisfactory progress in the preceding period. Longer funding periods will be considered in exceptional circumstances. Applications for less than £500 are not normally considered.

The WWF aims to match funds secured from other sources such as the statutory agencies. Applicants are always encouraged to look for funding elsewhere. Organisations are expected to approach bodies such as the Countryside Commission, English Nature, Countryside Council for Wales, Scottish Natural

Heritage, before or at the same time, as an approach is made to WWF UK. It is unlikely that WWF will release funds until the results of approaches to these other organisations are known.

Whilst land purchase may be assisted this is now exceptional and only considered for sites of great importance under serious or immediate threat. The maximum level of funding for purchase remains at 25% up to a limit of £5,000. The minimum grant is £1,000. Only a small proportion of grant-aid is now applied for land purchase.

Applications for loans can also be considered. Usually these are for six months, interest free.

Organisations applying for support are expected to supply an organisational development plan or forward strategy for a project to be considered.

All grants are subject to a number of terms and conditions including acknowledgement to WWF, reporting, monitoring and evaluation.

Applications: All applicants are advised to discuss potential projects by telephone before submitting an application. Two forms are available – for the general category and for land purchase. Guidance notes on completing these forms are also produced. Whenever possible, applications should be submitted to, or discussed with, WWF by the end of the year in order to be considered as part of the planning and budgeting process for the Conservation Programme which takes place in the first few months of each year. Nevertheless, applications are still accepted at any time and are eligible for the unprogrammed part of the budget set aside for urgent, unforeseen and innovative projects. These projects are circulated for assessment to the UK Project Allocation Group every other month.

Youth Clubs Scotland

Balfour House, 19 Bonnington Grove, Edinburgh EH6 4BL
Tel: 0131-554 2561; Fax: 0131-555 5223
Contact: Project Co-ordinator

Policy: There are two programmes, sponsored by BP, Scottish Natural Heritage, the National Lottery Charities Board and various trusts for different age groups.

The Grizzly Challenge is for 14-18 year olds, the Gruff Kids for 10 to 13 year olds. Both schemes are open to any group of 3 to 5 young people in Scotland. Grants of £100 are available, and participating teams are funded to appoint a support worker to provide guidance and support. All participating teams win a residential adventure experience and the winning team in each age group will receive a holiday of a lifetime.

Projects have included redecorating community halls, clearing paths, building children's playgrounds and constructing a floating bird sanctuary. Projects are assessed on preparation and planning, originality and innovation, realistic challenge, youth led, benefit to the environment and spark and enthusiasm.

Applications: Initial entries should be submitted during February to April for projects to be completed in the summer.

APPENDIX

Supportive Organisations

INTRODUCTION

The following organisations can often provide invaluable advice and publications. The list has to be limited. The Environment Council produces a '*Who's Who in the Environment*' which provides comprehensive directories of organisations, large and small, throughout the UK (Tel: 0171-834 2626).

People starting new projects are particularly advised to obtain:

A Guide to Good Practice in Managing Environmental Projects published by the Department of the Environment, Transport and the Regions, 1997. Whilst it is aimed specifically at groups availing themselves of the Local Projects Grants of the Environmental Action Fund (see entry) it is relevant for all new community projects. *Free* from: DETR, Blackhorse Road, London SE99 6TT Fax: 0181-694 0099.

Alphabetical Index of Supportive Organisations

SUPPORTIVE ORGANISATIONS

Action with Communities in Rural England (ACRE)

– see Rural Action

Somerford Court, Somerford Road, Cirencester, Gloucestershire GL7 1TW
Tel: 01285-653477; Fax: 01285-654537

The national association of Rural Community Councils works to improve the quality of life of local rural communities, especially of the disadvantaged. They provide a comprehensive advisory and information service.

Association of Community Technical Aid Centres

64 Mount Pleasant, Liverpool L3 5SD
Tel: 0151-708 7607; Fax: 0151-708 7606
Contact: Miles Sibley, Director

ACTAC is the umbrella organisation co-ordinating a national network of community technical aid services for both rural and urban areas. ACTAC's multi-disciplinary approach offers the skills of architects, landscape architects, planners, surveyors and community artists to community groups engaged in building and environmental improvement. The services are reinforced by information, training and mediation for development partnerships involving public, private and voluntary sector representatives, and also by research, training, publications and conferences on tenant participation, community environmental action and community organising. Full ACTAC members are not-for-profit organisations providing a service to those sections of the community which would not otherwise have access to technical services.

British Overseas NGOs for Development Group (BOND)

c/o Regent's Wharf, 8 All Saints Street, London N1 9RL
Tel: 0171-713 6161; Fax: 0171-837 4220
Contact: Richard Bennett, Co-ordinator

This network of over 150 UK-based organisations aims via information-sharing, training and advocacy work to enhance the effectiveness of international development. It publishes a quarterly newsletter and a Directory of Members.

British Trust for Conservation Volunteers (BTCV) – see also Millennium Awards

36 St Mary's Street, Wallingford, Oxfordshire OX10 0EU
Tel: 01491-839766; Fax: 01491-839646

Promotes practical conservation work by volunteers throughout the UK. It is one of the major providers of environmental training in the UK, running a programme of over 600 courses each year.

British Urban Regeneration Association (BURA)

33 Great Sutton Street, London EC1V 0DX
Tel: 0171-253 5054; Fax: 0171-490 8735

BURA aims to identify examples of best practice in urban regeneration both in the UK and abroad and so provide a platform for the exchange of successful initiatives. It co-ordinates workshops, seminars, conferences, exhibitions and regional and international visits.

Business in the Environment

44 Baker Street, London WC1M 1DH
Tel: 0171-224 1600; Fax: 0171-486 1700

BiE was initiated in 1989 by Business in the Community. Its mission is to devise and promote practical steps that will encourage understanding and apply the principles of sustainable development through action and partnership between business and its stakeholders.

It has produced various publications on aspects of environmental practice for companies.

Civic Trust

17 Carlton House Terrace, London SW1Y 5AW
Tel: 0171-930 0914; Fax: 0171-321 0180

To work with partners to improve the quality of life and the built environment in cities, towns and villages. It undertakes research, advice and training. It promotes the formation of local amenity societies and has partners in the north east England, Scotland and Wales.

In 1998 the trust launched its Millennium Fund Award Scheme, "Civic Champions". Approach the address above for further information.

Common Ground

Seven Dials Warehouse, 44 Earlham Street, London WC2H 9LA
Tel: 0171-379 3109; Fax: 0171-836 5741

This imaginative organisation forges links between the arts and the conservation of nature and our cultural landscapes. It offers ideas and information through publications, exhibitions and projects.

Community Development Foundation (CDF)

60 Highbury Grove, London N5 2AG
Tel: 0171-226 5375; Fax: 0171-704 0313

CDF demonstrates how to involve people effectively in the regeneration of their communities. It provides a range of services including consultancies, research and evaluation, conferences and seminars, training, publications and an information service.

Community Enterprise UK

Community Business Scotland Ltd, Unit 25, West Calder Workspace, Society Place, West Calder, West Lothian EH55 8AA
Tel: 01506-871370; Fax: 01506-873079

CEUK is a national organisation with regional representatives of individual community businesses. It promotes the development of regional networks to stimulate acceptance of community enterprise as an essential part of urban policy.

Community Links

105 Barking Road, London E16 4HQ
Tel: 0171-473 2270; Fax: 0171-473 6671
Contact: David Robinson

Community Links runs an independent social action centre with a range of projects, and the development of a national network – principally the "Ideas Annual" and National Tower Blocks Network.

The national work is co-ordinated from the Training and Development Unit (contact Sara Gowen, Community Links, 237 London Road, Sheffield S2 4NF 0114-258 8822).

Community Matters (National Federation of Community Organisations)

8/9 Upper Street, London N1 0PQ
Tel: 0171-226 0189; Fax: 0171-354 9570

Community Matters expands the support provided to community organisations and ensures that they are represented effectively at the local and national level. It runs an advisory service including a community consultancy service. It also provides training, advocacy and a range of publications.

Conservation Foundation

Royal Geographical Society, 1 Kensington Gore, London SW7 2AR
Tel: 0171-591 3111; Fax: 0171-591 3110
Contact: David Shreeve, Executive Director

The foundation organises award schemes (see Ford European Conservation Awards) and special grants to groups engaged in conservation throughout the world such as the Disney Award Scheme for Children. It also publishes a monthly environmental media diary service and runs a range of environmental and conservation initiatives. It publishes "Network 21" twice a year which is distributed to local authorities, environmental organisations, politicians and business people throughout Europe.

Council for Environmental Education

University of Reading, London Road, Reading RG1 5AQ
Tel: 01189-756061; Fax: 01189-756264

The council brings together about 80 national organisations including teacher and other professional associations, statutory authorities and voluntary bodies.

It provides a range of information services for teachers, youth workers and all those involved with environmental education.

Council for the Protection of Rural England (CPRE)

Warwick House, 25 Buckingham Palace Road, London SW1W OPP
Tel: 0171-976 6433; Fax: 0171-976 6373

CPRE works to influence decisions shaping the countryside through research and lobbying. It provides guidance and advice on rural issues to MPs, peers, the media and other organisations.

Development Trusts Association

20 Conduit Place, London W2 IHZ
Tel: 0171-706 4951; Fax: 0171-706 8447;
E-mail: 100607.542@compuserve.com
Contact: Angela Monaghan, Director

An independent membership organisation which encourages and advises on the creation of new development trusts, promotes their achievements and advocates on their behalf at regional, national and European levels. It runs training courses, conferences and seminars and publishes *Networker*, its useful newsletter.

It also has a Development Fund aimed at small and emerging trusts and established organisations facing difficulties

Earthwatch Europe

Belsyre Court, 57 Woodstock Road, Oxford OX2 6HU
Tel: 01865-311600; Fax: 01865-311383
Contact: Brian Walker, Director

Earthwatch Europe, set up with Earthwatch USA, resources scientific field work by finding members of the public prepared to share in both the costs and labour of field research. Special emphasis is given to projects addressing environmental and sustainable development issues. A funding force and a work force in one, Earthwatch team members share the cost of mobilising research expeditions. For two or three weeks, team members may learn to excavate, map, photograph, gather data, make collections, assist diving operations, and share other field chores associated with professional expedition research. Research priorities vary from year to year.

Application forms and further information are available for research proposals and individuals wanting to volunteer their time and money to carry out projects. See also its Millennium Award scheme under the Lottery section.

EIRIS – Ethical Investment Research Services

504 Bondway Business Centre, 71 Bondway, London SW8 1SQ
Tel· 0171-735 1351; Fax: 0171-735 5323;
E-mail: ethics@eiris.win-uk.net
Contact: Peter Webster, Executive Director

EIRIS, set up in 1982 with the help of a group of churches and charities, is one of the first organisations dedicated to helping people to invest according to their ethical principles. Its aims: to provide information to help investors apply ethical criteria to investment; to help people identify and chose between different types of ethical investment; to promote a wider understanding of, and debate on, corporate responsibility.

It has a database on over 1,000 UK and several hundred European Companies. A newsletter, *The Ethical Investor*, is published bi-monthly (£12.00 pa).

Energy Advice Centres

These local advice centres have been sponsored by the Energy Saving Trust. By 1998 there were 50 centres throughout the UK giving free and impartial advice on energy saving measures.

Ring 0800-512 012 and the call will be directed straight to the Energy Advice Centre nearest the caller.

European Environmental Bureau

34 boulevard de Waterloo, 1000 Brussels, Belgium
Tel: 00 32 2 539 0037/289 1090

The bureau has a membership of environmental organisations throughout Europe. Fifteen members are based in the UK. In early 1998 the director of the CPRE held a co-ordinatory role as UK representative in this country.

Going for Green Limited

Churchgate House, 56 Oxford Street, Manchester M60 7HJ
Tel: 0161-272 5221; Fax: 0161-272 5200;
Website: http:www.gfg.iclnet.co.uk
Contact: Professor Graham Ashworth, Chairman and Chief Executive

This public awareness campaign was initiated by the Department of the Environment. with a commitment of £1.5 million providing this sum be matched from private sector sources.

The campaign, with all-party support, aims to promote its five-point Green Code: Cutting down waste; Saving energy and natural resources; Travelling sensibly; Preventing pollution; Looking after the local environment.

Sustainable Communities Projects are being trialled in five local authorities (county, borough and district) across England and Wales in both rural and urban communities.

Campaign materials (six colour A3 posters for £5.00 a set or in a mini postcard sized version sponsored by Esso free in batches of up to 1,000) are available for general display. Exhibition equipment is also loaned.

Contact: Going for Green, PO Box 2100, Manchester M60 3GN.

Eco-schools Awards: Schools are encouraged to register their intention to achieve awards and a Green Eco-Flag in this European wide scheme. It is funded by Going for Green and managed by the Tidy Britain Group from its Wigan HQ.

Contact: Sue Rigby, Eco-schools Manager, the Tidy Britain Group, The Pier, Wigan WN3 4EX Tel: 01942-824788; Fax: 01942-824788

Groundwork Foundation and Trusts

85-87 Cornwall Street, Birmingham B3 3BY
Tel: 0121-236 8565; Fax: 0121-236 7356
Contact: Tony Hawkhead, Chief Executive

The Groundwork Foundation is an umbrella body for 48 autonomous trusts. It was established in 1981 and by 1998 was active in England, Wales and Northern Ireland. It is funded by central government and local authorities as well as other sources. It has an entrepreneurial role developing partnerships between the statutory, private and voluntary sectors. Its approach is to develop programmes which link environmental, social and economic regeneration and help to create communities in which "people are proud to live and work". Programmes concentrate on three themes:

◆ creating new landscapes e.g. finding new uses for land and buildings, in housing estates to abandoned parcels of land, children's playareas or industrial estates.
◆ involving local communities. Programmes create opportunities for people to participate in action for the environment.
◆ strengthening local economies. Work includes carrying out environmental reviews, improving business sites, and creating opportunities for local businesses to be involved in local communities for example through school-business links.

Landlife

The Old Police Station, Lark Lane, Liverpool L17 8UU
Tel: 0151-728 7011; Fax: 0151-728 8413
Contact: Jonathan Delf, Director

Landlife runs wildflower nurseries and a native landscape design service. It also produces educational publications.

Learning through Landscapes

3rd Floor, Southside Offices, The Law Courts, Winchester, Hants SO23 9DL
Tel: 01962-846258; Fax: 01962-869099

This national charity, launched in 1990, aims to improve the quality and educational use of school grounds. It works with schools, designers, local authorities and environmental organisations to develop imaginative landscapes to meet young people's needs, to promote the use of school grounds in the national curriculum, to strengthen community links, and to involve children in positive change and social interaction.

It produces a free information pack and a range of excellent educational materials.

Liaison Committee of Development NGOs to the European Union

10 Square Ambiorix, 1000 Brussels, Belgium
Tel: 00 32 2 743 8760; Fax: 00 32 2 732 1934; E-mail:mvalenti@clong.be Website: www.one.world.org/liaison
Contact: Massimo Valenti

The NGO-EU Liaison Committee represents more than 800 European Non Governmental Organisations (NGOs) working in the field of development or humanitarian aid and grouped in 15 national "platforms".

The Liaison Committee, co-ordinated by the Brussels Secretariat, provides information, and dialogue on EU policies and budgetary funds regarding development issues affecting the developing world. Membership, via the 15 national platforms, is open to all NGOs based in an EU member states and active in the various fields of International solidarity work, particularly, development, emergency relief and development education. The organisation functioning and the status of each national platform are decided at national level (see UK contact below). However national representative groups meet in response to the generally felt need for participation by all national platforms in certain areas: funding and education. Expert groups also work on particular policy areas.

Publications: *Liaison News Bulletin, monthly; NGO Handbook*, published annually. Essential information about the organisation and functions of the EC, The European Commission Parliament and Council, and Community Funds open to NGOs. It includes a table of budget lines open to NGOs and a 4-page section on the Environment under its information on Sectoral budget Lines.

United Kingdom – the EC-NGO Network

c/o Save the Children Fund, 17 Grove Lane, London SE5 8ED Tel: 0171-703 5400; Fax: 0171-793 7610; Nick Gallagher, Co-ordinator

Media Natura

137-149 Goswell Road, London EC1V 7ET
Tel: 0171-253 0880; Fax: 0171-253 0343

Media Natura is a registered charity, run by a board and council representing the media industry and the conservation movement. A sister company, Media Natura Limited, conducts contract work, the profits of which are devoted to the trust's work.

It describes its role as follows "Media Natura links two sets of expertise: the knowledge and the campaigning edge of the conservation movement, and the skills and facilities of the media industry. It functions rather like a dating agency. Media Natura's 'sponsors' pledge a certain amount of time, or facilities, or materials or ideas. The details are held on a central register. Conservation groups come up with projects that are needed; they might include responsible consuming, highlighting a key issue, launching an idea or making tangible the intangible. Others too can suggest projects. Media Natura then puts together the necessary media resources, draws up the contract and a management schedule, and sees that the conservation client and the media sponsors complete their collaboration smoothly and effectively."

Neighbourhood Initiatives Foundation

The Poplars, Lightmoor, Telford, Shropshire TF4 3QN
Tel: 01952-590777; Fax: 01952-591771
Contact: Donald Burrows, Director

NIF aims to involve residents of neighbourhoods in identifying and realising the needs of their communities, enabling local people to play a full part in planning the regeneration of their own neighbourhoods. It provides training for residents and officers in "planning for real" and other hands-on techniques; advice and information for community groups; self-build advisory service; carries out surveys and feasibility studies; organises residents conferences and facilitates participation and consultative exercises.

Pan London Community Regeneration Consortium

c/o BASSAC, First Floor, Winchester House, 11 Cranmer Road, London SW9 6EJ
Tel: 0171-820 3943; Fax: 0171-735 0804;
E-mail: bassac@mcrl.poptel.org.uk
Contact: Austen Cutten, Development Officer

The consortium is an SRB Challenge funded partnership (deriving from a Round 2 SRB bid) set up in response to the fact that very few successful bids were coming from the voluntary sector. It aims to:

◆ help London voluntary and community organisations play a greater role in regeneration partnerships;
◆ assist local regeneration partnerships to become more responsive to the needs of local communities.

Services provided include: information on partnerships; training and consultancy to develop partnership links; technical support for partnership bid preparation; training and development for community partners; professional assistance and training; extending opportunities for black and minority ethnic groups.

Sustrans Ltd

35 King Street, Bristol BS1 4DZ
Tel: 0117- 926 8893; Fax: 0117-929 4173
Contact: John Grimshaw, Director

Sustrans aims to promote low-pollution modes of transport. It works for the construction of the national cycle network, ensuring access for pedestrians and wheelchair users as well as cyclists. It designs and constructs traffic-free routes for pedestrians, cyclists and wheelchair users. It also provides consultancy advice to local authorities on promotion of the national cycle network.

Television Trust for the Environment

Prince Albert Road, London NW1 4RZ
Tel: 0171-586 5526; Fax: 0171-586 4866
Contact: Robert Lamb, Director

The aim of TVE is to provide videos on environment and development to NGOs in low and middle income countries free of charge and to raise funding for film-makers in the developing world to make these programmes. It provides a video distribution service and "Moving Pictures" bulletins and catalogues, distributed worldwide.

Tidy Britain Group
see also Going for Green

The Pier, Wigan, Lancashire WN3 4EX
Tel: 01942-824620; Fax: 01942-824778;
Website: http://freespace.virgin.net/tidy.britain

Contact: Professor Graham Ashworth, Director General

The group aims to protect and enhance the amenities of town and country by promoting the prevention and control of litter. It runs campaigns, education programmes, projects, consultancy and advisory services. Its award schemes include Britain in Bloom and the Seaside Awards for clean beaches. It also runs the "People and Places" programme, a local authority scheme for litter abatement.

Town & Country Planning Association

17 Carlton House Terrace, London SW1Y 5AS
Tel: 0171-930 8903; Fax: 0171-930 3280

The TCPA aims to influence central and local government and public opinion in matters relating to planning. In particular it campaigns for more local initiatives and decentralisation of decision-making. Its activities include: making representations on planning policy to government departments and other public bodies; organising conferences, seminars and study tours on all aspects of town and country planning policy and administration; running a specialist planning bookshop.

Trust for Urban Ecology

Stave Hill Ecological Park, Timber Pond Road, London SE16 1AG
Tel: 0171-237 9165; Fax: 0171-237 9165
Contact: Clifford Davy, Director

The trust promotes the conservation, use and appreciation of nature in urban areas by all sectors of the community. It provides advice, training and information on the design and management of urban greenspaces.

UK 21 – Community Network for Sustainability Practitioners

c/o Projects in Partnership, Tea Warehouse, 10a Lant Street, London SE1 1QR
Tel: 0171-407 8585 Fax: 0171-407 9555;
E-mail: pip.ltd@easynet.co.uk
Contact: Lindsey Colbourne

"A network connecting and supporting people in the UK who are enabling inclusive, community-based approaches to Local Agenda 21 and sustainability....and developing a strategic framework for their activities."

Over 200 organisations have supported this development of this network which aims to launch in June 1998. Its first three chosen priorities are: links to other initiatives; practical examples; tool kits of techniques.

Urban and Economic Development Group (URBED)

19 Store Street, London WC1E 9NT
Tel: 0171-436 8050; Fax: 0171-436 8083
Contact: Dr Nicholas Falk, Director

URBED is a non-profit making consultancy, research and training group, which specialises in finding practical solutions to the economic problems of run-down areas and creating new work. Its activities include: advising local authorities on how to revitalise run-down areas and helping to set up environmental and enterprise trusts; assisting small and medium-sized businesses to develop and

grow through training; advising community groups on re-using industrial buildings and raising finance. It also carries out research into the changing nature of industry and the management of urban regeneration.

Urban Wildlife Partnership
see *Wildlife Trusts*

The Green, Witham Park, Waterside South, Lincoln LN5 7JR
Tel: 01522-544400; Fax: 01522-511616
Contact: Chris Gordan, Community Officer

The Urban Wildlife Partnership is an independent organisation that acts as an umbrella for a range of 100 urban groups from Groundwork to Local Authority Rangers schemes. It provides advice and information for its members.

Waste Watch

Gresham House, 24 Holborn Viaduct, London EC1A 2BN
Tel: 0171-248 1818; Fax: 0171-248 1404
Contact: Jo Gordon, Director

Waste Watch is an independent charity sponsored by Shell UK Ltd and the Department of the Environment supporting action on waste reduction, re-use and recycling. It helps community-based recycling groups and local authorities through information packs, training and publications. It works nationally to persuade industry and government to reduce waste reduction and increase recycling. It also provides a consultancy service.

Wasteline provides public advice and information on recycling (0171-248 0242).

Wildlife Trusts
Formerly the Royal Society for the Promotion of Nature

The Green, Witham Park, Waterside South, Lincoln LN5 7JR
Tel: 01522-544400; Fax: 01522-511616

The Wildlife Trusts are a network of 48 autonomous local trusts working to conserve rural and urban wildlife. It also runs a junior branch, Wildlife Watch and hosts the Urban Wildlife Partnership, an independent umbrella organisation (see separate entry).

Women's Environment Network

87 Worship Street, London EC2A 2BE
Tel: 0171-247 3327; Fax: 0171-247 4740

The network addresses environmental issues that specifically affect women and informs, educates and empowers women who care about the environment. It has run campaigns as well as seminars, workshops and public meetings.

World Wide Fund for Nature
(See Other Grants and Award Schemes)

INDEX